WORLDCOMP'13
July 22-25, 2013
Las Vegas Nevada, USA
www.world-academy-of-science.org

PROCEEDINGS OF THE 2013 INTERNATIONAL CONFERENCE ON DATA MINING

DMIN 2013

Editors

Robert Stahlbock
Gary M. Weiss

Associate Editors

Mahmoud Abou-Nasr
Hamid R. Arabnia

FIREWALL MEDIA
(An Imprint of Laxmi Publications Pvt. Ltd.)
An ISO 9001:2008 Company
BENGALURU • CHENNAI • COCHIN • GUWAHATI • HYDERABAD
JALANDHAR • KOLKATA • LUCKNOW • MUMBAI • RANCHI • NEW DELHI
BOSTON (USA) • ACCRA (GHANA) • NAIROBI (KENYA)

This volume contains papers presented at The 2013 International Conference on Data Mining (DMIN'13). Their inclusion in this publication does not necessarily constitute endorsements by editors or by the publisher.

Branches

Branch	Phone	
Bengaluru	080-26 75 69 30	
Chennai	044-24 34 47 26,	24 35 95 07
Cochin	0484-237 70 04,	405 13 03
Guwahati	0361-254 36 69,	251 38 81
Hyderabad	040-27 55 53 83,	27 55 53 93
Jalandhar	0181-222 12 72	
Kolkata	033-22 27 43 84	
Lucknow	0522-220 99 16	
Mumbai	022-24 91 54 15,	24 92 78 69
Ranchi	0651-220 44 64	

Published in India by

An ISO 9001:2008 Company
113, GOLDEN HOUSE, DARYAGANJ,
NEW DELHI - 110002, INDIA
Telephone : 91-11-4353 2500, 4353 2501
Fax : 91-11-2325 2572, 4353 2528
www.laxmipublications.com info@laxmipublications.com

C—
Printed at:

Foreword

We are pleased to present this collection of papers submitted to the 9th International Conference on Data Mining 2013, DMIN'13 (www.dmin-2013.com), July 22-25, 2013, The New Tropicana Hotel, Las Vegas, Nevada, USA.

Data mining is a relatively young discipline that is critically important if we want to effectively learn from the tremendous amounts of data that are routinely being generated in science, engineering, medicine, business, and other areas. Data mining attracts innovative and influential contributions to both research and practice, across a wide range of academic disciplines and application domains. DMIN conferences seek to acknowledge and facilitate excellence in research and applications in the area of data mining. DMIN conferences are held annually within WORLDCOMP, the largest annual gathering of researchers in computer science, computer engineering and applied computing. WORLDCOMP'13 assembles a spectrum of 22 affiliated research conferences, workshops, and symposiums into a coordinated research meeting. Each conference has its own program committee as well as referees and own indexed proceedings. Attendees have full access to all 22 conferences' sessions, tracks, and tutorials. DMIN seeks to reflect the multi- and interdisciplinary nature of data mining and to facilitate the exchange and development of novel ideas, open communication and networking amongst researchers and practitioners in different research domains. As in 2012 and the years before, we hope that the 2013 International Conference on Data Mining will provide a forum for you to present your research in a professional environment, exchange ideas, and network and interact across research areas. DMIN actively supports students and beginning researchers from lesser developed countries by funding registration and accommodation, in order to allow for a truly international networking and understanding. The 2013 conference has provided an international and multicultural experience with contributions from 26 different countries. We consider the resulting diversity in attendees and the mixture of established and starting researchers as a particular advantage of an engaging conference format.

DMIN'13 attracted a large number of submissions of theoretical research papers as well as industrial reports and case studies on applications. The program committee would like to thank all those who submitted papers for review. We strived to establish a review process of high quality. To ensure a fair, objective and transparent review process all review criteria were published on the website. Papers were evaluated regarding their relevance to DMIN, originality, significance, information content, clarity, and soundness on an international level. Each aspect was objectively evaluated, with alternative aspects finding consideration for application papers. Each paper was refereed by at least two researchers in the topical area, taken the reviewers' expertise and confidence into consideration, with most of the papers receiving three reviews. The review process was competitive. The overall paper acceptance rate for papers was 45%.

We are very grateful to the many colleagues who helped in organizing the conference. In particular, we would like to thank the members of the DMIN'13 program committee. Their continuing support has been essential to further improve the quality of accepted submissions and the resulting success of the conference. The DMIN'13 program committee members are (in alphabetical order):

Mahmoud Abou-Nasr, Lamine M. Aouad, Jérôme Azé, Souhaib Ben Taieb, Daniel Berrar, James Buckley, Alina Campan, Peng Chen, Paulo Cortez, Christian Dawson, Qin Ding, António Dourado, Mengling Feng, Philippe Fournier-Viger, Shunkai Fu, Peter Géczy (JP), Corani Giorgio, Zahid Halim, Tzung-Pei Hong, Yo-Ping Huang, Ulf Johansson, Rikard König, Madjid Khalilian, Sebastian Klenk, Terje Kristensen, Philippe Lenca, Chuan Li, Wen-Yang Lin, José M. Merigo Lindahl, Tanja Magoc, Jun Meng, Sergey Morozov, Hossein Peyvandi, Torsten Reiners, Lotfi Ben Romdhane, Gerald Schaefer, Sabrina Senatore, Xuequn Shang, Victor Sheng, Yong Shi, Vijendra Singh, Robert Stahlbock, Shun-Hung Tsai, Nicole Vincent, Baoying Wang,

Chamont Wang, Fan Wang, Simon Wang, Xuewei Wang, Gary M. Weiss, Zijiang Yang, Yun Zhai, Defu Zhang, and Shang-Ming Zhou.

We would also like to thank our publicity co-chairs Ashu M. G. Solo (Fellow of British Computer Society, Principal/R&D Engineer, Maverick Technologies America Inc., Intelligent Systems Instructor, Trailblazer Intelligent Systems, Inc.), and Sven F. Crone (Lancaster University, UK) for circulating information on the conference..

Considering the increasing efforts of all towards the quality of the review process, the conference sessions and the social program of DMIN'13 we are confident that you can look forward to participating and attending a leading and reputable international conference. It is a particular pleasure to provide data mining oriented invited talks and tutorials presented by the following esteemed members of the data mining community: Vladimir Cherkassky (University of Minnesota, USA), Peter Geczy (AIST, Japan), and Alfred Inselberg (Tel Aviv University, Israel).

The DMIN'13 conference organizers are also thankful to a number of co-sponsors, without whom the conference would not have been possible. The conference was sponsored and or supported by the US Chapter of World Academy of Science (http://www.world-academy-of-science.org/); Computer Science Research, Education, and Applications Press (CSREA); Aldebaran Robotics Inc., USA; Taylor & Francis, United Kingdom. In addition, a number of university faculty members and their staff (names appear above and also on the cover of the proceedings), several publishers of computer science and computer engineering books and journals, chapters and/or task forces of computer science associations/organizations from 5 countries, and developers of high-performance machines and systems provided significant help in organizing the conference as well as providing some resources.

We are also grateful for support by the Institute of Information Systems at Hamburg University, Germany (www.uni-hamburg.de/IWI) and the Business Intelligence Laboratory, B I^{3}S lab, Hamburg, Germany (www.bis-lab.com). Furthermore, we would like to thank all members of the steering committee of the 2013 congress: Dr. Selim Aissi, (formerly: Chief Strategist - Security, Intel Corporation, USA), Senior Business Leader & Head of Global Enterprise Security Architecture, Visa Corporation, USA; Prof. Nizar Al-Holou, Professor and Chair, Electrical and Computer Engineering Department, Vice Chair, IEEE/SEM-Computer Chapter, University of Detroit Mercy, Detroit, Michigan, USA; Prof. Hamid R. Arabnia, Professor of Computer Science, Editor-in-Chief of The Journal of Supercomputing (Springer), Elected Fellow of Int'l Society of Intelligent Biological Medicine (ISIBM), The University of Georgia, Georgia, USA; Prof. Babak Akhgar, Fellow of the British Computer Society, CITP, Professor of Informatics, Co-Director of CENTRIC (Centre of Excellence in Terrorism, Resilience, Intelligence & organised Crime research), Sheffield Hallam University, Sheffield, UK; Prof. Kevin Daimi, Director, Computer Science and Software Engineering Programs, Department of Mathematics, Computer Science and Software Engineering, University of Detroit Mercy, Detroit, Michigan, USA; Prof. George Jandieri, Chief Scientist, The Institute of Cybernetics, Georgian Academy of Science, Georgia, Editorial Board Member of International Journal of Microwaves and Optical Technology, The Open Atmospheric Science Journal, American Journal of Remote Sensing, Georgian Technical University, Tbilisi, Georgia; Prof. Dattatraya V. Kodavade, Head of Computer Science and Engineering, D.K.T.E Society's Textile & Engineering Institute, Ichalkaranji, Maharashtra State, India; Prof. George Markowsky, Professor and Associate Director, School of Computing and Information Science, Chair of International Advisory Board of IEEE IDAACS, Director 2013 Northeast Collegiate Cyber Defense Competition, Chair Bangor Foreign Policy Forum, President Phi Beta Kappa Delta Chapter of Maine, Cooperating Professor Mathematics and Statistics Department UMaine, Cooperating Professor School of Policy & International Affairs UMaine, University of Maine, Orono, Maine, USA; Prof. G. N. Pandey, Vice-Chancellor, Arunachal University of Studies, Arunachal Pradesh, India and Adjunct Professor, Indian Institute of Information Technology, Allahabad, India; Prof. Fernando G. Tinetti, Co-editor of Journal of Computer Science and

Technology (JCS&T), Professor, School of Computer Science, Universidad Nacional de La Plata, La Plata, Argentina; Dr. Predrag Tosic, Microsoft, Washington, USA; Prof. Vladimir Volkov, The Bonch-Bruevich State University of Telecommunications, Saint-Petersburg, Russia.

Most importantly, we wish to express again our sincere gratitude and respect towards Professor Hamid R. Arabnia (Univ. of Georgia, USA; Elected Fellow, ISIBM; Editor-in-Chief, The Journal of Supercomputing (Springer); Member), General Chair and Coordinator of the federated congress, for his excellent and tireless support, organization and coordination of all affiliated events. His exemplary and professional effort in 2013 and all the years before in the WORLDCOMP steering committee makes these events possible!

Thank you all for your contribution to DMIN'13! We hope that you will experience a stimulating conference with many opportunities for future contacts, research and applications.

Robert Stahlbock
DMIN'13 General Conference Chair

Gary M. Weiss

Steering Committee DMIN'13
www.dmin-2013.com

Contents

SESSION: REAL-WORLD DATA MINING APPLICATIONS, CHALLENGES, AND PERSPECTIVES

SESSION: SEGMENTATION, CLUSTERING, ASSOCIATION + WEB / TEXT / MULTIMEDIA MINING

SESSION: REGRESSION AND CLASSIFICATION

SESSION: FILTERING, FEATURE SELECTION, INTEGRATION, ENSEMBLES

SESSION

REAL-WORLD DATA MINING APPLICATIONS, CHALLENGES, AND PERSPECTIVES

Chair(s)

Drs. Mahmoud Abou-Nasr
Robert Stahlbock
Gary M. Weiss

Maintenance Knowledge Management with Fusion of CMMS and CM

[1]Sten-Erik Björling, [1]Diego Galar, [2]David Baglee, [1]Sarbjeet Singh, [1]Uday Kumar
[1]Division of Operation and Maintenance Engineering, Luleå University of Technology, Sweden
[2]Institute for Automotive and Manufacturing Advanced Practise, Department of Computing, Engineering and Technology, University of Sunderland, UK
seb@ltu.se, diego.galar@ltu.se, David.baglee@sunderland.ac.uk
Sarbjeet.singh@ltu.se, uday.kumar@ltu.se

***Abstract*- Maintenance can be considered as an information, knowledge processing and management system. The management of knowledge resources in maintenance is a relatively new issue compared to Computerized Maintenance Management Systems (CMMS) and Condition Monitoring (CM) approaches and systems. Information Communication technologies (ICT) systems including CMMS, CM and enterprise administrative systems amongst others are effective in supplying data and in some cases information. In order to be effective the availability of high-quality knowledge, skills and expertise are needed for effective analysis and decision-making based on the supplied information and data. Information and data are not by themselves enough, knowledge, experience and skills are the key factors when maximizing the usability of the collected data and information. Thus, effective knowledge management (KM) is growing in importance, especially in advanced processes and management of advanced and expensive assets. Therefore efforts to successfully integrate maintenance knowledge management processes with accurate information from CMMSs and CM systems will be vital due to the increasing complexities of the overall systems.**

Low maintenance effectiveness costs money and resources since normal and stable production cannot be upheld and maintained over time, lowered maintenance effectiveness can have a substantial impact on the organizations ability to obtain stable flows of income and control costs in the overall process. Ineffective maintenance is often dependent on faulty decisions, mistakes due to lack of experience and lack of functional systems for effective information exchange [10]. Thus, access to knowledge, experience and skills resources in combination with functional collaboration structures can be regarded as vital components for a high maintenance effectiveness solution.

Maintenance effectiveness depends in part on the quality, timeliness, accuracy and completeness of information related to machine degradation state, based on which decisions are made. Maintenance effectiveness, to a large extent, also depends on the quality of the knowledge of the managers and maintenance operators and the effectiveness of the internal & external collaborative environments. With emergence of intelligent sensors to measure and monitor the health state of the component and gradual implementation of ICT) in organizations, the conceptualization and implementation of E-Maintenance is turning into a reality. Unfortunately, even though knowledge management aspects are important in maintenance, the integration of KM aspects has still to find its place in E-Maintenance and in the overall information flows of larger-scale maintenance solutions. Nowadays, two main systems are implemented in most maintenance departments: Firstly, Computer Maintenance Management Systems (CMMS), the core of traditional maintenance record-keeping practices that often facilitate the usage of textual descriptions of faults and actions performed on an asset. Secondly, condition monitoring systems (CMS). Recently developed (CMS) are capable of directly monitoring asset components parameters; however, attempts to link observed CMMS events to CM sensor measurements have been limited in their approach and scalability. In this article we present one approach for addressing this challenge. We argue that understanding the requirements and constraints in conjunction - from maintenance, knowledge management and ICT perspectives - is necessary. We identify the issues that need be addressed for achieving successful integration of such disparate data types and processes (also integrating knowledge management into the "data types" and processes).

Keywords: CMMS, CM, Maintenance Knowledge Management, Experience Management, I-Maintenance

I. INTRODUCTION

The production and process industry are passing through a continuous transformation and improvement for last couple of decades, due to the global competition coupled· with advancement of information and communication technology (ICT). The business scenario is focusing more on e-business intelligence to perform transactions with a focus on customers' needs for enhanced value and improvement in asset management. Such prognostic business requirement compels the organizations to minimize the production and service downtime by reducing the machine performance degradation. The above organizational requirements necessitate developing proactive maintenance strategies to provide optimized and continuous process performance with minimized system breakdowns and maintenance. Implementing solutions from the business world concepts such as e-intelligence, e-factory, e-automation, E-Maintenance, e-marketing and e-service have emerged.

E-Maintenance provides the organization with intelligent tools to monitor and manage assets (machines, plants, products, etc.) proactively through ICT, focusing on health degradation monitoring and prognostics, instead of fault detection and diagnostics. Maintenance effectiveness depends on the quality, timeliness, accuracy and completeness of information, knowledge and earlier experiences related to machine degradation state and support processes, based on which decisions are made. This translates into a number of key requirements: preventing data and information overload, ability to differentiate and prioritize data and actions (during collection as well as reporting), to prevent, as far as possible, the occurrence of information islands and to effectively communicate status and vital information to relevant actors. Integration and inclusion of maintenance knowledge management (MKM) into the processes and infrastructures of E-Maintenance creates the foundation for a more comprehensive approach to ICT-based maintenance solutions which one can call I-Maintenance ("Intelligence-based Maintenance"). The I-Maintenance approach not only aim at integrating maintenance knowledge management into the solutions but also offer integration of collaborative environments, remote computational services, ontology's for effective tagging of resources, solutions etc. all designed to be effectively used across different levels of the organization and between organizations.

CMMS and CM are the most popular repositories of information in maintenance, where most of deployed technology is installed and unfortunately isolated information islands are usually created. While using CMMS and CM technology as isolated systems can bring the achievement of maintenance goals, combining the two into one seamless system can have exponentially more positive effects on maintenance group's performance than either system alone might achieve. The combination of the strengths of an effective top-notch CMMS (preventive maintenance (PM) scheduling, automatic work order generation, maintenance inventory control, and data integrity) with the wizardry of a leading edge CM system (multiple-method condition monitoring, trend tracking, and expert system diagnoses) allows work orders to be generated automatically based on information provided by CM diagnostic and prognostic capabilities. Over the last 15 years, linking CMMS and CM technology was mostly a vision easily dismissed as infeasible or at best too expensive and difficult to warrant much investigation. Now, the available technology in CMMS and CM solutions has made it possible to achieve such a link relatively easily and inexpensively. Integration of a MKM component with the CMMS and CM environments introduces risks of creating additional information islands and complexities if not properly designed, developed and implemented. One promising approach for integrating MKM into overall solutions that also integrates CMMS and CM data is utilization of SOA (Service Oriented Architectures) in combination with implementation of software agents. The danger of trying to intimately integrate MKM, collaborative structures, CMMS and CM into one unified solution is that the overall solution with a high probability will be sub-optimized if not planned and implemented properly. This is especially dangerous when implementing solutions with a high rate of change in structure and processes – MKM is one of these types of solutions. Currently the most viable route for integrating CMMS, CM and I-Maintenance modules and solutions is to integrate at the end-user level, utilizing a combination of application servers with end-user environments that allows for modular integration of different information sources, services and functions.

A high specification CMMS can perform a wide variety of functions to improve maintenance performance. It is the central organizational tool for World-Class Maintenance WCM, primarily designed to facilitate a shift in emphasis from reactive to preventive maintenance. It achieves this shift by allowing maintenance professionals to set up automatic PM work order generation. A CMMS can also provide historical information that is then used to adjust a PM system to minimize repairs that are unnecessary, while still avoiding run-to-failure repairs. PMs for a given piece of equipment can be set up on a calendar schedule or a usage schedule based on measurements and readings. A fully featured CMMS also includes inventory tracking, workforce management, purchasing, in a package that stresses database integrity to safeguard vital information. The final result can be optimized equipment up-time, lower maintenance costs, and better overall plant efficiency dependent on the ability of the maintenance staff to use the systems and processes, factors highly dependent on the knowledge level and experience of the maintenance staff. On the other hand, CM system should accurately monitor real-time equipment performance, and alert the maintenance professional to any changes in performance trends. There are a variety of measurements that a CM package might be able to track including vibration, oil condition, temperature, operating and static motor characteristics, pump flow, and pressure output. These measurements are squeezed out of equipment by monitoring tools including ferrographic wear particle analysis, proximity probes, triaxial vibration sensors, accelerometers, lasers, and multichannel spectrum analyzers. The preferred CM systems are expert systems that can analyze measurements such as vibration and diagnose machine faults. Expert system analysis can place maintenance procedures on hold until absolutely necessary, thus extracting maximum equipment up time. In addition, expert systems should offer diagnostic fault trending where individual machine fault severity can be observed over time.

MKM allows for effective dissemination of experiences, manuals, collaborative structures for access of internal and external specialists and knowledge resources. In the context of support for the CMMS the MKM can integrate management of documentations, instructions, access to remote servicing, decision support and experience capture and management. In the context of support for CM the MKM can support the analysis processes of CM data by access of collaborative structures for internal and external specialists, in addition provide access to external CM analysis tools / computational engines and interaction with external vendors specialized support structures. The MKM component can be instrumental in the ability of the maintenance staff to properly interpret the results from the measurements and computations.Both CMMS and CM systems have strong suits that make them indispensable to maintenance operation improvements. CMMS is a great organizational tool, but cannot directly monitor equipment conditions. A CM system excels at monitoring those equipment conditions, but is not suited to organizing your overall maintenance operation. The logical conclusion, then, is to combine CMMS and CM technologies into a seamless system that avoids catastrophic breakdowns, but eliminates needless repairs to equipment that is running satisfactorily. The MKM environment can have a strong role in improving the accuracy and quality of the analysis and the resulting decisions. MKM also has an important role in minimizing the risk for mistakes and human error in the implementation of the decisions and the quality of the maintenance work performed on the work floor or in the field. It also allows for improved quality of the decisions made over time due to more accurate feedback of experiences and observations by the maintenance operators.

Technology providers are trying to develop advanced tools while the maintenance departments often struggle with daily problems of implementing, integrating and operating such systems. MKM systems can have a vital role in speeding up effective implementation of these more advanced ICT centric solutions by integrating competence resource structures into the solutions, allowing the end-users of different types to get support and instructions optimized for their own work roles and work contexts. MKM systems can supply infrastructures for experience capture and management supporting the maintenance departments to manage ever-increasing complexities in assets and process flows. The CMMS and CM technology providers or the users do generally not know the feasibility of applying CMMS or CM technologies, but apparently they seem to improve the efficiency of the maintenance activities. The users combine their experience and heuristics in defining maintenance policies and in usage of condition monitoring systems – an approach that can be effectively supported by a well functioning MKM implementation. The existing maintenance systems seem to be a heterogeneous combination of methods and systems in which the integrating factor of the information and business processes is the maintenance personnel, personnel that often cannot utilize the full functionality of the underlying systems. The information in the maintenance systems goes through these human minds forming an organizational information system and creating a high reliance on the expertise of the maintenance staff. Thus, increasing the support for the human component in the overall system to perform their work more accurately, securely and more effective improves the overall maintenance processes and the effectiveness of the overall operations. In this context MKM has an important role to fill at the same time as the vulnerability for the organization due to loss of vital staff can decrease [9].

With emergence of intelligent sensors to measure and monitor the health state of the component and gradual implementation of information and communication technologies (ICT) in organizations, conceptualization and implementation of E-Maintenance is turning into a reality [1]. While E-Maintenance techniques can provide benefits to an organization, seamless integration of information and communication technologies (ICT) into the industrial environment still remains a challenge. It is necessary to understand and address the requirements and constraints from the maintenance as well as the ICT standpoints in parallel. Thus, increasing the support for the human component in the overall system to perform their work more accurately, securely and more effective improves the overall maintenance processes and the effectiveness of the overall operations. In this context MKM has an important role to fill.

II. AN INTEGRATED APPROACH TO ASSET MANAGEMENT

Two main maintenance information sources found in the industries to be merged: Computer Maintenance Management systems (CMMS) and Condition Monitoring (CM). CMMS uses context-specific textual data to record information such as asset load and usage, component failures, servicing or repairs, and inventory control. Although for a given platform, there may exist several different implementations, the underlying structure is typically heavily regulated, allowing for a large base of consistently structured data. These systems are the core of traditional scheduled maintenance practices and rely on bulk observations from historical data to make modifications to regulated maintenance actions. CM systems collect component-specific quantitative data to assist maintenance crews in the identification of failures that are imminent or have already occurred. Typically there exists no standardization in the way data is collected across platforms or vendors, primarily because the technology is still in its infancy. There is still a need to investigate and debate on the type of information required for asset health diagnostics and information used to meet CBM objectives. CMMS environments do not today effectively support client platforms. More advanced resources such as multimedia and integrated collaborative environments, are useful for effective remote support and interaction with internal and external specialists. Core functionalities for effective experience capture are not present in current CMMS environments - the main challenge is the lack of effective meta-data management. CMMS, CM and MKM have to be linked. The measurements and analysis implementations supported by MKM and made by a CM package must be available to maintenance planners who work with a CMMS for the purpose of scheduling predictive and other types of work orders, these maintenance planners are also supported by MKM. In the past, maintenance organizations that used both CMMS and CM technologies linked the two systems by inputting CM data manually into the CMMS. While this is an acceptable way to transfer data for the purpose of scheduling predictive maintenance work orders, it is also time-consuming. Another CM data transfer method that has been used recently is a passive data exchange, which involves writing pertinent CM data to a specified local or network directory. Relevant data to be exchanged includes equipment identification, date and time stamps, repair priority, repair recommendations, and observations.

The CMMS program would routinely check this directory, and if a transfer file is found, the CMMS reads it and imports it into the CMMS database. Historically, this method of data transfer has been very specific to formal cooperation between various manufacturers of CM and CMMS software. The passive data transfer method is better than manual data entry, but still falls well short of the total automation and instant access to information that is possible when the CMMS and CM program are totally integrated. Integration of MKM solutions can support effective training and learning of the staff responsible for the data capture (increasing the quality), the staff responsible for the analysis and the information / experience exchange between internal and external specialists when developing the CM processes and results implementation. In future scenarios the CM analysis can be performed remotely, eventually by different companies with different specializations. A MKM environment can aid the internal analysis staff in selecting the correct CM analysis & modeling vendor / analysis approaches and handle the eventual initial training efforts needed for the services and analysis efforts. Integration has been addressed this far largely from the view point of representing the collected information to the end-user (operator or manager) in an effective manner, i.e., bridging the gap between information collected from plants and equipment and the enterprise resource planning (ERP) platforms. A major initiative has been the development of information integration specifications to enable open, industry-driven, integrated solutions for asset management. However, some of the efforts to standardize the E-Maintenance platforms currently underway are: Machinery Information Management Open Systems Alliance (MIMOSA) [2], GEM@WORK [3], CASIP [4] and PROTEUS [5].

Such platforms provide an information schema at the application-level and an application programming interface (API) to communicate with the underlying protocol stack. To our knowledge, existing communication technologies are not well-suited for reliable and timely delivery of appropriate data between distributed end-systems in industrial environments; this, in our opinion, remains a critical missing link in the seamless integration vision. Added to this is the current lack of effective integration of knowledge management structures into the overall maintenance environments. Effective integration of MKM solutions will become vital over time due to the increasing complexity of processes and products in combination with increased competition for knowledgeable staff and specialists.The main challenge for future maintenance systems is to effectively support the end-users of different types in their efforts to manage a complex work environment, complex and advanced assets and processes and management of their overall work situation to decrease stress and risks.

A. Integration of data sources

The first step of integrating a CMMS, CM and MKM packages into an automatic system is setting up a way for the systems to communicate. In the case of CMMS and CM technologies the first step can be to set up consistent data in each system that will allow them to communicate using a common base of information. Next, there must be a system of data cross-references between the sensors, meter tags, or other measurement tools in a CM system and the appropriate module in the CMMS that associates readings in one system with readings in the other. Meter readings or alarm triggers that are out of the acceptable range set up in the CMMS should trigger a pre-defined work order. Any discrepancy in this cross-reference for a piece of equipment will nullify the link for that piece of equipment, making the ability to predict problems problematic. This makes the initial planning of data entry rules and database setup a critical part of the pre-integration process. The third step is to provide a direct link between the systems' data tables. This is referred to as an "active exchange" of data. In today's environment, CMMS databases feature open architecture such SQL, Oracle and others. The most obvious obstacle in the integration of CMMS, CM and MKM data and information is the disparate nature of the data types involved, and attempts to remedy this problem have been met with inconsistent implementation and limited scalability. The first such technique is to assign the qualitative CMMS data with quantitative indexing, allowing for CM data to be separated into discreet maintenance states. Integration of MKM systems and environments has not been a factor at all in these earlier implementations due to the specialization of the vendors of the CMMS and CM system vendors – Knowledge Management has been seen as a separate area with its own markets and usage contexts and not viable to integrate in an efficient manner into CMMS and CM environments. It is the responsibility of the maintainer to correctly insert the appropriate fault or work code into the maintenance logs, which to date has not been done with sufficient accuracy or consistency to be deemed reliable. The example presented in figure 1, is a demonstrator of an integrated end-user environment supporting modular and work context-centric approach to information management for multiple organizational layers in an I-Maintenance structure. This demonstrator presents the ability to support end-user adaptation of the overall work environment depending on work roles, deployment environment and user access control structures. It also presents a concept for end-user controlled mash-up (systems able to present and manage information from many disparate information sources and services – all presented in one unified end-user environment). This demonstrator is based on research covering end-user environments for qualified maintenance of advanced technical systems (military fighters) allowing integration of knowledge / practices / experiences / standards management into a unified and integrated environment [8].

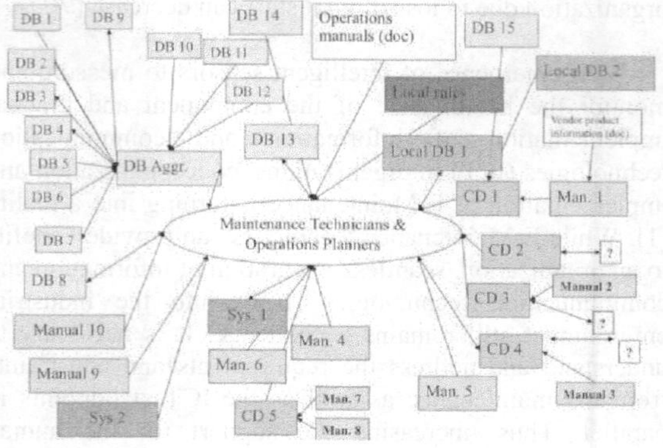

Figure 1: Integration of CM/CMMS/MKM and support for multiple work contexts. Courtesy of Enviro Data, Sweden

The above demonstrator is developed in response to information logistics and knowledge support challenges for maintenance planners and staff supporting advanced systems. Figure 2 presents an anonymized schema of different information and data sources needed for maintenance planning and work for this system. The same scenario is present in many other contexts, organizations and processes. The main challenge for managing this is to create productive and effective end-user environments to allow management and handling of all these disparate information and competence resource sources and access methods. This is a good example of the challenges for integrate CMMS, CM and MKM resources and in parallel allow for effective collaboration.

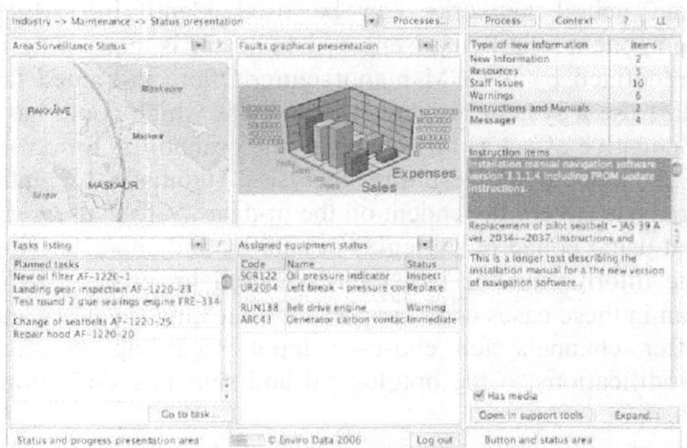

Figure 2: Example of an information sources map for a maintenance operations planner

B. Definition of Integration / Relation Process

Although there have been many recent efforts to collect and maintain large repositories of CMMS and CM data but there have been relatively few studies to identify the ways these two datasets could be related. There are even less examples of how the CMMS, CM and MKM resources can be linked and managed in effective work contexts. It is only logical to assume that written histories of maintenance records are linked to the measurements of onboard sensors, and it is in the interest of CBM research to develop a means by which these data sets can be consistently and reliably merged. At the same time relevant competence resources connected to the asset has to be effectively managed and updated in end-user environments that do not introduces additional complexities for the users during their most prevalent work contexts and processes. A full integration of CMMS and CM datasets requires a more advanced form of interfacing which more appropriately models the real-world relationships between observed maintenance and sensor data. Case studies to date have been generated by individuals who identify related events based upon their knowledge of the systems involved. For example, an abrupt change in a vibration sensor on a gearbox is assumed to be related to a recorded replacement of a nearby part. Taking an analytical approach to this decision making process is rather complex, since the determination of causality and dependence is often performed through a highly subjective process. MKMs can in this case increase the accuracy of the analysis by effectively supplying earlier experiences, faults and conclusions and at the same time speed up the processes by allowing faster access to external specialists and competence resources of different types. An MKM environment can also support wider and more complex analysis of overall process dependencies and more complex logging of faults and corrective actions than those allowed by the current selection of CMMS's.

The overall goal of an enhanced interfacing should seek to automate the complex process of linking events from different datasets – preferably utilizing SOA to guarantee the security of the data. Developing this system begins with a four-step investigation: historical data collection, importation into a single database, data abstraction, and data analysis. Using a wealth of historical information in combination with knowledge of system components, software agents are under development that attempts to bridge the gap between the data types by allowing for the proximity, severity, and rarity of events across datasets to be evaluated. Figure 3 describes a process utilizing direct integration of datasets, not SOA-based interaction. Through an integrated CM and CMMS system, identifying instances where CM data is reflected by real-world events can be performed regularly. This allows for an objective determination of asset parts prone to failure and an evaluation of CM effectiveness in monitoring those regions. Based upon these evaluations feedback can be given to CMMS and CM developers to refine the means by which the data is collected, and a strategy for the next generation of fully-integrated CBM systems can be devised. This can be one of the tasks for MKM environments – acting as a collaborative platform for collecting, evaluating and analyzing earlier experiences, mitigation methods and processes and support for internal practices development.

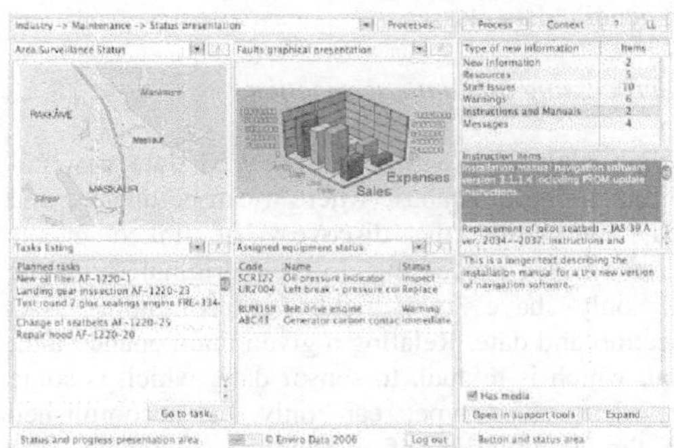

Figure 3. Depiction of the four-stage integration process

C. Data source collection

The history of Maintenance Management Systems predates the information age, it has traditionally been delegated to the unit-level for implementation. Collecting data for investigation studies has required the permission of various units, thus limiting the scale of CMMS research to date. As a result, efforts to centralize CMMS data have been slow to materialize therefore; data collection for early integration studies remains a small sample of the future capabilities of a centralized CBM system. In contrast, CM developers have relied on automated data centralization to evaluate and validate their systems since their inception. In order to minimize risk for un-intended sabotage of the measurement data due to faulty installation routines and low experience of handling the measurement equipment the organization can utilize MKM structures to integrate effective training efforts and eventual certification processes into the overall installation and maintenance of the measurement equipment.

D. Relational data importation

Modern CMMS information is stored in large relational, or tabular, databases. This format is appropriate for an integration investigation since there are a large number of software tools available to query and investigate the tables. For the historical analysis, only certain fields are required, thus allowing for the previously mentioned sensitive data to be removed or filtered. The data subset still contains a full history of component faults and related actions, providing a comprehensive maintenance history profile while alleviating security concerns.

Importing CM data into a relational database is somewhat more challenging, since each type of sensor generates different data classes, sampling rates, and number of compiled indicators. Furthermore, each manufacturer stores the collected information in unique proprietary formats, requiring platform-specific importation software to be written. This software allows the CM data to be exported from the original interface so that it can be expanded and generalized. Once this is accomplished, the benefits are tremendous: multiple manufacturer and cross-platform data can be viewed as through generic data classes.

E. Pre-processing and data abstraction

Although both the CMMS and the CM data now co-exist within a single database where it can be queried and explored, automating the discovery of linked events requires additional processing. In their original form, the datasets only have two fields in common: asset identification and date. Relating a given maintenance fault or action, which is textual, to sensor data, which is some arbitrary data class type, can only be accomplished through the compilation of overlapping metadata. The fields that are generated characterize the location and significance of events, creating a quantified set of parameters by which the disparate data can be compared.
Since CMMS is textual, it is processed using artificial intelligence (AI) tools applied to language processing (LP), [6]. LP is a subfield of both artificial intelligence as well as linguistics with a large variety of applications. It covers a many of topics ranging from machine translation to speech recognition and often focuses on a computer's ability to interpret and respond to natural human languages. A recent success in LP has been auto-summarization and information extraction. Due to the specific context of maintenance management data, in which descriptions of assets faults and performed actions are stored, the lexical domain is highly restricted and text CMMS fields can be analyzed separately to create a set of interpreters which extract key information from the fault or action description. The AI LP tool outputs which component the record is in reference to and a list of other descriptor keywords. Categorical statistical analyses are performed to characterize the rarity of a given record, and a pre-programmed scoring chart assigns each record a severity based on the available keywords. One additional level of abstraction of data for CM records is generated differently depending on the data class involved. Identifying anomalies can be performed using statistical distribution analysis and in the case of multidimensional data neural networks can be used identifying which component a particular sensor or indicator is monitoring is predefined by the CM manufacturer.Often un-trained the staff use a system for semantic analysis which could have a negative effect as this increases the probability for errors and faults in the resulting analysis. Automatic semantic analysis is very dependent on the in-data -> if the users are not using coherent strategies in naming and characterizing the information the larger the potential for errors. MKM can in these cases offer support for educating the users and offer channels for end-user input regarding eventual modifications to the ontological and semantic definitions used.

F. Analysis and Correlation

The metadata is then extracted from all the available records into a single events table containing asset identification, component name, event time, a rarity parameter, and a severity parameter. The simplest method of determination of event-relatedness is accomplished through a proximity study of the metadata. The results of this analysis could then be categorized by component and identify parts of the assets where CM devices have a high success rate in identifying component faults or reflecting maintenance actions. Known problematic subsystems that do not have a high count of related CMMS and CM events indicate that revision to the sensing strategy or changes in indicator definition are needed. For these components, further analysis can be performed on the raw data to discover new algorithms for condition indicator computation. However this computation is extremely complex due to the multi-location structure of many companies with lots of information systems related to maintenance in each of them (CMMS, CM, phones, PDA, laptops, SCADA, ERP…). Replication of all data in order to perform this correlation is not feasible and would require enormous computation resources, that is why the concept of cloud computing is seen as the answer in creating these metadata from all available information.

The analysis and correlation steps demands high levels of competence and experience - which is tricky to achieve when the number of equipment is high, very large number of variants exists and there are not enough units of a specific kind to locally create high expertise on the units in question. A MKM environment can offer structures for collaboration between the specialists and maintenance staff covering the fault modes, mitigating efforts, experiences and practices. A MKM can also offer collaborative environments for collective assistance in faults analysis and CM analysis.

III. CONCLUSIONS

Organizations can benefit greatly by integrating and synthesize information coordinated and managed from CMMS and CM systems and processes. This example of information logistics that is often characterized as E-Maintenance cannot as the research has shown fully deliver on its promises without integration and coordination with environments for management of knowledge, practices and experiences in combination with collaborative structures. This combination and integration of CMMS, CM, MKM environments (including practices and experience management) and collaborative / simulation tools and infrastructures can be labeled I-Maintenance – Intelligence-based Maintenance. I-Maintenance aims at integrating the knowledge and skills of the operators and maintenance planners into the processes to minimize costs, risks and increasing the overall performance.

This paper has shown the importance of providing maintenance managers with accurate and up to date information and insights using Maintenance knowledge systems, information and insights that will assist in the further implementation of IT in their processes and more accurately evaluate the IT systems and their contribution to the overall organizational performance. The ongoing efforts to simplify integration and coordination of systems by utilizing Service Oriented Architectures (SOA) will also allow for a faster and more effective implementation of I-Maintenance systems.

The final I-Maintenance system will manifest itself as an automated maintenance exploration interface in combination with end-use adaptable interfaces to a large number of different information sources and internal / external services. Users will be able to quickly identify possible diagnoses of faults and quickly retrieve historical maintenance actions that were effective in resolving the problem and exchange new ideas and practices for future use. Such a system would be easily scalable across several CM platforms, several asset types, and several locations, allowing for maintainers to have information on a variety of practices being performed across the field and with parallel access to a wide range of competence resources, experiences and collaboration with external and internal specialists. The majority of CMMS vendors recognize the necessity to move forward quickly. Because of this, all attempts to integrate CMMS, CM and MKM are going to be a key part of maintenance technology in the future. Currently, this integration consists of a common framework for data exchange. No real relations and context information is extracted from the huge amount of data included in these warehouses.

References

1. A. Parida and U. Kumar, (2004), Managing Information is the key to Maintenance Effectiveness, e-Proceedings of Intelligent Maintenance System, Arles, France, 15-17
2. Kahn, J and Klemme-Wolf, H (2004), Overview of MIMOSA and the Open System Architecture for Enterprise Application Integration," Proceedings of the 17th European Maintenance Congress,. 333-341,
3. X. Wang, C. Liu and J. Lee, (2004), Intelligent Maintenance Based on Multi-sensor Data Fusion to Web-enabled Automation Systems, e-Proceedings of Intelligent Maintenance System, , Arles, France, 15-17
4. J. Baptiste, (2004), A case study of remote diagnosis and E-Maintenance information system, e-Proceedings of Intelligent Maintenance System, , Arles, France, 15-17.
5. B. Thomas, R. Denis, S. Jacek, T. Jean-Pierre and Z. Noureddine,(2004), PROTEUS – An Integration Platform for Distributed Maintenance Systems, e-Proceedings of Intelligent Maintenance System' (IMS' 2004), , Arles, France, 15-17.
6. Manning, C. and Schutze , H.,(1999), Foundations of Statistical Natural Language Processing.. Press, Cambridge, MA
7. M. A. Vouk,(2008) Cloud computing Issues, research and implementations. In 30th International Conference on Information Technology Interfaces (ITI 2008). Cavtat/Dubrovnik, Croatia, , 31-40.
8. S-E Björling, Uday Kumar,(2009),ICT Concepts for Managing Future Challenges in E-Maintenance, COMADEM 2009, San Sebastian, Spain
9. Ivana Rasovska · Brigitte Chebel-Morello · Noureddine Zerhouni (2008)A mix method of knowledge capitalization in maintenance, Journal of Intelligent Manufacturing, 19:347–359
10. Mattias Holmgren, Maintenance-related incidents and accidents – Aspects from Hazard Identification, Doctoral Thesis, Luleå University of Technology

Sentimental Analysis on Turkish Blogs via Ensemble Classifier

Sadi Evren SEKER
Dept. of Business Administration
Istanbul Medeniyet University
academic@sadievrenseker.com

Khaled Al-NAAMI
Computer Science Department
The University of Texas at Dallas
kma041000@utdallas.edu

ABSTRACT
Sentimental analysis on web-mined data has an increasing impact on most of the studies. Sentimental influence of any content on the web is one of the most curios questions by the content creators and publishers. In this study, we have researched the impact of the comments collected from five different web sites in Turkish with more than 2 million comments in total. The web sites are from newspapers; movie reviews, e-marketing web site and a literature web site. We mix all the comments into a single file. The comments also have a like or dislike number, which we use as ground proof of the impact of the comment, as the sentimental of the comment. We try to correlate the text of comment and the like / dislike grade of the proof. We use three classifiers as support vector machine, k-nearest neighborhood and C4.5 decision tree classifier. On top of them, we add an ensemble classifier based on the majority voting. For the feature extraction from the text, we use the term frequency – inverse document frequency approach and limit the top most features depending on their information gain. The result of study shows that there are about 56% correlation between the blogs and comments and their like / dislike score depending on our classification model.

Keywords
Data Mining, Sentimental Analysis, Big Data, Text Mining

1. INTRODUCTION
The data set on this study is collected from internet for one of the high-circulating newspapers, a movie review web page with highest comments, an e-marketing web site with highest comments and a literature web site holding poems and novels all in Turkish. The properties of the dataset will be explained in the experiments section. We have processed the comments with text mining approach called term frequency - inverse document frequency (TF-IDF), which will be explained in the methodology section. On the other hand, we have accepted the number of like or dislike as the ground proof of the impact of the comment. Finally we have investigated the correlation between the features extracted from text mining and signal processing to compare the effect of signal processing outputs into the economy news. During this correlation study, we have implemented k-nearest neighborhood (KNN), C4.5 decision tree (C4.5) and support vector machine (SVM) algorithms, which are discussed in the section of classification. Moreover we have implemented an ensemble classifier over those three classifiers, which is based on majority voting (MaVL), which will also be explained in the background section. Finally, this paper holds the implementation details and the methodology of evaluation over classification results, which are held in the evaluation section.

2. PROBLEM STATEMENT
This study is the first time to address the correlation effect of the comment text and like / dislike count of comments for Turkish data sources.

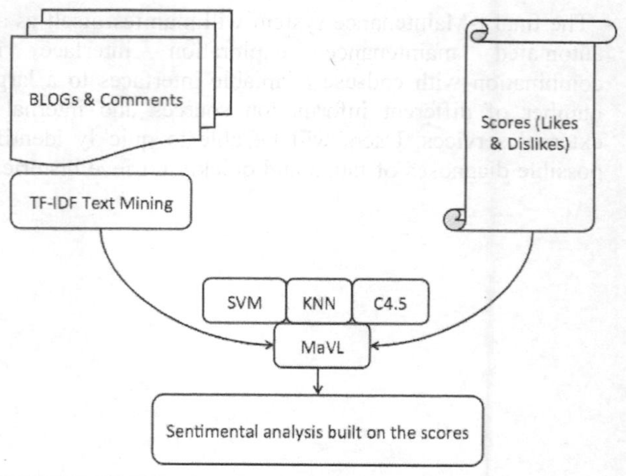

Figure 1. Overview of Study

One of the difficulties in this study is dealing with natural language data source, which requires a feature extraction. The other difficulty is dealing with large number of comments, which can be accepted as big data problem. The dataset holds 131,248 distinct words and when the feature vector of each economy news item is collected, the total size of the feature vector is over 32.5 GByte, which is beyond the computation capacity of a single computer with these classification algorithms. For a simple SVM implementation the required RAM is slightly more than 1TB.

3. RELATED WORK

Current studies on sentimental analysis on web-mined data has a great impact for the both content authors and publishers. For example the impact of a politician's speech can now be monitored real-time by the help of current studies[1]. For example, the researchs on Arabic Spring and the effect of social media on the Tunisian case [1] or French Presidental Election and social media research [2] or Iran Green Movement from the twitter data [3] or research on UK 2010 election and effect of social media [4] are only a few researches on the topic.

In most of the researches, the data is collected from the social media like Twitter [1-4] or Facebook [5] or e-learning environments mixed with social networks[6]. All of these studies have a text mining part. Zhai[7] shows that the studies based on TF-IDF has a higher success than suffix tress or n-gram based approaches for Chinese case with the SVM classifier.

Some of the reseraches prefers using the metrics built on the social network itself. For example in Twitter, it is possible to get the number of followers and following and such information may be useful to calculate the political views of people depending on who they follow as in UK Election research [4] where the feature extraction is built on the followers/following. Or on some other researches, text mining approaches like bag of words, interjection of emotics, part of speech tagging methods are implemented together [6].

4. BACKGROUND

We have implemented TF-IDF and classification methods as already explained in the introduction; this section will discuss these methods in detail. Also one of the difficulties is the number of words we are dealing with. We have implemented the information gain calculation for eliminating some of the features. Finally the evaluation and error calculation methods will be explained in detail.

4.1. Term Frequency – Inverse Document Frequency

TF-IDF is one of the text mining methods used for feature extraction from natural language data sources[7,8,9].

For the TF-IDF calculation is given in equation (1).

$$tfidf(t,d,D) = tf(t,d)x\ idf(t,D) \quad (1)$$

Where t is the selected term, d is the selected document and D is all documents in the corpus. Also TF-IDF calculation in above formula is built over term frequency (TF) and inverse document frequency (IDF), which can be rewritten as in equation (2).

$$tf(t,d) = \frac{f(t,d)}{\max\{f(w,d): w \in d\}} \quad (2)$$

where f is the frequency function and w is the word with maximum occurrence. Also the formulation of IDF is given in equation (3).

$$id(t,D) = log\frac{|D|}{|\{d \in D : t \in d\}|} \quad (3)$$

where $|D|$ indicates the cardinality of D, which is the total number of documents in the corpus.

4.2. Information Gain

The information gain of all the terms is calculated and ordered in descending order. Let *Attr* be the set of all attributes and E_x be the set of all training examples, *value(x,a)* with $x \in E_x$ defines the value of a specific example x or attribute $a \in Attr$, H, specifies the entropy. The information gain for an attribute $a \in Attr$ is defined as in equation (4).

$$IG(Ex,a) = H(Ex) - \\ - \sum_{v \in v(a)} \frac{|x \in Ex|v(x,a)|}{|Ex|} H(x \in Ex|v(x,a)) \quad (4)$$

Also entropy in the information gain calculation can be rewritten as in equation (5).

$$H(X) = \sum_{i=1}^{n} P(x_i)I(x_i) = \sum_{i=1}^{n} P(x_i)\log_b\left(\frac{1}{P(x_i)}\right) \\ = \sum_{i=1}^{n} P(x_i)\log_b(P(x_i)) \quad (5)$$

4.3. K- Nearest Neighborhood (KNN)

The k, c-neighborhood (or k, c(x) in short) of an U-outlier x is the set of k class c instances that are nearest to x (k-nearest class c neighbors of x).

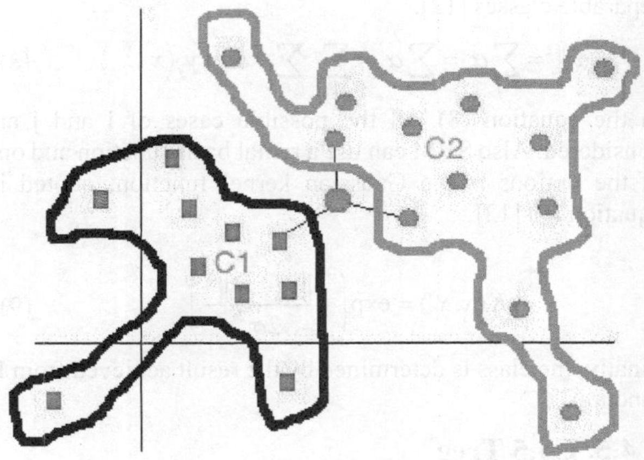

Figure 2. Visualization of K-NN

The K-NN [10] is explained in Figure 2. Here k is a user defined parameter. For example, k, $c_1(x)$ of an U-outliers x is the k-nearest class c_1 neighbors of x.

Let $\overline{D}_{Cout,q}(x)$ be the mean distance of a U-outlier x to its k-nearest U-outlier neighbors. Also, let $\overline{D}_{C,q}(x)$ be the mean distance from x to its $k,c(x)$, and let $\overline{D}_{Cmin,q}(x)$ be the minimum among all $\overline{D}_{C,q}(x)$, c ∈ {Set of existing classes}. In order words, k , c_{min} is the nearest existing class neighborhood of x. Then k-NSC of x is given in equation (6).

$$k-NSC(x)=\frac{\overline{D}_{C\min,q}(x)-\overline{D}_{Cout,q}(x)}{\max(\overline{D}_{C\min,q}(x),\overline{D}_{Cout,q}(x))} \quad (6)$$

4.4. Support Vector Machine (SVM)

The reason of applying SVM method as in Figure 3 over the dataset is determining the boundaries between classes [11.

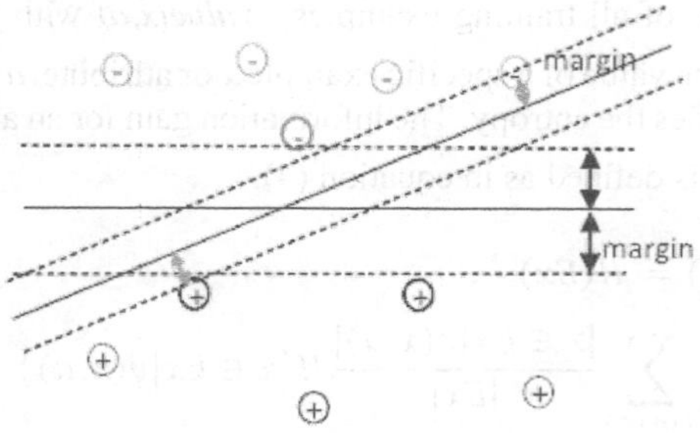

Figure 3. SVM boundary and margins

SVM aims to classify the samples into groups and define a boundary between the groups. SVM also tries to find out the maximum margin possibility between the groups [11].

$$\| \omega \| = \sum_{i=1}^{n} \alpha_i y_i x_i \quad (7)$$

The margin between the classes is symbolized by ω symbol in equation (7) and SVM seeks to maximize the value of ω. The above formula can be rewritten as below for the linearly separable classes [12].

$$\| \omega \|^2 = \sum_{i=1}^{l} \alpha_i = \sum_{iSVs} \alpha_i = \sum_{iSVs} \sum_{iSVs} \alpha_i \alpha_j y_i y_j \langle x_i, x_j \rangle \quad (8)$$

In the equation (8), all the possible cases of i and j are considered. Also SVM can use a radial basis function and one of the options is the Gaussian kernel function, quoted in equation (9) [12].

$$K(x,x') = \exp\left(-\frac{\|x-x'\|^2}{2\sigma^2}\right) \quad (9)$$

Finally, the class is determined by the result achieved from K function.

4.5. C4.5 Tree

C4.5 method [13] is a decision tree based classification algorithm. The tree is built by using the information gain of each feature in the feature vector.

The algorithm starts with a training data set S where S= { s_1, s_2 , … s_n } where each sample s_i has a p dimensional feature vector, FV.

For each sample s_i, FV = { x_{1i}, x_{2i}, … x_{pi} } and the information gain of each values would be IG = { ig(x_{1i}), ig(x_{2i}), … ig(x_{pi})}.

The algorithm creates a decision tree where each node defines a decision to either side.

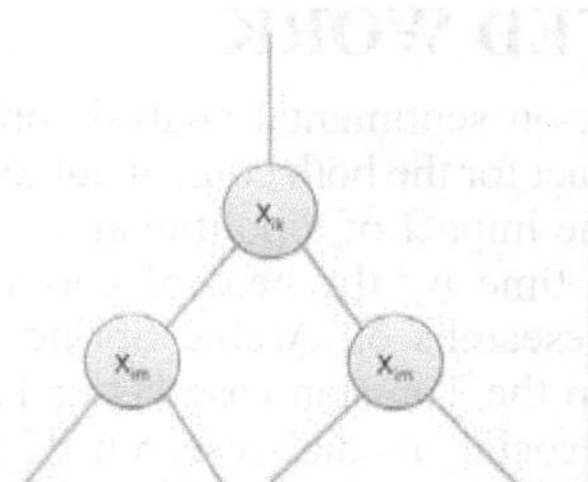

Figure 4. C4.5 Tree Demonstration

The highest information gain value is selected for the top most decision node and the second is get the decision criteria on the next level. Let ig (x_{ik}) > ig (x_{im}) for the Figure 4. The tree is constructed by following the similar approach for the next levels. Finally at the leaves, the samples are placed after the training.

In the time of testing, the features extracted from test samples are questioned via the decision nodes in the tree from root to leaves. The final leaf is accepted as the class of the test sample.

C4.5 has an advantage on other decision trees, since it uses the information gain and normalization and also it uses the prunning for the time performance.

4.6. Ensemble Classification

We have implmented a majority vote learning (MaVL or Marvel) [16] based ensemble method to combine three different classification methods. MV can be considered as a meta classifier which works over the classifiers like KNN, C4.5 or SVM in our case.

Let $S_i \in S$ where S is the set of classifiers and let $C_i \in C$ where C is the set of classes,

$$C(x) = argmax_i \sum_{j=1}^{B} w_j I(S_j(x) = i) \quad (10)$$

Where w_j is the weight of each indicator function I(•) which is added into the equation for normalization and the weights of each classifier is equal in our model.

Marvel, gets the summation for each of the classifier's vote and the sample is classified into the class with the highest vote.

4.7. Error Rate Calculation

The error rate of the system is calculated through root mean square error (RMSE). The calculation of RMSE is given in equation (11) [14].

$$x_{rmse} = \frac{\sqrt{x_1^2 + x_2^2 + \ldots + x_n^2}}{n} \quad (11)$$

For this study, above x values are the results achieved from the implementation of the algorithm. The RMSE result of 0 is considered ideal and lower values close to 0 are relatively better.

By the results fetched from the output layer and the calculation of RMSE, the algorithm back propagates to the weight values of the synapses.

Also the results are interpreted by using a second error calculation method RRSE (Root Relative Squared Error) and the calculation is given in equation (12) [15].

$$x_{rrse} = \sqrt{\frac{\sum_{j=1}^{n}(P_{ij} - T_j)}{\sum_{j=1}^{n}(T_j - \bar{T})^2}} \quad (12)$$

Where P_{ij} is the value predicted for the sample case j, T_j is the target value for sample case $_j$ and $\bar{T}$ is calculated by equation (13) [17].

$$\bar{T} = \frac{1}{n}\sum_{j=1}^{n} T_j \quad (13)$$

The RRSE value ranges from 0 to ∞, with 0 corresponding to ideal.

The third error calculation method is RAE (Relative Absolute Error) and the calculation is given in equation (14) [15].

$$E_i = \frac{\sum_{j=1}^{n} |P_{(ij)} - T_j|}{\sum_{j=1}^{n} |T_j - \bar{T}|} \quad (14)$$

$P_{(ij)}$ is the value predicted by the individual program i for sample case j (out of n sample cases), T_j is the target value for sample case j, and $\bar{T}$ is given by the equation (15) [15]:

$$\bar{T} = \frac{1}{n}\sum_{j=1}^{n} T_j \quad (15)$$

For a perfect fit, the numerator is equal to 0 and E_i=0 So, the E_i index ranges from 0 to infinity, with 0 corresponding to the ideal.

Also the success rate of prediction and expectation can be measured as the f-measure method. The f-measure method is built on the Table 1.

Table 1. f-measure method

		Predictions	
Expectations		Positive	Negative
	True	True Positive	True Negative
	False	False Positive	False Negative

The calculation of f-measure can be given as in equation (16) depending on the Table 1.

$$F_{measure} = \frac{2TP}{2TP + FN + FP} \quad (16)$$

5. EXPERIMENTS

In this study the dataset is in natural language and some preprocessing for the feature extraction from the data source is required. The first approach is applying the TF-IDF for the all terms in the data source. Unfortunately the hardware in the study environment was not qualifying the requirements for the feature extraction of all the terms in data source which is 139,434.

5.1. Dataset

We have implemented our approach and Table 2 demonstrates the features of the datasets.

Table 2. Properties of the Dataset

	News
# of News	9871
Authors	6881
Texts per Author	Mean (μ) : 44.05 Stddev(σ) : 535.52
Average word length	~6.7

The above dataset is collected from the web site of a high-circulating newspaper in Turkey. The data is collected directly from a database so the noisy parts on the web page like ads, comments, links to other news, etc. are avoided. Another problem is the noise of HTML tags in the database entries for formatting the text of news. The data has preprocessed and all the HTML tags are removed from the news and also all punctuations and stop words are removed in the preprocessing phase.

5.2. Feature Extraction

We have implemented a feature extraction algorithm 1 in order to extract two feature vectors.

Algorithm: Feature Extraction Methods

Let E be Economy News Corpus,
Let C be Closings of Stockmarket,
For each $E_i \in E$
For each $Term_j \in E_i$
if(count($Term_j$)>30)
T_j ← TF-IDF of $Term_j$
C_i ← closing_value(date(E_i)) $\in$ C
IG_{ij} ← Information Gain ($Term_j$, E_i)
V_1 ←Top300(sort(IG))
V_2 ←C

The above algorithm demonstrates the extraction of two vectors: one from the economy news corpus and another from the closing values of the stock market. We have limited the number of features to 300 and the Top300 function gets the topmost 300 features from the feature vector.

The V_2 feature vector is calculated easily by checking the closing value of the economy news on the date. There are some news items which are published during the time the stock market is closed like on weekends and we have considered these values as a third class besides the increase and decrease classes.

The correlation algorithms run over the two vectors V_1 and V_2 extracted via the Algorithm 1.

During the execution of algorithm, the execution requires more memory than the available hardware, where we run the algorithms on a intel 7 cpu and 8GByte of RAM. The required memory is calculated in equation (17).

Memory Requirement = 139,434 words x 9871 news x 6.7 average word length x 2 bytes for each character =~17GByte (17)

As a solution we have limited the number of words with the highest occurences. The number of occurences on our implementation is 30 and a word is taken into consideration after this number of occurences. The words appearing above this threshold value are 2878 and the memory required is reduced to 700MByte which is easier to handle in the RAM.

The feature vector extraction is about 56 minutes on average for the economy news.

5.3. Evaluation

The results of executions can be summarized in Table 3.

Table 3. Error and Success Rates of Classification Methods

	f-measure Average	RMSE	RAE	Correctly Classified
Random Walk	0.497	0.4182	0.9921	52.37%
RSI	0.501	0.4404	0.9930	50.70%
MACD	0.491	0.4174	0.9892	52.52%
Bollinger Band	**0.504**	**0.4141**	**0.9810**	**53.49%**

The success rate in Table 3 is the percentage of correctly classified instances. For example, the success rate of Random Walk with length=2 can be considered as the 37% of the instances are correctly classified to predict an increase, decrease or no change in the stock market value depending on the economy news processed.

The time series analysis method, "acceleration" should not be considered because of its unsuitable data output. The acceleration values calculated are either 0 or so close to 0, so the data set expectation was not realistic. This is the reason of high success rate on the acceleartion analysis. On the other hand rest 9 methods are suitable for the correlation and the highest success is achieved from the Bollinger Band with 52% correctly classified news. The success rate achieved in this study is much better than the previous studies[15].

The value of success is highly related with the market structure so the success rate here should not be understood as the success rate of the methodology or the classifier. The success rate in the table is the correlation between economy news and the stock market closing values.

6. CONCLUSION

During this study, it is first time the effect of time series anlaysis methods over the stock market closing values and their correlation with the economy news in the Turkey case has been studied. The feature extraction method and classification methods are kept simple and the study is mainly focused on the time series analysis. The analysis has shown that the success of Bollinger band is higher than the rest.

We believe this study would help to understand the market strength in Turkey from a financial perspective and also the study can help further research with other classification algorithms and feature extraction methodologies.

7. REFERENCES

[1] Younus, A.; Qureshi, M.A.; Asar, F.F.; Azam, M.; Saeed, M.; Touheed, N., "What Do the Average Twitterers Say: A Twitter Model for Public Opinion Analysis in the Face of Major Political Events," Advances in Social Networks Analysis and Mining (ASONAM), 2011 International Conference on , vol., no., pp.618,623, 25-27 July 2011 doi: 10.1109/ASONAM.2011.85 [2] Braun, H. 1987. Predicting stock market behavior through rule induction: an application of the learning-fromexample approach. Decision Sciences, vol. 18, no. 3, pp. 415-429.

[2] Wegrzyn-Wolska, K.; Bougueroua, L., "Tweets mining for French Presidential Election," Computational Aspects of Social Networks (CASoN), 2012 Fourth International Conference on , vol., no., pp.138,143, 21-23 Nov. 2012 doi: 10.1109/CASoN.2012.6412392

[3] Khonsari, K.K.; Nayeri, Z.A.; Fathalian, A.; Fathalian, L., "Social Network Analysis of Iran's Green Movement Opposition Groups Using Twitter," Advances in Social Networks Analysis and Mining (ASONAM), 2010 International Conference on , vol., no., pp.414,415, 9-11 Aug. 2010 doi: 10.1109/ASONAM.2010.75

[4] Boutet, A.; Hyoungshick Kim; Yoneki, E., "What's in Twitter: I Know What Parties are Popular and Who You are Supporting Now!," Advances in Social Networks Analysis and Mining (ASONAM), 2012 IEEE/ACM International Conference on , vol., no., pp.132,139, 26-29 Aug. 2012 doi: 10.1109/ASONAM.2012.32

[5] Neri, F.; Aliprandi, C.; Capeci, F.; Cuadros, M.; By, T., "Sentiment Analysis on Social Media," Advances in Social Networks Analysis and Mining (ASONAM), 2012 IEEE/ACM International Conference on , vol., no., pp.919,926, 26-29 Aug. 2012 doi: 10.1109/ASONAM.2012.164

[6] Martin, J.M.; Ortigosa, A.; Carro, R.M., "SentBuk: Sentiment analysis for e-learning environments," Computers in Education (SIIE), 2012 International Symposium on , vol., no., pp.1,6, 29-31 Oct. 2012

[7] Zhongwu Zhai; Hua Xu; Jun Li; Peifa Jia, "Sentiment classification for Chinese reviews based on key substring features," Natural Language Processing and Knowledge Engineering, 2009. NLP-KE 2009. International Conference on , vol., no., pp.1,8, 24-27 Sept. 2009

doi: 10.1109/NLPKE.2009.5313782

[8] Zhai, Y., Hsu, A., and Halgamuge, S. 2007.Combining News and Technical Indicators in Daily Stock Price Trends Prediction. Lecture Notes in Computer Science. 1087-1096.

[9] Fung, G., Yu, J., and Lam, W.2002. News sensitive stock trend prediction. Lecture Notes in Computer Science, vol. Volume 233, 481– 493.

[10] Masud, M. M., Al-Khateeb, T. M., Khan, L., Aggarwal, C. C., Gao, J., Han, J., and Thuraisingham, B. M.2011. Detecting recurring and novel classes in concept-drifting data streams. In *Proceedings of the 2011 IEEE 11th International Conference on Data Mining*.(Vancouver, Canada, December 11-14, 2011)IEEE Computer Society Washington, DC, USA , 1176–1181. DOI= http://dx.doi.org/10.1109/ICDM.2011.49

[11] W. H. Press, S. A. Teukolsky, W. T. Vetterlinga and B. P. Flannery , Numerical recipes: the art of scientific computing, Cambridge University Press, New York, 2007.

[12] S. R. Gunn, Support vector machines for classification and regression, University of Southamtpon, Technical Report, 1998.

[13] Yahia, M.E. and Ibrahim, B. A. 2003. K-nearest neighbor and C4.5 algorithms as data mining methods: advantages and difficulties. In Proceedings of Computer Systems and Applications, 2003. Book of Abstracts. ACS/IEEE International Conference on. (Tunis, Tunisia, July 14-18, 2003)

[14] K. V. Cartwright, Determining the effective or RMS voltage of various waveforms without calculus, Ph.D. Thesis, School of Sciences and Technology College of the Bahamas, Bahamas, 2007.

[15] Seker, S. E.;Ozalp N. ; Al-Naami, K. ; Mert C. ; Khan, L. , "Correlation Between Turkish Stock Market and EconomyNews", *Reliability Aware* Data Fusion, held along with SIAM International Conference on Data Mining 2013 (*SDM* 2013), May 2013, Austin, TX, USA

Reliable Probabilistic Classification of Mammographic Masses using Random Forests

Hechmi Shili[1,2], **Lotfi Ben Romdhane**[1,3], **and Béchir el Ayeb**[2]
[1]MARS Research Group, Faculty of Sciences of Monastir
[2]University of Monastir, Monastir, Tunisia
[3]High School of Sciences and Technology, Hammam-Sousse, University of Sousse

Abstract— *Mammography is the most effective method for identifying breast cancer in its earliest stages. Random forests (RF) have been successfully used for the task of classification with good performance, but without information about the reliability in classifications. In this paper, we present a novel reliable probabilistic approach to classify mammographic masses as benign, malignant and normal tissues. The main aim of this paper is to improve the performance of Random forests by introducing a recently developed algorithmic framework, namely the Venn Probability Machine, for making reliable decisions in the face of uncertainty.*

Keywords: Mammography, Probabilistic classification; Random forests; Venn prediction.

1. Introduction and Background

Breast cancer is the most common cause of cancer-related death in women worldwide, with some 327 000 deaths each year. Nearly 1.4 million cases of breast cancer were diagnosed across the world in 2008, compared with about 500 000 cases in 1975. This represents about 11% of all new cancer cases and 23% of all female cancers. It is predicted that the number of cases will rise to 1.7 million by 2020 [6]. Primary prevention seems impossible since the causes of this disease are still remaining unidentified. Early detection is the key to the ultimate survival rate for breast cancer patients. For women whose tumors were discovered early, the five year survival rate was about 82%, as opposed 60% that not been found early [6].

Mammography is still the most effective screening method for detecting breast cancer in its early, most treatable stages. However, the low positive predictive value of breast biopsy examinations resulting from mammogram interpretation leads to approximately 70% unnecessary biopsies performed on benign lesions. Computer-aided diagnosis (CADx) systems have been developed to assist the radiologist in the discrimination of benign and malignant breast lesions and thus to reduce the high number of unnecessary biopsies. It is important to realize that the classification of suspicious abnormalities in digital mammograms is an extremely challenging task for a number of reasons. First, it is a challenge to select a good feature set for the classification of mammogram. Second, abnormalities are often occluded or hidden in dense breast tissue, which makes detection difficult. Finally, symptoms of abnormal tissue may remain quite subtle. For example, speculated masses that may indicate a malignant tissue within the breast are often difficult to correctly diagnose, especially at the early stage of development.

As such, an increasing number of researchers have focused on the classification of suspicious masses in mammograms. Quite a lot of researchers apply the classification techniques to classify the marked region in the mammogram. Classifiers like decision tree classifiers [15], [8], Support Vector Machines [9], [16], k-nearest neighbors [12] and Artificial Neural Network [7], [1] have performed better in mass classification.

Most of the methods mentioned previously provide too little insight as to the importance of variables to the predictor derived. The transparency is very important in some application areas such as medical decision support. By contrast, classification and regression trees are known for their transparency. Decision tree have been widely and successfully used in mammographic mass classification.

In [15], the authors used a method based on binary trees for the classification of mammograms. Global feature extraction from different levels wavelet decomposition of normal and abnormal images was also used in this work. This classifier is then used to classify whether an entire whole-field mammogram is normal. However, in such a binary tree classifier, errors may accumulate from one level to another, thus making the classification erroneous. Hence, this method resulted in false positive in more than 50% of the cases, making it unreliable.

In [8], the authors discusses the effectiveness of using decision trees for mass classification in mammography. Different costs for type I and type II misclassification were applied for the experiments. The results obtained using algorithms based on decision trees were compared with that produced by neural network which was reported giving the higher classification rate than statistical models, with higher standard deviation. It is concluded that the decision trees are very promising for the classification of breast masses in digital mammograms. However, decision trees are rather unstable: small changes in the training set can result in different trees and different predictions for the same validation examples. It has been demonstrated that this problem can be mitigated by applying bagging [4]. Random Forests (RF) proposed by Breiman [4] is a combination of the random subspace method and bagging.

In [17], an approach using Random Forests Decision Classifier (RFDC), involving regression trees, has been used in mammogram classification. The technique in [17] yielded an accuracy of nearly 90%. However, this method is not very reliable as features are randomly selected in the tree induction process.

In [10], the authors investigated the usage of Random forests classifier for the classification of masses with geometry and texture features. The experiments are tested using a database of 236 clinical mammograms. This method achieved an average area under the ROC curve of 0.86 with Support Vector Machines (SVM) and 0.83 with Random forests. The experimental result shows that Random forests is a promising method for the diagnosis of masses.

Meyer et al. [11] compared 17 classifiers on 21 datasets obtained from the above-mentioned repository. RF outperformed neural network in terms of average test set errors in 15 cases, SVM in 7 cases. The authors concluded that ensemble methods - such as RF - proved very competitive, and often produce adequate results "out of the box", whereas SVM react very delicately to parameter tuning.

However, like most machine learning algorithms, Random forests outputs the label predictions for new instances without indicating how reliable the predictions are. The applicability of these classifiers is limited in critical domains where incorrect predictions have serious consequences, like medical diagnosis. Further, the default assumption of equal misclassification costs is most likely violated in medical diagnosis. This paper addresses the importance of reliability and confidence for classification, and presents a novel method based on a combination of Random forests, and Venn Prediction (VP) [18].

Venn Prediction is an extension of the original conformal predictor (CP) framework , which can be used for making multiprobability predictions [18]. In particular multiprobability predictions are a set of probability distributions for the true classification of the new example. This set can be summarized by lower and upper bounds for the conditional probability of the new example belonging to each one of the possible classes. The resulting bounds are guaranteed to contain well-calibrated probabilities (up to statistical fluctuations). Again, like with CPs, the only assumption made for obtaining this guaranty is that the data are are generated independently by the same probability distribution (i.i.d). The VP framework has until now been combined with the k-nearest neighbours algorithm in [18], [5], with SVMs in [19] and more recently with Neural Networks in [13].

This work is aimed at improving performance of the current mass classification methods using Random Froest classifiers. The novelty of this research is in exploiting the superiority of Venn prediction to produce probability estimates that are guaranteed to be well calibrated. The rest of this paper is organized as follows: Section 2 describes about the Random forests method. Section 3, details the Venn Prediction framework. Section 4 presents our proposed Algorithm for classifying masses in breast. Section 5 describes the experiments that have been conducted on benchmark data set. Finally, Section 6 presents some concluding remarks.

2. Random Forests

Random Forests (RF) is an ensemble learning technique developed by Breiman [4]. This technique combines many decision trees to make a prediction, giving as output the class that is the mode of the classes output by individual trees.

RFs is a family of methods, made of different decision tree ensemble induction algorithms, such as the Breiman Forest-RI method often cited as the reference algorithm in the literature [4]. In this algorithm, the training set for each individual tree in a Random forests is constructed by sampling N examples at random with replacement from the N available examples in the dataset. This is known as bootstrap sampling, and bagging describes the aggregation of predictions from the resulting collection of trees. As a result of the bootstrap sampling procedure, approximately one third of the available N examples are not present in the training set of each tree. The "out-of-bag" predictions are those predictions derived from non-bootstrapped observations which built that particular tree.

In this induction algorithm, a feature subset is randomly drawn for each node, from which the best splitting criterion is then selected according to the Gini index (Breiman et al., [3]), which measures the likelihood that an example would be incorrectly labelled if it were randomly classified according to the distribution of labels within the node. For a binary split, the Gini index of a node n may be expressed as $I_G(n) = 1 - \sum_{c=1}^{2} p_c^2$, where p_c is the relative proportion of examples belonging to class c present in node n. Thus, the Forest-RI Algorithm grows a decision tree using the following process :

Let T be the number of trees to build, for each of $|T|$ iterations

1) Select a new bootstrap sample from training set.
2) Grow an un-pruned tree on this bootstrap.
3) At each internal node, randomly select try m predictors and determine the best split using only these predictors.
4) Output overall prediction as the majority vote from all individually trained trees.

Figure 1 illustrates the workflow for random forests, where y_1, y_2, ...; y_c are class labels. As more trees are added to RF, the generalization error converges to a limiting value, thus there is no over-fitting in large RFs [4].

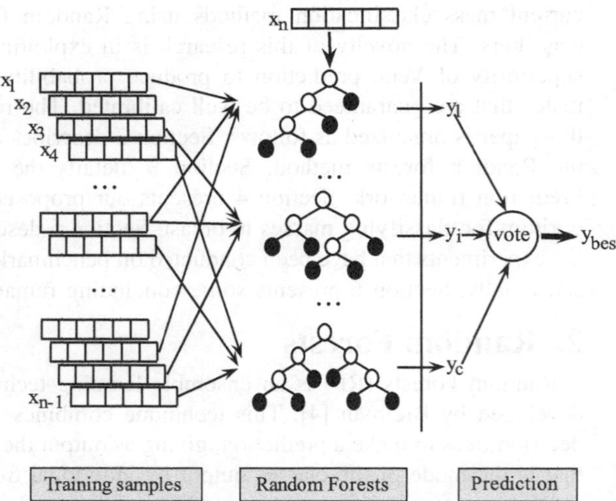

Fig. 1: General architecture of RF classifier.

The main advantage of Random Forests over other techniques such as Artificial Neural Networks, Support Vector Machines, Linear Discriminant Analysis, etc. is the robustness of this technique regarding solution over fitting, tending to converge always when the number of trees is large.

To assess the importance of a specific predictor variable (feature), the values of the variable in the out-of-bag samples are randomly permuted and then the modified out-of-bag samples are passed down the tree to get new predictions. The increase of estimation error for the modified and original out-of-bag data provides a useful measure for determining the feature importance, although feature selection is not needed in RF (Breiman and Cutler, [2]).

3. The framework of Venn machines

This section provides a brief overview of the Venn prediction mechanism; for more details the interested reader is referred to [18].

Let us consider a training set consisting of examples $Z = \{(x_i, y_i)\}_{i=1}^{n-1}$, where each $x_i \in \mathbb{R}^d$ is the vector of attributes for example i and $y_i \in Y = \{y_j\}_{j=1}^{c}$ is the class label of that example. Let x_n be a new unclassified example. Our task is to predict the probability of this new example belonging to each class $y_j \in Y$ based only on the assumption that all (x_i, y_i), $i = 1, 2, \cdots$ are generated independently by the same probability distribution (i.i.d).

The essential idea of Venn prediction is to divide all examples into a number of categories based on their similarity and calculate the probability of x_n belonging to each class $y_j \in Y$ as the frequency of y_j in the category that contains it. Then since we do not know the true labels of the new object x_n, we try every possible label as a candidate for its label. In each try, we calculate a probability distribution for the true class of x_n based on the examples

$$\{(x_1, y_1), \cdots, (x_{n-1}, y_{n-1}), (x_n, y_n)\}. \tag{1}$$

To divide each set (1) into categories we use a *taxonomy function*. $A_n : \mathbf{Z}^{n-1} \times \mathbf{Z} \to T, n \in \mathbf{N}$, which classifies the relation between an example and the bag of the other examples:

$$\begin{aligned}\tau_i =& A_n((x_i, y_i), \{(x_1, y_1), \cdots, (x_{i-1}, y_{i-1}), \\ & (x_{i+1}, y_{i+1}), \cdots, (x_n, y_n)\}).\end{aligned} \tag{2}$$

Values τ_i are called categories and are taken from a finite set $T = \{\tau_i, \tau_i, \cdots, \tau_k\}$. Equivalently, a taxonomy function assigns to each example (x_i, y_i) its category τ_i, or, in other words, groups all examples to a finite set of categories.

Typically each taxonomy is based on a traditional machine learning algorithm, called the *underlying algorithm* of the Venn predictor. The output of this algorithm for each attribute vector $x_i, i = 1, \cdots, n$ after being trained either on the whole set (1), or on the set resulting after removing the pair (x_i, y_i) (2), is used to assign (x_i, y_i) to one of a predefined set of categories. At this point it is important to emphasize the difference between the classes of the problem and the categories of a Venn taxonomy. These categories are assigned examples based on the output classification label of the underlying algorithm and not on the true class to which each example belongs. There fore the category corresponding to a given classification label y_j will contain the examples that the underlying algorithm "believes" to belong to class y_j, which are not necessarily the same as the examples that actually do belong to that class since the underlying algorithm might be wrong in some cases.

The conventional way of using Venn ideas was as follows. Categories are formed using only the training set. For each non-empty category τ, the empirical probabilities of an object within category τ to have a label y_j are found as

$$P_\tau(y_j) = \frac{N_\tau(y_j)}{N_\tau}. \tag{3}$$

Where N_τ is the total number of examples from the training set assigned to category τ, and $N_\tau(y_j)$ is the number of examples within category τ that are labelled with y_j.

Now, given a new object x_n with the unknown label y_n, one should assign it somehow to the most likely category of those already found using only the training set; let τ^* denote it. Then the empirical probabilities $P_{\tau^*}(y_j)$ are considered as probabilities of the object x_n to have a label y_j. The idea of confidence machines allows us to construct several probability distributions of a label y_j for a new object. First we consider a hypothesis that the label y_n of a new object x_n is equal to y $(y_n = y)$. Then we add the pair (x_n, y) to the training set and apply the taxonomy function A to this extended sequence $\{(x_1, y_1), \cdots, (x_{n-1}, y_{n-1}), (x_n, y)\}$. Let

$\tau^*(x_n, y)$ be the category containing the pair (x_n, y). Now for this category we calculate, as previously, the values N_{τ^*}, $N_{\tau^*}(y_j)$ and empirical probability distribution

$$P_{\tau^*(x_n,y)}(y_j) = \frac{N_{\tau^*}(y_j)}{N_{\tau^*}}, y_j \in Y. \quad (4)$$

This distribution depends implicitly on the object x_n and its hypothetical label y. Trying all possible hypotheses of the label y_n being equal to y, we obtain a set of distributions $P_y(y_j) = P_{\tau^*(x_n,y)}(y_j)$ for all possible labels y.

The taxonomy used is still very important as it determines how efficient, or informative, the resulting predictions are. We want the diameter of multiprobability predictions and therefore their uncertainty to be small, since saying that the probability of a given classification label for an example is between 0.8 and 0.9 is much more informative than saying that it is between 0 and 0.9. We also want the predictions to be as close as possible to zero or one, indicating that a classification label is highly unlikely or highly likely respectively.

The maximum and minimum probabilities obtained for each classification label y_j define the interval for the probability of the new example belonging to y_j:

$$\left[\min_{y\in Y} P_{\tau^*(x_n,y)}(y_j), \max_{y\in Y} P_{\tau^*(x_n,y)}(y_j)\right]. \quad (5)$$

To simplify notation the lower bound of this interval for a given class y_j will be denoted as $L(y_j)$ and the upper bound will be denoted as $U(y_j)$. The Venn predictor outputs the best class $\hat{y}$ for x_n where:

$$\hat{y} = \arg \max_{j=1,\cdots,c} \overline{P(y_j)}. \quad (6)$$

and $\overline{P(y_j)}$ is the mean of the probabilities obtained for y_j:

$$\overline{P(y_j)} = \frac{1}{|Y|} \sum_{y\in Y} P_{\tau^*(x_n,y)}(y_j). \quad (7)$$

This prediction is accompanied by the interval:

$$[L(\hat{y}), U(\hat{y})]. \quad (8)$$

as the probability interval of it being correct. The complementary interval

$$[1 - L(\hat{y}), 1 - U(\hat{y})]. \quad (9)$$

gives the probability that $\hat{y}$ is not the true classification label of the new example and it is called the error probability interval.

4. The Algorithm

The difference between alternative Venn Prediction methods is the taxonomy they use to divide examples into categories. Here a RF classifier defined which allocate examples into categories. This section describes our algorithm for reliable probabilistic classification of mammograhic masses. The main idea of the proposed Algorithm is to embed random forests in confidence machines. In this way, we expect designed Venn machines to inherit advantages of random forests.

First, we train a RF classifier, according to Forest-RI Algorithm, on the extended set (1). Second, we assign (x_i, y_i) to the corresponding category τ_i according to RF outputs $\{o_i^1, \cdots, o_i^l\}$. The predicted class of (x_i, y_i) is calculated by its majority vote of the out-of-bag predictions. Algorithm 1 presents the complete $RPRF$ algorithm.

Algorithm 1: Reliable Probabilistic Random forests (RPRF)

Input: Training set $Z = \{(x_i, y_i)\}_{i=1}^{n-1}$ in wich $x_i = \{x_i^1, \cdots, x_i^d\} \in \mathbf{R}^d$ and $y_i \in Y = \{y_1, \cdots, y_c\}$ the possible class for x_i, x_n a new example to be classified.

Result: The best class for x_n : $\hat{y} = \arg \max_{j=1,\cdots,c} \overline{P(y_j)}$, the probability interval for $\hat{y}$: $\left[\min_{y\in Y} P_{\tau^*(x_n,y)}(\hat{y}), \max_{y\in Y} P_{\tau^*(x_n,y)}(\hat{y})\right]$

```
begin
  for k ← 1 to c do
    Train a random forest (RF) classifier, according
    to Forest-RI Algorithm, on the extended set
    {(x_1, y_1), ..., (x_{n-1}, y_{n-1}), (x_n, y_k)};
    Supply the input patterns x_1, ..., x_n to the
    trained RF to obtain the output values
    {o_1, ..., o_n} based on the out-of-bag
    predictions;
    for i ← 0 to n do
      According to RF outputs {o_i^1, ..., o_i^c},
      assign (x_i, y_i) to the corresponding
      category τ_i.
    end
    Find the most likely category that contains
    (x_n, y_k), let τ* denote it.
    for j ← 0 to c do
      Compute the empirical probability
      P_{τ*(x_n,y_k)}(y_j) using equation (4).
    end
  end
  for j ← 0 to c do
    Compute the mean of the probability P(y_j)
    using equation (7).
  end
end
```

Applying a RF classifier that was trained on the whole

training data set (1), the examples are divided into categories for each assumed classification label $y_k \in \{y_1, \cdots, y_c\}$ of x_n and the process described in section 3 is followed for calculating the outputs of the Reliable Probabilistic Random Forests (RPRF). The predictions are based on the out-of-bag predictions from the RF.

In the next section, we will analyze experimentally our proposed model.

5. Experimentation

In this section, we will analyse experimentally our proposed model to well-known other proposals using a standard reference database. Experimental settings and results are described in the sequel.

5.1 Experimental settings

To evaluate our method, we used mammograms from the Mammographic Image Analysis Society (MIAS) database [14]. Films were taken from the United Kingdom National Breast Screening Program; digitized to 50 micron pixel edge, and presented each pixel with an 8-bit word. The MIAS database consists of totally 322 digital mammograms from 161 patients, which belong to three big categories: normal, benign and malign. There are 208 normal, 63 benign and 51 malign images. The normal ones are those characterizing a healthy patient, the benign ones represent mammograms showing a tumor, but that tumor is not formed by cancerous cells, and the malign ones are those mammograms taken from patients with cancerous tumors. This database provides for each mammogram a meta-data from radiologists about the characteristics of background tissue, the type and the severity of abnormality and the coordinates of center; etc. Using this informations, suspicious regions with the given centre and radius have been extracted as the Regions of Interest (ROIs).

We use a set which consists of totally 285 ROIs, which belong to three categories: normal, benign and malign. There are 130 normal, 75 benign and 80 malign ROIs. The images from the MIAS dataset are separated for training and testing. The training ratio is set as 80%, i.e. 80% of the samples for training and 20% for testing.

The computer classification results were validated using the following standard criteria: Accuracy (AC), Sensitivity (SE) or Recall, Specificity (SP), the area under the ROC curve (Az), F-measure (F1), Precision (Prec), Brier Score (BS) and Matthews's correlation coefficient (MCC). These measures are calculated from confusion matrix. The confusion matrix describes actual and predicted classes of the proposed method and shown in table 1. Calculations of those performance measures were carried out as follows:

$$SE = TPR = \frac{TP}{(TP+FN)} \quad (10)$$

$$SP = 1 - FPR = \frac{TN}{(TN+FP)} \quad (11)$$

$$AC = \frac{(TN+TP)}{(TN+TP+FN+FP)} \quad (12)$$

$$Prec = \frac{TP}{(TP+FP)} \quad (13)$$

$$F1 = 2 \times \frac{(Prec \times SE)}{(Prec + SE)} \quad (14)$$

$$MCC = \frac{(TP \times TN - FP \times FN)}{\sqrt{((TP+FP)(TP+FN)(TP+FP)(TN+FN)}} \quad (15)$$

where FP, FN, TP and TN denote false-positive, false-negative, true-positive and true-negative answers, respectively. Moreover, FPR and TPR denote false-positive rate and true-positive rate, respectively.

The Brier score, BS, is defined for a dichotomous event as the mean square error of the probability forecast:

$$BS = \frac{1}{M} \sum_{i=1}^{M} (p_i - o_i)^2 \quad (16)$$

where M is the total number of samples, p_i is the forecast probability, o_i is the verifying observation (1 if the event occurs, 0 if it does not).

5.2 Comparative analysis

The classification performance of the proposed system is compared with that of other three existing classifiers like Support Vector Machine (SVM) [16], Probabilistic neural network (PNN) [1] and Random Forests (RF) [17] classifiers. Numerical results are summarized in Tables 1 and 2.

Table 1 shows the confusion matrices for all used classifiers. This should be read as follows: rows indicate the object to be recognized (the true class) and columns indicate the label the classifiers associates at this object, thus obtaining the correct classified mammograms in the diagonal of the matrix. Therefore, the performance of this approach is 91.92%. We can see that the mammograms better classified are those belonging to normal class, while benign mammograms are the worst classified.

ROC curve is graphical display of sensitivity (TPR) on y-axis and (1 - specificity) (FPR) on x-axis with changing the decision threshold. This is generally depicted in a square box for convenience and its both axes are from 0 to 1. Figure 2 depicts the ROC curve for the proposed method. The area under the ROC curve is an important criterion for evaluating diagnostic performance. Usually it is referred as the Az index. Maximum Az = 1 and it means diagnostic test is perfect in differentiating diseased with non-diseased

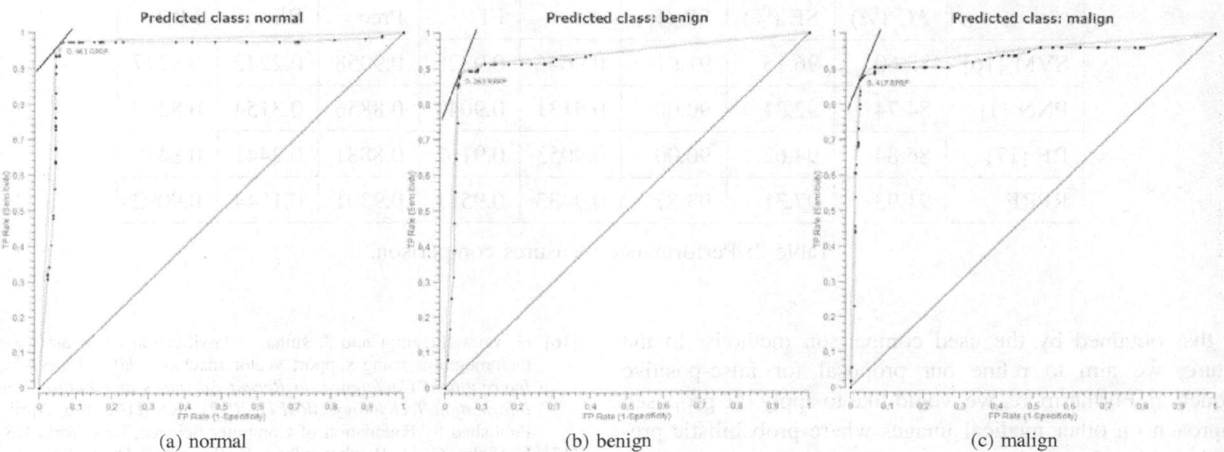

(a) normal (b) benign (c) malign

Fig. 2: The ROC curve for the proposed method.

		Assigned Class		
		normal	malign	benign
3*Actual Class	normal	250	4	6
	malign	10	142	8
	benign	16	21	113

(a) SVM [16]

		Assigned Class		
		normal	malign	benign
3*Actual Class	normal	253	2	5
	malign	9	140	11
	benign	10	9	131

(b) RPRF

		Assigned Class		
		normal	malign	benign
3*Actual Class	normal	246	6	8
	malign	15	133	12
	benign	16	18	116

(c) RF [17]

		Assigned Class		
		normal	malign	benign
3*Actual Class	normal	240	9	11
	malign	16	130	14
	benign	15	22	113

(d) PNN [1]

Table 1: Confusion matrices showing classification error results for (a) SVM, (b) RPRF, (c) RF and (d) PNN Classifiers.

subjects. The proposed methodology yielded an area under the ROC curve of 0.943.

Table displays the numerical results from the experiments. Classification Accuracy represents the overall performance of a classifier. It indicates the percentage of correctly classified positive and negative cases from the total number of cases. Our model yielded a higher accuracy rate, with a mean of 91.93% compared to SVM (88.6%), PNN (84.74%) and RF (86.84%). Sensitivity, also known as recall rate, measures the proportion of positives correctly identified. The proposed methodology yielded a higher sensitivity rate, with a mean of 97.31% compared to SVM (96.15%), PNN (92.31%) and RF (94.62%). The specificity measure represents the proportion of negatives that are correctly identified. Our model has a specificity of 93.87%. F-measure is widely used to evaluate classification techniques. It is a common evaluation metrics that combines precision and recall into a single value. Our proposed yields F-measure of 0.9511 which is only 0.9328 for SVM, 0.9040 for PNN and 0.9162 for RF. The Brier score is a well-known evaluation measure for probabilistic classifiers. It measures the average squared deviation between predicted probabilities for a set of events and their outcomes. The lower the Brier score of a model the better the predictive performance. Our proposed has a small Brier score 0.1544, explaining the good results of classification for this dataset.

As a summary to these simulations, it can be observed that the classification efficiency of the proposed classifier is better than other classifiers, for the mammogram classification problem of the database considered for the study.

6. Conclusion

In this paper, we have developed a reliable probabilistic algorithm for the classification of masses in Mammograms. The proposed method has acceptable performance compared

	AC (%)	SE (%)	SP (%)	Az	F1	Prec	BS	MCC
SVM [16]	88.60	96.15	91.61	0.9646	0.9328	0.9058	0.2242	0.8747
PNN [1]	84.74	92.31	90.00	0.9131	0.9040	0.8856	0.3154	0.8209
RF [17]	86.84	94.62	90.00	0.9053	0.9162	0.8881	0.2441	0.8432
RPRF	91.93	97.31	93.87	0.9433	0.9511	0.9301	0.1544	0.9092

Table 2: Performance measures comparison.

to that obtained by the used comparison methods. In the future, we aim to refine our proposal for false-positive reduction. Furthermore, we would like to apply the proposed approach on other medical images where probabilistic predictions are of great importance.

References

[1] A. T. Azar and S. A. El-Said. Probabilistic neural network for breast cancer classification. *Neural Computing and Applications*, pages 1–15, 2012.

[2] L. Breiman and A. Cutler. Random forests - classification manual. *http://www.math.usu.edu/ădele/forests/*, 2008.

[3] L. Breiman, J.H. Friedman, R.A. Olshen, and C.J. Stone. *Classification and Regression Trees*. Wadsworth Inc, 1984.

[4] Leo Breiman. Random forests. *Machine Learning*, 45(1):5–32, 2001.

[5] M. Dashevskiy and Z. Luo. Reliable probabilistic classification and its application to internet traffic. In *Advanced Intelligent Computing Theories and Applications*, volume 5226, pages 380–388, 2008.

[6] J. Ferlay, H. R. Shin, F. Bray, D. Forman, C. Mathers, and D. M Parkin. Globocan 2008 v1.2. cancer incidence, mortality and prevalence worldwide in 2008. *IARC CancerBase No. 10. Lyon, France: International Agency for Research on Cancer; 2010. [Accessed December 1, 2011]. at http://globocan.iarc.fr/*, 2008.

[7] M. J. Islam, M. Ahmadi, and M. A. Sid-Ahmed. Computer-aided detection and classification of masses in digitized mammograms using artificial neural network. *ICSI (2)'10*, pages 327–334, 2010.

[8] K. Kumar, P. Zhang, and B. Verma. Application of decision trees for mass classification in mammography. In *International conference on fuzzy systems and knowledge discovery, FSKD'06, China*, pages 366–376, 2006.

[9] P. Leod and B. Verma. Multi-cluster support vector machine classifier for the classification of suspicious areas in digital mammograms. *International Journal of Computational Intelligence and Applications*, 10(4):481– 494, 2011.

[10] J Liu, J Chen, X Liu, and J. Tang. An investigate of mass diagnosis in mammogram with random forest. In *Advanced Computational Intelligence (IWACI)*, pages 638 – 641, 2011.

[11] D. Meyer, F. Leisch, and K. Hornik. The support vector machine under test. *Neurocomputing*, 55(1-2):169–186, 2003.

[12] M. E. Osman, M. A. Wahed, A. S. Mohamed, and Y. M. Kadah. Computer aided diagnosis system for classification of microcalcifications in digital mammograms. In *26th National Radio Science Conference*, pages 1–6, 2009.

[13] H. Papadopoulos. Reliable probabilistic classification with neural networks. *Neurocomputing. Elsevier*, 2012.

[14] J. Suckling, J. Parker, D. Dance, S. Astley, I. Hutt, C. Boggis, I. Ricketts, E. Stamatakis, N. Cerneaz, S. Kok, P. Taylor, D. Betal, and J. Savage. The mammographic images analysis society digital mammogram database. *Experta Medica International Congress Series*, 1069:375–378, 1994.

[15] Y. Sun, C. F. Babbs, and E. J. Delp. Normal mammogram classification based on regional analysis. In *The 2002 45th Midwest Symposium on Circuits and Systems*, pages II–375 – II–378, 2002.

[16] G. vaira Suganthi and J. sutha. Classification of breast masses in mammograms using support vector machine. *IJCA Proceedings on International Conference on Recent Advances and Future Trends in Information Technology (iRAFIT 2012)*, iRAFIT(2):1–6, April 2012. Published by Foundation of Computer Science, New York, USA.

[17] L. Vibha, G. M. Harshavardhan, K. Pranaw, P. Deepa Shenoy, K. R. Venugopal, and Lalit M. Patnaik. Classification of mammograms using decision trees. In *Tenth International Database Engineering and Applications Symposium (IDEAS 2006), 11-14 December 2006, Delhi, India*, pages 263–266. IEEE Computer Society, 2006.

[18] V. Vovk, G. Alex, and G. Shafer. *Algorithmic Learning in a Random World*. Springer, 2005. Springer, New York.

[19] C. Zhou, I. Nouretdinov, Z. Luo, M. Adamskiy, N. Coldham, and A. Gammerman. A comparison of venn machine with platt's method in probabilistic outputs. In *EANN/AIAI (2)'11*, pages 483–490, 2011.

Identifying Patterns and Anomalies in Delayed Neutron Monitor Data of Nuclear Power Plant

Durga Toshniwal, Aditya Gupta
Department of Computer Science & Engineering
Indian Institute of Technology Roorkee
Roorkee, India
{durgatoshniwal, adityag} @gmail.com

Pramod K. Gupta, Vikas Khurana, Pushp Upadhyay
C&I and R&D-ES
Nuclear Power Corporation of India Ltd. Mumbai,
{pkgupta, vkhurana, pupadhyay} @npcil.co.in

Abstract— ***In nuclear fission, a delayed neutron is a neutron emitted by one of the fission products any time from a few milliseconds to a few minutes after the fission event. The counts of delayed neutrons constitute a time series sequence. The analysis of such time series can prove to be very significant for purpose of predictive maintenance in nuclear power plants. In this paper we aim to identify anomalies in neutron counts, which may be generated due to possible leaks in the nuclear reactor channel. Real world case data comprising of readings from Delayed Neutron Monitors (DNM) has been analyzed. The time sequences formed by the delayed neutrons have first been symbolically represented using Symbolic Approximation Algorithm (SAX), then anomaly detection and pattern detection algorithms have been applied on them.***

Keywords-Time Series; Anomaly Detection; Symbollic Approximate Algorithm; patterns; dataset; Delayed Neutron Monitor

I. Introduction

In nuclear engineering, a delayed neutron is a neutron emitted after a nuclear fission event, by one of the fission products (or actually, a fission product daughter after beta decay), any time from a few milliseconds to a few minutes after the fission event. Neutrons born within 10^{-14} seconds of the fission are termed "prompt neutrons."

If a nuclear reactor happened to be in critical state for prompt neutrons, the number of neutrons would increase exponentially at a high rate, and very quickly the reactor would become uncontrollable by means of cybernetics.

Delayed neutrons play an important role in nuclear reactor control and safety analysis [16]. The Nuclear reactors operate in subcritical state as far as only prompt neutrons are concerned. The delayed neutrons come a moment later, just in time to sustain the chain reaction when it is going to die out. In that regime, neutron production overall still grows exponentially, but on a time scale that is governed by the delayed neutron production, which is slow enough to be controlled (just as an otherwise unstable bicycle can be balanced because human reflexes are quick enough on the time scale of its instability). Thus, by widening the margins of non-operation and super criticality and allowing more time to regulate the reactor, the delayed neutrons are essential to inherent reactor safety and even in reactors requiring active control [16].

In nuclear reactors, the fuel is encased in metal rods which are mounted in groups in fuel assemblies which in turn are massed together to form the reactor core. Reactor coolant in the form of a fluid passed through the core to absorb heat generated by nuclear reactions in the fuel is typically circulated through several external heat transfer loops. The reactor coolant may be ordinary water, heavy water, a gas or any other material like liquid sodium [16].

In any case, the cladding on the fuel rods is subjected to high temperatures and internal stresses generated as a result of the nuclear reactions in the fuel which can lead to failures in the cladding. Such breaches in the fuel rod cladding introduce fuel into the reactor coolant which carries the contamination throughout the heat transfer loops. Identifying and locating the breached fuel rod in a timely manner is important in order that appropriate action might be taken prior to the time that operational or safety problems are created by the failure [16].

The counts of delayed neutrons (obtained from Delayed Neutron Monitors in nuclear reactors) constitute a time series. Time series is a sequence of data points, measured typically at successive points in time spaced at uniform time intervals. Time series data have a natural temporal ordering. This makes time series analysis distinct from other common data analysis problems, in which there is no natural ordering of the observations.

In this paper, we aim to identify anomalies in neutron counts generated due to possible leaks in the nuclear reactor channel or other reasons. Such situations are very critical and need continues monitoring and attention. The motivation of this study is to predict such conditions to avoid failures in the reactor and other unwanted events.

Two real world datasets have been used for the present study. The dataset's comprises of readings taken from Delayed Neutron Monitor (DNM) over a period of five years (2005-2010).

In order to find the anomalies and patterns in time series, we first convert our dataset into a symbolic representation. We have used symbolic aggregate approximation (SAX) algorithm for this purpose [1]. Then we apply anomaly detection and pattern finding algorithm on the symbolic representation

The remainder of the paper is organized as follows. Section 2 describes the related work. It includes description of SAX algorithm and anomaly detection algorithm. Following section, section 3 details the framework of our project. Section 4 describes the real world dataset that we have used. Next, section 5 describes the experimental results and discussions. Final conclusion is stated in section 6.

II. RELATED WORK

As with most problems in computer science, the suitable choice of representation of time series greatly affects the ease and efficiency of time series data mining. With this in mind, a great number of time series representations have been introduced, including the Discrete Fourier Transform (DFT) [8], the Discrete Wavelet Transform (DWT) [9], Piecewise Linear, and Piecewise Constant models (PAA) [11], (APCA) [12, 11], and Singular Value Decomposition (SVD) [11].

All the above methods are similar in terms of indexing power [13]; however, the representations have other features that may act as strengths or weaknesses. As a simple example, wavelets have the useful multi resolution property, but are only defined for time series that are an integer power of two in length [9].

One important feature of all the above representations is that they are real valued. This limits the algorithms, data structures and definitions available for them. For example, in anomaly detection we cannot meaningfully define the probability of observing any particular set of wavelet coefficients, since the probability of observing any real number is zero [14]. Such limitations have lead researchers to consider using a symbolic representation of time series. One main disadvantage is none of the above techniques allows a distance measure those lower bounds a distance measure defined on the original time series. For this reason, the various generic time series data mining approaches are of little utility.

We have used Symbolic Approximation Algorithm to represent out dataset in symbolic form. The main advantage of this algorithm is that it allows the lower bounding of the true distance. SAX also allows dimensionality/ numerosity reduction, and distance measures to be defined on the symbolic approach that lower bound corresponding distance measures defined on the original series. Now we can take advantage of the generic time series data mining model, and of a host of other algorithms, definitions and data structures which are only defined for discrete data, including hashing, Markov models, and suffix trees. The SAX algorithm is discussed in detail in section 2.

For anomaly detection in most real valued time series problems such as motif discovery [15], longest common subsequence matching, sequence averaging, segmentation, indexing [13], etc. have approximate or exact analogues in the discrete world, and have been addressed by the text processing or bioinformatics communities. For identifying time series anomalies in discrete datasets, Heuristically Ordered Time series is the best algorithm. The algorithm is discussed in section 2.

A. Symbollic Aggregate Approximation (SAX)

Symbolic Aggregate Approximation (SAX) algorithm [1] produces symbolic representation of time series. This representation is unique because it allows dimensionality/numerosity reduction, and it also allows distance measures to be defined on the symbolic approach that lower bound corresponding distance measures defined on the original series.

SAX allows time series of arbitrary length n to be converted into strings of length w such that $w<=n$. The alphabet size is also an integer a such that $a>=2$. Converting time series data into SAX representation is a two-step process. We first transform the data into the Piecewise Aggregate Approximation (PAA) [1] representation and then symbolize the PAA representation into a discrete string. There are two important advantages to doing this:

1. Dimensionality Reduction: We can use the well-defined and well-documented dimensionality reduction power of PAA [4, 5], and the reduction is automatically carried over to the symbolic representation.
2. Lower Bounding: Proving that a distance measure between two symbolic strings lower bounds the true distance between the original time series is non-trivial. The key observation that allows us to prove lower bounds is to concentrate on proving that the symbolic distance measure lower bounds the PAA distance measure. Then we can prove the desired result by transitivity by simply pointing to the existing proofs for the PAA representation itself [5].

So, to reduce the time series from n dimensions to w dimensions, the data is divided into w equal sized "frames." The mean value of the data falling within a frame is calculated and a vector of these values becomes the data-reduced representation. This representation is the PAA representation of the time series. Also we normalize each time series to have a mean of zero and a standard deviation of one before converting it to the PAA representation, since it is well understood that it is meaningless to compare time series with different offsets and amplitudes [6, 10].

Having transformed a time series database into PAA, we can apply a further transformation to obtain a discrete representation. It is desirable to have a discretization technique that will produce symbols with equal-probability. This is easily achieved since normalized time series have a Gaussian distribution [7]. Given that the normalized time series have highly Gaussian distribution, we can simply determine the "breakpoints" that will produce a equal-sized areas under Gaussian curve [7]. These breakpoints may be determined by looking them up in a statistical table. For example, Table 1 gives the breakpoints for values of a from 3 to 10.

Once the breakpoints have been obtained we can discretize a time series in the following manner. We first obtain a PAA of the time series. All PAA coefficients that are below the smallest breakpoint are mapped to the symbol "a," all coefficients greater than or equal to the smallest breakpoint and less than the second smallest breakpoint are mapped to the symbol "b," etc.

TABLE 1: A LOOKUP TABLE THAT CONTAINS THE BREAKPOINTS THAT DEVIDE A GAUSSIAN DISTRIBUTION IN A NUMBER (3 TO 10) OF EQUIPROBABLE REGIONS

β_i \ a	3	4	5	6	7	8	9	10
β_1	-0.43	-0.67	-0.84	-0.97	-1.07	-1.15	-1.22	-1.28
β_2	0.43	0	-0.25	-0.43	-0.57	-0.67	-0.76	-0.84
β_3		0.67	0.25	0	-0.18	-0.32	-0.43	-0.52
β_4			0.84	0.43	0.18	0	-0.14	-0.25
β_5				0.97	0.57	0.32	0.14	0
β_6					1.07	0.67	0.43	0.25
β_7						1.15	0.76	0.52
β_8							1.22	0.84
β_9								1.28

Figure 1 illustrates the three steps of SAX generation algorithm. 'C' is the name of the time series. First we obtain the PAA representation of C, which is represented by C-bar. Now we select alphabet size 3. So we introduce two breakpoints. The PAA points lying below the first breakpoint are labeled as 'a', the PAA points lying between the first and the second breakpoint are labeled 'b' and the points lying beyond the third breakpoint line are labeled 'c'.

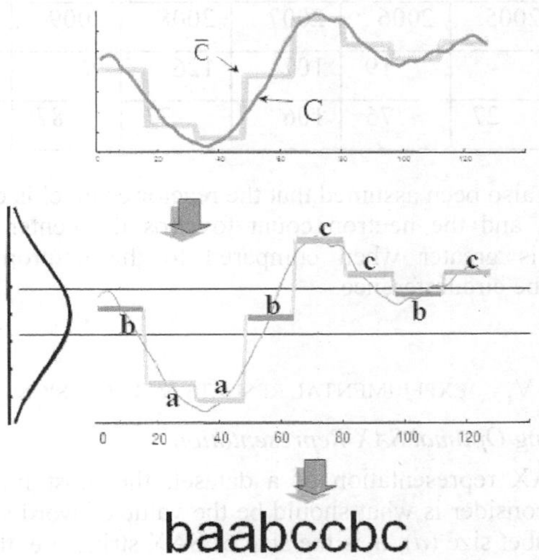

Figure 1: A time series is discretized by first obtaining a PAA approximation and then using predetermined breakpoints to map the PAA coefficients into SAX symbols. In the example above, with n = 128, w = 8 and a = 3, the time series is mapped to the word baabccbc

Now we have to define the distance measure on SAX representation. i.e. how do we calculate the distance between two SAX strings. The distance between two SAX strings can be calculated by Equation 1:

$$MINDIST(\hat{Q},\hat{C}) \equiv \sqrt{\tfrac{n}{w}}\sqrt{\sum_{i=1}^{w}\left(dist(\hat{q}_i,\hat{c}_i)\right)^2} \quad (1)$$

Where *dist()* function calculates the distance between two SAX coefficients. The dist() function can be implemented using a table lookup as illustrated in Table 2.

TABLE 2. LOOKUP TABLE USED BY MINDIST FUNCTION. THIS TABLE IS FOR AN ALPHABET OF CARDINALITY 4.

	a	b	c	d
a	0	0	0.67	1.34
b	0	0	0	0.67
c	0.67	0	0	0
d	1.34	0.67	0	0

The value in cell (r,c) for any lookup table can be calculated by the following Equation 2.

$$cell_{r,c} = \begin{cases} 0, & if\ |r-c| \le 1 \\ \beta_{\max(r,c)-1} - \beta_{\min(r,c)}, & otherwise \end{cases} \quad (2)$$

The question still remains, what values of *w* and *a* should we choose? There is a clear tradeoff between the parameter *w* controlling the number of approximating elements, and the value *a* controlling the granularity of each approximating element.

We choose the value of *a* and *w* such that the following ratio in equation 3 is maximized (close to 1).

$$Tightness\ of\ Lower\ Bound = \frac{MINDIST(\hat{Q},\hat{C})}{D(Q,C)} \quad (3)$$

So in order to choose the value of a and w, we conduct the following experiment. We find the tightness of lower bound for the time series by calculating the above ratio for every possible combination of substring possible and then averaging the ratio. The result of this experiment are shown in section 5.

B. Algorithm for detecting anomalies

Time series anomalies are subsequences of longer time series that are maximally different to all the rest of the time series subsequences. They thus capture the sense of the most unusual subsequence within a time series. Before discussing the algorithm, we must first discuss what are *non-self-match*. Given a time series T, containing a subsequence C of length n beginning at position p and a matching subsequence M beginning at q, we say that M is a non-self match to C at distance of Dist(M,C) if | p – q| >=n. [2]

The brute force algorithm for finding anomalies is simple and obvious. We simply take each possible subsequence and find the distance to the nearest non-self match. The subsequence that has the greatest such value is the discord. This is achieved with nested loops, where the outer loop considers each possible candidate subsequence, and the inner loop is a linear scan to identify the candidate's nearest non-self match.The pseudo code for algorithm is shown in Figure2.

```
Function [dist, loc ]= Brute_Force(T, n)
 best_so_far_dist = 0
 best_so_far_loc = NaN

For p = 1 to | T | - n + 1                          // Begin Outer Loop
  nearest_neighbor_dist = infinity
  For q = 1 to | T | - n + 1                        // Begin Inner Loop
    IF | p - q | ≥ n                                // non-self match?
      IF Dist (t_p,..., t_p+n-1, t_q,..., t_q+n-1) < nearest_neighbor_dist
        nearest_neighbor_dist = Dist (t_p,..., t_p+n-1, t_q,..., t_q+n-1)
      End
    End                                             // End non-self match test
  End                                               // End Inner Loop
  IF nearest_neighbor_dist > best_so_far_dist
    best_so_far_dist = nearest_neighbor_dist
    best_so_far_loc = p
  End
End                                                 // End Outer Loop
Return[ best_so_far_dist, best_so_far_loc ]
```

Figure 2: Algorithm for identifying discords in time series

The advantage of this algorithm is that it requires only one parameter, that is the length of the subsequence as input and it finds the anomaly. The algorithm has square complexity. In order to improve the running time of the algorithm, we implement the following optimization: We don't really need to find the true nearest neighbor for every candidate. As soon as for any candidate, we find that its 'nearest neighbor distance' is less than 'best so far' we abandon the instance of the inner loop, safe in the knowledge that current candidate cannot be the time series discord. The algorithm in figure 2 allows several potential weaknesses for the sake of simplicity. First, it assumes a single anomaly in the dataset. Second, in the first few iterations, the measure needs to note the difference a small anomaly makes, even when masked by a large amount of surrounding normal data. A simple solution to these problems is to set a parameter W, for number of windows. We can divide the input sequence into W contiguous sections, and identify anomaly for each sensor in each of the windows. [3]

III. PROPOSED FRAMEWORK

In the proposed framework (Figure 3), symbolic aggregate approximation algorithm is applied on the raw dataset. This helps in discretizing the dataset, and allows us to use various algorithms used in text data mining.

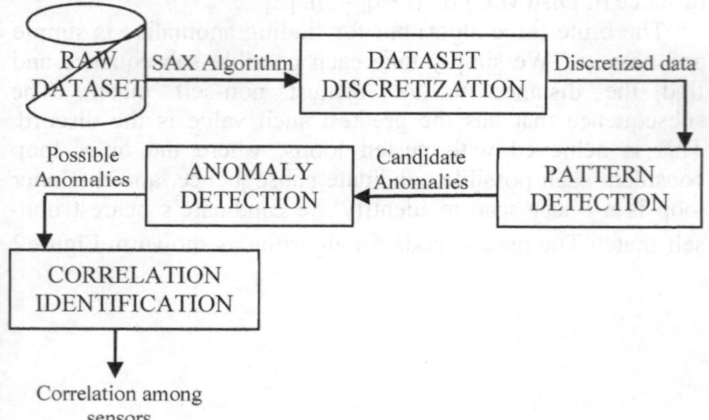

Figure 3. Framework for our experiment

After the dataset has been discretized, we apply the Heuristically Ordered Time series algorithm to find the anomalies in the dataset. We analyze the anomalies found and find the correlation among sensors, that is the probability of one sensor failing given that another sensor has failed.

IV. DATASET

There are two datasets that are analyzed. The first dataset (DP1) consists of readings for 5 years from 2006- 2010. The second dataset (DP4) consists of readings for 6 years 2006 – 2010. Each of these datasets contains readings recorded from 28 sensors on certain days.

Table 3 shows the number of days when readings are recorded in each of the dataset during the period of 2005-2010. For each of these days, a set of 14 readings have been considered for each of the 28 sensors deployed in the nuclear reactor. So in DP1 dataset, there are 434*14*28=1,70,128 (Days multiplied by number of readings each day) readings and in DP4 dataset there are 479*14*28=1,87,768 readings.

TABLE 3: NUMBER OF READINGS FOR EACH YEAR AND EACH DATASET

	2005	2006	2007	2008	2009	2010
DP1	-	19	107	126	96	86
DP4	27	76	106	77	87	106

It has also been assumed that the reactor channel is circular in shape, and the neutron count towards the center of the channel is greater when compared to the neutron count towards the circumference.

V. EXPERIMENTAL RESULTS & DISCUSSION

A. Finding Optimal SAX Representation

In SAX representation of a dataset, the most important point to consider is what should be the value of word size (w) and alphabet size (a). w is the size of SAX string, i.e. the time series string of length n is converted into SAX representation of length w. w is less than or equal to the length of original time series n. Very small values of w are not preferred as it leads to loss of accuracy. Also very large values of w are also avoided as then there is no reduction in the size of the dataset. [1]

Alphabet size a controls the granularity of each approximating element. So an alphabet size of 3 means that each approximating element can take 3 values i.e. 'a', 'b', 'c'.

One of the most important properties of SAX representation is that it lower bounds the distance of two symbolic representations when compared to the distance between the original series. Lower bounding means if A and B are original time series and distance between them is X ; Q and R are their symbolic approximations and distance between them is Y then Y lower bounds X. i.e. $Y \le X$ always! A lower bounding symbolic approach would allow us to use suffix trees, hashing, Markov models, text processing and bioinformatics algorithms on symbolic approximation.[1] The closer is Y to X more accurate is our approximation.

Hence we wish to choose variables a and w such that there is tightest possible lower bound between the symbolic approximation and time series. Equation 3 shows the equation for tightness of lower bound.

In this equation D and C are two time series subsections and D(Q,C) is the distance between these subsections. MINDIST(Q,C) finds the difference between the SAX approximations of Q and C. Hence we can see that the above equation will always be less than one, since MINDIST lower bounds D(Q,C) function.

In our experiment, we choose different values of *a* and *w* and for all possible combinations of time series subsequences find their *Tightness of Lower Bound.* Finally we take the mean for all the lower bounds to represent the property for a given *a* and *w*.

We performed such tests on DP1 dataset for year 2006. In all we found mean for lower bound for 171 subsequences of the data set. We averaged these results to find the final results. We conducted these experiments for all the sensors. Figure 4, Figure 5 and Figure 6 shows the results. In these results the tightness of lower bound is shown on z axis whereas x and y axis contain alphabet size and word size respectively.

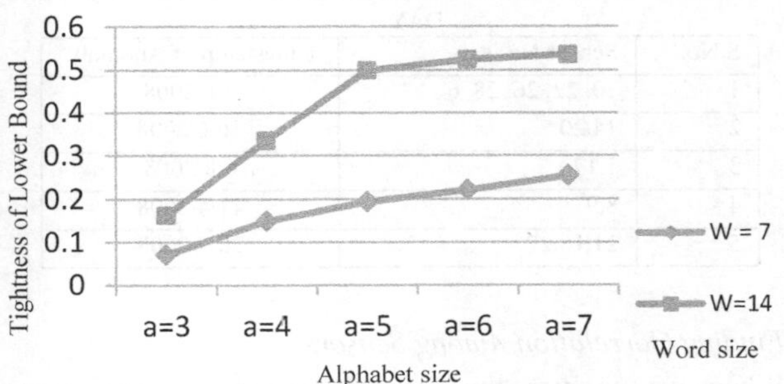

Figure 4: Tightness of Lower Bound for different values of alphabet sizes (a) and for word sizes of 7 and 14, when calculated for time series generated by SENSOR 1

The results suggest that using a low value for *a* results in weak bounds, but that there are diminishing returns for large values of *a*. The results also suggest that the parameters are not too critical; an alphabet size in the range of 5 to 7 seems to be a good choice.

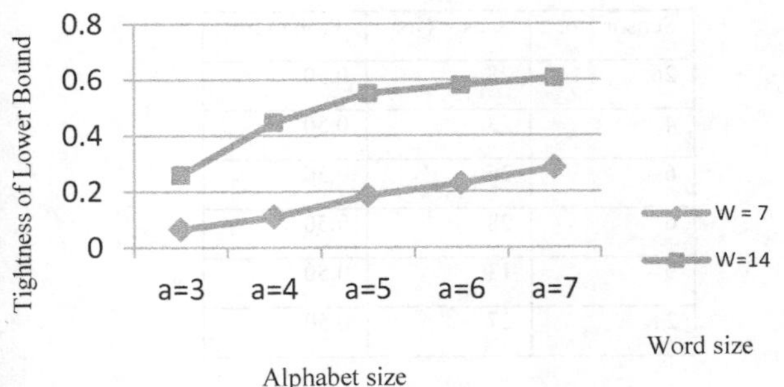

Figure 5 Tightness of Lower Bound for different values of alphabet sizes (a) and for word sizes of 7 and 14, when calculated for time series generated by SENSOR 26

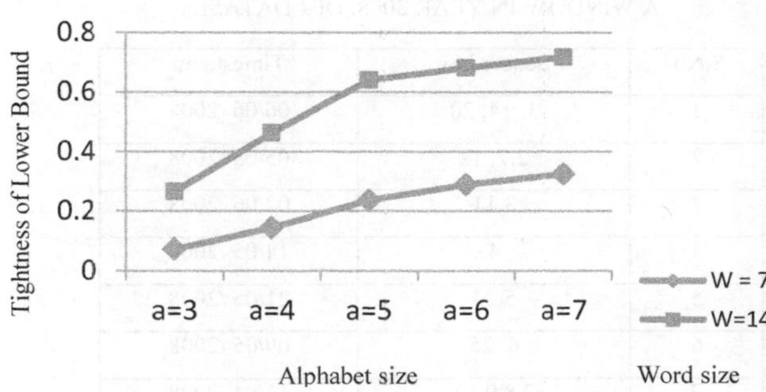

Figure 6 Tightness of Lower Bound for different values of alphabet sizes (a) and for word sizes of 7 and 14, when calculated for time series generated by SENSOR 12.

Based on these results we have chosen word size of 14 and alphabet size of 5 to represent the time series dataset by symbolic representation. Using the SAX algorithm we convert the entire dataset into symbolic representation.

B. *Finding Anomalies in the Dataset*

Once we have converted the time series dataset, we apply the algorithm discussed in section 2 to find the discords. It must be noted that this algorithm takes only the length of the anomaly as the input and identifies the subsequence of that length that is most different from other subsequences. We have performed our experiment for all anomaly sizes varying it from 3 to 14. We have found that strongest anomalies are detected for anomaly size of 11.

This algorithm has two potential weaknesses that we must solve. First, it assumes a single anomaly in the dataset. Second, in the first few iteration, the measure needs to note the difference a small anomaly makes, even when masked by a large amount of surrounding normal data. A simple solution to these problems is to set a parameter W, for number of windows.

We can divide the input sequence into W contiguous sections and apply our algorithm on each of these windows. In our experiment, we have taken the window size to be 17, hence we are finding the most anomalous subsequence of length 11 for each of the sensors in data taken across 17 days. It must be noted that, now in a time series there are 14 readings for each day and in all there are 17 days, so for each sensor we have 238 readings and we are trying to find the subsequence of length 11 that is most different from the others.

So we consider readings from each sensor to be part of a time series. We divide readings for each sensor in group of 17 days and apply the algorithm shown in figure 3. So for each sensor, we find the day when the sensor has been most anomalous (with respect to other 16 days in the window).

We repeat the above process for each window of each sensor. We get large number of results for our experiment, a snapshot of part of the results is shown below in table 4.

In all there are two datasets having data for a number of years. So we perform our experiment on the entire datasets.

TABLE 4: RESULT OF ANOMALY DETECTION ALGORITHM FOR A WINDOW IN YEAR 2008, DP4 DATASET

S.No.	Sensor No.	Timestamp
1	1, 14, 20	06/06 /2008
2	2,7, 12	05/05 /2008
3	3,11	02/06 /2008
4	4	14/05 /2008
5	5,24	21/05 /2008
6	6, 25	09/05 /2008
7	7,8,9,13	11/04 /2008
8	10	16/05 /2008
9	15, 22	28/05 /2008
10	18	07/04 /2008
11	19	26/05 /2008
12	21	18/04 /2008
13	23	4/9/2008

So as it can be seen above, in window of 17 days in year 2008, we have identified days when the sensor has been most anomalous. Also there are sensors that do not show any anomaly at all, for example sensor number 16, 17, 26, 27 and 28 don't show any anomaly!

In the second part of anomaly detection process, we try to identify a single day when each of the sensors has been most anomalous. In order to do this, we compare the most anomalous day in each window of set of 17 days. The results of this process for DP1 dataset for year 2008 are shown below in table 5.

TABLE 5: THE MOST ANOMALOUS DAY FOR EACH SENSOR DURING THE YEAR 2008 IN DP1 DATASET

2008- DP1	Days
Sensor 7	1/9/2008
Sensor 11	2/6/2008
Sensor 12	2/7/2008
Sensor 10	4/8/2008
Sensor 22	4/8/2008
Sensor 26	4/8/2008
Sensor 28	4/8/2008
Sensor 6	4/8/2008
Sensor 23	4/9/2008
Sensor 14	16/6/2008
Sensor 20	16/6/2008
Sensor 1	6/8/2008
Sensor 17	6/8/2008
Sensor 13	6/10/2008
Sensor 18	7/4/2008
Sensor 5	9/7/2008
Sensor 3	10/24/2008
Sensor 8	11/4/2008
Sensor 9	11/4/2008
Sensor 19	11/7/2008
Sensor 24	11/17/2008
Sensor 15	20/7/2008
Sensor 2	20/8/2008
Sensor 25	24/9/2008
Sensor 4	28/7/2008
Sensor 21	30/7/2008
Sensor 16	30/7/2008
Sensor 27	30/7/2008

From the above table, we derive a very useful result. We have derived the most anomalous day for each of the sensor independently. That is we considered data for each sensor as an independent time series, still there are group of days when multiple sensors are showing anomalies simultaneously. We can see that sensor 6, 10, 26, 28 and 22 show maximum anomalies on the same day. Below in table 6, we summarize this result. Hence we can deduce that there must be some correlation among sensors. That is, when one sensor fails, there is certain probability that other sensors with whom it has high correlation also fail. Hence in the next section we explore this and try to find sensors with high correlation.

TABLE 6: SENSORS SHOWING MAXIMUM ANOMALY ON SAME DAY

S.No.	Sensor No.'s	Timestamp of Anomaly
1	10, 22, 26, 28, 6	4/8/2008
2	14,20	16/6/2008
3	1,17	6/8/2008
4	8,9	11/4/2008
5	21,16,27	30/7/2008

C. *Finding Correlation Among Sensors*

When we analyze the discords found, we find some interesting patterns, like some sensors are related to each other. That is they show discords on same days. For these sensors, we find the probability of failure on same day. For example for DP4 dataset, and year 2008, we obtain the following observation as shown in table 7.

TABLE 7. PROBABILITY OF SENSORS FAILING SIMULTANEOUSLY

Sensor No.	Sensor No.	Probability
26	28	0.50
4	23	0.50
6	26	0.50
6	28	0.50
9	13	0.50
21	27	0.50

VI. CONCLUSION

The entire dataset has been discretized using SAX representation. Then anomaly finding algorithm was applied on the datasets. For both the datasets, days were identified when there is an anomaly in the neutron flow counts. These anomalies may be generated due to possible leaks in the nuclear reactor channels or other reasons.

Also correlation among sensors was found based on the result of anomalies. Hence the probability of two sensors showing anomalies simultaneously has been calculated. We have also ranked the sensors based on the mean of their readings and used the basic information given to us about dimensions of the devise to infer the locations of the sensors in the device.

In our future work, we will be applying motif discovery algorithms to identify patterns that repeat themselves in the dataset.

ACKNOWLEDGMENT

We would like to thank Department of Atomic Energy for providing the domain knowledge, dataset and for partially funding the research work and program. Research Project Grant Number DAE-603-ECD.

REFERENCES

[1] Jessica Lin , Eamonn Keogh , Stefano Lonardi , Bill Chiu, A symbolic representation of time series, with implications for streaming algorithms, Proceedings of the 8th ACM SIGMOD workshop on Research issues in data mining and knowledge discovery, June 13-13, 2003, San Diego, California.

[2] Eamonn Keogh , Jessica Lin , Ada Fu, HOT SAX: Efficiently Finding the Most Unusual Time Series Subsequence, Proceedings of the Fifth IEEE International Conference on Data Mining, p.226-233, November 27-30, 2005 [doi>10.1109/ICDM.2005.79]

[3] Eamonn Keogh , Stefano Lonardi , Chotirat Ann Ratanamahatana, Towards parameter-free data mining, Proceedings of the tenth ACM SIGKDD international conference on Knowledge discovery and data mining, August 22-25, 2004, Seattle, WA, USA [doi>10.1145/1014052.1014077]

[4] Keogh, E., Chakrabarti, K., Pazzani, M. & Mehrotra, S. (2001). Locally Adaptive Dimensionality Reduction for Indexing Large Time Series Databases. In proceedings of ACM SIGMOD Conference on Management of Data. Santa Barbara, CA, May 21-24. pp 151-162.

[5] Yi, B, K., & Faloutsos, C. (2000). Fast Time Sequence Indexing for Arbitrary Lp Norms. In proceedings of the 26st Int'l Conference on Very Large Databases. Sep 10-14, Cairo, Egypt. pp 385-394.

[6] Keogh, E. & Kasetty, S. (2002). On the Need for Time Series Data Mining Benchmarks: A Survey and Empirical Demonstration. In proceedings of the 8th ACM SIGKDD International Conference on Knowledge Discovery and Data Mining. July 23 - 26, 2002. Edmonton, Alberta, Canada. pp 102-111.

[7] Larsen, R. J. & Marx, M. L. (1986). An Introduction to Mathematical Statistics and Its Applications. Prentice Hall, Englewood, Cliffs, N.J. 2nd Edition

[8] Faloutsos, C., Ranganathan, M., & Manolopoulos, Y. (1994). Fast Subsequence Matching in Time-Series Databases. *In proceedings of the ACM SIGMOD Int'l Conference on Management of Data*. May 24-27, Minneapolis, MN. pp 419-429.

[9] Chan, K. & Fu, A. W. (1999). Efficient Time Series Matching by Wavelets. In *proceedings of the 15th IEEE Int'l Conference on Data Engineering*. Sydney, Australia, Mar 23-26. pp 126-133.

[10] Geurts, P. (2001). Pattern Extraction for Time Series Classification. In *proceedings of the 5th European Conference on Principles of Data Mining and Knowledge Discovery*. Sep 3-7, Freiburg, Germany. pp. 115-127.

[11] Keogh, E., Chakrabarti, K., Pazzani, M. & Mehrotra, S. (2001). Locally Adaptive Dimensionality Reduction for Indexing Large Time Series Databases. In *proceedings of ACM SIGMOD Conference on Management of Data*. Santa Barbara, CA, May 21- 24. pp 151-162.

[12] Datar, M. & Muthukrishnan, S. (2002). Estimating Rarity and Similarity over Data Stream Windows. In *proceedings of the 10th European Symposium on Algorithms*. Sep 17-21, Rome, Italy.

[13] Keogh, E. & Kasetty, S. (2002). On the Need for Time Series Data Mining Benchmarks: A Survey and Empirical Demonstration. *In proceedings of the 8th ACM SIGKDD International Conference on Knowledge Discovery and Data Mining*. July 23 - 26, 2002. Edmonton, Alberta, Canada. pp 102-111.

[14] Larsen, R. J. & Marx, M. L. (1986). An Introduction to Mathematical Statistics and Its Applications. Prentice Hall, Englewood, Cliffs, N.J. 2nd Edition.

[15] Chiu, B., Keogh, E. & Lonardi, S. (2003). Probabilistic Discover of Time Series Motifs. In the 9th SIGKDD Conference on Knowledge Discovery and Data Mining. pp 493-498.

[16] Locating a breached fuel assembly in a nuclear reactor on-line. **http://www.google.com/patents/EP0258958A1?cl=en**.

Alleviating the Class Imbalance problem in Data Mining

A. Sarmanova[1] and S. Albayrak[2]
[1]Computer Engineering, Yildiz Technical University, Istanbul, Turkey
[2] Computer Engineering, Yildiz Technical University, Istanbul, Turkey

Abstract - *The class imbalance problem in two-class data sets is one of the most important problems. When examples of one class in a training data set vastly outnumber examples of the other class, standard machine learning algorithms tend to be overwhelmed by the majority class and ignore the minority class. There are several algorithms to alleviate the problem of class imbalance in literature. In this paper the existing RUSBoost, EasyEnsemble and BalanceCascade algorithms have been compared with each other using different classifiers like C4.5, SVM, and KNN as the base learners. Several experiments have been done in order to find the best base learner and the algorithm which has the best performance according to the class distribution.*

Keywords: Class imbalance, binary classification, re-sampling, boosting.

1 Introduction

When learning from imbalanced data sets, machine learning algorithms tend to produce high predictive accuracy over the majority class, but poor predictive accuracy over the minority class [1]. In addition, generally the minority class is the class of interest.

There exist techniques to develop better performing classifiers with imbalanced data sets, which are generally called Class Imbalance Learning methods [2]. These methods divided into two categories, data level and algorithm level. Data level, involve preprocessing of training data sets in order to make them balanced. Preprocessing can be implemented in two ways: re-weighting or re-balancing. For example, for data-level methods can be given re-sampling, boosting and bagging. Data re-sampling has received much attention in research related to class imbalance. Data re-sampling attempts to overcome imbalanced class distributions by adding examples to or removing examples from the data set. The second approach is algorithm level, develops new algorithms that can handle class imbalance efficiently to improve the classification performance. This category includes cost-sensitive learning [3], kernel-based algorithms [4] and recognition based algorithms [5].

Re-sampling technique can be categorized into three groups to balance the training data sets. First, the over-sampling the minority class examples, second, the under-sampling the examples of the majority class and the third, hybrid methods that combine both sampling methods mentioned above. Under-sampling methods create a subset of the original data set by eliminating some examples from majority class instances; over-sampling methods, create a superset of the original data set by replicating some examples or creating new examples from existing ones.

Boosting is the preferred algorithm when class is imbalanced. Boosting method increases the performance of classification by focusing on examples that are difficult to classify. The examples which are misclassified currently will be assigned larger weight, in order to be more likely to be chosen as a member of training subset during re-sampling at next round. A final classifier is formed using a weighted voting scheme; the weight of each classifier depends on its performance on the training set used to build it.

In this paper, the existing RUSBoost, BalanceCascade and EasyEnsemble algorithms at data level will be analyzed to alleviate the problem of class imbalance.

This paper is organized as follows. Section 2 reviews related works and in Section 3, the algorithms used in the comparison are described. Section 4 presents the experimental setting while in Section 5 experimental results obtained by different existing algorithms and finally, in Section 6 the paper is concluded.

2 Related Work

Many techniques have been proposed in literature to alleviate the problem of class imbalance. One of the newest algorithms was presented by K.Nageswara Rao et al [2]. This is a new hybrid subset filtering approach for learning from skewed training data. An easy way to sample a dataset is by selecting examples randomly from all classes. However, sampling in this way can break the dataset in an unequal priority way and more number of examples of the same class may be chosen in sampling. To resolve this problem and maintain uniformity in example, they proposed a sampling strategy called weighted component sampling. Before creating multiple subsets, they created the number of majority subsets depending upon the number of minority instances. The ratio of majority and minority examples in the imbalanced data set is used to decide the number of subset of majority examples to be created. Subsets of majority examples are combined with minority subset and multiple balanced subsets are formed. Correlation based Feature Subset (CFS) filters is applied to reduce the class imbalance effects.

There are several algorithms specifically designed for learning with minority classes. One of them is SMOTEBoost, approach for learning from imbalanced data sets which was presented by N.V. Chawla et al. [6]. The proposed SMOTEBoost algorithm is based on the integration of the SMOTE algorithm within the standard boosting procedure. Unlike standard boosting where all misclassified examples are given equal weights, SMOTEBoost creates synthetic examples from the rare or minority class, thus indirectly changing the updating weights and compensating for skewed distributions. SMOTE was used for improving the prediction of the minority classes.

Hongyu Guo, Herna L Viktor [7] presented hybrid method, called DataBoost-IM, combining synthetic over-sampling and boosting. Compare to SMOTE-Boost, DataBoost-IM synthesize new examples for both majority and minority classes, but much more examples for the minority class. DataBoost-IM chooses the hard-to-learn examples to synthesize new examples. Initially, each example is assigned with an equal weight. In every iteration, the method first identifies the hard-to-learn examples based on their weights; then it generates synthetic data based on the set and also the class distributions; more minority synthetic examples are produced than majority ones such that new training sets are balanced after combing original data and synthetic data; next, the weak learner is applied to this new training set, and error rate and weight distribution are re-calculated accordingly.

3 Algorithms Used in the Comparison

In this parer existing three algorithms: RUSBoost, EasyEnsemble and BalanceCascade, which are good at dealing with class imbalance problem, have been chosen and described in details below.

3.1 RUSBoost

C. Seiffert et al. [8] present hybrid sampling/boosting algorithm, called RUSBoost, for learning from skewed training data. This algorithm provides a simpler and faster alternative and they utilized boosting by re-sampling, which resamples the training data according to the examples' assigned weights. It is this re-sampled training data set that is used to construct the iteration's model.

RUSBoost applies RUS, which is a technique that randomly removes examples from the majority class. The motivations for introducing RUS into the boosting process are simplicity, speed, and performance. RUS decreases the time required to construct a model, which is a key benefit particularly when creating an ensemble of models, which is the case in boosting. The loss of information, which is the main drawback of RUS, is greatly overcome by combining it with boosting.

In first step, the weights of each example are initialized to 1/m, where m is the number of examples in the training data set. In second step, T (number of classifiers in the ensemble) weak hypotheses are iteratively trained. RUS is applied to remove the majority class examples. For example, if the desired class ratio is 50: 50, then the majority class examples are randomly removed until the numbers of majority and minority class examples are equal. As a result, S'_t will have a new weight distribution D'_t. S'_t and D'_t are passed to the base learner, *WeakLearn*, which creates the weak hypothesis h_t. The pseudo loss $\mathcal{E}_t$ (based on the original training data set S and weight distribution D_t) is calculated. The weight update parameter α is calculated as $\mathcal{E}_t/(1-\mathcal{E}_t)$. Next, the weight distribution for the next iteration D_{t+1} is updated and normalized. After T iterations, the final hypothesis $H(x)$ is returned as a weighted vote of the T weak hypotheses. [8]

3.2 BalanceCascade

Under-sampling is an efficient strategy to deal with class imbalance. However, the drawback of under-sampling is that it throws away many potentially useful data. Xu-Ying Liu et al. [9] proposed two strategies to explore the majority class examples ignored by undersampling: BalanceCascade and EasyEnsemble.

BalanceCascade trains the learners sequentially, as new learners are built on examples that are filtered by previous learners. Initially, this method builds the first learner on a sampled subset containing partial majority class and the whole minority class; then a new sampled subset from majority class is filtered by such that the correct examples are removed and only incorrect ones are kept; with this refined majority subset and the minority set, a new ensemble learner is built. Iteratively, more learners are created on filtered sampling data set, and finally all learners are combined together. The BalanceCascade assumes the examples that have been correctly modeled are no longer useful on subsequent classifier construction. [9]

3.3 EasyEnsemble

EasyEnsemble samples several subsets from the majority class, trains a learner using each of them, and combines the outputs of those learners.

Given the minority training set P and the majority training set N, the under-sampling method randomly samples a subset N' from N, where |N'| < |N |. In this method, they independently sampled several subsets $N_1, N_2, ..., N_T$ from N. For each subset N_i ($1 \leq i \leq T$), a classifier H_i is trained using N_i and all of P. All generated classifiers are combined for the final decision. AdaBoost [10] is used to train the classifier H_i. [9]

4 Experimental Study

The experiments were conduct using eight real world benchmark data sets taken from the UCI Machine Learning Repository. The details of these datasets used in this study are shown in Table I. The experiments have been done using Matlab and WEKA. C4.5 (denoted J48 in WEKA) decision tree, support vector machine (SVM, denoted SMO in WEKA) and k-nearest neighbor (KNN, denoted Ibk in WEKA) algorithms are used as the base learners to validate the compared algorithms.

This paper uses three different performance metrics to evaluate the algorithms compared for our experiments, all of which are more suitable than the overall accuracy when dealing with class imbalance. In general, for binary class problems the performances of classifiers are evaluated by a confusion matrix (Table II). Based on the confusion matrix, three popular measures have been proposed: AUC, F-measure and G-mean. In our experiment these three evaluation measures are used to validate the compared methods. The classification methods are repeated ten times considering that the re-sampling of subsets introduces randomness. The AUC, F-measure and G-mean are averaged from these ten runs. These well known and widely used measures are defined in the Table III:

TABLE I. DATA SETS

Datasets	Size	Atribute	Majority	Minority
breast	699	10	458	241
bupa	345	7	200	145
haberman	306	4	225	81
hepatitis	155	18	123	32
ionosphere	351	35	225	126
pima	768	9	500	268
transfusion	748	5	570	178
wpbc	198	35	151	47

TABLE II. CONFUSION MATRIX

	Predicted class (Positive)	Predicted class (Negative)
Actual class (Positive)	True Positives TP	False Negatives FN
Actual class (Negative)	False Positives FP	True Negatives TN

TABLE III. EVALUATION MEASURES

False Positive Rate	FP_{RATE} (fpr) = FP/(FP+TN)
True Positive Rate	TP_{RATE} (Acc_+) = TP/(TP+FN)
True Negative Rate	TN_{RATE} (Acc_-) = TN/(TN+FP)
AUC	AUC = $(1+TP_{RATE}- FP_{RATE})/2$
G-mean	G− mean = $\sqrt{Acc_+ \times Acc_-}$
Precision	Precision = TP/(TP+FP)
Recall	Recall = Acc_+
F−measure	F-measure = (2×Precision×Recall)/(Precision+Recall)

5 Experimental Results

In this section the several experiments have been done using RUSBoost, BalanceCascade and EasyEnsemble algorithms. In subsection 5.1 the experiments have been done in order to find the best base learner among the C4.5, SVM and KNN and the best performed algorithm has tried to be found in subsection 5.2. In subsection 5.3 the experiments have been done with good performed algorithm according to the different class distribution.

5.1 Base Learners Performance

This section presents the results of our experiments with RUSBoost, BalanceCascade and EasyEnsemble. We investigated the performance of these techniques by different learners when classification models are trained using C4.5, SVM and KNN. We used AUC, F-measure, G-mean to evaluate the compared algorithms. The best results for the three algorithms have been obtained when the C4.5 is used as the base learner which we can observe from Fig. 1-9. The details are given below.

RUSBoost. When we calculated AUC (Fig.1) C4.5 has performed well on tree data sets and SVM has outperformed for four of eight data sets and KNN on one data sets. From Fig.2-3, we can see the results of RUSBoost in terms of F-measure and G-mean. When the C4.5 is used as the base learner it has outperformed for four of eight data sets, SVM has performed well on tree data sets and KNN on one data set.

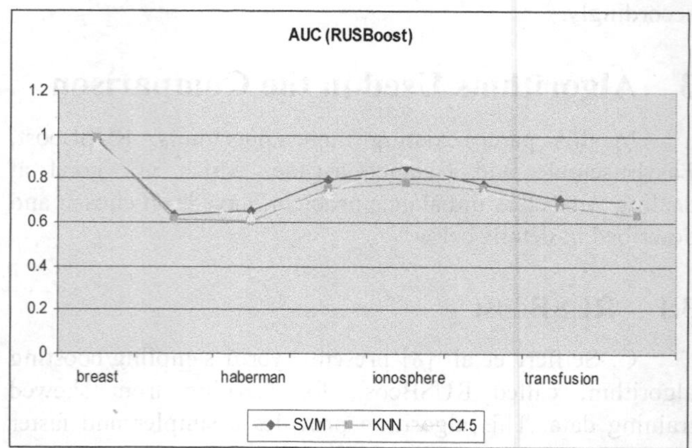

Fig. 1. AUC results of RUSBoost algorithm

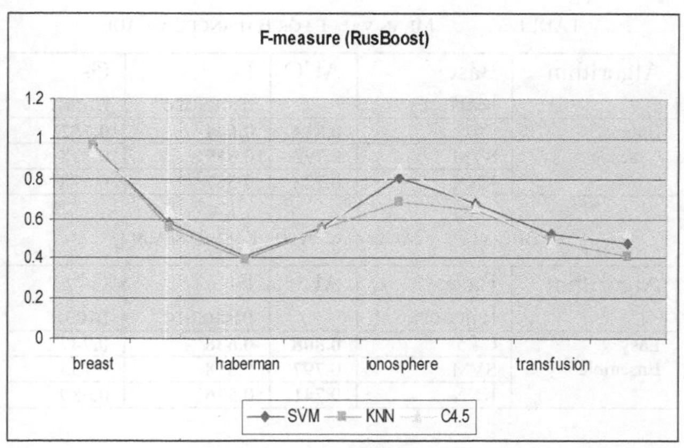

Fig. 2. F-measure result of RUSBoost algorithm

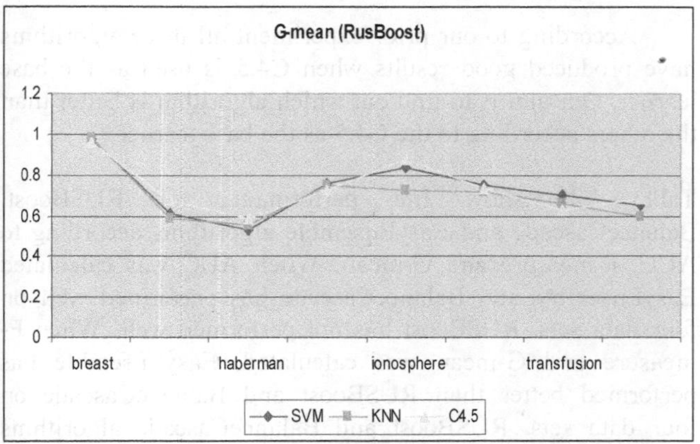

Fig. 3. G-mean results of RUSBoost algorithm

BalanceCascade. From Fig.4, we can observe the results of BalanceCascade algorithm in terms of AUC. When the C4.5 is used as the base learner the good results have been obtained in six out of eight data sets. When SVM is taken as the base learner it has been successful on two data sets. F-measure and G-mean (Fig.5-6) using C4.5 have been performed well over all data set. SVM and KNN are not performed well when they were used as the base learners.

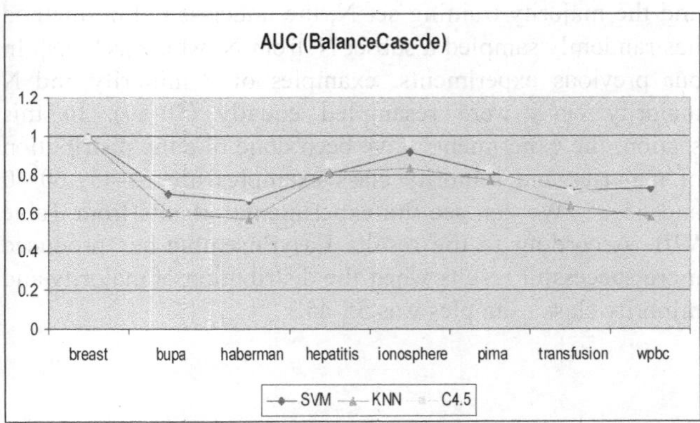

Fig. 4. AUC results of BalanceCascade algorithm

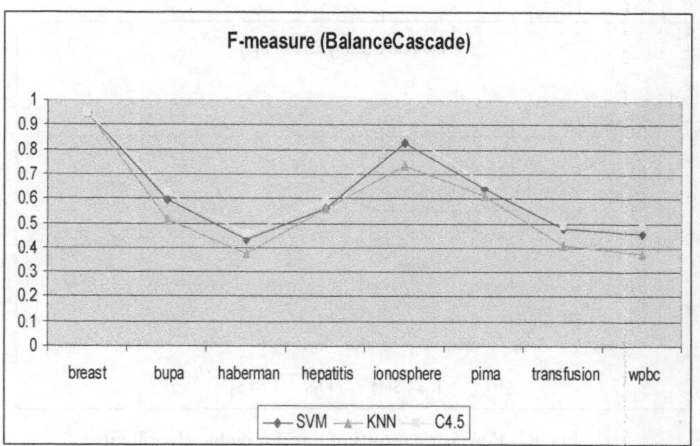

Fig. 5. F-measure results of BalanceCascade algorithm

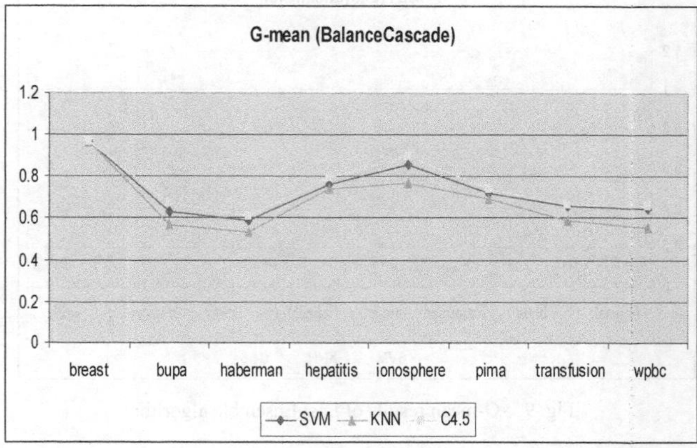

Fig. 6. G-mean results of BalanceCascade algorithm

EasyEnsemble. Fig. 7, 9 show the performance of EasyEnsemble algorithm as measured using AUC and G-mean. C4.5 has performed well in six out of eight data sets and SVM in two data sets. When using F-measure (Fig.8) to measure the performance using C4.5 it has been successful on five data sets and SVM on tree data sets. When KNN is selected as the base learner it has not performed well.

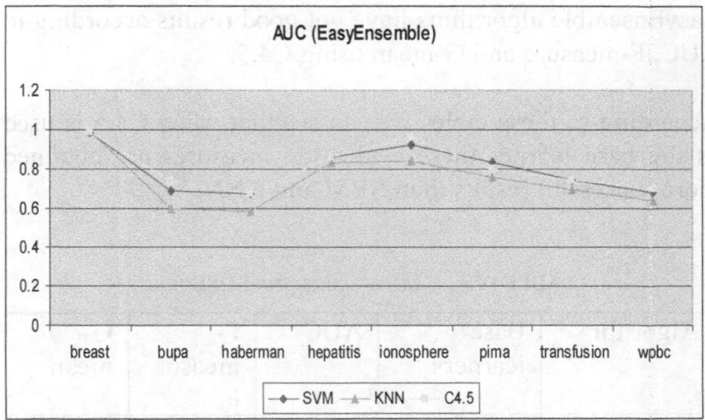

Fig. 7. AUC results of EasyEnsemble algorithm

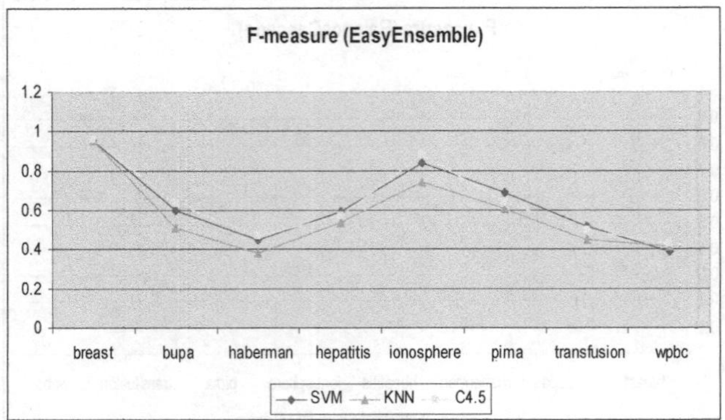

Fig. 8. F-measure results of EasyEnsemble algorithm

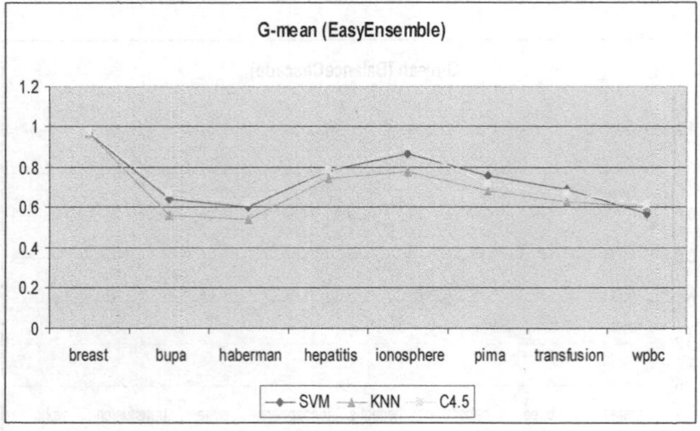

Fig. 9. G-mean results of EasyEnsemble algorithm

Tables IV-VI show the performance of C4.5, SVM and KNN using RUSboost, BalanceCascade and EasyEnsemble algorithms according to AUC, F-measure and G-mean, which are averaged over all data sets.

Table IV shows that the RUSBoost algorithm has got good results according to F-measure and G-mean using C4.5 and good AUC result using SVM.

Tables V, VI show that the BalanceCascade and EasyEnsemble algorithms have got good results according to AUC, F-measure and G-mean using C4.5.

According to these tables we can see that when C4.5 is used as the base learner these evaluation measures are obtained more successful results than SVM and KNN.

TABLE IV. MEAN VALUE FOR RUSBOOST

Algorithm	Base learners	AUC	F-measure	G-mean
RUSBoost	C4.5	0.7483	**0.6366**	**0.7345**
	SVM	**0.7625**	0.6234	0.7269
	KNN	0.7266	0.5863	0.6979

TABLE V. MEAN VALUE FOR BALANCECASCADE

Algorithm	Base learners	AUC	F-measure	G-mean
Balance Cascade	C4.5	**0.814**	**0.644**	**0.752**
	SVM	0.792	0.619	0.728
	KNN	0.723	0.567	0.678

TABLE VI. MEAN VALUE FOR EASYENSEMBLE

Algorithm	Base learners	AUC	F-measure	G-mean
Easy Ensemble	C4.5	**0.808**	**0.636**	**0.747**
	SVM	0.797	0.628	0.735
	KNN	0.741	0.576	0.689

5.2 Algorithm Performance

According to our prior experiment all three algorithms have produced good results when C4.5 is used as the base learner. Our aim is to find out which algorithm is better than the others according to the C4.5 as the base learner.

Table VII show the performance of RUSBoost, BalanceCascade and EasyEnsemble algorithms according to AUC, F-measure and G-mean. When AUC was calculated EasyEnsemble and BalanceCascade has performed well on four data sets, RUSBoost has not performed well. When F-measure and G-mean was calculated, EasyEnsemble has performed better than RUSBoost and BalanceCascade on four data sets. RUSBoost and BalanceCascade algorithms have been successful on two data sets.

The experiments show that the EasyEnsemble performs better than RUSBoost and BalanceCascade when C4.5 is used as the base learner.

5.3 Class Distribution Analysis

EasyEnsemble has been found as more successful algorithm according to our prior experiments. In EasyEnsemble there were given the minority training set P and the majority training set N, the under-sampling method has randomly sampled a subset N' from N, where |N'| <|N|. In our previous experiments, examples of P minority and N majority class were resampled equally (50-50). In this section, the experiments have been done like the distribution of majority and minority class examples are 55-45, 60-40 and 65-35. We can see the experimental results from Table VIII. According to the results EasyEnsemble has produced more successful results when the distribution of majority and minority class examples was 55-45.

TABLE VII. THE AUC, F-MEASUE AND G-MEAN RESULTS OF RUSBOOST, EASYENSEMBLE AND BALANCECASCADE ALGORITHMS USING C4.5

	AUC			F-measure			G-mean		
	RUSBoost	Balance Cascade	Easy Ensemble	RUSBoost	Balance Cascade	Easy Ensemble	RUSBoost	Balance Cascade	Easy Ensemble
Breast	0.9569	0.987	**0.993**	0.9380	0.951	**0.961**	0.9567	0.969	**0.975**
Bupa	0.6807	**0.745**	0.738	**0.6362**	0.626	0.636	**0.6778**	0.673	0.672
Haberman	0.6303	**0.677**	0.674	0.4487	0.454	**0.468**	0.5889	0.612	**0.623**
Hepatitis	0.7353	0.852	**0.862**	0.5375	**0.597**	0.573	0.7242	**0.797**	0.789
Ionosphere	0.8845	0.961	**0.963**	0.8567	0.875	**0.878**	0.8808	0.897	**0.904**
Pima	0.7413	**0.821**	0.797	0.6634	**0.666**	0.644	0.7360	**0.739**	0.720
Transfusion	0.6598	0.712	**0.741**	0.4832	0.493	**0.501**	0.6254	0.668	**0.674**
Wpbc	0.6978	**0.754**	0.697	**0.529**	0.488	0.431	**0.6858**	0.657	0.618
	0/8	***4/8***	***4/8***	2/8	2/8	***4/8***	2/8	2/8	***4/8***
	Number of the best performed data sets								

TABLE VIII. PERFORMANCE OF EASYENSEMBLE AVERAGED OVER ALL DATA SETS IN TERMS OF CLASS DISTRIBUTION

	Class distribution (majority – minority)			
	50-50	55-45	60-40	65-35
AUC	0.794	**0.801**	0.788	0.79
F-measure	0.596	**0.61**	0.595	0.59
G-mean	0.733	**0.738**	0.724	0.716

6 Conclusion

In this paper RUSBoost, BalanceCascade and EasyEnsemble algorithms have been compared in order to alleviate the problem of class imbalance, which is one of the most important problems faced in data mining, according to base learners performance and algorithm performance. Experiments have been done on real-world data sets using the C4.5, SVM and KNN as the base learners. The performances of classifiers have been compared using AUC, G-mean and F-measure. When C4.5 is used as the base learner it has given better results than SVM and KNN learners for all three algorithms. According to the results of the experiment EasyEnsemble algorithm has been found as the best algorithm to alleviate the problem of class imbalance and with class distribution 55-45 (majority - minority).

7 References

[1] N. Japkowicz. "Learning from imbalanced data sets: A comparison of various strategies, Learning from imbalanced data sets"; The AAAI Workshop 10-15. Menlo Park, CA: AAAI Press. Technical Report WS-00-05, 2000.

[2] K. Nageswara Rao, Prof. T. Venkateswara rao, Dr. D. Rajya Lakshmi, "A Novel Class Imbalance Learning Method using Subset Filtering". International Journal of Scientific & Engineering Research Volume 3, Issue 9, September-2012 1 ISSN 2229-5518.

[3] W. Fan, S. J. Stolfo, J. Zhang, "AdaCost: misclassification cost-sensitive boosting," Proc.Int. Conf. Machine Learning, Bled, Slovenia, June, 1999, pp. 97-105.

[4] Yuchun Tang, Yan-Qing Zhang, N. V. Chawla, "SVMs modeling for highly imbalanced classification," IEEE Trans. Syst., Man, and Cybern. - Part B, vol. 39, no. 1, pp. 281 - 288, Feb. 2009.

[5] Zhi-Qiang Zeng and Ji Gao, "Improving SVM classification with imbalance data set," Proc. 16th Int.Conf. Neural Information Processing (ICoNIP 2009), Bangkok, Thailand, 2009, pp. 389-398.

[6] N.V. Chawla, A. Lazarevic, L. O. Hall, and K.W.Bowyer, "SMOTEBoost: Improving prediction of the minority class in boosting," in Proc. Knowl. Discov. Databases, 2003, pp. 107–119.

[7] Hongyu Guo, Herna L Viktor, "Learning from Imbalanced Data Sets with Boosting and Data Generation: The DataBoost-IM Approach", ACM SIGKDD Explorations Newsletter, 2004.

[8] Seiffert C., Khoshgoftaar T. M., Van Hulse J., & Napolitano A., "RUSBoost: A Hybrid Approach to Alleviating Class Imbalance," IEEE Transactions on Systems, Man and Cybernetics, Part A: Systems and Humans, 40(1), 185-197, 2010.

[9] Xu-Ying Liu, Jianxin Wu, and Zhi-Hua Zhou, "Exploratory undersampling for class imbalance learning," IEEE Transactions on Systems, Man and Cybernetics, 39(2):539-550, 2009.

[10] R. E. Schapire, "A brief introduction to Boosting," in Proceedings of the 16th International Joint Conference on Artificial Intelligence, Stockholm, Sweden, 1999, pp. 1401–1406.

Efficiency of crop yield forecasting depending on the moment of prediction based on large remote sensing data set

Alexander Murynin[1], Konstantin Gorokhovskiy[2] and Vladimir Ignatiev[3]
[1] Dorodnicyn Computing Centre of RAS, Moscow, Russia
[2] Institute for Scientific Research of Aerospace Monitoring "AEROCOSMOS", Moscow, Russia
[3] Moscow Institute of Physics and Technology, Dolgoprudny, Russia

Abstract—*Agricultural yields can be predicted from detailed multi-year remote sensing image sequences using measured features of vegetation conditions. In this paper, the dependency between the moment of prediction and the accuracy of the forecast is studied. The linear model is selected as a basic approach of yield forecasting. Then, the model is extended with non-linear components (factors) in order to improve the accuracy of the forecasts. The extensions take into consideration long-term technological advances in agricultural productivity as well as regional variations in yields (fertility of the lands). The accuracy of the model has been estimated based on the time period between the moment of the forecast formation and the harvest time.*

Keywords: Image mining, crop yield forecasting, nonlinear regression.

1 Introduction

Effective and efficient yield forecasting is an important area of the research which helps in ensuring food security all around the world. Nowadays yield forecasting based on multi-year observations of the land surface from space is a subject of intensive research based on data mining techniques.

The principal idea of the approach is the following. Having two years with similar observations of informative features of vegetation condition one should expect similar yields. However, the complexity of vegetation models and incompleteness of observations provides a challenge in verification of any yield forecasting method. The level of noise makes it difficult to extract a useful signal. Only by analyzing a large dataset which contains several regions and spans over many years it is possible to estimate the accuracy of a yield forecast model and reliably compare it with any alternatives.

For these reasons it is required to use a source of data that can provide reliable and accurate spatial-temporal measurements of vegetation conditions. This data can be obtained from remote sensing using satellite imaging. Various sources of remote sensing information can be used for the purposes of the crop yields forecasting as complimentary to weather measurements as well as a sole source of data [3], [4], [5], [6].

There were attempts to develop a computational algorithm which uses different channels from the multispectral radiometers [4]. As an intermediate step the multispectral images were transformed into vegetation indices. These indices were used for droughts detection as well as the crop yields forecasting. The technique has shown promising results [7], [8], [9].

Rather than studying a general accuracy of the forecasts the authors of this study concentrated on finding a dependency between the moment of prediction and efficiency of yield forecasting for the selected model.

2 Forecasting model

The proposed model can be described as follows. Crop yield of a particular culture at a given region should be fairly reliably predicted by function whose parameters are averaged (by this region) values of vegetation indices during growth and ripening period of the crop. The better the historical track record of the indices is known, the better the forecast of crop yields can be made.

The model for forecasting crop yields is based on the history of vegetation indices, accumulated over a fixed period of the year but not earlier than the start of the growing season.

The model for crop yields forecasting in general looks like:

$$y_{kr} = f_{kr}\left(v(t), v(t+1), v(t+2), \ldots\right) \tag{1}$$

where

y_{kr} - predicted value of the yield at the end of the season for territorial region r and crop type k,

f_{kr} - unknown function of the yield forecast for the region and crop type,

$v(t)$ - vegetation index value for a region,

t - time of the start of the measurements in the current growing season, with $t+1$, $t+2$, ... corresponds to a discrete points in time when the measurements carried out during this season.

According to the recent studies in the field of crop yield forecasting there is a close correlation between vegetation indices obtained from multispectral images and productivity of plants [10], [11], [12]. In order to forecast the yield most of the studies require so called crop masks [13]. A reliable extraction of crop masks is organizationally difficult task. It requires close collaboration with farmers. Not to mention that is it often financially unfeasible activity. The proposed in this study method extracts the information from the overall condition of vegetation in the given area instead of using crop masks.

Regional administrative divisions are selected as units of the area. This choice is made due to the structure of available statistical information on the crop yields for previous years, which are officially provided by the government and publicly available. For example, the State Statistics Service of the Russian Federation allows obtaining historical information about the crop yields for all regions of the country [14]. Availability of this information makes it possible to adjust free parameters of a model to a specific region and crop type through learning process (or optimization).

From the available statistical data one can make a conclusion that the variability of the yield is small relative to its magnitude. Hence, after expansion of a yield model function in equation (1) into the Taylor polynomial the main contribution to the accuracy of the forecast will be made by the linear terms of the polynomial. As a simplification the non-linear terms of higher orders can be ignored. In this case, the model becomes linear, i.e. f_{kr} is a linear combination of $v(t)$.

2.1 Basic approach

As was mentioned earlier the model can be transformed into the linear one assuming that the soil and climate characteristics have a small variation for within (but ton between) the studied regions. The simplified linear model can be written as:

$$y_{rk} = \sum_{t=1}^{T} \alpha_{rk}(t) \cdot \langle v(t) \rangle_r \tag{2}$$

where

k - index indicating the crop type,

r - index pointing to a territorial region of the Russian Federation,

y_{rk} - crop yield estimate for a given area r, and crop type k,

$\langle v(t) \rangle_r$ - average value of the vegetation condition index for a given territorial region, $\langle \cdot \rangle_r$ is averaging operator by region r,

$\alpha_{rk}(t)$ - adjustable parameters of the model for individual time intervals of the vegetation period (or calendar year).

The insufficient amount of statistical information available for one region makes it difficult to adjust this simple model. Indeed, only a decade of yields data is available.

Thus, the model needs to be extended in order to be used in practical applications.

2.2 Resultant model with factor adjustment for regions and temporal trend

In the case when the amount of statistical data available for the adjustment of the individual models for each of the region is not sufficient it is required to reduce the number of adjustable parameters. Thus, in particular, one can assume that the main contributions to the difference in crop yields are made by the following factors:

- fertility of soils in a region,
- climatic differences between regions,
- amount of solar radiation, depending on the latitude of a region.

At the same time to build the model, we deliberately ignore the temporary displacement of growing season for various regions, for example, for the western part of the Russian Federation taken for this study. Using the above assumptions, the following formula can be suggested:

$$y_{rk} = C_{rk} \cdot \sum_{t=1}^{T} \alpha_k(t) \cdot \langle v(t) \rangle_r \tag{3}$$

where

k, r, y_{rk}, $\langle v(t) \rangle_r$ - were defined for equation (2),

$\alpha_k(t)$ - adjustable parameters of the model for crop type k but are now independent from the region

$\langle \cdot \rangle_r$ - averaging operator by region r,

C_{rk} - coefficient of performance of the region r for specific crop type k.

During the validation of the model described by the equation (3) was found that there are regular errors which depend from the year of the forecast. This observation was used to make a hypothesis about existence of a long-term trend in the yields. This trend hypothesis needed to be validated. In order to do that the original forecasting model has been modified to take into account the assumed trend as described further in the text.

Indeed, in the past few decades, there has been a stable growth of crop yields per unit of cultivated area [15] all over the globe. This is due to several factors. First of all, it is worth noting the progress in genetic engineering for crops improvement. Improved seeds are more resistant to drought, temperature changes and parasites. Another factor is the more efficient use of fertilizers. Progress in the field of agricultural technology has allowed to harvest with fewer losses. Improved methods of chemical treatment resulted in better control of pest populations.

Such improvements can be referred as a trend in crop yields. It is likely required to take it into account in order to improve the accuracy of the forecast. This trend may not continue but it is essential to (at least) remove this regular error from the training data.

Making an assumption that the yields changes are linearly dependent on time within the studied historic period it is possible to modify the previous model to predict the long-term increase in yields.

The average yield for the current year can be expressed from the yield of previous year by the following equation:

$$\frac{\langle y_{current}\rangle - \langle y_{start}\rangle}{\langle y_{start}\rangle} = \beta\cdot(Y_{current} - Y_{start})$$

where

$\langle y_{current}\rangle$ - average crop yield for the current year $Y_{current}$,

$\langle y_{start}\rangle$ - average crop yield in year of the beginning of observations Y_{start},

$\langle\cdot\rangle$ - averaging operator,

β - relative annual increase in productivity due to long-term trend.

Let us express $\langle y_{current}\rangle$ in terms of the other variables:

$$\langle y_{current}\rangle = [1+\beta\cdot(Y_{current} - Y_{start})]\cdot\langle y_{start}\rangle$$

The following nonlinear regression formula for the refined model of crop yields is obtained:

$$y_{rk} = [1+\beta\cdot(Y - Y_{start})]\cdot C_{rk}\cdot\sum_{t=1}^{T}\alpha_k(t)\cdot\langle v(t)\rangle_r$$

where

k, r, y_{rk}, $\langle v(t)\rangle_r$, $\alpha_k(t)$, C_{rk} - were defined for equations (2) and (3),

Y - current year for which the crop yields are evaluation,

Y_{start} - the year of the beginning of observations,

β - relative annual increase in productivity due to long-term trend.

Unlike initial linear approach this model can no longer be qualified as a linear but rather a factor model due to multipliers describing productivity of a region and the trend.

Authors made attempts to reduce this model back to linear one by adding coefficients C_{rk} and $[1+\beta\cdot(Y - Y_{start})]$ but the accuracy of the model has been reduced drastically in this case. It can be explained by significant variation of the above mentioned multipliers (which can be also called factors). For example the productivity (fertility) C_{rk} can differ by the factor of 2 between the regions.

On the other hand insufficient data per region makes it impossible to build separate linear model per individual region.

2.3 Forecast accuracy and the moment of the prediction

One can assume that the earlier in time we are making the forecast the less accurate it will be. In the contrary the closer we get to a harvest the more reliable forecasts we can achieve. Usually, it is required to know how reliable the forecast is depending on the date of the prediction. This study tries to provide the answer to this question for the described above model.

3 Results

The accuracy of the model was assessed using K-fold cross-validation method. The whole set of the input data has been partitioned several times into two subsets: the training subset and the testing subset. Each time the testing subset was different. In total 10 unique testing subsets were used so that the data for each year available were used as a testing subset at least once.

In addition, the dependency between the accuracy of the forecast and the moment of the forecast was studied. In each case it was assumed that the remote sensing data was available up to the moment of the forecast. That is: if, for example, a prediction takes place in August 13 one can assume that all the remote sensing data (for this year) prior to this date is already available for the analysis.

Cross-validation is used to evaluate the performance of the forecasting model in a manner similar to that which is commonly used for classifiers.

Due to insufficient amount of statistical data during the validation the chronological order of training data and validation data was not preserved. This does not jeopardize the validation for the following two reasons:

1) the forecasting scenario for each year is based on processing of the current year data and does not depend of the data from other (including previous) years.

2) the forecasting algorithm uses only data that strictly precede the forecasting time within the giving vegetation period (within the current year). In other words, the model uses only past observations for each forecasting moment and does not involve any future data within the considered year.

Remote sensing data for 14 regions of Russian Federation over span of 10 years (from 2000 to 2009) were used for training and validation of the model. Total data set used for training and validation consisted of more than 1500 images with dimensions 2400 x 2400 pixels each. The size of the images set was more than 54 GB. After the process of model training was complete the smaller set of images was used in the forecast for a given year. The images used in the forecast represent 7 separate moments in time with 16 days distance from each other. These images are 16 days cloudless composites snapshots with resolution of 500 meters captured by MODIS TERRA satellite.

For example, figure 1 shows the image with vegetation condition index (NDVI) for 3 regions of the Russian Federation: Ivanovo, Vladimir and Nizhny Novgorod regions. The image represents values of the index for 9 May 2007.

In order to simulate the change in prediction date the snapshots used in the model were selected in a "sliding window" manner. This is to maintain the number of snapshots constant and equal to 7. The constant number of observations was required to avoid model overfitting and preserve the ratio of the amount of training cases versus the number of coefficients in the model.

The resultant accuracies of prediction for two groups of cultures are shown in Table 1. Forecasting errors of crop yields is evaluated in the form standard deviation of forecasted values from the yield data available through the official statistics.

As can be seen from Table 1 the worst result is generated in late spring / early summer. This is due to the fact that information about vegetation condition in early stages of growth is less informative than in final stages. The visual representation of the forecasting errors is shown in Figure 2.

Fig. 1. The area in study: for Ivanovo (A), Vladimir (B) and Nizhny Novgorod (C) regions for 9 May 2007 (Vegetation index map).

It is worth noting that the proposed model does not require crop masks which are usually used in similar studies [13]. Our method extracts the required information from the overall condition of vegetation in the given area rather than condition of a given crop. The lack of crop mask may reduce the accuracy of the forecasts. Nevertheless, the comparison of our results with the results from other studies [13] shows that our model demonstrate competitive accuracy even without the crop mask or other information about cultivated areas such as soil types and weather conditions.

TABLE I

STANDARD DEVIATION OF THE FORECASTS CROP YIELDS FOR DIFFERENT CULTURES USING CROSS-VALIDATION FOR THE MODEL WITH FACTOR ADJUSTMENT FOR REGIONS AND TEMPORAL TREND FOR THE PERIOD 2000-2009. BEST ACCURACIES ARE MARKED WITH BOLD ITALIC FONT.

	Date of the forecast					
	June 10	June 26	July 12	July 28	August 13	August 29
Grain	16,1%	15,2%	13,7%	12,7%	***12,5%***	13,5%
Potato	19,8%	22,1%	20,4%	18,7%	18,0%	***16,9%***

4 Conclusion

This study introduces an approach to develop an efficient model for crop yield forecasting via extracting information from the large set of satellite images.

Also, the dependence between the moment of the forecast and its accuracy has been studied. It is shown the closer to the harvest the prediction is performed the better accuracy can be achieved. However, the useful forecast can be done even several months before the harvest.

The dependency of forecasting errors from the date of the forecast is shown in Figure 2 for the yields of grain and potatoes.

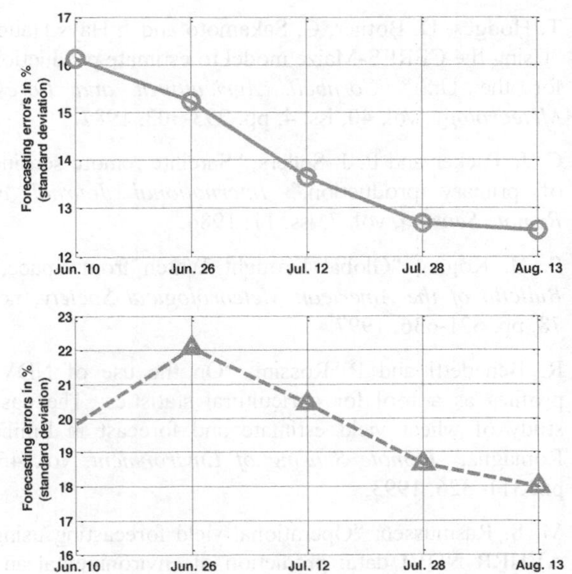

Fig. 2. Standard deviation of yield predictions for grain (top image) and potato (bottom image) cultures. As can be seen the accuracy of predictions improves gradually as we get closer to the harvest.

The main advantage of the suggested approach is the possibility to use free to access information, including satellite multispectral images and official statistical data.

It is shown that by finding out the appropriate form of forecasting function on the basis of remote sensing images and official government statistics data is possible to obtain fairly accurate results of yields forecasting.

Other advantage is that the proposed approach does not require any specific information about the cultivated areas. It minimizes the amount of the input data for practical implementation of the models. Specifically, this approach does not require crop masks. In other words the method uses overall condition of the vegetation in the given area rather than the condition of specific culture.

The analysis of the accuracy of forecasting crop yields using cross-validation method demonstrates the advantages and disadvantages of the proposed approach. The model with factor adjustment for regions and temporal trend allows obtaining forecasting errors from 12% to 22% depending on the culture, and the moment in time of the forecast. The closer we get to the harvest the better accuracy we can expect for such kind of forecasts.

We plan to continue this study with enhanced forecasting models in order to improve the accuracy and generality of the crop yield prediction as well as extend the forecasts to cover the more territorial regions.

References

[1] J. D. McQuigg, "Economic Impacts of Weather Variability," Atmospheric Science Dept University of Missouri, Columbia, 1975

[2] T. Hodges, D. Botner, C. Sakamoto and J. Hays Haug, "Using the CERES-Maize model to estimate production for the U.S." *Cornbelt. Agricultural and Forest Meteorology*, vol. 40, iss. 4, pp. 293-303, 1987.

[3] C. J. Tucker and P. J. Sellers, "Satellite remote sensing of primary production," *International Journal of Remote Sensing*, vol. 7, iss. 11, 1986.

[4] F. N. Kogan, "Global Drought Watch from Space," *Bulletin of the American Meteorological Society*, no. 78, pp. 621-636, 1997.

[5] R. Benedetti and P. Rossini, "On the use of NDVI profiles as a tool for agricultural statistics: The case study of wheat yield estimate and forecast in Emilia Romagna," *Remote Sensing of Environment*, vol. 45, pp. 311–326, 1993.

[6] M. S. Rasmussen, "Operational yield forecasting using AVHRR NDVI data: prediction of environmental and inter-annual variability," *International Journal of Remote Sensing*, vol. 18, pp. 1059–1077, 1997.

[7] L. S. Ungana and F. N. Kogan, "Drought monitoring and corn yield estimation in Southern Africa from AVHRR data." *Remote Sensing of Environment*, vol. 63, pp. 219–232, 1998.

[8] E. Aigner, I. Coppa and F. Wieneke, "Crop Yield Estimation Using NOAA – AVHRR Data and Meteorological Data in the Eastern Wimmera (South Eastern Australia)," *International Archives of Photogrammetry and Remote Sensing*, vol. 33, part B7, Amsterdam, 2000.

[9] Cs. Ferencz, P. Bogna, R. J. Lichtenberger, D. Hamar, Gy. Tarcsai, G. Timar, G. Molnar, Sz. Pasztor, P. Steinbach, B. Szekely, O. E. Ferencz and I. Ferencz-Arkos, "Crop yield estimation by satellite remote sensing," *International Journal of Remote Sensing*, vol. 25, no. 20, pp. 4113–4149, 2004.

[10] L. B. Phillips, A. J. Hansen and C. H. Flather, "Evaluating the species energy relationship with the newest measures of ecosystem energy: NDVI versus MODIS primary production." *Remote Sensing of Environment,* vol. 112, iss. 9, pp. 3538-3549, 2008.

[11] M.P. Kale, Sarnam Singh and P.S. Roy, "Biomass and productivity estimation using aerospace data and Geographic Information System" *Tropical Ecology*, vol. 43 no. 1, pp. 123-136, 2002.

[12] G. Edward, H. Alfredo, N. Pamela and N. Stephen, "Relationship Between Remotely-sensed Vegetation Indices, Canopy Attributes and Plant Physiological Processes: What Vegetation Indices Can and Cannot Tell Us About the Landscape," *Sensors 8*, no. 4, pp. 2136-2160, Mar. 2008.

[13] A. S. Islam and S. K. Bala, "Estimation of yield of wheat in greater Dinajpur region using Modis data," presented at 3rd International Conference on Water & Flood Management, ICWFM-2011, 2011.

[14] Regions of Russia. Social and Economic Indicators. 2011. Available: http://www.statbook.ru/eng/catalog.html?page=info&id=306

[15] R. A. Fischer, D. Byerlee and G. O. Edmeades, "Can Technology Deliver on the Yield Challenge to 2050?," presented at the Expert Meeting on How to Feed the World, Food and Agriculture Organization of the United Nations, Rome, 2009.

Neural Network Forecasting with the S&P 500 Index Across Decades

Mary Malliaris[1] and A.G. Malliaris[2]
[1]Information Systems & Operations Management, Loyola University, Chicago, IL, USA
[2]Economics, Loyola University, Chicago, IL, USA

***Abstract** - The purpose of this paper is to track the effectiveness of a neural network as a forecasting tool across six decades, using only information derived from closing prices. From 1950 through 2010, a neural network for each decade was trained on ten years of S&P 500 data and used to forecast the S&P 500's direction each day of the following year. The set of inputs and structure of the networks remained constant across time. Only the data sets used for training and forecasting changed. The results show that, with one exception over 60 years, the neural networks remained robust from training to validation sets and were correct more than 50% of the time.*

Keywords: Data Mining, S&P 500 Index, Financial Forecasting, Neural Networks

1 Introduction

Many different models have been used in predicting the S&P 500 stock index and its behavior. Some models use technical indicators and others add fundamental indicators or economic growth indicators. When neural networks are used, the focus is often on a short period of time with a network optimized for that period. The aim of this paper is to develop a neural network using only data based on the closing value of the S&P 500 Index and then apply it to six decades of data, using the same structure and set of inputs across decades. The objective is to see whether this small network with no outside information can be a viable guide for a trading strategy.

From the early 1970s, literature on the behavior of stock prices has been divided between theories supporting market efficiency and active portfolio management. Proponents of market efficiency believe that information is incorporated quickly into the market and that prices fully reflect this information. As a result, prices cannot be predicted because they are changed by the constant arrival of new information. Traders, on the other hand, maintain a belief that forecasting is possible. However, only a few of them have managed to outperform the market over decades. Thus, while market efficiency remains the dominant theory, much effort is expended both by money managers and academics in an effort to predict well over time. One common support on the side of trading comes from the use of technical analysis.

A varied sample of studies over the years that have examined the usefulness of technical analysis and active management strategies include [1], [2], [3], [4], [5], [6], [7], and [8]. These studies span the spectrum of findings. Some are critical of simple technical rules and find the random walk does as well; others find that, once transactions costs are included, the predictive advantage of trading rules is moderated; and finally, some find evidence that some technical indicators have significant ability to aid in predictions.

In a recent paper, Schulmeister [9] looked at technical trading strategies on the S&P500 futures and their ability at predicting returns. This paper found that, in the 1960s and 1970s, the use of daily stock data was profitable. But the same indicators from 2000-2006 had lessening results for those strategies. One possible explanation given by the author is that the trend to higher frequency in trading on technical indicators gives insufficient time to produce a profitable strategy.

Other papers have focused more on fundamental aspects and macroeconomic data when developing forecasting models. Doran, Ronn, Goldberg [10] found that short term expected returns were highly volatile. Avramov and Chordia [11] used firm specific factors to predict returns. Prominent factors for predicting S&P returns are the Treasury yield and dividend yield. However, this predictability holds best for small-cap stocks, growth stocks, and momentum stocks, and not the broader market. Hajizadeh,et al [12] used Garch and neural network models to successfully forecast the S&P volatility. Niaki and Hoseinzade [13] looked at 27 potential financial and economical variables from March 1994 through June 2008 and were successful forecasting using this large set of internal and external variables. Fukushima [14] followed a number of hybrid models on monthly data and recommended complex hybrid models as the best method for forecasting. Tsiah et al [15] had earlier developed a hybrid neural network and rule-based system that predicted effectively over a six-year period. This paper develops a number of specialized signals similar to those of technical analysis. Kara et al [16] used ten technical indicators as inputs in both an artificial neural network model and a support vector machines model and found that the ANN outperformed the SVM.

In this paper, rather than using technical indicators, fundamental aspects, or macroeconomic data, we build a network using variables derived only from the S&P 500 index daily prices. We then investigate the ability of this single network structure to forecast for over six decades. The next section describes the data and the network used. Section 3 details the results from this set of neural networks. We end with conclusions and recommendations for further research.

.

2 Data and Network Description

The data set began with the raw closing values of the S&P 500 from 1950 through 2010. These raw values were used to construct the other fields used as inputs. From the closing values, we calculated the percent the closing value changed, a four-day moving average of the closing values, and the percent change in these moving averages.

We then looked at the type of movement each day from the previous day, and logged it as having gone up or down. A string of two-day movement was formed by concatenating today's direction with yesterday's direction. For example, if the S&P 500 moved up yesterday and down today, the string UD was entered. In a similar fashion, strings of three, four and five days up and down movements were recorded. In Figure 1, we show, as an example, the percent of time over each decade that the possible four-day strings, DD, DU, UD, and UU have occurred. One interesting pattern we see is that, in every decade except the last one, the most often occurring string was UU. We also see that the string DD was on the rise from the 50s through the 70s, then decreased. Lastly, we see the increase over every decade of movement shifts. That is the percent of time that UD and DU occur increases from the 50s through the 00s. Charts for three, four, and five day patterns also indicate similarities in dominant patterns over the decades.

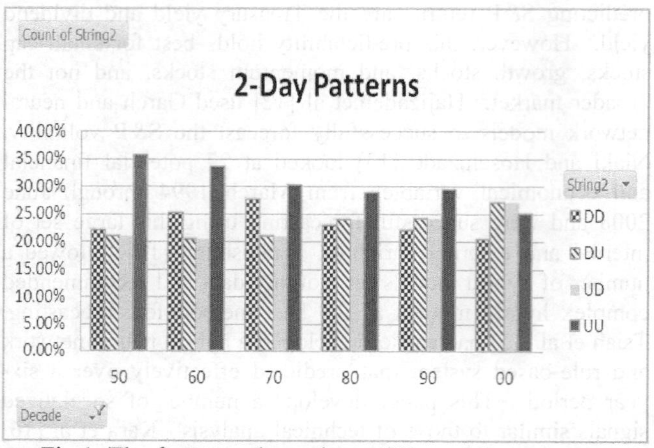

Fig 1 The four two-day strings of Up and Down across decades

Another ways of giving information to the networks is by condensing these directional movements to a count of the number of Up movements in strings of a given length. So we counted the number ups in strings of length 1 to 5 and used these as additional inputs. That is, our focus shifted from the exact pattern to a count of positive moves within a specific number of days. Figure 2 shows the result of converting the three days strings into this type of count. Within three days, it is possible to have 0, 1, 2, or 3 up movements. Looking at these counts across the decades, we see that the percent of times that three days in a row were all up has steadily decreased from the 50s through the 00s. In addition, there are more occurrences with exactly 2 ups than with exactly 1 up with three days. Last, the percent of times that three days were all down has been decreasing since the 70s.

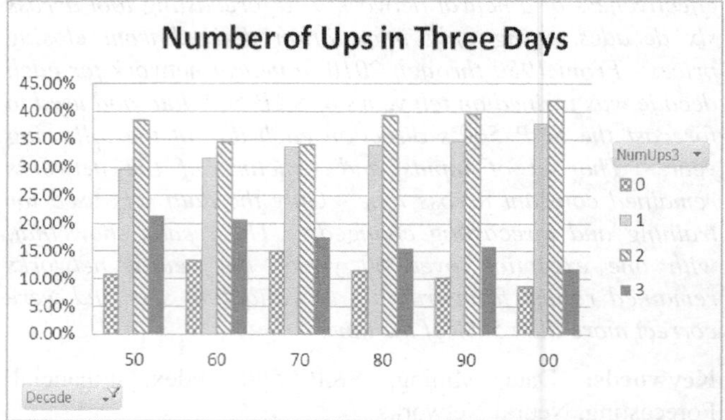

Fig 2. Count of Up Movements in Three Days, shown as percent within each decade.

The entire set of 14 inputs used in each of the networks is listed in Table 1. This table has a column with the label used for the input, an explanation of that input, and a sample value. The Target field, DirTp1, not shown in the table, was a prediction of the direction the S&P will move tomorrow, Up or Down.

After the columns were constructed for the entire data set, subsets were formed for the training and validation sets. A training set was fashioned for each of the decades where the entire ten years of data was available. We had a total of six training sets for the decades from 1950 through 2009. Validation sets were comprised of the entire year immediately following the associated training set. Specific dates for each of the training and validation sets are shown in Table 2.

All networks were developed and run in IBM's SPSS Modeler 14 software package. This package automatically selects an optimal network structure and settings. However, networks with alternate structures were also tested. Using the same inputs, networks with the recommended hidden layer of 9 nodes were tested against networks with hidden layers of 14 nodes and 20 nodes. The networks with hidden nodes of equal size and fan-out size did not improve the performance, so we used the Modeler suggested form with one hidden layer of nine nodes. Thus, for each multilayer perceptron, there were 14 inputs, one hidden layer with 9 nodes, and one output.

Table 1. Inputs for each network

Input	Explanation	Example
Close	Today's Closing Value	1132.99
PercChgClose	Percent Change in the Closing Value	1.60
CloseDir	Today's Closing Direction	U
MA4day	4 Day Moving Average of Closing	1137.08
PercChg4MA	Percent Change in the 4-day Mov. Avg.	-0.0593
NumUps1	Was today's close an Up move	1
NumUps2	Number of Up Closings in last 2 days	1
NumUps3	Number of Up Closings in last 3 days	2
NumUps4	Number of Up Closings in last 4 days	2
NumUps5	Number of Up Closings in last 5 days	3
String2	2-day Up and Down pattern	DU
String3	3-day Up and Down pattern	UDU
String4	4-day Up and Down pattern	DUDU
String5	5-day Up and Down pattern	UDUDU

Table 2. Data sets for each network.

Decade	Training/Testing Set	Validation Set
50s	Jan 1, 1950 -- Dec 31, 1959	Jan 1, 1960 – Dec 31, 1960
60s	Jan 1, 1960 -- Dec 31, 1969	Jan 1, 1970 – Dec 31, 1970
70s	Jan 1, 1970 -- Dec 31, 1979	Jan 1, 1980 – Dec 31, 1980
80s	Jan 1, 1980 -- Dec 31, 1989	Jan 1, 1990 – Dec 31, 1990
90s	Jan 1, 1990 -- Dec 31, 1999	Jan 1, 2000 – Dec 31, 2000
00s	Jan 1, 2000 -- Dec 31, 2009	Jan 1, 2010 – Dec 31, 2010

With this 14-9-1 structure, the value used for the random seed was 229176228 and 30% of the training set was used to prevent over-fitting. The training algorithm used by Modeler stops after 15 minutes, or when the error in the over-fit prevention set does not decrease after each cycle, if the relative change in the training error is small, or if the ratio of the current training error is small compared to the initial error. The structure of a typical network used for each of the decades is shown in Figure 3.

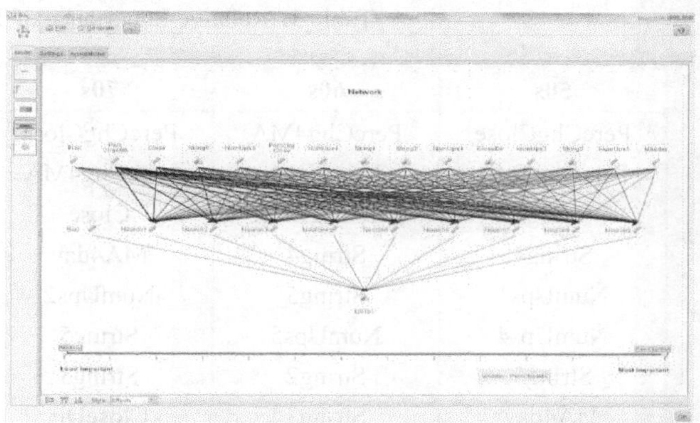

Fig 3. Structure of each of the neural networks.

3 Results

After training a network for each decade, Modeler allows us to look at the results in several ways. First, Modeler displays the 10 variables that have the greatest significance in determining the final value of the target. This is called the predictor importance, and indicates the relative importance of each predictor in estimating the model. All values assigned to these variables are relative to the variable's impact and their numeric values sum to 1.0. Predictor importance does not relate to model accuracy. It is the importance of each predictor in making a prediction, not whether the prediction is accurate. Predictor importance is calculated from the test partition and looks at the impact each variable has on changes in the target field. The relative importance of the ten highest variables for each network is shown in Table 3. Here we see that the percent change in the closing price and in the 4-day moving averages are highly ranked in most decades. We also see that the string of 5 days has a lot of impact every decade. In addition, the number of up movements within sets of four days occurs in many of the network lists.

In the outputs from Modeler, a matrix showing the count of correct and incorrect predictions is generated. We can also feed other sets through the trained network to generate counts of prediction accuracy on new data sets. Table 4 shows the overall percent of times that the network was correct on the training and validation sets. We see, in the decades of the 50s, 60s, and 70s, both the training and validation sets are correct close to sixty percent of the time. The 80s, 90s, and 00s show a drop in the overall ability to forecast with this methodology, but with the exception of the final validation set, all results are still better than 50%.

Table 5 breaks these forecasts down further into each direction. The rows show actual Down and Up values while the columns have the predicted Down and Up movements. The percent of predictions correctly matching the actual values are in the diagonal and shown in bold. The off-

Table 3. Relative Importance of Top Ten Variables in Each Network.

50s	60s	70s	80s	90s	00s
PercChgClose	PercChg4MA	PercChgClose	PercChg4MA	PercChg4MA	PercChg4MA
PercChg4MA	NumUps4	PercChg4MA	Close	NumUps5	NumUps4
String5	PercChgClose	Close	String5	PercChgClose	MA4day
String4	String4	MA4day	NumUps3	MA4day	String5
NumUps1	String5	NumUps2	PercChgClose	String3	Close
NumUps4	NumUps5	String5	NumUps4	String5	PercChgClose
String3	String2	String3	String4	String4	String4
MA4day	String3	CloseDir	String3	Close	String3
NumUps5	MA4day	String4	NumUps1	String2	NumUps1
NumUps3	Close	NumUps4	CloseDir	CloseDir	NumUps3

Table 4. Percent of Correct Forecasts in Training and Validation Sets

Decade	Tr Percent Correct	Val Percent Correct
50s	59.00%	59.92%
60s	59.90%	62.99%
70s	59.94%	58.10%
80s	55.18%	54.94%
90s	56.25%	52.78%
00s	52.96%	47.22%

Table 5. Comparison of Training Set and Validation Set Performance, Values as % of Column

		Training Set Predictions			Validation Set Predictions	
Actual Direction		Down	Up		Down	Up
50s	Down	**53.90**	39.05		**61.68**	41.38
	Up	46.10	**60.95**		38.32	**58.62**
60s	Down	**57.94**	39.00		**67.02**	39.38
	Up	42.06	**61.00**		32.98	**60.62**
70s	Down	**58.88**	39.06		**53.25**	39.77
	Up	41.12	**60.94**		46.75	**60.23**
80s	Down	**53.21**	43.84		**63.16**	45.73
	Up	46.79	**56.16**		36.84	**54.27**
90s	Down	**53.43**	42.02		**56.70**	49.68
	Up	46.57	**57.98**		43.30	**50.32**
00s	Down	**50.67**	44.99		**40.74**	45.30
	Up	49.33	**55.01**		59.26	**54.70**

diagonal numbers indicate the percent of incorrect predictions. For example, the training set of the 50s correctly predicted Down 53.9% of the time, and correctly predicted Up 60.95% of the time. The validation set used on this network correctly predicted Down 61.68% of the time, and Up predictions were correct 58.62% of the time.

For the training set data, we see that the percent of correct Up forecasts is greater than the percent of correct Down forecasts in every decade, even though there is a slight decrease over time in these values. In contrast, the percent of correct validation set forecasts are greater for the Down forecasts in four out of six decades. In particular, the last validation set, which had less than 50% accuracy overall on the validation set, turns out to do much better on the Up forecasts. It is only in trying to predict the Down days that the network falls below 50% correctness.

4 Conclusions

In this paper, we built a series of neural networks using information constructed only from the closing values of the S&P 500 Index. These networks covered over sixty years and included a training set for each decade followed by a one year validation set from the following decade. All networks used the same 14-9-1 topology, the same random seed, and a testing set with 30% of the data to prevent overtraining. In addition, each trained network was applied to a validation set of the entire following year. There were fourteen input variables based on the closing values and direction of movement in comparison to the previous day. From among the fields calculated by using the numeric closing values, those with greatest impact were the percent change in the closing price relative to yesterday and the percent change in the four-day moving average of closing prices. From among the up and down string patterns, the five-day pattern had the most consistent impact. Last, from the fields that counted the number of up days in strings of a given length, the four day count appeared higher up on the list in most of the networks. In every decade, the networks did better than 50% correct predictions on both training and validation sets, except in the last validation set. In this last set, the percent of correct forecasts in the up direction was almost 55%, while the down forecasts were correct only 41% of the time.

Other than retraining the network on each decade, no other changes were made to the neural network, and all information given to the network came from variables constructed using the daily closing price. It is interesting that this identical structure, using the same inputs, was useful for over six decades. Future research might investigate a smaller training time, say a rolling window of one or two years. This might enable us to see the importance of specific variables gradually shifting over time.

5 References

[1] Fama E, Blume M. « Filter Rules and Stock-Market Trading » ; J of Bus 39:226-241, 1966.

[2] Jensen M, Benington G. « Random Walks and Technical Theories: Some Additional Evidence » ; J of Fin 25:469-482, 1970.

[3] Brown D, Jennings R. « On Technical Analysis » ; The Rev of Fin Studies, 2:527-551, 1989.

[4] Brock W, Lakonishok J, LeBaron B. « Simple Technical Trading Rules and the Stochastic Properties of Stock Returns » ; J of Fin, 47:1731-1764, 1992.

[5] Blume L, Easley D, O'Hara M. « Market Statistics and Technical Analysis: The Role of Volume » ; J of Fin, 49:153-181, 1994.

[6] Gencay R « The Predictability of Security Returns with Simple Technical Trading Rules » ; J of Empirical Fin, 5:347-359, 1998.

[7] Allen F, Karjalainen R « Using Genetic Algorithms to Find Technical Trading Rules » ; J Fin Econ, 51:245-272, 1999.

[8] Lo A, Mamaysky H, Wang J. Foundations of Technical Analysis: Computational Algorithms, Statistical Inference, and Empirical Implementation. J of Fin 55:1705-1765, 2000.

[9] Schulmeister S. « Profitability of technical stock trading: Has it moved from daily to intraday data?, Review of Financial Economics, 18:4, pp : 190-201, October 2009.

[10] Doran J, Ronn E, Goldberg R. « A Simple Model for Time-Varying Expected Returns on the S&P 500 Index » ; Journal of Investment Management, 7 :47-72, 2009.

[11] Avramov D, Chordia T. « Predicting Stock Returns » ; Available at SSRN: http://ssrn.com/abstract=352980 or http://dx.doi.org/10.2139/ssrn.352980, March 23, 2005.

[12] Hajizadeh E, Seifi A, Fazel Zarandi M, Turksen I. « A hybrid modeling approach for forecasting the volatility of S&P 500 index return » ; Expert Systems with Applications, Vol 39:1, pp: 431-436, 2012.

[13] Niaki S, Hoseinzade, S. « Forecasting S&P 500 index using artificial neural networks and design of experiments » ; Journal of Industrial Engineering International, Vol 9:1, 2013.

[14] Fukushima A. « Hybrid forecasting models for S&P 500 index returns » ; The Journal of Risk Finance, Vol. 12 (4), pp.315 – 328, 2011.

[15] Tsaih R, Hsu Y, Lai C. « Forecasting S&P 500 stock index futures with a hybrid AI system » ; Decision Support Systems, 23 :2, pp: 161-174, 1998.

[16] Kara, Y., Acar Boyacioglu, M., & Baykan, Ö. K. « Predicting direction of stock price index movement using artificial neural networks and support vector machines: The sample of the Istanbul Stock Exchange » ; Expert Systems with Applications, Vol 38(5), 5311-5319, 2011.

Data Uncertainty Handling in High Level Information Fusion

R. Woodley[1], **M. Gosnell**[1], **and A. Fischer** [1]
[1]21st Century Systems, Inc., 6500 Prairie Ave, Omaha, Nebraska, USA

Abstract - *Situation/threat modeling and threat prediction require higher levels of data fusion to provide actionable information to the warfighter. A significant challenge to the fusion of information into higher levels of knowledge is the uncertainty in the underlying data. This uncertainty may be in the form of trust pedigree, sensor noise, and data relevancy. Handling these elements within the fusion structure is vital in order to develop high level information fusion (HLIF) systems for multi-sensory, multi-use applications. 21st Century Systems, Inc. has developed the initial concepts for what we call Fusion with Uncertainty Reasoning using Nested Assessment Characterizer Elements (FURNACE). FURNACE utilizes nested fusion loops building higher levels of information fusion without losing sight of the potential weaknesses of the underlying data. FURNACE uses advanced technologies in information filtering and reasoning to provide the levels of fusion. These reduce bias, disambiguate, and fill gaps in the data. FURNACE handles uncertainty through an innovative evidential reasoning technology that provides the necessary data to the analyst, such that they can account for the pedigree of the information supplied as it is aggregated and fused. Our preliminary results indicate this uncertainty handling scheme is capable of maintaining process standards such that actionable information is produced for the warfighter.*

Keywords: High Level Information Fusion (HLIF), Nested Fusion Loops, Situation Assessment and Modeling, Threat and Impact Assessment, Bias and Ambiguity and Uncertainty Handling

1 Introduction

The FURNACE effort is focused on the process and algorithms for high level data fusion with improved handling for bias, ambiguity, and uncertainty (BAU). Figure 1 shows our conceptual diagram of how FURNACE will support higher level fusion processes. FURNACE changes the paradigm in that it does not view the fusion levels as a sequential hierarchy. Instead, FURNACE parallels a meta-tagging scheme that adds the fused information as metadata to the existing data. Each level of FURNACE deals with the direct data plus the added metadata generated by each level of the fusion. FURNACE is able to account for data that is controlled by the analyst (i.e., a set of sensors or known data sources where the analyst can direct the content) as well as 'outsourced' data sources where the data is being repurposed for the analyst's needs and not collected specifically for those needs. The concept is applicable to all levels of data fusion. Initial work has developed the underlying algorithmic needs to produce a fusion system able to handle BAU, repurposed data, and do so in a cohesive manner. FURNACE creates the framework by which the user can connect feeds, define the domain, utilize repurposed data, and add context to information.

FURNACE takes a cue from the way human situational awareness is modeled to create an innovative data fusion system. By parallelizing the fusion process (i.e., getting away from the sequential hierarchy paradigm), the higher level fusion emerges from the data. The continual feedback

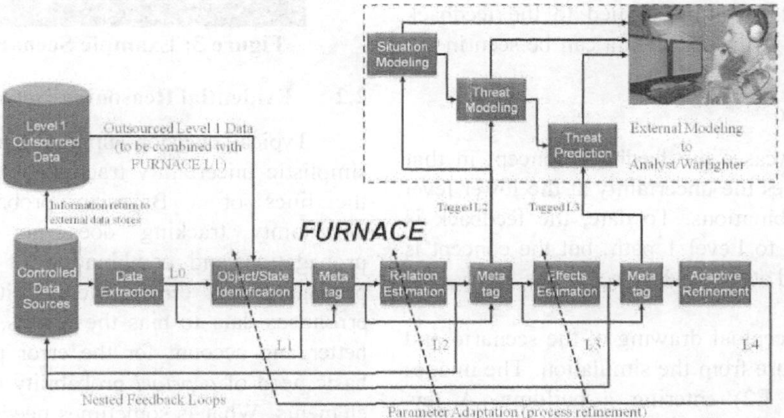

Figure 1: Conceptual diagram of the nested fusion loops.

bolsters true evidence, while ambiguous, or even fraudulent, data is suppressed. The structure of FURNACE provides a wealth of power to reduce bias and disambiguate data, but we also add filtering and fusion processes to the FURNACE concept. These algorithms help FURNACE further identify relevant data and helps fill in the gaps caused by missing data. A data uncertainty handling capability rounds out FURNACE's arsenal by helping the analyst understand the trustworthiness of the data so that proper decisions are made from the fused information FURNACE generates.

Our initial results show that the FURNACE concept is technically feasible. The resulting design and proof-of-concept form the basis for future development and a testbed to showcase FURNACE's abilities. We highlight here an example scenario from the Global Intelligence, Surveillance and Reconnaissance (GISR) domain to demonstrate the algorithms and concepts. FURNACE's design is different from previous fusion systems in that each fusion level bears symmetry with the other levels in the form and function of the design. Using a common fusion engine [1], [2], abstracted for both high and low level information fusion, provides a unique opportunity to setup an advanced nested feedback system that drives the reduction of BAU, as well as stabilizes the fusion results. This system is designed to handle BAU and repurposed data at an intrinsic level rather than treat it as an outside calculation. Given the period of performance constraint on initial Phase I work, we were able to show FURNACE operating up to Level 2. However, we show that the abstractions made in the design should be able to be adapted for any fusion level which we will show in Phase II development.

2 Example Scenario and Evidence Reasoning

We now describe the example scenario and data reasoning algorithm. The scenario is designed to test the data reasoning component of FURNACE. While the scenario is not overly complex, it does show where the data reasoning is able to modify the fusion results as it is applied to the feedback mechanism. The change in the fused data can be seen in the Results Section.

2.1 Example Scenario

This Scenario showcases the feedback concept in that higher level fusion reduces the uncertainty at the lower level to make additional combinations. To date, the feedback is designed for the Level 2 to Level 1 path, but the concept is general enough to be used at higher levels.

Figure 2 is the conceptual drawing of the scenario and Figure 3 is a screen capture from the simulation. The images show two entities (E1, E2) entering a building. A few minutes later two more entities (E3, E4) exit the building. The Area of Interest (AOI) is covered by three sensors. A GMTI-radar detects movement in a large area around the building. An EO-camera (EO1) has a Field of View (FOV) covering the front entrance. A second EO-camera (EO2) has a FOV covering the parking lot, but does not see the exit. E1 and E2 are detected by GMTI and EO1, while E3 is first detected by the GMTI and then EO2. E4 is only ever detected by the GMTI. There exists domain knowledge that no vehicle may enter the building. E1 and E3 have similar appearance, but there is no information about what happens inside the building to connect the two directly.

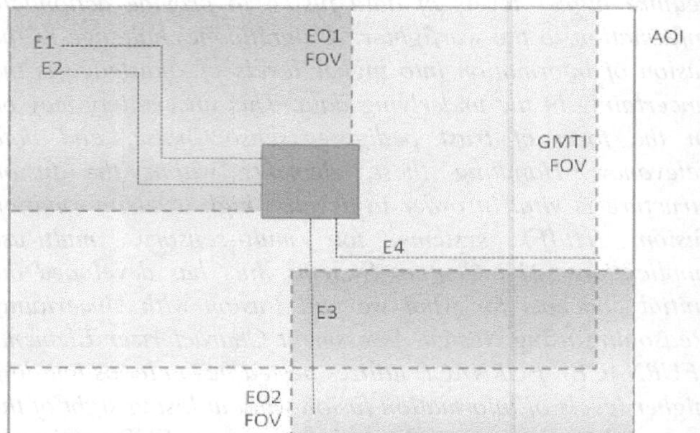

Figure 2: Concept drawing of Example Scenario

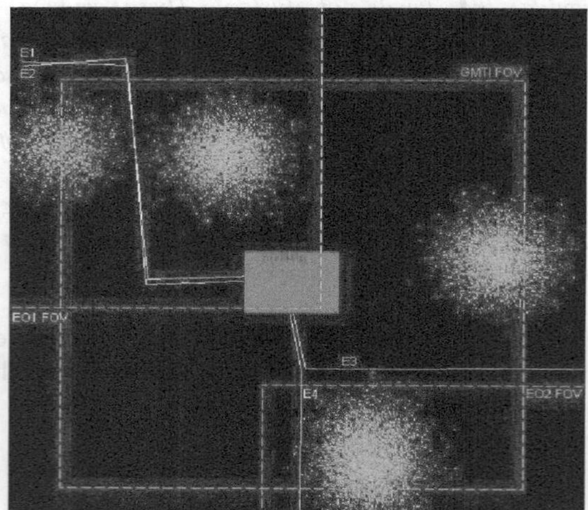

Figure 3: Example Scenario screen capture

2.2 Evidential Reasoning Network (ERN®)

Typical decision-support approaches will use either a simplistic uncertainty tracking method or something along the lines of a Bayesian probability approach. Simple uncertainty tracking does not fully account for the propagation and combination of uncertainty. It does not propagate the error whereby it may allow potentially erroneous data to bias the results. Bayesian approaches are better and account for the error propagation, but have the basic need of *a priori* probability measures on the uncertain elements. What is sometimes needed is a way to incorporate various degrees of uncertainty ranging from simple percent unknown up to probabilistic measures, where available. 21CSi's Evidential Reasoning Network (ERN®) technology is designed for this purpose.

ERN technology uses a belief algebra structure for providing a mathematically rigorous representation and manipulation of uncertainty within the evidential reasoning network. Since the introduction of the Dempster-Shafer Theory of Evidence [3], new evidential reasoning methods have been, and continue to be, developed, including fuzzy logic [4] and Subjective Logic [5], [6]. Recently, Mr. Steven O'Hara from 21CSi worked with Dr. Jøsang (creator of Subjective Logic) to develop Hypothesis Abduction using Subjective Logic (Analysis of Competing Hypothesis) [7], [8]. An evidential reasoning framework was needed to ensure that evidential reasoning expressions are coherent, consistent, and computationally tractable. 21CSi's Evidential Reasoning Network is a novel structure that addresses these needs. The two prime belief algebra operators required are *consensus* and *discount*. These operators allow the propagation of belief values through the network amongst various opinion generating authorities, such as human subject matter experts or software agents that perform some sort of data analysis, processing, and reasoning. The belief algebra structure is capable of using probabilistic belief mass assignments through the use of belief frames. The ERN Toolkit includes a Subjective Logic and Dempster-Shafer belief algebra implementation.

Subjective Logic (SL) [9] is a way of thinking about uncertainty that builds upon the basic ideas presented by Dempster and Shafer to incorporate the subjectivity of all observations. In Subjective Logic, we operate on opinions as opposed to facts. An *opinion* ω_x^A on a subject x by a party A is a 4-tuple of the belief (b_x^A), disbelief (d_x^A), uncertainty (u_x^A), and relative atomicity (a_x^A) (with respect to all possible states) about subject x. Note that $b_x + d_x + u_x = 1$, so while it is not necessary to specify all three of these values, it is convenient when performing certain calculations.

SL introduces the *consensus* operator to combine opinions and the *discount* operator to support the belief in the *source* of an opinion. It has been shown that the consensus combination rule generates more intuitively correct results than common variants of Dempster's rule [5], [6]. Subjective Logic can be viewed as an extension to binary logic and probability calculus.

The consensus between opinions ω_x^A and ω_x^B is defined by the formulas in Figure 4. In the case where we are dealing with dogmatic opinions (those with no uncertainty), then K=0, and a slightly different form of these equations is needed, and can be found in the referenced literature on Subjective Logic [9]. We use the $\oplus$ symbol to represent the consensus operator. The discount operator represents an

$$K = u_x^A + u_x^B - u_x^A u_x^B$$

$$b_x^{A,B} = \frac{b_x^A u_x^B + b_x^B u_x^A}{K}$$

$$d_x^{A,B} = \frac{d_x^A u_x^B + d_x^B u_x^A}{K}$$

$$u_x^{A,B} = \frac{u_x^A u_x^B}{K}$$

$$a_x^{A,B} = \frac{a_x^A u_x^B + a_x^B u_x^A - (a_x^A + a_x^B) u_x^A u_x^B}{K - u_x^A u_x^B}$$

Figure 4: Consensus Operation

opinion about another opinion, or the source of the opinion. The opinion ω_B^A represents the opinion of B by A. This is a model for the concept of trust, where an opinion/source you trust would be discounted slightly, while an opinion that is not trustworthy would be discounted greatly. Figure 5shows the SL Discount operator. We use a $\otimes$ symbol to represent a discount operator.

$$b_x^{A,B} = b_B^A b_x^B$$

$$d_x^{A,B} = b_B^A d_x^B$$

$$u_x^{A,B} = d_B^A + u_B^A + b_B^A u_x^B$$

$$a_x^{A,B} = a_x^B$$

Figure 5: Discount Operation

The expressivity of the belief algebra is important in a heterogeneous system that may be incorporating some mixture of probabilistic and evidential reasoning. When working in known probability measure spaces, the belief algebra should reduce to probability calculus to preserve the accuracy and functionality of the supporting probabilistic systems—and Subjective Logic is easily shown to do so.

3 Results

The design of the feedback mechanism has two components: the threshold function to determine if feedback is necessary and the uncertainty adjustment to produce the actual feedback information. The first thing that the feedback mechanism does is determine if there is need to send back any information. This is done for two reasons: First, since every relationship (including all primary, secondary, etc.) can potentially generate feedback, we would quickly create a logjam of data that would slow the process. By forcing the relationships to pass a threshold (i.e., a sniff-test to see if there is anything unusual that hampers the relationship (either in believability or uncertainty)) we only require the system to analyze that data and not everything. Second, we also eliminate many race conditions. By forcing the system to stabilize once it hits a threshold, feedback oscillations are attenuated while the system identifies and updates characteristics about an entity.

To calculate the threshold we utilize 21CSi's ERN technology. If we consider each relationship from the scenario as an opinion, then the data that forms the relationship is the evidence. Equation 1 shows an example of the calculation for relationship R1 based upon the entities E1 and E2 which form R1:

$$\omega_{R1}^{E1+E2} = \omega_{R1}^{E1} \wedge \omega_{R1}^{E2} \qquad \text{Eq. 1}$$

Equation 1, in belief algebra, says that the opinion on R1 is the opinion multiplication of the opinion of E1 about R1 and the opinion of E2 about R1. For our purposes, we are using the multiplication operator since the consensus operator is too sensitive to calculations with a dogmatic condition either in belief or disbelief. The opinion multiplication operator ^ is calculated as:

$$b_{x\wedge y} = b_x b_y + \frac{(1-a_x)a_y b_x u_y + a_x(1-a_y)u_x b_y}{1-a_x a_y},$$

$$d_{x\wedge y} = d_x + d_y - d_x d_y,$$

$$u_{x\wedge y} = u_x u_y + \frac{(1-a_y)b_x u_y + (1-a_y)u_x b_y}{1-a_x a_y},$$

$$a_{x\wedge y} = a_x a_y.$$

The opinion E1 about R1 takes into account how much E1 effects R1, the uncertainty of E1, and any additional domain knowledge that can affect the relationship. Then by analyzing the resulting opinion's disbelief (which is a function of both the level of dissimilarity and uncertainty in the opinion) we have a measure of the need for re-evaluating the entities that formed the relationship.

If the opinion about R1 has zero disbelief there is no need to re-evaluate the entities E1 and E2. However, if a relationship generates a feedback request, FURNACE would then determine what should be fed back. The relationships in the example are:

- R1: E1 – E2 spatial close
  E1 – E2 temporal close
- R2: E1 – Bg location close
- R3: E2 – Bg location close
- R4: E3 – Bg location close
- R5: E4 – Bg location close
- R6: E3 – E4 spatial close
  E3 – E4 temporal close

Suppose Relationship R5 reaches a threshold. With domain knowledge from the GISR examples stating that vehicles cannot exit the building, the opinion generated on R5 from the Building (Bg) will contain relatively high disbelief that E4 is a vehicle. Suppose E4 is initially classified as possibly vehicular (with high uncertainty). In this case, when the opinion multiplication combines the E4 and building opinions into R5, the disbelief reaches the threshold to be re-evaluated. When the updated R5 opinion is fed back, it forces the uncertainty that E4 is a human to decrease. When Level 1 processes the new uncertainty levels, it is able to determine that E4 is a human and not a vehicle.

The R1 opinion from Equation 1 is a primary relationship, dealing only with direct connections. Secondary relationships are harder to show and may or may not be useful. Table 1 shows a connectivity matrix example where the relationship label indicates a primary connection. If we look at the table, we see that E4 has primary connections to E3 and the building (Bg). However, Bg has primary connections to all four entities which implies that E4 has secondary connections E1 and E2. We can then form secondary opinion equations similar to Equation 1 using the opinion of E1 about E4 and so forth.

Table 1: Connectivity matrix

E1	-				
E2	R1	-			
E3			-		
E4			R6	-	
Bg	R2	R3	R4	R5	-
	E1	E2	E3	E4	Bg

The feedback due to primary connections affects the *entities* individually that formed the relationship. However, the secondary connections affect the *relationship* between the entities. Equation 2 shows the opinion of the secondary relationship between E1 and E3.

$$\omega_{E1,E3}^{R2+R4} = \omega_{E1,E3}^{R2} \wedge \omega_{E1,E3}^{R4} \qquad \text{Eq. 2}$$

When this is calculated it shows a high belief that a relationship exists between E1 and E3. The relationship is due to the secondary connection with building between the two entities as well as the similarity in appearance (which is obtained as metadata when processed in Level 1). This secondary connection opinion reaches the threshold to activate the feedback mechanism. This time, however, the feedback reduces the uncertainty such that the data for E1 and the data for E3 are the same entity. When Level 1 re-calculates the entities, it creates a new entity list.

Table 2: Base rate and probability expectation calculations

	Veh	person	Bldg	Irrelevant	Uncertainty
Person - E4	0.22	0.22	0.22	0.34	
E4(a)	0.15	0.2	0.05	0.6	
P(E4)	0.271	0.288	0.017	0.424	
Building B - E5			0.97		0.03
E5(a)	0.15	0.2	0.05	0.6	
P(E5)	0.0045	0.006	0.9715	0.018	

Table 3: Context truth table

Relationships	Veh	person	Bldg	Irrelevant	
Building A	T	T	F	T	Garage, can take cars and people
Building B	F	T	F	T	Regular building, only people can interact
Building S	F	T	F	F	Secure Facility, need to know everything
Person	T	T	T	T	
Vehicle	F	T	T	T	

Table 4: Relationship opinion calculation

Relationship Opinions - Building A

R5		B	D	U	A	P(x)
O1	E5 Opinion of R5	0.983	0.017		0.5	98%
O2	E4 Opinion of R5	1	0		0.5	100%
P(R5) = 98%	O1 ^ O2	0.98	0.02		0.25	**98%**

Relationship Opinions - Building B

R5		B	D	U	A	P(x)
O1	E5 Opinion of R5	0.712	0.288		0.5	71%
O2	E4 Opinion of R5	1	0		0.5	100%
P(R5) = 71%	O1 ^ O2	0.71	0.29		0.25	**71%**

The above example illustrates that the bias produced by the initially mislabeled entity E4 was reduced along with the uncertainty and ambiguity allowing the system to correctly classify the object. As the examples become more realistic and more complex we will be able to utilize the feedback system to iteratively correct the analysis and provide the best possible fusion results to the analyst. The actual calculations are somewhat more involved than portrayed above, but the principles still apply. Using data from the Example Scenario and the above analysis we calculate the base rate (Ex(a)) and probability expectation (P(Ex)) using the Evidential Reasoning Network for the entities involved in the relationship, shown in Table 2.

We next construct the *a priori* truth table of the possible context (which could possibly also be learned context). Table 3 shows three possible building types that could be included to extend this scenario. We will show first the calculation for a building (Type A) that would allow vehicles near it and then redo the calculation for the Type B building to illustrate the contextual aspect of FURNACE.

We can now calculate the opinion on the relationship as shown in Table 4. Note that when Entity E4 might be classified as a vehicle, the Type A building allows for vehicles, so it concludes that the relationship is 98% valid, so no feedback is needed. However, Type B does not allow vehicles and would trigger the feedback mechanism since the relationship is considered only 71% valid (see Table 4).

4 Conclusions

We investigated how a holistic fusion approach could be constructed and how uncertainty could be measured and then manipulated by the ERN technology. We also designed a feedback mechanism around the ERN technology which would help stabilize and prevent race conditions in the data feedback. By analyzing the level of disbelief in the fused output (along with its associated uncertainty) we could produce an intelligent threshold that would indicate if fused information is in need of additional processing. The actual feedback acts to either reduce or increase uncertainty such that lower fusion processes can make better decisions about the objects. Preliminary results show that the contextual information in the initial scenarios is successful in providing relevant feedback and reductions in uncertainty to provide fused output. These results indicate the approach to be feasible, but more work is needed to verify and increase the robustness of the concept through additional data and increasingly complex and higher level information fusion.

5 Acknowledgment

21st Century Systems, Inc. would like to acknowledge the support of the Office of the Secretary of Defense and the U.S. Air Force Research Laboratory (Contract No: FA8750-12-C-0168).

6 References

[1] R. Woodley, M. Gosnell, and A. Fischer, "High Level Information Fusion (HLIF) with Nested Fusion Loops," in *SPIE Signal Processing, Sensor Fusion, and Target Recognition XXII*, Baltimore MD.

[2] M. Hansen and C. Donahue, "Passive Sonar Fusion Multi-Model Ensemble Agents (MMEA)," 21st Century Systems, Inc, Technical Report, Oct. 2005.

[3] G. Shafer, *A mathematical theory of evidence*. Princeton NJ: Princeton University Press, 1976.

[4] P. Palacharla and P. Nelson, "Understanding relations between fuzzy logic and evidential reasoning methods," in *IEEE Proceedings of the Third IEEE Conference on World Congress on Computational Intelligence*, 1994, pp. 1933–1938.

[5] A. Jøsang, "A Logic for Uncertain Probabilities," *International Journal of Uncertainty, Fuzziness and Knowledge-Based Systems*, vol. 9, no. 3, pp. 279–311, Jun. 2001.

[6] A. Jøsang, "Subjective Evidential Reasoning," *International Conference on Information Processing and Management of Uncertainty in Knowledge-Based Systems (IPMU 2002)*, pp. 1671–1678, Jul. 2002.

[7] A. Jøsang, S. O'Hara, and K. O'Grady, "Base Rates for Belief Functions," in *Proc. Workshop on the Theory of Belief Functions (Belief 2010)*, 2010.

[8] A. Jøsang and S. O'Hara, "Product of Multinomial Opinions," in *Proc. International Conference on Information Processing and Management of Uncertainty in Knowledge-Based Systems (IPMU)*, 2010.

[9] A. Jøsang, *Subjective Logic: Draft*. Online at http://folk.uio.no/josang/papers/subjective_logic.pdf, 2013.

A Preliminary Approach to Study the Causality of Freezing of Gait for Parkinson's: Bayesian Belief Network Approach

A. Saad[1,3], A. Zeineldine[2], I. Zaarour[2], M. Ayache[1], D. Lefebvre[3], F. guerin[3], P. Bejjani[4]

[1]Islamic University of Lebanon, Engineering Faculty, Department of Biomedical, Beirut, Lebanon

[2]Lebanese University, Faculty of business and economical sciences, Doctoral school of Science and technology

[3]Laboratoire Groupe de Recherche en Electrotechnique et Automatique du Havre, Université du Havre France

[4]Director of Parkinson Center, Notre Dame de secours University Hospital, Beirut , Lebanon

Abstract - *Parkinson disease patients suffer from a disabling phenomenon called freezing of gait, which can be described as if their feet are 'frozen' or stuck, but that the top half of their body is still able to move. In this paper, we make a graphical probabilistic modeling study, "Bayesian Belief Network (BBN) approach" of a previously collected dataset that represents the measurements of acceleration sensors placed in the ankle, knee and hip of PD patients during their march. In an attempt to know if this is a traditional BBN model or a causal one, we built a FoG Model and tested it, first by forming an Epidemiological Approach, then, by inferring causal relations based on Additive Noise Models (ANM). Consequently, we built a Bayesian Naive Classifier Model related to FoG. The Bayesian belief Network classifier had the ability to identify the onset of freezing of PD patients, during walking using the extracted features. Promising results appeared into evidence when testing the BNC classifier models*

Keywords: Parkinson Disease, Freezing of Gait, Bayesian Network, Causality, Data Mining.

1 Introduction

Parkinson's disease (PD) is a common neurodegenerative disease. One of PD symptoms is freezing, which may occur during gait, speaking or a repetitive movement like handwriting. Freezing of gait (FoG) can be defined as "a brief, episodic reduction of forward progression of the feet despite the intention to walk", and is often described by patients as if their feet are glued to the floor for a short period of time [1]. FoG aspects of PD do not respond well to dopaminergic drugs, as it is one of the symptoms that often result from non-dopaminergic pathology [2]. Recent studies, investigated measuring features that may evaluate patterns of the handwriting and speech of PD patients and school children [3, 4], which can be used to detect writing and voice freezing episodes for PD patients. This study is oriented to the freezing of gait phenomenon of PD patients. Our proposal is a modeling approach that focuses on a specific class of Probabilistic Graphical Model (PGM), the directed[1]one, i.e. Bayesian Belief Network (BBN).The followed methodology consists of: (1) assessing the framework of the BBN model, we tried to identify if this is a traditional BBN case [5, 6] or a causal one [7, 8]. (2) By means of the assessed model a classification tool is built, to judge the FoG episodes of PD patients. This classification model can be inferred to diagnosis or forecasting issues. The following part of this paper discusses the explanation and background of the pre-collected dataset, and it gives a clear explanation of the modification done on the dataset. Next, we illustrated a brief state of the art in theories and concepts surrounding the *causality, as a background,* in order to assess a causal link between variables of interest, before building our BBN model. The machine learning approach is described in the fourth part, whereas the obtained results are described and illustrated in the fifth part of the paper. Finally the last part holds the general conclusion that is accomplished.

2 Data Preparation

2.1 Native Dataset

In previous studies, Marc Bächlin et al developed a wearable assistant for Parkinson's disease patients that detects FoG by analyzing frequency components inherent in the body movements, using measurements from on-body acceleration sensors [11]. They used three acceleration sensors positioned in different body parts (*ankle, knee and hip*) each sensor measures three components of acceleration(x: *horizontal forward axis*, y: *the vertical axis and z: the horizontal lateral axis*).Their detection algorithm was based on the principle illustrated by Moore et al that introduced a freeze index (FI) to evaluate the gait condition of PD patients. The FI is a ratio defined as the power in the 'freeze' band [3-8Hz] divided by

---

[1]The alternative classes of Probabilistic Graphical Model are Undirected Markov networks and Hybrid graphs [9], those families of classes are more adapted to statistical physics and computer vision [10].

the power in the 'locomotor' band [0.5-3Hz]. The FoG detection is performed by defining a 'freeze' threshold, where values above this threshold are considered as FoG events [12]. Referring to the data obtained by Marc Bächlin et al from 10 PD patients, we incorporated these values into our probabilistic model in an attempt to predict upcoming FoG episodes. The dataset is composed of separated files for each patient, although some patients have multiple files for each test done. Each file is composed of a matrix that contains measurement data of the three sensors in x, y and z directions. The last column contains the annotation, weather FoG occurred or not. These annotations was labeled by synchronizing the data by a video that recorded each patient run, which allowed to identify the exact start times, durations and end times of FoG episodes.

2.2 Employed features

Starting from the above described dataset, the freezing index for each acceleration measurement is calculated, using a sliding window that calculates the FI of a 256 samples of acceleration data. So we mapped the dataset from raw data to normalized data for generalization purposes in future work. The second step was to eliminate the data which is irrelevant to experiments done (Annotation 0), in order to constrain the classification between occurring of FoG and or NoFoG. Then we calculated the magnitude of the three components of the FIs. Accordingly, all of the measurements taken are represented in a low dimensional dataset, that it is ready to be introduced to our proposed machine learning model.

3 Causality

3.1 Epidemiological Approach

Inferring the causal structure of a set of random variables is a challenging task. In the causality domain, the variables of interest are not just statistically associated with each other, yet there is a causal relationship between them. The famous Slogan "correlation does not imply causation" is recognized and seems approved by researchers in empirical and theoretical sciences. For example, in analyzing a demographic database, we may find that the attributes representing the number of hospitals and the number of car thefts in a region are correlated. This does not mean that one causes the other. Both are actually causally linked to a third attribute, namely, population [2][13]. Formerly, authors in [14] quoted that "one *of the common aims of empirical research in social sciences is to determine the causal relations among a set of variables, and to estimate the relative importance of various causal factors*". Recently, the philosophical wise of this quote is broadly discussed, specifically in the medical and health science, more precisely in the context of Symptoms/Disease episodes [15, 16, 17, 18]. In particular, Lagiou et al. (p 565), mentioned that: *"A factor is a cause of a certain disease when alterations in the frequency or intensity of this factor, without concomitant alterations in any other factor, are followed by changes in the frequency of occurrence of the disease, after the passage of a certain time period (incubation, latency, or induction period"* [17]. In order to highlight the causal trends of our FoG problem, and from an epidemiological point of view, explicitly we will illustrate the FoG Model (Figure 1) by applying what so-called Hills Criteria of Causation [19], which is an old approach that outlines the minimal conditions needed to establish a causal relationship between two items. Hill's work has been recently validated by, Kundi (2006, p. 970) as a valuable tool, since both mechanistic and probabilistic aspects were considered [20]. Kundi applied Hill's criteria to the classic case of smoking and lung cancer. The first step for examining our causal proposal was to test if our study is consistent with Hill's criteria. Table I summarizes the nine criteria defined by Hill and the observations when applying it on the FoG case with respect to freezing index. It can be clearly observed that not all of the criteria hold in our case, where criteria (4 and 9) weren't applicable. On the other hand, the other criteria weren't as satisfactory as expected.

TABLE I. Observations based on Hill's criteria for FoG

Criterion	FoG correlation with freezing of index
1.Strength of Association	As FoG episodes occur, the value of the freezing index in higher than that when normal gait is happening.
2.Temporality	FoG in the vast majority of cases occurs when the freezing index increases.
3.Consistency	Several studies were applied on different patients, which produced the same results. The relationship also appeared for different genders.
4.Theoretical Plausibility	We don't have an explained biological theory stating a theoretical relationship between freezing index and FoG.
5.Coherence	The conclusion (that accretion of freezing index causes FoG) "made sense" given the knowledge about the algorithm for calculating the freezing index with respect to FoG occurrence.
6.Specificity in the causes	Freezing index is one of the clinical features (not the only one) that can be used to predict FoG.
7.Dose Response Relationship	Extracted data showed that there is a direct relationship between the value of the freezing index and the occurrence of FoG episodes.
8.Experimental Evidence	The experimental data collected clinically from patients made certain that FoG occurs when the freezing index increases.
9.Analogy	In this case, contrasting similar phenomena could not be applied, due to the fact that the approach of detecting causality of FoG is novel.

[2] This example is fully inspired from [13] p. 68

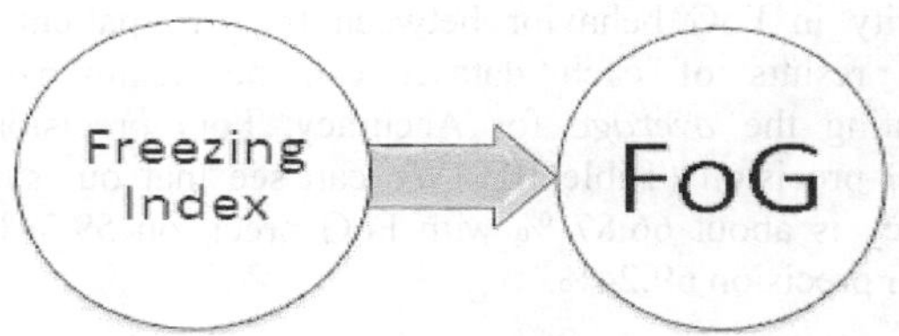

Figure 1. FoG causal model

3.2 BBN approach

The controversial debate on causality is still widely discussed in machine learning, probability theory and artificial intelligence. Several studies proposed causal discovery methods in the framework of BBN [8, 21, 22, 23, 24]. In this context, the causality issues have been studied by discovering the structure of BBN and it needs interventional data in cases where purely observational data is inadequate [10]; In general, the relation between causality and probability is based on a set of assumptions that allow the causal inference [25], and those assumptions are: (1) Causal sufficiency, (2) Markov, and (3) Faithfulness (definition of these assumptions are briefly mentioned in [10]). One of the known approaches to causal discovery is the So-called constraint-based approaches [8, 26], that select all direct acyclic graphs (DAGs) which satisfy the second and third assumption. In order to evaluate the causal link between our employed features we refer to a recent study that infers causal relations based on additive noise models (ANM). Jonas et al[27] published an algorithm that "able to distinguish between cause and effect, for a finite sample of discrete variables, and works both on synthetic and real data sets. The principle is that whenever the joint distribution P(X; Y) admits such a model in one direction, e.g. but does not admit the reversed model, one infers the former direction to be causal (i.e. X →Y)". Briefly, this algorithm tests whether the data admits an additive noise model by checking all possible functions and test whether they result in independent residuals. Applying Jonas et al causal inference method resulted that no causal relationships can be applied between any of our variables and between FoG.

4 Bayesian Naïve Classifier

Data mining is the science of extracting useful information from large data sets. It covers areas of machine learning, pattern recognition, artificial intelligence, and other areas [28]. One of data mining main objectives is prediction, which involves using some variables in data sets in order to predict unknown values of other relevant variables (*e.g. classification, regression, and anomaly detection*) [29].We already initialized the process of building a BBN model (section3.1 and 3.2) by studying the type of relationship between the Freezing Index concept and FoG episode via Hill's rule, and among features themselves via (ANM) model. Those two methodologies didn't validate the causality behavior between Freezing Index and FoG. Hence, we assume that BBN structure will depict a simple correlation between variables and FoG, and we will study the FoG episode via the simplest and traditional way of Classification Model where the FoG can be simply inferred to diagnosis or forecasting issues, specifically we tended to use the Bayesian Naïve Classifier (BNC), which is one of the most effective and popular classifiers in data mining techniques [13, 30]. It has been successfully applied to the different problem domains of classification task such as intrusion detection, image and pattern recognition, medical diagnosis, loan approval and bioinformatics [31].

4.1 Classification protocol

4.1.1 Learning

The first step of our learning protocol was to divide the previously described datasets (section 2.1), some for learning (9 datasets each for different patient) and the rest for testing. Thus, we built 9 BNC Models for nine different patients. For this purpose, 9 Belief network graphs were constructed (Figure 2), where the class node (FoG) will be the parent of the three FI nodes (FI nodes represents the magnitude of each acceleration sensor). Although, the data intended to learn each BNC model, was divided into 70% learning data and 30% testing data. The difference between the 9 BNC models is the conditional probability that will be learned according the training set introduced to the BNC model. Continuous variables have been discretized based on Akaike's criterion [32].The learning experiments were conducted with a random 10-fold validation; each fold takes a random 70% from the data set for learning and the remaining 30% for testing.

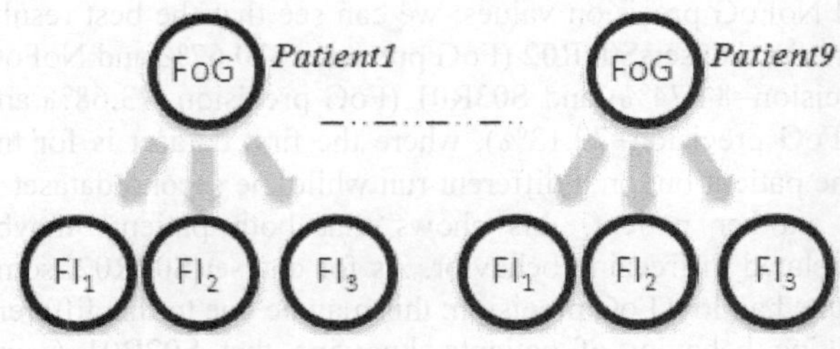

Figure 2. Nine BNC Models for each PD patient

4.1.2 Testing

After learning each fold, a confusion matrix was calculated (Table II) using the test data, the table represents the ***true positives*** (TP), ***false positives***(FP), ***false negatives***(FN) and the ***true negative*** (TN).From the confusion matrix, we evaluated three important values: FoG-precision, NoFoG-precision and Accuracy.

TABLE II. Confusion matrix calculated for each random fold.

	Model classification		
	FoG	True	False
Real classification	True	TP	FN
	False	FP	TN

Subsequently, and after calculating the above listed values for each fold, we choose the learning that holds the highest three values by referring to the priority of each value (starting by FoG-precision as highest priority followed by NoFoG-precision and finally Accuracy).After learning the nine BNC Model for 9 different patients, the rest datasets was introduced to each BNC model as testing datasets, for the purpose of testing the degree of generalization of our models. Also from each test dataset the confusion matrix, FoG-precision, NoFoG-precision and Accuracy were evaluated. In addition we made another testing approach, which is to enter each data sample as a parallel input to every one of the 9 BNC models, and the final decision that classifies whether a FoG or NoFoG is occurring, is based on the most likely decision made by all BNC models individually. For example, if 5 models decide that this sample is FoG and the rest do not, the final decision is taken as FoG.

5 Results

Following the learning and testing protocol, figure 3 summarizes the obtained result as function of FoG precession and NoFoG precision. Datasets were represented by "*S<patient number>R<test or run number>*".It is noticed when testing S01R01 (patient 1, first run) the FoG precision value was apparently high in all nine classifiers. Although the NoFoG precision values were low for some patients, yet this result showed that our classifier was able to detect every FoG episode with high precision with average of FoG precision 79.5%. In addition, if we take into consideration both FoG and NoFoG precision values; we can see that the best results were for datasetsS01R02 (FoG precision=70.67% and NoFoG precision=84.74%) and S03R01 (FoG precision=73.68% and NoFoG precision=79.13%), where the first dataset is for the same patient but on a different run while the second dataset is for another patient, this shows that both patients maybe correlated in freezing behavior. As for dataset S02R02, some results had low FoG precision; this may be due to the different walking behavior of patients, knowing that S02R01 (same patient but different run) showed an acceptable result for NoFoG precision and a very high result for FoG precision(92.85%).

Results for S05R02 showed that this patient may have a unique freezing behavior among the other learned patients, that's why none of the nine BNC models were able to differentiate this patient's freezing episodes from normal gait with high precision. Finally, for the dataset S06R01, some results had very good FoG precision about 89%. The best results were for S07R02 and S05R01 since they have moderate FoG and NoFoG precision. This may be due to the similarity in FoG behavior between the two patients. The testing results of each dataset can be summarized by calculating the *average* for Accuracy, FoG precision and NoFoG precision (Table III). We can see that our system's accuracy is about 66.87 % with FoG precision 59.34% and NoFoG precision 69.24%.

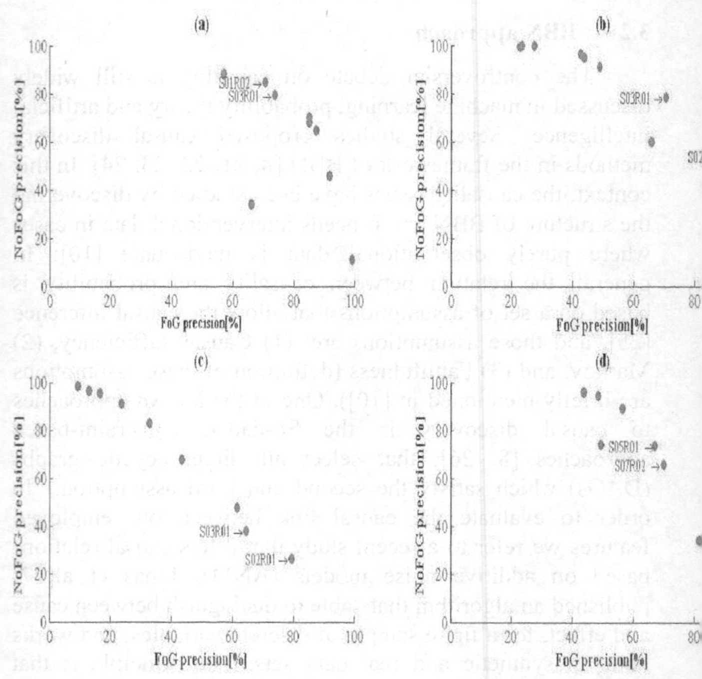

Figure 3. FoG precision vs. NoFoG precision results for testing datasets, (a)S01R01, (b)S02R01, (c)S05R02 and (d)S06R01.

Table IV shows the results for the second approach of testing which is making a decision based on the most likely one made by all BNC models individually. We can see that the accuracy and NoFoG precision increased and the FoG precision slightly decreased.

TABLE III. First approach averaged system accuracy.

Average	NoFoG precision (%)	FoG precision (%)	Accuracy (%)
S01R01	59.07	81.20	60.10
S02R02	85.22	50.31	80.87
S05R02	71.42	39.20	65.10
S06R01	61.23	66.66	61.40
System accuracy	**69.24**	**59.34**	**66.87**

TABLE IV. Second approach averaged system accuracy.

Average	NoFoG precision (%)	FoG precision (%)	Accuracy (%)
S01R01	65.21	85.71	66.16
S02R02	94.97	43.65	88.58
S05R02	83.03	33.74	73.36
S06R01	69.23	67.85	69.13
System accuracy	**78.11**	**57.74**	**74.31**

6 Conclusion

We have described a way for modeling freezing of gait phenomena of PD patients, based on BBN formalism. We made use of a dataset available online extracted from real PD patients while walking and having freezing episodes. The first approach, was studying the causality in the FoG/freezing index system, this was done by making an Epidemiological study followed by Causal inference one. This approach resulted in weak or no causality in FoG/Freezing Index system. Although, this can be further studied in future by calculating more features that may define FoG better. This result lead to a second approach which was applying Bayesian Naive classifier model to represent the datasets, we built 9 different BNC models for different patients, and the remaining datasets were introduced to each BNC model as testing datasets. This approach showed a fluctuating percentage of accuracy, FoG precision and NoFoG precision. Our classifier had the ability to detect FoG up to 99 %(FoG precision) if tested on the 9 BNC models locally, and up to 86% if tested globally. Some testing results were not as expected, we assume this was because of the different freezing behavior in different patient, knowing that when testing a specific BNC model related to a specific patient, with a dataset extracted from the same patient the result was significantly improved.

7 References

[1] N. Giladi, D. McMahon, S. Przedborski, E. Flaster, S. Guillory, V. Kostic, and S. Fahn, "Motor Blocks in Parkinson's Disease", PubMed, Neurology, Vol. 42, No.3, 1992.

[2] Rajesh Pahwa, Kelly E Lyons. Handbook of Parkinson's disease. 4thedition (2007).

[3] Ali Saad, IyadZaarour , Paul Bejjani , and Mohammad Ayache. Handwriting and Speech Prototypes of Parkinson Patients: Belief Network Approach. IJCSI International Journal of Computer Science Issues, Vol. 9, Issue 3, No 3, May 2012

[4] I. Zaarour, L. Heutte, PH. Leray, and J. Labiche, "Clustering and Bayesian Network Approaches For Discovering Handwriting Strategies of Primary School Children", International Journal of Pattern Recognition and Artificial Intelligence, Vol. 18, No. 7, 2004.

[5] Judea Pearl, "Fusion, Propagation, and Structuring in Belief Networks", Artificial Intelligence, Elsevier, Vol. 29, No. 3, pp.241-288, 1986.

[6] Judea Pearl, Probabilistic Reasoning in Intelligent Systems: Networks of Plausible Inference, Morgan Kaufmann Publishers Inc., San Francisco, A, USA, 1988.

[7] C. Glymour, and G. Cooper, "Computation, Causation, and Discovery", MIT Press, Cambridge, MA, 1999.

[8] Judea Pearl, "Causality: Models, Reasoning and Inference", Cambridge University Press, Cambridge, MA, 2000.

[9] Steffen L. Lauritzen, "Graphical Models", Clarendon Press, Oxford,UK, 1996.

[10] Montassar B. Messaoud, "SemCaDo: An Approach for Serendipitous Causal Discovery and Ontology Evolution", PhD thesis, Ecole Polytechnique de l'Université de Nantes, 2012.

[11] Marc Bächlin, Meir Plotnik, Daniel Roggen, InbalMaidan, Jeffrey M. Hausdorff, NirGiladi, and Gerhard Tröster, "Wearable Assistant for Parkinson's Disease Patients with the Freezing of Gait Symptom", IEEE Transactions on Information Technology in Biomedicine, Vol. 14 No. 2, pp 436-446, 2010.

[12] S. T. Moore, H. G. MacDougall, and W. G. Ondo, "Ambulatory Monitoring of Freezing of Gait in Parkinson's Disease," Journal of Neuroscience Methods, Vol. 167, No. 2, pp. 340-348, 2008.

[13] Jiawei Han, and Micheline Kamber, "Data Mining: Concepts and Techniques", 2nd Edition, University of Illinois at Urbana-Champaign, Morgan Kaufman Publishers, Elsevier Inc., USA, 2006.

[14] Spirtes Peter, Glymour Clark, and Scheines Richard, "Causality from Probability", Department of Philosophy, Report Paper 236, 1990.

[15] Federica Russo, and Jon Williamson, "Interpreting Causality in the Health Sciences", Research Project, International Studies in the Philosophy of Science Vol. 21, No. 2, pp. 157-170, July 2007.

[16] H. Frumkin, "Causation in medicine, Emory University, Rollins School of Public Health, Emory University, Atlanta, Georgia, 2006.

[17] P. Lagiou, H.O Adam., and D. Trichopoulos, "Causality in Cancer Epidemiology", European Journal of Epidemiology, Vo. 20, pp.565-574, 2005.

[18] P. Thagard, Explaining Disease: Correlations, Causes, and Mechanisms" Journal of Minds and Machines, Vol. 8, pp.61-78, 1998.

[19] B. Hill, "The Environment of Disease: Association or Causation?" Proceedings of the Royal Society of Medicine, Vol. 58, pp.295-300, 1965.

[20] M. Kundi, "Causality and the Interpretation of Epidemiological Evidence", Environmental Health Perspectives, Vol. 114, pp. 969-974, 2006.

[21] R.E. Neapolitan, "Learning Bayesian Networks", Prentice Hall Series in Artificial Intelligence, 1st Edition, 2003.

[22] J. Zhang, and P. Spirtes, "Detection of Unfaithfulness and Robust Causal Inference", Journal of Minds and Machines, Vol. 18, No.2, pp.239-271, June 2008.

[23] J. Pellet, and A. Elisseef, "Using Markov Blankets for Causal Structure Learning", Journal of Machine Learning Research, Vol. 9, pp.1295-1342, 2008.

[24] S. Nagl, M. Williams, and J. Williamson, "Objective Bayesian Nets for Systems Modeling and Prognosis in Breast Cancer", studies in computational sciences, Vol. 156, pp 131-167, Springer Berlin Heidelberg, 2008.

[25] Marek J. Drudzel, and Herbert A. Simon, "Causality in Bayesian Belief Networks", In Proceedings of the 9th Annual Conference on Uncertainty in Artificial Intelligence (UAI),1993.

[26] P. Spirtes, and C. Glymour, and R. Scheines, "Causation, prediction, and search", Lecture notes in statistics, New York, NY, Springer-Verlag, 1993.

[27] Jonas Peters, Dominik Janzing, and Bernhard Scholkopf, "Identifying Cause and Effect on Discrete Data using Additive Noise Models, Appearing in Proceedings of the 13th International Conference on Artificial Intelligence and Statistics (AISTATS) ,Vol. 9,2010.

[28] Adem Karahoca, "Data Mining Applications in Engineering and Medicine", 2012.

[29] F. Gorunescu, "Data Mining: Concepts, Models, and Techniques", India, Springer, 2011.

[30] R.Duda, and P. Hart, Pattern Classification and scene analysis, John Wiley & Sons, 1973.

[31] R. O. Duda et al, Pattern Classification, 2nd ed. Chichester, U.K.: Wiley-Interscience, 2000.

[32] D. Song, C. E. Henrik, K. Huebner, and D. Kragic, "Multivariate Discretization for Bayesian Network structure learning in robot grasping", in IEEE/RSJ International Conference on Intelligent Robots and Systems, 2011, Vol. 11. pp. 20-27.

Evaluation of Monte Carlo Subspace Clustering with OpenSubspace

David C. Hunn, Clark F. Olson[1]
[1]Computing and Software Systems, University of Washington, Bothell, WA, U.S.A.

Abstract - *We present the results of a thorough evaluation of the subspace clustering algorithm SEPC using the OpenSubspace framework. We show that SEPC outperforms competing projected and subspace clustering algorithms on synthetic and some real world data sets. We also show that SEPC can be used to effectively discover clusters with overlapping objects (i.e., subspace clustering).*

Keywords: subspace clustering, projected clustering, OpenSubspace

1 Introduction

Clustering algorithms attempt to divide objects in a data set into groups such that objects in a group are more similar to one another than to other objects in the data set. Similarity is usually based on distance. For data sets with few attributes, approaches such as k-means can be used to perform clustering in the full feature space. However, in many applications, data sets contain large numbers of attributes per object. For example, in some text processing applications each object is a term frequency vector whose length is equal to the number of terms under analysis. Such frequency vectors can have thousands of attributes depending on the size of the dictionary. As the dimensionality of data sets increases, traditional approaches that look for clusters in the full feature space start to fail. In part, the difficulty is that the longest and shortest distances in a data set will approach one another as the number of dimensions increases [1]. Thus, increasing dimensionality erodes the usefulness of distance metrics in determining the relative similarity of objects in a data set. A common solution is to use dimensionality reduction tools like principal component analysis (PCA) [2] to project the data set onto fewer dimensions. The resulting data set can then be clustered using traditional techniques. However, applying PCA produces a single subspace and in many applications, clusters exist in different subspaces of the full feature space. Thus, applying PCA may mask clusters and hide interesting results. One solution to these problems is subspace clustering. Subspace clustering aims to identify clusters of objects and their associated subspaces.

The most general aim of subspace clustering is to find all clusters in arbitrarily aligned subspaces. Unfortunately, this form of the problem has an infinite search space and finding clusters under these conditions is difficult. Instead, most approaches rely on heuristics to reduce the search space to something more practical. For example, in many applications, it is reasonable to assume that the attributes of the data are not correlated with one another. This enables one to restrict the search for clusters to only those that are axis-aligned—reducing the number of possible subspaces from infinite to 2^d, where d is the number of dimensions in the data set.

In this paper we evaluate an algorithm for performing projective clustering called Simple and Efficient Projective Clustering (SEPC) [3] using the OpenSubspace framework [4]. We present the results of a thorough evaluation of SEPC with both synthetic and real-world data sets including comparisons with competing approaches. We will also show that SEPC can be used to effectively discover clusters with overlapping objects (i.e., subspace clustering).

2 Related Work

For a thorough review of the current state of subspace and projected clustering, see [7]. We provide a brief overview of some historical and closely related algorithms to the current work.

CLIQUE [8] is often cited as the earliest subspace-clustering algorithm. In CLIQUE, the data set is discretized into ξ intervals of equal length. Units containing a sufficient number of points are considered dense. Adjacent dense cells are joined together to create clusters. The algorithm first discovers all one-dimensional dense units and then in a priori fashion searches for subspace clusters. The algorithm is made more efficient by leveraging the downward closure property of subspace clusters to prune the search space.

PROCLUS [9] is another approach to the problem of subspace clustering. Where CLIQUE is a bottom-up approach, PROCLUS builds clusters in a top-down fashion. PROCLUS is a k-medoid-like clustering algorithm. It partitions the data into k clusters with an average number of dimensions equal to l. In the first stage of the algorithm, a set of candidate medoids (M) is sampled from the data set. From M, k medoids are selected and the subspaces for each are determined by minimizing the standard deviation of the distances of the points in the neighborhood of the medoids to the corresponding medoid along each dimension. Then points are assigned to the medoid they are closest to using a distance metric that only considers the relevant subspaces for each medoid. In a refinement phase, medoids may be switched out for other members of M—the pool of medoids. The result is a strict partitioning of the data set into k parts along with a set of outlier points.

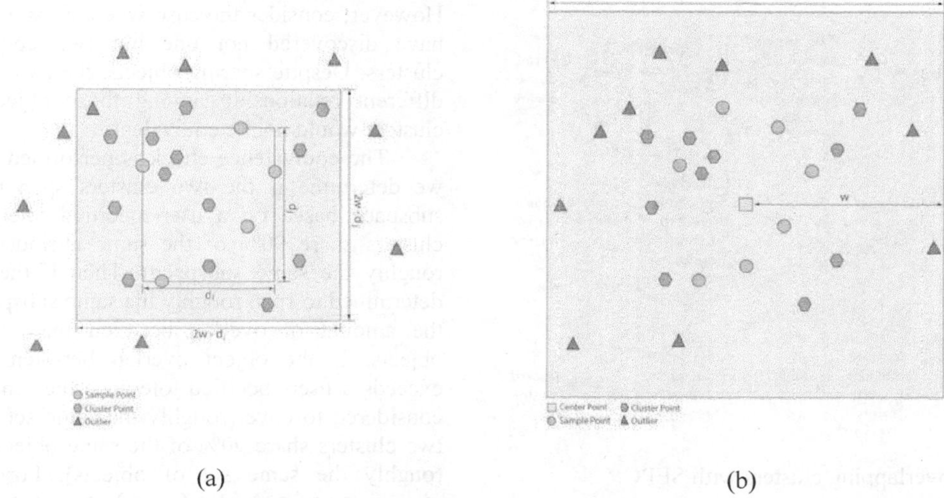

Fig. 1. A comparison between the SEPC and DOC algorithms for determining cluster dimensions and cluster points using a discriminating set. (a) The SEPC algorithm uses a sheath of width $\boldsymbol{w}$ to determine if a discriminating set congregates in a dimension. When the set congregates, a larger sheath with width between $\boldsymbol{w}$ and $\boldsymbol{2w}$ is used to determine additional data points that are added to the cluster. (b) The DOC and FastDOC algorithms use a sheath with width $\boldsymbol{2w}$ both to determine if the discriminating set congregates in a dimension and to find additional data points that are added to the cluster.

DOC [5] defines a global measure of cluster quality to determine an optimal cluster. Given a subspace cluster that contains a set of objects C and set of attributes D, the function $\mu(|C|, |D|) = |C|/\beta^{|D|}$ determines the quality of the cluster. β is a user defined constant that determines the tradeoff between objects and attributes in a cluster with the restriction $0 < \beta < 0.5$. The user must also specify a cluster width w, that is used to determine both the relevant attributes and object membership in the cluster. To discover clusters, the algorithm iteratively samples the data set in Monte Carlo fashion. DOC uses two loops to find an optimal cluster: an inner and outer loop. In the outer loop, it randomly samples medoids from the data set. Then in the inner loop, it randomly samples a small number of points from the data set. This small set of points is referred to as the discriminating set. The relevant dimensions of the hypothesized cluster are determined by calculating the distance between the medoid and the points in the discriminating set. This process is repeated many times and the highest quality cluster found is reported.

A closely related algorithm to DOC is MineClus [6]. MineClus uses a similar Monte Carlo framework to sample medoids from the data set. However, in MineClus the search for relevant subspaces is transformed into a frequent pattern tree growth method. This replaces the inner loop of DOC turning it into a determinative step. This replacement results in a significant decrease in running time compared to the DOC algorithm.

3 Approach

SEPC [3] is an iterative Monte Carlo algorithm inspired by DOC [5]. It inherited the cluster model as well as the quality function used by DOC. However, in SEPC, the outer loop in which DOC randomly samples the data set to determine a cluster medoid has been discarded. Instead, clusters are hypothesized using just the discriminating set.

In each trial, a small set of data points (the discriminating set) is sampled randomly from the data set. The minimum and maximum in each dimension of the discriminating set is determined. If the difference between the minimum and maximum value in a given dimension is less than a fixed width w, then a congregating dimension has been discovered. This results in a sheath of width w for determining the congregating dimensions. In contrast, the DOC algorithm uses two loops to generate a hypothetical cluster. In the first loop, seed points are sampled from the data set and in the second loop, a set of discriminating points is sampled from the data set. The distance along each dimension from the seed points to the points in the discriminating set is determined. The hypothesized cluster is said to congregate in the dimensions for which the distance is less than w. This results in a sheath of width $2w$ for determining congregating dimensions, twice as large in each dimension as the SEPC sheath. The narrower sheath of SEPC improves the detection of truly congregating dimensions. It also makes it possible to use values of $\beta > 0.5$ (DOC is limited to $\beta < 0.5$).

Once all congregating dimensions have been determined, the hypothesized cluster is populated with points from the data set. However, the distances calculated to determine the congregating dimensions cannot be used to determine which points belong to the hypothesized cluster, since they are generally too narrow to capture the extremal points in the cluster. Instead, the span of the sheath is determined in each congregating dimension by subtracting w from the maximum value and adding w to the minimum value. The length of the

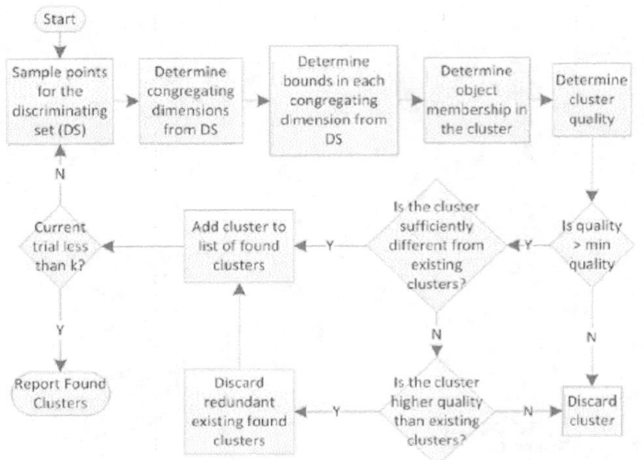

Fig. 2. Finding overlapping clusters with SEPC.

resulting range is $2w - d_i$, where d_i is the absolute difference between the minimum and maximum value in the discriminating set along dimension i. See Fig. 1 (a). In contrast, the DOC algorithm uses the same sheath width ($2w$) for determining congregating dimensions and point membership in the cluster. See Fig. 1 (b).

After point or object membership has been determined for a hypothesized cluster, its quality can be determined. If the quality is high enough, then it is retained. In disjoint mode, the points in the newly discovered cluster will be removed from consideration for membership in subsequently discovered clusters. Alternatively, if the user wishes to discover clusters with overlapping points, the hypothesized cluster will only be kept if it is qualitatively different from clusters that have already been discovered or if it is of higher quality than an existing cluster that it significantly overlaps with.

3.1 Soft Cluster Equality

Using the algorithm in non-disjoint mode is problematic if we do not remove duplicate clusters. Since points are not removed from consideration when they are assigned to clusters, the algorithm needs to check that each newly found cluster is unique and has not been previously discovered. When a new cluster is discovered, it is compared to existing found clusters. However, using a strict test for equality will result in a large number of clusters being discovered that are not very different from one another. To solve this problem, the algorithm allows the user to loosen the criteria for equality between clusters. This allows the user to tune the algorithm to yield only clusters that are truly unique.

Our test for cluster equality involves both the set of objects in each cluster as well as the subspaces spanned by each cluster. This dual check is necessary since a purely object-based method for determining cluster equivalence would be error prone. Consider two subspace clusters $C_1(O_1, S_1)$ and $C_2(O_2, S_2)$, with $O_1 \subseteq O_2$. Without considering the subspaces of the two clusters we may come to the conclusion that C_1 is redundant with respect to C_2. However, consider the case where $S_1 \neq S_2$. In this case, we have discovered not one but two conceptually distinct clusters. Despite sharing objects, the two clusters describe a different relationship among those objects, thus the two clusters would not be equivalent.

The equivalence check is performed in two steps: first we determine if the two clusters span roughly the same subspace based on a user-specified tolerance (e.g. if two clusters share 90% of the same attributes then they span roughly the same subspace). Then if the two clusters are determined to span roughly the same subspace, we determine the amount of overlap between their respective sets of objects. If the object overlap between the two clusters exceeds a user-specified tolerance then the two clusters are considered to cover roughly the same set of objects (e.g. if two clusters share 90% of the same objects then they cover roughly the same set of objects). Formally, given two clusters $C_i(O_i, S_i)$ and $C_j(O_j, S_j)$, $C_i = C_j$ if

$$\frac{|S_i \cap S_j|}{|S_j|} \geq Min\ Subspace\ Overlap \qquad (1)$$

and

$$\frac{|O_i \cap O_j|}{|O_j|} \geq Min\ Object\ Overlap. \qquad (2)$$

Where $Min\ Subspace\ Overlap$ and $Min\ Object\ Overlap$ are user specified values between zero and one. Note that this check is not commutative, since it determines the percent overlap of attributes and objects by dividing by the cardinality of one of the clusters.

3.2 Using Soft Cluster Equality

Since our check for subspace cluster equality is not commutative, we perform the check in both directions in the following way: each newly hypothesized cluster is checked against existing clusters using itself as the index. Therefore, each new cluster must be sufficiently unique with respect to existing clusters in order to be considered for inclusion in the clustering results. In other words, a user-specified percentage of a new cluster's subspace must be unique. Failing that, a user-specified percentage of the new cluster's set of objects must be unique. If a newly hypothesized cluster is determined to be redundant with respect to an existing cluster by this metric, then we discard the new cluster if its quality is lower than the existing cluster. If a newly hypothesized cluster is sufficiently unique (or of higher quality than redundant existing clusters) then we perform the equivalence check in the other direction. In this case, all existing clusters that are determined to be redundant with respect to the new cluster are removed from the clustering results. Fig. 2 depicts the process used by SEPC to discover overlapping clusters in a data set.

4 Quality Metrics

Some subspace clustering metrics used in OpenSubspace are object-based [4]. That is, they ignore the congregating dimensions of clusters in evaluating cluster quality. Instead, they rely entirely on how objects have been allocated into found clusters compared to the "true" allocation. This approach works sufficiently well when points belong to only one cluster. However, in some instances, it is advantageous to allow points to belong to multiple clusters that span different subspaces. In such cases, the above metrics will yield misleading results. For example, the synthetic data sets provided with the OpenSubspace framework typically have one or two clusters that, point-wise, are subsets of other clusters. However, the super- and sub-clusters span a different set of dimensions (typically, the larger cluster spans fewer dimensions). This causes problems for purely object-based metrics, because, the sub-clusters are not unique on a purely object basis. Thus, metrics like clustering error (CE) [7], account for the subspace spanned by each object.

For the following discussion, it is useful to define two types of clusters: *found clusters* and *hidden clusters*. A found cluster is returned as part of the results of running a clustering algorithm on a given data set. In contrast, a hidden cluster is known within a data set. In the case of synthetic data sets both the objects and subspace of hidden clusters are known, however, for real world data, we typically are limited to information about object membership in hidden clusters.

4.1 F1

In OpenSubspace, F1 is an object-based metric computed with respect to each hidden cluster. It is composed of two sub-metrics called recall and precision. A high recall corresponds to a high coverage of objects from a hidden cluster while a high precision denotes a low coverage of objects from other clusters. Prior to calculating F1, found clusters are mapped to the hidden cluster they overlap with the most. Then recall and precision are determined for each hidden cluster. The F1 scores for the hidden clusters are determined by taking the harmonic mean of their recall and precision scores. The overall F1 score is the average of the F1 scores of each hidden cluster.

Problems arise with the F1-measure when there are overlapping hidden clusters that span different subspaces. For F1, the trouble arises when found clusters are mapped to hidden clusters. Since, the mapping is done purely on a point or object basis, when one hidden cluster is a subset of another, there is a high likelihood that the smaller cluster will "capture" found clusters overlapping both the super- and sub-hidden clusters. This happens, because the overlap between a hidden and found cluster is normalized by the cardinality of the hidden cluster. This results in a bias towards smaller hidden sub-clusters.

4.2 Clustering Error

Clustering error (CE) [7] addresses the problem of overlapping clusters by taking into account the dimensions spanned by objects in a cluster. It does this by using *subobjects* in place of objects in its calculation. A subobject is the combination of an object together with the dimensions spanned by the cluster to which it belongs. This allows an object to belong to multiple clusters and still be unique for the purpose of quality measurement. CE measures the extent to which the subobjects in hidden clusters overlap with the subobjects in found clusters. However, before determining overlap between the two sets of clusters, an optimal mapping of found clusters to hidden clusters is performed, which may result in excess found clusters that are not mapped to any hidden cluster and vice versa. This solves a problem common to many subspace clustering quality metrics. Namely, many metrics fail to distinguish between the case where many found clusters overlap a single hidden cluster and, the case where only a single found cluster overlaps a hidden cluster. The second case is more desirable than the first.

One drawback to CE, is that in real world data sets, the congregating dimensions are often unknown, limiting this method's ability to judge a cluster's quality with respect to its subspace.

5 Experiments

We have reproduced the experiments performed in [8] using the SEPC algorithm and several competing algorithms. We have focused on examining the general properties of SEPC compared to several other subspace clustering algorithms. In [8], each experiment was conducted by trying many different parameter settings for each algorithm in an attempt to obtain the maximum possible performance for each. In addition, each run of an algorithm was limited to 30 minutes. For this evaluation, we used the same strategy. The following algorithms, as implemented in OpenSubspace, were used in this comparison: CLIQUE [9], DOC [5], MineClus [6], FIRES [10], PROCLUS [11], P3C [12], and STATPC [13]. Each algorithm has been tuned using the parameter settings provided by Mueller et al. [8]. The experiments were run on machines with 1.8GHz Dual-Core AMD Opteron™ 2210 processors and 2GB memory running Red Hat Linux 5.9.

5.1 Synthetic Data

OpenSubspace is packaged with three synthetic data sets, each intended to explore a different aspect of algorithm performance. These data sets enable evaluation over increasing dimensionality (number of attributes), over increasing data set size (number of objects), and over increasing amounts of noise (irrelevant objects). Additionally, all of the data sets contain overlapping hidden clusters. That is, they contain clusters that share objects, but span different subspaces. Thus, we applied SEPC in non-disjoint mode to maximize its possible achievable performance.

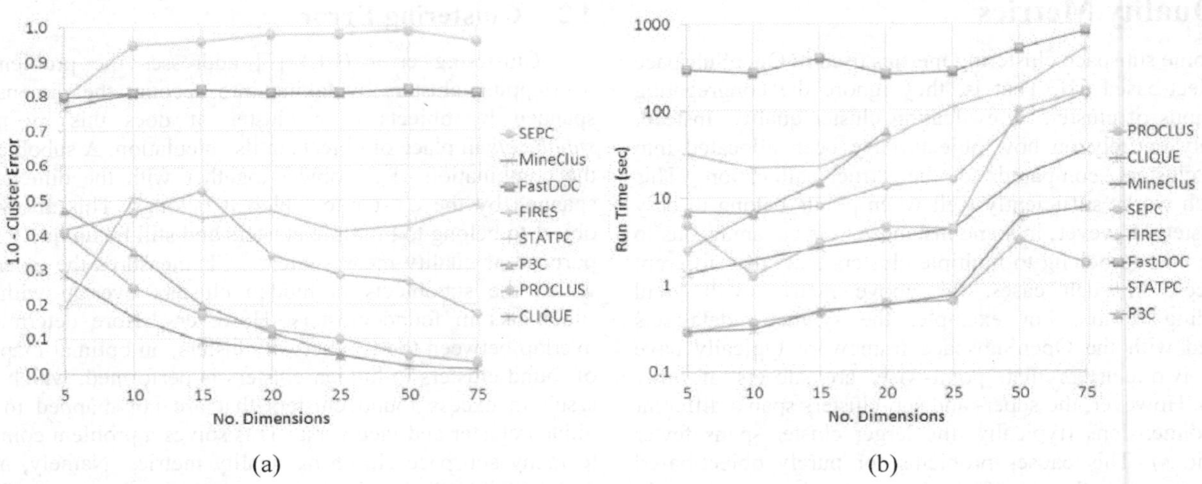

Fig. 3. Algorithm performance over an increasing number of dimensions measured by (a) clustering error and (b) run time.

As in [8], we used CE to examine the relative quality of the clustering results generated on these synthetic data by each algorithm. Since we have information about the relevant subspaces of the hidden clusters in the synthetic data; we can fully leverage the power of CE. Recall that the CE metric not only indicates that objects have been correctly assigned to clusters, but also penalizes redundancy (e.g. multiple found clusters covering the same hidden cluster) and splitting hidden clusters (many small found clusters covering the objects of a single hidden cluster). This also allows us to evaluate an algorithm's ability to discover clusters with overlapping objects. Since each of the synthetic data sets include overlapping clusters, algorithms that perform a strict partitioning of objects into clusters will not be able to score a perfect CE. For example, the maximum partitioned CE score for the object-count data sets is about 0.88. Recall that CE is determined using subobjects (objects combined with the subspace of the cluster to which it belongs). This means that according to the CE metric, an object may be assigned to multiple clusters, as long as those clusters span different subspaces. This also means that there can be more subobjects than objects in a data set. For example, the 1500-object data set has 1462 objects in its 10 hidden clusters. However, since some of these objects belong to more than one cluster, the data set contains 1663 subobjects. To determine the maximum possible CE results with single object assignment, we simply divide the number of objects by the number of subobjects, which yields approximately 0.88. Therefore, a CE score exceeding 0.88 on the 1500-object data set would indicate that the algorithm was successfully discovering overlapping clusters. The maximum disjoint CE value varies between the synthetic data sets. It is about 0.88 for all of the object-count and noise data sets, and about 0.8 for the dimension-count data sets.

We also examined the running times for each algorithm for each data set. For some algorithms, parameter settings may significantly affect running time. In such cases, we used consistent parameter settings to gather run time data even if it did not yield optimal CE results. In addition, some of the algorithms never completed within 30 minutes on some of the data sets for any parameter settings. For example, P3C did not finish within 30 minutes on any of the dimension data sets

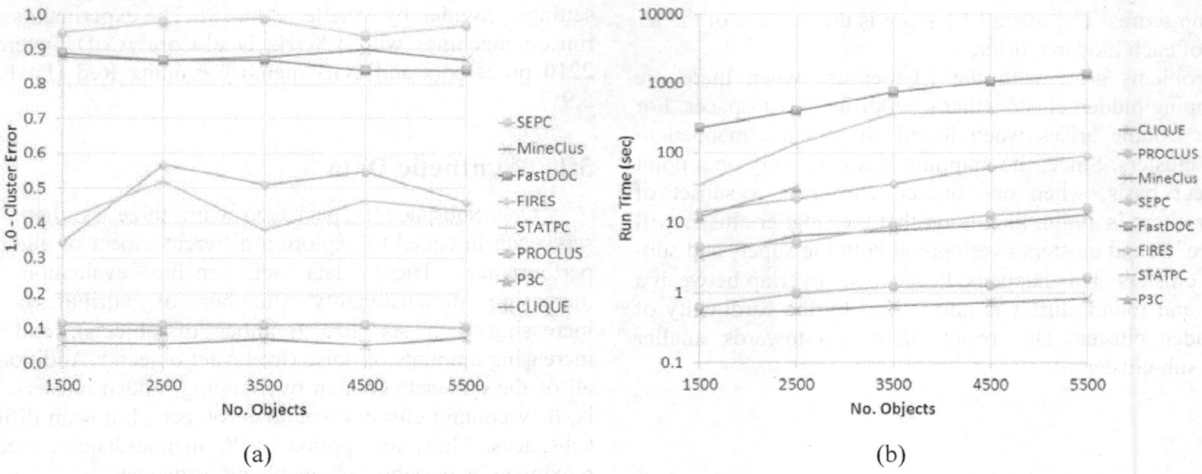

Fig. 4. Algorithm performance over an increasing number of objects measured by (a) clustering error and (b) run time.

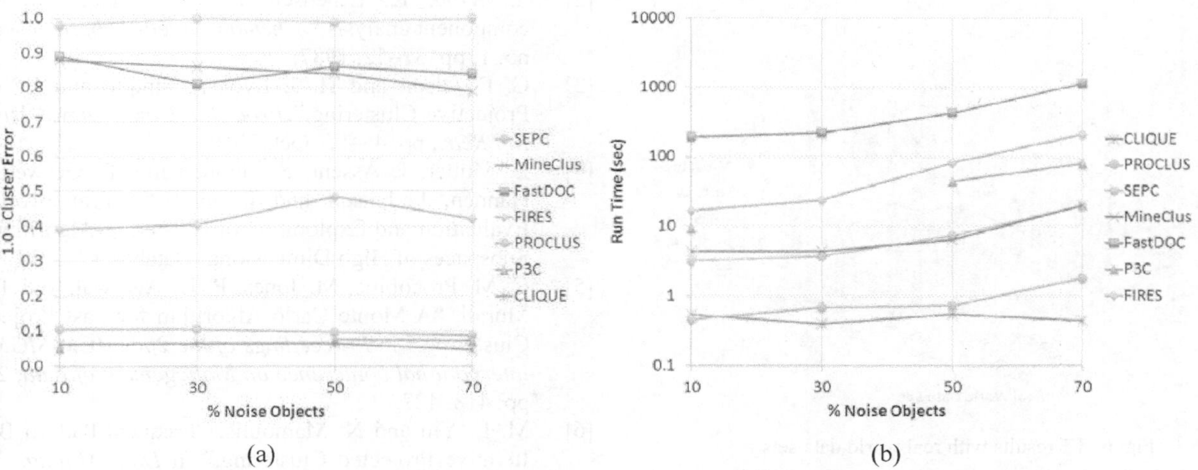

Fig. 5. Algorithm performance over increasing noise measured by (a) clustering error and (b) run time.

above 20 dimensions. This accounts for the missing data in Fig 3 (b), 4 (b) and 5 (b).

To evaluate the scalability of algorithms as the dimensionality of a data set increases, OpenSubspace includes data sets with dimensions varying from 5 to 75. Each data set includes ten subspace clusters that span 50%, 60%, and 80% of the full feature space. Fig. 3 shows the results of our evaluations of each algorithm on the dimension-based data sets. Our evaluation agreed closely with [8], in which Mueller and his team observed the best CE results for the cell-based approaches—particularly DOC and MineClus. In our evaluation, DOC and MineClus scored a CE value of approximately 0.8 across all dimensionalities. However, as can be seen in Fig 3 (a), SEPC exceeded these results for dimensionality of 10 or greater. At dimensionality 5, SEPC performs about as well as DOC or MineClus. However, as dimensionality increases, the CE score achieved by SEPC improves.

OpenSubspace also includes a set of synthetic data where the number of objects in each cluster varies, but the number of dimensions is constant. All of these data sets contain 20-dimensional objects, but they vary in size from about 1500 points up to about 5500 points. We used these data sets to evaluate algorithm performance over increasing data set size. The best results for DOC and MineClus varied between CE values of about 0.85 and 0.9. SEPC exceeded these results with a CE value of at least 0.94 (on the data set containing 4500 data points) and achieved a CE value of 1.0 for the data set containing 3500 data points. See Fig. 4 (a).

For noise-based experiments, OpenSubspace includes data sets where the percentage of noise objects increases from 10% noise up to 70% noise. These data sets were built by adding noise to the 20-dimensional data set from the first scalability experiments. For noise-based experiments, Mueller et al. reported CE results for DOC and MineClus of about 0.79 to 0.89. We saw similar results in our evaluation. We can see in Fig. 5 that the DOC and MineClus results exhibit a slight downward trend as the amount of noise in the data set increases. In contrast, the CE results for SEPC are consistent ranging from 0.95 to 0.97, with no degradation in performance with increasing amounts of noise.

Running time is an important factor to consider when evaluating subspace clustering algorithms. In addition to the CE data, we collected run time data on all of the synthetic data sets to compare SEPC to the other algorithms. See Fig. 3 (b), Fig. 4 (b), and Fig. 5 (b). From these graphs of run time data, we see that SEPC is significantly faster than DOC on all data sets. We also see that MineClus and SEPC have similar run times across all data sets. CLIQUE and PROCLUS are the fastest algorithms across all data sets. However, they also score among the lowest CE values.

SEPC consistently performed better than the other algorithms on each of the synthetic data sets with respect to the CE metric. Recall that the maximum disjoint CE scores for the object and noise data sets was 0.88 and 0.8 for the dimension data sets. SEPC scored CE results near 1.0 on all of these data sets (with the exception of the 5-dimensional data set). The high CE scores achieved by SEPC across all data sets indicate that it effectively discovered overlapping clusters. Overall, it appears SEPC's performance increases with scale. This was illustrated in the experiments with the dimensionality data sets. At 5 dimensions, SEPC performed as well as DOC and MineClus, but as the dimensionality of the data sets increased, SEPC's performance also increased. It appears that for very low dimensional data (less than 5), SEPC is comparable in performance to DOC and MineClus. However, the performance of DOC and MineClus stays the same for large dimensional data, while SEPC improves. SEPC runs much faster than DOC and in similar time to MineClus.

6 Real World Data

In addition to synthetic data, we used the real world data packaged with OpenSubspace to evaluate SEPC against other subspace clustering algorithms. These publicly available data sets from the UCI archive [14] have typically been used in classification tasks and thus the data have class labels. The class labels are assumed to describe natural clusters in the

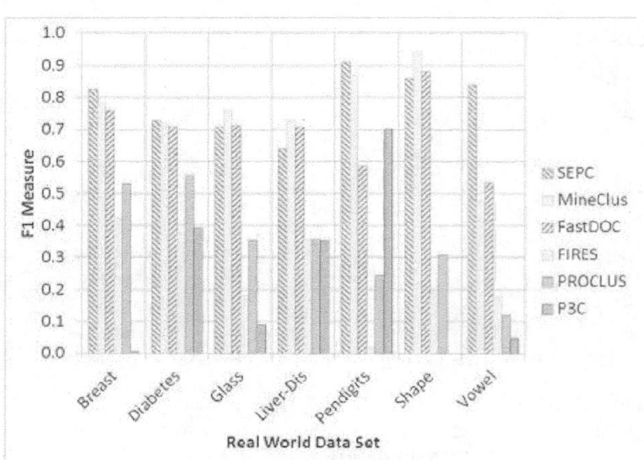

Fig. 6. F1 results with real world data sets.

data. However, no information about the subspaces of the clusters is known. This limits the usefulness of CE, since it can only be applied at the object level. Thus, we have followed the lead of [8] and optimized each algorithm with respect to F1. Also, since all of the clusters in the real world data sets are disjoint, SEPC was run in disjoint mode.

SEPC was compared with MineClus, DOC, PROCLUS, FIRES, and P3C. See Fig. 6 for a chart summarizing the F1 results obtained by each algorithm for each of the seven real world data sets. SEPC yielded the highest F1 score on four out of the seven data sets.

7 Conclusions

SEPC outperformed all other algorithms on synthetic data in terms of clustering quality measured by CE. The high CE scores achieved on the synthetic data sets show that the algorithm effectively identifies clusters even when they share objects. Thus, demonstrating SEPC can be rightly called a subspace clustering algorithm.

The experiments using the synthetic data sets reveal some possible areas where differences in algorithm performance might be more visible. For example, both DOC and MINECLUS, exhibit steady CE results of about 0.8 over an increasing number of dimensions, while the CE results for SEPC started at about 0.8, then increased to values closer to 1.0. Similar results were observed for data containing significant amounts of random noise. Experiments with larger data sets (both in the number of objects and in the number of dimensions), as well as with noisier data, would likely yield more interesting comparisons of performance between algorithms. We also demonstrated that SEPC can be used to achieve high quality results on real world data.

8 References

[1] C. Aggarwal, A. Hinneburg, and D. Keim, “On the Surprising Behavior of Distance Metrics in High Dimensional Space,” *Database Theory—icdt 2001*, pp. 420–434, 2001.

[2] S. Wold, K. Esbensen, and P. Geladi, “Principal component analysis,” *Chemom. Intell. Lab. Syst.*, vol. 2, no. 1, pp. 37–52, 1987.

[3] C. F. Olson and H. J. Lyons, “Simple and Efficient Projective Clustering,” *Proc. Int. Conf. Knowl. Discov. Inf. Retr.*, pp. 45–55, Oct. 2010.

[4] E. Müller, I. Assent, S. Günnemann, P. Gerwert, M. Hannen, T. Jansen, and T. Seidl, “A Framework for Evaluation and Exploration of Clustering Algorithms in Subspaces of High Dimensional Databases,” 2011.

[5] C. M. Procopiuc, M. Jones, P. K. Agarwal, and T. M. Murali, “A Monte Carlo Algorithm for Fast Projective Clustering,” in *Proceedings of the 2002 ACM SIGMOD international conference on Management of data*, 2002, pp. 418–427.

[6] M. L. Yiu and N. Mamoulis, “Frequent-Pattern Based Iterative Projected Clustering,” in *Data Mining, 2003. ICDM 2003. Third IEEE International Conference on*, 2003, pp. 689–692.

[7] A. Patrikainen and M. Meila, “Comparing Subspace Clusterings,” *Knowl. Data Eng. Ieee Trans.*, vol. 18, no. 7, pp. 902–916, 2006.

[8] E. Müller, S. Günnemann, I. Assent, and T. Seidl, “Evaluating Clustering in Subspace Projections of High Dimensional Data,” *Proc. Vldb Endow.*, vol. 2, no. 1, pp. 1270–1281, 2009.

[9] R. Agrawal, J. Gehrke, D. Gunopulos, and P. Raghavan, “Automatic Subspace Clustering of High Dimensional Data for Data Mining Applications,” in *Proceedings ACM SIGMOD International Conference on Management of Data*, Seattle, WA, 1998, vol. 27.

[10] H. P. Kriegel, P. Kroger, M. Renz, and S. Wurst, “A Generic Framework for Efficient Subspace Clustering of High-Dimensional Data,” in *Data Mining, Fifth IEEE International Conference on*, 2005, p. 8–pp.

[11] C. C. Aggarwal, J. L. Wolf, P. S. Yu, C. Procopiuc, and J. S. Park, “Fast Algorithms for Projected Clustering,” *Acm Sigmod Rec.*, vol. 28, no. 2, pp. 61–72, 1999.

[12] G. Moise, J. Sander, and M. Ester, “P3C: A Robust Projected Clustering Algorithm,” in *Data Mining, 2006. ICDM'06. Sixth International Conference on*, 2006, pp. 414–425.

[13] G. Moise and J. Sander, “Finding Non-Redundant, Statistically Significant Regions in High Dimensional Data: A Novel Approach to Projected and Subspace Clustering,” in *Proceeding of the 14th ACM SIGKDD international conference on Knowledge discovery and data mining*, 2008, pp. 533–541.

[14] “UCI Machine Learning Repository.” [Online]. Available: http://archive.ics.uci.edu/ml/. [Accessed: 05-Mar-2013].

MineTool-3DM²: An Algorithm for Data Mining of 3D Simulation Data

Tamara B. Sipes and Homa Karimabadi[1,2]
[1] University of California San Diego, La Jolla, CA
[2] SciberQuest, Inc., Del Mar, CA
tsipes@ucsd.edu, homa@eng.ucsd.edu

ABSTRACT

Scientific simulations are a valuable discovery tool in a variety of sciences, especially is space physics where scientific observation and *in situ* measurements are not always possible. Recent advances in kinetic simulations running on petascale computers have enabled 3D simulations of a variety of important scientific processes. **However, knowledge extraction from massive and complex data sets generated from petascale simulations still poses a major obstacle to scientific progress.** We propose a new approach to solving this problem by utilizing an innovative feature extraction technique in combination with a specialized classification algorithm which can be applied to 3D simulation datasets. In our previous work [12] we showed how data from 2D simulations as well as many other real life examples can be represented in a form of multivariate time series. In this work, we have adapted our multivariate time series analysis data mining technique to handle 3D simulation data. The technique extracts global features and metafeatures in a 3D simulation dataset in order to capture the necessary time-lapse information. The features are then used to create a static, intermediate data set that is suitable for analysis using the standard supervised data mining techniques. The viability of the new algorithm called MineTool-3DM² is demonstrated through its application to the problem of automatic detection of flux transfer events (FTE) in the 3D simulation data. MineTool-3DM2 built model led to a high FTE classification model accuracy of 96.7% correctly classified instances where the model produced one of three outputs of non-FTE, across-cut-FTE, and tangent-cut-FTE. For comparison, two other means of treating the time series data including a common summary statistics technique yielded much lower accuracies of 47% and 63% correctly classified instances, and 95.56% accuracy in the 2D simulation case. The low accuracy achieved using standard techniques (such as summary statistics) demonstrates the high level of complexity of this problem and the need for advanced techniques to handle such data.

Keywords

Multimedia Mining, Temporal and Spatial Data Mining, Multivariate Time Series Classification, Regression/Classification

1. INTRODUCTION

Scientific simulations have been used to enable further scientific advances in a variety of fields. Simulation can serve as a powerful tool to aid the understanding of a variety of scientific processes and enable scientific discovery. This is especially true in space sciences, where progress relies on use of computer simulations in close ties with *in situ* and remote spacecraft measurements. The arrival of petascale computing has led to a significant increase in the size of the simulations. In computing, **petascale** refers to a computer system capable of reaching performance in excess of one petaflops, i.e. 10^{15} or one quadrillion floating point operations per second. As a comparison, the average consumer computer runs at anywhere from 0.25 gigaflops to 7.5 gigaflops, or 10^9 floating point operations/sec.

Our largest simulations include over 3.2 trillion particles, and 15 billion cells, and are run for several days using 200 K cores on Jaguar, for example. Data analysis and data mining of these complex and massive data sets is a major holdup to progress in a variety of scientific fields today. *There is a prominent need for automated, intelligent methods to enable fast and accurate analysis and knowledge discovery in simulation data.*

Tracking an event in large simulation data repositories by human eye is time-consuming and error-prone. An alternative would be to think of a simulation as a series of images, and analyze a 'time series' of image data. This approach would require an image representation that would encompass the important areas of the image, and presenting it in a series. Another approach would be to concentrate on the particular area of the simulation that is of interest and focus on the features being created and changed in time. In our previous work on data mining of 2D simulation data [12] we adopted the later approach, as it decreases the complexity of the problem. Our approach entailed collecting a certain spatial and temporal information, or features of the event in the simulation window (as in a series of point coordinate values (x,y)), in addition to the other variables available, that describe the (x,y) simulated measurements. These features, or set of points being tracked over time, in effect add another dimension to the time series data at the input.

In this paper, we expand the 2D simulation data capabilities to 3D simulation data. In the sections below we describe how we devise and collect the 3D simulation features as a series of data points, or "cuts" in the example simulation domain, and utilize intelligent data mining classification tools to extract knowledge from them. The paper is organized as follows. Section 2 discusses the simulations: 2D and 3D; Section 3 discusses the time series analysis and the underlying algorithm of MineTool-TS. Section 4 describes the application to 3D simulation data. Summary and discussion are presented in Section 5.

2. SIMULATION DATA

Magnetopause reconnection is the primary mechanism for transfer of energy, momentum, and mass from the solar wind into the Earth's magnetosphere and is the focus of many space physics studies. Early observations of the magnetopause indicated that reconnection can sometimes be quasi-steady [5] but at other times transient (resulting in so-called flux transfer events) [11]. Despite progress, many very basic questions regarding magnetopause reconnection remain not well understood: What is the relative importance of the two types of reconnection to magnetic flux transport (at the magnetopause)? What is the generation mechanism of flux transfer events (FTEs) and are there different mechanisms involved depending on the solar wind and magnetosheath conditions? Do FTEs interact? There are also open questions regarding the size, extent, internal structure, magnetic topology, evolution and orientation of FTEs.

Research in this area has been stimulated by recent advances in the area of kinetic simulations (where all the particles are modeled as kinetic particles) running on petascale computers that have enabled 3D global hybrid simulations of the magnetosphere as well as 3D local fully kinetic simulations of the reconnection process. This new capability allows us to study and achieve closure on many aspects of magnetopause reconnection that have been out of reach up to now.

The simulation data example that we consider here are the 3D global hybrid simulations (in which electrons are modeled as fluid particles, and ions as fully kinetic) of the Earth's magnetosphere [8][9] where interaction of the solar wind plasma and magnetic fields impinging on the Earth's dipole field is modeled. The simulations are 3D in a sense that the spatial variations of the parameters are given in three dimensions and all three components of the vectors such as the magnetic field are kept.

One feature of particular interest in the simulations is the so-called flux transfer events [5] which were first observed in spacecraft data and are thought to be magnetic flux ropes formed at the Earth's magnetopause (Figure 1 illustrates the 3D full particle simulation of the primary and secondary flux rope formation). Many details regarding the FTEs remain poorly understood but peta-scale simulations are enabling us to finally settle many questions regarding their formation, structure, and evolution.

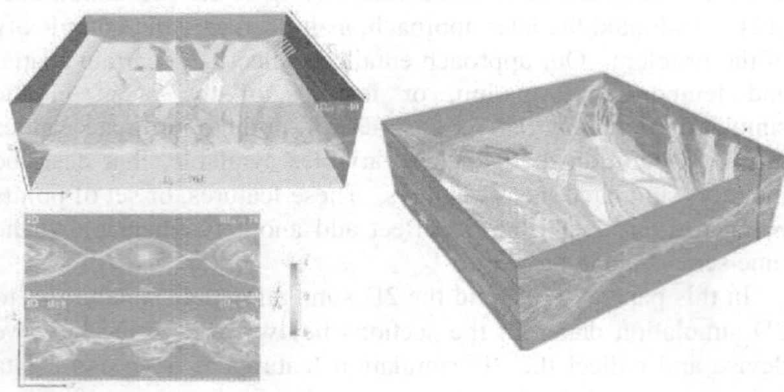

Figure 1. Left - Primary and secondary flux rope formation. 3D full particle simulation with mass ratio of 100 and 1 trillion particles. At early time, the linear tearing leads to formation of flux ropes over a rather small range of angles. At later time, secondary islands lead to a turbulent structure whereas in 2D the layer remains laminar. Right - Plot of sum of electron energy bands covering 4-6 times the thermal energy.

Figure 2 shows a simulation window of a 3D global simulation of magnetosphere, whereas Figure 3 illustrates several examples of FTEs in a 2D slice of a 3D global simulation. The simulation box is 2000 x 2000 ion skin depths or about 20 earth radii in each direction. The size of FTEs is small compared to the overall size of the magnetosphere and they appear as regions with density enhancements in this figure. FTEs also have complex structures in velocity and magnetic field variables. *Simulations have one major advantage to spacecraft observations* in that one has in effect a very good spatial coverage of FTE at any given time and can track its evolution in time. In contrast, a single spacecraft or even four-spacecraft as in the case of Cluster mission, have limited spatial coverage. Figure 3 shows three sample spacecraft trajectories.

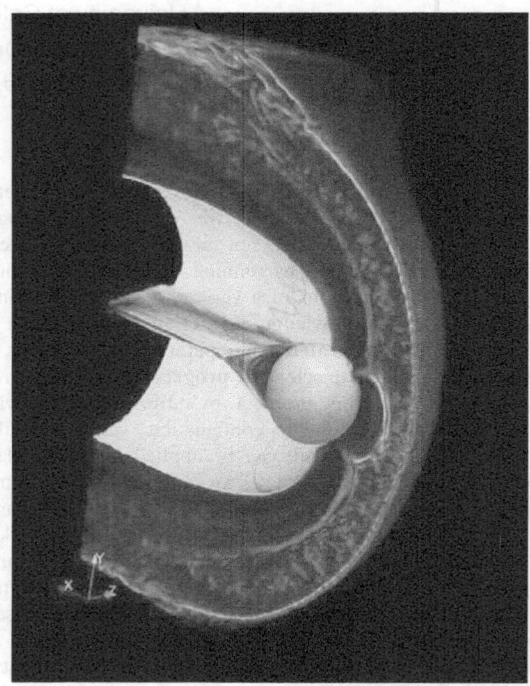

Figure 2. 3D global simulation of magnetosphere.

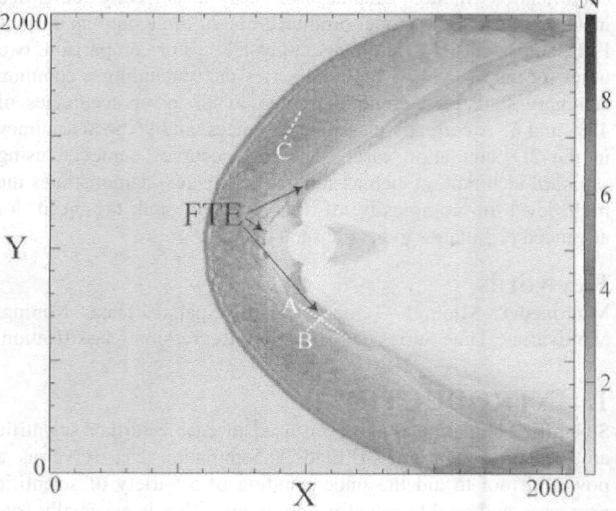

Figure 3. 2D slice of the 3D simulation of the Earth's magnetosphere showing three examples of FTEs, and the three sample spacecraft trajectories (A, B and C).

Our goal in this particular study was to determine whether data mining algorithms can distinguish between these different cuts which include cuts scheming the surface of the FTE (cut-A), across an FTE (cut-B), or cuts away from FTEs (cut-C). We were able to accomplish this in the simplified 2D simulation study [12]. In this paper, our goal is to determine if we can achieve this in the full 3D simulation. If successful, this would imply that data mining algorithms can equally be applied to *spacecraft data* to distinguish among these three cuts. It would also imply that there are distinct features among the variables that, for example, would enable the algorithm to distinguish between cuts across and along an FTE.

3. TIME SERIES DATA ANALYSIS

3.1 Multivariate Time Series Data

In the recent years we introduced a technique called MineTool [10] with distinct advantages over standard data mining techniques. Besides offering high accuracy of the resulting predictive models, a key advantage of MineTool-like approach is that it makes data mining more accessible, by offering a self-contained step by step procedure for model building. MineTool was created to handle static (non-time series) data and further expanded to a multivariate time series analysis technique which is naturally incorporated into the MineTool modeling process, suitable for time series data analysis. Some of the immediate applications of the resulting method, called MineTool-TS (for MineTool-TimeSeries), include multiple event detection and event classification [11].

In time series forecasting, one is interested in deciphering and quantifying temporal patterns in the data. In multi-variate time series data analysis, the relationship among the variables, each represented by a time series, can also be important. Time series analysis has become one of the most important branches of mathematical statistics and data mining, and a variety of techniques have been developed. The techniques range from a single time series forecasting (e.g., using the ARIMA method), to time series modification to allow certain patterns to be observed more easily (e.g., using FFT in signal processing), to multivariate time series classification. The latter is the focus of our work presented here.

3.2 Multivariate Time Series Classification

A data mining technique called MineTool-TS was introduced which captures the time-lapse information in multivariate time series data through extraction of global features and metafeatures [11]. In this paper we expand MineTool to handle not only static and time series data, but image, and simulation data as well, and call it MineTool-M^2 for MineTool-MultiMedia.

Time series data containing multiple variables (i.e. multivariate time series data) commonly occurs in a wide variety of fields including biology, finance, science and engineering. A time series (or more generally temporal data) is a sequence of measurements that follow non-random orders and can be generated either from a fixed point measurements at several time intervals or a convolved spatial-temporal variations as measured from a moving detector. Multivariate time series analysis is used when one wants to model and explain the interactions among a group of time series variables such as the field and plasma variables in the space physics domain. Much of the scientific data is in form of multivariate time series. Examples include ECG measurements, *in situ* field and plasma measurements of bow shock crossings, flux transfer events, turbulence in the solar wind, sign language hand movements, among others.

Multivariate time series classification attempts at classification of a new time series based on past observations of time series examples, rather than providing an analysis of a single-variate time series. Just like in any other classification problem, we are given examples of labeled data in order to build a predictive model. Historically, Hidden Markov Models (HMMs), recurrent Artificial Neural Networks (recurrent ANNs) and Dynamic Time Warping (DTW) have been used to build predictive models of multivariate time series data for classification tasks [15][21][24]. Even though these techniques are useful for certain tasks, they have several disadvantages which make them impractical for large datasets. In case of HMMs, for example, the number of parameters that needs to be set and examined is very large, even for small HMMs, determining the number of states for a certain dataset is just an educated guess, leading to many iterations of examining and setting the parameters. HHMs also do not handle continuous values very well, and make several major assumptions not readily available in a real-world scientific dataset. Recurrent ANNs suffer from several of the same problems as HMMs and require the user to experiment and choose many parameters and decide on the appropriate network architecture. The result is also in the form of a black-box which makes it difficult to understand.

If one could replace the time series by a static data consisting of variables that capture the relevant and interesting features (e.g., number of zero crossings, slope, and extreme values) of the time series, then the standard MineTool technique could be used. Two ideas for reduction of time series data immediately come to mind. First, one can randomly select several time instances of the data and treat each instance as a static data. The number of instances selected can be smaller than the total number of time instances available. Second, one can create summary statistics data, i.e., the time series data is replaced by its statistical measures such as the mean, standard deviation, minimum and maximum values, etc. As we will show shortly, even though these techniques are somewhat successful for a small number of simple datasets and problems, neither of these two approaches yields high accuracy results in modeling real life, complex time series data. Instead we use a more sophisticated approach to extract features from multivariate time series data that yields much higher accuracy [7][11].

3.2.1 MineTool for Static Data

The core data mining algorithm that underlies MineTool-TS is MineTool [10]. The advantages of MineTool over traditional algorithms such as support vector machine and artificial neural net (ANN) are its automated steps that make it more accessible and applicable in a variety of domains, accuracy, robustness and the analytical form of the model at the output.

An important algorithmic issue in data mining is how to find the optimal complexity of the model or the fitting function. Too much complexity in the model can result in overfit, whereas not enough complexity can result in underfit. The mathematical foundations of MineTool are based on considerations to balance the competing dangers of underfit and overfit to identify the level of model complexity that guarantees the best out-of-sample prediction performance without ad hoc modifications to the fitting algorithms themselves [14][17][18][26]. MineTool creates a predictive model architecture that is linear in the parameters. The algorithm searches for a model M that best relates rows of the input variable values Xij to the appropriate target value yi (yi = M(Xij)), where i = 1,…,N and j = 1,…,K. The model parameters are either linear combinations of the input ($\mathbf{X_i}'\boldsymbol{\alpha}$, where prime indicates transpose of the vector, index i refers to the ith observation), linear transformations of the input variables ($\zeta(Xi)$), or highly non-linear transformations of the input ($\Psi(Xi,\gamma)$). Equation 1 describes the general form of a MineTool model:

$$y_i = \mathbf{X}_i'\boldsymbol{\alpha} + \sum_{p=1}^{P} \zeta(\mathbf{X}_i)'\boldsymbol{\delta}_p + \sum_{q=1}^{Q} \boldsymbol{\Psi}(\mathbf{X}_i, \boldsymbol{\gamma}_q)'\boldsymbol{\beta}_q \qquad (1)$$

In its simplest form, the model would be a linear combination of the input parameters (i.e. a linear regression model). MineTool goes beyond a simple linear model by introducing the linear (such as level-1 and level-2 transformations producing cross-products, ratios, squares, cubes etc.) and non-linear transformation of the input variables, if their addition increases the model accuracy. The non-linear transforms Ψ are single hidden layer feed forward Artificial Neural Net (ANN)-like transforms, just like the ANNs of the same architecture, with the difference that the non-linear transformed inputs are combined into a linear model.

3.2.2 *Metafeature and Global Feature Detection*

To be able to process a (time) series dataset (represented with multiple rows of data describing one instance or observation) using MineTool, the data needs to be "flattened," or made static. Nevertheless, this needs to be accomplished without losing the important information incorporated in sequential measurements varying with time. Historically, this has been done either by summarizing the data and writing only the mean of the different row values of one observation, or recording the difference between the pairs of rows and then treating them as single instance entries. These techniques work somewhat well on just a limited set of time series problems. For real life, complex scientific datasets, these approaches are most often too weak to incorporate the important time changes in the data. The MineTool-TS solution to this problem is to collect the important time-changing information that can occur in one of the time series variables. While a value varies with time, it most often increases, decreases or stagnates. There are other, more complex features one can record, that consist of the three basic changes, such as bipolar signature (relevant in case of flux transfer events), where a value goes up, then goes down crossing the axis, and goes up again (the sinusoid function has a demonstrates the bipolar behavior, for example). Global features, just like the metafeatures, are used to extract the information from all the rows representing one observation. Global features describe one instance rows using one measurement, such as: the maximum value, minimum values, mean, mode or the number of zero crossings. Some of the metafeatures and global features included in the MineTool-TS algorithm are following:

- **Increasing Metafeature**— An increasing metafeature is recorded for all the consecutive rising time-series measurements. For each increasing event, we record its start point, duration, gradient and average value, so that the increasing events can be used for analysis and comparison.
- **Decreasing Metafeature**— A decreasing metafeature is recorded for all the consecutive reducing time-series measurements. For each decreasing event, similarly to the increasing events, we record starting point, duration, gradient (which is negative in this case) and average value.
- **Plateau Metafeature**— A plateau metafeature is recorded for all the consecutive non-changing time-series measurements. MineTool-TS allows for a small amount of noise to be ignored, so that the true plateaus are captured.
- **Bipolar Signature Metafeature**— A bipolar signature metafeature is recorded for all the consecutive time-series measurements that increase, decrease and cross the zero, and increase again.
- **Global Minimum**—For each single variable, the global minimum feature extracts the minimum value of all of the time observations belonging to one time series instance for the variable, and records it as the global minimum feature for that input channel.
- **Global Maximum**—The maximum value of all of the time observations belonging to one time series instance for the variable, and is recorded as the global maximum feature for that variable.
- **Mean** —The average value of all of the time observations belonging to one time series instance for the variable, and is recorded as the global mean feature for that specific variable.
- **Mode** —The mode value of all of the time observations belonging to one time series instance for the variable, and is recorded as the global mode feature for that specific input variable.
- **Number of Zero Crossings** —Lastly, the number of zero crossings occurring during the time observation recorded measurements is written down as the number of zero crossings global feature.

Next, once all the requested features are collected, the MineTool-TS algorithm performs the feature space segmentation to group similar features and make them have a higher predictive value for data mining. More details on the algorithm can be found in [11].

3.3 MineTool-3DM^2 Extension for Multimedia Data Mining

The time series classification algorithm needed to be adapted to handle simulation (and other multimedia) data. This is accomplished by a tailored data preparation of multimedia (3D simulation) data and then feeding such prepared data to the basic time series analysis algorithm described in [11] and the different length time series addition described in [12].

3.3.1 *Simulation Data Preparation*

The simulation data needs to be converted into a series dataset as the algorithm is designed for time series data. To prepare simulation data for being entered in MineTool-3DM^2 we perform a preprocessing step that converts the multimedia data into a series data set. Section 4.2 details our feature extraction step that converts the simulation data into a series "cuts" data and enables further analysis.

In the following section we illustrate the application of MineTool-M^2 to the Flux Transfer Event (FTE) simulation data.

4. APPLICATION TO SIMULATION DATA

To demonstrate the effectiveness of MineTool-3DM^2 to mining time series multimedia data, we looked at the problem of automatic detection of Flux Transfer Events (FTE) in 3D simulation data of the Earth's magnetosphere.

FTEs are typically identified on the basis of clear isolated bipolar signatures in the B_n component of the magnetic field (in the LMN coordinate system). The Cluster spacecraft magnetic field observations of 4-s resolution from the Fluxgate Magnetometer (FGM) [1] and plasma observations of 4-s resolution from the Cluster Ion Spectrometry (CIS) instrument [22] are commonly used for Cluster magnetopause crossings and FTE identifications. The measurements include a total of 11 input variables: B_x, B_y, B_z, |B|, N_p, V_x, V_y, V_z, $T_{||}$, $T_{\perp}$, T_t However, simulation is used to enable visualization of what the collected measurements mean, how these events occur in magnetosphere, and assist the scientist in evaluating novel algorithms and attaining better understanding of these events.

4.1 Description of the Test Problem

The goal of the data analysis and modeling was to build a model that will be able to distinguish the cuts across the FTEs from the cuts tangent to FTEs (two classes), as well as differentiate non FTEs. This is a challenging three-class, multivariate data series classification problem. In FTE observations, scientists can identify FTEs only by looking at signatures tangent to FTEs and our goal is to, using simulation and the presented MineTool-3DM² approach to data mining of multimedia time series data, improve this approach.

4.2 Data Collection and Preparation: "3D Cuts" Feature Extraction

To analyze simulation data in tracking an event, we chose to select and concentrate on a particular area of the 3D simulations that is of interest. We wanted to focus on the features being created and changing in time. In this manner, we are able to emphasize the FTE events in order to describe them, model and classify them. We introduced the *"cut" feature* [12], a novel computer vision feature extraction method that enables us to collect the important characteristic of the area of interest within simulation data window, while decreasing the complexity of the data selected for further analysis. In this paper, we extend this feature to the "3d cut' feature that "slices" the data in the 3D simulation window. A "3D cut" or a "3D slice feature" is a line drawn at the site of the feature of interest, or at the site of the feature non-existence. ***"Cuts" are modeled based on the spacecraft trajectories and, in effect, simulate what a spacecraft would observe while on a trajectory near an event or non-event.*** Our goal here was to determine whether data mining algorithms can distinguish between these different cuts. We have devised a cutting routine for making "cuts" or "slices" in the simulation data and creating a data file to be used in analysis and modeling. Figures 4a, 4b and 4c show three sample spacecraft trajectories-guided cuts or slices in the 3D simulation data which include cuts scheming the surface of the FTE (cut-A), across an FTE (cut-B), or cuts away from FTEs (cut-C). The variables that were observed in the cuts included:

X, Y, Z, B_X_slice, B_Y_slice, B_Z_slice, Density_slice, T_{PAR}_slice, T_{PERP}_slice, T_{TOTAL}_slice, V_{IX}_slice, V_{IY}_slice, V_{IZ}_slice, B_{TOTAL}, event

The simulation FTE data has been labeled with three labels: a) cuts tangent the FTE, b) cuts across to the FTE, and c) non-events. The dataset consists of series data and does not have to have the same length. In this phase of the project, we collected 30 of each of the types of FTE events, giving 90 total events, or streams of data. Each of our events had up to 1000 data points representing one cut, however the length was varying. We have prepared the data and converted in the form suitable for mining using our MineTool-3DM² method for multivariate classification of multimedia time series data.

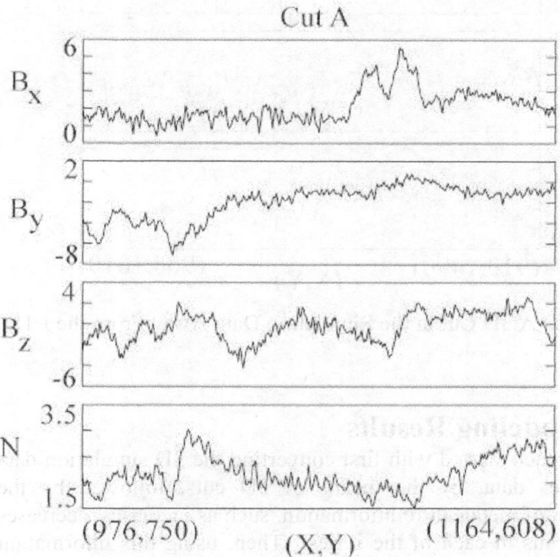

Figure 4a. A 3D Cut in the Simulation Data Tangent to the FTE.

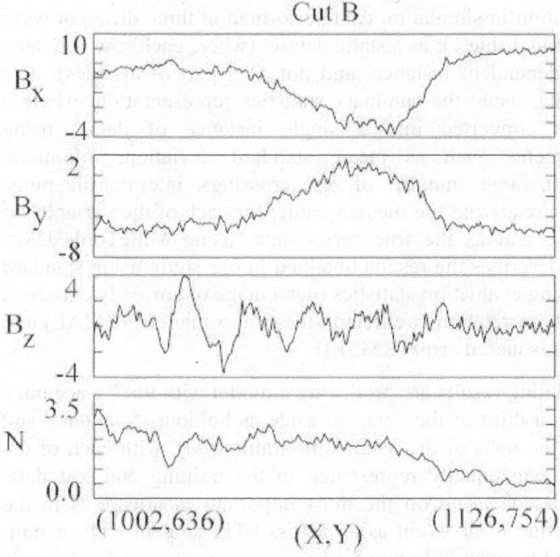

Figure 4b. A 3D Cut in the Simulation Data Across the FTE.

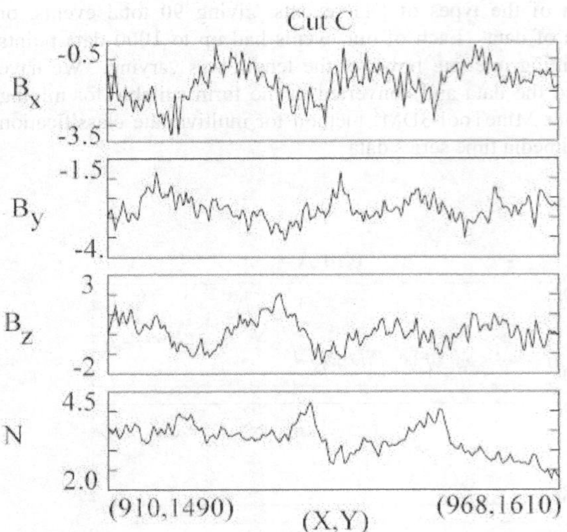

Figure 4c. A 3D Cut in the Simulation Data Away From the FTE.

4.3 Modeling Results

Our approach started with first converting the 3D simulation data into series data, by the means of 3D cuts, followed by the collection of metafeature information, such as increases, decreases and plateaus in each of the series. Then, using this information each of the series was "flattened" into a static row of data and fed into the intermediate dataset. This was completed for each of the 90 event examples. The flattened, static dataset was then fed into our MineTool algorithm, to discover the correlations among the input variables to the output variables.

We contrast the modeling results of the flux transfer event (FTE) classification in simulation data performed in three different ways (as listed in Table 1): as a static dataset (where each row is treated as an independent instance, and not as a part of a series), as a series data, using the summary statistics representation, where a series is converted into a single instance of data using measurements such as mean, standard deviation, minimum, maximum, range, number of zero crossings, interquartile range (or, the spread) and the median value, for each of the variables in the data), and as the true series data, using MineTool-3DM^2. Table 1 describes the results obtained in our study using standard data mining evaluation statistics (percentage of correctly classified instances, correlation coefficient, mean absolute error (MAE) and root mean squared error (RMSE)).

The modeling results are producing a model with 96.7% accuracy tested on a third of the data, set aside as holdout (test) data, and built on the 66% of the data as the training set, with each of the classes being equally represented in the training and test data. The model picks up on the most important metafeatures in the classification of an event as an across FTE, tangent FTE or non-event, and is given in Figure 5.

The predictive model created by the MineTool data mining method is in an analytical form, enabling insight into the most important metafeatures and global features detected by the algorithm in appropriately classifying a time series instance of data. The model in Figure 5 shows that the specific total magnetic field (B_{TOTAL}) together with the specific decrement in Y (which is a level-1 cross product linear transformation $\zeta(Xi)$) from the Eq. 1) negatively correlates to a series cut variable being classified as an FTE, while if the Density_avg * Vx_avg (a simple linear combination of the input variable $X_i'\alpha$) is detected, it positively correlates with an FTE event (there were no highly non-linear transformations $\Psi(Xi,\gamma)$ in the model chosen by the method). The model is also able to very accurately distinguish between an event label 1 and 2 (across and tangent FTE).

```
event = 0.352845
        -0.000164373*ttotal_avg*y_Dec_7
        -0.0667911*viy_avg*bz_avg
        -0.0133856*den_avg*y_Dec_7
        +0.196831*den_avg*vix_avg
        -0.00154025*Btotal_Inc_5*y_Dec_7
        -0.0627191*viy_avg*tperp_avg
        +0.00893886*by_avg*vix_avg
        -0.0429279*by_avg*den_avg
        ...

 Where :
 y_Dec_7 represents a time series feature
 with the following average description:
        average value of -> 462.253
        mid time value of -> 499.073
        gradient value of -> -0.103184
        duration of -> 942.273

 Btotal_Inc_5 represents a time series
 feature with the following average
 description:
        average value of -> 5.93243
        mid time value of -> 451.282
        gradient value of -> 0.0343282
        duration of -> 16.2183

 etc.
```

Figure 5. The Predictive Model of FTEs.

Table1. Comparative analysis of MineTool-M^2 vs. other methods.

Type of Analysis	Correctly Classified	Correlation coefficient	MAE	RMSE
Static Data Analysis	47.1%	0.3621	0.5732	0.6911
Summary Statistics Analysis	62.7%	0.5534	0.4912	0.6351
MineTool-3DM2	96.7%	0.935961	0.24502	0.29506

Table 2 compares the accuracy of different models built using a subset of variables, and illustrates their predictive ability. This type of analysis can be very revealing to the expert in the field, as it pinpoints which individual variables and/or combinations of variables lead to more or less accurate models of FTEs.

Table2. Comparative analysis of different variable models.

Variables used in the model	CC	%correctly classified
BxByBzDensTparTperTtotVxVyVzBtot	0.935961	96.7742%
BxByBz	0.885411	86.6667%
Bx	0.399886	43.3333%
By	0.688911	76.6667%
Bz	0.737009	70%
VxVyVz	0.807528	90%
TparTperTtot	0.854785	86.6667%
dens	0.575214	56.6667%
Btot	0.671588	66.6667%

5. SUMMARY AND DISCUSSION

In this paper we aim to contribute to the urgent need to understand and learn from the often massive, constantly increasing, complex, multimedia data, often collected or created in the form of simulation data, in an automated fashion.

We adapt our multivariate time series analysis data mining technique to handle simulation data. We extract the important information from the simulation data by introducing a novel computer vision feature extraction operator named "cuts" that collect the cuts-type of data in the simulation window. The cuts-data are then converted into a series data and input into MineTool-3DM^2 for analysis and modeling. We also expand the method to allow for uneven lengths of the series data at the input. The technique extracts global features and metafeatures in the 3D simulation dataset in order to capture the necessary time-lapse information. The features are then used to create a static, intermediate data set that is suitable for analysis using the standard supervised data mining techniques.

The capability of the new algorithm called MineTool-3DM^2 is demonstrated through its application to the problem of automatic detection of flux transfer events (FTE) in the simulation data. MineTool-3DM^2 built model led to a high FTE classification model accuracy of 96.7% correctly classified instances where the model produced one of three outputs of across cut FTE, tangent cut FTE, and non-FTE. For comparison, two other means of treating the series data including a common summary statistics technique yielded much lower accuracies of 47% and 63% correctly classified instances, illustrating the imminent need for advanced techniques, such as MineTool-3DM^2, to handle such data.

Our future work will encompass the expansion of MineTool-3DM^2 to other multimedia data as well. By applying and extending ideas from data mining, image and video processing, statistics, and pattern recognition, we are developing a new generation of computational tools and techniques that are being used to improve the way in which scientists extract useful information from data.

6. ACKNOWLEDGMENTS

The tools/techniques were developed at SciberQuest, Inc. and the application to 3D data was supported by the NSF Peta grant at UCSD. Simulations were performed on Kraken, a Cray XT5 system provided by the National Science Foundation at the National Institute for Computational Sciences, and on NASA' s Pleiades, which is provided by the NASA High-End Computing (HEC) Program.

7. REFERENCES

[1] Balogh A, Dunlop MW, Cowley SWH, Southwood DJ, Thomlinson JG, Glassmeier KH, Musmann G, Luhr H, Buchert S, Acuna MH, Fairfield DH, Slavin JA, Riedler W, Schwingenschuh K, Kivelson MG, The Cluster magnetic field investigation, *Space Sci. Rev.*, 79, 65-91, 1997.

[2] Candes, E.. *Ridgelets: Theory and Applications*. PhD thesis, Stanford University, Department of Statistics, 1998.

[3] Cortes C. and Vapnik V. Support-Vector Networks, *Machine Learning, 20, 1995.*

[4] Dempster, A., Laird, N., and Rubin, D. (1977). Maximum likelihood from incomplete data via the EM algorithm. *Journal of the Royal Statistical Society, Series B*, 39(1):1-38.

[5] R. C. Elphic. Observations of Flux Transfer Events: A Review. the American Geophysical Union, 1995.

[6] Hartley, H. (1958). Maximum likelihood estimation from incomplete data. *Biometrics*, 14:174–194.

[7] Kadous, M. W. *Temporal Classification: Extending the Classification Paradigm to Multivariate Time Series*. PhD thesis, School of Computer Science & Engineering, University of New South Wales, 2002.

[8] Karimabadi, H., and J. Dorelli, H. X. Vu, B. Loring, Y. Omelchenko, Is quadrupole structure of out-of-plane magnetic field evidence of Hall reconnection?, to appear in *Modern Challenges in Nonlinear Plasma Physics*, editor D. Vassiliadis, AIP conference, 2010.

[9] Karimabadi, H., H. X. Vu, D. Krauss-Varban, Y. Omelchenko, Global Hybrid Simulations of the Earth's Magnetosphere, *Numerical Modeling of Space Plasma Flows: Astronum-2006*, vol. 359, 257, 2006.

[10] Karimabadi, H., Sipes, T. B., White, H., Marinucci, M., Dmitriev, A., Chao, L.K., Driscoll, J., Balac, N. (2007). Data Mining in Space Physics: 1. The MineTool Algorithm, *J. Geophys. Res.*, 112, A11215, doi:10.1029/2006JA012136.

[11] Karimabadi, H., Sipes, T. B., Wang, Y., Lavraud, B. and Roberts, A. (2009). A new multivariate time series data analysis technique: Automated detection of flux transfer events using Cluster data, *J. Geophys. Res., Vol 114, A06216, doi:10.1029/2009JA014202, 2009*

[12] Sipes, T. B. and Karimabadi, H. (2012). MineTool-M2: An Algorithm for Data Mining of 2D Simulation Data,

Proceedings of the International Conference on Data Mining, Las Vegas, July 2012.

[13] Looney, C. G., Pattern recognition using neural networks, Theory and algorithms for engineers and scientists, Oxford University Press, 1997.

[14] Marinucci, M., Automatic Prediction and Model Selection,Ph.D. Thesis, Departamento de Fundamentos del Analisis EconomicoII, Facultad de Ciencias Economicas, Universidad Complutense de Madrid 2007.

[15] Myers, C. S. and Rabiner, L. R. A comparative study of several dynamic time-warping algorithms for connected word recognition. The Bell System Technical Journal, 60(7):1389-1409, September 1981.

[16] McLachlan, G. and Krishnan, T. (1997). *The EM algorithm and extensions*. Wiley series in probability and statistics. John Wiley & Sons.

[17] Pérez-Amaral, T., Gallo, G. M. and White, H., A Flexible Tool for Model Building: the Relevant Transformation of the Inputs Network Approach (RETINA), *Oxford Bulletin of Economics and Statistics*, 65 (s1), 821-838, 2003.

[18] Pérez-Amaral, T., Gallo, G. M. and White, H., A Comparison of Complementary Automatic Modeling Methods: RETINA and PcGets," *Econometric Theory*, 2005.

[19] Powell, M. J. D. *Radial basis functions for multivariate interpolation: A review*. In Algorithms for Approximation, J. C. Mason and M. G. Cox, Eds. Clarendon Press, Oxford, 1987.

[20] Ross Quinlan (1993). C4.5: Programs for Machine Learning. Morgan Kaufmann Publishers, San Mateo, CA.

[21] Rabiner, L. R. and Juang, B. H. An introduction to hidden markov models. IEEE Magazine on Acoustics, Speech and Signal Processing, 3(1):4-16, 1986.

[22] Reme, H. and C. Aoustin and J. M. Bosqued and I. Dandouras, B. Lavraud, et al., First multispacecraft ion measurements in and near the Earth's magnetosphere with the identical Cluster ion spectrometry (CIS) experiment, *Annales Geophysicae*, 19, 1303-1354, 2001.

[23] Ripley, B.D., Pattern Recognition and Neural Networks, Cambridge University Press; 1996.

[24] Schmidhuber, J., Graves, A., Gomez, F. and Hochreiter, S. Recurrent Neural Networks, Cambridge University Press, 2012.

[25] White, H., Approximate nonlinear forecasting methods, in *Handbook of Economic Forecasting*, Volume 1, Edited by Elliott, Granger and Timmermann, Elsevier, Amsterdam, 2006.

[26] White, H., Personnel Readiness: Neural Network Modeling of Performance-Based Estimates, *Final Report to the Office of Naval Research, Contract #: N00014-95-C-1078*, 1999.

[27] R. J. Vidmar. (1992, August). On the use of atmospheric plasmas as electromagnetic reflectors. *IEEE Trans. Plasma Sci.* [Online]. *21(3)*. pp. 876—880. Available: http://www.halcyon.com/pub/journals/ 21ps03-vidma

Actions Ontology System for Action Rules Discovery in Mammographic Mass Data

Angelina A. Tzacheva[1], Erik A. Koenig[1], and Justin R. Pardue[1]
[1]Department of Informatics, University of South Carolina Upstate, Spartanburg, SC 29303, U.S.A.

Abstract - *Actionable knowledge is a golden nugget within the data mining research field. Action rules describe possible transitions of objects in an information system - from one state to another more desirable state, with respect to a distinguished attribute. In this paper we propose an improved method for generating action rules by incorporating an additional ontology layer on top of the information system. It contains nodes of higher-level actions knowledge, which are linked with individual terms at the lower levels. The system shows the likely changes within classification attributes, with respect to a decision attribute of our interest. We experiment with Mammographic Mass DataSet in attempts to re-classify tumors from malignant to benign. In addition to medical domain, application areas include financial, and industrial domain.*

Keywords: Action rules, Ontology, Mammography

1 Introduction

An action rule is a rule extracted from a decision system that describes a possible transition of objects from one state to another with respect to a distinguished attribute called a decision attribute [13]. We assume that attributes used to describe objects in a decision system are partitioned into stable and flexible. Values of flexible attributes can be changed. This change can be influenced and controlled by users. Action rules mining initially was based on comparing profiles of two groups of targeted objects - those that are desirable and those that are undesirable [13]. An action rule was defined as a term $[(\omega) \wedge (\alpha \rightarrow \beta)] \Rightarrow (\varphi \rightarrow \psi)$, where ω is a conjunction of fixed condition features shared by both groups, $(\alpha \rightarrow \beta)$ represents proposed changes in values of flexible features, and $(\varphi \rightarrow \psi)$ is a desired effect of the action. The discovered knowledge provides an insight of how values of some attributes need to be changed so the undesirable objects can be shifted to a desirable group. How to identify an *action* which triggers the desired changes of flexible attributes and which is not described by values of attributes listed in the decision system is a difficult problem. In this paper, we propose locating such *actions* in an ontology [3] layer. We therefore call this layer - *actions ontology*.

Clearly, there has to be a link between the *actions* and the changes they trigger within the values of flexible attributes in the decision system. Such link can be provided either by an ontology [3] or by a mapping/linking *actions* with changes of attributes values used in the decision system. For example, one would like to find a way to improve his or her salary from a low-income to a high-income. Another example in business area is when an owner would like to improve his or her company's profits by going from a high-cost, low-income business to a low-cost, high-income business. Action rules tell us what changes within flexible attributes are needed to achieve that goal.

2 Previous work

Action rules have been introduced in [13] and investigated further in [16], [14], [10], [17], [15], [4], and [9]. Paper [6] was probably the first attempt towards formally introducing the problem of mining action rules without pre-existing classification rules. Authors explicitly formulate it as a search problem in a support-confidence-cost framework. The proposed algorithm has some similarity with Apriori [1]. Their definition of an action rule allows changes on stable attributes. Changing the value of an attribute, either stable or flexible, is linked with a cost [17]. In order to rule out action rules with undesired changes on attributes, authors designate very high cost to such changes. However, in this way, the cost of action rules discovery is getting unnecessarily increased. Also, they did not take into account the correlations between attribute values which are naturally linked with the cost of rules used either to accept or reject a rule. Algorithm ARED, presented in [7], is based on Pawlak's model of an information system S [8]. The goal was to identify certain relationships between granules defined by the indiscernibility relation on its objects. Some of these relationships uniquely define action rules for S. Paper [11] presents a strategy for discovering action rules directly from the decision system. Action rules are built from atomic expressions following a strategy similar to ERID [2]. Paper [18] introduced the notion of *action* as a domain- independent way to model the domain knowledge. Given a data set about actionable features and a utility measure, a pattern is actionable if it summarizes a population that can be acted upon towards a more promising population observed with a higher utility. Algorithms for mining actionable patterns (changes within flexible attributes) take into account only numerical attributes. The distinguished (decision) attribute is called utility. Each *action Ai* triggers changes of attribute values described by terms [$a \downarrow$], [$b \uparrow$], and [c (don't know)]. They are represented as an influence matrix built by an expert. While previous approaches used only features - mined directly from the decision system, authors in [18] define actions as its foreign concepts. Influence matrix shows the link between actions and changes of attribute values and the same shows correlations between some attributes, i.e. if [a $\downarrow$], then [b $\uparrow$]. In this paper, we propose an additional ontology layer, which contains the link between actions and changes of attribute values. Clearly, expert does not know correlations between classification attributes and the decision attribute. Such correlations can be described as action rules and they have to be discovered from the decision system. Authors in [18] did not take into consideration stable attributes and their classification attributes are only numerical. In this paper, for simplicity reason, we use only symbolic attributes. Numerical attributes, if any, are discretized before action rules are discovered.

3 Information systems and actions

In this section we introduce the notion of an information system and actions.

By an information system [8] we mean a triple $S = (X, At, V)$, where:

1. X is a nonempty, finite set of objects
2. At is a nonempty, finite set of attributes, i.e. $a : U \rightarrow V_a$, where V_a is called the domain of a
3. $V = \cup\{ V_a : a \in A \}$.

For example, Table 1 shows an information system S with a set of objects $X = \{x_1, x_2, x_3, x_4, x_5, x_6, x_7, x_8\}$, set of attributes $At = \{a, b, c, d\}$, and a set of their values $V = \{a_1, a_2, b_1, b_2, b_3, c_1, c_2, d_1, d_2, d_3\}$.

TABLE I
INFORMATION SYSTEM S

	a	b	c	d
	a_1	b_1	c_1	d_1
x_1	a_2	b_1	c_2	d_1
x_2	a_2	b_2	c_2	d_1
x_3	a_2	b_1	c_1	d_1
x_4	a_2	b_3	c_2	d_1
x_5	a_1	b_1	c_2	d_2
x_6	a_1	b_2	c_2	d_1
x_7	a_1	b_2	c_1	d_3

An information system $S = (X, At, V)$ is called a decision system, if one of the attributes in At is distinguished and called the decision. The remaining attributes in At are classification attributes. Additionally, we assume that $At = A_{St} \cup A_{Fl} \cup \{d\}$, where attributes in A_{St} are called *stable* and in A_{Fl} *flexible*. Attribute d is the decision attribute. "Date of birth" is an example of a stable attribute. "Interest rate" for each customer account is an example of a flexible attribute.

By *actions* associated with S we mean higher level concepts modeling certain generalizations of actions introduced in [18]. *Actions*, when executed, can influence or trigger changes in values of some flexible attributes in *S*. They are specified by expert. To give an example, let us assume that classification attributes in *S* describe teaching evaluations at some school and the decision attribute represents their overall score. *Explain difficult concepts effectively*, *Speaks English fluently*, *Stimulate student interest in the course*, *Provide sufficient feedback* are examples of classification attributes. Then, examples of *actions* associated with S will be: *Change the content of the course*, *Change the textbook of the course*, *Post all material on the Web*. Clearly, any of these three *actions* will not influence the attribute *Speaks English fluently* and therefore its values will remain unchanged. It should be mentioned here that an expert knowledge concerning *actions* involves only classification attributes. Now, if some of these attributes are correlated with the decision attribute, then the change of their values will cascade to the decision through the correlation. The goal of action rule discovery is to identify possibly all such correlations.

4 Action rules

In earlier works in [13], [16], [14], [10], and [15] action rules are constructed from classification rules. This means that we use pre-existing classification rules or generate them using a rule discovery algorithm, such as LERS [5] or ERID [2], then, construct action rules either from certain pairs of these rules or from a single classification rule. For instance, algorithm ARAS [15] generates sets of terms (built from values of attributes) around classification rules and constructs action rules directly from them. In [12] authors present a strategy for extracting action rules directly from a decision system and without using pre-existing classification rules.

Let $S = (X, At, V)$ be an information system, where $V = \cup \{V_a : a \in At\}$. First, we recall the notion of an atomic action set [11]. By an *atomic action set* we mean an expression $(a, a_1 \rightarrow a_2)$, where a is an attribute and $a_1 , a_2 \in V_a$. If $a_1 = a_2$, then a is called stable on a_1. Instead of $(a, a_1 \rightarrow a_2)$, we often write (a, a_1) for any $a_1 \in V_a$.

By *Action Sets* [11] we mean a smallest collection of sets such that:

1. If t is atomic action set, then t is an action set.
2. If t_1, t_2 are action sets, then $t_1 \wedge t_2$ is a candidate action set.
3. If t is a candidate action set and for any two atomic action sets $(a, a_1 \rightarrow a_2)$, $(b, b_1 \rightarrow b_2)$ contained in t we have $a \neq b$, then t is an action set .

By the domain of an action set t, denoted by $Dom(t)$, we mean the set of all attribute names listed in t. For instance, assume that $\{(a, a_2), (b, b_1 \rightarrow b_2)\}$, $\{(a, a_2), (b, b_2 \rightarrow b_1)\}$ are two collections of atomic action sets associated with *actions* A_1, A_2. It means that both A_1, A_2 can influence attributes *a*, *b* but attribute *a* in both cases has to remain stable. The corresponding action sets are: $(a, a_2) \wedge (b, b_1 \rightarrow b_2)$, $(a, a_2) \wedge (b, b_2 \rightarrow b_1)$.

Consider several *actions*, denoted $A_1, A_2, \ldots, A_n$. An *action* can influence the values of classification attributes in *At*. We assume here that $At - \{d\} = At_1 \cup At_2 \cup \ldots \cup At_m$. The influence of these *actions* on classification attributes in *At* is specified by the *actions ontology*.

By an *action rule* we mean any expression $r = [t_1 \Rightarrow t_2]$, where t_1 and t_2 are action sets. Additionally, we assume that $Dom(t_1) \cup Dom(t_2) \in At$ and $Dom(t_1) \cap Dom(t_2) = \emptyset$. The domain of action rule *r* is defined as $Dom(t_1) \cup Dom(t_2)$.

Now, we give an example of action rules assuming that the information system *S* is represented by Table 1. *a*, *c*, *d* are flexible attributes and *b* is stable. Expressions (a, a_2), (b, b_2), $(c, c_1 \rightarrow c_2)$, $(d, d_1 \rightarrow d_2)$ are examples of *atomic action sets*. Expression $(c, c_1 \rightarrow c_2)$ means that the value of attribute *c* is changed from c_1 to c_2 . Expression (a, a_2) means that the value a_2 of attribute *a* remains unchanged. Expression $r = [[(a, a_2) \wedge (c, c_1 \rightarrow c_2)]) \Rightarrow (d, d_1 \rightarrow d_2)]$ is an example of an *action rule*. The rule says that if value a_2 remains unchanged and value *c* changes from c_1 to c_1 , then it is expected that the value *d* will change from d_1 to d_2. We recall that *d* is the distinguished (decision) attribute, which the user is interested in. The domain *Dom(r)* of action rule *r* is equal to *{a, c, d}*. We extract candidate *action rules* by using algorithm ARD[11].

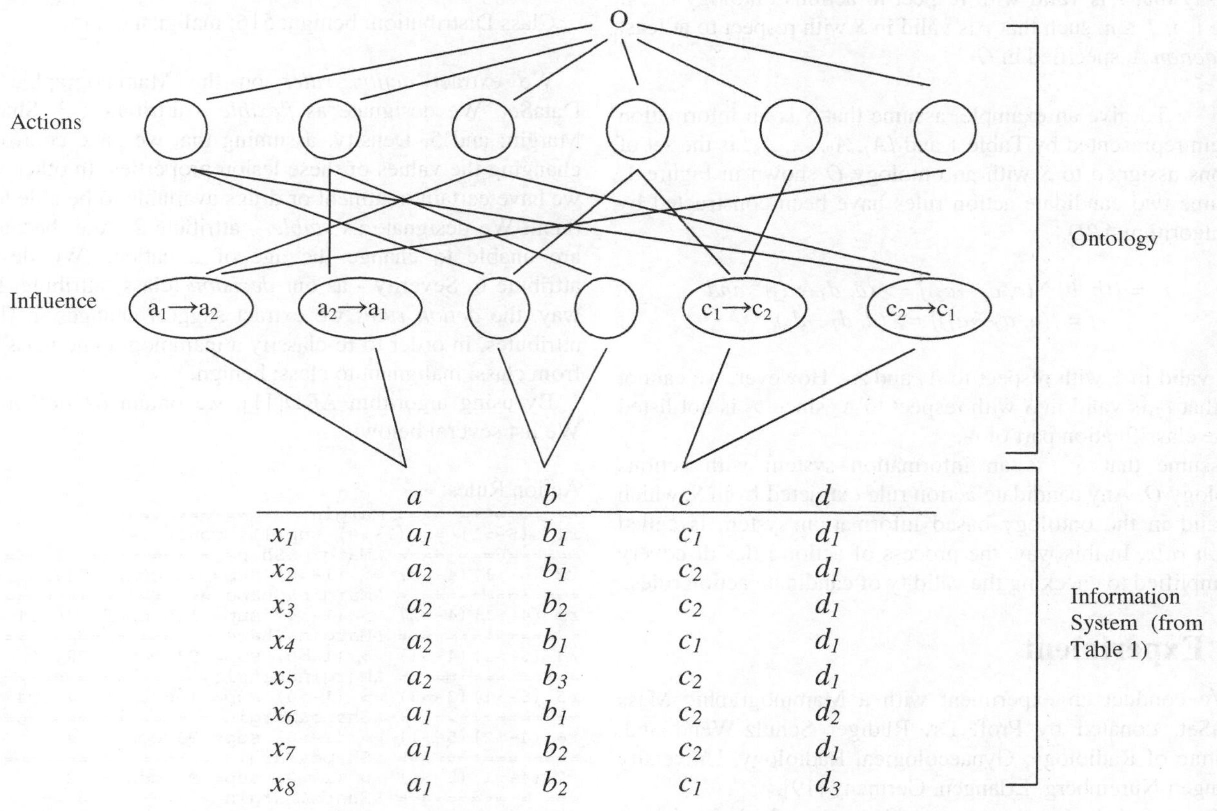

	a	b	c	d
x_1	a_1	b_1	c_1	d_1
x_2	a_2	b_1	c_2	d_1
x_3	a_2	b_2	c_2	d_1
x_4	a_2	b_1	c_1	d_1
x_5	a_2	b_3	c_2	d_1
x_6	a_1	b_1	c_2	d_2
x_7	a_1	b_2	c_2	d_1
x_8	a_1	b_2	c_1	d_3

Fig. 1. *Ontology Based Information System.*

5 Action rules discovery through actions ontology

An *ontology* [3], which is a system of fundamental concepts, that is, a system of background knowledge of any knowledge base, explicates the conceptualization of the target world and provides us with a solid foundation on which we can build sharable knowledge bases for wider usability than that of a conventional knowledge base. From knowledge-based systems point of view, it is defined as "a theory(system) of concepts/ vocabulary used as building blocks of an information processing system" by Mizoguchi [3]. Ontologies are agreements about shared conceptualizations. A very simple case would be a type hierarchy, specifying classes and their subsumption relationships.

Actions ontology associated with *S* is used to identify which candidate action rules, extracted by the algorithm *ARD*, are valid with respect to our *actions* and hidden correlations between classification attributes and the decision attribute.

Assume that: $S = \{X, At \cup \{d\}, V\}$ is an information system; $At - \{d\} = a \cup b \cup ... \cup z$; $\{A_1, A_2, ..., A_n\}$ are *actions* associated with *S*; $O\{[A_1, A_2, ..., A_n, [I_{i,j} : 1 \leq i \leq n, 1 \leq j \leq m]\}$ is the *ontology*, where $I_{i,j}$ is the influence of these *actions* on *S*; and, $r = [(a, a_1 \rightarrow a_2) \wedge (b, b_1 \rightarrow b_2) \wedge ... \wedge (z, z_1 \rightarrow z_2)] => (d, d_1 \rightarrow d_2)$ is a candidate *action rule* extracted from S . We assume that $At_{[i,j]}(A_i) = I_{i,j}$, where value $I_{i,j}$ is either an atomic action set, or *NULL* (undefined). By ontology based information system, we mean a couple consisting of: the information system *S*, and the *ontology O*. The ontology contains the *actions*, and the influence $I_{i,j}$ they have on *S*.

We say that *r* is valid in *S* with respect to action A_i , if the following condition holds:

$$\text{if } [At_{[i,j]}(A_i) \text{ is defined}]$$
$$\text{then } (At_{[i,j]}, At_{[i,j]} \rightarrow At_{[i,k]}) = (At_{[i,j]}, I_{i,j})$$

We say that *r* is valid with respect to actions ontology *O* , if there is *i*, $1 \leq n$, such that *r* is valid in *S* with respect to at least one *action* A_i specified in *O* .

To give an example, assume that *S* is an information system represented by Table 1 and $\{A_1, A_2, ..., A_n\}$ is the set of actions assigned to *S* with an ontology *O* shown in Figure 1. Assume two candidate action rules have been constructed by the algorithm *ARD*.

$$r_1 = [(b, b) \wedge (c, c_1 \rightarrow c_2)] => (d, d_1 \rightarrow d_2) \quad and$$
$$r_2 = [(a, a_2 \rightarrow a_1)] => (d, d_1 \rightarrow d_2).$$

r_1 is valid in *S* with respect to A_4 and A_5. However, we cannot say that r_2 is valid in *S* with respect to A_2 since b_2 is not listed in the classification part of r_2.

Assume that *S* is an information system with actions ontology *O*. Any candidate action rule extracted from *S*, which is valid in the ontology based information system is called *action rule*. In this way, the process of action rules discovery is simplified to checking the validity of candidate action rules.

6 Experiment

We conduct an experiment with a Mammographic Mass DataSet, donated by Prof. Dr. Rüdiger Schulz-Wendtland, Institute of Radiology, Gynaecological Radiology, University Erlangen-Nuremberg, Erlangen, Germany [19].

Mammography is the most effective method for breast cancer screening available today. This data set is used to predict the severity (benign or malignant) of a mammographic mass lesion from BI-RADS attributes and the patient's age. It contains a BI-RADS assessment, the patient's age and three BI-RADS attributes together with the ground truth (the severity field) for 516 benign and 445 malignant masses that have been identified on full field digital mammograms collected at the Institute of Radiology of the University Erlangen-Nuremberg between 2003 and 2006. Each instance has an associated BI-RADS assessment ranging from 1 (definitely benign) to 5 (highly suggestive of malignancy) assigned in a double-review process by physicians. Assuming that all cases with BI-RADS assessments greater or equal to a given value (varying from 1 to 5), are malignant and the other cases are benign.

The dataset contains 961 instances, and has 6 attributes (1 goal field, 1 non-predictive, 4 predictive attributes). The attributes are:

1. BI-RADS assessment: 1 to 5 (ordinal)
2. Age: patient's age in years (integer)
3. Shape: mass shape: round=1 oval=2 lobular=3 irregular=4 (nominal)
4. Margin: mass margin: circumscribed=1 microlobulated=2 obscured=3 ill-defined=4 spiculated=5 (nominal)
5. Density: mass density high=1 iso=2 low=3 fat-containing=4 (ordinal)
6. Severity: benign=0 or malignant=1 (binominal)

Class Distribution: benign: 516; malignant: 445;

We extract *action rules* on the Mammographic Mass DataSet. We designate as *flexible* – attributes: 3. Shape; 4. Margin; and 5. Density; assuming that we have control over changing the values of these lesion properties. In other words, we have certain treatment or drugs available to be able to alter them. We designate as *stable* – attribute 2. Age; because we are unable to change the age of a patient. We designate attribute 6. Severity - as our *decision* (class) attribute. In this way, the *action rules* we extract suggest changes in flexible attributes, in order to re-classify a mammographic mass lesion from class: malignant to class: benign.

By using algorithm ARD[11], we obtain 64 *action rules*. We list several below:

Action Rules:

```
=============== Margin ===============
r1  (5->1)  =>  (1->0)  sup=114  conf= 74.19
=============== &Margin&Shape =================
r2 (5->1)(4->2)  =>  (1->0)  sup= 93  conf= 74.35
=============== &Margin&Shape =================
r3 (4->1)(4->2)  =>  (1->0)  sup= 149  conf= 70.11
=============== &Margin&Shape =================
r4 (5->1)(4->1)  =>  (1->0)  sup= 93  conf= 72.90
=============== &Margin&Density ===============
r5 (5->1)(3->3)  =>  (1->0)  sup= 106  conf= 73.94
=============== &Shape&Margin ===================
r6 (4->2)(5->1)  =>  (1->0)  sup= 93  conf= 74.35
=============== &Shape&Margin ===================
r7 (4->1)(5->1)  =>  (1->0)  sup= 93  conf= 72.90
=============== &Shape&Margin ===================
r8 (4->2)(5->1)  =>  (1->0)  sup= 93  conf= 74.35
=============== &Shape&Margin ===================
r9 (4->1)(5->1)  =>  (1->0)  sup= 93  conf= 72.90
==============&Margin&Shape&Density============
r10 (5->1)(4->2)(3->3)  =>(1->0)  sup= 89  conf= 71.62
```

To clarify, let us consider for example, *action rule 2* above. By *r2* = Margin(5->1) & Shape(4->2) => Class(1->0) sup= 93 conf= 74.35 we mean that: IF Margin is changed from value 5 (spiculated) to -> value 1 (circumscribed) AND Shape is changed from 4 (irregular) to -> 2 (oval) THEN class of tumor (severity) is changed from 1(malignant) to -> 0 (benign). The support of this *action rule* is = 93 instances in the dataset, and our confidence in this rule is = 74%.

Based on the rest of the *action rules* we discovered, the following are desirable influences $I_{i,j}$ we would like to have on objects in the system S:

I_1 : A change in the margin from spiculated to circumscribed
I_2 : A change in the margin from spiculated to circumscribed AND a change in shape from irregular to oval
I_3 : A change in the margin from spiculated to circumscribed AND a change in shape from irregular to round
I_4 : A change in the margin from ill-defined to microlobulated AND a change in shape from irregular to oval
I_5 : A change the shape from irregular to oval AND a change in the margin from ill-defined to circumscribed

The *actions* we are willing or able to undertake, in order to trigger these desired influences on the tumors (objects) are defined or specified by experts; assuming that we have control over changing the values of these lesion properties. For example, action A_1 may involve *administering certain treatment*; action A_2 may be to *take particular drug*.
These actions, along with the changes they trigger within the flexible (classification) attributes are included in an Ontology Layer placed on top of the DataSet, resulting in an intelligent Mammographic Mass Information System.

7 Conclusions

We have introduced an ontology based information system, which is a couple consisting of: the information system S, and the *ontology O*. The ontology contains the *actions*, and the influence $I_{i,j}$ they have on S. Actions ontology is used as a postprocessing tool in action rules discovery. The influence $I_{i,j}$ shows the correlations among classification attributes triggered off by *actions*. If the candidate action rules are not in agreement with the *actions*, then they are not classified as *action rules*. However, if the actions ontology does not show all the interactions between classification attributes, then still some of the resulting action rules may fail when tested on real data. We have applied the proposed system to a Mammographic Mass DataSet. We discoverd 64 action rules, and associated actions suggesting ways to re-classify tumors from class: malignant to class:benign. The proposed system can be applied with other medical datasets, such as: diabetes or heart disease; as well as financial, and industrial data.

8 References

[1] R. Agrawal, R. Srikant. "Fast algorithm for mining association rules", *Proceeding of the Twentieth International Conference on VLDB*, 487-499. 1994.

[2] A. Dardzi´nska, Z. Ras. "Extracting rules from incomplete decision systems", in *Foundations and Novel Approaches in Data Mining, Studies in Computational Intelligence*, Vol. 9, Springer, 143-154. 2006.

[3] R. Mizoguchi. "Tutorial on ontological engineering - Part 1: Introduction to Ontological Engineering", *New Generation Computing*, OhmSha&Springer, Vol.21, No.4, pp.365-384. 2003.

[4] S. Greco, B. Matarazzo, N. Pappalardo, R. Slowinski. "Measuring expected effects of interventions based on decision rules", *Journal of Experimental Theoretical Artificial Intelligence*, Vol. 17, No. 1-2, 103-118. 2005

[5] J. Grzymala-Busse. "A new version of the rule induction system LERS", *Fundamenta Informaticae Journal*, Vol. 31, No. 1, 27-39. 1997.

[6] Z. He, X. Xu, S. Deng, R. Ma. "Mining action rules from scratch", *Expert Systems with Applications*, Vol. 29, No. 3, 691-699. 2005.

[7] S. Im, Z.W. Ras. "Action rule extraction from a decision table: ARED", in Foundations of Intelligent Systems, *Proceedings of ISMIS'08, A. An et al. (Eds.)*, Toronto, Canada, LNAI, Vol. 4994, Springer, 160-168. 2008.

[8] Z. Pawlak. "Information systems - theoretical foundations", *Information Systems Journal*, Vol. 6, 205-218. 1981.

[9] Y. Qiao, K. Zhong, H.-A. Wang and X. Li. "Developing event-condition-action rules in real-time active database", Proceedings of the 2007 ACM symposium on Applied computing, ACM, New York, 511-516. 2007.

[10] Z.W. Ras, A. Dardzinska. "Action rules discovery, a new simplified strategy", *Foundations of Intelligent Systems*, LNAI, No. 4203, Springer, 445-453, 2006.

[11] Z.W. Ras, A. Dardzinska. "Action rules discovery without pre-existing classification rules", *Proceedings of the International Conference on Rough Sets and Current Trends in Computing (RSCTC 2008)*, LNAI 5306, Springer, 181-190. 2008.

[12] Z.W. Ras, A. Dardzinska, L.-S. Tsay, H. Wasyluk. "Association Action Rules", *IEEE/ICDM Workshop on Mining Complex Data (MCD 2008)*, in Pisa, Italy, Proceedings, IEEE Computer Society. 2008.

[13] Z.W. Ras, A. Wieczorkowska. "Action-Rules: How to increase profit of a company", in Principles of Data Mining and Knowledge Discovery, *Proceedings of PKDD 2000*, Lyon, France, LNAI, No. 1910, Springer, 587-592. 2000.

[14] Z.W. Ras, A. Tzacheva, L.-S. Tsay, O. Gurdal. "Mining for interesting action rules", *Proceedings of IEEE/WIC/ACM International Conference on Intelligent Agent Technology (IAT 2005)*, Compiegne University of Technology, France, 187-193. 2005.

[15] Z. Ras, E. Wyrzykowska, H. Wasyluk. "ARAS: Action rules discovery based on agglomerative strategy", in *Mining Complex Data, Post-Proceedings of 2007 ECML/PKDD Third International Workshop (MCD 2007)*, LNAI, Vol. 4944, Springer, 196-208. 2007.

[16] L.-S. Tsay, Z.W. Ras. "Action rules discovery system DEAR3", in *Foundations of Intelligent Systems, Proceedings of ISMIS 2006*, Bari, Italy, LNAI, No. 4203, Springer, 483-492. 2006.

[17] A. Tzacheva, Z.W. Ras. "Constraint based action rule discovery with single classification rules", in *Proceedings*

of the Joint Rough Sets Symposium (JRS07), Toronto, Canada, LNAI, Vol. 4482, Springer, 322-329. 2007.

[18] K. Wang, Y. Jiang, A. Tuzhilin. "Mining Actionable Patterns by Role Models", in *Proceedings of the 22nd International Conference on Data Engineering*, IEEE Computer Society, 16-2516-25. 2006.

[19] A. Frank, A. Asuncion. "UCI Machine Learning Repository" [*http://archive.ics.uci.edu/ml*]. Irvine, CA: University of California, School of Information and Computer Science. 2010.

GDP Forecasting through Data Mining of Seaport Export-Import Records

H Raymond Joseph†

***Abstract*—With the ever increasing ubiquitousness of globalization through international trade, principally on sea, there seems to be a direct correlation to a nation's Gross Domestic Product(GDP). Traditionally, in literature, structural models have predicted GDP correlation with the export-import tonnage on a cross-section of commodities. In this paper, machine learning and data mining techniques on publicly available, export and import tonnage of commodities at sea ports of the nation in question are analysed. Algorithms are then considered that output real GDP forecasts for the fiscal. The dataset for the exercise consists of daily export and import tonnage at a given port. Several ports in the country of interest are then considered. With data for several years and the accompanying GDP forecast on a daily basis, the question provides a challenging supervised learning problem to be analysed, with an appropriately sized data set, that is expected to generalize.**

***Index Terms*—GDP Forecasting, Seaport Data Analysis, Export-Import Analysis, Machine Learning and Macroeconomics.**

I. Introduction

For the purpose of definition, GDP is the total market value of all final goods and services produced in a country in a given year, equal to total consumption, investment and government spending, plus the value of exports, minus the value of imports.[1]

Correlations drawn between Export-Import volumes and real GDP have been widely researched in Economics and Econometrics literature. There also exist quantitative models that seek to model the correlational behavior between these two Macroeconomic variables. Meanwhile, the large data-set available on tonnage and volume of Exports and Imports at a nation's Seaports and the corresponding GDP forecasts make the problem appropriate to be considered within the purview of Machine Learning and Data Mining. For instance, Owokuse investigates "Causality Between Exports, Imports and Economic Growth".[2] Ben-David and Loewy[1998] argue that an increase in exports means:Increase in employment in export sector industries which, in turn, increase income and GDP, reallocating resources from less productive sectors to exports industry and enhancing capacity utilization exports growth promotes GDP growth.[3]

Traditionally, GDP forecasts have been produced and utilised by several agencies ranging from Investment Banking Corporations, Ratings Agencies and Governments.[4] Many such agencies make forecasts about the expected GDP and make appropriate changes pertaining to spending, capital utilisation and leverage. Spending on GDP analytics forms an important part of research spending in these organisations. Such forecasts have been made from time to time to reflect dynamic changes in the economy.

As mentioned, there is an observed correlation between GDP and Export-Import. The nature of this dependency is not very clear, and very few mathematical models exist, that explicitly relate these quantities. Hence, the problem is bought within the purview of Machine Learning and Data Mining.

II. Application Context for GDP Forecasting Using Machine Learning on Export and Import Data

A. Importance of GDP forecasting

- Economic forecasts of GDP are very important for determining monetary and fiscal policy.[5]
- If the GDP is really expected to increase, then inflation may pick up and the Banks may need to raise interest rates. If the GDP is likely to continue to shrink, the Banks may need to pursue further quantitative easing.
- Another issue for any national monetary authority is that interest rate changes can take up to 18 months to have an effect. Therefore when interest rates are changed, they are trying to set the optimal rates for the future economic situation.

B. Machine Learning on Export and Import Data

The machine learning algorithm employed is expected to give various factors weights. For instance the weights for categories in codes 39 – 40, Plastics and Rubbers, (see table) may be very different from those for categories 72−83, Metals. Hence the algorithm is expected to assign appropriate weights.

Another important aspect to be noted is that, for most countries, Exports and Imports in all the categories may not necessarily be non-zero. There may exist several goods and commodites that are not traded at all by the country. Our model is able to allow for this.

C. Correlation between Export-Import and GDP

Disagreements persist in the empirical literature regarding the causal direction of the effects of trade openness on economic growth and hence the GDP. Michaely (1977), Feder (1982), Marin (1992), Thornton (1996) found that countries exporting a large share of their output seem to grow faster than others.[6] The growth of exports has a stimulating influence across the economy as a whole in the form of technological spillovers and other externalities. Models by

†The Author wishes to thank the Shastri-Indo Canadian Institute and the DFAIT, Canada, for generous funding.

Grossman and Helpman (1991), Rivera-Batiz and Romer (1991), Romer (1990) posit that expanded international trade increases the number of specialized inputs, increasing growth rates as economies become open to international trade.[7] Buffie (1992) considers how export shocks can produce export-led growth.[8] Export growth is often considered to be a main determinant of the production and employment growth of an economy and its GDP. Similarly, Import growth is expected to have adverse effects on GDP. Export expansion and openness to foreign markets is viewed as a key determinant of economic GDP growth because of the positive externalities it provides. For example, firms in a thriving export sector can enjoy the following benefits: efficient resource allocation, greater capacity utilization, exploitation of economies of scale, and increased technological innovation stimulated by foreign market competition. [9]

III. The Problem Formulation - Learning Data and Prediction Output Structure

The problem data-set is an N dimensional data vector, where$N$ is the number of classes of commodities considered. Each dimension of the data vector class is a $2-$tuple numerical - volume exported and volume imported. Hence, we have several data vectors for several days under consideration. The problem data-set is expected to consider 25 or more years for the purpose of sampling. Therefore, the data-set is large enough for Machine Learning purposes (365×25 data vectors). The classification system for commodities is the widely used International Harmonic System. A brief table of the classification is outlined as shown below in Table 1.[10]

Table 1: International Harmonic System of Classification.[10]

Code	Commodity
01-05	Animal & Animal Products
06-15	Vegetable Products
16-24	Foodstuffs
25-27	Mineral Products
28-38	Chemicals & Allied Industries
39-40	Plastics / Rubbers
41-43	Raw Hides, Skins, Leather, & Furs
44-49	Wood & Wood Products
50-63	Textiles
64-67	Footwear / Headgear
68-71	Stone / Glass
72-83	Metals
84-85	Machinery / Electrical
86-89	Transportation
90-97	Miscellaneous
98-99	Service

The Table 1 is presented only for the purpose of completeness. Note that $N = 16$ for this case. For the purpose of GDP forcasting, the factors may need to be weighted, within a data vector. For example, commodities entailed within section 72-83 (Metals) may be given more weights, as assigned by the learning algorithm. Corresponding GDP forecasts made are available for use by the learning algorithm. Hence, the problem reduces to a supervised learning problem.

At this point it must be borne in mind that for predicting GDP on day $t+t'$the Export-Import trade has to be forecasted on day $t + t'$. This setback is underscored by the fact that International Export-Import trades are predictable - contract agreements are entered into well before the goods are actually delivered. However, this can also be viewed as a sub-problem of forecasting trade volumes at time $t+t'$, given trade volumes upto time t. This complication will not be considered since, by the earlier assumption, trade volumes of commodities are considered to be predictable. Also, the apparent diificulty in predicating Import-Export trades is underscored by a causality relationship between these factors.

The problem formulation in qualitative term, alongwith dependencies is represented below pictorially:

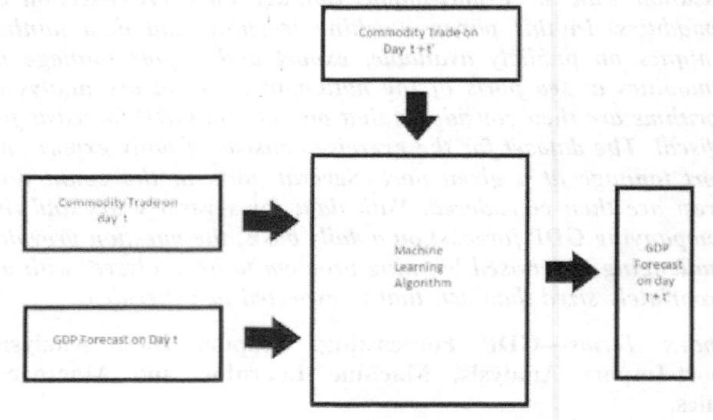

Figure 1: Pictorial Representation of the Problem Formulation.

IV. A Closer Look at The Data - Structure and Frequency

Presented in this section is a data-set example. The country considered is India. In particular, this is the data for the Chennai Port, on 16^{th}March, 2013.

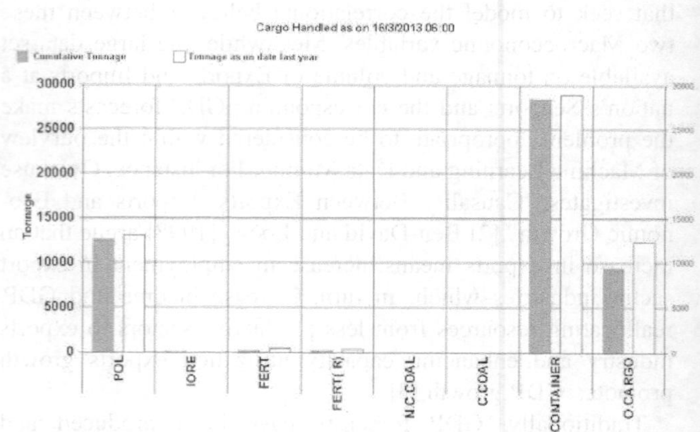

Figure 2: Data-Set Example.

V. Possible Algorithms and the Learning Process

Several algorithms can be considered for the purpose of this learning process. As such in this section their applicability is discussed.

A. Support Vector Machines - Multi-Class SVM approach

Support Vector Machine (SVM) ia very specific type of learning algorithms characterized by the capacity control of the decision function, the use of kernel functions and the sparsity of the solution. Established on the unique theory of the structural risk minimization principle to estimate a function by minimizing an upper bound of the generalization error, SVM is shown to be very resistant to problems of over-fitting thus, achieving an high generalization principle. Also, SVM is equivalent to solving a linearly constrained quadratic programming problem, so that the solution of SVM is always unique and globally optimal, unlike neural networks training which requires nonlinear optimization with the danger of bumping into a local minima.

A pictorial representation of the problem formulation for using an SVM approach is given in Figure 3.

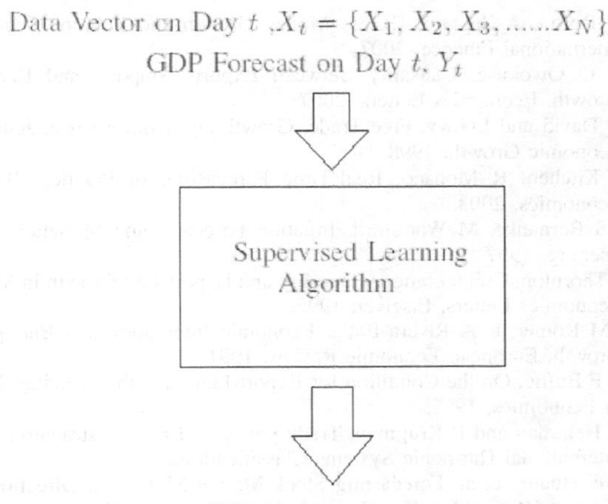

Figure 3: SVM Approach.

- The data vector is a vector of Nelements, where each element consists of Export and Import data on a given commodity.
- Hence, the problem becomes a N-dimensional supervised learning problem, with the supervising data aspect being the GDP on that day, corresponding to data within the data vector.
- The problem is reformulated as several binary classification problems.
- Each problem is such that it classifies all points over either a short-range of GDP or over the rest of the GDP range.
- The learning algorithm constructs a set of best-fit hyperplanes that separate these points.
- The GDP forecast varies over a short range, while the cargo tonnage has a larger variational range.
- This makes it simpler to have 'Pockets' wherein, Export-Import data vector falling within a certain accepted tolerance is mapped on to some GDP forecast.

Consider the problem of separating the set of training vector belonging with GDP forecasts,

$$G = \{(X_t; Y_t); t = 1, 2, ..., T\}$$

with the hyperplane

$$wF(X) + b = 0 \; ;$$

where, $X_t \in \mathbb{R}^{2N}$is the input vector on th t^{th}day, $y_i \in \{0, 8\}$is the known % GDP forecast.

Since the considered methodology is that of a Multi-Step SVM, notice that the classification SVM description is a binary classification problem. At the first classification, the classifier classifies the vectors of observed data into binary sets of (say) GDP growth forecast $>= 4\%$and GDP growth forecast $< 4\%$.

Then the classified data is once again input to the classifier but this time with constraints - $>= 2\%, <= 4\%$ and $< 2\%$ as one set and another set of $>= 4\%, <= 6\%$ and $>= 6\%, <= 8\%$ and so on. The classification continues until the forecast granularity reaches a desired stage such as 0.1%. [11]

B. Fuzzy Set Based Genetic Learning Algorithms

The genetic algorithms (GAs) are the procedure that searches the space of character strings of the specified length to find strings with relatively high fitness [12]. In preparing to apply the GAs to a particular problem, the first step involves determining the way to represent the problem in the chromosome-like language of GAs. An immediate question arises as to whether it is possible to represent many problems in a chromosome-like way. For this, we make use of fuzzy systems and the FAM matrix (Fuzzy Associative Memory).

Fuzzy systems are comprised of fuzzy sets, defined by their membership functions and fuzzy rules, which determine the action of the fuzzy system. The fuzzy rules can be concisely represented with one or more FAM matrices. The FAM matrix entries mainly depend on the subjective decision of an expert in each situation. GAs will then be used to adapt the FAM matrix entries so that the performance of a fuzzy system fits the desired behavior.

To apply genetic optimization to FAM matrix adaptation, we string the matrix entries together into a single long vector. The result is a very long binary vectors end to end. This is the chromosome upon which the GAs operate.

Here's a brief description of the algorithm:

- A single FAM matrix is used that deals with all the $16(N)$ classifications within the input data vector, as prescribed in the International Harmonic System.
- For the purpose of this method, each entry which comprised of Export and Import tonnage is made one entry which gives the signed difference between Import and Export.
- If we use r fuzzy sets for each input, i.e the possible GDP forecast interval $(0, 8)$ is divided into r partitions, then we will have r^{16}entries. Writing this as an appended vector from end to end, we will have $16 \times r^{16}$entries.
- The GA operates on the $16 \times r^{16}$entries.

From the preceding analysis, it is very clear that this number grows rapidly with r. However the analysis can be simplified by reducing N. The justification for reducing N lies in the arguments that:

- A certain country may not be either an Exporter or an Importer of all 16 categories of traded goods.

- Also, a number of commodities traded on the shores may be shown to economically have very little effect due to the volume in which it's traded in.

For the purpose of considering the workability, incorporating the above arguments, assume $N = 5$. Also, consider that$r = 10$. Then the number of entries for the GA to operate are, 5×10^5, which is still within reasonable limits for the Genetic algorithm to yield generalization. A pictorial representation of the Algorithm is as in Figure 4.

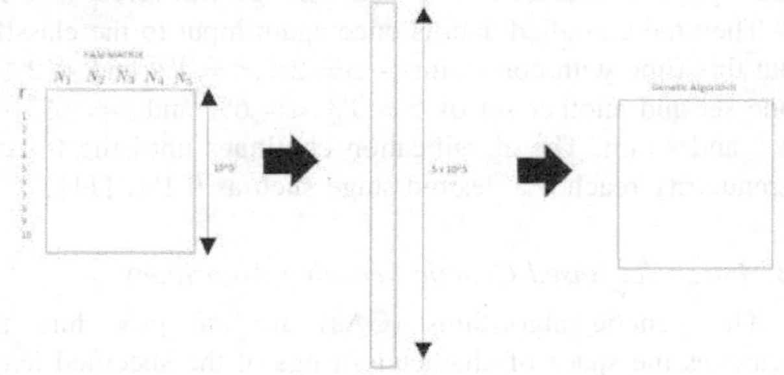

Figure 4: Using Genetic Algorithms.

C. Artificial Neural Networks

In recent times, much research has been carried out on the application of artificial intelligence techniques to the load forecasting problem.However, the models that have received the largest share of attention are undoubtedly the artificial neural networks (ANNs). The first reports on their application to the load forecasting problem were published in the late 1980's and early 1990's [13]. However, the models that have received the largest share of attention are undoubtedly the artificial neural networks (ANNs).

Artificial neural networks are mathematical tools originally inspired by the way the human brain processes information. Their basic unit is the artificial neuron. The neuron receives (numerical) information through a number of input nodes (four, in this example), processes it internally, and puts out a response. The processing is usually done in two stages: first, the input values are linearly combined, then the result is used as the argument of a nonlinear activation function. The combination uses the weights w_i attributed to each connection, and a constant bias term θ, with a fixed input equal to 1. The activation function must be a nondecreasing and differentiable function; the most common choices are either the identity function , or bounded sigmoid (s-shaped) functions, as the logistic one $y = \frac{1}{(1+e^{-x})}$. [14] Figure 5, shows the application of this learning model to the problem in hand.

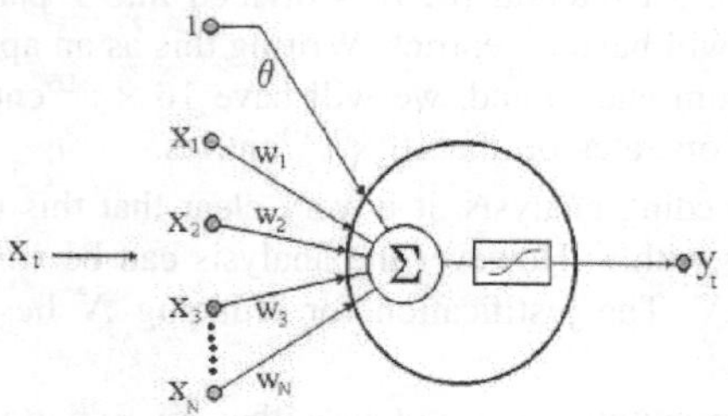

Figure 5: Artificial Neural Networks Approach.

VI. Conclusion

In this paper the problem of GDP forecasting was analysed with Seaport Export-Import data records as the learning resource. The usability of Learning Algorithms and problem formulation for these methods have also been discussed. The importance of GDP forecasting has been rightly emphasized in this paper, and hence it's utility. This paper can also be viewed as a quantitative indicator of the effect of Export-Import tonnage injected, on the economy of a nation.

The learning algorithms discussed are the Support Vector Machines, Fuzzy Set Based Genetic Learning Algorithms and also the Artificial Neural Network methods. Future research being carried out could focus on hybrid of these algorithms to yield more accurate forecasting.

References

[1] B Roffia, A Zaghini, Excess Money Growth and Inflation Dynamics, International Finance, 2007.

[2] T O Owokuse, Causality Between Exports, Imports and Economic Growth, Economics Letters, 2007.

[3] B David and Loewy, Free Trade, Growth and Convergence, Journal of Economic Growth, 1998.

[4] J Kitchen, R Monaco, Real-Time Forecasting in Practice, Business Economics, 2003.

[5] BS Bernanke, M Woodford, Inflation Forecasts and Monetary Policy, nber.org, 1997.

[6] J Thornton, Cointegration, Causality and Export-Led Growth in Mexico, Economics Letters, Elseiver, 1996.

[7] PM Romer, L A Rivera-Batiz, Economic Integration and Endogenous Growth, European Economic Review, 1991.

[8] E F Buffie, On the Condition for Export-Led Growth, Canadian Journal of Economics, 1992.

[9] E Helpman and P Krugman, Trade policy and market structure, 1985.

[10] International Harmonic Systems Classification.

[11] Wei Huang, et al, Forecasting Stock Market Movement Direction with Support Vector Machine, Computers and Operations Research, 2005.

[12] . Goldberg, D. E., Genetic Algorithm in Search, Optimization, and Machine Learning, Addison-Wesley, 1989.

[13] T. Czernichow, A. Piras, K. Imhof, P. Caire, Y. Jaccard, B. Dorizzi, and A. Germond, Short Term Electrical Load Forecasting with Artificial Neural Networks, Engineering Intelligent Syst., vol. 2, pp. 85–99, 1996.

[14] Henrique Steinherz Hippert, Carlos Eduardo Pedreira, and Reinaldo Castro Souza, Neural Networks for Short-Term Load Forecasting: A Review and Evaluation, IEEE Transactions on Power Systems, Vol. 16, February 2001.

Association Rule Mining for finding correlations among people

V.B. Nikam[1], Nimai Buch[2], and Yash Botadra[2] B.B. Meshram[3]
[1,2,3]Department of Computer Engineering and Information Technology
Veermata Jijabai Technological Institute
Mumbai, Maharashtra, India

Abstract – *Data mining is the process of extracting interesting, non-trivial, implicit, previously, unknown and potentially useful information or patterns from large information repositories. This paper focuses on Association Rule Mining on large image datasets. ARM is largely applied on datasets containing text, but we shall exploit its capabilities to mine images to get interesting and useful correlations and determine the degree of togetherness among faces in the video. Video processing generates a very large dataset which makes it difficult to analyze it manually. Our research model presented in this paper combines two of the most actively researched areas of computer science: Computer Vision and Data Mining.*

Keywords: Data mining, Association Rule Mining, Computer Vision, Face detection, Face recognition

1 Introduction

Data mining is known as one of the core processes of Knowledge Discovery in Database (KDD) as shown in Fig 1.

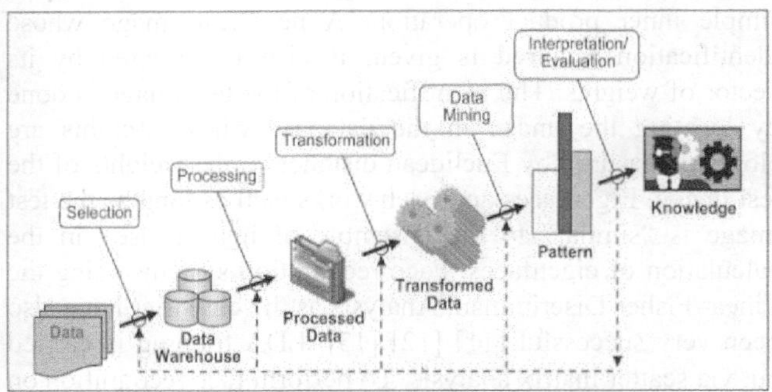

Figure 1 : Knowledge Discovery in Databases

A wide range of industries including retail, finance, health care, manufacturing, transportation and aerospace etc are already using data mining tools and techniques to take advantage of historical data for analysis and predictions for betterment of decision processes. Data mining helps analysts to recognize significant facts, relationships, trends, patterns, exceptions and anomalies that might otherwise go unnoticed. Association rule mining is one of the most important and well researched techniques of data mining to extract interesting correlations, frequent patterns, associations or casual structures among the sets of items in the transaction databases or other data repositories.

Association rule mining concludes to generate association rules from those large itemsets with the predefined confidence "ρ", say, large itemset $L_k = \{I_1, I_2, \ldots, I_k\}$, where $I_1, I_2, \ldots I_n \in I$, the rule can be $\{I_1, I_2, \ldots, I_{k-1}\} \rightarrow \{I_k\}$. Applying confidence, this rule can be determined as interesting or not, and so on. This can be iterated until all the frequent itemsets are over. Though association rules mining is well researched on structured datasets, certainly it can be extended on multimedia datasets also, as there are video and image based applications [2][3] which are in huge demand. In this paper, we have proposed a model for finding togetherness among people in videos using data mining methodologies. In this model we have focused on three major tasks as listed below: 1) Face Detection 2) Face Recognition and Tagging 3) Association Rule Mining on Tagged frames & face. Our model takes a video input since it is a multimedia data type, usually composed of images and audio. As we are processing only on the image portion, we have completely ignored the audio component. We apply association rule mining on the detected faces from the video to find correlations between people in the video.

2 Motivation

Association rule mining has been proved effective for structured datasets. However data mining on the unstructured data sets, especial face image is a hot research area these days. Boosting algorithms reduce the number of computations needed to mine face/non face drastically. The algorithms perform very well even on CPU platform. However, higher resolution images may create a bottleneck for the performance. Some research work optimized the well known computer vision library OpenCV to run not only on Intel platforms, but also on the Cell BE processor. For face detection using Haar-like features and AdaBoost algorithm, their implementation speeds-up computation up to 11x times for 640x480 video resolutions. Ghorayeb et al. proposed a hybrid implementation of AdaBoost for face detection, has not used Haar-like features [4]. Along with the obvious applications in the fields of biometrics, video surveillance, human computer interaction and image database management, the proposed technology has a wider scope for more interesting applications too. In the current scenario where crimes are increasing and so are the number of criminals, technologies like these can prove to be valuable in finding and recognizing accomplices of criminals. This may also find great relevance in social media and networking, where, on analyzing images, the closeness among friends can be determined. Using this information, appropriate suggestions can be made to users and people. The current technology and the plethora of applications of facial detection, recognition and analysis has been a motivator to perform further research in this speedily growing area of computer science.

3 Literature Review

3.1 Data Mining

Data Mining is the process of discovering interesting knowledge from large amounts of data using various algorithms [5].

Association Rules: An association rule is an implication of the form $X \rightarrow Y$, where $X, Y \in T$, and $X \cap Y = \Phi$. T is the set of objects, also referred to as items. X is called the antecedent and Y is called the consequent of the rule. In general, a set of items, such as the antecedent or the consequent of a rule, is called an itemset.

Support: Each itemset has an associated measure of statistical significance called support. For an itemset $X \in T$, Support(X)=S, if the fraction of records in the database containing X equals S.

Confidence: A rule has a measure of its strength called confidence, defined as the ratio,

$$\frac{support(X \cup Y)}{support(X)} \tag{1}$$

In association rule mining all the generated rules qualify support and confidence greater than minimum support threshold "σ" and minimum confidence thresholds "ρ" respectively. The algorithm mainly has two components,

a. All itemsets that have support above "σ", are called the frequent itemsets. All others are said to be non-frequent or small.

b. For each frequent itemset, all the rules that have minimum confidence, support are generated as,

$$\frac{support(X)}{support(X-Y)} \geq \rho \tag{2}$$

Then the rule, $(X\text{-}Y) \rightarrow Y$ is a valid rule for large itemset X and any $Y \in X$.

Algorithms such as: Apriori, AprioriTid, AIS [1] were proposed for mining all association rules. SETM was proposed to mine association rules using relational operations. These algorithms achieved significant improvements over the previous algorithms. Efficient algorithms like Eclat[6], FP-Growth[7], COFI[8], etc [9] for mining association rules are fundamentally different from Apriori algorithm. These algorithms not only reduce the I/O overhead significantly but also have lower CPU overhead for most of the cases.

3.2 Face Detection and Recognition

Face Detection and Recognition from images and videos is emerging as an active research area. Paul Viola and Michael Jones presented a framework for face detection that is capable of processing with high efficiency and accuracy [10]. There are three key contributions, 1. The introduction of a new image representation called the "Integral Image", which allows the features used by the detector to be computed very quickly. 2. A simple and an efficient classifier which is built using the AdaBoost Learning algorithm. 3. A method for combining classifiers in a "cascade" which allows more computation on promising face-like regions rather than background regions.

Definition: Integral Image: The integral image at location (x,y) is the sum of the pixel values above and to the left of (x,y) inclusive.

Eigen pictures (eigenfaces) are used for face recognition. Given the eigenfaces, every face in the database can be represented as a vector of weights. The weights are obtained by projecting the image into eigenface components by a simple inner product operation. A new test image whose identification required is given, is also represented by its vector of weights. The identification of the test image is done by locating the image in the database whose weights are closest, measured by Euclidean distance to the weights of the test image. Eigenfaces approach works well as long as the test image is "similar" to the ensemble of images used in the calculation of eigenfaces. Face recognition systems using the Linear/Fisher Discriminant Analysis as the classifier have also been very successful [11] [12] [13]. LDA training is carried out via scatter matrix analysis. To perform face recognition on a large face dataset but with very few training face images available per class, a holistic face recognition method based on subspace LDA is proposed.

4 Proposed methodology

Our work aims at finding relationship strength between people seen together in a video. This is done by detecting faces present in video frames, recognizing them if seen in earlier part of video, and finally using association rule mining algorithms to find the association rules for finding togetherness among the people in the video. We perform the image processing tasks using OpenCV, the open source Computer Vision library. The Viola Jones method for facial detection makes use of a cascade of Haar classifiers. These detected faces are then tagged and recognized using Principal Component Analysis (PCA) method, which makes use of eigenfaces and eigenvectors. The recognized faces are a data set of faces in each frame. We finally mine the data set using Association Rule Mining model. The block diagram shown in Fig 2 is a representation of a step-wise execution of our model, taking a raw video as input and generating the correlated group of people using association rules mining as the final output.

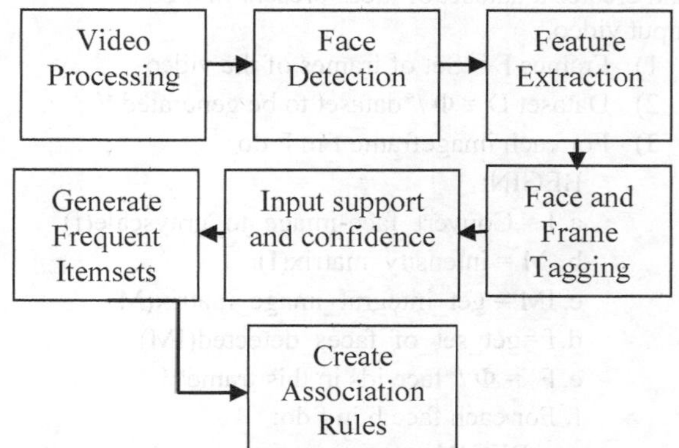

Figure 2: Block diagram of the model

The modules shown in the block diagram are as follows:

4.1 Video processing

The model takes a video as input, on which the face detection and recognition algorithm works. During this step, the video is split into a number of frames on which the Viola Jones algorithm work. The number of frames per second(fps) depends on the quality of the video and the video format (.avi, .wmv, .mp4 etc).

4.2 Face detection

For our model, we make use of the Haar-like cascade of classifiers to detect a face in an image. The cascade of binary classifiers as shown in Fig 3 is applied to check if the portion of the image in the rectangular window qualifies as a face or non face.

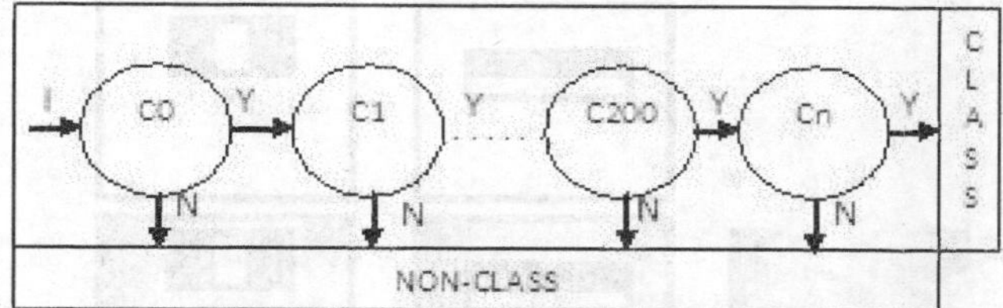

Figure 3: Cascade of binary classifiers

In this image, C_0, C_1, C_2, ..., C_n, is a cascade of "n" classifiers applied over the 24x24 pixel window. Even if the rectangular window does not conform to one of the classifier's requirements, it is not checked any further and is qualified as a non-face.

The basic, weak classifier is based on a very simple visual feature (often referred to as "Haar-like features"). There are four basic Haar features as shown in Fig4.

Haar-like features consist of a class of local features that are calculated by subtracting the sum of a sub-region of the feature from the sum of the remaining region of the feature.

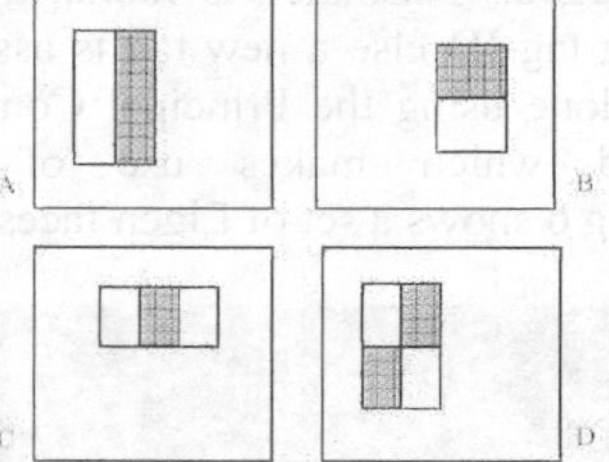

Figure 4 :Basic Haar features

$$f(x, a) = \sum_{i=0}^{n} pb_i \tag{3}$$

If the subtraction of these two regions exceeds the specified threshold value, then the image successfully passes that classifier and a new classifier is applied over it. The process continues for all "n" classifiers and if the image passes successfully through each, it is classified as a face.

4.3 Feature extraction

Feature extraction is the process of applying the Haar feature sub-window of a base size of 24x24 over the image as show in Fig 5. Each of the four feature types are scaled and shifted across all possible combinations.

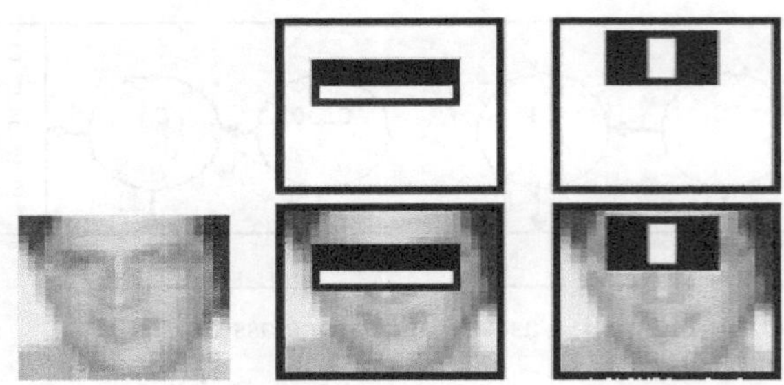

Figure 5 :Applying Haar features over an image

In a 24x24 pixels sub window, there are ~160,000 possible features to be calculated. These possibilities are reduced to an achievable level using Adaboost techniques [6]. Once the features such as nose, eyes etc are extracted, it becomes relatively easy to detect a face from an image.

4.4 Frame and face tagging

This is the face recognition step, where the detected faces in each frame are compared with a database of faces already detected and tagged. If a match is found, the face is tagged with an existing tag ID else a new tag is assigned to it. Face recognition is done using the Principal Component Analysis (PCA) method which makes use of eigenface and eigenvectors. Fig 6 shows a set of Eigen faces.

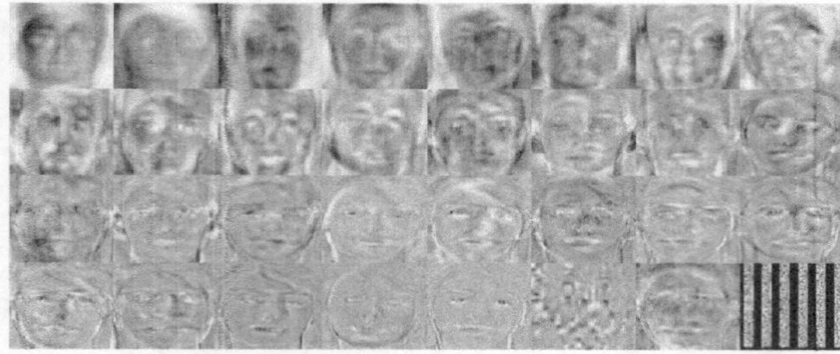

Figure 6: Set of Eigen faces

4.5 Support and confidence

The dataset containing faces and the respective frames of the faces is given as input to the association rule mining algorithm. The first step here is to input the Support(s) and Confidence(c) values required to find frequent itemset, and later rule generation for finding co-relations among the faces in the video. Intuitively, a set of faces that appears together in "many" frames is said to be frequent. To define the term "many" we use support "σ" threshold.

4.6 Generate frequent itemsets

The frequent photos are often presented as a collection of if–then rules, called association rules. The form of an association rule is I→j, where I is a set of items and j is an item. The implication of this association rule is that if all of the items in I appear in some basket, then j is "likely" to appear in that basket as well. We formalize the notion of "likely" by defining the confidence of the rule I→j to be the ratio of the support for "I U {j}" to the support for "I". That is, the confidence of the rule is the fraction of the baskets with all of "I" that also contain "j". Using these rules, we can determine the closeness among the people in the video.

Pseudo codes

Detect_And_Recognize_Faces(Video V)

```
Input: Video
Output: Dataset of Faces in the Video
// This procedure performs operations on videos
// and creates a dataset of faces present in the
// input video.
  1) Frames F = Set of frames of the video
  2) Dataset D = Φ /*dataset to be generated*/
  3) For each imageframe f in F do
       BEGIN:
       a. I = Convert_face-image_to_grayscale(f)
       b. M = intensity_matrix(I)
       c. IM = get_integral_image_matrix(M)
       d. f =get_set_of_faces_detected(IM)
       e. F' = Φ /*face ids in this frame*/
       f. For each face þ in f do:
          BEGIN
            a)fid=Recognize_from_Database(þ)
            b)If þ is not recognized, fid=assign new id to
              þ
            c)F' =F' U fid
          END
       g. D=D U F'
       END
  4) Return D
```

Generate_Association_Rule(Dataset D, Support S, Confidence C)

```
Input : Dataset D of Faces, Support S, Confidence C
Output: Togetherness among people
// This procedure performs association rules mining
// operations on distinct tagged faces of each frame of
// video, and finds the co-relations among people in the
// video.
  1) FIS = Association_Rule_Mining_Algorithm(D,S)
  2) R=Φ /*Set of Rules*/
  3) For each frequent item set fis' in FIS do
       BEGIN
       a. For each non empty c in fis' do
          BEGIN
          a)If support(fis')/support(c) ≥ C
                Then R= R U {c → (fis'- c)}
          END
       END
  4) Return R
```

The above pseudo-code describes the general outline of the proposed model, which can be further extended and refined while implementing the same.

5 Conclusion and Future Scope

The KDD process concludes with some knowledge generated from the source data. When finding correlations among the people in a video becomes manually infeasible, association rule mining on video datasets provide results faster. Video processing involves feature extraction and then processing the features for mining. This generates a very huge data set which is practically impossible to process without parallel processing, especially if the video is long and the time required to get output is expected to be very less. However, the same can be achieved with a GPU or cloud like scalable and massively parallel [3][14] processing environments. Our model processes videos to extract correlations among the people in the video. We tag the frames and faces, before we process for co-relation determination. The image indexing can also be extended as a future research direction, which may speed-up the performance of overall processing. The percentage accuracy of the face matching is the further challenge which can be separately addressed in future scope.

6 References

[1]. R. Agrawal, T. Imielinski and A. Swami. "Mining association rules between sets of items in large databases", *International Conference on Management of Data*, Proceedings of ACM SIGMOD, pages 207–216, Washington, DC, May 26-28 1993.

[2]. V.B. Nikam, B.B. Meshram, V.J. Kadam, Image Compression Using Partitioning Around Medoids Clustering Algorithm, InternationalJournal of Computer Science Issues,Vol.8, Issue6, Nov2011, ISSN (Online): 1694-0814.

[3]. V.B. Nikam, Kiran Joshi, B.B. Meshram, "An Approach For System Scalability for Video on Demand", Interface,2011

[4]. Ghorayeb, H., Steux, B., Laurgeau, C., "Boosted algorithms for visual object detection on Graphics Processing Units", Proceedings of the 7th Asian conference on Computer Vision, ACCV'06, Volume Part II, Pages 254-263

[5]. V. B. Nikam, B. B. Meshram, "Scalability Model for Data Mining", ICIMT2010, Dec 28-30, 2010, 978-14244-8882-7/2010, IEEE

[6]. Christian Borgelt, "Efficient Implementations of Apriori and Eclat", Proceedings of the IEEE ICDM Workshop on Frequent Itemset Mining Implementations (FIMI), Melbourne, Florida, 2003/11/19

[7]. Christian Borgelt, "An Implementation of the FPgrowth Algorithm", Proceedings of the 1st international workshop on open source data mining: frequent pattern mining implementations, ACM 2005/8/21

[8]. Mohammad El-hajj , Osmar R. Zaïane , "COFI Approach for Mining Frequent Itemsets Revisited",DMKD '04 Published in roceedings of the 9th ACM SIGMOD workshop on Research issues in data mining and knowledge discovery, Pages 70–75, ISBN:1-58113-908, ACM

[9]. A. Savasere, E. Omiecinski, and S. Navathe, "An efficient algorithm for mining association rules", Proceedings of the VLDB Conference, pages 432– 444, Zurich, Switzerland, September 1995.

[10]. Paula Viola and Michael Jones, "Robust Real Time Face Detection", International Journal of Computer Vision, 57(2),137–154, 2004.

[11]. D. L. Swets, J. Weng, "Discriminant Analysis and Eigenspace Partition Tree for Face and Object Recognition from Views", Proceedings of International Conference on Automatic Face and Gesture Recognition, 1996 pp. 192-197.

[12]. W. Zhao, R. Chellappa, A. Krishnaswamy, "Discriminant Analysis of Principal Components for Face Recognition", Proceeedings of International Conference on Automatic Face and Gesture Recognition, 1998 pp. 336-341.

[13]. W. Zhao,R. Chellappa, N. Nandhakumar, "Empirical Performance Analysis of Linear Discriminant Classifiers", Proceedings of IEEE Conference on Computer Vision and Pattern Recognition, 1998 pp. 164-169

[14]. V.B. Nikam, B.B. Meshram, "Scalable Frequent Itemset Mining using Heterogeneous Computing: ParApriori Algorithm", Submitted for Publication

Toward Sustainable High-Yield Agriculture via Intelligent Control Systems

Brian McLaughlan and James Brandli
Brian.mclaughlan@uafs.edu, jbrand01@uafortsmith.edu
University of Arkansas – Fort Smith
5210 Grand Ave
Fort Smith, AR 72904
(479) 788-7824

***Abstract* -- Hunger ranks as the number one health risk facing the world today, with scarcity of natural resources playing a key part in the problem. Aquaponics has the potential for high-yield plant and animal production but has parameters that are substantially more difficult to maintain. To prevent failure and ensure maximum yields for minimal outside input, this paper proposes AI-based data mining to learn and maintain proper environmental conditions. Experiments are conducted that determine the appropriateness of various AI techniques for this project. These AI techniques are being applied in a real-world aquaponics farm.**

Keywords: artificial intelligence, agriculture, aquaponics

I. Introduction

With approximately 870 million malnourished people in the world today, hunger tops the list of the worst health risks facing mankind (FAO, 2011). This problem is being addressed from multiple directions, including technological developments, policy implementation, education improvements, and financial assistance (Sanchez, 2009; Bratspies, 2012).

One cause of hunger is scarcity of natural resources, particularly water and fertile ground. Aquaponics has shown potential as a method of overcoming this problem by completely eschewing the use of soil and needing only 2 to 10% of the water required by traditional farming methods.

The term *aquaponics* is a portmanteau of the terms *aquaculture* (raising aquatic animals such as fish) and *hydroponics* (cultivating plants in water). In such a system, plants and animals exist in a symbiotic relationship, nourishing each other and removing toxins harmful to the other. In its most basic form shown in Figure 1, bacteria break down the toxins created by fish and provide nourishment to the plants in the form of nitrogen compounds. The plants then filter out the nitrogen and provide a beneficial habitat for the fish.

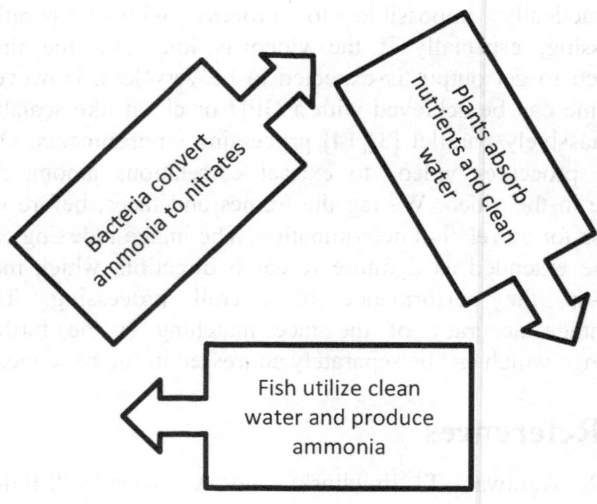

Figure 1: Aquaculture Cycle

One complication with the use of aquaponics is the margin of error restrictions when compared to traditional farming techniques. While traditional farming can be successful under a variety of conditions, aquaponics is far less forgiving. If the margin of error in traditional farming could be compared to the width of a two-lane highway, the margin of error in hydroponics is a six-foot sidewalk, and aquaponics' is a narrow footpath. Thus, constant monitoring must be provided to maintain ideal conditions lest the system break down with disastrous results.

In its most basic form, this monitoring could be performed manually by humans. However, as the size and complexity of the aquaculture system increases, the chance of human error increases. In fact, the complexity of the system could prevent humans from even noticing correlations between events occurring in seemingly unrelated portions of the structure. This problem increases as modern sensor technology is added; although sensors provide round-the-clock monitoring, the significance of particular details in massive amounts of data can easily be obscured.

This paper proposes the use of artificial intelligence to provide data mining of relevant sensor data in an aquaponics system. The AI could discover growing parameters that are most successful in the farm's particular climate and maintain those parameters once reached. The experiments in this paper aim to isolate AI techniques that pertain to this goal.

The remaining portions of this paper are as follows. Section 2 explores the history of aquaponics and current research on the topic. Section 3 examines potential methods for modeling the farm and AI. Section 4 details our experimentation and results. Section 5 describes our on-going real-world work on this topic.

II. Aquaponics Background

Aquaponics has been in use for many centuries, notably in ancient Central American and Southeast Asian cultures. However, recent developments in large-scale deployment have been pioneered by researchers at the University of the Virgin Islands (Rakocy, 2013). Many other tropical countries and islands have followed suit, attracted to the prospect of food production in resource-poor regions. Unfortunately, these efforts have focused on tropical climates where plant growth is at its most ideal.

Modern aquaponics consists of two separate components, one for fish and one for plants. The separation prevents the fish from eating plants destined for human consumption. Fish are further separated between young fish fry and older fish that may eat the fry.

The system in which the plants and fish are raised is a closed loop. This would generally limit the inclusion of no more than a few plants or fish before the system became toxic. However, the synergistic properties of plants and fish, combined with aggressive oxygen dissolution, allow a much higher concentration of agriculture yield than would normally be found in nature.

While many different species of plants and fish are possible, certain types are more commonly used. Tilapia are commonly grown fish, while leafy vegetables such as lettuce appear to perform well in an aquaponics system (Pantanella, et al, 2010).

There are several high-tech hobbyists who have begun to integrate sensors into aquaponics (ManyLabs, 2013; Robb, 2012). However, these systems are exclusively for monitoring conditions and alerting the operator to out-of-bounds conditions. They provide no control systems, nor do they quantify the effect of their sensors on the food yield (e.g., fewer dead fish leading to increased number that reach maturity).

Variations on the system are possible. Some could include additional small animals such as rabbits and chickens. The waste products of these animals can be used for fertilizer while the unused portions of their carcasses can be ground into meal for cross-feeding to the other species of animals in the system. In nutrient-poor conditions, additional fertilizer could be safely composted from many different types of waste materials, including sewage if necessary.

III. Methodology

Our real-world aquaculture farm utilizes many measurements taken from a number of locations. However, our data gathering experiments only those measurements that are provided by automated sensors. These sensors include sensors in both water and air. Air sensors are limited to brightness and temperature. Water sensors include clarity (brightness), temperature, dissolved oxygen, pH, nitrogen, and water current. These sensors are located at the entrance and exit of each tank in the aquaponics system.

Additional inputs come from human operators that designate when certain maintenance functions are performed. These include adding new fish, extracting healthy fish for food production, presence of dead or sick fish, addition of fish food, addition of water, addition of nutrients, and addition or removal of plant material. The location of each of these events is also recorded. Finally, the user records a range of times and dates where the system appears to be working well or poorly and assigns a confidence in the score.

We examined several potential methods for extracting relevant information from the data. Of particular interest for this paper were two AI techniques: artificial neural networks and nearest neighbor models. Each of these techniques should be able to utilize the user's assessments of times and dates as training data for future decisions.

IV. Experimentation and Results

Utilizing simulation recommendations from other researchers in environmental information systems (Boote, et al, 2010) and data generated from existing sensors, we built a simple agriculture simulator to determine which, if either, of our methodologies would show potential capability for predicting events and determining appropriate behaviors in our aquaponics system.

We implemented the nearest neighbor model (Stanfill and Waltz, 1986) using a k-d tree, allowing it to search in $O(\log N)$ time and allowing real-world data to logged and used as training data at the same time. Accuracy was boosted by utilizing a support vector machine (Boser, et al, 1992) to kernalize the algorithm. This model did a good job of recognizing situations that were similar to known events, labeling them properly, and determining appropriate actions. However, solution time was over 100 times slower than a simulated neural network as shown in Figure 2. A neural network implemented in hardware would show significant improvements.

The neural network was implemented as a basic multilayer feed-forward network utilizing back-propagation for inputting the training set. This method had success rates lower than the nearest neighbor model, but the results were returned significantly faster.

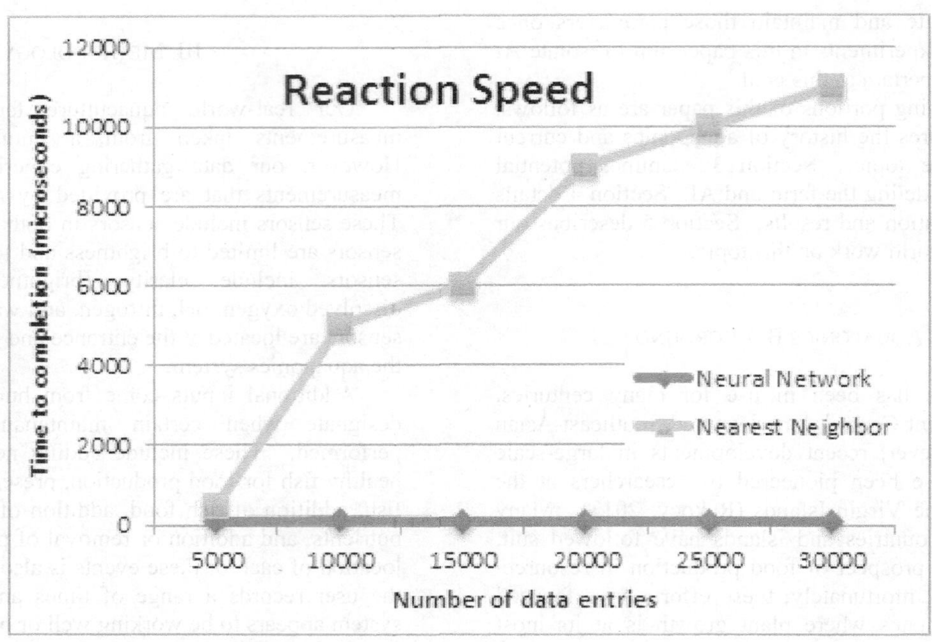

Figure 2: Reaction speed of Algorithms

Errors in the returned data were most likely caused by errors in the recorded times for events. If operators over- or under-estimate the time in which an event occurred (such as dying fish), unrelated data would be erroneously accused of being involved in the event.

Examination via qualitative analysis of these two algorithms provides similarly murky conclusions.

The slower speed of nearest neighbor doesn't appear to be a significant problem in an aquaponics system. While poor conditions can quickly kill fish stock, these times are measured in hours, not minutes or seconds. Thus, the slower speed should not impact our decision.

The nearest neighbor algorithm is also able to continuously learn from new data. This allows it to incorporate unforeseen events into its knowledge base. The neural network would require its operator to manually feed the new event data back into the AI as additional training information. On the other hand, the neural network's lack of a growing database allows for much cheaper memory requirements.

Additionally, the neural network can be implemented in much simpler hardware than the nearest neighbor algorithm. While the nearest neighbor algorithm may seem to be the clear winner, the reality is that the aquaponics system will likely be deployed in "rugged" conditions where maintenance of a complex computer system is not feasible. The neural network would be implemented as a simple "black box" control circuit.

It appears the best solution would be a neural network with a limited data memory. If a new training case was encountered, the data memory would allow the information to be fed back into the network for additional training. This capability should be provided in a very simple user interface, ideally with two dials to set the time range to include and a button to execute the retraining. Thus, the basic neural network could be trained for a general climate, with future modifications adjusting it to the local microclimate.

V. On-going and Future Work

This sensor network is currently being implemented on a farm in western Arkansas. One initial goal is to determine if such a system can boost the yield of an actual aquaculture system in a temperate zone. The farm has been in place for a year and has produced an average of over 3.5 pounds of food per square foot, a significant improvement over traditional farming at almost 0.25 pounds per square foot. Experiments will show if the AI can actually improve those numbers further. Experiments are currently being performed on tilapia and lettuce, but future trials will be performed on beans and roses.

Future experimentation will focus on association rule learning to allow an AI to determine appropriate actions for complex systems without requiring human input. For example, feeding fish may trigger a chain reaction that alters the pH of the hydroponic plant tanks. If the relationship is discovered, the AI could take pre-emptive measures to level the pH and prevent a spike whenever the fish are fed.

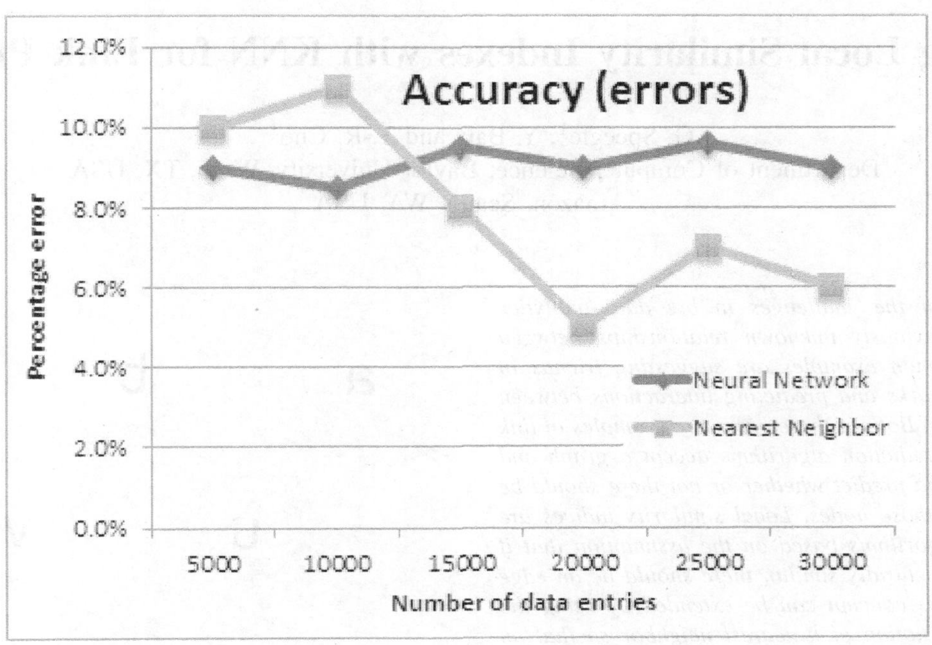

Figure 3: Error rate of algorithms

On the engineering side, steps will be taken to ruggedize the components for use by non-technical personnel.

Regarding quality assurance, steps can be taken to allow this system to degrade gracefully. Experiments will be run which will intentionally limit the capabilities of components to see if the system can be made to successfully adapt.

VI. References

Boote, K.J., Jones, J.W., Hoogenboom, G., White, J.W. (2010). "The Role of Crop Systems Simulation in Agriculture and Environment" International Journal of Agricultural and Environmental Information Systems. 1(1): 41-54.

Boser, B., Guyon, Il, and Vapnik, V.N. (1992). "A training algorithm for optimal margin classifiers." In *COLT*-92.

Bratspies, R.M., "Food, Hunger, and Technology" (2012). City University of New York – School of Law report.

Food and Agriculture Organization. (2011). "The State of Food Insecurity in the World 2011". Yearly report.

ManyLabs (2013) "Aquaponics project documentation" www.manylabs.org/docs/project/aquaponics/, accessed April 1, 2013.

Pantanella, E., Cardarelli, M., Colla, G., Rea, E., Marcucci, A. (2010). "Aquaponics vs. Hydroponics: Production and Quality of Lettuce Crop" In proceedings of *XXVIII International Horticultural Congress on Science and Horticulture for People: International Symposium on Greenhouse 2010 and Soilless Cultivation.*

Rakocy, J.E.; Shultsz, R.C., Thoman, E.S. (2013). "Update on Tilapia and Vegetable Production in the UVI Aquaponic System" University of the Virgin Islands Agricultural Experiment Station.

Robb, J. (2012) "One way to make aquaponics easier." http://www.resilientcommunities.com/one-way-to-make-aquaponics-easier/ , accessed April 1, 2013.

Sanchez, P.A. (2009). "A Smarter Way to Combat hunger" Nature Weekly International Journal of Science, March 11, 2009.

Stanfill, C. and Waltz, D. (1986) "Toward memory-based reasoning" *CACM*, 29(12), 1213-1228.

Extending Local Similarity Indexes with KNN for Link Prediction

G. Speegle[1], Y. Bai[2] and Y.-R. Cho[1]
[1]Department of Computer Science, Baylor University, Waco, TX, USA
[2]Amazon, Seattle WA, USA

Abstract— *One of the challenges in big data analytics is discovering previously unknown relationships between objects. Two common examples are suggesting friends in social media networks and predicting interactions between biological proteins. Both of these cases are examples of link prediction. Link prediction algorithms accept a graph and a pair of nodes and predict whether or not there should be an edge between those nodes. Local similarity indices are link prediction algorithms based on the assumption that if two nodes are structurally similar, there should be an edge between them. This concept can be extended by using the machine learning notion of k-nearest neighbor so that an edge from u to v is predicted if nodes similar to u have an edge to v, or nodes similar to v have an edge to u. It is straightforward to extend local similarity indices to k-nn versions of the algorithms, and with suitable selection of k accuracy is improved. Although there is additional computational cost, it can be amortized such that operations such as finding all predictions have similar computation time.*

Keywords: Link Prediction, k-nearest neighbor, Graphs

1. Introduction

Graphs are used to represent relationships between real world objects. For example, graphs can represent the distance between two cities, whether or not two people are friends in a social media network, or the interaction between two proteins. However, graphs do not always contain all the information from the real world. If two people are not friends on Facebook, it does not mean they are not friends in real life. Two proteins may interact in a way that has not yet been discovered. Thus, certain edges are "missing" in the graph. Suggesting missing edges is called *link prediction*.

The literature contains many link prediction algorithms. In [9], the algorithms are called indexes and are divided into categories. We are interested in similarity indices, and in particular, local similarity indices. Local similarity indices make a prediction on an edge (u, v) by using the properties of the nodes u and v. In theory, nodes with similar properties are more likely to have an edge than nodes that do not. Local similarity indices are computationally very efficient and reasonably good at predicting edges.

This work focuses on extending the theory behind local similarity indices in a natural way. The concept that two nodes are similar implies an edge between them only uses a portion of the information available. We consider a set of k nodes similar to u (and respectively, v). The more similar nodes that have an edge to v (or u), the more likely (u, v) is to exist. This technique is commonly known as k-nn. However, in order to avoid confusion between the similar nodes and the nodes adjacent in a graph, we use the term k-similarity to refer to the former case.

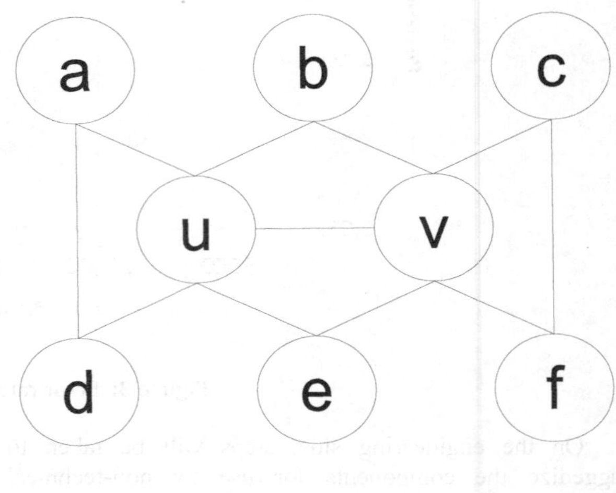

Fig. 1
A SIMPLE GRAPH WITH EIGHT NODES. THE LINK (u, v) IS OF INTEREST. NODES u AND v HAVE TWO COMMON NEIGHBORS, b AND e.

To see the difference between local similarity indices and k-similarity consider the simple graph in Figure 1. A key measurement for local similarity is the number of common neighbors between two nodes. Nodes u and v have two neighbors in common, specifically, nodes b and e.

Finding the k-similarity nodes to u and v is more complex. Table 1 shows how the similarity would be computed for the graph using common neighbors as the similarity criterion. Given a value for k, k-similarity can be computed from the table. For example, with $k = 1$, the most similar node to u is v and the most similar node to v is u. Since neither the edge (v, v) nor (u, u) is in the graph, the score for k-similarity using common neighbors and k=1 for (u, v) would be zero. Note that $k = 2$ results in a tie, which is arbitrarily broken. Assume a is selected as the second most similar node to u. Since (a, v) is not in the graph, the number of similar nodes to u that are neighbors of v is still zero. However, if a is

Table 1
THE k-SIMILARITY CALCULATIONS FOR FIGURE 1 USING COMMON NEIGHBORS AS THE SIMILARITY CRITERION. U SHARED IS THE NUMBER OF NEIGHBORS IN COMMON BETWEEN u AND THE NODE. V SHARED IS SIMILAR FOR v.

Node	Neighbors	U Shared	V Shared
u	a,b,d,e,v	5	2
v	b,c,e,f,u	2	5
a	d,u	1	1
b	u,v	1	1
c	v,f	1	1
d	a,u	1	1
e	u,v	1	1
f	c,v	1	1

selected as the second most similar node to v, since (a, u) is in the graph, the number of similar nodes to v that are neighbors of u is now one, and the reported score is one.

Using k-similarity with local similarity indices is very straightforward. Once the framework is in place, creating a k-similarity version of the index requires writing one method with typically no more than a few lines of code. As shown in Section 3, with appropriate selection of k, the k-similarity version can perform better than the native version for predicting links in biological graphs. However, sometimes the k-similarity version performs significantly worse, leading to speculation as to what properties of the indices can be exploited by k-similarity.

The notation in this paper extends the typical graph notation in order to simplify discussions. A graph G is defined as $G = (V, E)$ such that V is the set of vertices (or nodes) in the graph, and E is the set of edges. Let U be the set of all possible edges in G. The link prediction problem, as defined in [9], is to find the edges in $U - E$ that should be in G. Let the neighbors of a vertex $v \in V$ be denoted $\Gamma(v)$. The degree of a vertex v is d_v. When needed, the k-similarity vertices to v are denoted $K(v)$. The graph used in this work is modified from the BioGRID Interaction Database [14]. The graph consists of 6,186 nodes and 192,474 unique edges. The graph has been modified from [14] to remove redundant edges and self-loops.

This paper proceeds by providing background information on models for link prediction in graphs. Next, the paper describes the development of k-similarity algorithms and the experiments showing the impact of k-nn versus native applications of the local similarity indexes. Some surprising issues are discussed in Section 4. The conclusion and future work ends the paper.

2. Related Work

Link prediction is a popular research topic. In [9], the link prediction techniques are divided into similarity based algorithms, maximum likelihood methods and probabilistic models. Similarity based algorithms assume that an edge (u, v) is more likely if the nodes u and v are similar, based on some criteria. Clearly, k-nn methods are similarity based. Maximum likelihood methods assume the graph has an underlying structure, so that edges which contribute towards the structure are favored over edges that do not. Examples include the dendrogram in [4] and block models [2]. The probabilistic approaches attempt to model the underlying graph structure and predict the missing edges based on the probability of the link given the model. See [9] for more about maximum likelihood and probabilistic methods.

More recently, matrix factorization has been used for link prediction [10]. Matrix factorization is similar to k-similarity in that it incorporates other prediction models. As with k-similarity, matrix factorization does not ensure a better result than using the native version of the similarity index. Also, as with k-similarity, the matrix factorization model can be optimized for AUC, and this is done in [10]. Fundamentally, the matrix factorization model is a supervised learning technique which combines the graph topology with side information. It requires training linear in the number of possible edges, or quadratic in the number of vertices, which is similar to k-similarity for making all predictions.

The work by Lu and Zhou [9] further divides similarity methods into local, global and quasi-local indices. A local index uses structural information such as the number of common neighbors. Global similarity are typically based on properties of the entire graph, such as the number of moves two random walkers starting at u and v make before they meet. Quasi-local indexes perform trade-offs between the high computational complexity of global indexes versus the generally weaker predictive power of local similarity indices. For example, one quasi-local method considers not only the common neighbors, but also all common nodes within a distance of 2 from each node [15].

Within the hierarchy in [9], the extension of local similarity indexes to k-nn methods is best represented as a quasi-local index, in that more than local information is used, but with optimization it is possible to consider only information in a small portion of the graph.

2.1 Local Similarity Indices

Ten similarity measures (called indices in [9]) are used to test the application of k-similarity for link prediction. We describe each of the algorithms in detail in this section. The similarity measures are presented in alphabetical order for easier reference.

2.1.1 Adamic-Adar

Abbreviated AA, this similarity measure originally presented in [1], is based on shared items on web pages. If two students have many items in common, they are more likely to be friends. Additionally, rare shared items, contribute more to the similarity score. The similarity score is modified slightly in [8] to consider common neighbors as the shared items. The modified formula is

$$s^{\mathrm{AA}}(x, y) = \sum_{z \in \Gamma(x) \cap \Gamma(y)} \frac{1}{\log d_z}$$

2.1.2 Common Neighbors

Abbreviated CN, this similarity measure is one of the most basic, but performs very well. It is used in [11] to show that the probability of scientists collaborating increases with the number of collaborators they have in common. For nine of the ten local similarity measures in [9], the absence of common neighbors yields a similarity score of zero.

$$s^{\text{CN}}(x,y) = |\Gamma(x) \cap \Gamma(y)|$$

2.1.3 Cosine Similarity

Abbreviated cos, it is labeled as the Salton Index in [9]. The cosine similarity is based on the cosine of the angle between two vectors. By representing the neighbors as bit vectors of nodes, the cosine can be computed. Alternatively, the cosine similarity can be calculated directly from the properties of the nodes as

$$s^{\text{cos}}(x,y) = \frac{|\Gamma(x) \cap \Gamma(y)|}{\sqrt{d_x * d_y}}$$

2.1.4 Hub Depressed Index

Abbreviated HDI, this similarity measure is new in [9]. It is analogous to HPI, except hubs are depressed due to their large degree. The similarity formula is

$$s^{\text{HDI}}(x,y) = \frac{|\Gamma(x) \cap \Gamma(y)|}{\max(d_x, d_y)}$$

2.1.5 Hub Promoted Index

Abbreviated HPI, this similarity appears in [13] as the topological overlap between two nodes. Collections of nodes with high topological overlap tend to represent biologically interesting modules. The similarity formula is

$$s^{\text{HPI}}(x,y) = \frac{|\Gamma(x) \cap \Gamma(y)|}{\min(d_x, d_y)}$$

2.1.6 Jaccard Index

Abbreviated J, this similarity measure was defined by Paul Jaccard over 100 years ago. It is a statistic for comparing the similarity of two sets, and it is applied here by comparing the sets of neighbors between two nodes. The formula is

$$s^{J}(x,y) = \frac{|\Gamma(x) \cap \Gamma(y)|}{|\Gamma(x) \cup \Gamma(y)|}$$

2.1.7 Leicht-Holme-Newman Index

Abbreviated LHN, this similarity measure in [7] can be considered a near inverse of k-similarity. Vertices u and v are similar if either has a neighbor w that is similar to the other. Consider 1-NN, in which if the most similar node to u is a neighbor of v, then u and v are similar. The significant distinction is that LHN reports similarity if any neighbor is similar, while k-similarity reports similarity if any similar node is a neighbor. Since link prediction is defined by similarity between two vertices, the simplified formula in [7] is used in which the number of common neighbors is divided by the expected number of neighbors. It is proportional to the formula:

$$s^{\text{LHN}}(x,y) = \frac{|\Gamma(x) \cap \Gamma(y)|}{d_x * d_y}$$

2.1.8 Preferential Attachment

Abbreviated PA, this local similarity method does not use common neighbors. Over ten years ago, the concept was used to note that new edges tended to be incident on high density nodes more often than low density nodes [3]. A similarity measure based on this concept is used in several applications (see [9] for a listing) and is defined as

$$s^{\text{PA}} = d_x * d_y$$

2.1.9 Resource Allocation

Abbreviated RA, this similarity measure is based on the flow of resources in a graph [12]. Resources leaving one node flow into all of its neighbors. The amount of the resource that flows into the target represents the resource allocation. Specifically, the similarity formula is [9]

$$s^{\text{RA}}(x,y) = \sum_{z \in \Gamma(x) \cap \Gamma(y)} \frac{1}{d_z}$$

2.1.10 Sorensen

Abbreviated S, [9] states this similarity measure is primarily used for ecological community data. The formula is

$$s^{S}(x,y) = \frac{2 * |\Gamma(x) \cap \Gamma(y)|}{d_x + d_y}$$

3. K-Similarity Extensions to Local Similarity Indexes

Adapting a local similarity index to a k-similarity approach is straightforward. The prediction of an edge (x, y) is the greater number of elements in the k-nn of each node that are neighbors of the other node in G.

$$s^{K}(x,y) = \max(|\{v|v \in K(x) \wedge (v,y) \in E\}|, \\ |\{v|v \in K(y) \wedge (v,x) \in E\}|)$$

Making a single prediction with k-similarity is significantly slower than using the local index alone. Finding the k-similarity of a node requires $O(|V|)$ local similarity calculations, while just using the index requires only one. However, since the k-similarity of a node can be calculated once and saved, making all of the predictions for a graph requires $O(|V|^2)$ local similarity calculations, identical to the number when using the index alone. Thus, for finding the edges most likely to be missing from a graph, the k-similarity approach is not prohibitively slow.

3.1 K Selection

One of the challenges for using k-similarity is the selection of k. The general wisdom is selecting k does not significantly alter the effectiveness of the algorithm, so long as k is not too small. In [6] optimal values for k can be efficiently determined as long as the error can be incrementally calculated. For link prediction, AUC is used as the scoring factor, enabling a $O(|V|^2)$ algorithm to determine the optimal k.

The maximum reasonable value for k is $\sqrt{|V|}$ [6], [5]. Call this value maxK. The algorithm for calculating the best k uses a maxK $\times$ maxK matrix M. M_{ij} is the percentage of edges with a predicted score of j or less when using the i-nearest neighbors. Thus, it is a cumulative distribution and when $j \geq i$, $M_{ij} = 1.0$. To efficiently generate M, the algorithm iterates over the edges in the graph. The maxK nodes are found for each node incident on the edge and the appropriate M_{ij} is incremented. In one pass over the matrix, the cumulative values are computed and each cell is divided by the total number of edges.

The error for a particular k can be computed by considering all of the non-edges ($(u, v) \in U - E$). The k-similarity score j is calculated for each nearest neighbor set of size $1 \leq i \leq$ maxK. The error for (u, v) with i-nearest neighbors is the number of actual edges with a lower score ($M_{i(j-1)}$) plus one-half the number of actual edges with the same score (M_{ij}). The results are in Figure 2. The indexes are split into two charts for clarity.

From Figure 2, it is clear that the error improves with increasing k. In fact, for nine of the ten indexes, the lowest error occurs with $k = 79$. However, it is also clear that each error improves only marginally after some point. We use the least k such that the error improves by less than 1% as worthy of investigation.

3.2 Area Under the Curve

Our next experiments show the impact of different values of k within the k-similarity framework on AUC, a common measurement of link prediction algorithms. Experiment 1 calculates the AUC using only the native local similarity index. The second through fourth experiments use different values of k. Experiment 2 uses an arbitrarily chosen value of 10. Experiment 3 uses the first k such that the error never improves by more than 1%. Experiment 4 uses the k with the least error. Table 2 shows the results. It should be noted that although increasing k increases the work done, it does not incur any additional index computations, which are the most expensive operations. Therefore, the runtime for each index is similar for different values of k.

It is interesting to note that while using k-similarity is generally helpful, it does not always improve the performance of the index. In particular, HPI performs very badly as a k-similarity index (see Section 4.1 for an explanation) . Conversely, HDI is exceptionally powerful as a k-similarity index, outperforming all other techniques. Also, note that the improvement between Experiment 3 and Experiment 4

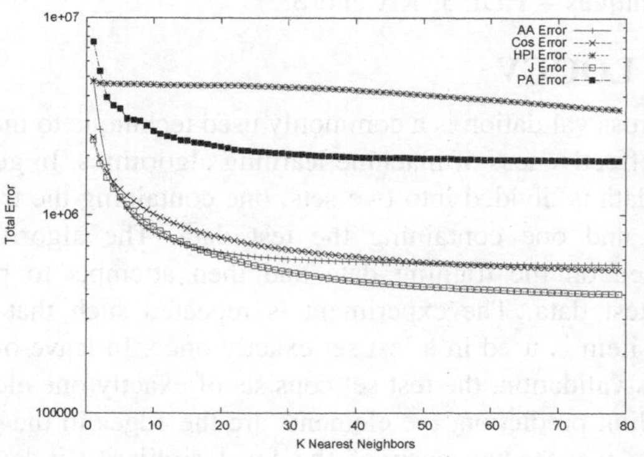

(a) The k-nn error for five of the local indexes: AA, cos, HPI, J and PA.

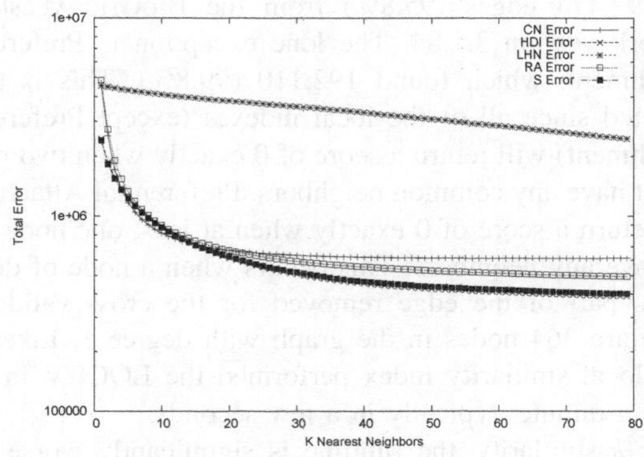

(b) The k-nn error for five of the local indexes: CN, HDI, LHN, RA and S.

Fig. 2
THE ERROR FOR THE LOCAL SIMILARITY INDEXES IN [9].

Table 2
THE AUC FOR THE TEN LOCAL SIMILARITY INDEXES IN [9] UNDER FOUR EXPERIMENTS. THE FIRST USES THE SIMILARITY INDEX ALONE. THE NEXT THREE USE THE k-SIMILARITY APPROACH. IN EXPERIMENT 2, $k = 10$. IN EXPERIMENT 3, THE k IS INCLUDED IN THE RESULTS. IN EXPERIMENT 4, THE k IS 79 EXCEPT FOR COMMON NEIGHBOR WHERE THE BEST k VALUE IS 68. THE VALUES ARE THE AVERAGES OF 5 EXECUTIONS. THE BEST RESULTS FOR EACH EXECUTION IS IN BOLD.

Index	Exp 1	Exp 2	Exp 3	Exp 4
AA	0.906	0.912	0.934 (22)	0.937
CN	0.903	**0.917**	0.928 (20)	0.933
Cos	0.839	0.895	0.934 (31)	0.944
HDI	0.824	0.907	0.951 (38)	**0.958**
HPI	0.819	0.520	0.512 (10)	0.646
J	0.833	0.911	**0.952** (38)	0.957
LHN	0.669	0.569	0.565 (10)	0.745
PA	0.895	0.720	0.772 (23)	0.797
RA	**0.910**	0.908	0.941 (30)	0.953
S	0.836	0.913	0.948 (38)	**0.958**

is typically small, especially under the better performing techniques – HDI, J, RA and S.

3.3 LOOCV

Cross validation is a commonly used technique to measure the effectiveness of machine learning algorithms. In general, the data is divided into two sets; one containing the training data and one containing the test data. The algorithm is trained on the training data and then attempts to predict the test data. The experiment is repeated such that every data item is used in a test set exactly once. In leave-one-out cross-validation, the test set consists of exactly one element. For link prediction, the elements are the edges in the graph. Thus, we execute each of the local similarity indexes on a graph with an edge removed and see if it predicts the existence of the edge.

Natively, nine of the local indexes found 184,357 of the 192,474 edges (95.8%) from the BioGrid yeast PPI network version 3.1.84. The lone exception is Preferential Attachment, which found 192,110 (99.8%). This is to be expected since all of the local indexes (except Preferential Attachment) will return a score of 0 exactly when two nodes do not have any common neighbors. Preferential Attachment will return a score of 0 exactly when at least one node does not have any neighbors. This occurs when a node of degree one is part of the edge removed for the cross validation. There are 364 nodes in the graph with degree 1. Likewise, each local similarity index performed the LOOCV in well under a minute, typically in a few seconds.

For k-similarity the runtime is significantly worse with indexes requiring 24-48 hours. Since the graph changes for each edge removed, the optimization of computing the k-similarity of each node once and saving it for later use is not possible. As a simple example, consider again the graph in Figure 1. Removing the edge (u, v) changes the common neighbors. The three most similar nodes to u are now v, a and d. None of these nodes have an edge to v. Similarly, the three most similar nodes to v are u, c and f. None of these nodes have an edge to u. Therefore, under LOOCV, the score for the k-similarity using common neighbors would be zero, indicating the node is not found. Recall the score for the node with (u, v) included is likely to be above zero, depending on the tie breaking process.

Using the k-similarity version of the local similarity index resulted in better LOOCV performance for three of the indexes (AA, RA and CN), slightly worse performance for four of the indexes (Cosine, HDI, Jaccard, PA and Sorensen) and terrible performance for HPI and LHN. Table 3 has the results of the LOOCV experiments.

3.4 Testing Predictions

The genome information is constantly evolving, creating the need for new link predictions. We can exploit this to provide another mechanism for testing the local similarity indexes and the impact of using k-similarity. For this experiment, we use version 3.1.73 of the yeast PPI data

Table 3
THE NUMBER OF EDGES FOUND DURING LEAVE ONE OUT CROSS-VALIDATION FOR BOTH LOCAL SIMILARITY INDEXES AND THE k-SIMILARITY VERSION OF THE INDEX. NINE OF THE INDEXES FOUND 184,357 (95.8%) OF THE EDGES IN THE BIOGRID YEAST PPI NETWORK VERSION 3.1.84.

Index	LOOCV	LOOCV with KNN
AA	184357	191539 (99.5%)
CN	184357	191815 (99.7%)
Cosine	184357	168267 (87.4%)
HDI	184357	173017 (89.9%)
HPI	184357	19401 (10.1%)
Jaccard	184357	173226 (90.0%)
LHN	184357	5579 (2.9%)
PA	192110 (99.8%)	191969 (99.7%)
RA	184357	191815 (99.7%)
Sorensen	184357	173226 (90.0%)

from BioGRID (last modified 2011-01-31). Between version 3.1.73 and version 3.1.84, 28,974 edges were added to the yeast protein interaction graph.

The best predictions for each index, both used natively and with k-similarity are generated. Since the k-similarity approach does not differentiate between ties, all of the perfect scores are included in the experiment. For most indexes, relatively few links received a perfect score, so the top 100 predictions are used. However, Common Neighbors produced 271 "perfect" scores, while Adamic-Adar yielded 157. We then count the number of predicted links that are present in the newer data. The results are in Table 4. It is interesting to note that the local similarity indexes by themselves tend to be extremely successful or fail miserably with this experiment. Six of the native implementations did not predict any found links, while four predicted a number of links extremely unlikely to be found by chance. Only three of indexes did not make a successful prediction when combined with k-similarity but for many of the indexes, random chance could find the same number of links. It is interesting to note that the native Adamic-Adar index performs the best.

4. Issues with Extending Local Similarity Indexes with KNN

The results from Section 3 indicate using local similarity indexes within a k-similarity approach can be beneficial. However, there are some obvious issues. First, the surprisingly bad performance of the HPI index must be examined. Second, optimization of the running time of the approaches must be considered. Finally, the ease and power of creating new k-similarity approaches is demonstrated.

4.1 Hub Promoted Index Performance

The Hub Promoted Index (HPI) [13] is an effective local similarity index. Under our experiments in Section 3, HPI scored 0.819 on the AUC experiment (see Table 2). Although that is not particularly strong compared to the other local

Table 4

THE NUMBER OF PREDICTIONS FROM BIOGRID VERSION 3.1.73 THAT WERE DISCOVERED AS OF BIOGRID VERSION 3.1.84. THE NATIVE CHANCE AND KNN CHANCE COLUMNS REPRESENT THE PROBABILITY THE NUMBER OF EDGES COULD BE GUESSED RANDOMLY.

Index	Predictions	Native Found	Native Chance	KNN Found	KNN Chance
AA	157	14	7.8×10^{-15}	5	2.5×10^{-7}
CN	271	18	1.3×10^{-14}	6	1.3×10^{-7}
Cosine	100	0	1	3	8.5×10^{-5}
HDI	100	0	1	3	8.5×10^{-5}
HPI	100	0	1	0	1
Jaccard	100	0	1	1	0.08
LHN	100	0	1	1	0.08
PA	100	6	3.5×10^{-10}	0	1
RA	100	8	4.1×10^{-14}	0	1
Sorensen	100	0	1	1	0.08

similarity indexes, it is well above random chance and the index performed much better on the data in [9].

However, using HPI within our k-similarity framework performed exceptionally poorly. Using a k of 10, HPI scored 0.520 for AUC, barely better than random chance. Increasing k to the maximum (78) yields a score of 0.646, which is better, but still below any of the local similarity indexes by themselves. Likewise, the error score for HPI (Figure 2) improves very slowly. In fact, the first time the error improves by less than 1% is at $k = 3$.

Comparing HPI to the basic common neighbors approach sheds light on the reason it does not work well within a k-similarity framework. Recall the formula for HPI as

$$s^{\text{HPI}}(x, y) = \frac{|\Gamma(x) \cap \Gamma(y)|}{\min(k_x, k_y)}$$

where k_x is the degree of node x. Therefore, the best possible score for HPI is 1, and is achieved when either $\Gamma(x) \subseteq \Gamma(y)$ or $\Gamma(y) \subseteq \Gamma(x)$.

Now consider the score for the edge (u, v) within the k-similarity framework. We consider only u, as the case for v is identical. The most similar nodes to u would be those nodes x such that $\Gamma(x) \subseteq \Gamma(u)$. This is much more likely in cases where the degree of x is very low. In particular, if the degree of x is 1, then if the neighbor of x is also a neighbor of u, then the HPI score of (u, x) is 1. Given the existence of hubs within the yeast PPI network, it is very likely for a sufficiently large set of such nodes to exist. Note that since these nodes have a degree of 1, and their only neighbor is the hub, these nodes cannot have an edge to v, and thus fail to add to the score.

As a comparison, consider the common neighbors similarity index under k-similarity. A node of degree 1 is less likely to be the most similar because a node of high degree would be more likely to have two or more common neighbors. Of course, a node of high degree would also have many non-common neighbors, but in the basic approach, there is no penalty for uncommon neighbors.

4.2 Common Neighbor Optimization

Nine of the ten local similarity indexes (all but Preferential Attachment) use the number of common neighbors as a significant portion of the score calculation. In seven of these approaches (all but Adamic-Adar and Resource Allocation), the number of common neighbors serves as the numerator of the score function. In AA and RA, each common neighbor contributes to the score.

For the k-similarity framework, finding the k most similar nodes is a significant consumption of resources. In the naïve case, all other vertices must be checked. However, for the common neighbor based indexes, given a node u, only nodes with a distance of 2 or less may have a common node with u. Thus, only those nodes need to be considered. Given an adjacency matrix A, $A \cup A^2$ (where $a_{ij} \in A \cup B$ is true if the entry is true in A or B) can be precomputed to hold the possible common neighbors. Thus, we can find the k-similarity of a node without considering all possible nodes, potentially saving significant time. Table 5 shows the speedup to be 25-75%.

4.3 Extension from Native to KNN

The framework established allows very rapid development of both native and k-similarity local similarity indexes. For example, consider an unusual local similarity index developed for this paper called Asymmetric. This index is designed to work in both directed and undirected graphs, so the similarity for edge (u, v) is allowed to be different from the similarity for edge (v, u). Specifically, the score for (u, v) is defined as

$$1.0 - \frac{|\Gamma(u) - \Gamma(v)|}{|\Gamma(u)|}$$

.

For undirected graphs, the score of (u, v) is the maximum of the directed scores for (u, v) and (v, u).

To implement the AUC test for Asymmetric requires creating the class and implementing the prediction method. In this case, five new lines of code have to be added to

Table 5
COMPARISON OF THE TIME REQUIRED TO PERFORM k-SIMILARITY PREDICTIONS WHEN THE GRAPH IS PRE-PROCESSED SUCH THAT ONLY POSSIBLE NODES ARE SEARCHED AS OPPOSED TO THE ENTIRE GRAPH. PREFERENTIAL ATTACHMENT IS NOT INCLUDED SINCE THE OPTIMIZATION IS NOT APPLICABLE. THE k FROM EXPERIMENT 3 IN TABLE 2 IS USED. THE TIME IS IN MILLISECONDS.

	KNN		Optimized		
Index	Score	Time	Score	Time	Speedup
AA	0.934	1208440	0.934	970389	1.25
CN	0.928	166743	0.928	105703	1.58
cos	0.934	760410	0.934	430137	1.77
HDI	0.951	766940	0.951	434552	1.77
HPI	0.512	786422	0.513	444833	1.77
J	0.952	1326770	0.951	824168	1.61
LHN	0.565	766476	0.566	428172	1.79
RA	0.941	1200200	0.939	973598	1.23
S	0.948	763862	0.950	429719	1.78

implement Asymmetric (most of the local similarity indexes from [9] only needed one additional line of code). The test suite can then be executed on a given graph by simply passing parameters to the class. For example, the parameter -m indicates finding the best K, while -e finds the AUC for both the native and k-similarity implementation. It took less time to create the class than to run the experiments.

For the curious, the Asymmetric index has an AUC of 0.829 run natively, 0.952 with $k = 38$ and 0.960 with $k = 78$. After $k = 38$, the error improves by less than 1%, which is the cut-off used in Experiment 3 reported in Table 2. The Asymmetric index using k-similarity with $k = 78$ outperformed all of the other local similarity indexes under any conditions, *even though the native implementation was unimpressive.*. Thus, using the k-similarity framework can lead to new and improved algorithms for link prediction.

5. Conclusion

Local similarity indexes (see [9]) are quick tools for predicting links in graphs. Typically, these tools look at only the portion of the graph immediately connected to a node or to properties of the node. This allows large graphs to be processed efficiently and predictions to be made when more robust techniques would be too computationally expensive.

The machine learning technique k-nn can be applied by assuming that if the k most similar nodes to v have a link to u, then v should have a link to u. The challenge is to find the k most similar nodes. However, local similarity indexes are exactly intended to find similar nodes, leading to a natural integration between the local similarity indexes and k-nn.

We propose a framework in which given a local similarity index s, a prediction for edge (x, y) in graph G can be made. Based on s, the k most similar neighbors to x and y are found. The score of the link is

$$s^K(x,y) = \max(|\{v|v \in K(x) \land (v,y) \in E\}|, |\{v|v \in K(y) \land (v,x) \in E\}|)$$

For each index, the best k is found by following the techniques in [6].

Using an index in a k-similarity framework as opposed to native application produces unpredictable results. In some cases, the k-similarity version of the index performs considerably better than the native application, but in some cases the k-similarity version is far worse (see Table 2). For testing purposes, the k-similarity versions are significantly slower under AUC and unreasonable under LOOCV. However, when finding all possible predictions, the k-similarity versions required only twice as much time, indicating reasonable performance for some applications.

This work needs to be extended in several ways. There are additional graphs to be considered, such as co-authorship or social media. Social media applications with hundreds of millions of nodes would require the optimizations in Section 4.2 to run efficiently. Also, the use of k-similarity as a framework with reasonable performance opens the opportunity for similarly indexes which may perform poorly when applied natively. Thus, new similarity indexes can be developed. In particular, semantic similarity can be considered, as well as structural similarity.

References

[1] Lada Adamic and Eytan Adar. Friends and neighbors on the web. *Social Networks*, 25(3):211–230, 2003.

[2] Edoardo M. Airoldi, David M. Blei, Stephen E. Fienberg, and Eric P. Xing. Mixed membership stochastic blockmodels. *J. Mach. Learn. Res.*, 9:1981–2014, June 2008.

[3] A.-L. Barabasi and R. Albert. Emergence of scaling in random networks. *Science*, 286(5439):509–512, 1999.

[4] Aaron Clauset, Christopher Moore, and M.E.J. Newman. Hierarchical structure and the prediction of missing links in networks. *Nature*, 453:98–101, 2008.

[5] Anil K. Ghosh. On nearest neighbor classification using adaptive choice of k. *Journal of Computational and Graphical Statistics*, 16(2):482–502, 2007.

[6] G. Hamerly and G. Speegle. Best k for knn. In *Proceedings of the 27th British National Conference on Databases, BNCOD 27*, pages 37–54, June 2010.

[7] E. A. Leicht, Petter Holme, and M. E. J. Newman. Vertex similarity in networks. *Phys. Rev. E*, 73:026120, Feb 2006.

[8] David Liben-Nowell and Jon Kleinberg. The link prediction problem for social networks. In *Proceedings of the twelfth international conference on Information and knowledge management*, pages 556–559, 2003.

[9] L. Lu and T. Zhou. Link prediction in complex networks: A survey. *Physcia A: Statistical Mechanics and it Applications*, 390(6):1150–1170, 2011.

[10] A. Menon and C. Elkan. Link prediction via matrix factorization. *Machine Learning and Knowledge Discovery in Databases*, pages 437–452, 2011.

[11] M. E. J. Newman. Clustering and preferential attachment in growing networks. *Phys. Rev. E*, 64:025102, Jul 2001.

[12] Qing Ou, Ying-Di Jin, Tao Zhou, Bing-Hong Wang, and Bao-Qun Yin. Power-law strength-degree correlation from resource-allocation dynamics on weighted networks. *Phys. Rev. E*, 75:021102, Feb 2007.

[13] E. Ravasz, A. Somera, L. D. A. Mongru, Z. N. Oltvai, and A.-L. Barabasi. Hierarchical organization of modularity in metabolic networks. *Science*, 297:1551–1555, August 2002.

[14] C. Stark, B.J. Breitkreutz, A. Chatr-Aryamontri, and et al. The biogrid interaction database: 2011 update. *Nucleic Acids Research*, 39:D698–D704, 2011.

[15] T. Zhou, L. Linyuan, and Y.-C. Zhang. Predicting missing links via local information. *The European Physical Jounral B*, 71:623–630, 2009.

A New Simple Classification Algorithm enabling a New Approach for Identification of Virtual Bullying

K Burn-Thornton
University College
Durham University,
South Rd,
DURHAM DH1 3RW, UK.

T Burman
School of Engineering and Computer Science
Durham University,
South Rd,
DURHAM DH1 3LE, UK.

***Abstract*— In this paper we present a new, simple, classification algorithm which can be used to identify a change in virtual behaviour between a sender and recipient which could be used as an early indicator of virtual bullying or harassment. This application is not only, a novel application of Data Mining techniques but also, a new approach used to identify virtual bullying by virtue of identification of a change in behaviour.**

The approach which we have taken makes use of a new linear discriminant algorithm to classify normal and non-normal style(s) of email correspondence for each sender and recipient pair. A change in email style is taken to signify a change in relationship between the sender and recipient which could provide an early indicator of virtual harassment/bullying.

This approach has great potential for use in large organization where it is often appears to be hard to identify unacceptable information transmission between two colleagues – especially when one is in a more senior position.

By identifying behavior indicating a change in relationship between two colleagues it should be possible to instigate company anti bullying processes in a more timely manner and reduce the long term effect on those being bullied/harassed. This should ensure a more effective work force in terms of work place efficiency and reduction of stress related absence resulting from harassment or bullying.

We show that by regarding the contents of the emails as a set of Cascading Style Sheets, CSS, type files, which we call sender signature styles (SSSs), and accompanying information, it is possible to improve the identification of the number of sender signature styles contained within the email, irrespective of the length.

We also describe how, as a by-product of this work, a set of sender signature styles (SSSs) can be created during investigation of each email and hence be used as a library, containing increasing membership, for comparison with future emails sender by the same sender. By the nature of this task abnormal sender signature (ASSSs) files will also be created from virtual correspondence which has been known to be of concern, as well as that which has independently being identified as being indicative of being of possible concern

The implications of the use of SSSs, and ASSSs, for identification of future email interactions are discussed.

Keywords- Virtual Bullying, Data Mining, Novel approach.

I. INTRODUCTION

The current employment climate appears to have resulted in an increase in bullying and harassment experienced in the work place[1], This is indicated by the increase in the implementation of anti bullying/harassment procedures which have been put in place in company – as well as the proliferation of antibullying/harassment work place courses. This change in culture is also supported by many union web sites which proclaim on their site main page their success in fighting bullying cases which demonstrates its strong presence in a working environment [2].

Often this behavior is hard to identify, and eliminate, in large companies where such activity is readily facilitated by the virtual society in which this behaviour takes place by email and which can have a detrimental, and long-lasting, effect on those being bullied[3].

Approaches that have been taken to identify bullying behaviour and support those undergoing such behaviour include paper based 'tools' or process steps which require following[4].

Some software tools are also available but require virtual button pressing when bullying is taking place and are not an ideal approach for identification of one, or many, bulling or harassing emails. However, an approach which has not been taken is to make use of software to identify different nature, or construction, of emails which are sent from one sender to a recipient.

This paper describes a novel Data Mining approach, which enables a change in email style between a given sender recipient pair to be identified and hence provide a possible early indicator of virtual harassment/bullying by virtue of the change in virtual relationship.

The first section describes current approaches which are used to identify potential bullying/harassing behaviour in emails. This is followed by a discussion of two possible solutions which would enable email signature styles to be determined and a description of algorithms which may be gainfully employed in achieving each solution are then described.

An overview of the sub-tasks carried out by the algorithms which have been used to implement the proposed solution follows. The remaining sections discuss the investigations which were carried out in order to determine the effectiveness of the approach, the metrics which were used to determine the effectiveness and the results of the investigations for the CSS type solutions – the SSS(ASSS) based solution. Conclusions regarding the results of the investigations are then drawn with future profitable avenues for investigation being discussed.

II. EXISITING APPROACHES

The approach which is predominantly used in this area is that of the provision of reactive solutions when someone feels that they are being subject to cyber-bullying [5-6] and are not readily ideal to provide a solution to bullying/harassment from email.

These solutions range from papers based tools, or a series to steps to follow [4] , to software such as KnowDiss or CyberBully which are to all intents and purposes software in which the virtual pressing of a 'panic button' cause emails, or instant messaging, to be created to inform others what is happening or what is perceived to be happening [5-6].

In an ideal world a response to bullying behaviour should be proactive rather than reactive. If such an approach were to be taken the solution software would need to be able to identify bullying/harassing behavior as it were about to happen and not afterwards.

Such a proactive approach could be a solution which could detect a change in email style using a pattern matching approach based upon the fact that all emails have a unique signature style[2, 7, 8, 9](ASS) since all emails from the same sender should contain only one SSS or a variant on the same SSS in correspondence with the same recipient or group of recipients.

III. DOCUMENT (EMAIL) SIGNATURE STYLE

Document signature style makes the assumption that each individual has a unique writing style which is characterized by their individual use, and combination, of nouns, verbs and other features which include referencing[2, 8, 10, 11]. If the document signature style were to vary throughout the paragraphs of an email or between the sender and different recipients this could provide an indication that there was change in virtual behaviour between the sender and the recipient or recipients.

Such variation in style could be used as a basis for early instigation of any bullying/harassment in a company – something which is often hard to identify by the presence of hierarchical relationships and trans company support networks - especially if historical information could be used to show that early indications of a change in virtual behavior resulted in bullying/harassment behavior at a later date.

This approach could, if sufficiently accurate, prove to be a driver for facilitating a reduction in company sickness absence as well as progressing toward eliminating this unacceptable behaviour in a work place.

A Extraction of Signature Style

In order to determine the unique sender signature(s) present in the emails it is necessary to determine key elements of emails which can be used to determine a unique email signature created by each sender.

Initial analysis of over 1000 emails in one university School[9] suggested that the key elements of the signature required in order to determine whether, or not, an email is 'normal' or 'harassing/bullying' may be reduced to number of words in a sentence, number of lines in a paragraph, paragraph formatting, degree and use of grammar, type of language used and word spelling. These key signature features are concomitant with those proposed at ICADPR for instance those in [10] and [11].

The first two elements of the signature are self explanatory but the others may require some clarification. Degree and use of grammar to include the manner in which infinitives are used; use of, and types, of punctuation; use of pluarality. Type of language is taken to mean language style which in different types of English for instance UK and US. However, word spelling includes not only language spelling differences such as those found between UK & US, for example as in counsellor and counselor, but also frequency of typographical errors and spelling mistakes.

A solution to this analyzing this information would be an approach which is able to extract the key signature elements, and their values, from paragraphs, and compare them with others in the same email and with those extracted from other emails from the same sender. It could also be helpful if the approach used could be used, during any subsequent university formal procedures, to show how the email would have appeared if written in a 'non harassing/bullying' style by the sender. Such documentation would prove useful if additional proof 'virtual bullying', or change in virtual behaviour, towards a particular recipient, was required.

The following section describes two possible variants on such an approach.

IV. POSSIBLE APPROACHES

Both of the possible approaches suggested in this section make use of a modification of the approaches which we used in our web site maintainability tool[6] and multiple submission tool. The approaches make use of Cascading Style Sheets (CSS) or a combination of the eXtensible Markup Language (XML) in combination with the eXtensible Style Language (XSL) [13].

These approaches make use of information extraction and representation. Some commonality can be observed between the first steps of the approaches, which are described in the next section, and that of Ghani [14] and Simpson[15].

A CSS

If a CSS –based approach were used, a named sender signature style (SSS) could be defined which would describe the values assigned to the key signature features. Once the

SSS files were created, the signature of style of the sender could not only be compared with others within the same email but it could also be applied to any email section and the output compared with that contained within the current, or other, emails sent by the same sender. By using this approach the speed of investigation of emails could be minimized by the reduction in the size of file which is required in order achieve comparison [16].

In practice, each section of the email being investigated could be converted directly to a section of SSS containing the feature values. Such an approach would require the use of a measure of uncertainty when mapping the samples of document and related SSS code to named signature styles. Figure 1 provides an example of how a page of email text may be converted using such an approach.

Data Mining would appear to be able to provide a solution to this problem by making use of modified clustering techniques.

The only drawback to this approach is that a library of assignable values for each key signature feature will need to be defined initially. However, this library could be updated as part on an electronic backup process.

B XML

For an XML approach all content information would be contained in an XSL file with its companion XML file containing the ASS feature information which would be recursively applied to the XSL document.

Using the example from Figure 1 this approach would result in the production of a XML file containing a section of text that would be marked up as a reference name, and the XSL file would contain a template which could be applied reference names in that document. Such an approach would readily facilitate comparison of emails because it would be relatively easy to target comparison of emails by investigation of specific signatures, SSSs.

Rigid definitions do not exist for XML tags which means that any appropriately defined names will have to be used in the XML file as well as a library of attributable values of the signature features, as in the CSS approach. However, a major drawback of this approach would be the need of consistency for XML tags and the possibility of ongoing modification to a centrally accessed XML tag dictionary.

The requirements which will need to be fulfilled for the XML/XSL solution suggest that the CSS based solution may be the more accurate approach to use for the comparison of signature styles in emails. This is because even a slight variation is XML tags could result in a large discrepancy in ASS and hence identification of a document as containing more than one sender style when it does not.

The following section provides an introduction to Data Mining, which will be used as the basis of the CSS , or SSS, approach.

V. *SUITABLE DATA MINING APPROACHES*

The class of algorithms, or approach which we can utilize more effectively, appears to be from the statistical class of algorithms.

These are the same algorithms which were discussed for the task of web site maintainability [6]. The reasons behind the choice of algorithm for the task are discussed in the final sub-section.

The most appropriate algorithm for the conversion from sender email to CSS, SSS, from those listed above, is the k-NN algorithm, or a variant of such. The other algorithms are not appropriate because they either require too many samples with which to build an effective model from which to work effectively in this application (decision trees, Bayesian classifiers), require numerical data (Fisher's linear discriminants), or require prior knowledge of the classes (K Means).

However, k-NN can work effectively with a small number of samples, can work with categorical data given an appropriate function to compare two samples, and does not require any prior knowledge of the number of classes, or sender types.

The following sections describe the implementation of the CSS solution which has been described in this section.

VI. CSS SOLUTION

In order to implement the k-NN algorithm, or a slight variant therein, some means of finding a numeric difference between two samples of the senders emails and SSS is required. This can be achieved by determining the percentage of signature features in one sample which are not present in the other sample or samples.

A visual representation of the approach used to determine the difference between the two samples of SSS signature features, and their values, present in each sample signature, may be seen in Figure 2.

In order to achieve this each section of email needs to be represented by equivalent signature features and their values. In the same manner as presentation tags in HTML code these can be represented as signature tags. It is these adjacent signature tags which form clusters of tags and can be represented by a single SSS.

The first stage of the implementation of the k-NN type algorithm, kb-NN, is to create the signature tags from the original document and then each cluster of signature tags is converted to a SSS sample using a set of rules that are defined in a data file. This can be changed by the user as the SSS evolves, but a standard set of rules.

Each line is in the format:

Tag-name SSS-equivalent value

After each cluster is converted to an SSS the algorithm iterates through each sample and compares it to any that have already been classified. At the start of the loop, none will have been classified. Otherwise, a list of the other classified samples is created and ordered by difference to the new sample. If no sample is within a threshold distance, it is assumed that the new sample is not sufficiently similar to any previous classification, and so the user is prompted for a new classification for this sample. Otherwise, the closest k samples are taken from this list and the new sample is assigned the same classification as the majority of these k samples. An appropriate value of k can be found through trial and error during initial investigations.

For the final conversion of the classifications to a style sheet, an arbitrary sample from each classification is used to supply the definition of the style, and the name assigned to the classification is used as the name of the style. As each sample in the class should be very similar, it should not matter which sample is used for the style definition.

A slight modification was made to the kb-NN class so that it could be used to create an example document from an existing signature style. This modification was that a new sender signature is not created if no close match among the previously classified samples is found i.e. if a change in email style exists in the email. The contents of the style sheet are read in and set as the classified samples to provide the classification.

The same approach is used for finding groups of email paragraphs with the same style. The major differences in this case is that the methods used to represent each paragraph, and the differences between them – as well as the automatic naming procedure of a process which is to all intents and purposes completely unsupervised.

Each paragraph, is represented by a set of feature information, including a list of the number of times each one is used, and the distribution of the feature tags throughout the page or paragraph. The combination of this set of information gives a good overall impression of the written signature style of the sender.

The difference between two sets of information is found by the number of features, and values, that are not present in one set of information and is present in another, or those where the font is used more than twice as many times in one than in the other. The table distributions are compared using the chi-squared test. Each distribution is composed of 100 values, indicating the number of signature tags in that 100th of the section. The chi-squared value is calculated as the sum of the squares of the differences of each of these values, as given by the formula:

$$\chi^2 = \sum_{i=1}^{100} \frac{(x_i - y_i)^2}{y_i} \qquad \text{[equation 1]}$$

where

x is distribution of table tags in information1.
y is distribution of table tags in information2.

The set of this information provides an overall value for the difference between the two emails, or paragraphs.. This can then be directly compared to the value for any other emails. Again, if the email. or paragraph, being classified is not sufficiently similar to any previously classified section, a new classification, or SSS, is created for it.

The following section describes investigations which were carried out, using the new algorithm, to determine the effectiveness of the CSS methods to facilitate comparison of sender signature styles (SSS) in emails.

VII INVESTIGATIONS

In order to determine the effectiveness of the approach used, a set of metrics were defined which enabled the effectives of the solution to be determined on a wide range of emails sent.. This section describes the metrics used and the wide range of emails used.

A Measures of Effectiveness: Metrics Used

The effectiveness of the solution was determined by the ease, and effectiveness, of extraction of file information from the source email into a separate sender signature style sheet and the degree to which the content of the original emails remained unaltered once it has been produced by use of the style sheet.

The metrics of :- Number of sender signature styles produced and number of differences between the sender style features in the original email, or paragraph, in the email and that created using the SSS were also used to determine the effectiveness of the solution.

The following sections describe in detail the metrics and provides a justification for their use.

Metric 1 - A count of the sender (email) signature styles produced.

Sections of email paragraphs which are slightly different could potentially be converted to the same SSS style, because the data mining approach used allows for some fuzziness in the classification in line with a sender styles varying slightly within the paragraphs of an email. However, email paragraphs which vary greater than observed with one email should result in different SSS styles. This should be indicated by the number of styles produced. Therefore the number of styles produced is also an important measure of how easy it will be to determine commonality in sender signature style within paragraphs contained within an email.

Metric 2 – Information Differences

The key sender signature features emails created by the system, using the appropriate SSS, should identical to those contained within the original, or other, emails. This is tested by measuring the number of differences between the original and newly produced emails, assigning a score to each type of difference, and adding these scores together.

B Emails Investigated

Figure 3 provides examples of the wide range of emails which were investigated.

These emails were chosen as examples of their wide range of emails to which the new algorithms can be applied because they represent a cross section of the variation in sender styles contained with emails sent within a university school.

Sample 1 containing emails sent by an email sender who has never been known to be the subject of a complaint regarding harassment/bullying.

Sample 2 contains emails sent by a sender whose first language is not English and containing emails sent by an email sender who has never been known to be the subject of a complaint regarding harassment/bullying.

Sample 3 containing emails sent by an email sender who has been known to be the subject of a complaint regarding harassment/bullying.

This range of emails should enable the performances of the new algorithm on different styles of emails to be determined.

The following section describes the results from applying the metrics to the wide range of test emails.

VIII. Results

Simple plots are used to visualize the results. Figures 4 to 5 show the results of investigation of the two metrics.

A Count of the sender signature styles produced.

The number of sender styles produced is dependent of the written content of each email. Figure 4 shows that, on average, two styles are produced from a email known to have one sender signature style. The figure also shows that, on average, three styles are produced from an email of unknown type with the distribution of the number of styles produced being skewed towards the lower end. The new algorithm accurately determined the number of the sender email types from the emails known to be of bullying/harassing nature However, the figure shows that human determination was less accurate – especially for samples 2 those for which English was not a first language.

B Information Differences

These results shown in Figure 5 are consistent with that results of the SSS investigations in that information differences observed between the original, and key features of the, email are strongly correlated with the error in determining sender type. Thus suggesting that if the SSSs contained in the email can be determined then it is it possible to reform key features of the original email for comparison with other sender emails and with future emails by the same sender.

IX. Conclusions & Future Work

We have described a novel application of Data Mining in which a new linear discriminant algorithm, kb-NN, a variant on k-NN, , which enables an indicator of a change in virtual relationship between the sender and recipient, an hence an early indicator of possible virtual whether emails sent are of a bullying/harassment

The results presented in section VII show that the approach used facilitates accurate investigation of the nature of emails send by a specific sender and indicate whether virtual bullying/harassment may be occurring. Such results have the potential to be used in early instigation of anti harassment/bullying procedures..

Is intended that further work will be carried out investigating the three key metrics in email from other Faculties and universities. Work will also be carried out to modify the Data mining algorithm to maintain accuracy of indication of potential bullying/harassing emails across this new range of email documents.

ACKNOWLEDGEMENTS

Acknowledgement is made to Mark Carrington for his original project work in 2002 which led to development of this paper.

X. References

[1]www.bohrf.org.uk/downloads/bullyrpt.pdf, accessed 18/4/2012.

[2] www.ucu.org.uk/media/pdf/f/0/bully_harass_toolkit.pdf accessed 17/4/2012.

[3] http://www.Mind.org.uk accessed 18/4/12.

[4]www.nhs.uk/Livewell/workplacehealth/Pages/bullyingat work accessed 18/4/12.

[5] news.com.au, April 19, 2011 accessed 18/4/12.

[6] http://www.KnowDiss.com accessed 18/4/12.

[7] Cai J, Paige R and Tarjan R, More Efficient Bottom-Up Multi-Pattern Matching in Trees, Theoretical Computer Science, 106), pp.21-60,1992.

[8] Ninth International Conference on Document Analysis and Recognition (ICDAR 2007) Vol 1 Writer Identification in Handwritten Documents Curitiba, Parana, Brazil September 23-September 26ISBN: 0-7695-2822-8

[9] Information produced from Brunel University under FOI **Act.**

[10] Chaski, C. E. , 2007-07-25 "Multilingual Forensic Author Identification through N-Gram Analysis" Paper presented at the annual meeting of the The Law and Society Association, TBA, Berlin, Germany 2010-06-04 from http://www.allacademic.com/meta/p177064_index.html.

[11] Siddiqi I, Vincent N, "Writer Identification in Handwritten Documents," Document Analysis and Recognition, International Conference on, vol. 1, pp. 108-112, Ninth International Conference on Document Analysis and Recognition (ICDAR 2007) Vol 1, 2007.

[12] Kövesi B, Boucher JM, and Saoudi S, Stochastic K-means algorithm for vector quantization. Pattern Recognition Letters, 22,pp. 603-610, 2001.

[13] Wilde E, Wilde's WWW. Technical foundations of the World Wide Web. London: Springer, 1999.

[14] Ghani R, Jones R, Mladenic D, Nigam K and Slattery S, Data mining onsymbolic knowledge extracted from the web, in Proceedings of the Sixth International Conference on Knowledge Discovery and Data Mining (KDD-2000), Workshop on Text Mining.

[15]Simpson S http://www.comp.lancs.ac.ucomputing/users/ss/websitemgmt , accessed 10/2/12.

[16] Sommerville I, Software engineering 5th ed., International computer science series, Wokingham, England : Addison-Wesley, 1996.

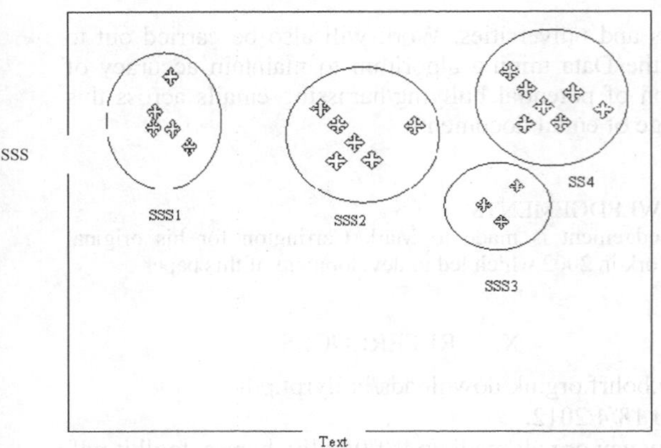

Figure 1- Clustering

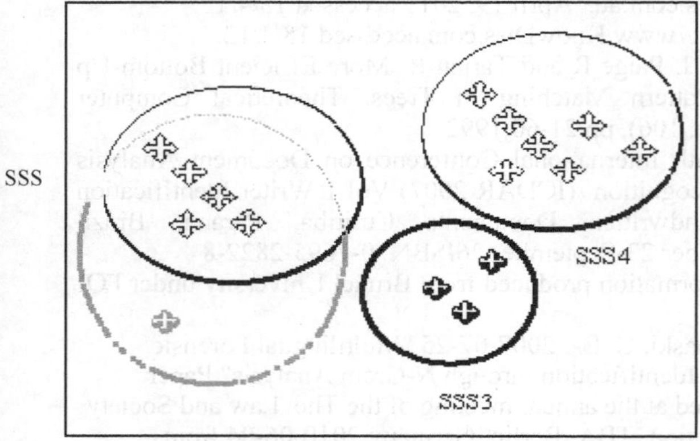

Figure 2 – kb-NN Classifying email

Sample	Staff	First Language	Number	Email Type
1	UK	English	100	Known 'Non Bullying/Harassing'
2	UK	Not English	100	Known 'Non Bullying/Harassing'
3	UK	English	100	Known ' Bullying/Harassing'

Figure 3 - Examples of email types.

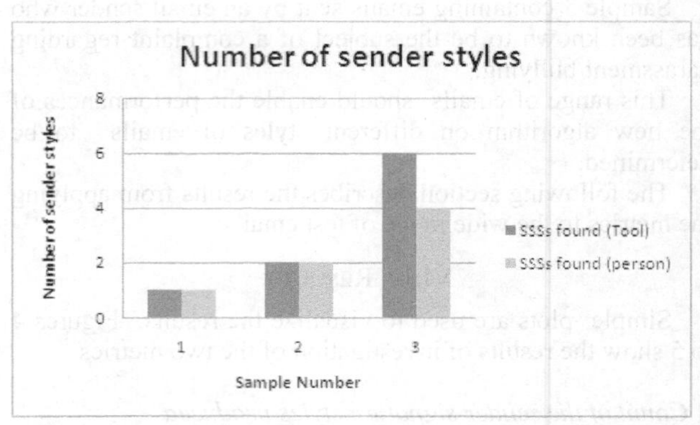

Figure 4 - A count of the sender signature styles produced.

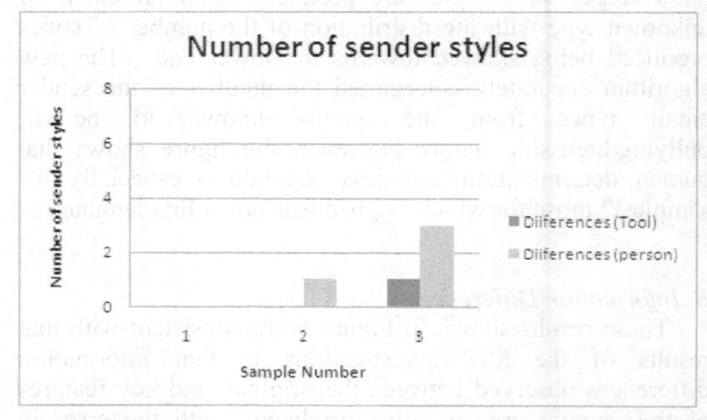

Figure 5- Information Differences between Original and Reformed Email

Using Data Mining to Analyze Donation Data for a Local Food Bank

S. Jiang, L. Davis, H. Tavares De Mleo, and J. Terry
Department of Industrial and Systems Engineering, North Carolina A&T State University, Greensboro, NC, USA

Abstract - *Food insecurity is one of the difficult situations a lot of American communities face today. Hunger, particularly experienced by children has serious impacts on the society. Fighting hunger cannot solely depend on the government assistance programs. Non-profit organizations such as Feeding America play a very important role in this effort. These organizations heavily rely on food donations. However, it is not easy to understand donation and hence presents challenges for those organizations to plan and manage their resources. In this research, data mining techniques were applied to analyze donation data from a local food bank and useful information was generated to help the food bank manage their resources.*

Keywords: Data Mining, Donation, Food Bank

1 Introduction

IT'S hard to imagine that one in six Americans struggle with food and many of them are children [1]. Everyday in America, millions of people are unable to provide proper meals for themselves, making food security or food insecurity - the availability of food and the accessibility to it [2] - a big concern. According to a recent research, in year 2011, about 17.9 million households (14.9% of US population) were food insecure, an increase of 4% from the year before [3]. Furthermore, 16.7 million children lived in food insecure household in 2011. Food insecurity problems vary among different states. According to Feeding America, a non-profit organization that fights hunger in America, seven states had statistically significant higher household food insecurity rates than the U.S. national average in 2009- 2011. The state of North Carolina with a rate of 17.1%, is one of them. In 2010, 27.6% of the North Carolina children lived in food insecurity households. Child hunger presents several problems including health, education, and workforce and job readiness problems [4]. US government has food assistance programs to help fight the hunger. The Supplemental Assistance Nutrition Program (SNAP), Women, Infants, and Children (WIC) and the Emergency Food Assistance Program (TEFAP), are the top three programs has the most participation. One in four Americans participates in at least one of the food assistance programs yearly [4]. Unfortunately, food insecurity problems are way more serious than government assistance programs alone can handle. A lot of non-profit organizations are also working hard to fight the hunger. Among them, Feeding America, formerly known as America's Second Harvest, is the nation's largest hunger-relief charity engaged in the fight to end hunger. Its mission is to feed hungry Americans through a network of associated food banks. The Feeding America organization assists local food banks in securing and distributing food, raising funds and acquiring more donors, sharing best practices amongst food banks and other agencies, as well as advocating and inspiring individuals and the government to take action in ending hunger. Over 200 food banks under the Feeding America network are serving counties across the country and are supplying food to over 37 million Americans.

North Carolina has several food banks that are a part of the Feeding America network. The North Carolina Association of Feeding America Food Banks consists of six food banks and one food shuttle organization: Food Bank of Albemarle, Food Bank of Central and Eastern North Carolina, Manna Food Bank, Second Harvest Food Bank of Metrolina, Second Harvest Food Bank of Northwest North Carolina, Second Harvest Food Bank of Southeast North Carolina, and the Inter-Faith Food Shuttle. The food banks of North Carolina communicate public awareness about hunger issues, initiate fundraising events to collect donations, as well as distribute such food donations statewide.

In 2011, the North Carolina Food Banks distributed over 121 million pounds of food to 10 million North Carolinians in need. The North Carolina Association of Feeding America Food Banks works in all 100 counties in the state and have nearly 2,700 partner agencies. These agencies include church pantries, soup kitchens, shelters for the homeless and abused, childcare facilities and programs, and senior meal programs. Practically 170,000 individuals receive assistance from one of those partner agencies every week. The utilization of food banks has been steadily increasing since the early 1980s [6]. The food bank that is the focus of this study is the Food Bank of Central and Eastern North Carolina (FBCENC) that serves the largest population in the state.

The Food Bank of Central and Eastern North Carolina (FBCENC) serves 34 of the 100 counties in North Carolina and is the largest food bank in the area. The FBCENC is comprised of six branches located in the Wilmington, Durham, Raleigh, Sandhills, Greenville, and New Bern areas. The New Bern branch was recently established within the past two years. The headquarters of the FBCENC is operated under the Raleigh branch and is located in Wake County. The FBCENC distributes over 150,000 pounds of food to 800 partner agencies. Partner agencies consist of emergency food programs such as soup kitchens, food pantries, homeless shelters, elderly nutrition programs and recognized churches. These partner agencies serve more than 500,000 individuals at risk of hunger across the 34 counties.

The donations received by the FBCENC are generated from local food drives, deliveries from partner food banks, and individual and business donations. The FBCENC also receives food and monetary donations from the government through the TEFAP and SNAP programs. In addition, the FBCENC will also purchase food to fulfill the unmet demand.

One of the challenges the FBCENC faces is to manage their resources to effectively fight the hunger. Although the FBCENC does receive food from various sources, majority of them are from donations as seen in Fig. 1.

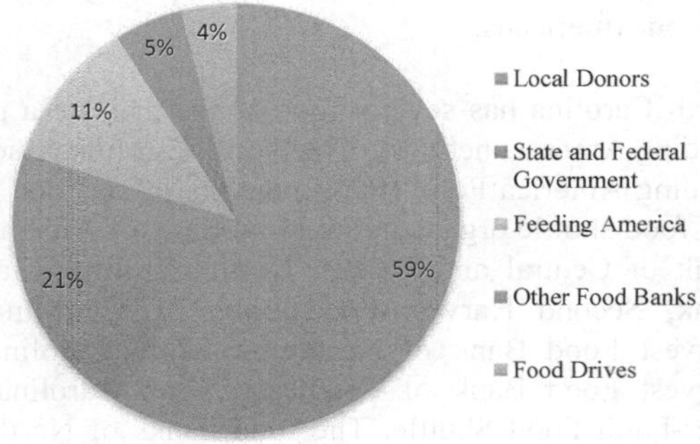

Fig. 1 FBCENC Food Sources

It is clearly from Fig. 1 that donations are very critical to the FBCENC mission. Therefore, understanding donations and detecting and discovering the trend of donation become a very important task for the FBCENC. Unfortunately, donation data are huge in volumes, and complex in nature, making them difficult to analyze. It is a typical data rich but information poor situation. Therefore, appropriate tools are needed to examine and analyze the donation data, and to discover important patterns.

Data Mining, an increasing important tool in extracting information from large amounts of data [7,8], can be applied in this situation.

This study aims to apply data mining techniques to explore the donation data and to use visualization tool present information to the food bank.

2 Method

2.1 Data collection

Historical donation data from FBCENC were retrieved. It contains 88,133 records of the food received by the Food Bank for the fiscal years of July 2006-07 to June 2010-11. To ensure only the donated records used, the data was filtered to remove the purchased records from the set. This decreased the records of food donations to 87,604. The key fields in the

TABLE 1
KEY FIELDS IN THE DATASET

Key Fields	Description
Posting Date	Date item received
Donor Name	Name or title of source
Gross Weight	Total mass of item
UNC_Product_Category_Code	Donor classification
UNC_Storage_Requirements_Code	Storage classification
FBC_Product_Type_Code	Food classification
Branch_Code	Branch
FBC_Product_Category_Code	Classification of receipt

dataset include: posting date, donor name, gross weight, Category code, storage code as seen in Table 1.

A closer look at the data revealed there are many issues that needed to be addressed before the analysis. For instance, on certain days, one donor might have a positive gross weight and on the same day the same number but negative gross weight would also appear. This would have an impact on the frequency of donation although the total gross weight remains the same. Other indications of potential data error entry can be seen as a negative weight of donation. Clearly, data needed to be preprocessed before any analysis could be done.

2.2 Data preprocessing

Screening process was conducted to examine the sample for any unusual observations, missing values, and outliers.

2.3 Exploratory data analysis

Although there have been many high powered and yet expensive data mining tools commercially available, a simple and cheap alternative us needed for this study. JMP® is such a tool [9]. Since the goal of this study was to explore the donation data and provide insights to the management of the food bank, an exploratory analysis was conducted using JMP®.

First, a frequency analysis was conducted since the food bank is interested in donation frequency. Specifically, they are interested in getting information on frequent donors, occasional donors, and one-time donors. Second, a trend analysis was done on the longitudinal data to detect any patterns that may exist.

2.4 Stochastic modeling

From the food bank's viewpoint, it would be useful if the number of new donors each month can be predicted. In this study, we applied Markov chain analysis in JMP® to solve this problem.

2.5 Cluster analysis

Cluster analysis is a widely used tool that can explore data and group observations into clusters based on certain criteria. Two types of cluster analysis are often used. The first is the hierarchical cluster analysis and the second is the k-means cluster analysis. Typically, hierarchical cluster analysis is used in the early stage of the research where exploration of data is the main concern. K-means cluster analysis, on the other hand, is an individual directed technique [7,8].

Given the large number of donors, it is useful to find a reasonable way to group them together. In this study, a cluster analysis was used. Both gross weight and frequency were selected as the criteria to get the clusters. Since we are exploring the donation data before further analysis can be done, hierarchical cluster analysis was used instead of k-means cluster analysis. Ward's minimum variance method was used for the hierarchical cluster analysis. Ward's method measures the distance between two clusters using the ANOVA sum of squares between the two clusters added up over all the variables. At each generation, the within-cluster sum of squares is minimized over all partitions obtainable by merging two clusters from the previous generation. The sums of squares are easier to interpret when they are divided by the total sum of squares to give the proportions of variance (squared semipartial correlations) [8]. JMP® was used to conduct the hierarchical cluster analysis.

3 Results

In this study, an exploratory analysis was conducted to examine the donation data for the local food bank. A stochastic model was also built to predict new donors for the food bank. Cluster analysis was done to study donors. The following provide detailed results of these analyses.

3.1 Frequency analysis

Donation data were examined to analyze the frequency. It can be seen from Fig.2 that majority of donors are occasional donors and only a few of them are frequent donors. To further investigate this, four groups were formulated as: (1) Group 1: the first 10% of the most frequent donors (145 times); (2) Group 2: between the 3rd quantile (36) and the first 10% of the most frequent donors (145); (3) Group 3: between 1 and the 3rd quantile (36) ; and (4) Group 4: One time donors (1).

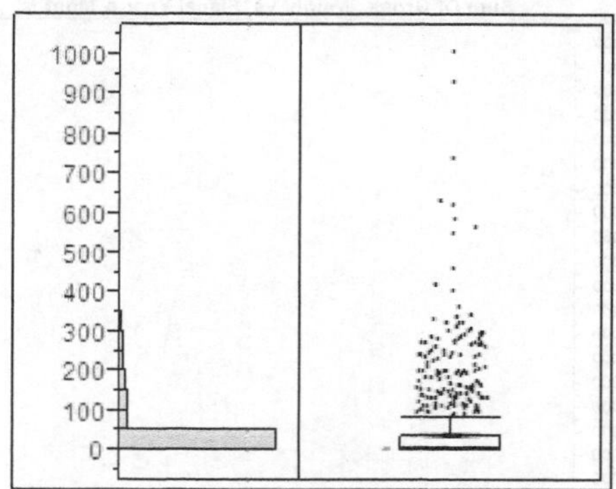

Fig. 2 Boxplot of donation frequency

Table 2 provides the descriptive statistics of the gross weight for each of the four groups. A visualization of the information as represented by a tree map can be seen in Fig. 3.

TABLE 2
DESCRIPTIVE STATISTICS OF GROSS WEIGHT BY EACH GROUP

Donor Group	Number of donors	Average	Standard Deviation	Percentage
Group 1	101	390793.41	944,09.76	20.31%
Group 2	153	677940.91	2509026.69	53.37%
Group 3	490	94471.78	154961.65	23.82%
Group 4	283	17252.60	65,832.58	2.51%

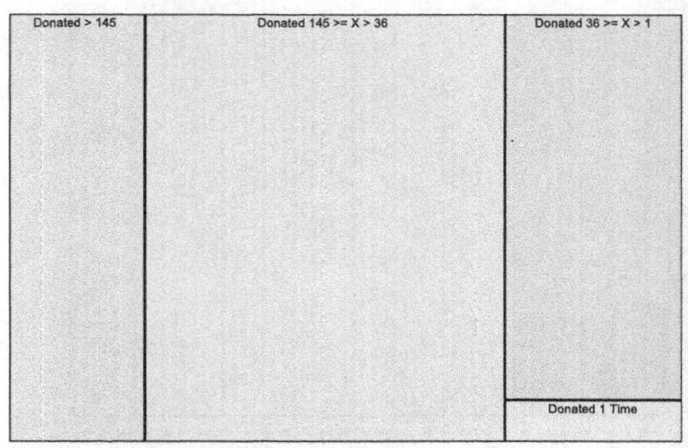

Fig. 3 Tree map of Gross_weight by each donor group

It is clear that more than half of the total gross weight came from Group 2 (between the 3rd quantile (36) and the first 10% of the most frequent donors). One-time donors (Group 4) only contributed about 2.5% of the gross weight even though there were 283 of them, ranking the second among four groups. Hence, caution needs to be taken when using frequency of donations as a measure.

3.2 Trend analysis

Given the data set spans five fiscal years, we also looked at the overall trend of amount (in terms of gross weight) of donation over the years as seen in Fig 4.

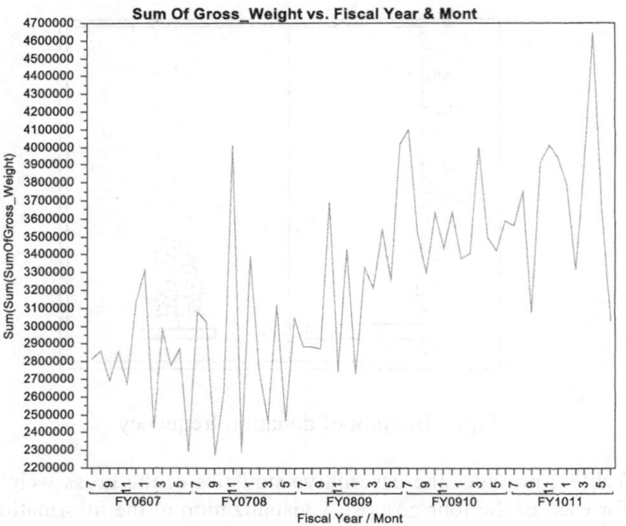

Fig. 4 Donation over the five years

Overall, there is an increasing trend in terms of amount of donation. However, large oscillation was found for data in certain years indicating more efforts need to be spent to investigate the story behind it. Another observation was made on the number of donations over the years as seen in Fig. 5.

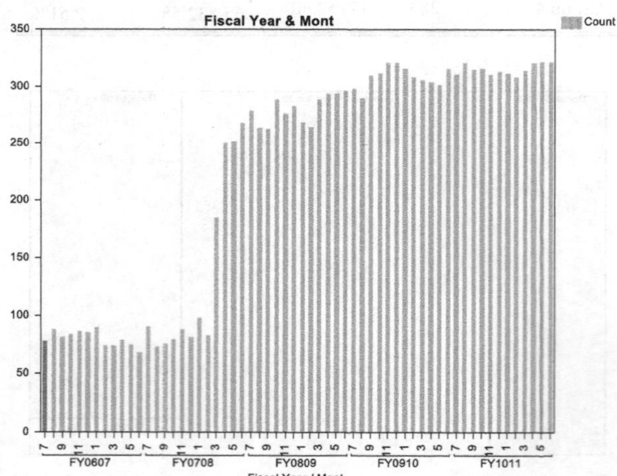

Fig. 5 Number of donations over the five years

There is an obvious jump from the first two years to the next three years in terms of the number of donations. Within the first two years, the number of donations each month is relatively the same and the same was noticed for the last three years. Further work is needed to discover the reason behind this. We also examined the total donations as measured by the gross weight. Figure 6 provides a snapshot of donation for each fiscal year. It clearly shows an upward trend which is consistent with the observation on the donation frequencies. Fig. 7 provides the monthly donation for each fiscal year.

From the graph, it seems that a similar pattern can be detected for each fiscal year since the lines seem to be parallel. This will be investigated further in the future research.

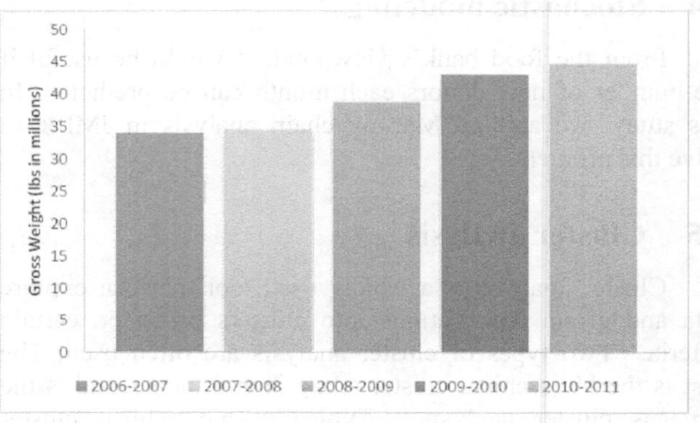

Fig. 6 Donations (Gross Weight) for each fiscal year

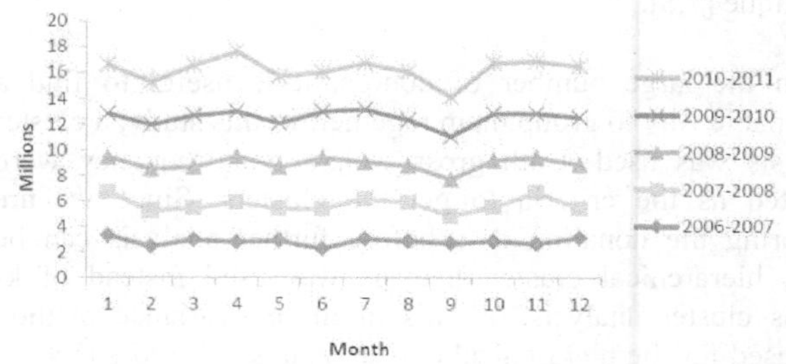

Fig. 7 Monthly Donations (Gross weight) over the five years

3.3 Stochastic modeling

Markov chain analysis was conducted to predict the number of new donors each month to help them plan and manage their resources more effectively. First, a transition matrix was developed. Since the goal is to predict the number of new donors, only one-time donor data were used. Four states were created based on the number of one-time donors in a month: State 1: no more than 2 donors; State 2: more than 2 but no more than 5 donors; State 3: more than 5 but no more than 8 donors; and State 4: more than 8 donors. Based on the data, a frequency matrix was generated as shown in Table 3. Using the frequency matrix, a transition matrix was then developed as seen in Table 4.

TABLE 3
FREQUENCY MATRIX

State	1	2	3	4
1	1	7	2	0
2	6	10	8	5
3	0	9	1	1
4	3	3	1	2

TABLE 4
TRANSITION MATRIX

State	1	2	3	4
1	0.1000	0.7000	0.2000	0.0000
2	0.2069	0.3448	0.2759	0.1724
3	0.0000	0.8182	0.0909	0.0909
4	0.3333	0.3333	0.1111	0.2222

Stationary vectors were acquired using MATLAB and results indicated that after some time (25), the system would be in a stationary state with the following probabilities:

Prob(State 1) = 0.1641;
Prob(State 2) = 0.4978;
Prob(State 3) = 0.2036;
Prob(State 4) = 0.1341.

This forecasting model will provide some insights to the food bank as they plan their resources in the future.

3.4 Cluster analysis

Hierarchical cluster analysis was conducted on the donation data to understand donors. Figure 8 shows the dendrogram based on the results. From the dendrogram, it can be seen 20 clusters can be obtained using the scree plot. Even though this is still a very large number, it is a good starting point given the complex nature of the donation data.

4 Discussion and Conclusion

Food insecurity and hunger are critical issues among the communities of the United States. Food banks such as the Food Bank of Central and Eastern North Carolina, aid the communities by providing food and other necessities to partner agencies whom then distribute to those in need. The survival of most food banks, including the FBCENC, rely heavily on receiving donations from the community. Being so, the amount of donations received fluctuates over time and can be difficult to predict. This instability increases the difficulty for a food bank to properly plan, distribute, and ration donations to the partner agencies. The purpose of this study was to apply data mining techniques to explore donation data and use visualization tools to provide meaningful information to the FBCENC.

Donation data were first preprocessed since the screening process revealed various problems with the data entry. Feedback has been given to the food bank to help improve data quality in the future. Although it is almost inevitable to have data errors given the large amount of data and human involvement in the entering process, it is still important to take some precautions to reduce those errors. With the recorded data, preprocessing them has proven to be important once again.

Exploratory data analysis was conducted to uncover data patterns. Frequency analysis revealed there exists relatively large number of one-time donors (the second largest group) and yet the total amount of donation from them only provides a small percentage of the total gross weight. We recommend the FBECNC to take this into consideration in their strategic planning.

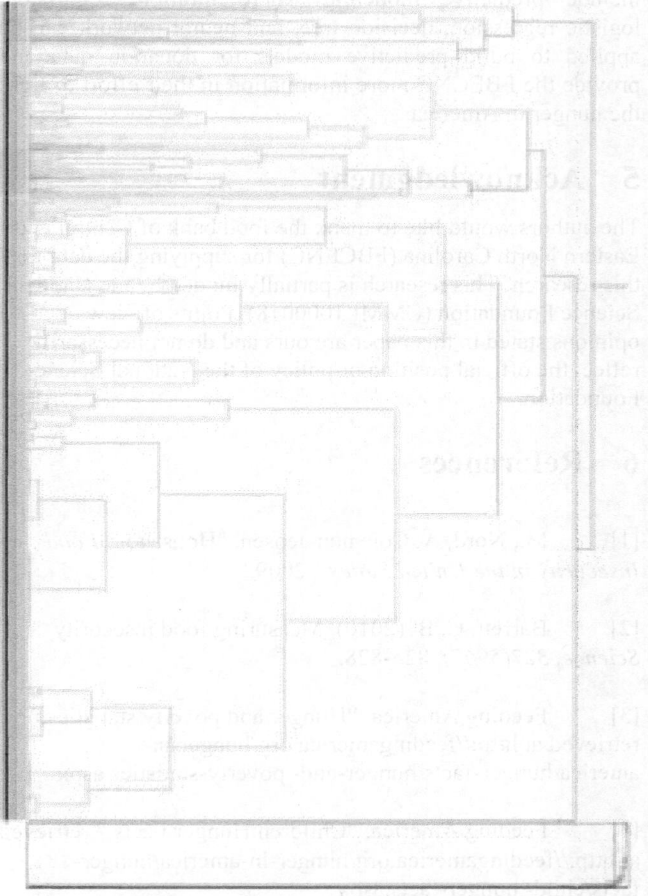

Fig. 8 Dendrogram of the cluster analysis

Trend analysis revealed an overall increasing trend in donations and yet large oscillation was observed for certain years. It is important to conduct further investigation on those data and adjust strategies accordingly. It is also interesting to notice that similar patterns were discovered from the monthly data for all five fiscal years. More research needs to be done to study those patterns since it will provide guidance for the FBCENC plan their resources in the monthly basis.

Markov chain analysis was conducted to predict number of one-time donors. Results indicated that a stationary system could be achieved over time. This will provide some insights to the FNCENC and help their strategic planning.

Finally, a hierarchical cluster analysis was conducted to understand donors. About 20 clusters were formulated based on the analysis. This number is still too large and yet did reveal useful information about donors. Further research need to consider revising selection criteria and with better understanding of donation data, a k-means cluster analysis may be needed. The goal of this study is to explore the donation data and provide initial thoughts on how these data can be used to help the FBECNC. Future research will also include predictive modeling where multiple regression, logistic regression, decision tree, and neural network can be applied to build predictive models for donation data and provide the FBECNC more information in their effort to fight the hunger in America.

5 Acknowledgment

The authors would like to thank the food bank of Central and Eastern North Carolina (FBCENC) for supplying the data for this research. This research is partially funded by the National Science Foundation (CMMI 1000018). Points of view or opinions stated in this paper are ours and do not necessarily reflect the official position or policy of the National Science Foundation.

6 References

[1] M., Nord, A. Coleman-Jensen, "Household *Food Insecurity in the United States*." 2009.

[2] Barrett, C. B. (2010). Measuring food insecurity. *Science, 327(5967),* 825-828.

[3] Feeding America. “Hunger and poverty statistics,” retrieved at http://feedingamerica.org/hunger-in-america/hunger-facts/hunger-and- poverty-statistics.aspx

[4] Feeding America. “Children Hunger Facts,” retrieved at http://feedingamerica.org/hunger-in-america/hunger-facts/child- hunger-facts.aspx

[5] Feeding America. “Hunger in America 2010 National Report”, retrieved at http://feedingamerica.issuelab.org/resource/hunger_in_america_2010_ national_report

[6] Tarasuk, V. S., and Beaton, G. H., 1999, "Household Food Insecurity and Hunger Among Families Using Food Banks," *Canadian journal of public health. Revue canadienne de sante publique,* **90,** 109-113.

[7] M. Kantardzic, “Data Mining: Concepts, Models, Methods, and Algorithms,” Wiley, 2011.

[8] J. Han, M., Kamber, J. Pei, “Data mining: concepts and techiques,” 3rd edition, Morgan Kaufman, 2011

[9] SAS Institute, “JMP 10 Modeling and Multivariate Methods,” 2012.

Flash reactivity : adaptative models in recommender systems

J. Gaillard[1], M. El-Beze[1], E. Altman[2] and E. Ethis[3]
[1] SFR Agorantic, University of Avignon, France
[2] Maestro, INRIA Sophia-Antipolis, France
[3] Norbert Elias Center, University of Avignon, France

Abstract— *Recommendation systems take advantage of products and users information in order to propose items to targeted consumers. Collaborative recommendation systems, content-based recommendation systems and a few hybrid systems have been developed. We propose a dynamic and adaptive framework to overcome the usual issues of nowadays systems. We present a method based on adaptation in time in order to provide recommendations in phase with the present instant. The system includes a dynamic adaptation to enhance the accuracy of rating predictions by applying a new similarity measure. We did several experiments on films data from Vodkaster, showing that systems incorporating dynamic adaptation improve significantly the quality of recommendations compared to static ones.*

Keywords: recommender systems, adaptive model, instantaneity, similarity measure, evaluation protocol

1. Introduction

This work has been carried out in partnership with the website Vodkaster[1], often considered as the Cinema social network in France. Users post *micro-reviews* (MR) to express their opinion on a movie and rate it. These reviews should not exceed 140 characters like on Twitter. More details on the corpus are given in section 5.

Though for the moment, we use only the users ratings, note that as future work, we intend to include the semantic level derivable from the reviews. In this perspective we will take into account for each pair movie-user both a rating and the textual argument associated to it. However, this is not the only reason we are working on the dataset provided by Vodkaster. In fact, we are interested in building a recommendation system relying on opinions expressed by a cinephilic community, exactly what Vodkaster offers.

Nowadays, classical Recommender Systems (RS) are able to suggest appropriate items to users from a large catalog of products. Those systems are individually adapted by using a profile for each user, itself made upon an analysis of past ratings. The most common techniques used in RS are Content-Based Filtering (CBF) and Collaborative Filtering (CF). Hybrid systems combine collaborative and content-based techniques, thus taking advantages from both methods.

However, whatever the technique used, one of the biggest issues remains reactivity [2]. The last decade has shown a historical change in the way we purchase and/or consume products. Nowadays, society demands having everything instantaneously. The needs have to be satisfied and change more and more quickly. This is mostly due to the growth of the Internet use and it is Internet itself that allows us to meet this legitimate expectation. It is therefore necessary to design RS adapting themselves instantaneously [5].

In this paper, we propose a new method that makes the system very fitted to dynamic behavior, reactivity and swift adaptivity. From this point of view we have to avoid the complete recalculation of models at each new incoming data or update, but only update a few relevant variables. In this way the system will be able to react promptly on the fly.

In the next section, we present the state of the art in recommendation systems and introduce our improvements. Then, we present our approach and define the methods corresponding to it. We describe the evaluation protocol and perform experiments. Finally we report our results and compare them to a baseline.

2. Related work and choice of a baseline

In this section, we present the methods used in most of classical recommender systems. [6] CF system uses logs of users, mainly user ratings on items, with dates. In these systems, the following hypothesis is made : if user a and user b rate n items similarly, they will rate other items in the same way [4]. This technique has many well-known issues such as the cold start problem, i.e when a new element (item or user) is created, it is impossible to make a recommendation, due to the absence of rating data. Other limitations of recommendation systems are the data sparsity problem, the scalability problem, overspecialization and domain-dependency.

In CBF systems it is supposed that users are independent [3]. Hence for a given user, recommendations will be made by taking into account items he previously liked. Metadata are compared to explicit or implicit user preferences. Unlike CBF, CF systems do not need a description of items to be recommended, a simple identifier number is enough.

[1] www.vodkaster.com

2.1 Similarity measures

The similarity measures between two entities (items or users) is a cornerstone of systems based on neighborhood methods and one well worth noting [11]. The Pearson (eq.1) correlation coefficient was one of the first similarity measure proposed by Resnick [1]. There exist other similarity measures such as Jaccard [12] [14], Cosine, similarity based on the Euclidian distance, etc.

Let T_i be the set of users who have rated item i, S_u the set of items rated by u, $r_{u,i}$ the rating of user u for item i and $\overline{r_x}$ the mean of x (user or item).

$$Pearson(i,j) = \frac{\sum_{u \in T_i \cap T_j}(r_{u,i} - \overline{r_i})(r_{u,j} - \overline{r_j})}{\sqrt{\sum_{u \in T_i \cap T_j}(r_{u,i} - \overline{r_i})^2 \sum_{u \in T_i \cap T_j}(r_{u,j} - \overline{r_j})^2}} \quad (1)$$

We choose the Pearson similarity measure as a baseline.

2.2 Rating prediction

Consider a given user u and a given item i. We assume the pair (u, i) is unique since generally, social networks may not allow one user to give multiple ratings for one item, and this rule is applied by Vodkaster. We define two rating prediction methods : one *user oriented* and the other *item oriented*. In the following, *Sim* will denote a similarity function.

$$rating(u,i) = \frac{\sum_{v \in T_i} Sim(u,v) \times r_{v,i}}{\sum_{v \in T_i} |Sim(u,v)|} \quad (2)$$

$$rating(i,u) = \frac{\sum_{j \in S_u} Sim(i,j) \times r_{u,j}}{\sum_{j \in S_u} |Sim(i,j)|}$$

Finally, we do a linear combination of $rating(u,i)$ and $rating(i,u)$.

$$\hat{r}_{u,i} = \beta \times rating(u,i) + (1-\beta) \times rating(i,u) \quad (3)$$

We add two components in order to balance and correct the prediction by taking into account $\overline{r_u}$ and $\overline{r_i}$. We combine these two averages ratings with two coefficients, m_i for $\overline{r_i}$ and m_u for $\overline{r_u}$., with $m_i + m_u = 1$. We call this new rating function weighted rating ($\hat{r}w$)

$$\hat{r}W_{u,i} = \gamma \hat{r}_{u,i} + (1-\gamma)(m_i\overline{r_i} + m_u\overline{r_u}) \quad (4)$$

In the case where $\hat{r}_{u,i}$ is not computable, we apply a backing off like strategy relying on $m_i\overline{r_i} + m_u\overline{r_u}$. It is possible that i (or u) has no ratings, hence $\overline{r_i}$ (or $\overline{r_u}$) does not exist. In the absence of either one of these two averages, we only rely on the other one.

3. Methods

In this section we present the methods we use and propose some of the improvements we have implemented in our system.

3.1 Distance of Manhattan

To derive a similarity measure from the distance of Manhattan, also known as the taxicab distance [13], we take the complement to one. Hence, the more ratings are close, the more the similarity tends to 1, and therefore the more the users or items are considered as alike. We normalize the results by dividing the sum by the maximum difference between two ratings ($MaxD$) times the number of elements in the intersection. In the remainder, this similarity function is used for both users and items. In the following k is either an item or user, x, y is a pair of items or users depending on the case.

$$Manhattan(x,y) = 1 - \frac{\sum_{k \in T_x \cap T_y} |r_{k,x} - r_{k,y}|}{|T_x \cap T_y| MaxD} \quad (5)$$

We add another component that takes into account the difference of the means $\overline{r_x} - \overline{r_y}$, with a coefficient F. This new component can be useful in some cases. For instance, let us look at the similarity between user a and user b. User a has a certain tendency to be very severe on items he rates. On the contrary, b is more indulgent. This difference of behaviors between a and b is somehow related to the difference of average ratings. In the end, this heterogeneity is taken into account in the similarity by a coefficient F.

$$Manhattan2(x,y) = 1 - \frac{\sum_{k \in T_x \cap T_y} |r_{k,x} - r_{k,y}| + F|\overline{r_x} - \overline{r_y}|}{(|T_x \cap T_y| + F) MaxD} \quad (6)$$

We use a coefficient proportional to the cardinality of the intersection $T_x \cap T_y$ as a confidence measure. Therefore we are giving more weight to items sharing a greater number of users. We call this similarity measure the Manhattan Weighted Corrected similarity (MWC).

$$MWC(x,y) = Manhattan2(x,y) \times \left(1 - \frac{1}{|T_x \cap T_y|^{\alpha}}\right) \quad (7)$$

3.2 Metadata

Metadata allows our system to overcome the cold start problem whenever a new item is added to the database and thus has not been yet rated. It is therefore impossible to compute the similarity with another item based on ratings of common users. The use of metadata can fix this problem, since we can now compare two items according to their metadata. In our case, we are dealing with movies. Metadata are for instance the director's name, main actors or genre. Such data can be found on IMDB[2] (Internet Movie DataBase) and can be downloaded.

[2]www.imdb.com

3.3 Dynamic adaptation with Manhattan

In this section we present the process used to attain a dynamic adaptation along time. The key idea follows the simple principle that each update or new pair (u, i) has to be taken into account instantaneously by the system. It cannot be delayed for some days since everything changes so fast. It could already be too late and thus mislead the following recommendations, especially the ones based on a small number of ratings. One log of rating can make the difference.

The similarity measure named Manhattan Weighted Corrected (eq. 7) is designed to allow us to update items-to-items and users-to-users similarities in a very efficient way. Indeed, unlike *Pearson* or *Cosine*, this method does not lead to a complete re-calculation of the pre-calculated models.

For instance, we look at the similarity between item a and item b. User $sarah$ has previously rated item a and now rates item b, that she has never rated before. $\overline{r_{sarah}}$ and $\overline{r_b}$ are updated very easily. Indeed, if we look at the details of the MWC function, we clearly see that in the numerator sum :

$$\sum_{u \in T_a \cap T_b} |r_{u,a} - r_{u,b}|$$

since $sarah$ is now belonging to $T_a \cap T_b$, we just need to add $|r_{sarah,a} - r_{sarah,b}|$ to the pre-calculated sum. We also have to increment the cardinality of the intersection by one. And we are done. With only four simple additions, we have updated the database. The same holds for items.

Taking advantage of this property, we ran the updating algorithm on the training corpus. The results are outstanding. The complexity has been reduced from $o(n^2)$ to $o(n)$ (square to linear). If we consider the whole set of updates, we reduced from $o(n^3)$ to $o(n)$.

Suppose now a new item is created and consequently has not been rated yet. It is thus impossible to predict a rating for this item, unless we take into account metadata. We define a new similarity measure based on metadata, namely Metadata Based similarity (MBS). Let M_x be the set of metadata of x (user or item). We then have the following :

$$MBS(x, y) = \frac{|M_x \cap M_y|}{|M_x \cup M_y|} \tag{8}$$

This ratio is also known as the Jaccard similarity coefficient, used to measure similarity between two sets.

In case the classical similarities cannot be calculated, MBS allows the system to make a prediction and therefore it increases the coverage. In other cases where an item has already been rated, the use of MBS enhances the prediction precision (see results).

4. Evaluation criteria

In this section we present our evaluation protocol. Since we cannot make online experiments with real users, we are not able to measure the impact of our recommendations, that should lead in the best case to an act of consumption with a good feedback (good rating). However, the key point in a recommender system is the rating prediction accuracy [10]. Hence, one could say that a recommender system could be evaluated on his ability to predict the rating of a given user u for an item i. From this perspective, we can test the system on predicting a rating for which we know the actual real rating. In other words, we compare $r_{u,i}$ and $\hat{r}_{u,i}$.

If a prediction $\hat{r}_{u,i}$ is less than a certain threshold r_{min}, we assume item i is not recommendable for user u. Therefore, any prediction below this threshold is not taken into account in the evaluation. On the contrary, when $\hat{r}_{u,i} > r_{min}$ and $r_{u,i} > r_{min}$, we consider our recommendation as successful.

Ideally we should be able to measure the quality and the performance of two functionalities expected from a recommender system. The first one is the ability to promote an item appreciated by a small number of amateurs to a maximum number of users themselves likely to appreciate it. The second one consists in recommending to an user the maximum number of items he is likely to appreciate. In this paper, we did a hybrid evaluation. We evaluate the system globally on each pair (u, i). Hence we are in between the promotion of items for users and the promotion of users for items.

4.1 Root Mean Squared Error

This measure namely *Root Mean Square Error* is often used to evaluate different methods applied in RS. It also has become popular with the Netflix Challenge [7]. Let R be the set of the predicted ratings, the RMSE is defined as follows :

$$RMSE = \sqrt{\frac{1}{|R|} \sum_{(u,i,r) \in R} (\hat{r}_{u,i} - r_{u,i})^2} \tag{9}$$

It is widely assumed that reducing the RMSE amounts to increasing the relevance and precision of the recommendations.

4.2 Mean Absolute Error

We also use the Mean Absolute Error (MAE) to evaluate how close our predictions are to the real ratings. The mean absolute error is given by :

$$MAE = \frac{1}{|R|} \sum_{(u,i,r) \in R} |\hat{r}_{u,i} - r_{u,i}| \tag{10}$$

5. Experiments

5.1 Corpus

The corpus contains over 50,000 MR. For each MR, we have : *an unique ID, the author's name, the text, the rating (0.5 up to 5), the date of the post, the film title, its country,* and its *release year*. We have split the corpus into three sub-corpuses : training, development and test. The date makes the corpus chronologically sortable. It is very important to note that in our experiments, we take into account the date since we work on dynamic adaptation. The chronological order, from old to recent is : training, development, test.

	Training	Development	Training+Development	Test
Size	57631	9999	68502	9999
Films	8680	3298	9428	3951
Users	1824	730	2080	737

	Development	Test
User unseen	2858	3274
Film unseen	2452	1895
User and Film unseen	446	375
User unseen different	244	235
Film unseen different	675	849
User and Film unseen different	442	375

Table 1: Statistics on the corpus

The second part of Table 1 shows how important the adaptation is. Indeed, the number of unseen users and unseen films is quite large (first two rows). Note that these users and films are re-appearing at least twice in the development (or test) corpus. In this case, adaptation makes even more sense. This is not the case when an unseen user or film appears only once (last 3 rows of the table). The worst case is when we have a two sided cold start, from the user's side and the film's side (user and film unseen).

5.2 Evaluating

To evaluate the system, we first create our item-users database from the training sub-corpus. (8680 items, 1824 users) Then, we go through the development sub-corpus. Each element in it is a pair user-item (u, i), containing the rating of user u on item i. In the remainder, an item (or user) that has been rated by users (resp. rated items) is considered has *seen*. Otherwise it is *unseen*. For each of the following cases, the system reacts differently.

a) u and i are seen: This is the simplest case in which we have rating data for i and u. We just use the weighted rating method (eq. 4).

b) u seen, i unseen: Item i is a new item and has not been rated yet. But u is seen. This means u has already rated at least one item. We can thus use the user oriented rating function with the metadata based similarity function. This rating function is based on similarities between i and the items already rated by u. It is hence not necessary for i to be seen (*i.e* rated).

c) u unseen, i seen: User u is new and has not rated any item yet. But i is seen. This means i has already been rated once. In that case, we use the item oriented rating function again with the metadata based similarity function. This rating function is based on similarities between u and the users that have already rated i. It is hence not necessary for u to be seen.

d) u unseen, i unseen: In this extreme case, we generally have access only to the metadata for items nor for users. It is then difficult to make a prediction.

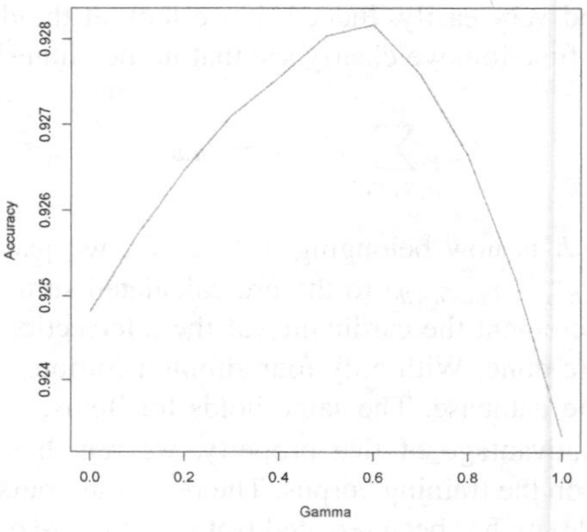

Fig. 1: Accuracy in function of γ at constant coverage (2200 predictions) on the development corpus. Optimal value is 0.6

We did several tests on the development corpus in order to determine the optimal γ. Recall that this coefficient weights the average in the weighted rating prediction formula (eq. 4). The results of these tests are shown on figure 1.

Figure 2 shows the effect of adaptation. We recall that the development corpus (and others too) is sorted chronologically, from older to newer ratings. Therefore in this graph, the closer we are to time zero, the closer we are to the training corpus, time speaking. The first observation we can make is the global tendency for accuracy to decrease as time goes by, that is as we go away from the training corpus in time. However, we also observe that the adaptation slows down this tendency and in some time ranges even reverse the trend (between 1500 and 1800).

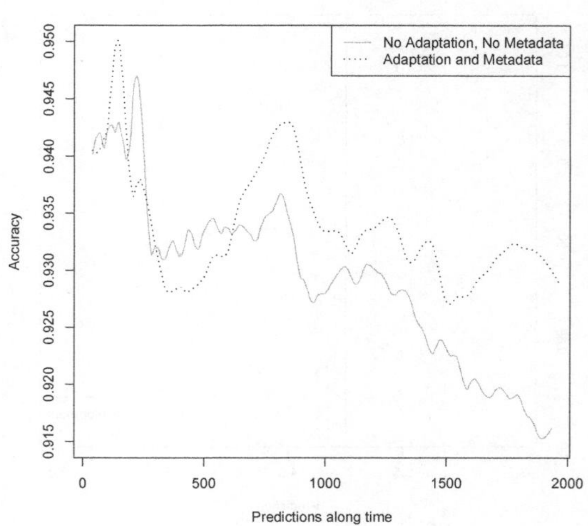

Fig. 2: Evolution in time at constant coverage (2100 predictions) with adaptation and metadata, and none of them (development corpus)

5.3 Results

To be able to compare different methods, we take a constant coverage (2200 predictions).

5.3.1 Pearson

We present here the results obtained with our baseline.

Corpus	Method	Score	RMSE	MAE
Development	No adaptation	84.36	0.93	0.73
Test	No adaptation	86.77	0.94	0.71

Table 2: Results with Pearson

We observe that the results are better on the test corpus than on the development corpus. This can be explained by the fact that the training corpus used for predicting the test is larger than the one used for predicting the development.

5.3.2 Manhattan Weighed Corrected

We present here the results with our method.

	Score	RMSE	MAE
No adaptation No metadata	91.09	0.90	0.70
Adaptation only	92.76	0.88	0.69
Metadata only	91.50	0.89	0.70
Metadata and Adaptation	92.93	0.87	0.68

Table 3: Results with MWC on the development corpus

Table III and Table IV show the effect of adaptation and metadata, together and separately. We can see that using metadata only is not as useful as expected. However, the

	Score	RMSE	MAE
No adaptation No metadata	89.6	0.98	0.75
Adaptation only	90.6	0.94	0.72
Metadata only	89.3	0.99	0.75
Metadata and Adaptation	90.7	0.94	0.73

Table 4: Results with MWC on the test corpus

adaptation combined with metadata allows a gain in accuracy greater than 1.5%.

5.4 Analysis

We present some examples of good recommendations and mistakes too.

- *The Hobbit : An Unexpected Journey* (2011, USA) recommended to user *Zarai.*

	#ratings in training	#ratings in test	Average
The Hobbit	0	7	3.76
Zarai	0	87	4.4

Predicted rating	5	Real rating	5

We are able to recommend a film that has not been rated yet to an user unseen in the training. Thanks to adaptation, this becomes possible and the prediction is a very good one.

- *Le Père Noël est une ordure* (1982, France) recommended to user *Fernand.*

	#ratings in training	#ratings in test	Average
Le Père Noël...	14	2	4.1
Fernand	0	45	4.2

Predicted rating	5	Real rating	5

We recommend this film seen 14 times in the training corpus to an user named Fernand unseen in the training corpus (does not include any movie rated by him). However, at the moment we recommend this movie, we can take into account all of his ratings found in the test so far. This example is a good proof of the interest of a short-term adaptation.

- *The Nightmare Before Christmas 3D* (2006, USA) recommended to user *Bart.*

	#ratings in training	#ratings in test	Average
The Nightmare...	2 ($r = 1, 3$)	2 ($r = 4.5, 5$)	3.4
Bart	0	31	4.68

Predicted rating	4.7	Real rating	2.5

This is the first error observed when the predictions values are sorted in decreasing order. The user has rated this movie 2.5. However, it has been well rated in the test and it's probably the main reason we have recommended it. Before the recommendation has been done, Bart's average rating was 4.68, which is very high. In this case, adaptation misleads the system.

5.4.1 Accuracy in function of coverage

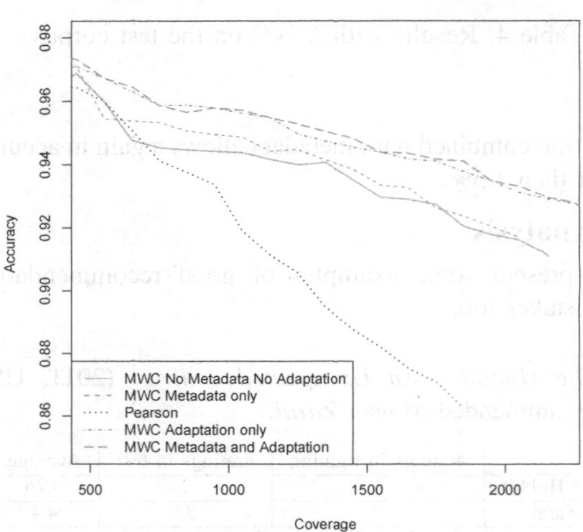

Fig. 3: Accuracy for Pearson and MWC in function of the coverage on the development corpus

Figure 3 depicts the difference of accuracy between a classical Pearson similarity measure and the Manhattan Weighted Corrected similarity at several levels of coverage. We can see that in the case of the MWC method, the accuracy stays very high (over 92.5%) even for large coverages (over 2000). On the contrary, the Pearson similarity leads to a very fast decrease in accuracy. Indeed, the accuracy is only 85.1% at a coverage of 2000, whereas the MWC gives 93.3%. Our method outperforms the baseline.

5.4.2 Robustness

As we can see in Fig. 4, the results obtained on the test and development corpus can be considered as similar since the confidence interval has been estimated to be 0.011 (i.e 1.1%).
Fig. 4 also depicts the fact that the knee of the curve, for both development and test experiments is around a prediction value of 3.75 (vertical line). Below this threshold, the accuracy level drops very quickly. However, predictions above the same threshold can be considered as trustworthy (see Table V).

	Threshold	Coverage	Accuracy	RMSE	MAE
Development	3.75	1537	94.5	0.84	0.65
Test	3.75	1455	92.4	0.92	0.69

Table 5: Accuracy at a preset confidence level

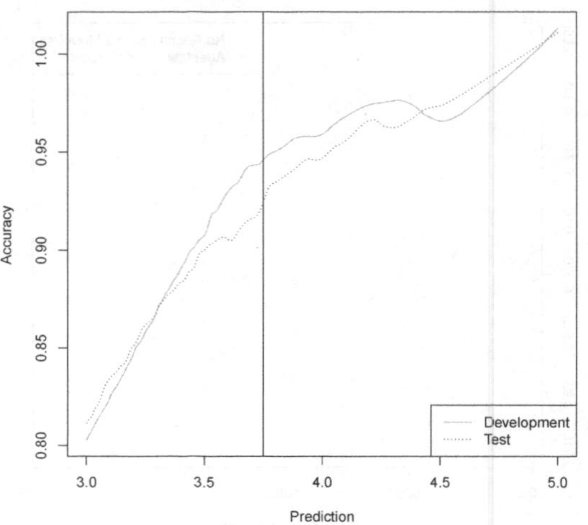

Fig. 4: Accuracy in function of the predicted ratings on development and test corpora

6. Conclusions and perspectives

In order to obtain a flash reactivity, we have proposed a new similarity measure based on the distance of Manhattan. This new measure named *Manhattan Weighted Corrected* similarity leads to a significant decrease in complexity and allows an instantaneous adaptation. Hence we are able to update the parameters of the recommender system step by step, whenever a new rating occurs. Thanks to this new method, we obtained results outperforming the one's obtained with a classical Pearson. Moreover, by applying the same algorithm during the training phase, we have dramatically reduced its complexity. We have also shown that this method allows us to perform a detailed analysis of the prediction errors (bad recommendations). This analysis could be used for future improvements of our system.
We are currently working on adding text content. The idea is to extract information about users movies taste (horror film, thriller, this actor, interested in soundtrack...) and films characteristics (good scenario, too long, great special effects...) as it is expressed in natural language in micro-reviews. Therefore, it will be possible to take into account the aesthetics tastes of users and not only their ratings.
We are also developing a new adaption method that adapts itself according to the users taste at a given moment in time. We will check whether it is worth or not to take into account the entire rating history. This is coherent with our conception of recommendation. We believe that nowadays recommender systems have to be instantaneous, giving the right recommendation at the right time, learning from their mistakes, and adapting the model not to repeat again and again the same errors.

Acknowledgment

The authors would like to thank Vodkaster for providing the data.

References

[1] P Resnick and R. Varian Hal, Recommender systems (introduction to special section). Communications of the ACM 40, 1997

[2] G. Adomavicius and A. Tuzhilin. Toward the Next Generation of Recommender Systems: A Survey of the State of the Art and Possible Extensions, IEEE Trans. Knowl. Data Eng, 17 (6), 2005, pp. 734-749.

[3] B. Mehta, T. Hofmann, and W. Nejdl. Robust collaborative filtering. In RecSys, 2007

[4] M. Deshpande and G. Karypis. Item based top-N recommendation algorithms. ACM Trans. Inf. Syst., 2004.

[5] N. Lathia. Evaluating Collaborative Filtering Over Time. PhD thesis, University College London, 2010.

[6] R. Burke, Hybrid Web Recommender Systems. The Adaptive Web, 2007, pp. 377-408

[7] R. Bell, Y. Koren and C. Volinsky. The BellKor 2008 Solution to the Netflix Prize The Netflix Prize, 2007.

[8] B.M Sarwar, Konstan J.A., Borchers, A., Herlocker, J., Miller, B., Riedl, J. Using filtering agents to improve prediction quality in the groupLens research collaborative filtering system. Proceedings of the ACM Conference on Computer Supported Cooperative Work, 1998.

[9] Schein, A.I., A. Popescul and L.H Ungar. Methods and metrics for cold-start recommendations. Proceedings of the 25th Annual International ACM SIGIR Conference on Research and Development in Information Retrieval, 2002.

[10] J. Herlocker, J.A Konstan, L. Terveen and J. Riedl. Evaluating collaborative filtering recommender systems. ACM Transactions on Information Systems (TOIS) 22 (1), 2004.

[11] C Ziegler, S.M McNee, J.A Konstan and G. Lausen. Improving recommendation lists through topic diversification Fourteenth International World Wide Web Conference, 2005.

[12] F. Meyer. Recommender systems in industrial contexts, PhD thesis, University of Grenoble, France, 2012.

[13] Eugene F. Krause. Taxicab Geometry. Dover, 1987.

[14] F. Meyer, F. Fessant. Reperio: A Generic and Flexible Industrial Recommender System, Web Intelligence and Intelligent Agent Technology (WI-IAT), 2011. pp. 502-505

Analysis of Truck Compressor Failures Based on Logged Vehicle Data

Rune Prytz, Sławomir Nowaczyk, Thorsteinn Rögnvaldsson, *Member, IEEE,* and Stefan Byttner

Abstract—**In multiple industries, including automotive one, predictive maintenance is becoming more and more important, especially since the focus shifts from product to service-based operation. It requires, among other, being able to provide customers with uptime guarantees. It is natural to investigate the use of data mining techniques, especially since the same shift of focus, as well as technological advancements in the telecommunication solutions, makes long-term data collection more widespread.**

In this paper we describe our experiences in predicting compressor faults using data that is logged on-board Volvo trucks. We discuss unique challenges that are posed by the specifics of the automotive domain. We show that predictive maintenance is possible and can result in significant cost savings, despite the relatively low amount of data available. We also discuss some of the problems we have encountered by employing out-of-the-box machine learning solutions, and identify areas where our task diverges from common assumptions underlying the majority of data mining research.

Index Terms—**Data Mining, Machine Learning, Fault Prediction, Automotive Diagnostics, Logged Vehicle Data**

I. Introduction

With modern vehicles becoming more and more sophisticated cyber-physical systems, increased software and system complexity poses new development and maintenance challenges. For commercial ground fleet operators, including bus and truck companies, the maintenance strategy is typically reactive, meaning that a fault is fixed only after it has become an issue affecting vehicle's performance.

Currently, there is a desire for truck manufacturers to offer uptime guarantees to their customers, which obviously requires a shift in the paradigm. New ways of thinking about component maintenance, scheduling and replacement need to be introduced. Statistical lifetime predictions are no longer sufficient, and workshop operations need to be planned and their results analysed at the level of individual vehicles.

At the same time, it is slowly becoming feasible to analyse large amounts of data on-board trucks and buses in a timely manner. This enables approaches based on data mining and pattern recognition techniques to augment existing, hand crafted algorithms. Such technologies, however, are not yet in the product stage, and even once they are deployed, a significant time will be required to gather enough data to obtain consistently good results.

In the meantime, it is necessary to explore existing data sources. One example of that is Volvo's "Logged Vehicle Database" (LVD), that collects statistics about usage and internal workings of every vehicle. This data is stored on-board Electronic Control Units during regular operation, and uploaded to a central system during visits in authorised workshops.

The LVD is just one database among many that are of interest for predictive maintenance purposes. Others that are being currently used in related projects include "Vehicle Data Administration" (VDA) and "Vehicle Service Records" (VSR). These databases each contain different, but complementary information: usage statistics and ambient conditions, up-to-date information regarding vehicle equipment, design and configuration specifications, as well as history of all maintenance and repair actions conducted at Volvo Authorised Workshops.

In a typical data mining study, the underlying assumption is that a lot of information is available. For example, it is common in fault prediction research to be able to continuously monitor the device in question. In this regard, the automotive domain is much more restrictive. We are only able to observe any given truck a couple of times per year, at intervals that are unknown *a priori* and difficult to predict even during operation.

In this project we have decided to focus on analysing two components: compressor and turbocharger. Due to lack of space, in this work we only present results related to the compressor, but most of our discussions are valid for both subsystems. The main motivation of predictive maintenance is the possibility to reduce the unplanned stops at the road side. They can be very costly, both for the customer and for the OEM.

If the truck is under warranty or service contract the following expenses could typically be incurred: towing, disruption of garage workflow, actual repair, rent of replacement truck and loss of OEM reputation. During a service contract all maintenance and service costs are covered by a fixed monthly fee. A secondary motivation is to minimise the amount of maintenance that is done on trucks under service contract while still guaranteeing required level of uptime towards the customer.

Additionally, certain components, such as the turbocharger or timing belt, cause significant collateral damage to the vehicle when they fail. Such components are often already either designed to last the full lifetime of the vehicle or scheduled for planned maintenance. In practice, however, this is not enough to prevent all unexpected failures. In these cases predictive maintenance would also be very effective in reducing the excess cost, even though the number of

Rune Prytz is with the Volvo Group Trucks Technology, Advanced Technology & Research Göteborg, Sweden (email: rune.prytz@volvo.com).

Sławomir Nowaczyk, Thorsteinn Rögnvaldsson and Stefan Byttner are with the Center for Applied Intelligent Systems Research, Halmstad University, Sweden (emails follow firstname.lastname@hh.se pattern).

breakdowns is low.

Obviously, predictive maintenance not only saves money, it also introduces additional expenses in terms of unnecessary repairs for the wrongly diagnosed vehicles as well as wasted component life. The latter comes from the fact that the still working component gets exchanged.

The importance of this factor varies greatly depending on particular application. In this study we disregard it completely, since both turbocharger and compressor are exchanged at most once during a vehicles lifetime.

The other cost factor, incorrectly diagnosed failures, can never be completely avoided, but is expected to be surpassed by the savings obtained from finding vehicles before they have an unexpected breakdown. This expense will be the major focus of our discussions in this work.

From classification point view, this can be directly linked to the ratio between True Positive examples and False Positive ones. As mentioned previously, the cost of one on-the-road breakdown is far greater than the cost of one unnecessary component replacement. It is also important to notice that the number of False Negatives is almost irrelevant in this application. They represent "wasted opportunity," i.e. money that could potentially be saved but was not, however they do not incur any direct expenses.

The predictive maintenance solution we are proposing in this paper is designed to be used as an aid in the garage. Whenever a truck is in the workshop for whatever reason, logged data is collected and analysed. The classification algorithm then marks the vehicle as either normal or in need of compressor replacement (within a specified prediction horizon). The workshop will then either exchange the compressor right away, perform additional diagnostics, or schedule another visit in the near future.

This paper is organised as follows. In the next section we describe in more detail the type of data we are working with, as well as present the business constraints that dictate how we state the problem and how are we trying to solve it. We follow by a discussion of related research in Section III. We present our approach in Section IV and results of experiments we have conducted in Section V. We close with conclusions in Section VI.

II. Data and constraints

A typical quality measurement in the automotive industry is the fault frequency of a component. It's percentage of components that fail within a given time: most typically, either a warranty or service contract period. However, that is not a representative measure for our case. Our data consists of a number of data readouts from each truck, spread over long time, but compressor or turbocharger gets replaced at most once.

Most of the vehicles never have a failure of the components we are interested in. Even for those that do, many of the readouts come from the time when the compressor is in good condition, and only in some cases there is a readout from the workshop visit when it is exchanged.

In order to get representative data, we need to select our examples from three scenarios: some of the data should come from trucks on which compressor never failed, some should come from readouts shortly before compressor failure, and some should come from trucks on which the compressor failed far in the future. In order to ensure that, we also consider the number of readouts that is available from each vehicle. Trucks that have too few readouts or do not contain all the data parameters we are interested in are discarded at this stage.

One of the topics of our analysis is to investigate how does the relative ratio of positive and negative examples in train and test datasets influence machine learning results. It is obvious that component failures are an exception rather than a norm. However, there are different ways of measuring the precise ratio between "faulty" and "good" cases. Nevertheless, the fault frequency in the vehicle population does not necessarily translate directly into exactly the same level of imbalance between examples.

We are not able to disclose any real fault frequency data. However, as a guidance, high fault frequency is between 5-10% while a good components may have fault frequency in the range of 0 to 3%. In this paper we will construct the dataset in such way that the baseline fault frequency is 5%. It is important to be aware, however, that there are many factors affecting this and under different circumstances, the data can look very different. Examples include truck configuration and age, usage patterns, geographical location and many more

As a simple example, we can easily imagine a predictive maintenance system being deployed and not applied to all vehicles, but only to those that service technicians consider "high risk". Similarly, while compressor is an important component to monitor, the methodology itself is fully general, and there are other parts that could be targeted. Some of them are designed to be replaced regularly, and thus could have failures that occur on almost all trucks. Therefore, in several places in this paper, we will discuss how different fault frequencies affect classification results.

The vehicles in our dataset are all Volvo trucks, from the same year model, but equipped with three different compressor types. They also vary with respect to geographical location, owner, and type of operation, for instance long-haul, delivery or construction.

We have selected 80 trucks which had compressor failures and at least 10 LVD readouts, with the right number of parameters available. In addition we have chosen 1440 trucks on which, so far at least, no compressor had failed. They all fulfil the same requirements on LVD data. We could easily obtain more "non-faulty" vehicles, but it is the ones with compressor failures that are the limiting factor.

A. Logged Vehicle Data

Logged Vehicle Data is a Volvo internal database which gathers usage and ambient statistics collected from Volvo vehicles. The data is downloaded from the truck when it is serviced at an authorised Volvo workshop, or wirelessly through a telematics gateway. The database is used for various tasks during product development, after market and even sales support.

A typical task for product development would be to support a simulation or validate an assumption with real usage statistics from the field. For instance, such questions could concern the relationship between average fuel economy and weight, altitude or engine type. During the sales process the database can provide usage statistics for already existing customers, which is helpful in configuring the right truck for a particular purpose.

This database contains data of varying types and has high number of dimensions. Typically a vehicle record contains hundreds of parameters and at most tens of readouts. The number of readouts directly depends on the availability of telematics equipment and on whether the vehicle has been regularly maintained at a Volvo workshop. For example, in our dataset the average number of readouts per vehicle is 4 per year. However, the variance is very high and many trucks have one or less readouts per.

There is also a problem with missing values, typically caused by connectivity issues or software updates. Modern on-board software versions log more parameters, which means that older readouts tend to include less data than newer ones.

Finally, the stored parameters are typically of cumulative nature. This means that the readouts are highly correlated and not *independently identically distributed*, as is usually assumed in machine learning. It could be interested to analyse, instead of the LVD data itself, the changes between subsequent readouts — but it can be complicated because there is a number of different aggregation schemes employed (for example, averages, accumulators and histograms).

B. VSR and VDA

The Volvo Service Records a database that keeps track of all maintenance and repair operations done on a particular vehicle. The database is mainly used by the workshop personnel for invoicing purposes, as well as for diagnostics, allowing to check previously carried out repairs.

A typical repair event contains date, current mileage, and a list of unique maintenance operation codes and exchanged part numbers. In addition to that there may be a text note added by the technician. For the purposes of this work, we are using VSR to find out whether and when a compressor was replaced on a given truck.

The VDA database contains vehicle specification for all vehicles produced by Volvo. It lists the included components such as gearbox model, wheel size, cab version, or engine and compressor type. All options have a unique label which makes it easy to use for classification.

III. Related Work

In a survey of Artificial Intelligence solutions being used within automotive industry, [1] discusses, among other things, both fault prognostics and after-sales service and warranty claims. An representative example of work being done in this area are [2] and [3], where authors present two data mining algorithms that extracts associative and sequential patterns from a large automotive warranty database, capturing relationships among occurrences of warranty claims over time. Employing a simple IF-THEN rules representation, the algorithm allows filtering out insignificant patterns using a number of rule strength parameters. In that work, however, no information about vehicle usage is available, and the discovered knowledge is of a statistical nature concerning relations between common faults, rather than describing concrete individual.

More recently [4] presented a survey of 150 papers related to the use of data mining in manufacturing. While their scope was broader than only diagnostics and fault prediction, including areas such as design, supply chain and customer relations, they have covered a large portion of literature related to the topic of this paper. The general conclusion is that the specifics of automotive domain make fault prediction a more challenging problem than in other domains: almost all research considers a case where continuous monitoring of devices is possible, e.g. [5] or [6].

It is more common to consider emergent solutions, where vehicles are able to communicate using telematic gateways. An early paper [7] shows a system architecture for distributed data-mining in vehicles, and discusses the challenges in automating vehicle data analysis. In [8] cross-fleet analysis, i.e. comparing properties of different vehicles, is shown to benefit root-cause analysis for pre-production diagnostics. In [9] and [10], a method called COSMO is proposed for distributed search of "interesting relations" among on-board signals in a fleet of vehicles, enabling deviation detection in specific components.

A method based on a similar concept of monitoring correlations, but for a single vehicle instead of a fleet, is shown in D'Silva [11]. In Vachkov [12], the neural gas algorithm is used to model interesting relations for diagnostic of hydraulic excavators. Contrary to our work, however, both the papers by D'Silva and Vachkov assume that the signals which contain the interesting relations are known *a priori*. In [13], a method for monitoring relations between signals in aircraft engines is presented. Relations are compared across a fleet of planes and flights. Unlike us, however, they focus on discovering relationships that are later evaluated by domain experts.

Even though not particularly recent, [14] and [15] are still excellent introductions to more general machine learning and artificial intelligence topics. In this paper we are also facing many challenges related to the imbalanced nature of diagnostics data. In order to make our initial investigations more widely accessible we have decided not to use any specialised solutions, but an overview of research on this area can be found, for example, in [16], [17] or [18].

IV. Approach

We have decided to base our initial analysis on using out-of-the-box supervised classification algorithms. From among the available attributes, 4 interesting VDA parameters and 8 LVD interesting parameters were chosen by experts within

Volvo. Those include, for example: compressor model, engine type, vehicle mileage, average compressed air usage per kilometre, etc.

At this stage of our research, we have decided to consider each data readout as a single learning example. Even though they definitely do not satisfy the basic *independent and identically distributed* assumption, this gives us flexibility in both the classifier choice and in deciding how to analyse actual faults.

When constructing the dataset we need to merge data from the three databases. First we find, in the VSR, all truck that had the compressor exchanged. To do that we use the unique maintenance code for compressor replacement. After that we find all the LVD and VDA data for the faulty vehicles, up to and until the aforementioned repair occurred. At this stage we discard some vehicles, either because they do not have sufficient number of readouts or because not all the interesting parameters selected by Volvo experts are available. After that we also select some number of "non-faulty" trucks.

For each LVD readout, we also create a new parameter denoting time to repair. It uses the timestamp of repair entry in VSR and this particular readout's date. In the case of non-faulty trucks we are assuming that they may break just after the latest readout available, so that the *time to repair* parameter can be calculated for all trucks. This parameter is later used for labelling examples as either positive or negative, based on the prediction horizon, but is of course not used for classification. This step is one of the areas where there is definitive room for improvement, since it is definitely not clear, however, when – if at all – the symptoms for the imminent failure become visible in the data.

When selecting examples for classification a prediction horizon and the desired fault rate must first be defined. The *time to repair* parameter is used to determine which readouts are considered as positive: those that fall within the prediction horizon. After that, at most two examples per vehicle are drawn to form the training and test datasets.

For the trucks marked as faulty, we select exactly one positive and one negative example, at random. Finally, we add one negative example from the remaining trucks until the desired fault frequency is archived. By selecting an equal (and small) number of positive and negative examples from each truck we avoid the problem of classifiers learning characteristics of individual vehicles rather than those of failing compressors.

The reason for choosing random readouts as examples is twofold. First of all, it is not entirely clear how to choose which data readout is the best one to use. It is important that there is sufficient distance between corresponding positive and negative example, in order for the data to be changed significantly. The further apart the two examples are, the larger the chance that symptoms of failing compressor are present in the positive example and are missing from the negative one. On the other hand, selecting dates close to the cutoff boundary would allow more precision in estimating *when* the components is likely to break.

The random approach avoids any systematic bias in either direction, but it means that actual training dataset only depends on the prediction horizon to a limited degree. It also means that we have no real control over how similar positive and negative examples actually are. It is an interesting question of how to find the appropriate cutoff point automatically, preferable on an individual basis.

In the final step, we remove 10% of the dataset, to be used as the test data, and use the rest as train data. Since we have few examples available, we use both out-of-bag evaluation on the training dataset, as well as the separate evaluation on the test data. In section V we sometimes present both evaluations, and sometimes only one of them, depending on which one is more appropriate for a particular purpose.

One of the issues with out-of-bag evaluations is that it is computationally intense. To speed up the processing, each classifier is only evaluated on a subset of the train data. The out-of-bag evaluation subset contains all the positive examples, but only a portion of negative examples. The resulting confusion matrix is then up-scaled for the *true negatives* and *false positives.*

As an evaluation of the business case for the predictive maintenance solution, we introduce measure of cost savings:

$$C_{save} = TP \cdot (C_u - C_p) - FP \cdot C_p$$

The method will be profitable if the correctly classified faulty trucks (i.e. *true positives TP*) save more money than the non-faulty trucks wrongly classified as faulty (i.e. *false positive FP* waste. Because an on-road *unplanned* breakdown costs (C_u) is much higher than the *planned* component replacement (C_p), every TP reduces costs.

A. Learning algorithms

In this work we have used the KNN, C5.0 and Random Forest learning algorithms. Each of them is evaluated in R using the Caret package as described in [19]. By default, the Caret package tunes the parameters of each classifier.

V. Experiments

In this section we present the results of early experiments we have performed. Throughout this presentation we have two main goals. First, we argue that those initial results are encouraging and promise a tangible business benefits, thus warranting further work, and hopefully inspiring others to investigate similar approaches in other applications. Second, we demonstrate difficulties we have encountered due to the type of data available and specifics of the domain.

As the first step towards familiarising the reader with our data, we present how the dataset size affects quality of classification. In Figure 1 we have plotted the classification accuracy, both using out-of-bag evaluation and a separate test set, for all three classifiers.

This figure is mainly useful to show the level of variance in classifier behaviour, since — even though it looks impressive — accuracy is not a particularly suitable measure for this

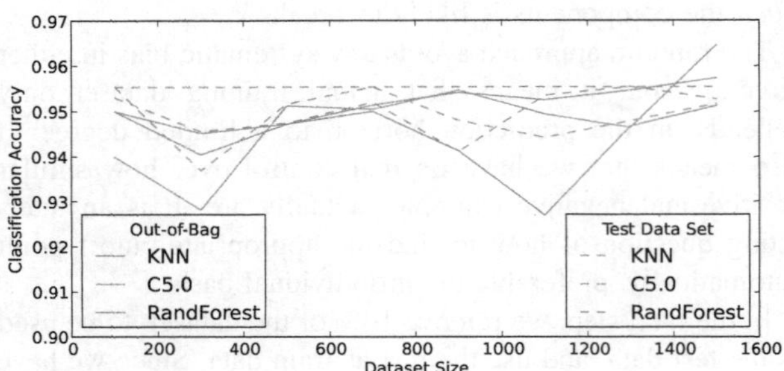

Fig. 1. Impact of dataset size on classification accuracy

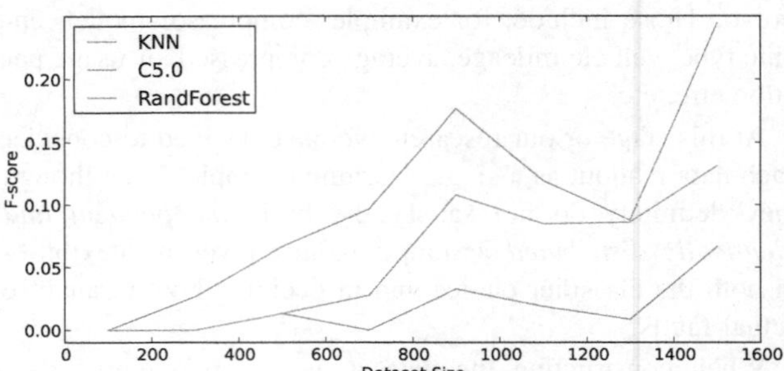

Fig. 2. Impact of dataset size on $F_{0.5}$-score

problem. As explained before, the baseline for our analysis is to assume 5% fault frequency, and this is the ratio between positive and negative examples in both training and test datasets.

Therefore, accuracy of 95% can be achieved in a very simple manner, by doing no generalisation whatsoever and simply answering "No" to every query. As can be seen from the plot, classification algorithms we are using are employing more complicated schemes, but only Random Forests consistently beats that simplest strategy, and only on the test data set — which in itself is not entirely conclusive, due to the limited size of the data we are working with.

Finally, this plot also shows that there is no significant difference in results between out-of-bag and test data evaluations. Therefore, in some of the subsequent plots we will limit ourselves to only presenting one of them, unless particular scenario makes both interesting.

In figure 2 we are presenting the F-score:

$$F = (1 + \beta^2)\frac{\text{precision} * \text{recall}}{\beta^2 * \text{precision} + \text{recall}},$$

as this is one of the most popular measures that is actually suitable for highly imbalanced data sets. In our case we have decided to use parameter $\beta = 0.5$, because in this application, precision is significantly more important than recall: every compressor that we do not flag as needing replacement simply maintains *status quo*, while every unnecessary repair costs money.

By analysing this plot it is clearly visible that the dataset we have currently access to is very small, only barely sufficient for the analysis. Even when using all the data as the training set, the F-score of the best classifier barely exceeds 0.2. On the other hand, this plot clearly shows that we have not yet reached saturation levels, and it is reasonable to assume that as more data becomes available, the quality of classification will continue to increase. This also means that most of the results presented subsequently can be expected to improve in the future.

One of the most interesting questions with regard to predictive maintenance is how early in advance can faults be detected. In order to answer that, we have performed an experiment where we were interested in evaluating the influence of prediction horizon on the classification quality.

In this case we have decided to present the results in Figure 3 for three different values of fault frequency (colours correspond to different classifiers, while line styles denote 5%, 20% or 50% class distribution). The imbalanced nature of the data is obviously a problem, but as we have discussed in section II, there is significant flexibility in how the final product will be deployed, and that allows us some freedom. Therefore, it is interesting to see prediction quality in a number of settings. That said, the performance on highly skewed data sets is still the most important one, because other solutions typically involve various kinds of cost-incurring tradeoffs. In order to not clutter the figure, we only include F-score evaluated using out-of-bag method.

In most diagnostic applications the prediction horizon is a very, if not the most, important measure. In out case, however, it is both less critical and more difficult to define precisely. The former comes from the fact that one is only expected to exchange compressor once in a lifetime of a vehicle. Therefore, the precise time of when is it done, as long as it is reasonable, does not directly influence the costs. There are, of course, some benefits of minimising wasted remaining useful life, but they are difficult to measure since they mainly relate to customer satisfaction.

The difficulty in defining the prediction horizon, however, is definitely something we are interested in investigating further. One idea would be to take into account individual usage

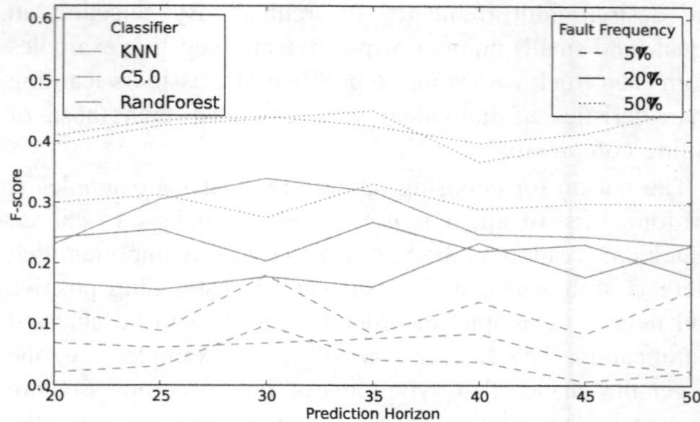

Fig. 3. $F_{0.5}$-score as a function of prediction horizon, for three different levels of fault frequency in vehicle population

patterns of trucks, for example by assuming that vehicles that are rarely in the workshop should have longer advance notice, while those that are maintained more regularly can wait until the failure is more imminent.

At the moment, however, we are treating all data readouts as individual and independent examples, and therefore each of them has to be marked as either positive or negative one. We use a very simple scheme of assuming that all examples closer to the failure than the prediction horizon are positive, and all examples further away are negative. This, however, makes analysing influence of prediction horizon on the classification quality more difficult, especially taking into account the irregular intervals at which we obtain vehicle data.

Moreover, during our first attempts of analysing the data (which we are not presenting here due to space constraints), we have encountered a situation that all machine learning algorithms learned to almost exclusively consider characteristics of particular trucks, instead of indicators of failing compressor. They would provide, for most of the vehicles, predictions that never changed over time. This resulted in classifiers that achieved good accuracy and F-score, but were completely useless from business point of view.

To this end we have decided to use exactly two data readouts from each vehicle on which we have observed compressor replacement: one positive and one negative example. This solves the aforementioned problem, since now there is no benefit to distinguishing individual, but it even further reduces the size of available data. In addition, it is not entirely clear how to choose which data readout to use, if we can only use one of them.

On the one hand, one would want to use readouts as close to the prediction horizon boundary as possible, to be highly precise in predicting wasted life of the components. On the other hand, it is not good to choose positive and negative examples that are too close in time, since it is very likely that the difference in logged data between those two points does not contain any new information about state of the compressor.

To this end, we have decided to choose one example from each side of the prediction horizon boundary at random. It means, however, that varying the prediction horizon only introduces small changes in the actual training and test datasets. It may even happen that for two significantly different values of the horizon, we end up with the same data. This explains the results that can be seen in Figure 3: prediction horizon has very little influence on the F-score.

Accuracy and F-score are important measures from research point of view. The inspiration for our work, however, arises from practical needs of automotive industry, and the major measure from the business perspective is clearly cost reduction. It is very expensive to have components fail during transport missions, because not only does it introduce disruptions in the workshop operations, it also incurs other costs, like towing, collateral damage, and customer dissatisfaction. Therefore, it is cheaper to replace components during

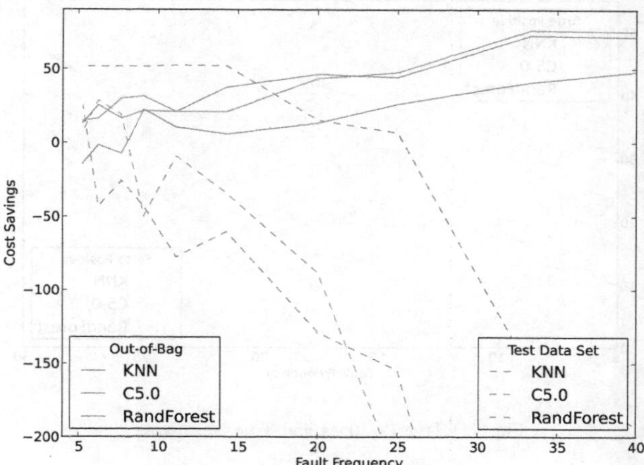

Fig. 4. Maintenance cost savings that can be achieved for varying fault frequency in training dataset (test set always has 5% of positive examples).

scheduled maintenance. The exact degree to which this is the case varies, of course, from component to component, and depends on which factors are taken into account: reputation, for example, is notoriously difficult to appraise.

Therefore, in order to be on the safe side, we have decided to use a factor of 2.5 to measure cost savings that can be provided by our solution. In other words, it costs on average two and a half as much to repair a truck in which compressor failed on the road, as it would cost to replace this component as a scheduled operation.

Figure 4 shows how the benefits of introducing our predictive maintenance solution depend on the fault rate in the vehicle population. The most interesting is, of course, the left side of the plot, because it shows that even the low quality classification results that we are able to obtain from our 1600 data samples are enough to offer tangible benefits. Both Random Forest and C5.0 classifiers are accurate enough to save expenses.

It is interesting to see how cost savings (at least looking at out-of-bag data) grow as the imbalance in the data decreases. This is consistent with results from Figure 2 and can be easily explained by the higher quality of classification.

On the other hand, the cost when measured on the test set drops very rapidly (except for the Random Forest classifier, the result which we are not able to explain just yet). The reason for this behaviour is that the test data always contains 95%–5% split of negative and positive examples. As the distribution of data in the training set become more and more different from the distribution in test set, the quality of classification drops.

Finally, in Figure 5 we present the relation between True Positives and False Positives, again as a function of fault frequency. We are only using out-of-bag evaluation here. This is the plot that actually contains the most information, since those are the two factors that directly affect the economical viability of our solution. As mentioned earlier, presence of False Negatives does not affect the cost in any direct way.

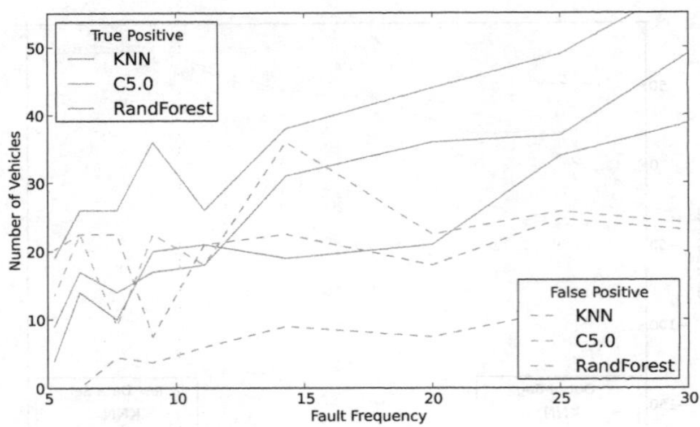

Fig. 5. True Positives and True Negatives

It is interesting to look at the differences between the three classifiers, and the potential tradeoffs that may be important from business perspective.

It is clear that KNN is not well-suited for this particular problem, although it can possibly be explained by the fact that we have not performed any data normalisation, and the large differences in absolute values of various parameters may be difficult for it to handle. Even for more balanced data sets, this classifier is struggling to obtain more True Positives than False Positives.

From the pure cost perspective, Random Forest seems to be better than C5.0, because the difference between True Positives and True Negatives is larger. On the other hand, C5.0 actually detects more faulty compressors, in simply makes more FP mistakes as well. In Figure 4 those two classifiers score very close, but if we would assume another relative costs for planned and unplanned component replacements, the difference between them could be significant. It would be interesting to investigate what is the reason for this difference, and possibly to identify parameters that would allow us to control this tradeoff.

VI. Conclusions and Future Work

The most important conclusion of this work is that using data mining based on Logged Vehicle Data as predictive maintenance solution in automotive industry is a viable approach. We will continue the work in this area, investigating more complex machine learning approaches. Current classification quality and cost avoidance is not great, but it is expected to increase as we get access to more data and as we replace generic algorithms with more specialised ones.

It is known that data availability will dramatically increase as the new Volvo truck reaches the customers. It is equipped with new and enhanced telematics platform, enabling larger and more frequent LVD readouts.

The second contribution of this paper is identifying a number of distinctive features of automotive industry, and discussion regarding to what degree do they fit typical machine learning and data mining research paradigms.

Ideas for future work include extending this analysis to other components, especially the ones where "exchange once in a lifetime" assumption does not hold, as well as evaluating known methods of dealing with imbalanced data sets.

It is also necessary to define the notion of prediction horizon in a better way, preferably allowing learning algorithm to choose the threshold in an individualised manner. Another approach to investigate is to use regression to predict *time to repair*. One possible solution would be to look at the differences between readouts, as this may decrease the correlation between examples and enhance classification performance.

Acknowledgement

Parts of this work have been supported by Halmstad University, Volvo GIB-T, VINNOVA (the Swedish Governmental Agency for Innovation Systems) and The Knowledge Foundation (KK-stiftelsen).

References

[1] O. Gusikhin, N. Rychtyckyj, and D. Filev, "Intelligent systems in the automotive industry: applications and trends," *Knowledge and Information Systems*, vol. 12, pp. 147–168, 2007.

[2] J. Buddhakulsomsiri, Y. Siradeghyan, A. Zakarian, and X. Li, "Association rule-generation algorithm for mining automotive warranty data," *International Journal of Production Research*, vol. 44, no. 14, pp. 2749–2770, 2006.

[3] J. Buddhakulsomsiri and A. Zakarian, "Sequential pattern mining algorithm for automotive warranty data," *Computers & Industrial Engineering*, vol. 57, no. 1, pp. 137 – 147, 2009.

[4] A. Choudhary, J. Harding, and M. Tiwari, "Data mining in manufacturing: a review based on the kind of knowledge," *Journal of Intelligent Manufacturing*, vol. 20, pp. 501–521, 2009.

[5] A. Kusiak and A. Verma, "Analyzing bearing faults in wind turbines: A data-mining approach," *Renewable Energy*, vol. 48, 2012.

[6] A. Alzghoul, M. Löfstrand, and B. Backe, "Data stream forecasting for system fault prediction," *Computers & Industrial Engineering*, vol. 62, no. 4, pp. 972–978, May 2012.

[7] H. Kargupta *et al.*, "VEDAS: A mobile and distributed data stream mining system for real-time vehicle monitoring," in *Int. SIAM Data Mining Conference*, 2003.

[8] Y. Zhang, G. Gantt *et al.*, "Connected vehicle diagnostics and prognostics, concept, and initial practice," *IEEE Transactions on Reliability*, vol. 58, no. 2, 2009.

[9] S. Byttner, T. Rögnvaldsson, and M. Svensson, "Consensus self-organized models for fault detection (COSMO)," *Engineering Applications of Artificial Intelligence*, vol. 24, no. 5, pp. 833–839, 2011.

[10] R. Prytz, S. Nowaczyk, and S. Byttner, "Towards relation discovery for diagnostics," in *Proceedings of the First International Workshop on Data Mining for Service and Maintenance*. ACM, 2011, pp. 23–27.

[11] S. D'Silva, "Diagnostics based on the statistical correlation of sensors," Society of Automotive Engineers (SAE), Tech. Rep., 2008.

[12] G. Vachkov, "Intelligent data analysis for performance evaluation and fault diagnosis in complex systems," in *IEEE International Conference on Fuzzy Systems*, July 2006, pp. 6322–6329.

[13] J. Lacaille and E. Come, "Visual mining and statistics for turbofan engine fleet," in *IEEE Aerospace Conf.*, 2011.

[14] T. M. Mitchell, *Machine Learning*. McGraw-Hill, 1997.

[15] S. Russell and P. Norvig, *Artificial Intelligence: A Modern Approach*, 2nd ed. Prentice Hall Series in AI, 2003.

[16] G. M. Weiss, "Mining with rarity: a unifying framework," *SIGKDD Explor. Newsl.*, vol. 6, no. 1, pp. 7–19, Jun. 2004. [Online]. Available: http://doi.acm.org/10.1145/1007730.1007734

[17] K. Napierala and J. Stefanowski, "Bracid: a comprehensive approach to learning rules from imbalanced data," *Journal of Intelligent Information Systems*, vol. 39, no. 2, pp. 335–373, 2012.

[18] J. Stefanowski, "Overlapping, rare examples and class decomposition in learning classifiers from imbalanced data," in *Emerging Paradigms in Machine Learning*, vol. 13. Springer, 2013, pp. 277–306.

[19] M. Kuhn, "Building predictive models in R using the `caret` package," *Journal of Statistical Software*, vol. 28, no. 5, pp. 1–26, 2008.

Proposed Business Intelligence Models for Medical Risk Assessment Case study of Venous Thrombosis Disease in Egypt

Dr. Edward Wadid[1], Dr. Nevine Makram Labib[2] and Prof. Sayed Abdel Wahab[1]

[1]Department of Computer and Information Systems
Faculty of Management Sciences,
Sadat Academy for Management Sciences
Cairo, Egypt
edwardwadid@gmail.com

[2]Department of Business Administration
Faculty of Business Administration, Economics and Political Science
The British University in Egypt, Egypt
nevmakram@gmail.com

Abstract— Risk assessment tools have been widely used in various fields such as Information Technology, Environmental studies as well as Healthcare. This paper explores the use of Business Intelligence tools in the healthcare industry in developing countries. In doing so, three different models using SQL Server 2008 Business Intelligence Tool were explored. These models are Naïve Bayes, Decision Trees and Neural Networks. Hence, a prototype Intelligent Risk Assessment Model, DVTRAM (Deep Vein Thrombosis Risk Assessment Model) is proposed. It applies different data mining techniques in order to uncover hidden patterns that may lead to medical complications such as Pulmonary Embolism (PE). Results showed that all of the three models were able to extract patterns in response to the predictable state. As for the performance of the models, they varied depending on the class value. In the future, the outcomes may constitute a good background for the development of a Medical Expert System in the domain of Internal Medicine.

Keywords- Business Intelligence (BI), Risk Assessment, , Data Mining (DM), Naïve Bayes, , Neural Networks, DVT, VTE

1. Introduction

Medical risk assessment has become a part of the daily activities of primary care physicians. It involves the identification of the risk factors, personal characteristics and test findings, which are associated with the increased incidence of a given disease, and the evaluation of the potential risk factors that may result out of it. The level of risk can be described either qualitatively (i.e. by classifying risk into categories as 'high', 'medium', or 'low') or quantitatively (with a numerical estimate).

The traditional risk assessment, using data analysis, has become insufficient, and methods for efficient computer-based analysis became essential. Examples of these methods are the Intelligent Data Analysis (IDA), Data Mining (DM) and Machine Learning.

As for Business intelligence (BI), it may be defined as "a set of mathematical models and analysis methodologies that systematically exploit the available data to retrieve information and knowledge useful in supporting complex decision-making processes"[1]. The BI tools are a type of application software designed to report, analyze and present the data previously stored in a data warehouse or data mart.

A BI system provides decision makers with information and knowledge extracted from data, through the application of mathematical models and algorithms. The rational approach typical of a BI analysis may be summarized in the following main characteristics. First, the objectives of the analysis are identified and the performance indicators that will be used to evaluate alternative options are defined. Then Mathematical models are developed by exploiting the relationships among system control variables, parameters and evaluation metrics and finally, what-if analyses are carried out to evaluate the effects on the performance determined by variations in the control variables and changes in the parameters. Some of the BI techniques are Data Mining (DM) that makes use of numerous methods for automatically searching large amounts of data for patterns and other interesting relations and Data Warehouses that use logical collections of information with structures that favor efficient data analysis (such as OLAP and Decision Support Systems (DSS) [2].

This research discusses the development of a risk assessment system using both Data Mining and Business Intelligence to support the specialists in defining the risk level of a certain disease. It investigates the potential of these data to predict the risk of a Venous Thrombosis (VTE) outcome for patients since an accurate risk prediction system may give clinicians an early indication of danger, thereby allowing enough time for medical

intervention or closer monitoring of the patient. While the medical aspect of this research is important, the central aim of this research is to present a practical approach and to investigate the exploitation of frequent patterns as an underlying technique for risk assessment purpose.
Hence, the goals of the research are to predict the risk level of DVT and to identify the significant influences and relationships in the medical inputs associated with the predictable state DVT.

2. Literature Review

As stated in one of the recent survey papers that dealt with the use of Data mining techniques in healthcare, for both the diagnosis and prognosis purposes, the following algorithms were found out to be of high performance: Decision Trees, Support Vector Machine, Artificial neural networks , Naïve Bayes and Fuzzy Rules. Analyses showed that it is very difficult to consider a single data mining algorithm as the most suitable for the diagnosis and/or prognosis of diseases since the performance of the algorithms depends mainly on the case as some of the cases require a combination of different algorithms in order to provide effective results [3].
Regarding the Deep Venous Thrombosis (DVT) disease, which is the main concern of this paper, a study made use of a genetic algorithm to construct decision trees model so as to predict the presence of the disease. It was found out that although the Decision trees are simple and practical as prediction models, they can be complex and incomprehensible [4].
Another study dealt with the task of predicting which patients are most at risk for post-hospitalization VTE, given a set of cases and controls. For this purpose, machine-learning methods were used to induce models for the prediction. Several risk factors for VTE that were not previously recognized were identified and the study showed that machine-learning methods were able to induce models that identify high-risk patients with accuracy that exceeds previously developed scoring models for VTE [5].
A third study investigated the DVT risk in patients with relapsed chronic lymphocytic leukemia treated with lenalidomide. It was found out that these data linked lenalidomide associated with DVTs with TNFα upregulation and endothelial cell dysfunction and suggested that aspirin may have a role for DVT prophylaxis in these patients [6].
A research reported an evaluation of a computerized tool to identify patients at high risk for VTE that found a sensitivity of 98% and positive predictive value of 99%. It also mentioned another computer program that was used to detect VTE and had a sensitivity of 92%, specificity of 99% and a positive predictive value of 97% to identify DVT and a sensitivity of 100%, specificity of 98% and positive predictive value of 89% to identify PE. It showed that these tools were found to provide a dependable method to identify patients at high risk for and with VTE [7].

3. Medical Problem of the Case Study

A deep-vein thrombus (blood clot) is an intravascular deposit that is composed of fibrin and red blood cells with a variable platelet and leukocyte component. Deep-vein thrombosis occurs when a thrombus forms (usually in regions of slow or disturbed blood flow) in one of the large veins, usually in the lower limbs, leading to either partially or completely blocked circulation.

A clot blocks blood circulation through these veins, which carry blood from the lower body back to the heart. The condition may result in health complications, such as fatal Pulmonary Embolism (PE) that can occur when a fragment of a blood clot breaks loose from the wall of the vein and migrates to the lungs, where it blocks a pulmonary artery or one of its branches. When that clot is large enough to completely block one or more vessels that supply the lungs with blood, it can result in sudden death. Deep Vein Thrombosis and PE are collectively known as Venous Thromboembolism (VTE). Since DVT has a high mortality rate, predicting it early is important [8].

4. Model Development Methodology

The proposed model, DVTRAM (Deep Venous Thrombosis Risk Assessment Model), uses the Cross-Industry Standard Process for Data Mining (CRISP-DM) methodology and the Data Mining Extensions (DMX), a SQL-style query language for data mining, for building and accessing contents of the models [9].

4.1. CRISP-DM Methodology

According to the CRISP DM Methodology, the DM process consists of three stages:

1. *Initial exploration:* that starts with the data preparation.
2. *Model building or pattern identification:* that involves considering various prediction models and choosing the best one based on their predictive performance.
3. *Deployment:* that involves using the model selected in the previous stage and applying it to new data in order to generate predictions and estimations of the expected outcomes.

4.2. Data Collection Methods

Two types of data collection methods were used. They are the following:

1. Literature review was conducted for the state of knowledge of risk factors of VTE.
2. Questionnaire: Based upon the evidence presented in the literature review and the experts' opinions, a

questionnaire was developed for medical specialists to collect their opinions concerning the estimation of risk levels for each risk factor. Another questionnaire was developed to collect patients' data, including risk factors, based upon the previous questionnaire and the experts' opinion. These data were the inputs of the mining models of the research.

Many problems have been faced, while trying to collect the needed data, such as the availability of medical data; as they were only available in a paper format since there were no medical records comprising such data.

The data were extracted from surveys taken from 6 Hospitals across Egypt and medical cases from some specialists of Hematology diseases. All data collected from hospitals conform to the patients' data privacy and security regulations. These data are considered de-identified. Identifiable means the data that is explicitly linked to a particular individual along with the data that include health information with data items that could reasonably be expected to allow individual identification. Hence, 600 patient cases have been collected in paper format then converted into digital format.

As for loading these data, Microsoft Excel Spreadsheets were used to enter data in a flat file as an initial phase then it was converted into a database using MS SQL 2008.

The database was then explored to be better acquainted before using these data in the core DM process. This exploration was done using simple SQL queries that consist of statistical analysis and aggregations, and graphical visualization.

4.3. Data Preparation Phase

This step was concerned about deciding which data will be used as input for DM methods in the subsequent step. Preparing data for the mining process consisted mainly of combining all of the relevant data in one table, or dataset, so that it acts as the source for the learning algorithms, and also dividing it properly between training and test sets. The training dataset was used to build several DM after being pre-analyzed so as to see how the attributes were represented in terms of their values in order to determine the initial input set of attributes.

5. Description Of Data

The database comprises the medical records of 408 patients (after being preprocessed) extracted from 6 hospitals. Each patient record includes a patient ID and a list of up to ten risk factors.

5.1. Initial Feature Selection

The analytical dataset is comprised of several attributes. However, some of them did not carry any relevant information from the analysis perspective. For instance, the attribute 'Long distance travel' for patient is missing as no data were available for this factor. In all of the cases there were no available data about genetic risk factors and other female risk factors such as pregnancy or hormone replacement therapy.

Table 1 reviews the attributes that have been selected for the analysis and those that have been rejected.

TABLE 1 Initial feature selection

Attribute	Accepted	Reason for Rejection
Gender	yes	
Age	yes	
BMI	yes	
Smoking	yes	
Immobility	yes	
Alcohol	No	No available data for such Attribute
Long distance travel	No	No available data for such Attribute
Medical illness	yes	
Minor Surgery	yes	
Major Surgery	Yes	
Family History	Yes	
Previous History	Yes	
Pregnancy	No	No available data for such Attribute
Oral contraceptives	No	No available data for such Attribute
Hormone replacement therapy	No	No available data for such Attribute

5.2. System Overview

Before explaining the individual components, a high-level preview of the entire DVTRAM framework is provided in Figure 1. Since the objective of the research was to develop a system that can help in estimating the risk levels of DVT, the following system components were used. They are illustrated in figure 2.

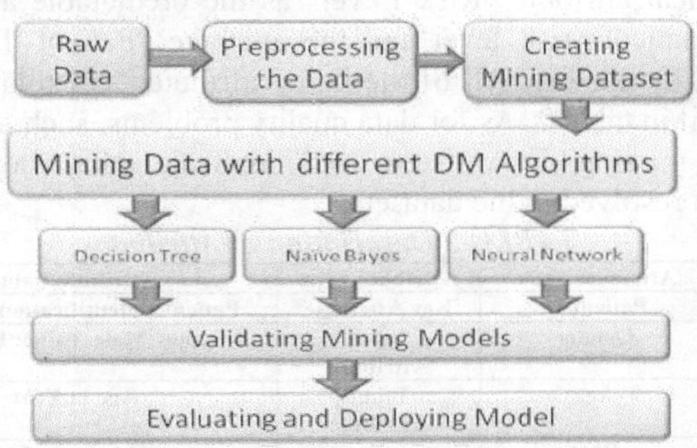

Figure 1 System Architecture

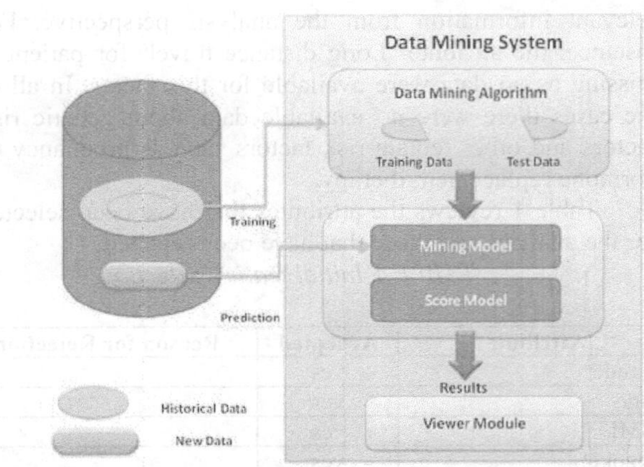

Figure 2 Components of Data Mining System

6. Mining Models with MS-SQL Business Intelligence

Microsoft SQL business intelligence tool has been selected for developing the different mining models for the proposed system.

6.1. Data Reception Phase (Analysis Module)

The records were split equally into two datasets: training dataset (204 records) and testing dataset (204 records). Records for each set were selected randomly to avoid bias. In this research, classification-modeling technique has been used as mining technique. The prediction model made use of three Data Mining model, Naïve Bayes, Decision Trees and Neural Networks. Naïve Bayes algorithm supports only categorical (discrete) attributes while Decision Trees and Neural network algorithms both support categorical and continuous attributes. To ensure consistency, categorical attributes have been used for all three models. We have identified the medical attribute "Risk Level" as the predictable attribute for patients risk level and the attribute "Patient-ID" was used as the key. All of the input attributes as explained in detail in table 2. As for data quality problems, such as noise and missing, inconsistent and duplicate data, they have been resolved in the datasets.

TABLE 2 Description of Attributes

S	Attribute name	Attribute Type	Attribute Value
1	Patient-Id	Key Attribute	Patient's identification number
2	Gender	Input Attribute	(value Male; value: Female)
3	Age	Input Attribute	Age in Year
4	BMI	Input Attribute	BIM in numbers
5	Smoking	Input Attribute	(value: Yes; value No)
6	Immobility	Input Attribute	
7	Hypertension	Input Attribute	(value Yes; value No)
8	Medical Illness	Input Attribute	Name of the medical illness
9	Minor surgery	Input Attribute	Name of the minor surgery
10	Major surgery	Input Attribute	Name of the major surgery
11	Family History	Input Attribute	(value Yes; value No, value don't know)
12	Previous History	Input Attribute	(value Yes; value 2 No)
13	Overall Risk	Predictable Attribute	Very low, Low, Moderate, High, Very High

The trained model was evaluated against the testing dataset for their accuracy and effectiveness before they were deployed in DVTRAM.

The two methods used for evaluating the mining models were the Classification Matrix, which is a matrix for each model that specifies the Input Selection; it can quickly see how often the model predicted accurately, and the Lift Chart which compares the accuracy of the predictions of each model, and can be configured to show accuracy for predictions in general, or for predictions of specific value. Following is the evaluation of each model.

6.2. Naives Bayes Model

The Microsoft Naive Bayes does not introduce any specific constraints other than for the numbers of attributes. These numbers are limited with the use of the model's parameters. Also the method requires the input attributes to be discrete. The model of the Naive Bayes was built with the default setting of the parameters. The exception is the "Minimum Dependency Probability = 0.005". Tests have shown that the outcome of the method was affected by the modification of the parameters, because they mostly concern the number of attributes and their states. Results are summarized in table 3.

Table 3 Classification Matrix by Percentages for Naive Bayes model

	High (Actual)	Low (Actual)	Moderate (Actual)	Very High(Actual)	Very Low (Actual)
High	73.97 %	0.00 %	20.55 %	41.03 %	0.00 %
Low	0.00 %	81.82 %	1.37 %	0.00 %	0.00 %
Moderate	10.96 %	0.00 %	76.71 %	0.00 %	0.00 %
Very High	15.07 %	0.00 %	0.00 %	58.97 %	0.00 %
Very Low	0.00 %	18.18 %	1.37 %	0.00 %	100.00 %
Correct	73.97 %	81.82 %	76.71 %	58.97 %	100.00 %
Misclassified	26.03 %	18.18 %	23.29 %	41.03 %	0.00 %

Figure 3 represents the accuracy chart for Naïve Bayes model. The blue line represents the 'no model', the red line is 'the ideal model' and the green line represent the

Naïve Bayes model. From the graph it could be seen that the Naïve Bayes model is quite near the ideal model.

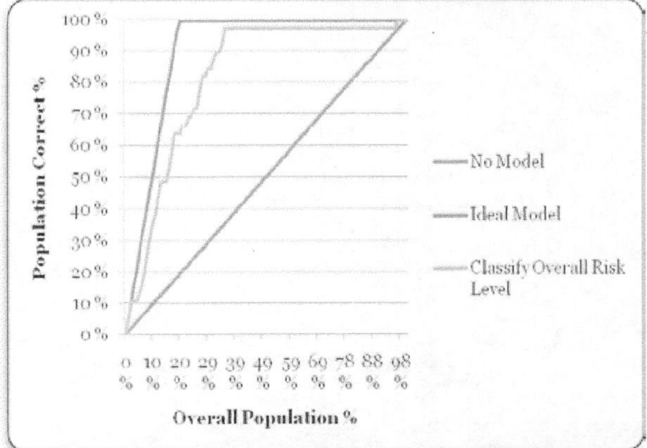

Figure 3 Accuracy Chart for Naive Bayes Model

6.3. Decision Tree Model

The Microsoft Decision Tree model incorporates features of the C4.5 and the CART algorithms. Thus, they are capable of performing predictions both in discrete and continuous problems. A tree can be grown on training data which contains errors. The algorithm does not implement pruning. Instead, the growth of a tree is controlled in two ways: Bayesian score – a score which stops further growth of a tree if the remaining data does not justify any more splits and Parameter COMPLEXITY_PENALTY – a parameter which takes values from 0 to 1, where the higher the value the smaller the tree as illustrated in table 4.

Table 4 Classification Matrix by Percentages for Decision Tree Model

	High(Actual)	Low(Actual)	Moderate (Actual)	Very High(Actual)	Very Low(Actual)
High	77.61 %	0.00 %	17.65 %	27.91 %	0.00 %
Low	0.00 %	85.71 %	11.76 %	0.00 %	31.58 %
Moderate	7.46 %	14.29 %	70.59 %	0.00 %	68.42 %
Very High	14.93 %	0.00 %	0.00 %	72.09 %	0.00 %
Very Low	0.00 %	0.00 %	0.00 %	0.00 %	0.00 %
Correct	77.61 %	85.71 %	70.59 %	72.09 %	0.00 %
Misclassified	22.39 %	14.29 %	29.41 %	27.91	100.0

6.4. Neural Network Model

The Microsoft Neural Network is an implementation of the feed-forward neural network (no cycles in the graph are allowed). There are two types of functions associated with each neuron: combination and activation. Following are the results of using Neural Network model.

TABLE 5 Classification Matrix by Percentages for Neural Network model

	High (Actual)	Low(Actual)	Moderate (Actual)	Very High(Actual)	Very Low (Actual)
High	70.15 %	0.00 %	17.33 %	29.27 %	0.00 %
Low	13.43 %	88.89 %	24.00 %	0.00 %	16.67 %
Moderate	2.99 %	0.00 %	53.33 %	2.44 %	33.33 %
Very High	10.45 %	0.00 %	1.33 %	65.85 %	0.00 %
Very Low	2.99 %	11.11 %	4.00 %	2.44 %	50.00 %
Correct	70.15 %	88.89 %	53.33 %	65.85 %	50.00 %
Misclassified	29.85 %	11.11 %	46.67 %	34.15 %	50.00 %

7. Results and Medical Assessment:

7.1. Models Validation

As mentioned before, the Microsoft SQL Server implements only two performance measure techniques: a Lift Chart and Classification Matrix techniques. The X-axis shows the percentage of the test dataset that is used to compare the predictions. The Y-axis shows the percentage of values predicted to the specified state. The blue and green lines show the random-guess and ideal models respectively. The purple, yellow and red lines show the Neural Network, Naïve Bayes and Decision Tree models respectively. The top line (red) shows the ideal model; it captures 100% of the target population for patients with DVT using 50% of the testing dataset. The bottom line (blue) shows the random line which is always a 45-degree line across the chart. It indicates that if we are to randomly guess the result for each case, 50% of the target population would be captured using 50% of the testing dataset. All three model lines (purple, green and Light-blue) fall between the random and ideal lines.

The following figures show that all three models had sufficient information to learn patterns in response to the predictable state. Figure 4 illustrates the lift chart validation for High risk level patients.

All of three models were able to extract patterns in response to the predictable state (High). The most effective model to predict patients who are likely to have a defined risk level for DVT disease appears to be Naïve Bayes followed by Decision Trees and Neural Networks. Figure 5 illustrates the lift chart validation for Low risk level patients. Also all of three models were able to extract patterns in response to the predictable state (low). The most effective model to predict patients who are likely to have a defined risk level for DVT disease appears to be Naïve Bayes followed by Neural Networks and finally Decision Trees.

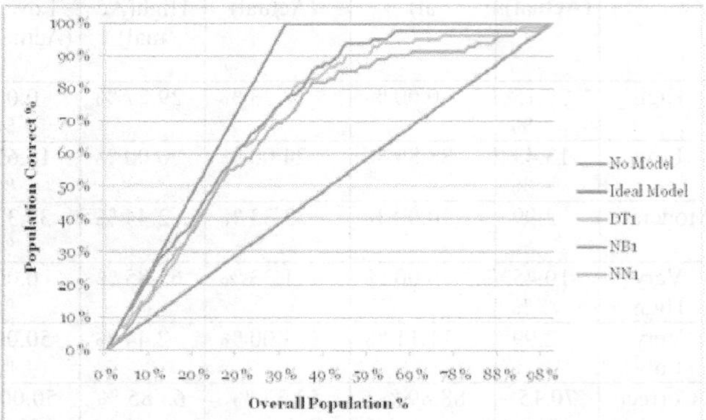

Figure 4 Lift Chart for High risk level patients

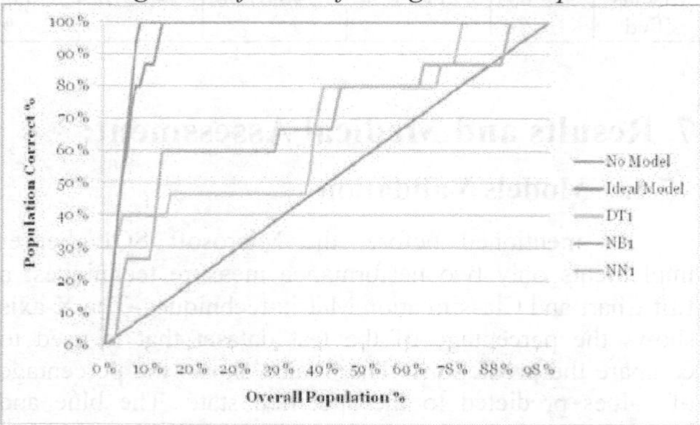

Figure 5 Lift Chart for low level risk

All three models achieved the objectives of the mining goals as they could provide good decision support to healthcare practitioners in assisting physicians and patients and discovering the medical factors associated with DVT disease.

7.2. Sample Case:

Hence, DVTRAM was able to support prediction queries based on "what if" scenarios. Users input values of medical attributes to diagnose patients with DVT disease. For example, entering the following attributes:

Gender = Male, Age = 71, BMI = 32, Smoking = Yes, Immobility = Use aid, Medical illness = Cancer, Minor Surgery = No, Major Surgery =No, Family History = No and Previous History = No into the models, would produce the results shown in Figure 6.

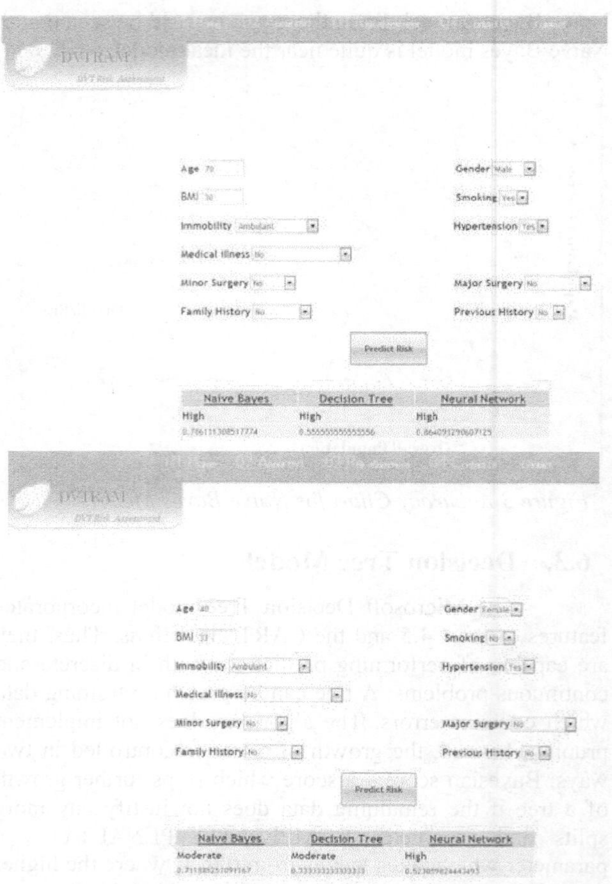

Figure 6 Result of DVTRAM system for a given data.

The three models ranked the person risk level within two risk levels. Naïve Bayes gave the Very High risk with probability (63%), the Decision Tree ranked in a High risk level with (43%) and Neural Network ranked in a High risk level with (64%). Based on these high figures, medical doctors can recommend that the patient is ranked between the high and very high risk level of DVT. Performing "what if" scenarios could thus help prevent a potential DVT occurrence.

7.3. Medical Assessment of the Results:

The previously mentioned results were revised by two Hematology specialists. They found them acceptable although they had some comments such as that the factors related to female gender they were concerned about did not appear in the assessment. In addition there was a clear confusion in the classification between Low and very Low risk levels and between High and Very High risk levels too. Some of the factors taken in consideration, such as major surgery and medical illness did not reflect the actual reality. As for Genetic characteristics, although they were the most important variables that determine the level of risk, they were summarized in a one factor, family history, which was not enough to clarify the relationship of different genetic factors with the disease. Therefore, this risk assessment system may be used as a kind of initial assessment only and specialists should be referred to in order to diagnose the situation carefully.

7.4. System Evaluation:

The mining goals, previously mentioned, were evaluated against the three-trained models.

Concerning the first goal, all three models were able to predict the risk level of DVT given patients' medical profiles using the singleton query and batch or prediction join query. As for the second goal, the system was able to identify the significant influences and relationships in the medical inputs associated with the predictable state DVT. The Dependency viewer in Decision Trees and Naïve Bayes models showed the results from the most significant to the least significant medical predictors. The most significant factor is Age followed by Medical Illness. Decision tree model gave a significant relation to all input attributes while Naïve Bayes gave a low significance to BMI attribute.

8. Summary and Conclusions

A prototype DVT disease risk assessment system was developed using three Data Mining classification-modeling techniques. DMX query language and functions were used to build and access the models. The models were trained and validated against a testing dataset. Accuracy Chart and Classification Matrix methods were used to evaluate the effectiveness of the models.

8.1. Contribution of the Research:

The research offers a contribution to the field of Business Intelligence and Medical risk assessment since the proposed system provides a Data Mining Tool for classifying patient risk characteristics based on features extracted from their medical data and acts as an intelligent system for estimating the risk level of suspected DVT patients. Eventually, these information will help specialists to use their resources more effectively.

8.2. Problems Faced :

They were primarily concerned with the data collection as the data were unreliable and difficult to extract. In some cases, the noise present in the samples was very high. As for the number of samples, it was not adequate to train the different models properly.

8.3. Limitations of the Research:

Following are some limitations of the work presented in this research paper:

1. The current version of DVTRAM is based on thirteen attributes. The list needs to be expanded to provide a more comprehensive diagnostic system.
2. It only used categorical data while for some diagnostic cases, the use of continuous data may be necessary.

8.4. Benefits and Future work of the Research

The system may serve as a training tool to train nurses and medical students to estimate patients risk levels of DVT disease. It can also provide decision support to assist medical doctors to make better clinical decisions or at least provide a "second opinion." The web version of the system can be used to assist anyone to determine his risk level for developing DVT. As for future work, the following enhancements can be made:

1. DVTRAM can be further enhanced and expanded so as to incorporate other medical attributes.
2. It can also incorporate other data mining techniques. Continuous data can also be added.
3. Text mining can be integrated with Data Mining.
4. The risk assessment model may be applied on other medical conditions and diseases.
5. Using different mining tools to testing and validating results rather than the Microsoft Data Mining tools.

9. References

[1] Carlo Vercellis ,"Business Intelligence: Data Mining and Optimization for Decision Making", John Wiley and Sons Ltd. Publication, 2009.

[2] http://en.wikipedia.org/wiki/Business_intelligence

[3] Elma Kolçe (Çela) and Neki Frasheri, "A Literature Review of Data Mining Techniques used in Healthcare Databases", ICT Innovations 2012 Web Proceedings - Poster Session ISSN 1857-728.8

[4] Christopher Nwosisi, Sung-Hyuk Cha, Yoo Jung An, Charles C. Tappert, and Evan Lipsitz, "Predicting Deep Venous Thrombosis Using Binary Decision Trees", IACSIT International Journal of Engineering and Technology, Vol. 3, No. 5, October 2011.

[5] Emily Kawaler, Alexander Cobian, Peggy Peissig, Deanna Cross, Steve Yale, and Mark Craven, "Learning to Predict Post-Hospitalization VTE Risk from EHR Data", AMIA Annual Symposium Proceedings. 2012; 436–445.

[6] Georg Aue, Jay Nelson Lozier, Xin Tian, Ann Marie Cullinane, Susan Soto, Leigh Samsel, Philip McCoy, and Adrian Wiestner, "Inflammation, TNFα, and endothelial dysfunction link lenalidomide to venous thrombosis in chronic lymphocytic leukemia", American Journal of Hematology, 86(10): 835–840, October 2011.

[7] R. Scott Evans, James F. Lloyd, Valerie T. Aston, Scott C. Woller, Jacob, S. Tripp, C. Greg Elliot and Scott M. Stevens, "Computer Surveillance of Patients at High Risk for and with Venous Thromboembolism AMIA Annual Symposium Proceedings 2010; 217–221.

[8] "Deep-Vein Thrombosis: Advancing Awareness To Protect Patient Lives" , White Paper Public Health Leadership Conference On Deep-Vein Thrombosis Washington, D.C., 2011.

[9] S. Palaniappan and R. Awang, "Intelligent Heart Disease Prediction System Using Data Mining Techniques", IJCSNS International Journal of Computer Science and Network Security, Vol. 8, No.8, August 2008, p. 343.

Improve the Quality of Product Recommendation based on Multi-channel CRM for E-commerce

Chuen-He Liou
Center for General Education
National Taipei University of Nursing and Health Sciences, Taipei, Taiwan

Abstract—**In Internet age, more and more Web applications and services are developed for electronic commerce (EC). However, the quality of product recommendations is still not good for electronic commerce. There are hundreds of thousands products placed on EC websites, but low percentage of those products were purchased by customers even though they still purchased many products. Because the scattered products customers purchased, customer-product matrix is also very sparse. It is difficult to find customers with the similar product preferences and the quality of the traditional product recommendation – the collaborative filtering method is not good. In this paper, we tried to propose a multi-channel customer relationship management (CRM) approach to solve the sparse problem of customer-product matrix, which results in the poor quality of product recommendations due to the difficulty of finding customers with the similar product preferences. We considered not only the similar users of the Web channel, but also the similar users of the other channels (e.g. television and catalog) in a multi-channel retailer. By these similar users from the multiple channels, the recommended products were ordered by the weighted frequent counts of the most frequent items purchased by the similar users with the hybrid weights for the Web target user.**

I. INTRODUCTION

As the Internet becomes more popular, Web services and applications are getting more for electronic commerce (EC). However, the quality of product recommendations is still not good for electronic commerce. There are hundreds of thousands products placed on EC website, but low percentage of those products are purchased by customers even though they still purchased many products. Because the scattered products customers purchased, customer-product matrix is also very sparse. It is difficult to find customers with the similar product preferences and make good product recommendation.

Recommender systems are widely used to recommend various items, such as movies and music, to customers according to their interests [1, 2]. Generally, recommender systems are based on either collaborative or content-based filtering techniques. Collaborative filtering (CF), which has been used successfully in various applications, utilizes preference ratings given by customers with similar interests to make recommendations to a target customer [3, 4]. In contrast, content-based filtering (CBF) method derives recommendations by matching customer profiles with content features [5, 6]. Some studies have combined collaborative filtering and content-based filtering techniques as a hybrid recommendation method [7, 8].

The typical CF method relies on finding users with similar interests to make recommendations. However, it suffers from the sparsity problem, which arises because users rate very few items and the user–item rating matrix is very sparse; thus, the recommendation quality is poor due to the difficulty of finding users with similar interests [4]. For example, we could find the sparse customer-product matrix on the Web channel as shown in Fig. 1. Customer (C5) only purchased products (P3, P8) on Web channel. It is hard to find similar users by the sparse customer-product matrix, so the recommendation quality may be poor.

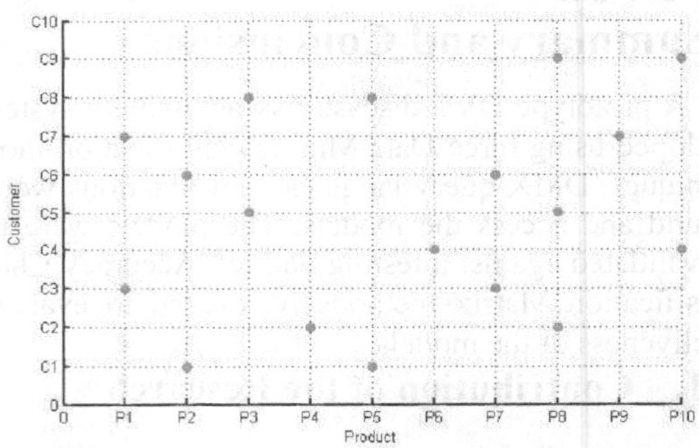

Fig. 1 Sparse customer-product matrix on the Web

In this paper, we tried to solve the sparsity problem on the Web by considering the consumption behaviors of multiple channels' users first. Customers could purchase products on the Web as well as the other channels (e.g. television, catalog) in a retailer. If we consider the consumption behaviors of all channels in a retailer, the customer-product matrix of all channels is more condensed than the individual Web channel, which is shown on Fig. 2. For example, customer (C5) purchased products (P3, P4, P5, P7, P8, P10) on all channels (e.g. Web, television and catalog channels) in a retailer. We could find more users with the similar interests in all channels. Thus, the recommendation quality of all channels may be better than the individual Web channel.

Furthermore, customer could purchase the different products in the individual channel (e.g. Web, television and catalog channel). For example, customers purchased products in multiple channels are shown in Fig. 3 as follows. Customer

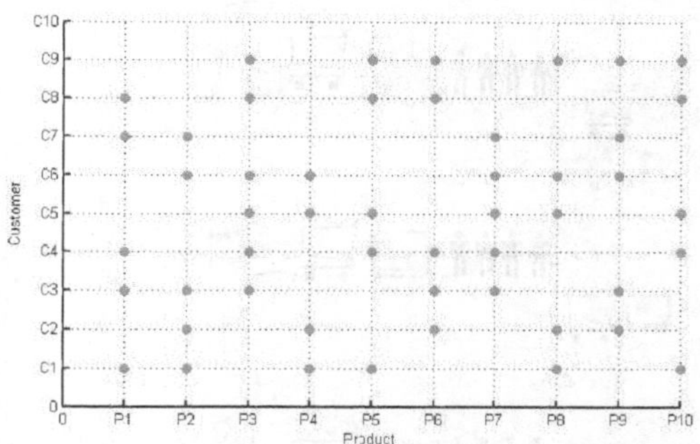

Fig. 2 Condensed customer-product matrix in all channels

(C5) purchased products (P3, P8) on the Web channel, purchased products (P4, P7) on the television channel, and purchased products (P5, P10) on the catalog channel. We could find similar users individually in each channel (e.g. Web, television and catalog channel) first, and then hybridize their consumption behaviors of the multiple channels.

It is interesting that the similar users of all channels might be not the same as the similar users of individual channel by considering the channel factor. The multiple channels' users might have the similar product preferences to the Web target user by their consumption behaviors on the multiple channels with the different weights. The hybrid weights indicate the relative importance of the consumption behaviors of the multiple channels' similar users to the Web channel users. The recommendation quality of the hybrid effect from the multiple channels might be better than all channels.

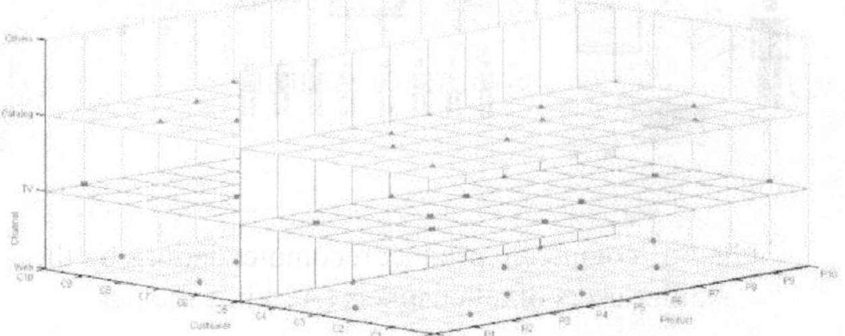

Fig. 3 Customers purchased products in multiple channels

Finally, we tried to propose a hybrid multi-channel method which adjusts the weights of the individual channel to address the difficulty of finding similar users on Web due to the sparsity problem inherent in typical CF systems for electronic commerce. The method finds the similar preference users of the multiple channels based on the similar product preferences, and the most frequent items of the individual channel similar users for the target Web user. Thus, the products were sorted by the frequencies of the frequent items with the hybrid weights of the individual channel to recommend to the target Web user.

The remainder of this paper is organized as follows. In Section II, we discuss the related work of our research. In Section III, we describe the proposed recommendation scheme and engine. In Section IV, we present the experiment evaluation. In Section V, we draw some conclusions.

II. RELATED WORK

A. *Multiple channels*

Multiple channels can be divided into physical channels (e.g., department stores) and virtual channels (e.g., the Web, catalogs, and television) [9]. In the past, most companies only provided single sales channels for customers to purchase products. However, because of advances in information technology and increased demand, companies now use multiple channels, i.e., physical and virtual channels, to provide customers with seamless services. In this way, companies create more value for their customers, e.g., greater choice and convenience. The channels can also be designed to allow customers to move from one channel to another seamlessly by reducing transaction costs during the purchase process [9-12]. Existing studies do not provide product recommendations for electronic commerce based on the consumption behavior of the multiple sales channels' similar preference users.

B. *Customer Relationship Management (CRM)*

CRM represents the abbreviation of "customer relationship management", some other studies use the terms "customer relationship marketing" or "information-enabled relation marketing" as the abbreviations [13]. CRM could identify, attract significant and profitable customers by managing relationships with them and develop their long-term relationships strategically [14, 15]. CRM could also be an e-commerce application of database marketing [16]. CRM is how businesses manage their customer relationship by interacting with their customers based on customers' past transactions; it could be a methodology, technology, and e-commerce application to manage their customer relationships [17]. CRM is also an one-to-one marketing for each customer based on how much you know about your customers [18]. Besides, multichannel integration could be one of key cross functional processes in CRM strategy development. Payne and Frow [19] discuss the strategic role of multiple channel integration in CRM.

C. *Most Frequent Item-based Recommendation Method*

The most frequent item-based recommendation method [4] counts the purchase frequency of each product by scanning the products purchased by the users in a cluster. Next, all the products are sorted by the purchase frequency in descending order. Finally, the method recommends the top N products that have not been purchased by the target customer.

D. *Collaborative Filtering*

Collaborative filtering (CF) [2, 3] utilizes the nearest-neighbor principle to recommend products to a target audience. The neighbors are identified by computing the similarity between customers' purchase behavior patterns or tastes. The similarity is measured by Pearson's correlation coefficient, which is defined as follows:

$$corr_P(c_i, c_j) = \frac{\sum_{s\in I}(r_{c_i,s} - \bar{r}_{c_i})(r_{c_j,s} - \bar{r}_{c_j})}{\sqrt{\sum_{s\in I}(r_{c_i,s} - \bar{r}_{c_i})^2 \sum_{s\in I}(r_{c_j,s} - \bar{r}_{c_j})^2}} \qquad (1)$$

where $\overline{r_{c_i}}$ and $\overline{r_{c_j}}$ denote the average number of products purchased by customers C_i and C_j respectively; variable I denotes the mix of the set of products; and $r_{ci,s}$ and $r_{cj,s}$ indicate, respectively, that customers C_i and C_j purchased product item S.

The *k*NN-based CF method utilizes k-nearest neighbors (*k*-NN) to recommend *N* products to a target user [4]. The k-nearest neighbors are identified by computing the similarity between customers' purchase behavior or tastes. The similarity is measured by Pearson's coefficient, as shown in (1). After the neighborhood has been formed, the *N* recommended products are determined by the k-nearest neighbors as follows. The frequency count of products is calculated by scanning the data about the products purchased by the *k*-nearest neighbors. The products are then sorted based on the frequency count, and the *N* most frequently occurring products that have not been purchased by the target customers are selected as the top-*N* recommendations.

III. Methodology

A. *Multiple Channel CF (MC-CF) based approach*

In Fig. 4, the similar users of multiple channels were found based on their product preferences and then provide recommendations by their product transactions for Web target user. The similar users of the other existing channels could be used to provide more transactions for the Web channel user. First, we found the similar users of each channel based on the users' similarity, which is measured by Pearson's correlation coefficient (1) of users' product preferences. For each target Web channel user, similar users are selected from the television, catalog, and Web channel users based on their product preferences in the corresponding channel. The method could find more similar users for the Web target user and would solve the sparsity problem of the Web channel to improve the quality of recommendations. The system then finds the most frequent items of the similar users of each channel based on their purchased transactions on each channel. The most frequent items of the hybrid multiple channels are determined, respectively, from the items of multiple channels using the weighted sum of the frequent counts with the different hybrid weights w_T, w_C, and w_W. The hybrid weights indicate the relative importance of the consumption behaviors of the multiple channels' similar users to the Web channel users on the Web, and are determined according to the best recommendation quality derived from the preliminary analytical data. Finally, the method uses the hybrid weights (w_W, w_T, w_C) to recommend products based on the most frequent-items approach.

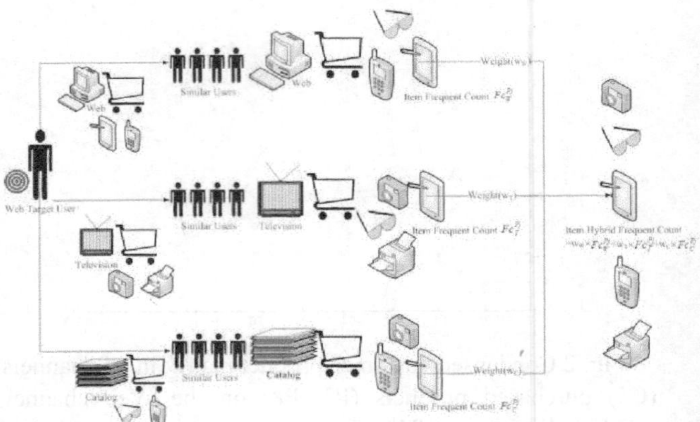

Fig. 4 E-commerce product recommendations by the similar users of the multiple channels (MC)

B. *All Channels CF (AC-CF) based approach*

We could solve the sparsity problem by considering the similar users of all channels in a multichannel retailer, which is shown on Fig. 5. The customer-product matrix of all channels could be more condensed than the individual Web channel. We could find more users with the similar interests in all channels. Thus, the recommendation quality of all channels may be better than the single Web channel.

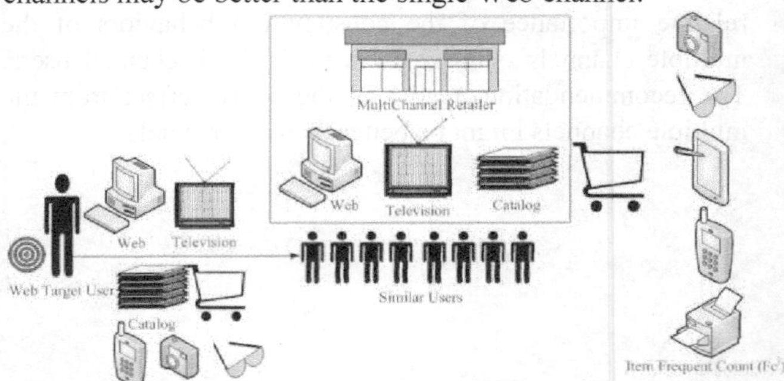

Fig. 5 E-commerce product recommendations by the similar users of all channels (AC) in a retailer

C. *The Recommendation Engine*

The proposed method derives recommendations based on the most frequent items approach. For the similar users of the multiple channels, the most frequent items are extracted from the product transactions in the individual channel. The recommendation engine is comprised of the most frequent items Y_M^{MF}, which is shown in Fig. 6. In the figure, M represents either T, C, or W, which denote the television, catalog and Web channels respectively.

Let $Y_M^{MF}, M \in \{T,C,W\}$ denote the set of most frequent items derived from the similar users in multiple channels for the target user u on the Web. Let $Fc_T^{P_j}, Fc_C^{P_j}$, and $Fc_W^{P_j}$ represent the frequency counts of an item Pj in Y_M^{MF}, respectively. Let Y_u^{MF} be the set of candidate products generated from the union of $Y_M^{MF} - X_u$. The products in Y_u^{MF} are ranked according to the weighted sum of their frequency counts calculated as (2).

$$Fc^{Pj} = w_T \times Fc_T^{Pj} + w_C \times Fc_C^{Pj} + w_W \times Fc_W^{Pj} \tag{2}$$

Finally, the selected products are the most frequent items ranked according to the frequency count of products purchased by the similar users in multiple channels. Then, products in Y_u^{MF} that have not been purchased by the user *u* are added to the recommended product list as the top-N recommendations.

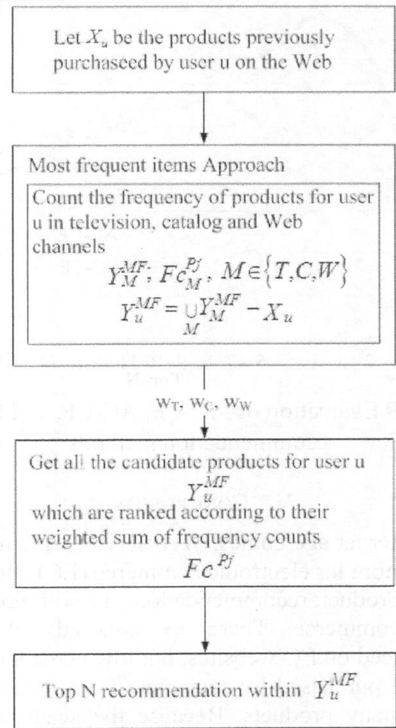

Fig. 6 The recommendation engine

IV. EXPERIMENTAL EVALUATION

A. Experiment Dataset

We use a data set obtained from a multi-channel company to conduct our experiment evaluation. The company is a home shopping company that owns television, catalog, Web and mobile channels in Taiwan. For the television channel, products are introduced on the channel and viewers can purchase the products by calling a toll-free number.

The experiment dataset were extracted from CRM system of the case company in 2007. To reduce the data quantity, the threshold of item purchased frequency is set to 10. There are 1,455 users who purchased 2,863 products on the Web. The products offered on the Web channel were also available on the other channels.

B. Evaluation Metrics

Two metrics, precision and recall, are commonly used to measure the quality of a recommendation. They are also used in the field of information retrieval [20, 21]. Product items can be classified into products that customers are interested in purchase and those that are of no interest. The recommendation method then suggests products of interest to the customers accordingly. The recall metric indicates the effectiveness of a method in locating products of interest, while the precision metric represents customers' levels of interest in the recommended product items.

Recall is the fraction of interesting product items located:

$$\text{Recall} = \frac{\text{number of correctly recommended items}}{\text{number of interesting items}} \quad (3)$$

Precision is the fraction of the recommended products that customers find interesting:

$$\text{Precision} = \frac{\text{number of correctly recommended items}}{\text{number of recommended items}} \quad (4)$$

The items deemed interesting to customers are the products that the customers purchased in the test set. Correctly recommended items are those that match the interesting items. Because increasing the number of recommended items tends to reduce the precision and increase the recall, the F1 metric is used to balance the tradeoff between precision and recall [21]. The F1 metric, which assigns equal weights to precision and recall, is calculated as follows:

$$\text{F1} = \frac{2 \times \text{recall} \times \text{precision}}{\text{recall} + \text{precision}} \quad (5)$$

C. The hybrid effect of the other channels on the Web

We compared the F1-metric qualities of one-channel with two-channel recommendation scheme. The scheme is a typical k-nearest neighbors (k-NN, k similar users) CF method, which finds similar users in individual channel and recommends top-N products are ranked according to their frequency counts of the most frequent items purchased by these similar users from one or two channels. We choose k = 20 as the number of nearest neighbors (NN) to find rapidly the hybrid effect of the other channels on the Web channel.

Fig. 7 demonstrated the hybrid effect of the other channels (Catalog and TV) on the Web channel. In the figure, the Web channel recommendation quality became better after considering the additional TV channel, but the quality became worse after considering the additional catalog channel. The recommendation quality of the products provided from the similar users of TV channel is better than the similar users from the catalog channel. The purchased transactions on TV channel are more important to the Web users than the catalog channel. Thus, the hybrid weight of TV channel for the Web channel may be larger than the catalog channel.

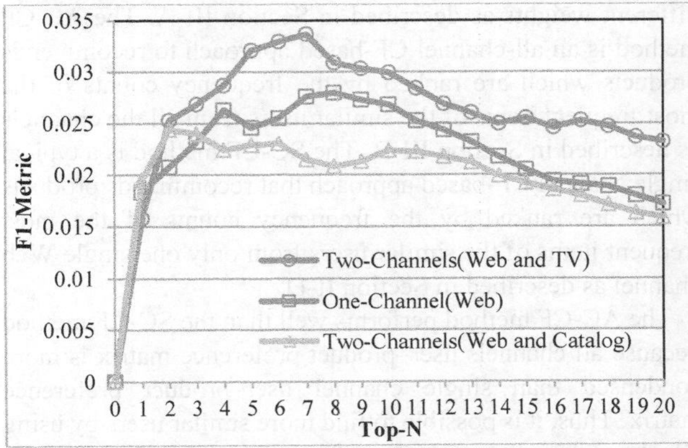

Fig. 7 The hybrid effect of the other channels on the Web

D. Determining the hybrid weights for the multi-channel recommendation scheme

The hybrid channel recommendation scheme is based on the weight ratios of the Web (w_W), television (w_T), catalog (w_C) channels (i.e., $w_W + w_T + w_C = 100\%$). The weights are derived as follows. First, the dataset is divided into a training dataset (55%), preliminary analytical dataset (25%) and a testing dataset (20%). We use the training dataset to derive the most frequent items, and use the preliminary analytical data to derive the weights. Second, the weights are determined according to the best recommendation quality that can be achieved under the different combinations of weight assignments for the preliminary analytical data. Because the monthly average number of products purchased on the Web is 5.7, which is calculated from the dataset. We use the top 6 recommendations to determine the hybrid weights of the multiple channels. We adjust the values of the channel weights systematically in increments of 10%. The qualities of the top 6 hybrid recommendations according to different hybrid weight combinations (w_W, w_T, w_C) are shown in Fig. 8. The best recommendation quality F1-metric of 0.02568 for the top 6 recommendations is derived when (w_W, w_T, w_C) = (90%, 10%, 0%). We use the weight ratios of the hybrid recommendation scheme in the experiment next section.

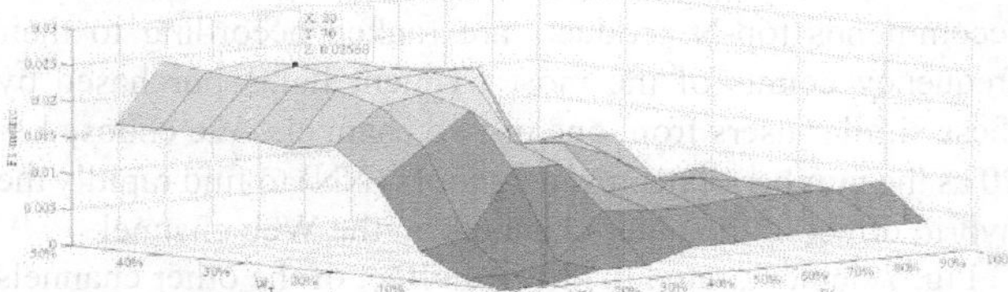

Fig. 8 Weight combinations of the hybrid recommendation

E. Evaluation of the multi-channel recommendation method

Figure 9 shows the evaluation results of the three recommendation methods. We compare the proposed multi-channel CF (MC-CF) recommendation method, with two methods, namely, all channels CF (AC-CF), and single channel CF (SC-CF) methods. The MC-CF method is a CF-based method to recommend products which are ranked by the weighted frequency counts of the most frequent items of the similar users from the multiple channels with the different weights as described in Section III-A. The AC-CF method is an all-channel CF-based approach to recommends products which are ranked by the frequency counts of the most frequent items of the similar users from all the channels as described in Section III-B. The SC-CF method is a typical single channel CF-based approach that recommends products which are ranked by the frequency counts of the most frequent items of the similar users from only one single Web channel as described in Section II-D.

The AC-CF method performs well than the SC-CF method because all channels user–product preference matrix is more condensed than single channel user–product preference matrix. Thus, it is possible to find more similar users by using all channels user–product preference matrix. The MC-CF method generates recommendations with the hybrid weighting ratio set at (w_W, w_T, w_C,) = (90%, 10%, 0%) for the top-N recommendations, as described in Section IV-D. The experiment results demonstrate that the proposed multi-channel CF-based (MC-CF) method performs well than the all channels (AC-CF) method and single channel (SC-CF) method for most of top-N recommendations.

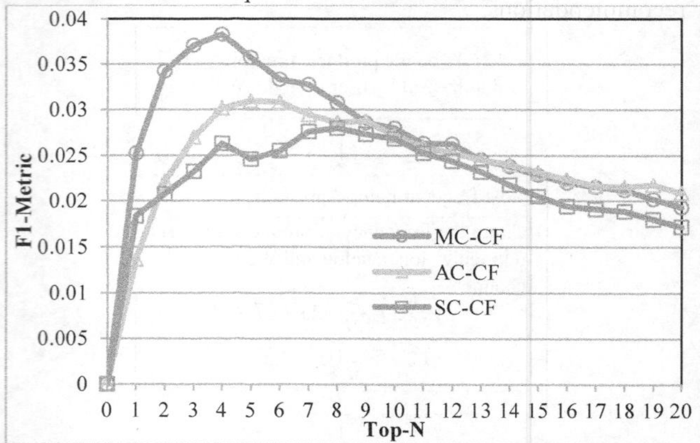

Fig. 9 Evaluation of MC-CF, AC-CF, and SC-CF recommendation methods

V. CONCLUSION

As the Internet age comes, Web services and applications are getting more for electronic commerce (EC). However, the quality of product recommendations is still not good for electronic commerce. There are hundreds of thousands products placed on EC websites, but low percentage of those products are purchased by customers even though they still purchased many products. Because the scattered products customers purchased, customer-product matrix is also very sparse. It is difficult to find customers with the similar product preferences from a single channel and provide good product recommendations.

Some multi-channel companies often use advertising and marketing campaigns to gather information about users' consumption behavior on the specific channel. However, businesses could also obtain such information from the CRM systems of existing channels. In this paper, we have proposed a multi-channel CRM method to solve the difficulty of finding similar users for electronic commerce. It is assumed that the consumption behavior of Web channel users correlates with the consumption behavior of the similar users from the multiple channels with the different weights.

Experiments were conducted to compare the multiple channel CF-based (MC-CF) method, all channel CF-based (AC-CF) method, and single channel CF-based (SC-CF) method. The AC-CF method performs well than the SC-CF method because all channels user–product preference matrix is not as sparse as single channel user–product preference matrix. Thus, it is possible to find more similar users by using all channels product preference matrix. The experiment results demonstrate that the proposed multiple channels (MC-CF) method performs well than AC-CF and SC-CF methods. The proposed method mitigates the sparsity problem and improves the recommendation quality by finding more similar users based on the consumption behavior patterns of users in multiple channels. The hybrid weighting ratio set at (w_W, w_T, w_C) = (90%, 10%, 0%) for the top-N recommendations. The consumption behaviors of the Web channel are most important to Web channel itself, and TV channel is more important than the catalog channel. It would be beneficial for the Web channel users by considering the additional consumption behaviors of TV channel users.

Our study has some limitation. For example, we did not consider the hybrid weight of the mobile channel because the purchased transactions of the mobile channel were not sufficient. The hybrid effect was not obvious and the weight of the mobile channel could be neglected. In the future, we will try more methods to apply other data mining techniques, e.g., clustering and association rules, to improve the qualities of product recommendations for e-commerce.

ACKNOWLEDGMENT

This research was supported in part by the National Science Council of the Taiwan under Grant NSC 101-2410-H-227-003.

REFERENCES

[1] W. Hill, L. Stead, M. Rosenstein, and G. Furnas, "Recommending and evaluating choices in a virtual community of use," presented at the Proceedings of the SIGCHI Conference on Human factors in Computing Systems, Denver, Colorado, USA, 1995.

[2] U. Shardanand and P. Maes, "Social information filtering: algorithms for automating "word of mouth"," presented at the Proceedings of the SIGCHI conference on Human factors in computing systems, Denver, Colorado, USA, 1995.

[3] P. Resnick, N. Iacovou, M. Suchak, P. Bergstrom, and J. Riedl, "GroupLens: an open architecture for collaborative filtering of netnews," presented at the Proceedings of the 1994 ACM Conference on Computer Supported Cooperative Work, Chapel Hill, North Carolina, USA, 1994.

[4] B. Sarwar, G. Karypis, J. Konstan, and J. Riedl, "Analysis of recommendation algorithms for e-commerce," presented at the Proceedings of the Second ACM Conference on Electronic Commerce, Minneapolis, Minnesota, USA, 2000.

[5] K. Lang, "Newsweeder: Learning to Filter Netnews," in *Proc. 12th Int'l Conf. Machine Learning*, 1995.

[6] M. Pazzani and D. Billsus, "Learning and Revising User Profiles: The Identification of Interesting Web Sites," *Machine Learning*, vol. 27, pp. 313-331, 1997.

[7] M. Balabanović and Y. Shoham, "Fab: content-based, collaborative recommendation," *Communications of the ACM*, vol. 40, pp. 66-72, 1997.

[8] M. Claypool, A. Gokhale, T. Miranda, P. Murnikov, D. Netes, and M. Sartin, "Combining Content-Based and Collaborative Filters in an Online Newspaper," in *Proc. ACM SIGIR '99 Workshop Recommender Systems: Algorithms and Evaluation*, 1999.

[9] B. Tiernan, *The hybrid company: reach all your customers through multi-channels anytime, anywhere*: Dearborn Trade, 2001.

[10] H. Schröder and S. Zaharia, "Linking multi-channel customer behavior with shopping motives: An empirical investigation of a German retailer," *Journal of Retailing and Consumer Services*, vol. 15, pp. 452-468, 2008.

[11] A. M. Chircu and V. Mahajan, "Managing electronic commerce retail transaction costs for customer value," *Decision Support Systems*, vol. 42, pp. 898-914, 2006.

[12] D.-R. Liu and C.-H. Liou, "Mobile commerce product recommendations based on hybrid multiple channels," *Electron. Commer. Rec. Appl.*, vol. 10, pp. 94-104, 2011.

[13] L. Ryals and A. Payne, "Customer relationship management in financial services: towards information-enabled relationship marketing," *Journal of Strategic Marketing*, vol. 9, pp. 3-27, 2001/01/01 2001.

[14] F. A. Buttle, "The CRM value chain," *Marketing Business*, pp. 52-55, 2001.

[15] J. Hobby, "Looking after the one who matters," *Accountancy Age*, vol. 28, pp. 28-30, 1999.

[16] S. Kutner and J. Cripps, "Managing the customer portfolio of healthcare enterprises," *The Healthcare Forum Journal*, vol. 4, pp. 52-54, 1997.

[17] M. Stone and N. Woodcock, "Defining CRM and assessing its quality.," *Successful customer relationship marketing*, pp. 3-20, 2001.

[18] D. Peppers, M. Rogers, and B. Dorf, "Is your company ready for one-to-one marketing?," *Harvard Business Review*, vol. 77, p. 151, 1999.

[19] A. Payne and P. Frow, "The role of multichannel integration in customer relationship management," *Industrial Marketing Management*, vol. 33, pp. 527-538, 2004.

[20] G. Salton and M. J. McGill, *Introduction to modern information retrieval*: McGraw-Hill, New York, USA, 1986.

[21] C. J. Van Rijsbergen, *Information retrieval*: Butterworth-Heinemann Newton, MA, USA, 1979.

Using Recursive Sorting to Improve Accuracy of Memory-based Collaborative Filtering Recommendations

Serhiy Morozov and Hossein Saiedian
Electrical Engineering and Computer Science
University of Kansas, Lawrence KS, USA

***Abstract*—Modern user behavior datasets contain millions of records, so quickly combining all potentially relevant ratings is often not feasible. Instead, we make suggestions from a small set of the most relevant ratings, so that the memory-based recommender systems could produce simple and accurate results. We propose a new instance selection algorithm that removes irrelevant data after sorting it twice, unlike the traditional approach where the data is only sorted once. The accuracy of the resulting recommendations on the Netflix dataset is considerably better than the standard approach.**

I. Introduction

Collaborative filtering systems recommend items that other users enjoyed, essentially automating "word-of-mouth" suggestions. The assumption is that one user's favorite items may be inferred by observing other users with similar interests. As the name implies, personalized recommendations are derived from filtering all available items through preferences of similar users [13]. However, user opinions are subjective and have little to do with content similarity. In fact, a pure collaborative filtering system has no knowledge of item content, which makes it ideal for abstract domains such as paintings, music, and poetry [13].

Memory-based collaborative filtering is simple and intuitive, does not require many tuning parameters or long training sessions, and can justify recommendations [3], [16]. The recommendation is a consensus of similar users or items, called neighbors. Because some neighbors are more influential than others, this method is often called the K Nearest Neighbors (KNN) approach [18]. To quantify a neighbor's influence, we measure its similarity to the user or item in question, i.e., the active vector [10], [16]. Depending on whether the dataset is a collection of user or item vectors it would be a user- or item-based approach.

The estimate for an active user u on active item a is a weighted sum of neighbors' ratings adjusted by their mean, $\bar{r}_i$.

$$P_{u,a} = \bar{r}_u + k\frac{\sum_{i=1}^{n} w(u,i)(r_{i,a} - \bar{r}_i)}{\sum_{i=1}^{n} w(u,i)}$$

In this formula, n is the neighborhood size, $w(u,i)$ is the influence of a neighbor i, and k is a tuning coefficient [5]. The bottom of this fraction is the sum of the neighbors' weights, which we call net weight. The neighborhood size may vary greatly. Also, some neighbors may offer little influence due to their low similarity. Therefore, the instance selection method that reduces the neighborhood has a large impact on the recommendation accuracy.

When predicting a known rating, the error of an estimate is $P_{u,a} - r_{u,a}$. The accuracy of the entire system may be summarized by the Root Mean Squared Error (RMSE), a popular metric that is especially sensitive to large errors. The goal of this work is to reduce the RMSE.

$$RMSE = \sqrt{\frac{\sum_{u \in U, i \in I} (P_{u,a} - r_{u,a})^2}{|P|}}$$

We evaluate our instance selection algorithms on the Netflix dataset. It contains over 100,000,000 ratings, representing over 17,000 items and over 480,000 users. To establish a point of reference for our experiments, we examine some of the well-known results from the Netflix website, `www.netflixprize.com`. It lists the typical prediction errors of many trivial recommendation approaches that suggest the same rating for every item. For instance, recommending a four star rating for each movie is the most accurate (RMSE = 1.1748), because each recommendation is close to the overall average rating of 3.6 stars. Likewise, recommending 3.6 stars for everyone gives an even smaller error of 1.1287. This value may be reduced further by recommending the movie or user average for each movie and user vector. This results in a typical error of 1.0533 for an average movie and 1.0651 for an average user approach. In general, recommendations with RMSE ¿ 1 are not worth the effort.

II. Recommendation Accuracy Problem

There is a demand for recommender systems that can consistently produce accurate recommendations, but there are few systems that successfully do so. On the one hand, humans are notoriously unpredictable, but on the other hand, there are processing and storage limitations that prevent extensive dataset analysis. Furthermore, user behavior data is not perfect, and there is usually little of it. However, it is often the only source of information available, so we need a way to infer user behavior patterns from sparse data. Many studies show dramatic recommendation quality improvements due to changes in the data [5], [9], [17]. In a sense, optimizing anything else is comparable to fixing the symptoms, while improving the data addresses the root of a problem.

The easiest way to reduce data sparsity is to add default ratings to the dataset. Some of the simplest default ratings include mean rating and majority rating [5]. However, aggregate defaults are usually poor approximations for the actual opinions [9], so they are often made neutral or negatively skewed to ensure a more conservative prediction.

Sometimes, default ratings come from external sources of actual opinions. For example, the MovieLens project populated missing values with existing ratings from a different movie dataset [17]. Likewise, Basu, Hirsh, and Cohen used the Internet Movie Database website to supplement their dataset [2]. Using external sources of default ratings is a simple and effective way to reduce data sparsity, but those sources may not always be available.

Missing data can also be inferred from a cluster of similarly classified vectors. For example, the GroupLens project clustered users based on their preferences and related news articles based on their topic [12]. As a result, each cluster appeared to have a rich rating history. Such clusters provide good default ratings, but require a way to determine vector membership. In order to group users with no expressed preferences, some systems consider additional properties like age, gender, and education [1]. Item clusters often use domain-specific knowledge, which is rarely available and may not have clear-cut boundaries. Clustering is an effective way to reduce sparsity and improve performance, but it sacrifices personalization.

One way to improve the quality of data, without supplementing the dataset, is to remove unnecessary ratings. Data reduction algorithms shrink a dataset without damaging it. They preserve the useful information, remove noise, and decrease the amount of computation necessary to complete a recommendation [7], [11]. Such algorithms are especially relevant when scaling up is not an option.

Instance selection is a common data reduction technique that has been traditionally used for data classification. The instance selection algorithm chooses the smallest possible portion of the available data, such that a successful classification may still occur [7], [11]. For example, some algorithms remove instances that do not affect other classifications [14] and some employ a ranking mechanism to eliminate irrelevant instances [6]. A memory-based recommendation is essentially a way to classify one's opinion, given a set of friends' opinions and a way to quantify their influence. Therefore, instance-based learning algorithms, like KNN, could benefit from instance selection.

Even though instance selection algorithms are meant to manage an overwhelming amount of data, the algorithms themselves do not scale well. In fact, most approaches exhibit at least quadratic complexity, which makes them unsuitable for many serious applications [7], [8]. Therefore, most instance selection algorithms do not apply to the problems that would benefit most from their use. However, recommendation accuracy improvement is considerable and we focus our research on this aspect of instance selection.

III. Instance Selection Algorithms

Before making a recommendation, we first identify all potentially relevant ratings. We locate all users who rated the active item and all items that were rated by the active user. Based on these two lists, we locate a set of ratings that are either on a related item (according to the active user) or given by a related user (according to the active item). The ratings are then placed in a matrix where items are rows and users are columns. Each cell contains a rating that is associated with a single user and an item. We refer to rows in such a matrix as item vectors and columns as user vectors. A transposed matrix would represent users as rows and items as columns, so we can produce user- and item-based recommendations from the same data.

The standard instance selection approach ranks neighbors based on every dimension. It compares every row of the matrix to the active vector and rearranges the rows in the order of decreasing similarity. As a result, the most influential vectors are concentrated at the top of the matrix because the active vector is the first row. Truncating such a matrix deletes only the least relevant data.

The recursive instance selection approach also sorts and truncates the matrix, except it does so in two passes. The first pass sorts and identifies the top 30 most similar dimensions. The second pass selects vectors with the highest similarities according to these dimensions. A single sort can establish the most similar dimensions, but not the nearest neighbors according to those dimensions. The recursive approach chooses the best neighbors according to the best dimensions.

Both methods eventually truncate the matrix to 30 rows, i.e., a neighborhood of at most 30 most similar vectors. Empirical results show this size to be particularly accurate [15], [16]. A truncated matrix contains enough data to establish the mean of a vector, which is used to support a particular recommendation, yet does not introduce unnecessary noise that causes over-fitting.

IV. Recursive Sorting Rationale

Collaborative filtering assumes that users who agreed in the past are likely to agree in the future. As a result, users who agree more tend to have a bigger influence. Ideally, the opinions are unanimous and every neighbor has a weight of 1. In the worst case scenario, everyone's weight is 0, which means that neighbors have no shared dimensions. Therefore, the total influence in a neighborhood of n vectors is between 0 and n. In reality, the net neighborhood weight is somewhere in the middle, because both instance selection algorithms require at least one shared dimension for all neighbors. Maximizing the net weight of a fixed size neighborhood more closely resembles the best case scenario.

Since neighborhoods are restricted to a fixed size, the only way to guarantee high net weights is to consider the most influential neighbors first. The first n vectors ordered by their influence will always produce a net weight greater than that of a random sample of neighbors. Sorting ensures that after truncation the neighborhood contains most similar vectors as opposed to a random sample of them. Truncating the neighborhood without sorting it first may still produce a high net weight, but such outcome is unlikely.

Another fundamental assumption of collaborative filtering is that similar users agree on most items, regardless of their domain. We refer to this type of comparison as "global similarity" because all common dimensions contribute to the similarity of any two vectors. Global similarity can identify very influential neighbors, which are extremely rare. Our approach requires two users to agree on a few of the most relevant items, not all of them. We refer to this type of comparison as "local similarity" because only a subset of all common dimensions contributes to the similarity.

Standard approach uses global similarity to rank vectors. Recursive approach first identifies a subset of dimensions and then ranks the vectors by their local similarity on those dimensions. For instance, two globally similar users may disagree on a few movies. As long as the number of such movies is sufficiently small, the global similarity remains high. However, local similarity according to these movies would conclude the two users to be less similar. Likewise, one may compare the two globally dissimilar users across the commonly liked movies and get a high local similarity.

Consider the following examples that demonstrate the changes in global and local similarity between two users. We use cosine similarity to quantify the strength of a relationship between two vectors. It is the baseline metric for many collaborative filtering systems [15]. In this case, both users have rated the same three movies. However, the similarity between user vectors may be established across all or just the first two common dimensions. In fact, the choice of common dimensions has a large effect on the perceived vector similarity.

$$u_1 = <1,2,3>; u_2 = <1,3,1>; cos(u_1, u_2) = 0.806$$

$$u_1' = <1,2>; u_2' = <1,3>; cos(u_1', u_2') = 0.990$$

$$u_1 = <1,2,3>; u_2 = <5,1,3>; cos(u_1, u_2) = 0.723$$

$$u_1' = <1,2>; u_2' = <5,1>; cos(u_1', u_2') = 0.614$$

Comparing two vectors on fewer dimensions could produce a higher similarity if the dimensions are sorted. Consider a case where we sort the matrix by rows and columns such that the most similar vectors are positioned closer to the top left corner of the matrix. Assuming that dimensions are sorted, comparing vectors on less similar dimensions will allow the outliers on a neighbor's rating scale to affect the similarity metric. Extreme opinions on different scales are less likely to agree, so the similarity of such vectors would decrease. If this is false, then considering an extra dimension will result in higher vector similarity, i.e., most of the rows agree on this column. If that were the case, the additional columns should be considered earlier, since columns for which the rows agree most often are placed first. However, this is impossible because the columns are considered in order of decreasing similarity.

To demonstrate this principle, consider five vectors with five dimensions $< a, b, c, d, e >$ in Figure 1. The net weight of such matrix is 3.56, where the weight of each vector is quantified by its Pearson's correlation to the active vector. In other words, we sum the similarities of the 1st row and the 2nd row, 1st row and 3rd row, 1st row and 4th row, etc. Then we delete one of the columns and recompute the similarities again. The net weights of four truncated versions of this matrix, with one of the dimensions removed, are as follows: no $e = 3.87$, no $d = 4.08$, no $c = 3.38$, no $b = 2.94$. Removing some dimensions increases the net weight, but how does one know which dimensions to remove?

a	b	c	d	e
3	4	2	1	3
2	3	1	1	3
3	4	3	3	4
4	4	2	2	4
3	3	2	3	2

Fig. 1. A 5 × 5 Matrix

Consider the similarity of each dimension to a: $a = 1.00, b = 0.65, c = 0.50, d = 0.35, e = 0.42$. The d and e dimensions are the least similar and removing them increases the net weight. Figure 2 shows the negative correlation between the similarity of a dimension and the net weight of a truncated matrix that does not contain it.

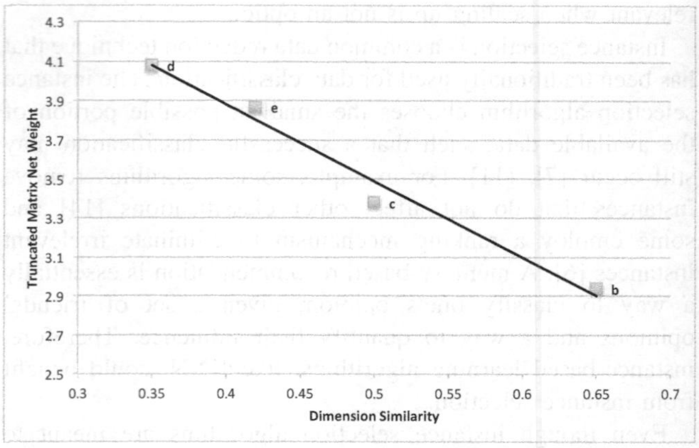

Fig. 2. Truncated Matrix Net Weights

To verify this phenomenon, we examined the neighbors identified by the two algorithms on the Netflix dataset. Figures 3 and 4 show typical similarities in an item and user-oriented neighborhood. In both cases, the recursive approach identifies neighbors with higher similarities and greater net weight, i.e., area under the curve.

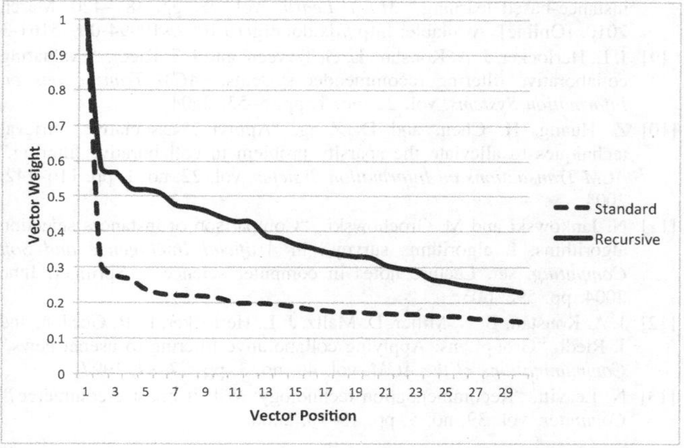

Fig. 3. Item Similarity Comparison

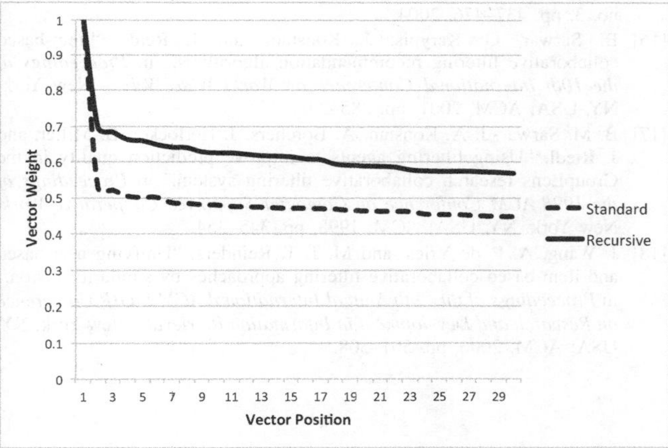

Fig. 4. User Similarity Comparison

V. Justification for Resorted Data

To further support the benefits of our recursive algorithm, we considered a statistical justification of this approach. The Rao-Blackwell theorem states that if $g(x)$ is an estimator for θ, then conditional expectation of $g(x)$ given a sufficient statistic $T(x)$ is a better estimator of θ and never worse [4]. This theorem employes a well-known relationship between conditional and unconditional variance, i.e., $var(E(g(x)|T(x)))$ $<=$ $var(E(g(x)))$. Smaller variance means smaller Mean Squared Error, which means higher overall system accuracy. Therefore, we can improve recommendation accuracy by employing estimators which are functions of the sufficient statistic. In other words, we need an instance selection algorithm that represents a sufficient statistic of the data.

In the context of our recommender system, x is a set of ratings in the dataset, $g(x)$ is the influence of a neighbor, $E(g(x))$ is the weighted average of neighbor's opinions scaled by their influence, $T(x)$ is a sufficient statistic computed from the original data, and $E(g(x)|T(x))$ is the conditional expected value of a rough estimator given a sufficient statistic. In other words, it is a weighted average of all ratings that have the same value for the sufficient statistic, i.e., local weights on dimensions selected by their global similarity ranking.

A sufficient statistic is a function of the data that describes it in such a way that a sample generated according to this statistic would be as useful as the original data for estimating θ, the actual rating we are trying to predict. The purpose of the sufficient statistic is to capture all of the useful information necessary for estimating θ, so that the data may be discarded in favor of the statistic. The list of the most relevant dimensions, established in the first step of the recursive algorithm, is a sufficient statistic of the data. Once we know the best dimensions, we no longer need the rest of them.

The first pass of the recursive algorithm decides which dimensions are the most relevant. It categorizes the matrix dimensions into two groups: top 30 and everybody else. Vectors from the first group receive a weight of $T(x) = 1$ and everyone else receives a weight of $T(x) = 0$. Ignoring dimensions from the latter group may improve the accuracy of an existing estimator $g(x)$. In fact, Rao-Blackwellisation of $g(x)$ is guaranteed not to make things worse.

We considered two alternative instance selection methods with cosine similarity as well as Pearson's correlation measures on 1,000 randomly chosen ratings from the Netflix Quiz dataset. Figure 5 shows that using Pearson's correlation is considerably better than cosine similarity. In fact, this approach had lower RMSE scores for both vector orientations. Also, resorting the data was more accurate for cosine as well as Pearson's similarities.

Even though Pearson's correlation is a more accurate way to compare vectors, the choice of a similarity measure is irrelevant for our instance selection process. The benefits of our approach come not from a particular weight metric, but from reducing the number of dimensions and deciding which dimensions should participate in the similarity computation.

Method	KNN-Item	KNN-User
Cosine Standard	1.301	1.305
Cosine Recursive	0.980	0.945
Pearson Standard	0.786	0.826
Pearson Recursive	0.423	0.465

Fig. 5. RMSE on the Netflix Quiz Dataset

VI. Conclusion

We believe that a small number of relevant ratings is sufficient to make an accurate recommendation. Such ratings may be chosen with a recursive approach that requires two neighbors to be similar in some, but not all, domains. It establishes more pertinent evidence for vector similarity, so that selected ratings are more relevant. To test this claim, we developed an algorithm that organizes ratings in matrices sorted by user/item similarities.

The main purpose of our instance selection algorithm is to produce small and dense matrices. It selects relevant data by recursively resorting the matrix, since local similarities of users and items are mutually dependent. The resulting vectors do not necessarily agree in every shared dimension, but they hold the most insight about the current recommendation. Our analysis shows that resorting the matrix can not decrease recommendation accuracy. Furthermore, our empirical study shows that the recommendation accuracy from resorted matrices is considerably better than the standard approach where the data is only sorted once.

References

[1] G. Adomavicius and A. Tuzhilin, "Toward the next generation of recommender systems: A survey of the state-of-the-art and possible extensions," *IEEE Transactions on Knowledge and Data Engineering*, vol. 17, no. 6, pp. 734–749, 2005. [Online]. Available: http://ieeexplore.ieee.org/xpls/abs_all.jsp?arnumber=1423975

[2] C. Basu, H. Hirsh, and W. Cohen, "Recommendation as classification: Using social and content-based information in recommendation," in *Proceedings of the Fifteenth National/Tenth Conference on Artificial Intelligence/Innovative Applications of Artificial Intelligence*. Menlo Park, CA, USA: American Association for Artificial Intelligence, 1998, pp. 714–720.

[3] R. M. Bell and Y. Koren, "Lessons from the netflix prize challenge," *ACM SIGKDD Explorations Newsletter*, vol. 9, no. 2, pp. 75–79, 2007.

[4] D. Blackwell, "Conditional expectation and unbiased sequential estimation," *The Annals of Mathematical Statistics*, vol. 18, no. 1, pp. 105–110, 1947. [Online]. Available: http://www.jstor.org/stable/2236107

[5] L. Candillier, F. Meyer, and M. Boullé, "Comparing state-of-the-art collaborative filtering systems," in *Proceedings of the 5th International Conference on Machine Learning and Data Mining in Pattern Recognition*, ser. LNCS, vol. 4571. Springer, 2007, pp. 548–562.

[6] C. de Santana Pereira and G. Cavalcanti, "Instance selection algorithm based on a ranking procedure," in *The 2011 International Joint Conference on Neural Networks (IJCNN)*, 31 2011-aug. 5 2011, pp. 2409 –2416.

[7] C. García-Osorioa, A. de Haro-Garcíab, and N. García-Pedrajasb, "Democratic instance selection: A linear complexity instance selection algorithm based on classifier ensemble concepts," *Artificial Intelligence*, vol. 174, no. 5-6, pp. 410 – 441, 2010.

[8] N. García-Pedrajas, J. A. Romero Del Castillo, and D. Ortiz-Boyer, "A cooperative coevolutionary algorithm for instance selection for instance-based learning," *Mach. Learn.*, vol. 78, pp. 381–420, March 2010. [Online]. Available: http://dx.doi.org/10.1007/s10994-009-5161-3

[9] J. L. Herlocker, J. A. Konstan, L. G. Terveen, and J. T. Riedl, "Evaluating collaborative filtering recommender systems," *ACM Transactions on Information Systems*, vol. 22, no. 1, pp. 5–53, 2004.

[10] Z. Huang, H. Chen, and D. Zeng, "Applying associative retrieval techniques to alleviate the sparsity problem in collaborative filtering," *ACM Transactions on Information Systems*, vol. 22, no. 1, pp. 116–142, 2004.

[11] N. Jankowski and M. Grochowski., "Comparison of instances selection algorithms: I. algorithms survey," in *Artificial Intelligence and Soft Computing*, ser. Lecture notes in computer science. Springer, June 2004, pp. 598–603.

[12] J. A. Konstan, B. N. Miller, D. Maltz, J. L. Herlocker, L. R. Gordon, and J. Riedl, "GroupLens: Applying collaborative filtering to usenet news," *Communications of the ACM*, vol. 40, no. 3, pp. 77–87, 1997.

[13] N. Leavitt, "Recommendation technology: Will it boost e-commerce?" *Computer*, vol. 39, no. 5, pp. 13–16, 2006.

[14] E. Marchiori, "Class conditional nearest neighbor for large margin instance selection," *IEEE Transactions on Pattern Analysis and Machine Intelligence*, vol. 32, pp. 364–370, 2010.

[15] N. Miller, Bradley, A. Konstan, Joseph, and J. Riedl, "PocketLens: Toward a personal recommender system," *ACM Trans. Inf. Syst.*, vol. 22, no. 3, pp. 437–476, 2004.

[16] B. Sarwar, G. Karypis, J. Konstan, and J. Reidl, "Item-based collaborative filtering recommendation algorithms," in *Proceedings of the 10th International Conference on World Wide Web*. New York, NY, USA: ACM, 2001, pp. 285–295.

[17] B. M. Sarwar, J. A. Konstan, A. Borchers, J. Herlocker, B. Miller, and J. Riedl, "Using filtering agents to improve prediction quality in the GroupLens research collaborative filtering system," in *Proceedings of the 1998 ACM Conference on Computer Supported Cooperative Work*. New York, NY, USA: ACM, 1998, pp. 345–354.

[18] J. Wang, A. P. de Vries, and M. J. T. Reinders, "Unifying user-based and item-based collaborative filtering approaches by similarity fusion," in *Proceedings of the 29th Annual International ACM SIGIR Conference on Research and Development in Information Retrieval*. New York, NY, USA: ACM, 2006, pp. 501–508.

SESSION

SEGMENTATION, CLUSTERING, ASSOCIATION + WEB / TEXT / MULTIMEDIA MINING

Chair(s)

Drs. Robert Stahlbock
Peter Geczy
Gary M. Weiss

Mining for Hydrologic Features in LiDAR Data

Rebecca Reizner, Eric Shaffer, and Brianna Birman, *University of Illinois at Urbana-Champaign*

Abstract—**Light Detection and Ranging (LiDAR) can generate 3D point data of terrains with high resolution and accuracy, enabling automated detection of important hydrologic features. This paper describes a method for detecting sinkholes in LiDAR data. Current methods of sinkhole detection are lengthy and labor intensive, requiring hours or days of manual work. The method demonstrated in this study can locate sinkholes in the same LiDAR data within minutes with no need for human intervention.**

I. Introduction

Automated detection of hydrologic features has become increasingly important for geologists. The ability to acquire high-resolution LiDAR data for large swaths of land means that much more data is available for analysis. The increased detail of LiDAR data over USGS topographic maps potentially allow up to 30% more sinkholes to be identified[8]. Unfortunately, traditional, mostly manual methods for landform analysis do not scale well. Sinkhole identification is an operation of particular interest, as sinkholes cause safety hazards to those living and working in areas exhibiting the potential for such formations. This is because sinkholes serve as a direct conduit to the underlying bedrock aquifer in the region creating a high potential for groundwater contamination[7].

II. Previous Work

Sinkhole detection and cataloging has been an important problem for decades. Previous methods have used seismic and acoustic emission/ microseismic(AE/MS) techniques[1], topographic maps, aerial photos[2], contouring[3], and LiDAR data visually inspected for sinkholes. A common approach to identifying sinkholes is to locate closed depression contours[8]. Even when computers are used for the contouring or slope analysis, people are still needed to accurately locate the sinkholes by hand.

A study by Young[5] has attempted to use LiDAR to ocate sinkholes in Jefferson County, West Virginia. He has created a DEM from the data and used a modification of the Terrain Shape Index to attempt to locate sinkholes. His algorithm found 94 sites. They were able to visit 55 of these to determine accuracy. Of these, 16.4% were definitely a sinkhole, 43.6% were probably a sinkhole, 25.5% were depressions, and 14.5% were not sinkholes. The geologists desired greater accuracy then this and when we tried a similar technique, our results were poorer.

While LiDAR data has been effectively used to segment many urban features[4], identifying landforms in LiDAR data has not been researched extensively.

III. Hydrologic Features

Sinkholes are one of the most studied hydrologic land features. They are formed when ground below the surface erodes away causing the land to collapse. This erosion is due to ground water slowly dissolving and washing away the underlying bedrock which is typically limestone or other carbonate rock. Sinkholes can vary in size dramatically from less than a foot deep to thousands of feet across. Shapes vary from circular to elongated to completely irregular. When first formed, the sides tend to be very steep and cylindrical. Over time, erosion cause the sinkholes to flatten out into more of a cone shape. Tools for automatic identification of sinkholes must be sophisticated in order to accurately analyze the immense variety of formations.

IV. Methods

Testing was done on a tract of land 20,000 by 35,000 feet in Waterloo, IL. This area is characterized by thousands of sinkholes. The LiDAR data was acquired by the Illinois State Geological Survey in April 2011. The sampling method had the contractor flying over the same area twice, once with a density of at least 1pt/m^2, and once at a lower altitutde with a point density of at least 4pts/m^2. This was to achieve improved vegetation penetration. LiDAR Class 2 points are classified as ground points. LiDAR Class 8 points are derived from LiDAR Class 2 points and are an interpolation of the key points. A combination of Class 2 and Class 8 points were the basis of the data used for our algorithm.

A digital elevation map (DEM) was created from this data at $\frac{1}{10}$ resolution. This operation effectively generated a regular spatial clustering of the original set of points and enabled interpolation within sparse areas.

As seen in Algorithm 1, an iterative process then segmented out all of the points that were in the lowest 1% of the heights. We created sets of points that were touching. If this set contained more than 20 cells it was temporarily labeled as a sinkhole. The exclusion of the smaller sinkholes prevented noise from the LiDAR data being counted as a sinkhole. The process was then repeated, segmenting out the lowest 2% of ground heights. This time the new sinkholes are compared to the old sinkholes. If one of the new sinkholes covers 2 or more old sinkholes that are larger than 100 cells, it is discarded. If the new sinkhole covers multiple sinkholes that are smaller than 100 cells, the smaller old sinkholes

Rebecca Reizner is with the Department of Computational Science and Engineering, University of Illinois, Urbana, IL 61801, USA (phone: 630-696-2456; email: reizner1@illinois.edu).

Eric Shaffer is with the Department of Computational Science and Engineering, University of Illinois, Urbana, IL 61801, USA (phone: 217-372-4190; email: shaffer1@illinois.edu).

Brianna Birman is with the Department of Computer Science, University of Illinois, Urbana, IL 61801, USA (email: birman1@illinois.edu).

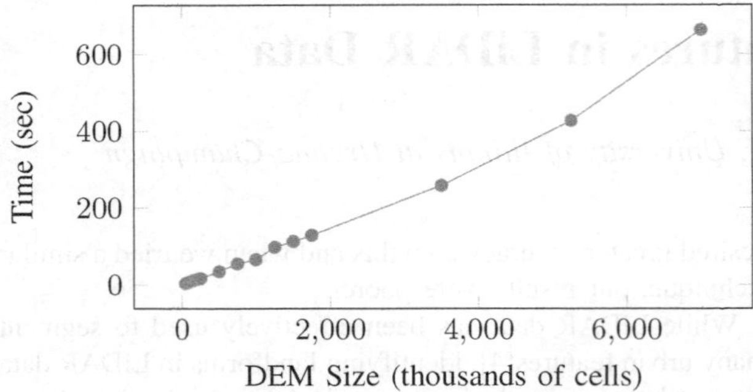

Fig. 1. Time vs Problem Size

are discarded, allowing the newer larger one to effectively absorb them. This value of 100 cells was used to mirror the manual process of segmenting sinkholes as performed by geologists. If a new sinkhole covers only one old sinkhole, the old sinkhole is replaced with the new one. If a new sinkhole does not cover an old sinkhole, it is simply added to the temporary list of sinkholes. This process is repeated up until 99% of the lowest elevation points in the DEM are segmented out and checked for sinkholes.

Algorithm 1 Find Sinkholes

Input: DEM
Output: List of sinkholes

Initialize SINKHOLES to empty list
for $i = 0.01; i < 1; i += 0.01$ **do**
  Flood DEM at i
  Add potential sinkholes to SINKHOLES
  if new sinkhole overlaps old sinkhole **then**
    if old sinkhole is smaller than 100 cells **then**
      remove old sinkhole
    else if new sinkhole overlaps 2 or more old sinkholes **then**
      remove new sinkhole
    end if
  end if
end for
return SINKHOLES

The algorithm is scalable, requiring linear time in the number of cells in the DEM. This theoretical time-bound has been verified from experimental timings, as seen in Figure 1.

V. Main Results

Our algorithm found 2564 sinkholes in the LiDAR data. The LiDAR data consists of 56 las files creating a total of 15.2 GB of data. The program takes under 10 minutes to complete running serially on a 2.00GHz Intel Xeon CPU with 126GB of memory. Figure 2 shows these sinkholes overlayed on the DEM we created. Segmenting the same data set by hand would require days.

To verify our results, we obtained shapefiles from geologists at ISGS that contained data for 2451 sinkholes found using the same LiDAR data. In comparison, this data took them several days to manually generate. To compare our results to the geologists', we filtered out the sinkholes that they found with a bounding box less than 2000ft^2. This is so they would be comparable to the sinkholes we found which only includes sinkholes that cover at least 20 DEM cells. It is necessary to have this lower bound to prevent larger error rates due to differences in interpolation between the LiDAR points. Using this method 83% of the sinkholes identified by the geologists were found with our algorithm. Furthermore, 96% of the sinkholes we found were sinkholes that geologist also found. Further refinement needs to be done in tandem with the geologists to clarify the properties of sinkholes and determine if our algorithm needs to be more or less selective.

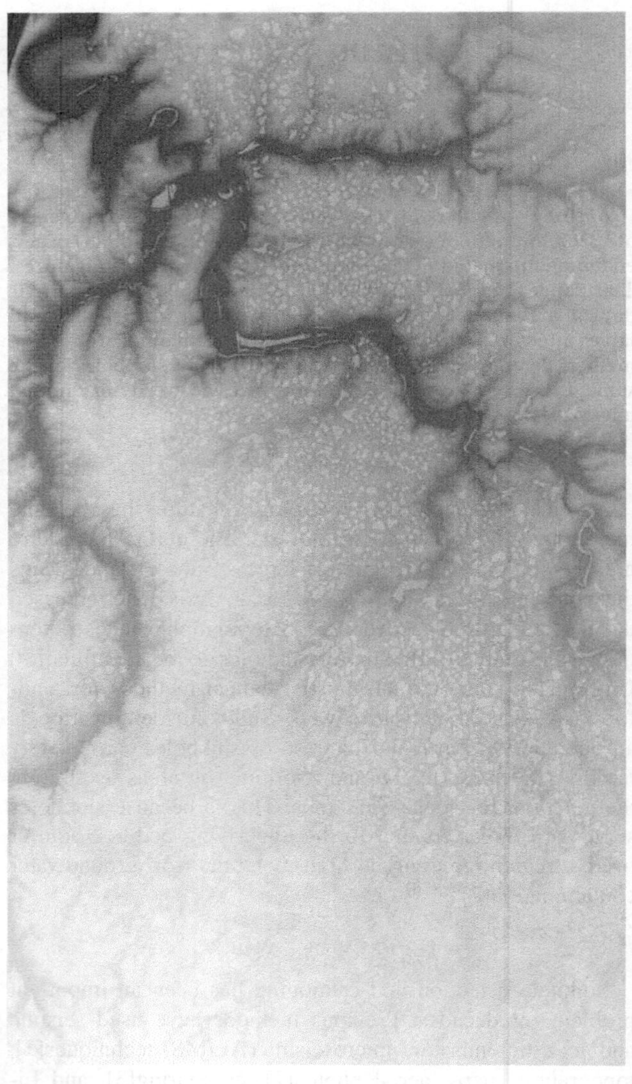

Fig. 2. Detected Sinkholes

VI. Further Filtering

After reviewing our sinkholes, we learned that our algorithm was identifying sections of streambed as sinkholes. We determined that one characteristic differentiating streambed from actual sinkholes is aspect ratio, because thin, long depressions are more frequently streambeds. A second differentiating metric is the fraction of the bounding box around the sinkhole is filled, with curving streambed depressions filling less of their bounding box. These metrics are scale-invariant, allowing them to be applied generally to the initial set of detected hydrologic features.

To employ these metrics as filters, we needed to determine threshold values for each that differentiate sinkholes from streambed. To do this, we manually created a training dataset with sinkholes and streambeds labeled and fed this data into Weka's[6] decision tree algorithm. We used the decision tree to determine the cutoff points for each of these ratios, and then used the learned ratios to perform streamed filtering on the rest of the data. The filtering algorithm proved quite effective, with a sampling of our results before and after streambed filtering shown in Figure 3 and Figure 4 respectively. This brought our false positives from 3.9% to 2.7%. However, this filtering also lowered the number of professionally identified sinkholes that our algorithm found from 84.5% to 83.3%.

Table I shows which of the sinkholes our algorithm found were also identified by the geologists with varying filters. The first is with no filtering. The second is with filtering out sinkholes that are smaller than 20 DEM cells. The third is with the same filter and the streambed filter. These are the same filters represented in Tables II, III, and IV. These three tables represent how many of the geologists sinkholes were found with our algorithm. Table II shows this data in reference to all of the geolgists' sinkholes. Table III represents only the geologists' sinkholes that have a bounding box greater than 2000m^2. Table IV shows only the geologists' sinkholes that have a bounding box greater than 4000m^2.

TABLE I
ACCURACY OF SINKHOLES

Filters	Total	Ours Verified	False Positives	Percent Accurate
None	2636	2315	321	87.8
> 20	2162	2077	85	96.1
> 20 & SF	2113	2056	57	97.3

TABLE II
COMPLETENESS OF ALL SINKHOLES

Filters	Found	Total	Percent Found
None	1837	2283	80.5
> 20	1658	2283	72.6
> 20 & SF	1628	2283	71.3

VII. Moving Towards Sinkhole Characterization

The ability to identify sinkholes in LiDAR data effectively allows the creation of a digital catalog of sinkholes. A next step is to look at what can be learned about sinkholes through

TABLE III
COMPLETENESS OF > 2000 SINKHOLES

Filters	Found	Total	Percent Found
None	1703	1930	88.2
> 20	1630	1930	84.5
> 20 & SF	1608	1930	83.3

TABLE IV
COMPLETENESS OF > 4000 SINKHOLES

Filters	Found	Total	Percent Found
None	1625	1807	89.9
> 20	1602	1807	88.6
> 20 & SF	1583	1807	87.6

analysis of such a catalog. Our software can compute some basic geometric characteristics of sinkholes such as perimeter and depth. We can also extract information about vegetation locations from LiDAR data. With this data, one can define multiple classes, such as dividing perimeter lengths into three classes of *small*, *medium*, and *large* and similar classes for depth. One interesting question is then how being in one class influences the probability of being in another class. We chose to use a Naive Bayesian Classifier to answer such questions. Clearly, there may be confounding variables that spoil the assumption of conditional independence. So, we must proceed understanding that high probabilities may be simply be indicative of the existence of such a confounding variable. The discovery of such a variable would be interesting in and of itself, making the investigation a worthwhile pursuit.

As an initial inquiry, we examined the relationship between the maximum relative depth (distance from the lowest point of the sinkhole to the top of the sinkhole) and the perimeter using a set of 2366 sinkholes. The perimeter characteristic is divided into three buckets: 0 - 60 feet is

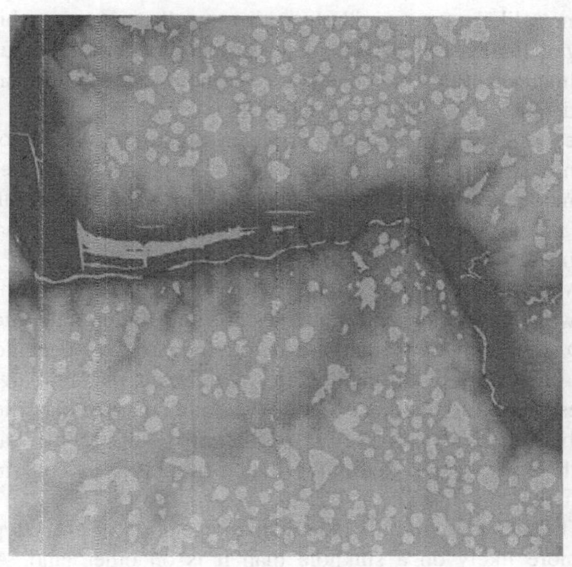

Fig. 3. Before Streambed Filtering

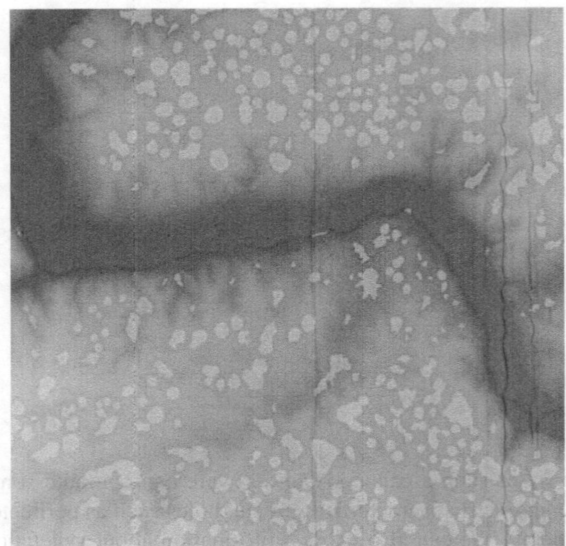

Fig. 4. After Streambed Filtering

small, 60 to 95 is *medium*, and greater than 95 is *large*. Depth is divided into the following buckets: 0 to 15 feet is *shallow*, 15 to 22 is *moderate*, and greater than 22 meters is *deep*. We then calculate the likelihood of a certain depth given the perimeter, producing the results in Table V.

TABLE V
PROBABILITY OF DEPTH GIVEN THE PERIMETER

	Small Perimeter	Medium Perimeter	Large Perimeter
Shallow	0.640083	0.376623	0.327273
Medium	0.287795	0.345083	0.246753
Deep	0.072122	0.278293	0.4259744

The table shows that some generalizations can be made about the geometric structure of sinkholes. A shallow depth is most likely for a sinkhole with a small perimeter, while *deep* is the least likely. The depth probabilities for a medium perimeter sinkhole are much less pronounced. Shallow and moderate depths are more likely than deep, but not by as much as it was for small perimeter sinkholes. A sinkhole with a large perimeter is most likely deep, and least likely of moderate depth, but like medium perimeter, the results are not as pronounced as the depth likelihoods for small perimeters.

A more intriguing exercise is to look at the relationship between vegetation and sinkholes. As part of pre-classified LiDAR data, points that are determined to be vegetation are divided into three categories: *low*, *medium*, and *high*. These vegetation points occur above points that are classified as bare earth. By projecting vegetation points to the bare earth level, we can determine if that vegetation is covering a sinkhole.

The results in Table VI show that vegetation of every type is more likely on a sinkhole than it is on other land. An overlay image of vegetation and sinkholes, seen in Figure

TABLE VI
PROBABILITY OF VEGETATION LEVEL GIVEN SINKHOLE EXISTENCE

	Over Sinkhole	Not Over Sinkhole
Low Vegetation	0.965995	0.888883
Medium Vegetation	0.987562	0.926441
High Vegetation	0.995783	0.939347

Fig. 5. Sinkholes with Detected Vegetation Overlaid

5 shows a portion of the analyzed area. It implies that this strong relationship stems from land without sinkholes being more often cleared for development.

VIII. CONCLUSIONS AND FUTURE DIRECTIONS

The algorithm presented in this paper provides an accurate, efficient, and automated way of identifying sinkholes from LiDAR data. This allows sinkholes to be cataloged and monitored, providing important information for land planning strategies. Future work will attempt to characterize the risk of sinkhole formation in an area through correlations between sinkholes and soil type. It may also be possible that the geometric pattern of emergent sinkholes, by exposing underlying geological lineation, can be used to predict where new sinkholes are likely to form.

ACKNOWLEDGMENT

The authors would like to thank Donald Luman and Samuel Panno from the Illinois State Geological Survey.

REFERENCES

[1] Hardy, H. R., Jr., Belesky, R. M., Mrugala, M., Kimble, E. J., & Hager, M. E. 1986, Pennsylvania State Univ. Report

[2] Mukherjee, Arindam, Pavlowsky, Robert T., and Gouzie, Douglas, "GIS Database for Sinkhole Hazard Assessment in Christian County, Missouri" Joint South-Central and North-Central Sections, both conducting their 41st Annual Meeting (1113 April 2007)

[3] Seale, L. Don, Brinkmann, Robert, and Vacher, H.L. "GIS Database for Sinkhole Hazard Assessment in Christian County, Missouri" Joint South-Central and North-Central Sections, both conducting their 41st Annual Meeting (1113 April 2007)

[4] Golovinskiy, Aleksey, Kim, Vladimir G., and Funkhouser, Thomas "Shape-based Recognition of 3D Point Clouds in Urban Environments"

[5] Young, John, "Using LiDAR to map sinkholes in Jefferson County, West Virginia" Eastern Panhandle West Virginia GIS Users Group Meeting (2009)

[6] Mark Hall, Eibe Frank, Geoffrey Holmes, Bernhard Pfahringer, Peter Reutemann, Ian H. Witten (2009); The WEKA Data Mining Software: An Update; SIGKDD Explorations, Volume 11, Issue 1.

[7] Merrick & Company, "Merrick Utilizes LiDAR in Large Sinkhole Plain" (March 07, 2013)

[8] Jacoby, Doug CMS, GISP; Luman, Donald PhD; "Sinkhole ID" (November, 1, 2012)

Role of Social Media in Early Warning of Norovirus Outbreaks: A Longitudinal Twitter-Based Infoveillance

Ahmed H. YoussefAgha, Wasantha P. Jayawardene, David K. Lohrmann

Abstract: The purpose of this study was to determine the trend in daily norovirus-related keyword utilization on twitter and to develop an experimental computational model that can accurately predict outbreaks in real-time. Data were collected from twitter within an accessible limit (1%) between February 1 and May 5, 2012 using seven keywords. Data were analyzed to determine the trend of daily norovirus-related keywords utilization on twitter on daily bases. Because of the trend lines on time were expected to be non-linear, a polynomial of degree five was used to model the trends in the norovirus hashtag separately by week. We also explored the correlation between norovirus hashtag utilization on twitter and other related hashtags. For categorical data analysis, each hashtag distribution was transformed into a binomial distribution. Nonparametric test of Wilcoxon Scores (Rank Sums) was used to compare norovirus days with different codes. Chi-Square test was used to explore associations between norovirus and other hashtags. Probability of the "norovirus" hashtags occurring above the daily mean on a day with "fever" hashtags above the daily mean was 0.467 (p=0.0433), whereas that for "outbreak" was 0.625 (p=0.027). "Norovirus" hashtag had the highest correlation with "fever" hashtag, followed by "outbreak", "throwing up", and "sick" hashtags. A statistically significant difference between "fever" and "sick" keywords was found in relation to utilization of the "norovirus" hashtag. A non-linear regression equation, using a polynomial of degree six, was formed for each of the four short term extrapolation periods.

Keywords: Norovirus; Outbreak; Twitter; Hashtags

I. INTRODUCTION

Acute gastroenteritis, usually accompanied by diarrhea, nausea, vomiting abdominal pain, and/or fever, is one of the leading causes of morbidity in the United States. Approximately 179 million cases of acute gastroenteritis leading to approximately 0.6 million hospital admissions and 5,000 deaths occur every year [1]. As detection of viruses, unlike bacteria, in foods is very difficult, the best way of identifying the causative agent in the majority of outbreaks is the epidemiological analysis of patients [2].

Transmission of noroviruses occurs mainly through the fecal-oral route, either directly from person to person [3] or indirectly through contaminated food [4] water [5], surfaces [6], or animals [7]. Airborne transmission of infectious droplets can also occur during vomiting [8]. Most norovirus outbreaks occur in locations with high density of susceptible individuals is high, such as hospitals [9], elderly homes [10], and military bases [11], as well as in settings where turnover of vulnerable individuals, such as hotels [12], restaurants [13], and cruise ships [14].

People with norovirus are contagious for three days from the onset of symptoms to, although contagiousness may persist for up to two weeks after recovery from symptoms. Major symptoms are vomiting (more common among children) and diarrhea (more common among adults) several times a day [15]. Nausea, abdominal cramps, headache, fever, chills, and myalgia may also present as associated symptoms [15]. Winter vomiting disease, a condition characterized with vomiting alone, can also occur [16]. Due to the nature of symptoms, people usually call norovirus infection "stomach flu" [14, 17] or sometimes "gastric flu" [12]. Most people recover from symptoms within 12-60 hours, although dehydration can be problematic among young children, the elderly, and people with debilitating illnesses [15]. Norovirus is not a nationally notifiable disease in the US, because testing for the disease is not generally available in hospitals and doctor's offices. Therefore, norovirus is usually diagnosed only when an outbreak of symptoms is reported to CDC [18]. A norovirus outbreak is defined as the occurrence of two or more similar cases that are linked epidemiologically; for example, ingestion of a common food [18].

Traditionally, newspapers, radio, and television are the major sources of information from public health agencies to the public and play a large role in risk communication during outbreaks [19]. However, internet was the most frequently used source of information about the H1N1 pandemic in 2009 [20]. The type of disease surveillance that utilizes online contents is called infoveillance [21]. Because twitter has short text status updates with <140 characters (tweets) that users share with followers, it's a candidate for longitudinal infoveillance text mining [19]. Longitudinal mining of tweets allows identification of changes in public responses [19], as well as early warning and detection of outbreaks, such as swine flu [22].

Ahmed H. YoussefAgha is with Department of Epidemiology and Biostatistics, School of Public Health Bloomington, Indiana University; Address: SPHB C108, 1025 E 7th Street, Bloomington, IN 47405, USA; Tel: 1-812-369-9798; E-mail: ahmyouss@indiana.edu

Wasantha P. Jayawardene (corresponding author) is with Department of Applied Health Science, School of Public Health Bloomington, Indiana University; Address: SPHB C116, 1025 E 7th Street, Bloomington, IN 47405, USA; Tel: 1-812-272-9136; E-mail: wajayawa@indiana.edu

David K. Lohrmann is with Department of Applied Health Science, School of Public Health Bloomington, Indiana University; Address: SPHB C116, 1025 E 7th Street, Bloomington, IN 47405, USA; Tel: 1-812-856-5101; E-mail: dlohrman@indiana.edu

II. METHODS

A. *Purpose of the Study*

The main purpose of our study is to investigate the trend of norovirus-related keyword utilization via twitter on daily basis and to develop an experimental computational model that can accurately predict outbreaks in real-time. A norovirus outbreak was identified and tracked through longitudinal mining and analysis of twitter data. Based on findings from previously published studies, tweets between 02/01/2012 and 05/02/2012 were archived for analysis.

B. *Methodology*

Our intent was to develop an infectious diseases monitoring system comprised of four dimensions: (1) a tweet classifier, which instantly monitored and analyzed an incoming tweet to determine whether it was disease-related; (2) a disease classifier, which extracted all disease features from each relevant tweet and identify which disease is being tracked; (3) a named entity recognition analyzer, which was responsible for extracting text available on web-sites that are referred to by twitter users; and (4) a data mining and alert generator - a software component that will generate disease alerts when necessary along with periodical reports.

The tweet classifier was responsible for performing two tasks (1) capturing live tweets in real-time and (2) analyzing captured tweets to determine whether a tweet was relevant to the scope of this project. Tweet classifier was trained by analyzing manually selected tweets using a machine learning algorithms to be discussed later. As result of the classification process, irrelevant tweets were ignored and relevant tweets were filtered in and stored for further multi-category classification.

The disease classifier processed the relevant tweets and mapped them into their most related disease. Therefore, each tweet was analyzed to extract disease features. However, to be able to classify a tweet as being related to one disease or another we developed a manually large training set that had sufficient data about the symptoms of the diseases we were monitoring. For each disease of interest, a profile was developed using tweet features and literature features.

The named entity recognition analyzer was responsible for extracting text available on web-sites referred to by Twitter users. Though not all tweets will have an embedded URL, we took advantage of this available detailed information when it was provided. News articles, for example, revealed the name of a disease that was tracked. It was very important also to identify the other entities (organism, person, percentage, quantity, and location) mentioned in a news article and then link them to the literature, the host organism, and the place of occurrence.

The data mining and alert generator was the most important component for our system. After tweets were classified and weather data was tracked for the subject region of the tweets, a series of data mining events executed to predict whether the disease was going to spread. The data mining and alert generator predicted the magnitude of spread given the location of the disease and rate of spread. We used statistical data mining methods and techniques to accomplish this task and accessed extensive computational resources to derive a complex model that enabled analysis of the resources needed to generate appropriate alerts.

C. *Keywords*

The "#" symbol in twitter is called a hashtag, used to mark keywords or topics in a tweet. It is created organically by twitter users as a way of classifying messages. According to the literature, "diarrhea", "throwing up", "nausea", "stomach pain", "fever", "headache", and "body ache" were chosen as hashtags for this twitter study. Additional hashtags, with similar meanings, i.e., "stomach flu", "sick", "throw up", and "outbreak", were also included.

D. *Data Collection*

We subscribed to the services available at Indiana University Pervasive Technology Institute for our system as a high performance application. Data were collected from twitter within an accessible limit (1%) between February 1, 2012 and May 5, 2012 using the keywords mentioned above. A sample size of 27 days was determined as the number needed to study the disease trend in four weeks. Therefore, a period of four weeks between February 1st and May 5th was randomly selected. Twitter messages sent within four week time frame were subjected to investigation.

E. *Analysis*

Data were analyzed to determine the trend of norovirus-related keywords utilization via twitter on a daily bases. Because the trend lines on time were expected to be non-linear, polynomial of degree five was used to model the trends of the norovirus hashtag separately for each week. So, for non-linear short term extrapolation and/or interpolation, each polynomial required 6-7 points (i.e., 6-7 days) to be developed. The non-linear polynomial of degree six can be used for short term extrapolation. The ability to access greater amounts of data (currently limited to 1% of all twitter) would have enhanced the extrapolation.

First, four conditional probabilities were evaluated:

a) pr (dayswithnorovirus>mean|dayswithfever>mean)
b) pr (dayswithnorovirus>mean|dayswithsick>mean)
c) pr (dayswithnorovirus>mean|dayswithvomiting>mean)
d) pr (dayswithnorovirus>mean|dayswithoutbreak>mean)

Then, the correlation between norovirus hashtag utilization on twitter with the other related hashtags was explored. For categorical data analysis, each hashtag distribution was transformed into a binomial distribution (table-1). For each selected study day, if a keyword hashtag frequency was less than or equal to the mean value of the same keyword, it was coded 1, and if the frequency was greater than the mean value, it was coded 2. Nonparametric test of Wilcoxon Scores (Rank Sums) was used to compare norovirus days with code 2 to norovirus days with code 1. Chi-Square test was used to assess associations between norovirus days (coded 1 or 2) and other hashtag (coded 1 or 2) such as fever, sick, outbreak, and vomiting.

III. RESULTS

A mean frequency of over 1700 hashtags (table-2) of "throwing-up", "sick", "headache", and "fever" per day were found. Daily mean of other hashtags were between 14 and 27, except "diarrhea", which was reported only 32 times during the 27-day period. The probability that more than 15 norovirus hashtags (daily mean for "norovirus") occurred on a day with "fever" hashtag frequency exceeded 155 (daily mean for "fever") was 0.467 and was statistically significant (p=0.0433). Similarly, the probability that more than 15 "norovirus" hashtags occurred on a day with "outbreak" hashtag frequency exceeded 23 (daily mean for "outbreak") was 0.625 (p=0.027). However, none of the remaining norovirus-related hashtags (diarrhea, sick, headache, throwing-up, vomiting) had a statistically significant association with norovirus hashtags.

"Norovirus" hashtag had a moderate correlation with the seven other related hashtags collected during the four-week period (table-3). "Norovirus" hashtag had the highest correlation with "fever" hashtag (r=0.396), followed by correlations with "outbreak" (r=0.374), "throwing up" (r=0.281), "sick" (r=0.277), "headache" (r=0.258), "diarrhea" (r=0.180), and "vomiting" (r=0.155) hashtags.

Nonparametric test Wilcoxon Scores found that each of the "fever" and "sick" keywords significantly differed (p<0.05) for the days grouped by code 1 and the days grouped by code 2 in relation to utilization of "norovirus" hashtag. If at least two conditions of "fever">155, "sick">5395, and "vomiting">76 were satisfied, and at the same time, if "outbreak"≤23, then the probability of "norovirus" hashtag being greater than 15 was 77.8%.

TABLE 1
TRANSFORMATION OF HASHTAG FREQUENCY INTO A BINARY DISTRIBUTION

Day*	Norovirus (μ=15)	Diarrhea (μ=1.4)	Fever (μ=155)	Sick (μ=5395)	Headache (μ=1718)	Throwing up (μ = 5420)	Vomiting (μ=26)	Outbreak (μ=23)
1st Feb	1	1	1	1	1	1	1	1
2nd Feb	1	2	1	1	1	1	1	1
3rd Feb	1	1	2	2	2	1	2	2
:	:	:	:	:	:	:	:	:
10th Feb	2	2	2	2	2	2	1	2
11th Feb	2	1	1	2	2	2	1	1
:	:	:	:	:	:	:	:	:

* Only a sample of the 27-day study period is shown in the table

TABLE 2
MEAN AND STANDARD DEVIATION OF NOROVIRUS AND OTHER RELATED HASHTAGS PER DAY

	Norovirus	Diarrhea	Fever	Sick	Outbreak	Headache	Throwing - up	Vomiting
Total	405	32	4194	145669	618	46379	145852	704
Mean	15	1.2	155	5395	23	1718	5402	26
SD	22	1	68	2137	27	603	1994	11

TABLE 3
CORRELATIONS AMONG NOROVIRUS AND OTHER RELATED HASHTAGS

	Norovirus	Diarrhea	Fever	Sick	Outbreak	Headache	ThrowingUp
Diarrhea	0.180	1					
Fever	0.396	0.309	1				
Sick	0.277	0.301	0.930	1			
Outbreak	0.374	0.000	0.472	0.246	1		
Headache	0.258	0.312	0.890	0.943	0.349	1	
ThrowingUp	0.281	0.214	0.775	0.841	0.413	0.927	1
Vomiting	0.155	0.247	0.695	0.762	0.319	0.812	0.832

Four periods of surveillance using the hashtags between February 1, 2012 and May 5, 2012: February 1–8, February 9–14, February 29–March 5, April 26–May 2 (figure 1). A non-linear regression equation was formed for each of the four periods for short term extrapolation; long term extrapolation was impossible as the trend was non-linear. A non-linear polynomial of degree six could be used for short term extrapolation. If the study could be expanded to access more than 1% of all twitter, the extrapolation would be enhanced.

IV. DISCUSSION

When twitter-based systems first appeared in epidemic surveillance, they were criticized for the possibility of producing exaggerated or misleading reports, lack of specificity (false positives), and extreme sensitivity to external forces such as unpredictable media interests. These condemnations are still valid, although they are recognized and adjusted to the extent possible. Despite these limitations, twitter-based epidemic surveillance is an irreplaceable resource for early warning of emerging outbreaks because of its sensitivity, availability, convenience, and transparency. Therefore, twitter has become a useful tool in the worldwide epidemic surveillance system. Moreover, findings of this study are highly compatible with the norovirus-related keyword search in "Google Trends" during the first half of 2012.

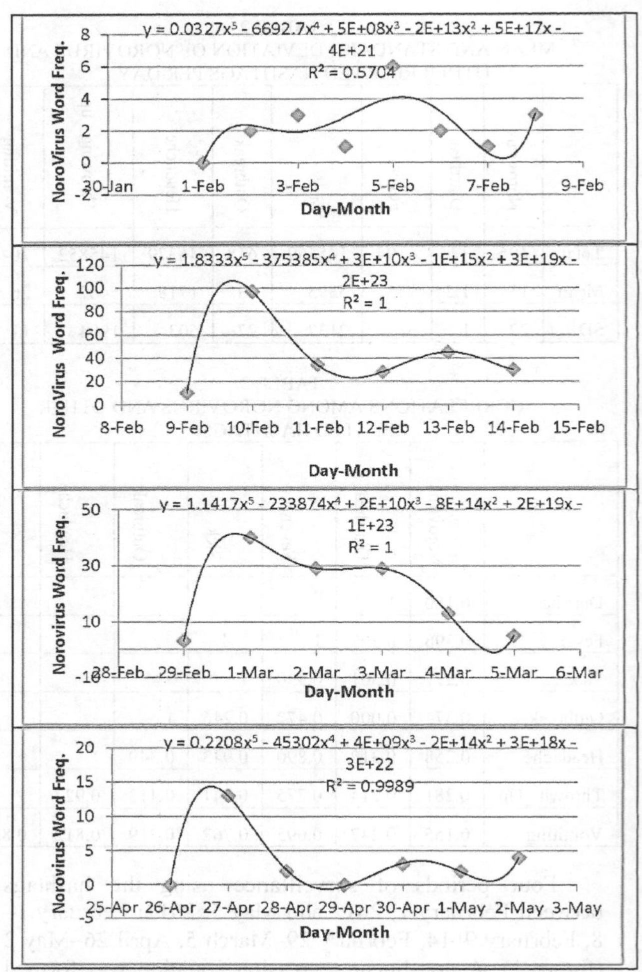

Figure 1: Short Term Extrapolation with Non-Linear Regression Equations for Each of the Four Periods between February 1, 2012 and May 2, 2012.

Several tweets-related challenges exist. High volumes of tweets are generated by millions of users tweeting in real-time simultaneously. This in turn required a high computational power to store and process incoming tweets. At its core, our model relied on the classification algorithms of tweets so that any tweet could be identified as relevant and, when relevant, could be further classified as to what disease was tracked. Finally, multi-lingual tweets are a challenge, because tweet users don't necessary share their status updates in English. Millions of twitter users share information in various languages, such as Spanish, French, Arabic, etc. More importantly, many users used less formal languages, acronyms, and even short hand. As a first step, we only focused on the tweets that were in English.

The geographic location, timing, and size of each norovirus outbreak may vary, complicating efforts to produce reliable and timely estimates of norovirus activity using traditional time series models. Epidemics are difficult to anticipate. Using actual tweet contents, which often reflected the user's perceived discomfort, when they were tweeting about their symptoms, we devised an estimation method based on well-understood statistical methods. The accuracy of the resulting real-time norovirus outbreak forecasting demonstrated that the subset of tweets identified and used in the models applied in the current study contained data associated with norovirus activity.

The current twitter-based model attempted to forecast norovirus activity. Because results generated by the current study could be available to public health officials as soon as the data are captured online, the forecast is potentially available at a much earlier time than ordinary public health alerts. Although it is possible to gather epidemic data in real time from hospital visits, drug purchase at pharmacies, and from school absenteeism, doing so at a national level would require combining data from different geographic areas and from multiple institutions/firms, a considerable data collecting burden. In contrast, twitter data are easily and efficiently collected and processed automatically in real time.

Despite these findings, this study has several limitations. First, the use of twitter is neither uniform across regions or time. Usually, Mondays are the busiest day for twitter traffic, while the lowest number of tweets is observed on Sundays. Large cities on east and west coasts produce far more tweets per person than cities in the Midwest or in other countries. In places where tweets are less frequent, the accuracy of our model may be low. Another limitation is that we only had 27 days of sampled data. Inclusion of more seasons, especially non-epidemic seasons, should help improve the accuracy of our norovirus estimates. Moreover, no comparable data, such as survey results, are available to validate our results. For example, absence of a detectable signal may indicate an apathetic public or a lack of knowledge. Therefore, we propose future studies to confirm our results with autocorrelated data.

The exact demographics of the twitter population are different from the general population. "Pew Research Center's Internet and American Life Project - Winter 2012 Tracking Survey, January 20 – February 19, 2012" (N=2,253), which coincided with the period of current study, showed that 15% of internet-users used twitter at some time and 8% of internet-users used twitter on a typical day. On a typical day, 20% of people in 18-24 year age group used twitter, with the percentage gradually decreasing with increasing age: 11% in 25-34 age group, 9% in 35-44 age group, 3% in 45-54 age group, 4% in 55-64 age group, and 1% in 65+ age group. According to the same survey, 15% of women and 14% of men used twitter, whereas 28% of non-Hispanic blacks, 14% of Hispanics, and 12% of non-Hispanic whites used it. People with no high school diploma had the highest twitter usage (22%), followed by college graduates (17%), persons with some college education (14%), and high school graduates (12%). Highest twitter usage was reported in urban areas (19%), followed by suburban areas (14%), and rural areas (8%). The demographics of the twitter population that would tweet about health related concerns, is unknown. Characteristics of twitter usage in relation to age, race, education level, and locality can affect the generalizability of findings.

V. CONCLUSION

Probability of “norovirus” hashtags occurring above the daily mean on a day with “fever” hashtags above daily mean were statistically significant. “Norovirus” hashtag had the highest correlation with “fever” hashtag, followed by “outbreak”, “throwing up”, and “sick” hashtags. “Fever” and “sick” keywords had a statistically significant difference in relation to utilization of “norovirus” hashtag. A non-linear regression equation, using a polynomial of degree six, can be formed for short term extrapolation of norovirus incidence. Twitter-based epidemic surveillance is an irreplaceable resource for early warning on emerging outbreaks because of their sensitivity, availability, convenience, and transparency.

REFERENCES

[1] A. J. Hall, M. Rosenthal, N. Gregoricus, S. A. Greene, J. Ferguson, O. L. Henao, *et al.*, "Incidence of Acute Gastroenteritis and Role of Norovirus, Georgia, USA, 2004-2005," *Emerging Infectious Diseases,* vol. 17, pp. 1381-1388, 2011.

[2] I. Barrabeig, A. Rovira, J. Buesa, R. Bartolomé, R. Pintó, H. Prellezo, *et al.*, "Foodborne norovirus outbreak: the role of an asymptomatic food handler," *BMC Infectious Diseases,* vol. 10, pp. 269-275, 2010.

[3] A. S. Chapman, C. T. Witkop, J. D. Escobar, C. A. Schlorman, L. S. DeMarcus, L. M. Marmer, *et al.*, "Norovirus outbreak associated with person-to-person transmission, U.S. Air Force Academy, July 2011," *Msmr,* vol. 18, pp. 2-5, 2011 2011.

[4] A. Yilmaz, K. Bostan, E. D. A. Altan, K. Muratoglu, N. Turan, D. Tan, *et al.*, "Investigations on the Frequency of Norovirus Contamination of Ready-to-Eat Food Items in Istanbul, Turkey, by Using Real-Time Reverse Transcription PCR," *Journal of Food Protection,* vol. 74, pp. 840-843, 2011.

[5] O. Zacheus and I. T. Miettinen, "Increased information on waterborne outbreaks through efficient notification system enforces actions towards safe drinking water," *Journal of Water and Health,* vol. 9, pp. 763-772, Dec 2011.

[6] J. C. M. Heijne, M. Rondy, L. Verhoef, J. Wallinga, M. Kretzschmar, N. Low, *et al.*, "Quantifying Transmission of Norovirus During an Outbreak," *Epidemiology,* vol. 23, pp. 277-284, Mar 2012.

[7] M. Summa, C.-H. von Bonsdorff, and L. Maunula, "Pet dogs—A transmission route for human noroviruses?," *Journal of Clinical Virology,* vol. 53, pp. 244-247, 2012.

[8] B. A. Lopman, A. J. Hall, A. T. Curns, and U. D. Parashar, "Increasing Rates of Gastroenteritis Hospital Discharges in US Adults and the Contribution of Norovirus, 1996-2007," *Clinical Infectious Diseases,* vol. 52, pp. 466-474, 2011.

[9] R. Fretz, D. Schmid, S. Jelovcan, R. Tschertou, E. Krassnitzer, M. Schirmer, *et al.*, "An outbreak of norovirus gastroenteritis in an Austrian hospital, winter 2006-2007," *Wiener Klinische Wochenschrift,* vol. 121, pp. 137-143, Feb 2009.

[10] L. Hualiang, N. Sammy, C. Shelley, C. Wai Man, K. C.K. Lee, S. C. Ho, *et al.*, "Institutional risk factors for norovirus outbreaks in Hong Kong elderly homes: a retrospective cohort study," *Bmc Public Health,* vol. 11, pp. 297-303, 2011.

[11] M. Wadl, K. Scherer, S. Nielsen, S. Diedrich, L. Ellerbroek, C. Frank, *et al.*, "Food-borne norovirus-outbreak at a military base, Germany, 2009," *BMC Infectious Diseases,* vol. 10, pp. 1-10, 2010.

[12] A. Doménech-Sánchez, C. Juan, J. L. Pérez, and C. I. Berrocal, "Unmanageable norovirus outbreak in a single resort located in the Dominican Republic," *Clinical Microbiology & Infection,* vol. 17, pp. 952-954, 2011.

[13] Centers for Disease Control and Prevention, "Multisite Outbreak of Norovirus Associated with a Franchise Restaurant -- Kent County, Michigan, May 2005," *MMWR: Morbidity & Mortality Weekly Report,* vol. 55, pp. 395-397, 2006.

[14] Reuters, "Hundreds on QE 2 Sick with Suspected Stomach Flu," in *Reuters*, ed, 2007.

[15] U. Parashar, E. S. Quiroz, A. W. Mounts, S. S. Monroe, R. L. Fankhauser, T. Ando, *et al.*, ""Norwalk-like viruses". Public health consequences and outbreak management," *MMWR. Recommendations and reports : Morbidity and mortality weekly report. Recommendations and reports / Centers for Disease Control,* vol. 50, pp. 1-17, 2001 Jun 2001.

[16] A. L. Greer, S. J. Drews, and D. N. Fisman, "Why "Winter" Vomiting Disease? Seasonality, Hydrology, and Norovirus Epidemiology in Toronto, Canada," *Ecohealth,* vol. 6, pp. 192-199, Jun 2009.

[17] E. Peter and M. Blake, "26,500 school cafeterias lack required inspections," ed.

[18] N. C. f. I. a. R. D. Division of Viral Diseases, Centers for Disease Control (CDC). (2012, March 18, 2012). *Norovirus* Available: http://www.cdc.gov/ncidod/dvrd/revb/gastro/norovirus.htm

[19] C. Chew and G. Eysenbach, "Pandemics in the Age of Twitter: Content Analysis of Tweets during the 2009 H1N1 Outbreak," *Plos One,* vol. 5, Nov 2010.

[20] J. H. Jones and M. Salathe, "Early Assessment of Anxiety and Behavioral Response to Novel Swine-Origin Influenza A(H1N1)," *Plos One,* vol. 4, Dec 2009.

[21] G. Eysenbach, "Infodemiology: tracking flu-related searches on the web for syndromic surveillance," *AMIA ... Annual Symposium proceedings / AMIA Symposium. AMIA Symposium,* pp. 244-8, 2006 2006.

[22] P. Kostkova, E. de Quincey, and G. Jawaheer, "The potential of social networks for early warning nad outbreak detection systems: the swine flu Twitter study," *International Journal of Infectious Diseases,* vol. 14, pp. E384-E385, Mar 2010.

Spatial-Temporal Clustering of a Self-Organizing Map

Carlos Enrique Gutierrez[1], **Prof. Mohamad Reza Alsharif**[1], **Prof. Katsumi Yamashita**[2]
Rafael Villa[3], **He Cuiwei**[1], **Prof. Hayao Miyagi**[1]
[1]Department of Information Engineering. Univ. of the Ryukyus. Okinawa, Japan.
carlosengutierrez@yahoo.com.ar, asharif@ie.u-ryukyu.ac.jp, hecuiwei0924@gmail.com, miyagi@ie.u-ryukyu.ac.jp
[2]Graduate School of Engineering. Osaka Prefecture University. Osaka, Japan. yamashita@eis.osakafu-u.ac.jp
[3]Regional Public Goods. InterAmerican Development Bank. Washington DC. USA. rafaelv@iadb.org

Abstract - *In this paper we explore the spatial and temporal properties of a set of news published after a natural disaster by using SOM (Self-organizing Maps). SOM develops a low-dimensional representation of the input data space by mapping high dimensional vectors into a 2-dimensional grid. Training stage produces a visual representation and a set of quantization points that can be considered as groups of spatially related news. Temporal dependency is detected by analyzing SOM units' activation over the time, discovering temporal associations between data items. Our SOM stores information throughout its grid in a way such that space and time structures of the input data set are discovered and stored. First it has no knowledge, but after learning it develops spatial-temporal representations.*

Spatial-Temporal relations can be used for predictive modeling, search of sequential patterns, and mostly used for understanding. In our case, discovered dependencies describe the causes or context that precede a topic, showing how it evolved and moved over the time.

Keywords:, neural networks, self-organizing map, temporal clustering, principal component analysis.

1. Introduction

Data mining can be applied on various sources of data such as on-line newspapers, social networks, blogs, etc; to discover groups or clusters of related events, having as disadvantage that it implies to manage high-dimensional data. If we take in account that each single word represents a variable, it is very complex to process the full set of variables and visualize events' relationships, fortunately, groups of variables often move together in time and space; one reason for this is that more than one variable might be measuring the same driving principle governing the system's behavior.

But besides the events' relationships that can be found by a computation of a "distance" between vectors; one of the most interesting problem is to find an effective and simple method able to discover temporal relations as well.

The purpose of this paper is to create a practical method based on artificial neural networks, to find spatial-temporal representations within raw data. In particular, we use a type of self-organizing map (SOM) called Kohonen's network, which is applied to uncover and visualize the inherent structure and topology of a set of news. If the data form clusters in the input space, i.e. if there are regions with very frequent and at the same time very similar data, the self-organizing process will ensure that the data of a cluster are mapped to a common localized domain in the map. Moreover, the process will arrange the mutual placement of domains in such a way as to capture as much of the overall topology of the cluster arrangement as possible. In this way, even hierarchical clustering can be achieved. The temporal factor is added to the map by the analysis of temporal dependencies between units, with the introduction of a time-dependent matrix that stores unit-to-unit and neighborhood-to-unit temporal relations.

In our work, a set of news published between March 11th and March 18th 2011 (March 11th is sadly remembered as the day where multiple earthquakes triggered a huge tsunami in Japan) are encoded as numeric vectors by using PCA. Secondly, a SOM is trained to build an organized representation of the input space. Next, a second training stage is applied to find temporal clusters. Finally, temporal representations are interpreted and analyzed, showing topics evolving over the time.

2. Input Data Encoding

Our data set contains 421 text files (news available at CNN web site). At this step, our aim is to develop a suitable representation of the input data as a numerical matrix. An implementation in C++ was developed to extract from each file the words, create a dictionary and compute words frequency. Special characters, numbers, symbols, and meaningless words such as conjunctions, prepositions and adverbs were removed. In addition, our implementation includes a Porter stemming algorithm [10]. Stemming is the process for reducing inflected (or sometimes derived) words to their stem, base or root form. The general idea underlying stemming is to identify words that are the same in meaning but different in form by removing suffixes and endings; for instance, words such as "expanded", "expanding", "expand", and "expands" are reduced to the root word, "expand ". The output was a dictionary of words (vector l of 9961 elements) and a matrix X of 421x9961 (news x words), where each element $x_{i,j}$ is a number equal to the frequency of $word_j$ at news i. As expected, the result is a high-dimensional matrix.

By using principal component analysis is it possible to transform a set of observations of possibly correlated variables into a set of values of linearly uncorrelated variables called principal components. Each principal component is a linear combination of the original variables, and all of them are orthogonal to each other, so there is no redundant information. By this method it is possible to compress the data by reducing the number of dimensions, without much loss of information [8]. Let X and Y be $m \times n$ matrices related by a linear transformation P $(n \times n)$; m indicates the observation number with n variables; X is the initial data set and Y is a re-representation of X. PCA re-express the initial data as a linear combination of its basis vectors:

$$Y = XP \tag{1}$$

p_i are column vectors of P.
x_i are row vectors of X.

Each row of Y has the form:

$$y_i = [x_i p_1 \cdots x_i p_n] \tag{2}$$

We recognize that each coefficient of y_i is a dot product of x_i with the corresponding column in P, in other words, the jth coefficient of y_i is a projection on to the jth column of P. By assuming linearity, the problem reduces to find the appropriate change of basis, the columns vectors p_i of P, also known as the principal components of X.

But first, let's define S_x as the covariance matrix of X. S_x is a simple way to quantify redundancy by calculating the spread between variables. X is in mean deviation form because the means have been subtracted off or are zero.

$$S_x = \frac{1}{n-1} X^T X \tag{3}$$

S_x is a square symmetric $n \times n$ matrix. Its diagonal terms are the variance of particular variables. The off-diagonal terms are the covariance between variables. From S_x the eigenvectors with their corresponding eigenvalues are calculated. Eigenvectors are a special set of vectors associated with a linear system of equations (i.e., a matrix equation), also known as characteristic vectors, proper vectors, or latent vectors [11]. Each eigenvector is paired with a corresponding factor so-called eigenvalue by which the eigenvector is scaled when multiplied by its matrix. A non-zero vector p_i is an eigenvector of the covariance matrix S_x if there is a factor λ_i such that:

$$S_x p_i = \lambda_i p_i \tag{4}$$

Generalizing:

$$S_x P = \Lambda P \tag{5}$$

The full set of eigenvectors is as large as the original set of variables. In PCA, the eigenvectors of S_x are the principal components of X. Matrix P ($n \times n$) contains n eigenvectors, arranged in a way such as p_1 is the principal component with the largest variances (the most important, the most "principal"); p_2 is the 2nd most important, and so on. In addition, the eigenvalues contained in diagonal matrix Λ are arranged in descending order $\lambda_1 > \lambda_2 > \cdots > \lambda_n$ and they represent the variance of X captured by the principal components. This last relation is used for dimensionality reduction.

$$S_x p_i = \sigma_i^2 p_i \quad \text{with} \quad \sigma_1^2 > \sigma_2^2 > \cdots > \sigma_n^2 \tag{6}$$

From matrix X, after subtracting off the mean for each variable, the covariance matrix and its principal component are computed. As result, the full set of 9961 principal components, matrix P, and the corresponding 9961 eigenvalues, diagonal matrix Λ, are obtained.

Principal components with larger associated variances have important dynamics; while those with lower variances represent noise. It is common to consider only the first few principal components whose variances exceed 80% of the total variance of the original data. In our case, the first 362 principal components (out of 9961) describe almost all the variability of the data set. Let's take, for instance, the $l = 362$ largest eigenvalues $\lambda_1 > \lambda_2 > \cdots > \lambda_l, (l < n)$; and truncate the matrix P at column l. That means, we are taking only the first l principal components of P. It implies a strong dimensionality reduction, in the order of 96%. This reduced $(n \times l)$ matrix is called $\hat{P}$. The original data set X $(m \times n)$ is re-expressed then as Y $(m \times l)$ by using matrix $\hat{P}$ $(n \times l)$:

$$Y = X\hat{P} \tag{7}$$

Equation (7), as a dot product, shows how matrix Y compresses X and contains the distribution of the news along the most important l components. Rows of matrix Y will be the input vectors of the Self-Organized Map used to discover spatial-temporal relations.

3. Spatial Relations Uncovering by Self-organizing maps (SOM).

At this stage, our work seeks to generate an understandable spatial map of the input space. To achieve it, we use matrix Y to feed a 2-dimensional 10x10 SOM network; each row y_i of Y represents a news. Considering the 421 training vectors, we assume that a grid of 100 units may produce a reasonable amount of quantization points and a suitable visualization. Generally, in SOM, variables are normalized by dividing each column of Y by its standard deviation, however, in our case; we consider that representation by PCA has homogenized the input data.

A SOM consists of components called units, cells or neurons. Associated with each unit there is a weight vector of the same dimension as the input data and a position vector in the map space. In learning stage an input vector is presented to the SOM at each step. These vectors constitute the "environment" of the network. SOM includes a competitive and unsupervised learning able to find clusters from the input data. Competitive learning means that a number of units are comparing the same input signals with their internal parameters, and the unit with the best match, the winner, is tuned itself to that input affecting also its neighbors. Therefore, different units learn different aspects from the input.

Some requirements are needed for self-organization: i) the units are exposed to a sufficient number of different inputs; ii) for each input, the synaptic input connections to the exited group of units are only affected; iii) similar updating is imposed on many adjacent neurons; iv) the resulting adjustment is such that it enhances the same responses to a subsequent, sufficiently similar input.

The most popular model of SOM is the model proposed by Teuvo Kohonen[5] called Kohonen network. Kohonen algorithm introduces a model that is composed of two interacting subsystems. One of these subsystems is a competitive neural network that implements the winner-take-all function. The other subsystem modifies the local synaptic plasticity of the neurons in learning [6]. Kohonen learning uses a neighborhood function ϕ, whose value $\phi = (i,k)$ represents the strength of the coupling between unit i and unit k during the training process. The learning algorithm is as follows [6]:

- Start: n-dimensional weight vectors $w_1, w_2, \ldots, w_m$ for the m computing units are selected at random. An initial radius of the neighborhood r, a learning constant η, and a neighborhood function ϕ are selected. The neighborhood function $\phi = (i,k)$ is defined as:

$$\phi(i,k) = \exp\left(-\left(\frac{|i-k|}{r}\right)^2\right) \quad (8)$$

Where i is the position of the ith unit and k is the position of the unit with the maximum excitation. The neighborhood function ϕ changes according to a schedule, producing larger corrections at the beginning of the training that at the end.

- Step 1: Select an input vector y using the desired probability distribution over the input space.
- Step 2: The unit k with the maximum excitation is selected (that is, for which the Euclidean distance between w_i and y is minimal, $i = 1,2,\ldots,m$).
- Step 3: The weight vectors are updated using the neighborhood function ϕ and the following rule:

$$w_i \leftarrow w_i + \eta\phi(i,k)(y - w_i) \text{ for } i = 1,2,\ldots,m \quad (9)$$

- Step 4: Stop if the maximum number of iterations has been reached; otherwise modify η and ϕ as scheduled and continue with step 1.

By repeating this process several times, it is expected to arrive to a uniform distribution of weight vectors for the input space. We perform 3000 iterations, at each one the complete set of training vectors is entered into the network once. The result is a nonlinear projection of the input space onto a map (Figure 1). A main property of the map is that, the distance relationships between the input data are preserved by their images in the map as faithfully as possible. However, a mapping from a high-dimensional space to a lower-dimensional one will usually distort most distances and only preserve the most important neighborhood relationships between data items. Figure 1 shows the SOM map after training and the 95 quantization points generated as gray dots. The size of the dots represents the amount of input vectors captured by weight vectors. For instance, w_{36} at coordinates (6,4) captures more inputs than w_{18} at (8,2). Within a quantization point the news are spatially related; therefore, a quantization point is by itself a group and represents a sub-set of input vectors.

Convergence of the network is evaluated empirically; it gets stable state after 3000 iterations, at this stage the map doesn't change and weight vectors experiment very small updates.

The obtained SOM mainly reflects metric distance relations between input vectors. In order to give a semantic-meaningful component to the map, we present, after the spatial training the context where the input data may be located, in that way the map reflects logic or semantic similarities. Context is a background, environment, framework, setting, or situation surrounding an event or occurrence. In linguistic it is defined as words and sentences that occur before or after a word or sentence and imbue it with a particular meaning.

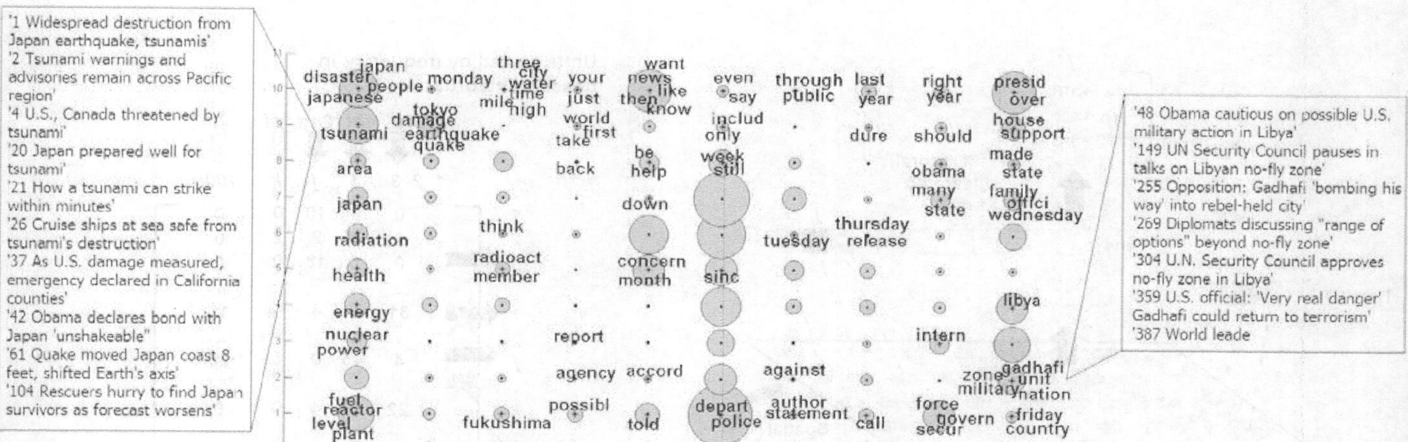

Figure 1. SOM map after training and the 95 quantization points generated as gray dots. The size of the dots represents the amount of input vectors captured by weight vectors. Most frequent words are mapped to give a semantic characteristic to the discovered structure.

We assume that the most frequent words have strong correlations with contexts that surround events described in our set of news. Hence we choose to represent each most frequent *k-th* word by a *n*-dimensional vector, whose *k-th* component has a fixed value equal to *k-th* word's total frequency and whose remaining components are zero. Each vector then is compressed by equation (7) that reduces their dimensionality by using *l* principal components. The words are presented to the network and the strongest responsive units are detected and labeled with the words. The responses on the map show how the network captured the spatial relations among the news. News related to earthquake-tsunami in Japan are distributed on the left side, while those related to Middle East and Libya on the right. Middle units captured a variety of topics, unit w_6 at (6,1) for example, captured several news related to crime.

Earthquake-tsunami news are differentiated in sub-categories, corresponding to more specialized items such as radiation, health, energy, etc. The labels uncover the semantic relation between items; they show the contexts where the news items are located. Each news incorporates frequent words in its representation as vector; with a sufficient amount of training the inputs leave memory traces on the same units at which later the words individually converge.

Therefore, a meaningful topographic spatial map is obtained by adding 100 most frequent words, showing logical similarities among inputs. It is possible to add more words which will enrich the map and will add more details to the semantic relations, but for simplicity and good visualization, we chose only 100 words.

4. Temporal Learning:

Previous section described how SOM's units stored spatial patterns. At this section temporal dependency analysis is performed to find significant temporal associations between data items or events. The main idea is to identify temporal sequences of spatial patterns that are likely to occur one after another.

Our spatially-trained SOM is fed once more with the input data set and temporal sequences of activated units are monitored and stored in a time-dependent matrix. The temporal aspect comes from movements or changes of the input data. Every time a unit *k* fires, our model creates a vector *d* of dimension *m*, where *m* is the total amount of SOM units. The element *d(k)* has a fixed value equal to 1 and the remaining components are zero. Vectors *d* are the inputs of the time-dependent matrix denoted as *T*.

In order to analyze the temporal proximity of units, the matrix *T* is created with *m* rows and *m* columns and its elements are initialized to 0. Rows correspond to units activated at time *(t-1)* and columns to the units at time *(t)*. Our model memorizes the previously activated unit, in a way such that for an input *d* at time *t*, the matrix *T* is updated by increasing *T(i,j)* an amount equal to *a*, where *i* is the unit fired on time *(t-1)*, and *j* is the unit fired on time *(t)*. The value added to *T(i,j)* corresponds to a transition value from the past unit to the current unit. Neighbors of unit *i* are also considered, the reasoning is that if unit *j* is frequently followed by unit *i*, the model considers that there is a high probability that neighbors of *i* follow unit *j* as well. For this last case, matrix *T* is updated by a scale down increment $(a^* \beta)$ in elements *T(Ni,j)*, where *Ni* denotes neighbors of *i*.

In that way time-dependent matrix *T* receives inputs and learns temporal relations among units over the time (Figure 2).

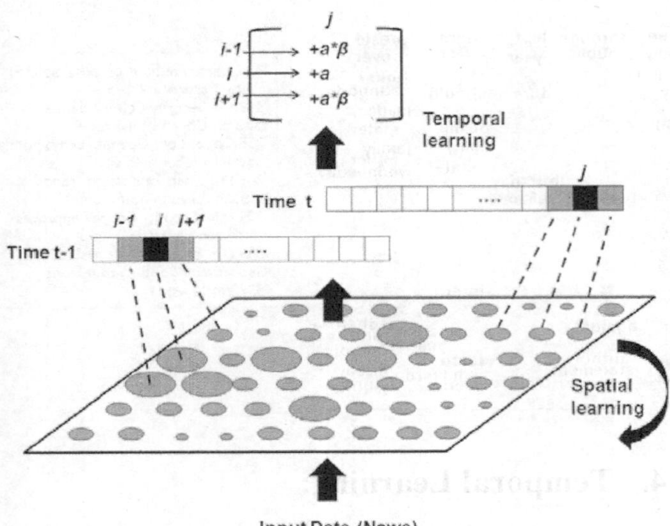

Figure 2. After spatial training, units activated are represented as vectors. They are the inputs of a time-dependent matrix T that learns over the time temporal relations among units

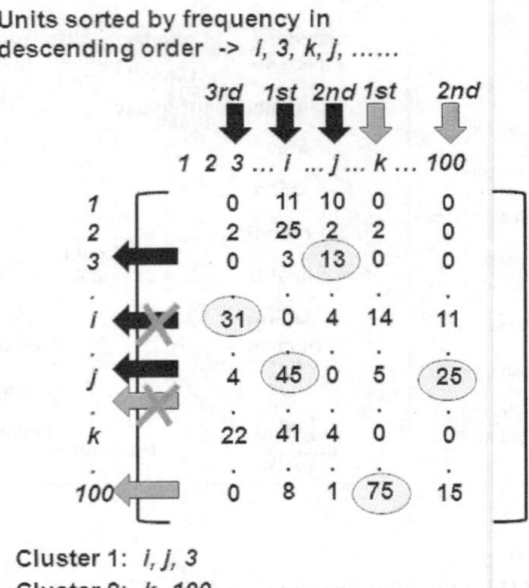

Figure 3. Temporal clustering example. 1st cluster start with column i (most frequent unit), taking most-connected unit j after 1st loop. During 2nd loop unit j takes unit 3. This last unit takes unit i at 3rd loop, but it is already in the cluster, therefore cluster 1 is closed.

5. Temporal Clustering:

After T is built, the process continues by clustering matrix T. The aim is to generate coherent clusters, which means, we seek to detect clusters where the units have high probability to follow each other through the time; these clusters are called temporal clusters and they contain groups of units that are likely to represent the evolution on time of a certain topic or event.

Vector C of dimension m, where m is the total amount of SOM units, stores the number of news pooled for each unit of the SOM. C and matrix T are used by the algorithm described below to detect temporal clusters. Figure 3, in addition, illustrates the process:

- Step1: Find from vector C the most frequent unit that is not yet part of a cluster. The most frequent unit is the one with the highest corresponding value in C.
- Step 2: Pick the unit that is most-connected to the most frequent unit. The model finds the most-connected unit by finding the highest value in the column of matrix T that corresponds to the current unit. Add the most connected unit to the cluster only if it is not part of a cluster.
- Step 3: Repeat step 2 for the most connected unit. Then recursively computes step 2 on its most connected unit, and so on, until no new unit is added.
- Step 4: All these units are added to a new temporal cluster.
- Step 5: Go to step 1 and find the most frequent unit that is not yet part of a cluster.

Once temporal clusters are formed, they are interpreted as frequent news topics and events evolving over the time. Each unit captures a subset of news; therefore, the five most frequent words are taken from each unit as a description of the unit's topic, results are shown in table below:

Temporal Cluster (Units coordinates frequently activated, in temporal order)	5 most frequent words for each unit in temporal order
(5,7), (6,2), (6,1)	'lodg', 'sweat', 'trial', 'particip', 'ray' 'court','charg', 'attorney', 'case', 'judg' 'polic', 'investig', 'depart', 'alleg', 'suspect'
(2,9), (1,9), (6,7)	'tokyo', 'earthquak', 'power', 'japan', 'quak' 'tsunami', 'japan', 'earthquak', 'warn', 'area' 'moon', 'year', 'last', 'look', 'zune'
(6,8), (5,10)	'seavey', 'bike', 'week', 'appl', 'kate' 'your', 'like', 'want', 'peopl', 'just'
(5,1), (10,10)	'investig', 'crash', 'driver', 'polic', 'william' 'aristid', 'haiti', 'spend', 'return', 'elect'
(9,1), (1,1), (6,3), (6,4)	'bahrain', 'forc', 'govern', 'secur', 'saudi' 'reactor', 'plant', 'radiat', 'fuel', 'nuclear' 'yale', 'school', 'clark', 'polic', 'sentenc' 'polic', 'accord', 'offic', 'baghdad', 'video'
(10,2), (2,4), (3,8), (10,4), (9,7), (10,3)	'zone', 'gadhafi', 'council', 'unit', 'resolut' 'nuclear','plant', 'power', 'japan', 'disast' 'earthquak', 'japan', 'school', 'might', 'peopl' 'gadhafi', 'govern', 'libyan', 'presid', 'libya' 'state', 'unit', 'hispan', 'medic', 'marijuana' 'gadhafi', 'zone', 'forc', 'libyan', 'libya'
(7,1), (4,1), (3,1), (10,6)	'palestinian', 'isra', 'author', 'hama', 'gaza' 'reactor', 'meltdown', 'nuclear', 'possibl', 'radiat' 'reactor', 'plant', 'nuclear', 'explos', 'tuesday' 'afghanistan', 'diplomat', 'petraeus', 'pakistan', 'court'
(1,6), (1,3)	'radiat', 'japan', 'airlin', 'nuclear', 'flight' 'nuclear', 'plant', 'power', 'energi', 'reactor'

(3,2), (8,1), (9,3)	'plant', 'reactor', 'nuclear', 'japan', 'agenc' 'protest', 'forc', 'govern', 'demonstr', 'secur' 'forc', 'bahrain', 'govern', 'gadhafi', 'intern'
(2,2), (1,7)	'power', 'nuclear', 'reactor', 'plant', 'daiichi' 'japan', 'food', 'govern', 'japanes', 'spaniard'
(2,1), (7,4)	'reactor', 'plant', 'japanes', 'report', 'nuclear' 'offici', 'defens', 'peopl', 'rain', 'civil'
(8,6), (7,6)	'releas', 'record', 'anonym', 'execut', 'donat' 'right', 'inmat', 'maryland', 'bill', 'california'
(8,9), (8,7)	'head', 'earli', 'educ', 'start', a'childhood' 'obama', 'conyer', 'presid', 'kenni', 'critic'
(7,3), (4,10)	'lucia', 'attack', 'accord', 'anti', 'baker' 'citi','just','parad', 'your', 'peopl'

Table 1. Main temporal clusters detected by proposed model.

Temporal clusters represent a high-level perception of meaning, knowledge, logic, etc, over the time. They can be interpreted as an image or memory of frequent sequences of topics. Main topics, those that remain in the time, come to light, while volatile topics are not displayed. For instance, temporal cluster of units (1,6), (1,3) shows that topic ('radiat', 'japan', 'airlin', 'nuclear', 'flight') follows frequently to topic ('nuclear', 'plant', 'power', 'energi', 'reactor'). We can infer that, during the disaster, there was a transition from issue "nuclear-radiation-flights" to issue "energy-power-reactor", and that transition was frequently mentioned.

Our SOM developed automatically the formation of a spatial-temporal "memory" in a way that its layout forms an image of the most important relations.

6. Conclusion and future work

Our application demonstrates that plain text sources can be represented as a numerical matrix, compressed and transformed to serve as input data for a SOM network. A SOM has been trained producing a spatial representation of the news set into a 2 dimensional map. This representation is a finite number of quantization points that group similar input vectors. Frequent words on map enabled to form a semantic structure. Time dimension was considered on SOM temporal learning, where groups of units were discovered having a high time-dependency. Temporal clusters detection was possible by the utilization of a time-dependent matrix that stores the transitions from a SOM unit to another; this matrix is the model's perception of frequent events over the time.

Although our data set was relatively small, the proposed model was able to discover temporal dependencies. We believe that results are improved and determined largely by what model is exposed to. Enough input must change and flow continuously through time for a suitable learning. The model can be scaled exponentially with diverse input data without complexity due its finite set of quantization points. SOM also can be modified as a self-growing map working "on demand".

Our time-dependent matrix also can be modified assigning a memory to it, in a way that it doesn't remember only the last fired unit at time *(t-1)*, but the last *k* units fired at times *(t-1), (t-2), (t-3), ..., (t-k)* , expanding its ability to detect unknown temporal relations. Another improvement to consider is that neighbors of unit *i* fired at time *(t-1)* that follow unit *j* fired at time *(t)* are considered, but we do not evaluate the potential temporal relation among neighbors of *i* with neighbors of *j*.

In addition, when matrix *T* is updated by a scale down increment $(a*\beta)$ in elements $T(Ni,j)$, where *Ni* denotes neighbors of *i*, we assign empirical amounts to transition value *a* and parameter *β*. If a memory is provided to matrix *T*, *a* and *β* should vary on time. Temporal clustering algorithm also can be improved considering, for example, not only the most-connected unit, but the 2nd most-connected, the 3rd most-connected.

Temporal clusters can be used to make predictions. The model computes for a new input *x* a spatial distribution on its *m* units, and a temporal distribution on its *c* temporal clusters.

Our application emphasizes the spatial-temporal arrangement of the units and the segregation of the information into separate areas. Temporal clusters give an idea of how frequent events evolve over the time, although in a high level it does completely on unsupervised way.

7. References

[1] C.E. Gutierrez, M.R. Alsharif, H. Cuiwei, M. Khosravy, R. Villa, K. Yamashita, H. Miyagi, Uncover news dynamic by principal component analysis. Shanghai, China, ICIC Express Letters, vol.7, no.4, pp.1245-1250, 2013.

[2] C.E. Gutierrez, M.R. Alsharif, H. Cuiwei, R. Villa, K. Yamashita, H. Miyagi, K. Kurata, Natural disaster online news clustering by self-organizing maps. Ishigaki, Japan, 27th SIP symposium, 2012.

[3] C.E. Gutierrez, M.R. Alsharif, R. Villa, K. Yamashita, H. Miyagi, Data Pattern Discovery on Natural Disaster News. Sapporo, Japan, ITC-CSCC, ISBN 978-4-88552-273-4/C3055, 2012.

[4] H. Ritter, T. Kohonen, Self-Organizing Semantic Maps. Biological Cybernetics. Springer-Verlag 61, pp. 241-254, 1989.

[5] T. Kohonen, Self-Organization and Associative Memory. Berlin, Springer, 1984.

[6] R. Rojas, Neural Networks. Berlin, Springer-Verlag, 1996.

[7] X. Wu, V. Kumar, J.R. Quinlan, Top 10 algorithms in data mining. London , Springer-Verlag, 2007.

[8] L. I. Smith, A tutorial on Principal Components Analysis. 2002.

[9] J. Shlens, A tutorial on Principal Component Analysis: Derivation, Discussion and Singular Value Decomposition. 2003.

[10] M.F. Porter, M.F. An algorithm for suffix stripping, Program, vol.14, no.3, pp.130–137, 1980.

[11] M. Marcus and H. Minc, Introduction to linear algebra. New York: Dover, pp.145-146, 1988.

[12] R. Yan and L. Kong, Timeline generation through evolutionary trans-temporal summarization. Conference on Empirical Methods in Natural Language Processing, Edinburg, Scotland, pp.433–443, 2011.

[13] Y. Zhang and L. E. Ghaoui, Large-Scale Sparse Principal Component Analysis with Application to Text Data. Advances in Neural Information Processing Systems (NIPS). 2011.

[14] O. Vikas, A. K. Meshram, G. Meena and A. Gupta, Multiple document summarizations using principal component analysis incorporating semantic vector space model. Computational Linguistics and Chinese Language Processing. vol.13, no.2, pp.141-156, 2008.

An Evolutionary Associative Contrast Rule Mining Method for Incomplete Database

Kaoru Shimada and Takashi Hanioka
Fukuoka Dental College, 2-15-1 Tamura, Sawara, Fukuoka, 814-0193, Japan

Abstract—*A method for associative contrast rule mining from incomplete database is demonstrated to find interesting differences between two incomplete data sets. The method extracts rules like "if X then Y" is interesting only in the focusing class. The method has been developed using a basic structure of the evolutionary graph-based optimization technique and adopting a new evolutionary strategy to accumulate rules through its evolutionary process. The method can realize the association analysis between two classes of the incomplete database using chi-square test. We evaluated the performance of the evolutionary method for associative contrast rule mining for the incomplete database. In addition, the evaluation of the mischief for the rule measurements by missing values is demonstrated.*

Keywords: association rules, missing values, evolutionary computation and genetic algorithms, contrast mining

1. Introduction

Association rule mining is the discovery of association relationships or correlations among a set of attributes (items) in a database. Association rule in the form of 'if X then Y ($X \rightarrow Y$)' is interpreted as 'the set of attributes X are likely to satisfy the set of attributes Y'. Many techniques for association rule mining and its applications have been proposed, which achieve quite effective performances [1], [2]. However, previous approaches cannot handle incomplete database. An incomplete database includes missing values in some instances. For example, the database of questionnaires probably includes missing data such as age, income, and so on. In the case plural databases are joined, missing data would also appear because attributes in each database are not the same. Conventional rule mining methods regard the database as complete, or disregard instances including missing values. Instances including missing data are deleted for rule mining or filled in with the mean values or frequent category [3], [4]. When the data sets have a huge number of instances, it is easy to take these policies. However, the data mining for dense database like medical data is different from the situation. Experimental data sets probably include missing values caused by the failure of the experiments or extraordinary values. It is not possible for these cases to fill the missing values with mean values or frequent categories.

We have already proposed an association rule mining method for incomplete database using an evolutionary computation technique [5], [6]. The method extract rules directly without constructing the frequent itemsets used in the previous approaches. Available attribute values in an instance including missing values are used for the calculation of rule measurements. The method has been developed using a basic structure of Genetic Network Programming (GNP) and adopting a new evolutionary strategy to accumulate rules through its evolutionary process. GNP is one of the evolutionary optimization techniques, which uses the directed graph structures as genes [7], [8]. Conventional Genetic Algorithm (GA) based methods extract a small number of rules optimizing a given fitness function [9], [10]. On the other hand, in the GNP based method, rules satisfying given conditions are accumulated in a rule pool through GNP generations and extracted rules are reflected in genetic operators as acquired information. GNP individuals evolve in order to store new interesting rules into the pool as many as possible, not to obtain the individual with highest fitness.

In this paper, the GNP based rule mining method is extended to the associative contrast rule mining to find interesting differences between two incomplete data sets. The associative contrast rule is defined as follows: although $X \rightarrow Y$ satisfies the given importance conditions within Database A, however, the same rule $X \rightarrow Y$ does not satisfy the same conditions within Database B [7]. The method can realize the association analysis between two classes of the incomplete database using χ^2 test. When we use the conventional rule extraction methods, it is not easy to extract such rules, because we have to check the combinations of rules one by one. In [5], the algorithm for rule mining from incomplete database was proposed, however, such as the comparison of the performance of the rule extraction and the mischief for the rule measurements by missing values were not evaluated sufficiently. In this paper, we describe the performance of the evolutionary method of associative contrast rule mining for incomplete database. In addition, the evaluation of the mischief for the rule measurements by missing values is demonstrated.

This paper is organized as follows: in the next section, some related concepts on associative contrast rules in the incomplete database are presented. In Section 3, an algorithm capable of finding the associative contrast rules from the incomplete database is described. Experimental results are presented in Section 4, and conclusions are given in Section 5.

2. Associative Contrast Rules

Let A_i be an attribute in the database and C be the class labels. The attribute values of tuples are indicated by 1 or 0 as shown in Table 1 (a). The absence of item A_i is described as $A_i=0$ and missing data (lack of information) are indicated as 'm' different value from 1 and 0. For example, $ID=4$ in Table 1 (a) misses the data of attribute A_2. In this paper, we use database form like Table 1 (a). Suppose that the class label is $C=1$ or $C=0$, that is, the database is divided into two classes, and the database has no missing data in the class label.

X and Y denote the following combinations of attributes: $X=(A_j=1)\wedge\cdots\wedge(A_k=1)$, $Y=(A_m=1)\wedge\cdots\wedge(A_n=1)$, $X\cap Y=\emptyset$. X is represented briefly as $A_j\wedge\cdots\wedge A_k$. An association rule is an implication of the form $X\rightarrow Y$. X is called antecedent and Y is called consequent of the rule. If the number of tuples containing X in the database equals x, then we define $\alpha=support(X)=x/N$, where, N is the total number of tuples for the rule evaluation. Let $\beta=support(Y)=y/N$ and $\gamma=support(X\wedge Y)=z/N$ using y and z, the number of tuples containing Y and $X\wedge Y$, respectively. The rule has measures of its frequency called *support* and its strength called *confidence* defined by

$$support(X\rightarrow Y)=\frac{z}{N}, confidence(X\rightarrow Y)=\frac{z}{x}.$$

In addition, the significance of association via the chi-square test for correlation used in classical statistics is also used for the measurement. χ^2 value of the rule $X\rightarrow Y$ is given as

$$\chi^2(X\rightarrow Y)=\frac{N(\gamma-\alpha\beta)^2}{\alpha\beta(1-\alpha)(1-\beta)}. \quad (1)$$

In the case of the rule extraction from incomplete database, the number of tuples for measurement calculation is different rule by rule [5]. For example, let $(A_1=1)\wedge(A_2=1)\wedge(A_3=1)\rightarrow(A_4=1)$ be a candidate rule in Table 1. It is clear that the tuple $ID=1$ in Table 1 does not satisfy this rule by $A_2=0$. When at least one of the values of A_1, A_2, A_3 or A_4 equal 0, it is sure that the tuple does not satisfy the rule. Therefore, $ID=4,5$ and 6 are available to judge for the rule even if they have missing values. These tuples are available for the calculation of rule measurements. However, tuples $ID=7$ and 8 are not available, because we cannot judge whether the tuples satisfy the rule or not by missing values. Therefore, the tuples whose attribute values equal 1 or m, but not the tuples whose all attribute values equal 1 should be excluded. Measurements of the above rule are

$$support((A_1=1)\wedge(A_2=1)\wedge(A_3=1)\rightarrow(A_4=1))=\frac{1}{6},$$

$$confidence(A_1=1)\wedge(A_2=1)\wedge(A_3=1)\rightarrow(A_4=1))=\frac{1}{1}.$$

In this paper, missing rate is defined as the ratio of the number of missing values and the total number of attribute values. In Table 1, for example, 8 missing values are found

Table 1: An example of incomplete database.

(a)

ID	A_1	A_2	A_3	A_4	C
1	1	0	1	0	0
2	1	1	1	1	1
3	1	1	0	0	1
4	0	m	1	1	0
5	0	m	m	1	0
6	m	m	1	0	1
7	1	1	1	m	1
8	m	1	1	m	1

(b)

$A_1\wedge A_2\wedge A_3\rightarrow A_4$
not satisfy
satisfy
not satisfy
not satisfy
not satisfy
not satisfy
cannot judge
cannot judge

within 32 values of A_1, A_2, A_3 and A_4, then, missing rate is 8/32=0.25 (25%). M value and Y value introduced in [5] are used for the measurements calculation of rules as follows. M value represents the number of tuples whose attribute values for the rule are equal 1 or m, and Y value represents the number of tuples whose attribute values for the rule are all equal to 1. N value which is the number of available tuples is also defined for the rule measurement calculation. For example, M value for the above rule equals 3 ($ID=2,7$ and 8). Y value is 1 ($ID=2$) and N value is 6. These values satisfy the following formula:

$$N \text{ value} = N_T-(M \text{ value} - Y \text{ value}),$$

where, N_T is the total number of tuples in the database. When the database is complete, N value equals N_T.

In the case of data mining from the dense database, such as the medical data, differences between two data sets gathered by different conditions are more interesting than support-confidence framework. The following rule showing difference between class labels [7] is considered.

[Associative contrast rule] Although $X\rightarrow Y$ satisfies the given importance conditions within $C=1$, $X\rightarrow Y$ does not satisfy the conditions within $C=0$.

For example, conditions of importance for associative contrast rules are defined using chi-square value as follows:

$$\chi^2(X\rightarrow Y)_{(C=1)}\geq\chi^2_{min} \quad (2)$$

$$\chi^2(X\rightarrow Y)_{(C=0)}<\chi^2_{max} \quad (3)$$

$$support(X\rightarrow Y)_{(C=1)}\geq supp_{min}, \quad (4)$$

$$support(X\rightarrow Y)_{(C=0)}\geq supp_{min}, \quad (5)$$

where, χ^2_{min} and χ^2_{max} ($\chi^2_{min}\geq\chi^2_{max}$) and $supp_{min}$ are the threshold values given by users in advance. $C=1$ and $C=0$ represent the focused class label for the rule. It is not easy for the conventional frequent itemset based methods to extract the above rules, because we have to check the combinations of rule measurements one by one.

Instead of (2) and (3), like the following conditions on the threshold for *confidence* could be used.

$$confidence(X\rightarrow Y)_{(C=1)} - confidence(X\rightarrow Y)_{(C=0)}>\delta \quad (6)$$

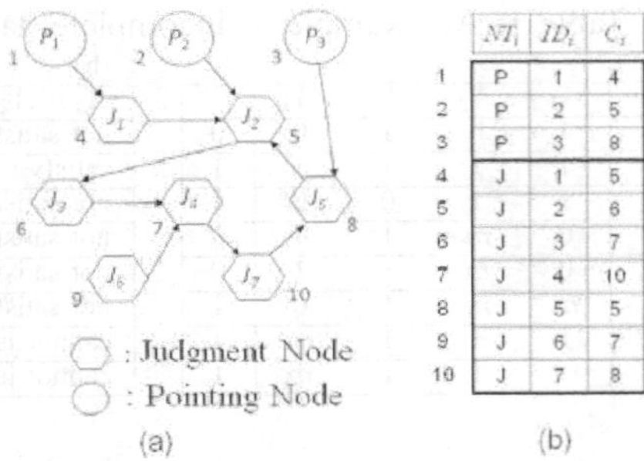

	NT_i	ID_i	C_i
1	P	1	4
2	P	2	5
3	P	3	8
4	J	1	5
5	J	2	6
6	J	3	7
7	J	4	10
8	J	5	5
9	J	6	7
10	J	7	8

Fig. 1: Basic structure of individual in GNP-based method.

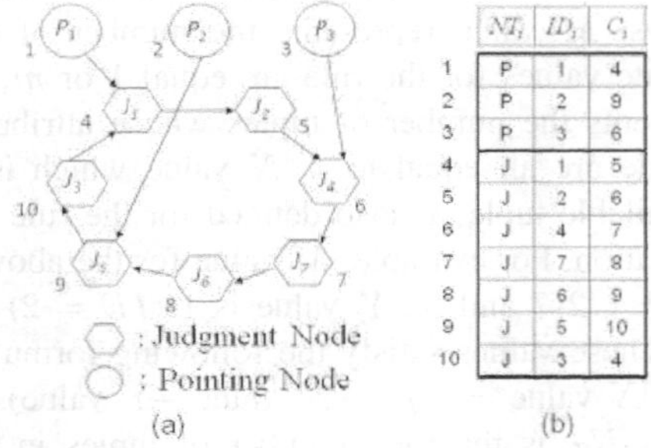

	NT_i	ID_i	C_i
1	P	1	4
2	P	2	9
3	P	3	6
4	J	1	5
5	J	2	6
6	J	4	7
7	J	7	8
8	J	6	9
9	J	5	10
10	J	3	4

Fig. 2: Basic structure of individual in ring structure method.

$$confidence(X \rightarrow Y)_{(C=0)} - confidence(X \rightarrow Y)_{(C=1)} > \delta \quad (7)$$

where, δ is a constant expressing the threshold of the difference of $confidence$.

3. Evolutionary Rule Mining Method

In this section, the associative contrast rule mining method for incomplete database based on evolutionary computation is described [5]. The form of rules and conditions of threshold values for interestingness are given by users in advance. Rule representations and fitness function are designed based on the users objects. The task for rule extraction is done accumulatively through evolutionary process, not to obtain elite individual at the final generation.

3.1 Structure of Individuals

The basic structure of the GNP individual is shown in Fig. 1. the individual is composed of two kinds of nodes: Judgment node and Pointing node (Processing nodes in [5] are renamed as *Pointing nodes*). P_1 is a Pointing node and is a starting point of rules. Each Pointing node has an inherent numeric order ($P_1, P_2, \ldots, P_s$) and is connected to a Judgment node. Each Judgment node has two connections: Continue-side and Skip-side. The Continue-side of the node is connected to another Judgment node. The Skip-side of the node is connected to the next numbered Pointing node. The Skip-side of Judgment nodes are abbreviated in Fig. 1 (a).

The gene structure of the GNP individual is shown in Fig. 1 (b). NT_i describes the node type and ID_i is an identification number of functions. C_i denotes the nodes ID which are connected from node i as Continue-side. All individuals in a population have the same number of nodes.

In this paper, *Ring structure* method and *Random network* method are introduced for the purpose of the comparison. *Ring structure* utilizes an individual using the same settings as GNP except the Judgment node connection is restricted to make ring structure, that is, one ring form is composed using all the Judgment nodes (See Fig. 2). *Random network* utilizes an individual using the same settings of GNP except the evolutionary mechanism. The connections and functions of Judgment nodes are initialized every generation.

3.2 Basic Idea of Rule Representation

Rules are represented as the connections of nodes in an individual. Attributes and their values correspond to the functions of Judgment nodes. Fig. 3 (a) shows a sample of the node connection in the individual. '$A_1 = 1$', '$A_2 = 1$', '$A_3 = 1$', '$A_4 = 1$' and '$A_5 = 1$' in Fig. 3 (a) denote the functions of Judgment nodes. The connections of these nodes represent rules like $(A_1 = 1) \rightarrow (A_2 = 1)$ and $(A_1 = 1) \wedge (A_2 = 1) \rightarrow (A_3 = 1)$.

Judgment nodes can be reused and shared with some other rule representations because of the GNP's feature. GNP individual generates many rule candidates using its graph structure. The kinds of the Judgment node functions equal the number of attributes in the database.

If a rule symbolized by node connections is interesting, then the rules symbolized by after changing the connections or functions of nodes could be candidates of interesting ones. We can obtain these rule candidates effectively by genetic operations for individuals, because mutation or crossover operation change the connections or contents of the nodes.

3.3 Node Transition in the Individual

Individuals examines the attribute values of each tuple using Judgment nodes and calculates the measurements of rules using Pointing nodes. Judgment node determines the next node by a judgment result. When the attribute value equals 1, then we move to the Continue-side. On the other hand, in the case that the attribute value equals 0, the Skip-side is used for the transition. For example, in Table 1 (a), the tuple $1 \in ID$ satisfies $A_1 = 1$ and $A_2 = 0$, therefore, the node transition from P_1 to P_2 occurs in Fig. 3 (a). When the attribute value is missing, then, move to the Continue-side. If the transition to Continue-side connection continues and the number of the Judgment nodes from the Pointing node becomes a cutoff value (given maximum number of attributes in rules, $MaxLength$), then, the connection is transferred to the next Pointing node using the Skip-side

(a) An example of node connection.

(b) Change of Pointing node connection.

Fig. 3: An example of node connection for rule mining.

obligatorily. Skip-side of the Judgment node is connected to the next numbered Pointing node. Then, another examinations of attribute values start at the next Pointing node. If the examination of attribute values from the starting point P_s ends, then the individual examines the tuple $2 \in ID$ from P_1 likewise. Thus, all tuples in the database are examined.

3.4 Calculation of Rule Measurements

Y value and M value are obtained as the numbers of tuples moved to the Continue-side at each Judgment node. These values are counted up and stored in memories. In addition, each Judgment node examines the case of $C = k(k = 0, 1)$ at the same time. In Fig. 3 (a), $Y_a(k)$, $Y_b(k)$, $Y_c(k)$, $Y_d(k)$ and $Y_e(k)$ are the numbers of tuples which belong to class $C = k$ and move to the Continue-side at each Judgment node satisfying that all the attribute values are equal to 1 from the pointing node (Y value). On the other hand, $M_a(k)$, $M_b(k)$, $M_c(k)$, $M_d(k)$ and $M_e(k)$ are the number of tuples at each Judgment node satisfying that the attribute values are equal to 1 or missing values (M value). Using these values, N values, that is, the number of available tuples for the rule measurements calculation are calculated as follows:

$$N_x(k) = N_T - (M_x(k) - Y_x(k)) \quad (8)$$

where, x is a position of the Judgment node. For example, $N_d(k)$ is obtained as $N_d(k) = N_T - (M_d(k) - Y_d(k))$.

Rule measurements are calculated using the above numbers. For example, in the case of $Rule : (A_1{=}1) \wedge (A_2{=}1) \rightarrow (A_3{=}1) \wedge (A_4{=}1)$, the measurements for $C{=}k$ are

$$support(Rule_{(C=k)}) = \frac{Y_d(k)}{N_d(k)},$$

$$confidence(Rule_{(C=k)}) = \frac{Y_d(k)}{Y_b(k) - (N_b(k) - N_d(k))}.$$

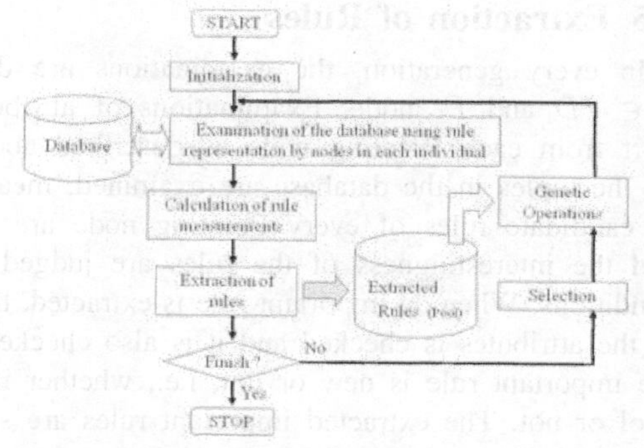

Fig. 4: Flow of the GNP-based rule extraction.

Table 2: Measurements of rules within $C = k$ $(k = 0, 1)$.

Association Rules	Support	Confidence
$A_1 \rightarrow A_2$	$\frac{Y_b(k)}{N_b(k)}$	$\frac{Y_b(k)}{Y_a(k)-(N_a(k)-N_b(k))}$
$A_1 \rightarrow A_2 \wedge A_3$	$\frac{Y_c(k)}{N_c(k)}$	$\frac{Y_c(k)}{Y_a(k)-(N_a(k)-N_c(k))}$
$A_1 \rightarrow A_2 \wedge A_3 \wedge A_4$	$\frac{Y_d(k)}{N_d(k)}$	$\frac{Y_d(k)}{Y_a(k)-(N_a(k)-N_d(k))}$
$A_1 \wedge A_2 \rightarrow A_3$	$\frac{Y_c(k)}{N_c(k)}$	$\frac{Y_c(k)}{Y_b(k)-(N_b(k)-N_c(k))}$
$A_1 \wedge A_2 \rightarrow A_3 \wedge A_4$	$\frac{Y_d(k)}{N_d(k)}$	$\frac{Y_d(k)}{Y_b(k)-(N_b(k)-N_d(k))}$
$A_1 \wedge A_2 \wedge A_3 \rightarrow A_4$	$\frac{Y_d(k)}{N_d(k)}$	$\frac{Y_d(k)}{Y_c(k)-(N_c(k)-N_d(k))}$

$N_b(k) - N_d(k)$ is the number of tuples including missing data for $(A_3 = 1) \wedge (A_4 = 1)$ within $Y_b(k)$. Because the difference of the number of tuples including missing data between $(A_1{=}1) \wedge (A_2{=}1) \wedge (C{=}k)$ and $(A_1{=}1) \wedge (A_2{=}1) \wedge (A_3{=}1) \wedge (A_4{=}1) \wedge (C{=}k)$ equals to $N_b(k) - N_d(k)$.

The measurements of each rule for every class are calculated at the same time. Therefore, the rules showing the difference between classes in the database can be evaluated. Table 2 shows an example of measurements of rules in $C = k$. Using both measurements for $C = 1$ and $C = 0$, we can extract associative contrast rules.

In order to obtain the χ^2 value of the rules, we consider changes of the connection of Pointing nodes in each generation. For example, if the connection of P_1 is changed from '$A_1{=}1$' node to '$A_3{=}1$' node as shown in Fig. 3, we are able to calculate the support of $(A_3{=}1)$, $(A_3{=}1) \wedge (A_4{=}1)$ and $(A_3{=}1) \wedge (A_4{=}1) \wedge (A_5{=}1)$ in the next examination. In Fig. 3 (b), $Y_p(k)$, $Y_q(k)$ and $Y_r(k)$ are the numbers of tuples belonging to class k and moving to the Continue-side at each Judgment node satisfying that all the attribute values are equal to 1 from the Pointing node P_1. $M_p(k)$, $M_q(k)$ and $M_r(k)$ are also calculated at the same time. Then, the N values like $N_p(k)$, $N_q(k)$ and $N_r(k)$ are obtained using (8). When we calculate the χ^2 value of the rule $X \rightarrow Y$ in the incomplete database, we can use the N value of $X \cup Y$ instead of N in (1). α, β and γ in (1) are calculated by using Y values and N values. The operation changing the connections of the Pointing node can be repeated like a chain operation in each generation. A consequent of the rule can be the antecedent of another rule using this operation.

3.5 Extraction of Rules

In every generation, the examinations are done from $1 \in ID$ and P_1 node. Examinations of attribute values start from each Pointing node as described above. After all the tuples in the database are examined, measurements of candidate rules of every Pointing node are calculated and the interestingness of the rules are judged by given conditions. When an important rule is extracted, the overlap of the attributes is checked and it is also checked whether the important rule is new or not, i.e., whether it is in the pool or not. The extracted important rules are stored in a rule pool all together through the evolutionary process. Fig. 4 shows the flow of the rule extraction.

3.6 Genetic Operations and Fitness

Individuals are replaced with new ones by a selection rule in each generation [5]. The individuals are ranked by their fitnesses and upper 1/3 individuals are selected. The number 1/3 is determined experimentally, which is not so sensitive to the results. After that, they are reproduced three times for the next generation, then the following three kinds of genetic operators are executed to them; crossover with the probability of P_c, mutation-1 with the probability of P_{m1} (changes the connection of nodes) and mutation-2 with the probability of P_{m2} (changes the function of Judgment nodes). The operators are executed for the gene of Judgment nodes. All the connections of the Pointing nodes are changed randomly in order to extract new rules efficiently. $P_c = 1/5$, $P_{m1} = 1/3$ and $P_{m2} = 1/5$ is an effectual setting and was used in the experiments in Section 4. Information of the extracted rules like frequency of the appearances of attributes in the rules can be used for genetic operations. The more concrete explanation of the operations are described in [7].

Fitness of the individual can be defined depending on the problems. The capacity for extraction of new rules should be considered. Following functions were used in Section 4.

Fitness for associative contrast rule mining using χ^2 threshold is defined by

$$F_d^{\chi^2} = \sum_{r \in R} \{\chi^2_{(C=1)}(r) + 10(n_X(r) - 1) + 10(n_Y(r) - 1) + \alpha_{new}(r)\} \quad (9)$$

where, R: set of suffixes of extracted rules satisfying (2), (3), (4) and (5) in the individual, $\chi^2_{(C=1)}(r)$: χ^2 value of rule r in $C = 1$. $n_X(r), n_Y(r)$: the number of attributes in the antecedent and in the consequent of rule r, respectively. $\alpha_{new}(r)$: additional constant defined by

$$\alpha_{new}(r) = \begin{cases} \alpha_{new} & \text{(rule } r \text{ is new)} \\ 0 & \text{(otherwise).} \end{cases} \quad (10)$$

Constants are set up empirically. $\chi^2_{(C=1)}(r)$, $n_X(r)$, $n_Y(r)$ and $\alpha_{new}(r)$ are concerned with the importance, complexity and novelty of rule r, respectively.

Table 3: Averaged number of extracted rules (30 trials).

	missing rate (%)			
	0	2	5	10
GNP-based Method	3450.5	2356.4	1269.8	580.1
(Interesting rules)	(614.4)	(528.2)	(379.4)	(147.8)
(Unexpected rules)	(0.0)	(400.6)	(397.6)	(331.2)
Ring structure	3333.2	2297.1	1250.2	602.7
(Interesting rules)	(601.8)	(517.0)	(378.8)	(156.6)
(Unexpected rules)	(0.0)	(382.2)	(384.7)	(340.4)
Random network	1416.9	1117.2	785.2	491.0
(Interesting rules)	(289.1)	(342.1)	(260.8)	(118.9)
(Unexpected rules)	(0.0)	(208.1)	(270.9)	(296.1)

Fitness for using $confidence$ threshold is defined by

$$F_d^{conf} = \sum_{r \in R} \{10 \times |conf(r)_{(C=1)} - conf(r)_{(C=0)}| + (n_X(r) - 1) + (n_Y(r) - 1) + \alpha_{new}(r)\} \quad (11)$$

where, R: set of suffixes of extracted rules satisfying (4), (5) and (6) or (7) in the individual, $conf(r)_{(C=k)}$: $confidence$ of rule r in $C = k$.

4. Experimental Results

Experiments were executed using artificial incomplete data sets by the following viewpoints.

- Evaluation of the performance of the associative contrast rule extraction from the incomplete database.
- Evaluation of the mischief for the rule measurements by missing values.

We used the same dataset named SNP_{com} used in [5]. SNP_{com} has 100 attributes and 270 instances and has no missing data. The original data is The Mapping 500K HapMap Genotype Data Set (Affimetrix)[1]. This database contains Single Nucleotide Polymorphism (SNP) information of 270 people. 100 SNPs were picked up at random and constructed the dataset SNP_{com}. Support values of 100 SNPs are between 0.1 and 0.6. The original data has 4 class labels: YRI, JPT, CHB and CEU. Datasets including artificial missing values were generated randomly from SNP_{com} using given missing rates, i.e., 2%, 5% and 10%. For every missing rate, 30 incomplete data sets were generated and named $SNP_2(i)$, $SNP_5(i)$, and $SNP_{10}(i)$ $(i = 1, \ldots, 30)$, respectively. In addition, we made a complete dataset having 200 attributes named as SNP_{com200} based on the above.

The population size for evolutionary rule accumulation mechanisms is 120. The number of Pointing nodes and Judgment nodes in each individual are 10 and 100, respectively. The number of changing the connections of the Pointing nodes in each generation is 5. The condition of termination is 500 generations for evolution. All algorithms were coded in C. Experiments were done on a 1.80GHz Intel(R) Core2 Duo CPU with 2GB RAM.

[1] http://www.affymetrix.com/support/technical/sample_data/500k_hapmap_genotype_data.affx

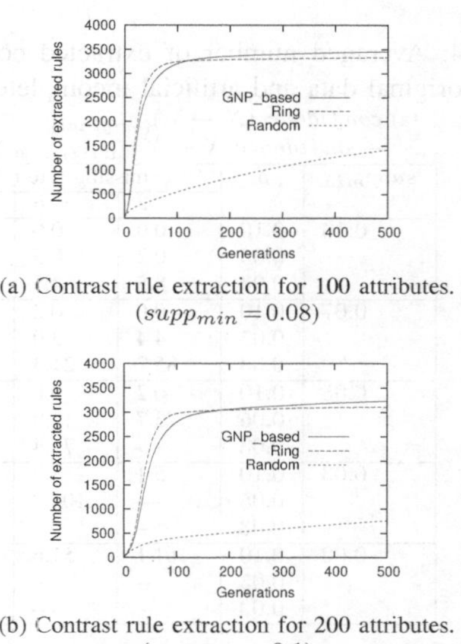

(a) Contrast rule extraction for 100 attributes. ($supp_{min}=0.08$)

(b) Contrast rule extraction for 200 attributes. ($supp_{min}=0.1$)

Fig. 5: Averaged number of extracted contrast rules.

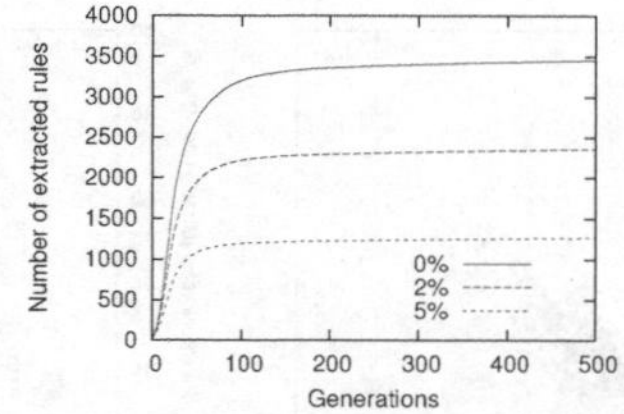

(a) Averaged number of extracted rules.

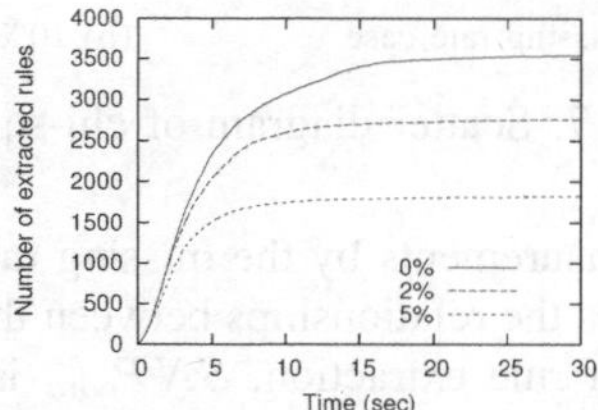

(b) Run-time versus number of extracted rules.

Fig. 6: Number of extracted contrast rules in the pool.

First of all, the contrast rule mining in the SNP_{com} were evaluated. Instances were divided into 2 classes as follows; $C=1$ in the case of YRI or JPT (135 instances), $C=0$ in the case of CHB or CEU (135 instances). This class division has no scientific meaning, only intention was to make a dataset for the estimation use. The associative contrast rules defined by (2), (3), (4) and (5) were extracted. $supp_{min}=0.08$, $\chi^2_{min}=6.63$, $\chi^2_{max}=1.0$, $1 \leq n_X(r) \leq 4$, $1 \leq n_Y(r) \leq 4$ and $\alpha_{new}=150$ were used. In order to obtain the whole identified rules in the SNP_{com} satisfying the given conditions, 10000 independent rule extractions were done and obtained 4248 identified rules.

Fig. 5 (a) shows the averaged number of extracted rules over 30 data sets in the rule pool versus number of generations for the evolution. *GNP-based*, *Ring* and *Random* denote the methods described in Section 3. This demonstrates that the evolutionary rule accumulation based methods can extract most of the contrast rules within 100 generations. Fig. 5 (b) shows the same experiment in the case of using SNP_{com200}. In this experiment, $supp_{min}=0.1$ was used. *Ring* tends to converge in early generations.

Fig. 6 (a) shows the averaged number of extracted rules over 30 data sets. Associative contrast rules were extracted from SNP_{com} and $SNP_m(i)$ ($m=2,5$, $i=1,\ldots,30$), respectively. 0% denotes using SNP_{com}. 2% and 5% denote the missing rates. Fig. 6 (b) shows a sample of run-time in the same experiment as Fig. 6 (a). It shows that the most of the contrast rules were extracted within 10 seconds. In this experiment, 500 generations were set as the terminal condition, however, users can set the maximum calculation time instead and quit the rule extraction.

Table 3 shows the averaged number of total associative contrast rules obtained at the final generation. It is found that the method can extract rules based on χ^2 values from the dense incomplete database. The number of extracted rules tends to decrease by increasing the missing rate, this can be caused by the decrease of the N value in (1). In this experiment, *interesting rule* was defined as the rule extracted from SNP_{com} and satisfying additional conditions, that is, $\chi^2(X \rightarrow Y)_{(C=1)} \geq 10.0$, $support(X \rightarrow Y)_{(C=1)} \geq 0.1$ and $support(X \rightarrow Y)_{(C=0)} \geq 0.1$. The number of interesting rules in SNP_{com} is 642. It is found that 95% of the *interesting rules* are covered in each rule extraction using GNP-based method. In addition, *unexpected rule* was defined as the rule excluded from the rule extraction of SNP_{com}. A percentage of the number of *unexpected rules* tends to increase by the missing values.

Fig. 7 (a) shows the scatter diagram of χ^2 values of extracted rules in $C=1$ in the original data case and in the 5% missing rate case. Plots show the χ^2 values of all the rules obtained in the two rule extractions. 69% of the rules extracted in the 5% missing rate case are found in the rule pool of the original data case. It is found that most of the rules having high χ^2 value in the original data set are also extracted in the artificial incomplete data set using 5% missing rate. Fig. 7 (b) shows the scatter diagram for the 10% missing rate case. It shows the weak correlation of the χ^2 values of the rules compared with Fig. 7 (a). 43% of the rules extracted in the 10% missing rate case are found in the rule pool of the original data case. In this experiment, χ^2 values were used for the both classes as one of the conditions of interesting rules. This result suggests that 10% missing rate cause the different feature of rule extraction from the original data set in a detailed analysis.

Next, the associative contrast rule extraction between SNP_{com} and $SNP_m(i)$ ($m=2,5,10$, $i=1,\ldots,30$) were examined based on (6) and (7) to evaluate the mischief for

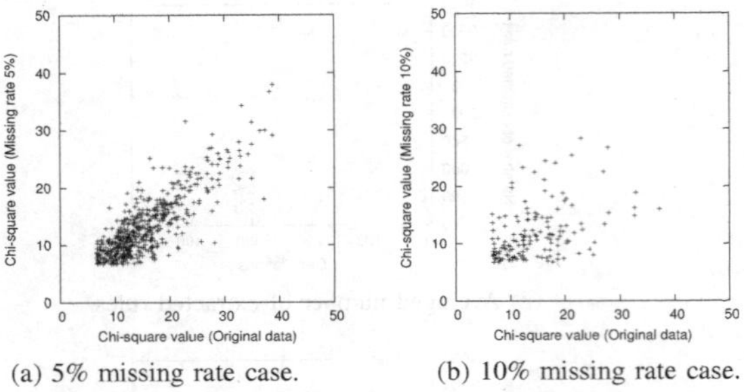

(a) 5% missing rate case. (b) 10% missing rate case.

Fig. 7: Scatter diagram of chi-square values.

the rule measurements by the missing rate. This experiment demonstrates the relationships between the missing rates and reliability of rule extraction. SNP_{com} is set at class $C=1$ and $SNP_m(i)$ is set at $C=0$. If many rules are extracted, then the missing values affects for the rule measurements, because $SNP_m(i)$ have different features from SNP_{com}. This experiment was executed using GNP-based method. δ = 0.03, 0.05, 0.10 and 0.15 for (6) and (7) were used. The maximum number of extracted rules in the pool was set as 5000 and we quit the rule extraction by this condition. $1 \leq n_X(r) \leq 4$, $1 \leq n_Y(r) \leq 4$ and $\alpha_{new}=30$ were used.

Table 4 shows the total number of extracted rules at 500 generation. '—' describes that the number of extracted rule is more than 5000. In this experiment, a huge number of candidate rules are examined, however, only a small number of contrast rules are extracted in many cases. The associative contrast rule mining method can be used for the difference detection between two data sets.

Table 4: Averaged number of extracted contrast rules between original data and artificial incomplete data.

(a) $confidence(X \rightarrow Y)_{(original)} - confidence(X \rightarrow Y)_{(artificial)} > \delta$

$supp_{min}$	δ	missing rate (%)		
		2	5	10
0.10	0.10	0.0	0.0	0.0
	0.05	0.2	0.5	0.0
	0.03	8.5	4.5	0.5
0.07	0.10	0.0	0.2	0.0
	0.05	4.4	3.0	0.4
	0.03	85.7	21.4	2.7
0.05	0.10	0.2	0.6	0.2
	0.05	23.7	13.9	3.1
	0.03	—	75.4	10.4
0.03	0.10	5.1	7.7	2.3
	0.05	—	104.7	22.6
	0.03	—	—	57.9
0.02	0.10	61.1	51.6	14.3
	0.05	—	—	76.4
	0.03	—	—	152.6

(b) $confidence(X \rightarrow Y)_{(artificial)} - confidence(X \rightarrow Y)_{(original)} > \delta$

$supp_{min}$	δ	missing rate (%)		
		2	5	10
0.20	0.15	0.0	0.0	0.4
	0.10	0.0	0.2	25.3
	0.05	1.9	100.4	409.3
0.18	0.15	0.0	0.1	1.9
	0.10	0.0	2.2	63.1
	0.05	9.0	251.2	732.6
0.15	0.15	0.0	0.8	18.5
	0.10	0.0	17.1	374.3
	0.05	56.6	1242.6	2418.0
0.12	0.15	0.1	6.0	167.8
	0.10	1.2	134.7	2161.4
	0.05	419.6	—	—
0.10	0.15	0.2	28.0	855.0
	0.10	7.3	749.2	—
	0.05	1746.7	—	—

5. Conclusions

A method for associative contrast rule mining from incomplete databases has been demonstrated using a graph-based evolutionary method. An incomplete database includes missing data in some instances, however, the method can extract rules satisfying given conditions. The performances of the associative contrast rule extraction have been evaluated using artificial incomplete data sets in the medical field. The results show that the method has a potential to realize association analysis. In addition, the evaluation of the mischief for the rule measurements by missing values is demonstrated. We are studying applications of the method to information processing in the medical science field.

Acknowledgment.

This work was partly supported by JSPS KAKENHI Grant Number 24500191.

References

[1] R. Agrawal and R. Srikant, "Fast Algorithms for Mining Association Rules", in *Proc. of the 20th VLDB Conf.*, pp. 487–499, 1994.

[2] J. Han, J. Pei, Y. Yin and R. Mao, "Mining Frequent Patterns without Candidate Generation: A Frequent-Pattern Tree Approach", *Data Mining and Knowledge Discovery*, Vol. 8, pp. 53–87, 2004.

[3] J. W. Grzymala-Busse and W. J. Grzymala-Busse, Handling Missing Attribute Values Data Mining and Knowledge Discovery Handbook, 2nd ed., O. Maimon, L. Rockach (eds.), Springer, pp.33–51, 2010.

[4] M. Saar-Tsechansky and F. Provost, Handling Missing Values when Applying Classification Models, Journal of Machine Learning Research 8, pp.1625-1657, 2007.

[5] K. Shimada and K. Hirasawa, "A Method of Association Rule Analysis for Incomplete Database Using Genetic Network Programming", in *Proc. of the Genetic and Evolutionary Computation Conference 2010 (GECCO 2010)*, pp. 1115–1122, 2010.

[6] K. Shimada, "An Evolving Associative Classifier for Incomplete Database", Springer LNAI 7377: Advances in Data Mining, Perner P.(Ed.). pp.136–150, 2012.

[7] K. Shimada and K. Hirasawa, "Exceptional Association Rule Mining Using Genetic Network Programming", in *Proc. of the 4th International Conference on Data Mining (DMIN 2008)*, pp. 277–283, 2008.

[8] S. Mabu, C. Chen, N. Lu, K. Shimada and K. Hirasawa, "An Intrusion-Detection Model Based on Fuzzy Class-Association-Rule Mining Using Genetic Network Programming", IEEE Trans. on Systems, Man, and Cybernetics - Part C-, Vol. 41, pp.130–139, 2011.

[9] A. A. Freitas, "Data Mining and knowledge Discovery with Evolutionary Algorithms", Springer, 2002.

[10] A. Ghosh and L. C. Jain, "Evolutionary Computing in Data Mining", Springer, 2005.

HIERARCHICAL VIDEO INDEXING AND RETRIEVAL SYSTEM

Mohammed Yassine Kazi Tani*, Abdelghani Ghomari*, Lamia Dali Youcef**
*Université of Oran
Computer Science Department
Research on Industrial Informatics and Networks Laboratory (RIIR)
BP 1524, El-M'Naouer 31000 - Oran, Algeria
{yassine.kazi@gmail.com; ghomari65@yahoo.fr}
** Abou Bakr Belkaid University of Tlemcen
GEE Department
Systems and Technologies of Information and Communication Laboratory (STIC)
B.P 230, Chetouane- Tlemcen-
lamiadaliyoucef@mail.univ-tlemcen.dz

Abstract

In this paper we will improve a previous system named: Semantic Retrieval of Event from Indoor Surveillance Video Database by adding a hierarchical indexing approach. The aim of our work is to improve the initial result provided by the system and taking into account moving studies of objects in video documents of videosurveillance applications.

Key words: video document, indexing and retrieval video surveillance, indexing approach, Semi- automatic annotation.

1. Introduction

Nowadays, the existence of multiple sources of video capture (Phone, Videosurveillance…) attracted several researches in the field of modeling, indexing and retrieval video. The importance size of video documents requires new compressing methods to facilitate their use on the large network like Internet. For this, many standards of compression exists like: MPEG1, MPEG2, MPEG4 [2] and MPEG7 [3] that change the context of compression for standardizing the description of multimedia document content. MPEG21 [4] is also a standard of compression that describes the method of multimedia documents production and the consumption of their content.

The large scale of video databases used actually in many applications domains such as the videosurveillance require an efficient indexing system for videos retrieval.

For this purpose, there exist in the literature two approaches of indexing and retrieval video documents: the first one is based on textual annotations and the second one is based on the visual content (segmentation and analysis of the different structural units content) [7].

So, to overcome the problematic of indexation in video documents, a semi-automatic annotation technique exists which benefits of manual and automatic annotations advantages [5, 6].

In this paper, we try to improve a work called "Semantic retrieval of events from indoor surveillance video database" [18] by giving our point of view (the system is presented in the section 3 and 4 and its implementation is being done). At the same time, we try to highlight other points such as related works (Section 2) and the conclusion (Section 5).

2. Related Works

2.1 Video documents

2.1.1 Components of video documents

Content and container terms are essential to know in a multimedia document. The content is written on a text medium and the paper is the container [1]. Concerning video documents, the indexing is focused on the video sequences that can be a Plan or a Scene that compose the video documents (figure1).

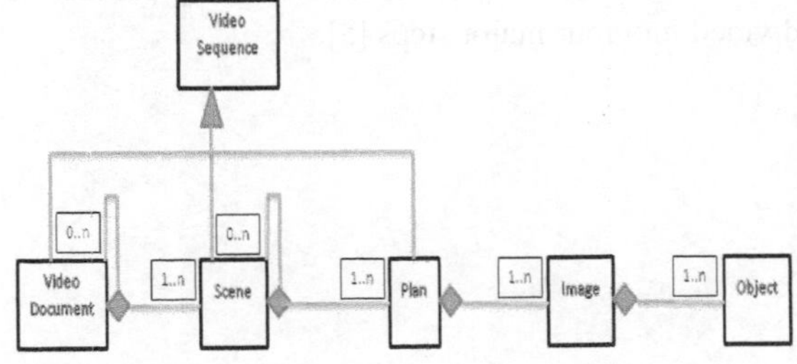

Figure 1 Structural unit of video documents

2.1.2 Characteristic of video documents

We can divide these features in three categories:

1. Media data: The video document itself, and the information about the compression format, the size of the video;
2. Metadata: The information about the video content, such as visual features (color, texture,...) and spatio-temporal characteristics;
3. Semantic data: This means the textual annotations that define the content of the video.

Thus, from these categories, the features of video documents are shown as follows [7] :

- Physical features: we can find the format (.Mpg), the type of compression (MPEG1, MPEG2, MPEG4 etc.), the size and the speed (number frames/second) NTSC (30 frames/second), the length and the name of video;

- Visual features: also called low-level features, like colors represented by a color scheme, texture (measure RGB values of a pixel relative to the other neighboring pixels), shapes and contour;

- Semantic features: also called high-level features, where we find the notion of annotations that define the content of the video.

2.1.3 Video documents indexing

The importance size of video documents manipulated in many critical applications like videosurveillance requires an efficient indexing system for videos retrieval.

The indexing process represents an operation that interprets, describes and characterizes a document or a part of a document for a future use.

According to the figure 2, the indexing process is divided into four major steps [5]:

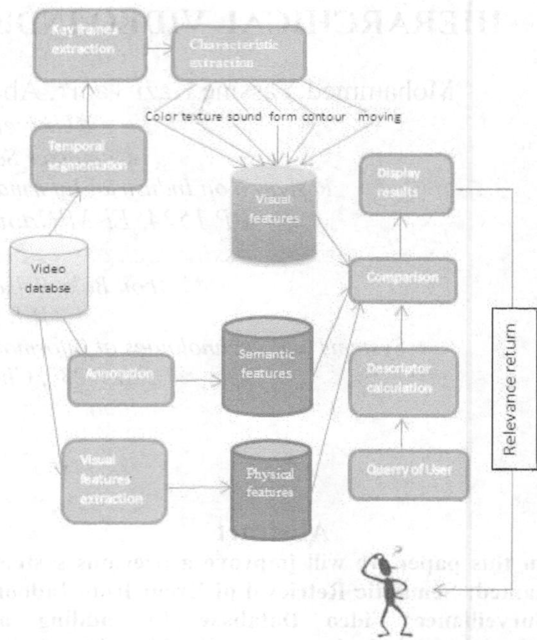

Figure 2 A video indexing and retrieval system

- **Segmentation:** It consists in dispatching the whole video into several parts "plan or scenes" as needed and especially to keep the same semantic aspect of the scene or plan in order to facilitate their indexing (figure 3). As a result, several methods exist for video segmentation [14, 15, 16, 17], the difference from pixel to pixel, the comparison of color histograms, motion estimation, and so on....

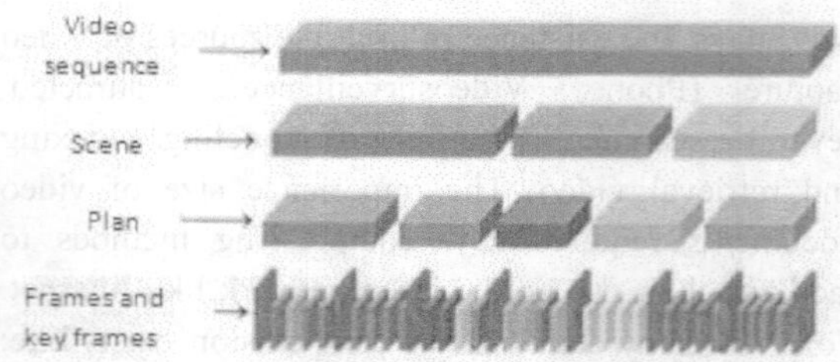

Figure 3 Temporal segmentation of video sequences

- Representation and classification

After the segmentation step, different types of features "Physics, Semantics, visual" also called digital signatures are extracted and assigned to different video sequences for two purposes: interpretation or description.

- Index creation

The most widely common methods for index creation are those based on the annotation with its different forms: *manual annotation, automatic annotation* and *semi-automatic annotation*. The annotation expresses two distinct aspects "description and interpretation". In the description of the video, we can find all concepts that explain the video content (objects, people, places, events ...), and interpretation gives a point of view to explain a given sequence or any other part of the video [13].

- *Manual annotation*: is done by a human being who will annotate the various videos in the database with its own semantics and its own way of interpretation. The advantage of this method is to be accurate but when the database is very large, the annotation process is very heavy for the annotator as he/she will be obliged to browse the entire database to annotate it.
- *Automatic annotation*: Unlike manual annotation, automatic annotation is made by a machine that consists of extracting the different features of video and then spreading them in order to annotate other related videos that have the same features in the database. The automatic annotation has the advantage of annotating a large database, but its biggest flaw is that it is unable to give satisfactory results when the videos contain several objects, several movements, many people….
- Semi-*automatic annotation:* To overcome the problems presented by the both previous methods, semi-automatic annotation is based on the accuracy of manual annotation to annotate a part of its database and then use the advantage of automatic annotation in the purpose of annotating a very large database by comparing all video that have the similar visual features.

- Retrieval and interactivity

Retrieval step represents the final goal in the indexing process. Therefore, present retrieval systems [5] allow expressing the user query in four different ways:

1. *Retrieve by physical features*: the user can formulate his query by physical features such as modification date, size and number of images...
2. *Retrieve by semantic features*: the most common of all keywords retrieve represents the most used in the world as used for example by YouTube and allows the user to express his query based on keywords that represent the semantic of the video.
3. *Retrieve by visual features*: This type of retrieve is performed by inserting a video key by the user with which the system performs a comparison of low-level features with existing videos in the database.
4. *Retrieve by features combination*: This is the type of research that gives more satisfaction as far as the accuracy is based on the three types of features (physique, visual and semantic).

Interaction represents the dialogue interface between the user and the indexing system which expresses queries with different existing types.

2.2 SHIATSU (Tagging and Retrieving Video without Worries)

SHIATSU [6] is a semi-automatic system that covers the problems due to the use of only textual annotation like the semantic gap. The existence of synonyms (indexed by a synonym of the keyword in the query formulated by the user), homonymy/polysemy (two synonyms' words). The architecture of SHIATSU system is based on three ideas:

1. *The hierarchical annotation*: makes two levels of indexing and starting with the sequences that make up the video and then proceed after that to indexing the entire video with summarizing the different indexes sequences;
2. *The similarity-based labeling*: Assign previously existing indexes to different videos that have the same visual features;
3. *The indexing and retrieval based on multidimensional taxonomy*: A system which implies the existence of several dimensions (root retrieval).

To perform indexing videos, SHIATSU is based on:

2.2.1 Shot detection

In order to separate the video sequences, SHIATSU is based on the balance approach. It exploits the color histogram and the object border for comparing two successive frames.

Color histogram HSV (hue, Saturation and Value): the distance between two consecutive frames k and k +1 « d_{HSV} (k, k+1) » is defined by:

$$d_{HSV}(k, k+1) = \frac{1}{6N} \sum_i |h_k[i] - h_{k+1}[i]|$$

N is the number of pixels, h_k represents the histogram of the image k.

The resulting distance is compared to a threshold θ_{HSV} :

$$\Theta_{HSV} = \frac{\beta_{HSV}}{M/f} \sum_{i=M-M/f+1}^{M} L_{HSV}(i)$$

β_HSV is a sensitivity parameter (by default, it is at 1), M is the total number of images in the video, f is the frame rate in the video and L_{HSV} represents the list of ascending values HSV away from all consecutive sequences.

ECR "Edge Change Ratio": Change report between two frames k, k+1 is calculated as follows:

$$ECR(k, k+1) = \max\left(\frac{X_k^{out}}{\sigma_k}, \frac{X_{k+1}^{in}}{\sigma_{k+1}}\right)$$

σ_k is the number of pixels edge and k, X_k^{out}, X_{k+1}^{in} represent respectively pixels of existing and new edges in the frames k and k +1.

The change ratio is compared to a threshold Θ_{ECR} :

$$\Theta_{ECR} = \frac{\beta_{ECR}}{2M/f} \sum_{i=M-2M/f+1}^{M} L_{ECR}(i)$$

β_{ECR} is a sensitivity parameter (by default, it is 1) L_{ECR} and represents order list crossing ECR values. Whenever the two values (d_{HSV} (k, k +1)) and ECR (k, k +1)) exceed their thresholds, there will be a cut to separate the two video sequences consecutively.

2.2.2 Indexing video

There are two levels of video indexing, sequences indexing and then the entire video indexing, because the system SHIATSU [6] is based on hierarchical annotation.

Sequences indexing: is based on different key frames that compose it. The process of selecting key frames can be done in three different ways:

- Select the first frame of each sequence;
- Select the first, the middle and the last frame of each sequence;
- Select a depending number on the sequence length L (s), N (k) = C. L(s)/ f, where C is a constant.

We can define the indexing process video sequences as follows:

After extracting key frames of each video sequence, each of them will pass through the extractor of visual features to extract color and texture. These features are then used by the annotation module to search from the database the frames that have the same features. Indexes are then proposed for this key frame and this is repeated for all key frames sequences and we take only the terms which recur most in the majority of key frames.

In the end, the user can choose the indexes proposed by the system or introduce its own indexes.

Hierarchical indexing: In order to index the whole video, we proceed as follows: We first compute the relevance of each sequence "S" length in relation to the whole video.

$$W(s) = \frac{L(s)}{L(V)}$$

Then, we calculate the rank R (t) of each sequence index.

$$R(t) = \frac{1}{N_s} \sum_s W(s) A(t, s)$$

N_s is the total number of video sequences and A (t, s) is the relevance of the index "t" in relation to the sequence "S" (A (t, s) = 0 when the sequence "S" has not the index "t").

In the end, we take the top 10 R (t) as an index of the whole video sequence.

2.2.3 Retrieval method

In the literature, we can find the most used retrieval system such as SHIATSU [6] that offers three ways:

- KS (keyword retriever) ;
- FS (frame retriever) ;
- KFS (keyword and frame retriever): that represents the retrieve by combining the two previous methods.

2.2.4 Semantic retrieval of events from indoor surveillance video database

Here, we focus our interest to the main goal of this work [18] which guides users to find required sequences in database of video surveillance. At this end, several steps are required:

- *Preprocessing*: the raw video is analyzed by segmenting videos into CAIs [19] and tracking semantic objects (human) in them.
- *Trajectory modeling*: in each CAI, trajectories are further modeled with the sliding window technique.
- *Event modeling*: In this study, an event model for two people fighting is built, and the feature vectors of human objects at consecutive time point are extracted.
- *Initial retrieval*: When the user submits a query, the system performs an initial query based on some heuristics specific to the event type, and returns the initial retrieval result to the user.

• *Interactive learning and retrieval*: the user responds to the retrieval results by giving his/her feedbacks and refines the retrieval results in the next iterations until a satisfactory result is obtained.

The CAVIAR [20] videos database is used and the results of this framework are shown in the following graph (figure 4):

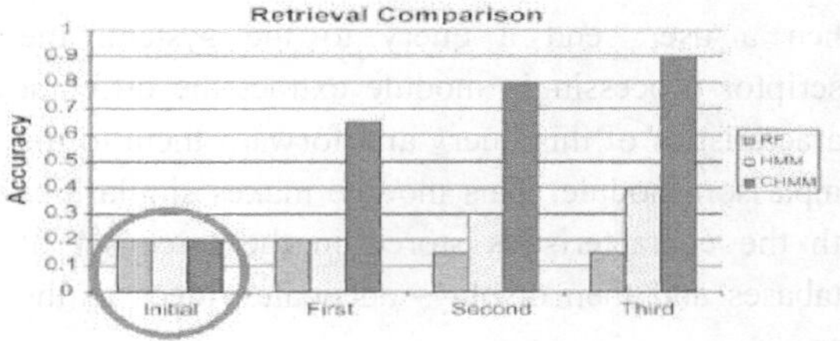

Figure 4 Accuracies of "meeting and fighting" events across iterations

From this graph, we can see the accuracy of the initial results returned to the user and this accuracy of 0.2/1 is very low. For this purpose, our approach is based on a hierarchical indexing to improve the initial results returned to the user.

3. Our hierarchical video indexing and retrieval approach

After having seen and analyzed the graphs resulting from the experiments done by the work of "Semantic retrieval of event from indoor surveillance video database" [18], we have noticed that during the initial iteration, there was a little relevance in the result returned by the indexing system according to the query of the user. Therefore, there was a continuous need to do the relevant feedback "RF" in order to improve the final result. For this purpose, our approach (figure 5) is to improve the initial iteration accuracy. This is possible when we include a hierarchical indexing [6] in the step of "event modeling". So, the proposed approach is as follows:

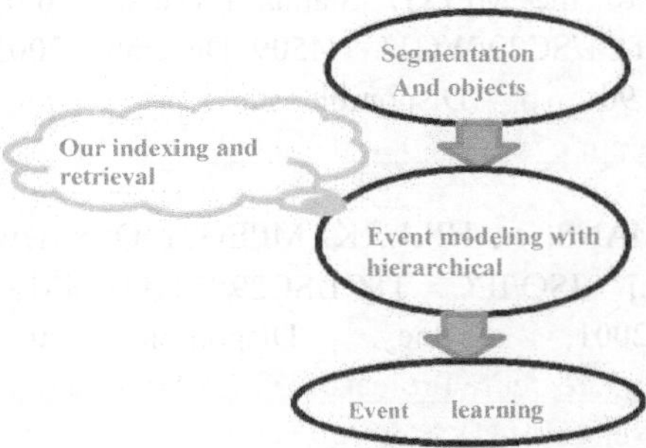

Figure 5 Our video indexing and retrieval approach

3.1 Video segmentation and objects tracking

In this step, we used the CAIs technique "Common Appearance Interval" for segmentation [19] (figure 6):

Figure 6 Video segmentation with CAIs

As for object tracking, a method called Simultaneous partition and Class Parameter Estimation (SPCPE) associated with Background learning and Subtraction methods are used.

3.2 Event modeling

In order to improve the indexing process, we propose a hierarchical annotation thanks to indexing the different CAIs (normal or abnormal human interaction) before annotating the whole video sequence.

First, for annotating the different CAIs, we need to extract the three properties for normal human interaction:

• Dist: distances between two objects in the SP (Sequence Pair);

• Θ : degree of alignment of two objects (i.e. M1 and M2 are the motion vectors of two objects at time t) (figure 7);

Figure 7 The degree of alignment

• Vdiff: changes of velocities of the two objects between two consecutive frames.

In addition, another propriety that is the magnitude of motion change of each object which can be analyzed by Optical Flow needs to be taken into account for abnormal human interactions "meeting and fighting" or "robbing and chasing".

After annotating the different CAIs, the indexing process is improved thanks to a hierarchical indexing which indexes the whole video. We proceed as follows:

We first compute the relevance of each CAIs "C" length in relation to the whole video.

$$W(c) = \frac{L(c)}{L(v)}$$

L(v) represents the length of the whole video. Then, we calculate the rank R (t) of each CAIs index.

$$R(t) = \frac{1}{N_c} \sum_c W(c)\ A(t, c)$$

N_c : is the total number of CAIs and A (t, c) is the relevance of the index "t" in relation to the CAIs "C" (A(t, c) = 0 when the CAIs "C" has not the index "t"). And last, we take the R (t) that has the most occurrences as an index of the whole video sequence.

3.3 Event learning and retrieval

In this step, we keep the same learning algorithm CHMM *"Coupled Hidden Markov Model"* [18] and we also use the relevant feedback after the initial query of the user if necessary.

In our approach, we think that it would be the least possible necessary to use the relevant feedback "RF" and the result of initial query will be performed.

4. Our video indexing and retrieval system

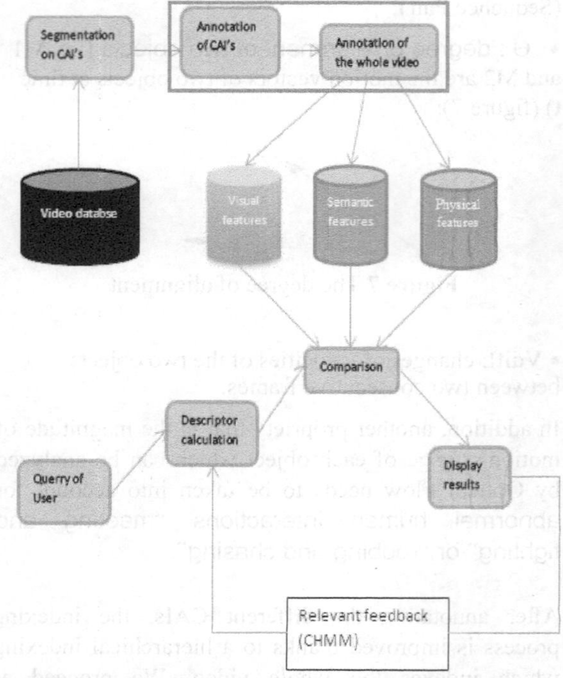

Figure 8 Our video indexing and retrieval systems

The system working proceeds as follows: we segment the videos from video database (Figure 8) using the (CAIs) technique. Then, to improve the initial result feedback of the system cited in [18], we annotate the different CAIs segments to get a set of index that contribute to annotate the whole video. This process represents the hierarchical indexing. Hereafter, we store the result of the annotations in three sets of databases: visual, semantic and physical. When a user send a query to the system, the descriptor processing's module extract the different characteristics of this query and forward them to the comparison module. This module makes similarities with the characteristics stored in the three set of databases and then displays adequate videos to the user.

The aim of our approach is to maximize the user satisfaction in the initial query to avoid relevant feedbacks of the CHHM algorithm.

5. Conclusion

In this paper, we discuss our proposed video indexing and retrieval approach by explaining the hierarchical indexing technique to improve the initial results obtained in [18]. Our video indexing and retrieval system is under development in the RIIR Laboratory and will be experimented by using the CAVIAR video database in the future.

References

[1] " Assistance Intelligente a la RI", book chapter: Indexation multimédia, Rédigé par Bruno Bachimont.

[2] LEE, H .Standard coding for MPEG1, MPEG2 and advanced coding for MPEG4. [En ligne] Rapport EE8205, 6 juin 1997, 15 p. Disponible sur : http://citeseer.nj.nec.com/lee97standard.html

[3] International Organisation for Standardisation. Overview of the MPEG7 Standard (version 6.0). ISO/IEC/JTC1/SC29/WG11 N4509. December 2001 , Pattaya, 90 p . Disponible sur : http://mpeg-industry.com/mp7a/w4980_mp7_overview1.html

[4] BORMANS, J., HILL, K. MPEG21 Overview. [En ligne] ISO/IEC JTC1/SC29/WG11/N4318. Juillet 2001, Sydney. Disponible sur : http://ipsi.fhg.de/delite/Projects/MPEG7/Documents/mpeg21-Overview4318.htm

[5] Un système pour l'annotation semi-automatique des vidéos et application à l'indexation, université du Québec, Aout 2009.

[6] M. Patella . C. Romani, l. Bartoloni. "SHIATSU: tagging and retrieving video without worries", Springer Science+business Media, LLC, 2011.

[7] Contribution aux techniques orientées objets de gestion des séquences vidéo pour les serveurs web, Mihaela SCUTURUCI, 2002.

[8] CHAN, S.S.M., WU, Y., LI, Q., ZHUANG, Y. A Hybrid Approach to Video Retrieval in a generic video Management and Application Processing Framework. [En ligne] Proceedings of the Second IEEE International Conference on Multimedia and Expo (ICME'01). August 22-25, 2001, Tokyo, Japan. Disponible sur: http://citeseer.nj.nec.com/chan01hybrid.html

[9] F SOUVANNAVONG, « Indexation et recherche de plan Vidéo par le contenu Sémantique », Thèse sur le traitement de signal et des images, Ecole Nationale Supérieure des Télécommunications, Paris, pp. 141, juin 2005.

[10] S LEFEVRE, J. HOLLER, N. VINCENT, « Segmentation Temporelle de Séquences d'images en Couleurs » Laboratoire d'Informatique, Université de Tours, France.

[11] A. HANJALIC, R. L. LAGENDIJK, and J. BIEMOND, "Automated High-Level Movie Segmentation for Advanced Video-Retrieval Systems", IEEE Transactions on Circuits and Systems for video Technology, pp. 580-588, juin 1999.

[12] R, BRUNELLI, O. MICH, and C. M. MODENA, "A Survey on the Automatic Indexing of Video Data", Journal of Visual Communication and Image Representation, ITC-irst, I-38050 Povo, Trento, Italy, pp. 78-112, Juin 1999.

[13] A. SALWAY, "Video Annotation: the Role of Specialist Text", Thesis, Departement of Computing, School of Electronic Engineering, Information technology and Mathématics, University of surrey, Guildford, United Kingdom, pp. 188, December 1999.

[14] P. WU, "A Semi-automatic Approach to Detect Highlights for Home Video Annotation", IEEE International Conference on Acousctics, Speech, ans Signal Processing, Montreal, Quebec, Canada, vol. 5, pp. 957 – 960, Mai 2004.

[15] IIARIA Bartoloni, Marco Patella, Corado Romani, SHIATSU, tagging and retrieving videos without worries, 2011

[16] Jacobs A, Miene A, Ioannidis GT, Herzog O (2004) Automatic shot boundary detection combining color, edge, and motion feautures of adjacent frames. In: TRECVID 2004, Gaithersburg, MD, pp 197-206.

[17] Qu Z, Liu Y, Ren L, Chen Y, Zheng R(2009) A method of shot detection based on color and edges features. In: SWS 2009, Lanzhou, China, pp 1-4.

[18] Semantic retrieval of event from indoor surveillance video database, Chengcui Zhang *, Xin Chen, Liping Zhou, Wei-Bang Chen, Journal homepage: www.elsevier.com/locate/patrec , available online 18 May 2009.

[19] L. Chen, M.T Ozsu, "Modeling of video Objects in a video database". IEEE Conference on Multimedia, Lausanne, Switzeland pp , 2002.

[20] Caviar video database, http://homepages.inf.ed.ac.uk/rbf/CAVIAR.

A Novel Query Suggestion Method Based On Sequence Similarity and Transition Probability

Bo Shu[1], Zhendong Niu[1], Xiaotian Jiang[1], and Ghulam Mustafa[1]
[1]School of Computer Science, Beijing Institute of Technology, Beijing, China

Abstract— *Query suggestion plays an important role in search engines which helps to improve user experience by suggesting related terms. Conventional query suggestion methods usually employ pair-wise contextual correlation evaluation or complete sequence matching. However, when confronted with a long or newly appeared sequence, these methods cannot guarantee satisfied performance. This paper presents a novel query suggestion method to solve this problem. We first evaluate the similarities between current query sequence and each sequence in the training set, then calculate the transition probabilities from each sequence to its subsequent query. We can calculate relevance of each candidate query to the current query sequence with these interim results and retrieve the most relevant candidates for suggestion. We evaluated our method against four commonly used methods with a dataset from a commercial search engine. The experimental result shows that our method provides more relevant suggestion queries and offers better recall and precision.*

Keywords: Query suggestion, sequence similarity, transition probability

1. Introduction

Search Engines help users retrieve interesting documents. But users often input too few keywords [1] [2] and contain insufficient information for search engines to understand their intention. This is because users usually do not have a clear concept about what they want, or they use improper words to describe it. Besides, the polysemy phenomenon of words also makes it more difficult to get the exact user requirement.

Query suggestion technology solves these problems by suggesting several related query candidates to users according to their input queries, assisting them to use proper keywords to describe their search intents, and reducing the search attempts unnecessary.

There are two steps in query suggestion process: query candidates extraction, and contextual correlation evaluation. Query candidates can be extracted from both documents and query logs. When selected from documents, we often choose terms co-occurred with the current query in high ranked documents [3] [4]. This method suffers from high complexity, and the queries input by users is not employed to refine the candidates. While selected from query logs [5] [6] [7] [8], the advantages include: representing the intent of user directly, reflecting the modification process of user input queries, querying log data concisely, being easier to analysis, etc.

After selection, we need to rank the candidates in order to provide users with several of the most relevant ones, where similarity evaluation method plays an important role. There has been many researches on evaluating the correlation between query and its candidates, such as by user information [9], user feedback [10] [11] [12], arch [13], content [14], user intention [15], etc. Some methods evaluate the correlation between two queries by constructing bipartite graph with click-through data, existing user queries, and the clicked URLs [2] [6] [16] [17]. Other methods, like [18], use queries, URLs, terms to evaluate the correlation between the query and terms in document. Because the query log are very sparse, only a few popular queries link to a few high ranked URL and most URL has no query associated.

The rest of this paper is organized as follows. Section 2 discusses related works. In Section 3, we proposed our algorithm. In Section 4, we compared our method with three other existing methods, and demonstrate the experimental results. At last, we drew conclusions in Section 5.

2. Related Work

Many methods use session to cluster queries and generate query candidates [5] [19] [20] [21]. These methods need to define and identify the session [22] [23], then cluster queries with sessions and other property, such as content [24], submit time [25] [26] [27], clicked URL [28], searching topic [28], etc.

Yanan Li, et al [29] use query trace graph to calculate transition probability of queries and obtain candidates according to the probabilities. [30] improved this method with time information. However, both of the methods only calculate the transition probability of consecutive query pairs. The scarcity of taking all the prefix sequence into consideration lead to a decreasing precision in recommending queries with a long sequence.

Qi He, et al [31] proposed a new method to generate candidates. They first use the training set to generate Mixture Variable Memory Markov model, then select the candidate based on the resemblance between the user input query sequence and historical query sequence models retrieved from search engine logs.

In [31], a statistic shows that 34.34% of session patterns (specialization, generalization, parallel movement, and others) is related to the order of query session. To find out the relation between the length of sequence and the session pattern, we employed similar categories and performed similar experiments for each of the length from 2 to 5. The session set we used contains 2,000 unique sessions. Figure 1 illustrates a similar result from that in [31], which shows that 34.34% of session patterns are related to the order of query session (spelling change, generalization, and specialization). Figure 1 support the following observations: as the session length increases, roughly the proportion of specialization pattern tends to decrease, the proportion of parallel movement pattern tends to increase, the generalization pattern stays low, and the proportion of other patterns keeps fluctuating.

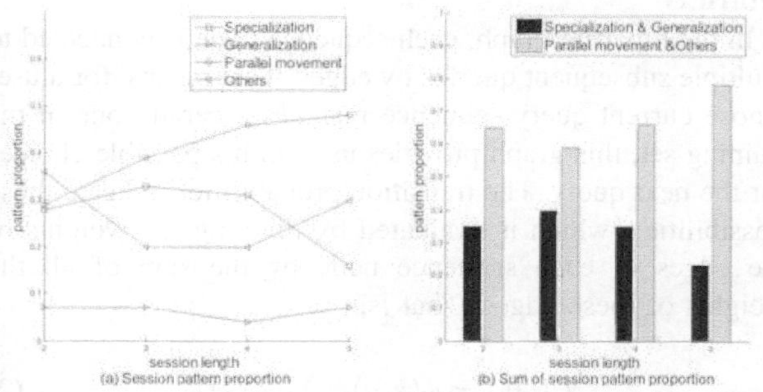

Fig. 1: Relationship between session length and session patterns

In our approach, we follow the idea of retrieving query candidates from query logs for its effectiveness and high efficiency. Some methods, such as variable memory Markov model [31], if cannot find completely matching sequence, will discard the head of sequence and try to match the rest. For example, if sequence $[q_1, q_2, \cdots, q_{i-1}]$ cannot be found in the training dataset, they remove its first element and try again to match the remaining sequence $[q_2, \cdots, q_{i-1}]$. However, according to Figure 1, relying only on complete sequence matching is not enough. Also, we need to consider the order of elements in the sequence, for the similar sequence may also provide contextual information for subsequent query suggestion. Instead of complete sequence matching along, our approach searches all the similar sequences, and measure the correlation between query sequences with similarity measures. Early researches showed that the usage of N-gram model tends to increase accuracy [31]. We also use this method and generalize it to suit the circumstance of variable length sequence - query transition probability.

We propose a novel method based on query sequence similarity and transition probability. Our method first calculate the similarity between input query and existing query sequences in the training set, then calculate the transition probability from each query to their subsequent query. After accumulating the products of each pair of similarity and transition probability to a certain subsequent query, the recommendation score of it can be obtained. According to these scores, we list the most contextual related queries to the input query as candidates.

3. Algorithm

3.1 Notation and Problem Statement

Let Q be the set of unique queries, $Q = \{q_1, \cdots, q_n\}$, S be the set of distinct sequence formed by elements in Q, $S = \{S_1, \cdots, S_m\}$, where $S_i = [q_{i1}, \cdots, q_{ij}, \cdots, q_{ik}]$, $q_{ij} \in Q$. For example, a user u may input query "computer", "DELL computer", "DELL OPTIPLEX 755", "DELL OPTIPLEX 755 price" sequentially. The query sequence of user u is S_u, $S_u = [q_1, q_2, q_3, q_4]$, q_1 is "computer", q_2 is "DELL computer", and q_3 is "DELL OPTIPLEX 755", etc.

The problem of query suggestion is to recommend candidate queries to users based on their historical query sequence. This process can be divided into 3 steps: (1) calculate the similarity between current user's input sequence and the sequence in the training set; (2) calculate the transition probability from a given query sequence to a query (both of them are in the training set); (3) for each candidate query in the training set, accumulate the products of each pair of sequence similarity and the transition probability to this query, so we can obtain the queries with the highest score as suggested queries. In the following sub-sections, we will elaborate each step in detail.

3.2 Similarity of Sequence

Many measures can be adopted to calculate the similarity of two sequences, such as Cosine Distance, Jaccard Coefficient, Hamming Distance, Minkowski Distance (including Manhattan distance and Euclid distance), Levenshtein Distance, Damerau-Levenshtein Distance, etc. Among these measures, Cosine Distance and Minkowski Distance do not concern about position information; Hamming Distance only evaluates the distance between the sequences with the same length and only adopts substitution operation; Levenshtein Distance has no transposition operation; Only Damerau-Levenshtein Distance, which is a special type of edit distance, has insertion, deletion, substitution, and adjacency transposition operation, which often been used by search engine users to modify their original input query strings. Besides, we have two other considerations: first, when two pairs of query sequences have same length, the longer common sequence the pair of query sequence has, the higher similarity it has; second, when two pairs of sequence have common sequence of the same length, the pair of sequence with the larger length has the lower similarity. Based on the above-mentioned considerations, we define the similarity between two query sequences based on Damerau-Levenshtein Distance as:

$$sim(s_a, s_b) = 1 - (DL(s_a, s_b)/MaxLen(s_a, s_b)) \quad (1)$$

where $sim(s_a, s_b)$ is the similarity between s_a and s_b, $DL(s_a, s_b)$ is the Damerau-Levenshtein Distance between s_a and s_b, and $MaxLen(s_a, s_b)$ is the length of the longer sequence of s_a and s_b. The range of this similarity measure is $[0, 1]$ and a larger value means the two query sequences are more similar. Similar to [24], we set the threshold to 0.4, which means we regard the two sequences having a similarity less than 0.4 as completely irrelevant sequences and do not choose those sequences for the further calculation.

3.3 Transition Probability from sequence to query

By analyzing query logs, we can observe one query sequence may be followed by different queries, while different query sequences may lead to the same subsequent query. This can be depicted in a sequence-query bipartite graph with vertices representing query sequences and their subsequent queries.

The bipartite graph can be constructed with the following approach: (1) First, segment and extract sessions from query log, then convert each session into a query sequence; (2) For each sequence, we extract each possible pair of sub-sequence and subsequent query. Supposing we have the sequence $[q_1, q_2, q_3, q_4, q_5]$. It can be decomposed into the following 10 sequence-query pairs, with each of them having an occurrence weight of 1: $\langle [q_1], q_2 \rangle$, $\langle [q_1, q_2], q_3 \rangle$, $\langle [q_1, q_2, q_3], q_4 \rangle$, $\langle [q_1, q_2, q_3, q_4], q_5 \rangle$, $\langle [q_2], q_3 \rangle$, $\langle [q_2, q_3], q_4 \rangle$, $\langle [q_2, q_3, q_4], q_5 \rangle$, $\langle [q_3], q_4 \rangle$, $\langle [q_3, q_4], q_5 \rangle$, $\langle [q_4], q_5 \rangle$. (3) Search each of the pairs in the bipartite graph. If the sub-sequence or its subsequent query does not exist, we add this node in the graph. Then we attempt to add an edge to connect the sub-sequence node to the subsequent query node with the weight of 1; but if both of them are already in the bipartite graph, we simply increase the weight of their edge by 1. A brief algorithm of the bipartite graph construction process is formalized as below.

Algorithm 1: Query sequence subsequent query bipartite graph construction

Input:
T: Session training set.

Output:
G: Sequence-query transition probability bipartite graph.

Notation:
s: Session sequence in training set.
l_s: Length of sequence, i.e. the number of queries in session s.
$node\,[s]$: Node of sequence s.
$node\,[q]$: Node of query q.
$edge\,\langle s, q\rangle$: Edge from sequence s to query q.
$\phi\,\langle s, q\rangle$: Weight of the edge from sequence s to query q.

for each s in T
  for $i = 0, \ldots, (l_s - 2)$
    for $j = 2, \ldots, l_s - i$
      for $k = i, \ldots, j + i - 2$
        retrieve $[q_i, \cdots, q_{(j+i-2)}]$ as query sequence
        retrieve $q_{(j+i-1)}$ as subsequent query
        if $node\,[q_i, \cdots, q_{(j+i-2)}]$ **not exist in** G
          add $node\,[q_i, \cdots, q_{(j+i-2)}]$ to G
        if $node\,[q_{(j+i-1)}]$ **not exist in** G
          add $node\,[q_{(j+i-1)}]$ to G
        if $edge\,\langle [q_i, \cdots, q_{(j+i-2)}], q_{(j+i-1)}\rangle$ **not exist in** G
          add $edge\,\langle [q_i, \cdots, q_{(j+i-2)}], q_{(j+i-1)}\rangle$ to G
          $\phi\,\langle [q_i, \cdots, q_{(j+i-2)}], q_{(j+i-1)}\rangle = 0$
        $\phi\,\langle [q_i, \cdots, q_{(j+i-2)}], q_{(j+i-1)}\rangle$ ++

return G

In the bipartite graph, each sequence node is connected to multiple subsequent queries by edges. That means, for a user whose current query sequence matches a certain one in the training set, this graph provides us with his possible choices for the next query. The transition probabilities indicate these possibilities, which is evaluated by dividing the weights of the edges of each sequence node by the sum of all the weights of these edges. That is,

$$P(q|s) = \phi(s, q)/(\sum \phi(s)) \quad (2)$$

where the $P(q|s)$ is the transition probability from sequence s to its subsequent q, $\phi(s, q)$ is weight of edge from s to q, $\phi(s)$ is the weight of edge out of s. For example: the occurrence number of a sequence-query tuple $< s, q >$ is x and the occurrence number of sequence S in all sequence-query tuples is y, then in bipartite graph $\phi(s, q)$ is x and $\sum \phi(s)$ is y. The transition probability from s to q is x/y. The range of transition probability is $[0, 1]$. A larger transition probability means the user who has input a certain query sequence is more likely to choose the query connected by this edge as subsequent query.

3.4 Recommendation Score of a Query to a Sequence

The recommendation score $R\,(s, q)$ of a query to a current user query sequence is formed by accumulating the products of each pair of the similarity between the current sequence and the sequence in the training set and the transition probability from the sequence in training set to this query. Formalized by the following formula:

$$R\,(s, q) = \sum_{s_t \in T} sim\,(s, s_t) \times (sim\,(s, s_t))^{\rho - 1} \times (P\,(q|s_t)) \quad (3)$$

where the $R(s,q)$ is the recommendation score of query q to the user inputted query sequence s, s_t is a query sequence in training set T. ρ is the case amplification power [32]that modifies the influence of the similarity to the score by punishing low similarity and reducing noise. Typical $\rho \geq 1$. A large ρ makes the similarity factor less influential to the recommendation score. In this paper we set ρ to 2.5 according to [32] [33].

The diagram of sequence similarity model is shown in Figure 2. We can see that it is a directed acyclic graph and the recommendation score of a query for a input sequence is equal to the sum of path products that from input sequence to this query in training set.

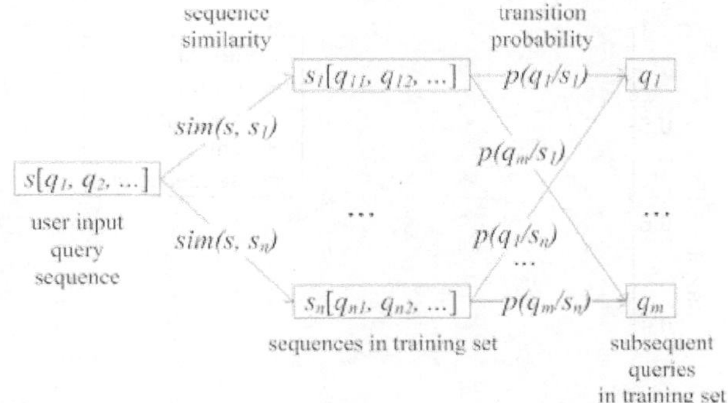

Fig. 2: Evaluation model of sequence similarity model

4. Experiment Result

We evaluated the performance of our method against four other existing query suggestion methods: text similarity [24], co-occurrence [5], query trace graph [29], and VMM[31].

4.1 Train Data Set

We employed a 30 days query log extracted from a commercial search engine (http://www.sogou.com/labs/dl/q-e.html. Corpus Search Engine Click-through Log(SogouQ). 2012-12-15.) to test our suggestion model. This is a chinese search engine and most of queries in the log are in chinese. Table 1 shows its format. Among them user ID is automatically assigned by the search engine according to the Cookie information when the users get access to it.

The input queries in the period from a user's start browsering to end has the same unique user ID. We only use user ID and query content fields in our experiment. In this 30 days query log data, we use the earlier 25 days log data as the training set and the rest as the test set.

Table 2 summarizes the statistics of the training dataset and the test dataset. The number of unique queries is the number of total query records after removing the adjacent same query records and a few unrecognizable code.

Table 1: Format of query log.

user ID	query content	...	clicked URL	...
xxx	q_1	...	www.a.com	...
yyy	q_2	...	www.b.com	...

Table 2: Statistic of query log.

Data	Searches	Unique queries	Query sequences
training	18,506,239	9,203,195	6,043,848
test	2,920,724	1,492,460	973,976

4.2 Session Segmentation and Selection

Session is defined as a sequence of queries input by a user for a specific search purpose [5]. Sessions are identified by cookie information. A cookie includes user ID, access timestamps, query text, clicked URL, etc. In practice, a session can be retrieved from search log of a search engine system, or from the query sequence by input a user with a terminal in the period from starting a browser to closing it. We identify a query sequence by user ID, and consider the query sequence as a session.

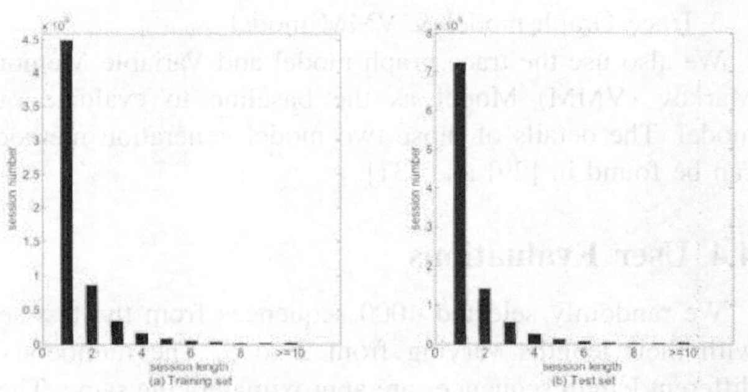

Fig. 3: Relationship between the counts and the length of the sequences in training set and test set

Figure 3 shows the relationship between the counts and the length of sequences in the training set and test set. We can see from it that the number of sequences decreases as the length of sequence goes up. 74% of sequences contain only one query. The proportions of the Sequences whose length larger than 5 are less than 1%. The sum of proportions of sequences whose length large than 5 is less than 2%, which can be safely discarded. So we selected the sequences with the length varying from 2 to 5 for training and test.

4.3 Baseline Methods

In order to evaluate the performance of the proposed method, we implement four widely-used query suggestion methods as baselines: text similarity [24], co-occurrence [5], trace graph [29], and VMM [31].

1 Text Similarity

For each query sequences we use (1) [24] to calculate the similarity between queries, where s_a and s_b denote query strings instead of query sequence. Then we select the queries that have high similarity with the user input query as the suggestion query candidates. Only the last query of the user input query sequence is considered. In the following experiment, when evaluating the recall and precision of text similarity method, we set the threshold to 0.4 [24]. That means if the similarity of a query in the training set and the user query is less than 0.4, then the former query will not be considered as a candidate.

2 Co-Occurrence

The method in [5] only evaluates the pair-wise similarity between two queries. However, in our experiment we need to evaluate the recommendation score of a query to a test sequence. So when choosing recommendation queries, we only search the queries that had co-occurred with all the queries that appears in the test query sequence in the training set. We sum up the co-occurrence between the recommendation query and each query in test query sequence as the recommendation score of recommendation query, then we select the queries with high recommendation score as candidates.

3 Trace Graph model & VMM model

We also use the trace graph model and Variable Memory Markov (VMM) Model as the baseline to evaluate our model. The details of those two model generation methods can be found in [29] and [31].

4.4 User Evaluations

We randomly selected 4000 sequences from the test set, with their lengths varying from 2 to 5. The numbers of different length sequences are approximately the same. Then we discarded the last query of each sequence to form test sequences. For each test sequence, we calculated its recommendation score with each of the five methods and chose up to 5 the most recommendable queries (Some methods, such as co-occurrence, might not generate enough candidates for a long sequence) that did not appear in the test sequence for suggestion.

20 volunteers had been chosen to evaluate the suggested queries. Each of them selected one twentieth of the total query suggestion results. After their inputting the test sequence as user query sequence, if they think the user will choose the suggested queries, then they approve it; otherwise they reject it. The volunteers not only need to consider the contextual or semantic relation between test sequence and the suggested queries, but also the intention of users after inputting the sequence. For example, the user is likely to select "DELL OPTIPLEX 755" after inputting "computer" and "DELL computer", but they seldom select "computer" after inputting "DELL computer" and "DELL OPTIPLEX 755", although they have semantic or contextual relationship.

We use the standard metrics - precision and recall - to evaluate the performance of the five query suggestion methods. Precision is defined as the ratio of the number of queries approved by volunteers over the number of all candidates. Recall is defined as the ratio of the number of queries approved by volunteers over the expected number of candidates.

4.5 Query Suggestion Recall

Figure 4 shows the recall measure achieved by the five query suggestion methods. From the results, we make the following analysis:

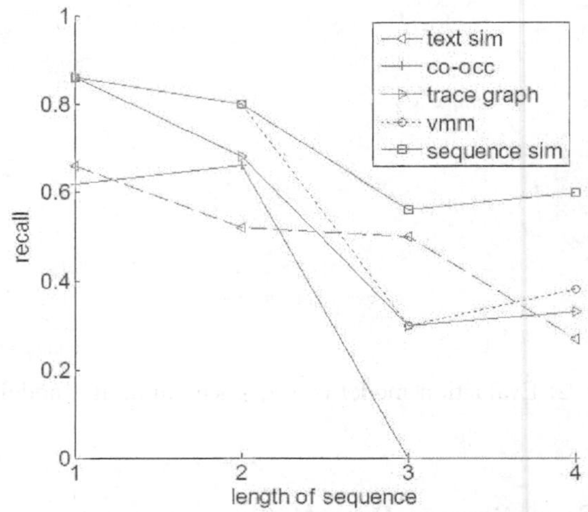

Fig. 4: Recall of five query suggestion models

1. When the length of sequence is equal to 1, the best recall is achieved by sequence similarity, trace graph, and VMM methods with the value of 0.86 because they apply the same candidate generating method.

2. As the length of sequence get larger, the recall of co-occurrence method decreases. That is ascribed to the decreasing occurrence probability of a number of queries occurred in a session as the number of queries increases. The recall of text similarity method continuously decreases, for the text similarity method only considers the last query, but a text similar query to the last query has less contextual relation with a long sequence. The trace graph, VMM, and sequence similarity methods share the same change trend. When session length is larger than two, the recall of trace graph and VMM methods are very close. That indicates VMM method tends to degenerate to trace graph method when it is more difficult to find the complete matching sequence with the increasing sequence length.

3. Sequence similarity method achieves the best recall across all sequence lengths. Because sequence similarity method will search similar sequences if it cannot find the

complete matching sequence. Thus it can always find enough candidates.

4. When the length of sequence is larger than 2, the recall of co-occurrence method drops to 0. Further analysis shows this is because co-occurrence method can find no sequence in the training set that has all the queries appeared in test sequence and still has a query that is different from the queries in test sequence for suggestion.

4.6 Query Suggestion Precision

Figure 5 shows the precision achieved by five query suggestion methods. From the results, we make the following analysis:

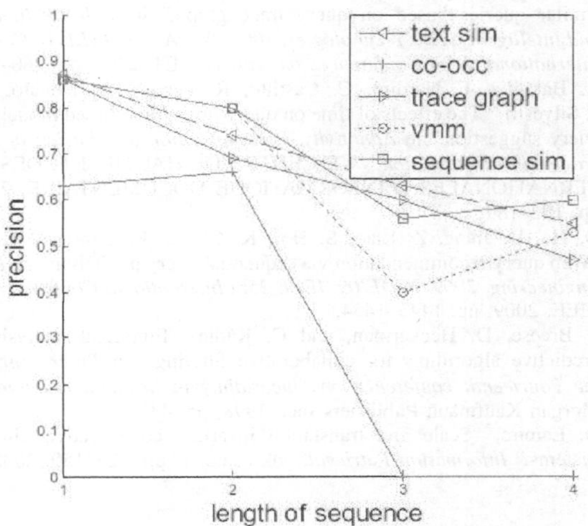

Fig. 5: Precision of five query suggestion models

1. The precision of each method has a downtrend as the length of sequence increases. Co-occurrence method has the lowest precision. When the length of sequence is larger than 2, its precision drops to 0 due to the same reason mentioned in the previous sub-section.

2. The precisions of sequence similarity, text similarity, trace graph, and VMM methods are very close when the length of sequence is equal to 1. Combining with the recall analysis, we know that is because the other three methods retrieved fewer candidates than that of the sequence similarity method. They may merely have few hits, but the less quantity of suggested queries gets their precisions raised.

3. The sequence similarity and VMM method have roughly the same change trend, because they all adopt the sequence information to generate candidates. The sequence similarity method has a higher precision due to its more flexible matching strategy.

Figure 6 shows the overall precision and recall of the user evaluation on the five query suggestion methods. We can see that although the precision of sequence similarity, text

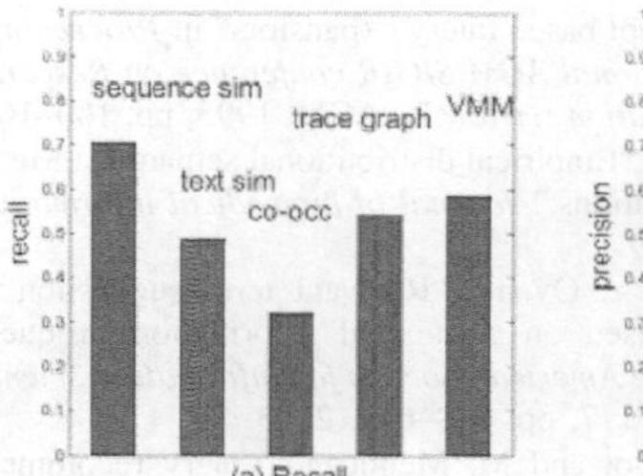

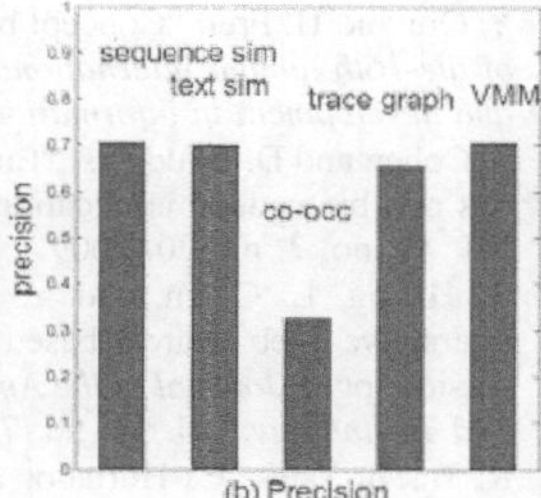

Fig. 6: Precision and Recall of volunteers' evaluation of five query suggestion models

similarity, trace graph, and VMM models are very close, the recall of sequence similarity method has an obvious advantage over the other four methods. The sequence similarity model has an outstanding comprehensive performance. We also can see from Figure 4 and Figure 5 that with the increase of the length of query sequences, the advantage of our method is more obvious.

5. Conclusions

In this paper, we present a novel method based on sequence similarity and transition probability for query suggestion. We evaluated the performances of our method with a dataset by comparing with four other existing methods. The experiment result shows that our method has both high precision and recall. This is because we adopt not only the query position information in a sequence and transition probability from query sequence to the subsequent query, but also employ a more flexible sequence matching strategy.

As future work, we will test our method with a larger training set and then extend our similarity calculation by adopting more attributes such as the time, IP, region of a user's query submission etc. Using more attributes of a query makes it more precise to evaluate the similarity between sequences.

Acknowledgment

This work is supported by the National Natural Science Foundation of China (no. 61250010), the Program for Beijing Municipal Commission of Education (grant no.1320037010601), the 111 Project of Beijing Institute of Technology and the New Century Excellent Talents in University(grant no. NCET-06-0161).

References

[1] B. Jansen, A. Spink, and T. Saracevic, "Real life, real users, and real needs: a study and analysis of user queries on the web," *Information processing & management*, vol. 36, no. 2, pp. 207–227, 2000.

[2] J. Wen, J. Nie, and H. Zhang, "Clustering user queries of a search engine," in *Proceedings of the 10th international conference on World Wide Web*. ACM, 2001, pp. 162–168.

[3] Y. Qiu and H. Frei, "Concept based query expansion," in *Proceedings of the 16th annual international ACM SIGIR conference on Research and development in information retrieval.* ACM, 1993, pp. 160–169.

[4] T. Cohen and D. Widdows, "Empirical distributional semantics: Methods and biomedical applications," *Journal of biomedical informatics*, vol. 42, no. 2, p. 390, 2009.

[5] C. Huang, L. Chien, and Y. Oyang, "Relevant term suggestion in interactive web search based on contextual information in query session logs," *Journal of the American Society for Information Science and Technology*, vol. 54, no. 7, pp. 638–649, 2003.

[6] R. Baeza-Yates, C. Hurtado, and M. Mendoza, "Query recommendation using query logs in search engines," in *Current Trends in Database Technology-EDBT 2004 Workshops.* Springer, 2005, pp. 395–397.

[7] C. Huang, L. Chien, and Y. Oyang, "Clustering similar query sessions toward interactive web search."

[8] S. Jiang, S. Zilles, and R. Holte, "Query suggestion by query search: a new approach to user support in web search," in *Web Intelligence and Intelligent Agent Technologies, 2009. WI-IAT'09. IEEE/WIC/ACM International Joint Conferences on*, vol. 1. IET, 2009, pp. 679–684.

[9] P. Chirita, C. Firan, and W. Nejdl, "Personalized query expansion for the web," in *Proceedings of the 30th annual international ACM SIGIR conference on Research and development in information retrieval.* ACM, 2007, pp. 7–14.

[10] L. Fitzpatrick and M. Dent, "Automatic feedback using past queries: social searching?" in *ACM SIGIR Forum*, vol. 31, no. SI. ACM, 1997, pp. 306–313.

[11] M. Magennis and C. van Rijsbergen, "The potential and actual effectiveness of interactive query expansion," in *ACM SIGIR Forum*, vol. 31, no. SI. ACM, 1997, pp. 324–332.

[12] Y. Song and L. He, "Optimal rare query suggestion with implicit user feedback," in *Proceedings of the 19th international conference on World wide web.* ACM, 2010, pp. 901–910.

[13] R. Kraft and J. Zien, "Mining anchor text for query refinement," in *Proceedings of the 13th international conference on World Wide Web.* ACM, 2004, pp. 666–674.

[14] J. Wen, J. Nie, and H. Zhang, "Query clustering using user logs," *ACM Transactions on Information Systems*, vol. 20, no. 1, pp. 59–81, 2002.

[15] M. Strohmaier, M. Kröll, and C. Körner, "Intentional query suggestion: making user goals more explicit during search," in *Proceedings of the 2009 workshop on Web Search Click Data.* ACM, 2009, pp. 68–74.

[16] D. Beeferman and A. Berger, "Agglomerative clustering of a search engine query log," in *Proceedings of the sixth ACM SIGKDD international conference on Knowledge discovery and data mining.* ACM, 2000, pp. 407–416.

[17] H. Cao, D. Jiang, J. Pei, Q. He, Z. Liao, E. Chen, and H. Li, "Context-aware query suggestion by mining click-through and session data," in *Proceeding of the 14th ACM SIGKDD international conference on Knowledge discovery and data mining.* ACM, 2008, pp. 875–883.

[18] M. Diligenti, M. Gori, and M. Maggini, "Users, queries and documents: A unified representation for web mining," in *Proceedings of the 2009 IEEE/WIC/ACM International Joint Conference on Web Intelligence and Intelligent Agent Technology-Volume 01.* IEEE Computer Society, 2009, pp. 238–244.

[19] B. Fonseca, P. Golgher, B. Pôssas, B. Ribeiro-Neto, and N. Ziviani, "Concept-based interactive query expansion," in *Proceedings of the 14th ACM international conference on Information and knowledge management.* ACM, 2005, pp. 696–703.

[20] R. Jones, B. Rey, O. Madani, and W. Greiner, "Generating query substitutions," in *Proceedings of the 15th international conference on World Wide Web.* ACM, 2006, pp. 387–396.

[21] B. Fonseca, P. Golgher, E. De Moura, B. Pôssas, and N. Ziviani, "Discovering search engine related queries using association rules," *Journal of Web Engineering*, vol. 2, no. 4, pp. 215–227, 2003.

[22] D. He, A. Göker, and D. Harper, "Combining evidence for automatic web session identification," *Information Processing & Management*, vol. 38, no. 5, pp. 727–742, 2002.

[23] A. Jansen, B. J. Spink, C. Blakely, and S. Koshman., "Defining a session on web search engines," *Journal of The American Society for Information Science and Technology*, vol. 58, no. 6, pp. 862–871, 2007.

[24] X. Shi and C. Yang, "Mining related queries from search engine query logs," in *Proceedings of the 15th international conference on World Wide Web.* ACM, 2006, pp. 943–944.

[25] S. Chien and N. Immorlica, "Semantic similarity between search engine queries using temporal correlation," in *Proceedings of the 14th international conference on World Wide Web.* ACM, 2005, pp. 2–11.

[26] Q. Mei, D. Zhou, and K. Church, "Query suggestion using hitting time," in *Proceedings of the 17th ACM conference on Information and knowledge management.* ACM, 2008, pp. 469–478.

[27] R. Baraglia, C. Castillo, D. Donato, F. Nardini, R. Perego, and F. Silvestri, "Aging effects on query flow graphs for query suggestion," in *Proceedings of the 18th ACM conference on Information and knowledge management.* ACM, 2009, pp. 1947–1950.

[28] D. Widyantoro and J. Yen, "Using fuzzy ontology for query refinement in a personalized abstract search engine," in *IFSA World Congress and 20th NAFIPS International Conference, 2001. Joint 9th*, vol. 1. IEEE, 2001, pp. 610–615.

[29] Y. Li, B. Wang, S. Xu, P. Li, and J. Li, "Querytrans: Finding similar queries based on query trace graph," in *Web Intelligence and Intelligent Agent Technologies, 2009. WI-IAT'09. IEEE/WIC/ACM International Joint Conferences on*, vol. 1. IET, 2009, pp. 260–263.

[30] R. Baraglia, F. Nardini, C. Castillo, R. Perego, D. Donato, and F. Silvestri, "The effects of time on query flow graph-based models for query suggestion," in *Adaptivity, Personalization and Fusion of Heterogeneous Information.* LE CENTRE DE HAUTES ETUDES INTERNATIONALES D'INFORMATIQUE DOCUMENTAIRE, 2010, pp. 182–189.

[31] Q. He, D. Jiang, Z. Liao, S. Hoi, K. Chang, E. Lim, and H. Li, "Web query recommendation via sequential query prediction," in *Data Engineering, 2009. ICDE'09. IEEE 25th International Conference on.* IEEE, 2009, pp. 1443–1454.

[32] J. Breese, D. Heckerman, and C. Kadie, "Empirical analysis of predictive algorithms for collaborative filtering," in *Proceedings of the Fourteenth conference on Uncertainty in artificial intelligence.* Morgan Kaufmann Publishers Inc., 1998, pp. 43–52.

[33] D. Lemire, "Scale and translation invariant collaborative filtering systems," *Information Retrieval*, vol. 8, no. 1, pp. 129–150, 2005.

SESSION

REGRESSION AND CLASSIFICATION

Chair(s)

Drs. Robert Stahlbock
Gary M. Weiss

A Multi-scale Nonparametric/Parametric Hybrid Recognition Strategy with Multi-category Posterior Probability Estimation

Zhao Lu[1], **Zheng Lu**[2], **and Haoda Fu**[3]
[1]Department of Electrical Engineering, Tuskegee University, Tuskegee, AL, USA
[2]Astella Pharma Global Development, Inc., Northbrook, IL, USA
[3]Eli Lilly and Company, Indianapolis, IN USA

Abstract — *The synthesis of an effective multi-category nonlinear classifier with the capability to output calibrated posterior probabilities to enable post-processing is of great significance in practical recognition situations in that the posterior probability reflects the assessment uncertainty. In this paper, a multi-scale nonparametric and parametric hybrid recognition strategy is developed for this purpose. Based on the binary tree representation for nested structure, a new nonlinear polychotomous classification algorithm with the capability of estimating posterior probability is developed on the strength of kernel learning and Bayesian decision theory. In particular, by capitalizing on the intrinsic conexus between hierarchical structure and multi-scale analysis, the polychotomous multi-scale Bayesian kernel Fisher discriminant is implemented for building the classifier at different scales for different levels. Finally, the performance of the proposed classification and posterior probability estimation algorithm is validated by designing a multi-category Bayesian kernel Fisher discriminant classifier for a satellite images dataset.*

Keywords: Kernel Fisher Discriminant; Binary Tree; Posterior Probability; Inter-class Separability; Class-conditional density function; Multi-scale.

1 Introduction

In the realm of pattern recognition and statistical learning, most of existing schemes can be categorized into parametric or nonparametric approaches. Parametric methods assume specific parametric models, while nonparametric methods usually do not require any postulations for the model and utilize the sampled data directly for model representation. Both parametric and nonparametric methods have their own strengths and limitations [1], and the complementarity between them has aroused considerable research endeavours in fusing non-parametric and parametric methods for targets tracking, nonlinear systems identification, classifier construction and modeling, etc [1−6]. In this paper, as a stride towards the fusion of kernel-based nonparametric computational learning methods and parametric density estimation methods, a multi-scale multi-class recognition strategy is developed, where the kernel Fisher discriminant (KFD) is employed for feature extraction and parametric class-conditional density estimation is used for Bayesian classification.

In real world, most of classification problems encountered comprise multiple categories, i.e., polychotomous classification problem, such as automatic target recognition, optical character recognition, face recognition, etc. In general, the issue of polychotomous classification is much more involved than dichotomic classification. With the burgeoning of various kernel learning algorithms since 1990s [7−9], such as support vector machine (SVM), kernel Fisher discriminant (KFD) and kernel principal component analysis (KPCA) and so on, the synthesis of multi-category nonlinear kernel classifier with superior generalization capability has become a focus of research in the past decade [10−16]. The conventional approaches for extending binary classifier to polychotomous classifier fall into two categories, i.e., the direct method and 'divide-and-combine' approach. The direct method is a straightforward generalization of the corresponding dichotomic algorithms, and all data are considered in one optimization formulation, which may result in prohibitively-expensive computing cost for solving a nonlinear optimization problem with a large number of variables.

In contrast to the direct method, the methodology of 'divide-and-combine' usually decomposes the multi-category problem into several subproblems that can be solved by using binary classifiers. Two widely used 'divide-and-combine' methods are pairwise and one-versus-rest. In the approach of pairwise, an n-class problem is converted into $n(n-1)/2$ dichotomic problems which cover all pairs of classes. Then, the binary classifiers are trained for each of pairs, and the classification decision for a test pattern is given on the aggregate of output magnitudes. Apparently, in pairwise methods, the number of binary classifiers built increases rapidly with the increasing of the number of classes, which easily leads to onerous computational task. This problem is alleviated in the one-versus-rest method, where only n binary classifiers are needed for n-class problem and each of them is trained to separate one class of samples from all others.

However, all training data have to be involved in constructing each binary classifier and one-versus-rest method is not capable to yield the optimal decision boundaries. In particular, both methods can result in the existence of unclassified regions.

Recently, as a new member in the family of 'divide-and-combine' methods, the multi-category classifier with hierarchical tree structure has aroused extensive interest in the community of pattern recognition and machine learning [16−19]. As a natural hierarchical representation for nested structure, the binary tree usually organizes information into different levels, which enables the multi-scale implementation so that the higher in the hierarchy a level is the finer scales the information is processed in.

Moreover, compared to the conventional approaches in constructing the multi-category classifiers, the polychotomous classifiers with hierarchical structure are advantageous in improving computational tractability and classification accuracy, diminishing the amount of data involved in training each binary classifier and eliminating unclassifiable regions. Also, the hierarchical structure invoked empowers the design and implementation of multi-scale polychotomous classification algorithms to take care of local as well as global complexity of the input-output map. For constructing the hierarchical tree structure, non-metric distance functions for measuring the inter-class separability was developed in Refs. [17−18, 20]. The significance of no-metric distance function in image classification and computer vision has been investigated in [21], and the raison d'etre of non-metric distance function is also corroborated by some research in psychology suggesting the ubiquity of non-metric distance in human similarity judgments [22].

On the other hand, the synthesis of a multi-category nonlinear classifier with the capability to produce a calibrated posterior probability $P(class|input)$ to enable post-processing is of great significance in practical recognition situations. For instance, a posterior probability allows decisions that can use a utility model. Posterior probabilities are also required when a classifier is making a small part of an overall decision, and the classification outputs must be combined with other sources of information for decision-making, such as example-dependent misclassification costs, the outputs of other classifiers or domain knowledge [23−25]. For the nonlinear kernel classification algorithms, albeit some endeavours have been devoted to convert the output of support vector classifier into the posterior probability by fitting some predefined mapping functions [23−27], such as logistic link function and sigmoid function, these schemes are empirical per se and the building of classifier is irrespective of the estimation of posterior probability.

Compared to the algorithm of support vector classification, which directly generates geometric decision boundary for dichotomy with an uncalibrated value, a crucial advantage of the KFD is that the produced outputs can easily be transformed into the posterior probabilities, i.e., the class membership. In other words, the output values imply not only whether a given test pattern belongs to a certain class, but also the probability of this event [7, 28]. Some recent researches have revealed the essence of KFD in nonlinear classification [29] and the equivalence between linear SVC and sparsified Fisher discriminant analysis [30]. Although the algorithm of Fisher discriminant can be generalized to $n-$ class feature extraction and dimension reduction problem by directly projecting the data onto a $(n-1)$ dimensional space [31], this direct method is obviously unable to be used when the number of classes is greater than the dimensionality of the input space. While, for the algorithm of polychotomous KFD developed in Ref. [17], it can be used for multi-category problem regardless of the dimensionality of the input space, and in particular the hierarchical tree structure synthesized provides a natural framework for evaluating the multi-class posterior probabilities. Herein, in the line of our previous arguments [17−18], the problem of evaluating multi-class posterior probability is approached by an innovative multi-scale polychotomous Bayesian kernel Fisher discriminant algorithm developed in this paper. The proposed algorithm primarily rests on two pillars: class-conditional density function estimation and binary tree representation for nested structure. The former enables the evaluation of posterior probability for the dichotomic subproblems, and the latter empower us to convert the multi-category classification problem into $(n-1)$ dichotomic subproblems and thereby implement the multi-scale classification.

The rest of this paper is organized as follows. In the next section, the kernelized group clustering algorithm used in [17] for binary tree induction is briefly reviewed. Following that, the polychotomous Bayesian KFD on the strength of Lindeberg-Feller central limit theorem is discussed in Section 3. In Section 4, the algorithms for estimating class conditional probability densities and multi-class posterior probability are presented. The simulation study on satellite image data classification is conducted in Section 5, with concluding remarks in Section 6.

The following generic notations will be used throughout this paper: non-boldface symbols such as $y, k, P, \cdots$ refer to scalar valued objects, lower case boldface symbols such as $\boldsymbol{x}, \boldsymbol{\varphi}, \boldsymbol{\beta}, \cdots$ refer to vector valued objects, and capital boldface symbols such as $\boldsymbol{N}, \boldsymbol{K}, \boldsymbol{A}, \cdots$ will be used for matrices and sets.

2 Macro-class partition algorithm for binary tree synthesis

The strategy of determining the topology of binary tree by dividing the multiple classes to be recognized into two smaller macro-classes at each non-leaf node has been developed in Refs. [17−18]. Apparently, there exist many possibilities to split the multiple classes into two smaller macro-classes; hence the macro-class partitioning algorithm plays a vital role in the success of this strategy. Albeit the hierarchical divisive clustering method may be a natural choice for macro-class partitioning [32], the challenge is posed for defining the appropriate distance function capable of measuring the inter-class separability in feature space for clustering classes in the scenario of nonlinear classification.

In Ref. [20], the sum of minimum distances function d_{md} was proposed for measuring the inter-class separability

$$d_{md}(\boldsymbol{A},\boldsymbol{B})=\frac{1}{2}\left(\sum_{a_i\in A}\min_{b_j\in B}\left\|\boldsymbol{a}_i-\boldsymbol{b}_j\right\|+\sum_{b_j\in B}\min_{a_i\in A}\left\|\boldsymbol{a}_i-\boldsymbol{b}_j\right\|\right) \quad (1)$$

where $\boldsymbol{A}=\{\boldsymbol{a}_i \mid i=1,2,\cdots,p\}$ and $\boldsymbol{B}=\{\boldsymbol{b}_i \mid i=1,2,\cdots,q\}$ are training datasets of two different classes. Compared to the well-known Hausdorff metric, which is defined as the maximum distance between any point in one shape and the point that is closest to it in the other, the distances function d_{md} defined by (1) is non-metric and advantageous due to its capability of taking into account the overall structure of the points set. Further, for measuring inter-class separability in the feature space induced by nonlinear mapping $\boldsymbol{\varphi}(\cdot)$, the sum of minimum distance function was kernelized to the following form in Ref. [17–18]

$$\tilde{d}_{md}(\boldsymbol{A},\boldsymbol{B})=\frac{1}{2}\left(\sum_{a_i\in A}\min_{b_j\in B}\sqrt{2-2k(\boldsymbol{a}_i,\boldsymbol{b}_j)}+\sum_{b_j\in B}\min_{a_i\in A}\sqrt{2-2k(\boldsymbol{a}_i,\boldsymbol{b}_j)}\right) \quad (2)$$

where $k(\boldsymbol{a}_i,\boldsymbol{b}_i)=\boldsymbol{\varphi}(\boldsymbol{a}_i)^T\boldsymbol{\varphi}(\boldsymbol{b}_i)$ is the kernel function such that $k(\boldsymbol{x},\boldsymbol{x})=1$, and obviously the kernelized distance function $\tilde{d}_{md}$ in (2) can be evaluated without explicitly knowing the nonlinear mapping $\boldsymbol{\varphi}(\cdot)$.

Before training the dichotomic classifiers at non-leaf nodes, the topology of the binary tree needs to be determined firstly by partitioning the classes to be recognized into two smaller macro-classes at each non-leaf node from top to down. This procedure specifies the training datasets used for training each binary classifier and therefore is critical to the recognition performance of the hierarchical classification algorithm.

In the hierarchical classification algorithm, it is obvious that the degeneration of classification performance at higher level has greater impact on the overall classification performance than that occurred at lower levels. Therefore, the upper level the more separable classes should be partitioned, i.e., maximizes the degree of separability while partitioning the multiple classes into two macro-classes from top to down.

With the kernelized distance function $\tilde{d}_{md}$ for measuring the inter-class separability, the macro-class partition algorithm implemented by invoking the hierarchical divisive clustering can be applied for each non-leaf node from top to down, where the classes in one macro-class are recursively divided into two macro-classes belonging to left-node and right-node respectively. Initially, the macro-class partition algorithm starts from the root node, where the macro-class includes all classes to be recognized. Firstly, the kernelized sum of minimum distance function $\tilde{d}_{md}$ between all pairs of the classes in one macro-class are evaluated, and then partition the pair of classes between which the distance is maximal into the left-node and right-node as the prototype classes of the child nodes, respectively. Subsequently, assign the remaining classes in the non-leaf node into the child node whose prototype class is the closest to it in the sense of kernelized distance function $\tilde{d}_{md}$. Thus, two smaller macro-classes, either of which may also consist of multiple classes, are formed in the left child node and right child node, respectively. Iterating this procedure from top to down for every non-leaf node until only one individual class is left in each leaf node produces a hierarchy of nested macro-classes, and thereby determines the topology of the binary tree. Apparently the number of leaf nodes equals to the number of classes.

3 Estimation of class-conditional PDF of projected data in kernel feature space

The binary tree synthesized via macro-class partition algorithm offers a skeleton where the dichotomic classifier can be trained at each non-leaf node for implementing a decision rule that separates the macro-class into its left child node and its right child node. Thus, the n-class polychotomous classifier can be constructed by training $(n-1)$ binary classifier at non-leaf nodes, which is less than the number of dichotomic classifiers trained in pairwise and one-versus-rest methods. Also, as learning proceeds from top to down, the amount of data involved in the subsequent training processes decrease rapidly. These substantially improve the computational tractability. In this section, following a briefly review for KFD algorithm, the estimation of the underlying class-conditional PDF for the projections generated via KFD in feature space will be discussed.

Given a set of m– dimensional input vectors $\boldsymbol{x}_j$, $j=1,\cdots,\ell$, ℓ_1 input vectors in the subset $\boldsymbol{D}_1$ labeled ω_1 and ℓ_2 input vectors in the subset $\boldsymbol{D}_2$ labeled ω_2. In the algorithm of KFD, the generalized Rayleigh quotient is maximized in the feature space in order to find the projection direction $\boldsymbol{w}$ which maximizes the between-class variance and minimizes the within-class variance for the projections on it. In feature space, the generalized Rayleigh quotient becomes

$$J(\boldsymbol{w})=\frac{\boldsymbol{w}^T\boldsymbol{S}_B\boldsymbol{w}}{\boldsymbol{w}^T\boldsymbol{S}_W\boldsymbol{w}}, \quad (3)$$

where

$$\boldsymbol{S}_B=(\boldsymbol{m}_2-\boldsymbol{m}_1)(\boldsymbol{m}_2-\boldsymbol{m}_1)^T,$$

$$\boldsymbol{S}_W=\sum_{i=1}^{2}\sum_{x_j\in D_i}(\boldsymbol{\varphi}(\boldsymbol{x}_j)-\boldsymbol{m}_i)(\boldsymbol{\varphi}(\boldsymbol{x}_j)-\boldsymbol{m}_i)^T,$$

$$\boldsymbol{m}_i=\frac{1}{\ell_i}\sum_{x_j\in D_i}\boldsymbol{\varphi}(\boldsymbol{x}_j).$$

Define the matrices $\boldsymbol{N}$ and $\boldsymbol{M}$ as follows

$$\boldsymbol{N}=(\boldsymbol{\vartheta}_2-\boldsymbol{\vartheta}_1)(\boldsymbol{\vartheta}_2-\boldsymbol{\vartheta}_1)^T,$$

$$M = \sum_{i=1}^{2}\left[K_i K_i^T - \ell_i \vartheta_i \vartheta_i^T\right]$$

where ϑ_i is the ℓ – dimensional column vector with components

$$(\vartheta_i)_r = \sum_{x_j \in D_i} \frac{k(x_r, x_j)}{\ell_i}$$

and K_i are the kernel matrices with entries $(K_i)_{rj} = k(x_r, x_j)$. With the vital ansatz that $w = \sum_{j=1}^{\ell} \beta_j \varphi(x_j)$, the generalized Rayleigh quotient (3) can be reformulated in terms of kernel function in the feature space as [33]

$$J(\beta) = \frac{\beta^T N \beta}{\beta^T M \beta}. \quad (4)$$

The expansion coefficients vector β can be obtained by maximizing the $J(\beta)$ in (4), and several effective algorithms for that have been available and discussed in [7]. Thereby, the projections of the mapped data points $\varphi(x_j)$ onto the discriminant w in feature space can be calculated as

$$y = w^T \varphi(x) = \sum_{j=1}^{\ell} \beta_j \varphi^T(x_j)\varphi(x) = \sum_{j=1}^{\ell} \beta_j k(x_j, x) \cdot \quad (5)$$

From equation (5), it is reasonable to treat the projection $y = w^T \varphi(x)$ as a scalar random variable, which is the weighted summation of all components of the data points $\varphi(x)$ mapped into the high-dimensional feature space. It is noteworthy that the feature spaces induced by kernel functions are usually very high-dimensional, and for instance, the dimension of the feature space induced by Gaussian RBF kernel is infinite. Hence, according to the celebrated Lindeberg-Feller Central Limit Theorem, this fact implies that the set of projections y of the mapped data in each class tends to be distributed normally, i.e.

$$p(y \mid \omega_i) \sim N(\mu_i, \sigma_i) \quad (6)$$

where

$$N(\mu_i, \sigma_i) = \frac{1}{(2\pi\sigma_i^2)^{1/2}} exp\left\{-\frac{(y-\mu_i)^2}{2\sigma_i^2}\right\},$$

is the univariate Gaussian probability density function. Thus, the estimation of the class-conditional density function $p(y \mid \omega_i)$ for the projections y_j is boiled down to the issue of estimating the parameters μ_i, σ_i of Gaussian PDFs, which can be readily solved by the methods of maximum likelihood or Bayesian inference. In this paper, the method of maximal likelihood estimation is exerted for calculating the parameters of class-conditional Gaussian PDF, and the details of maximal likelihood estimation algorithm can be referred to [31–32]. The availability of class-conditional density functions makes it possible to build the classifier upon the Bayesian decision theory, which is a fundamental statistical approach, whose power, coherence, and analytical nature when applied in pattern recognition make it among the elegant formulations in science.

4 Multi-category posterior probability estimation & multi-scale discriminant

With the estimated class-conditional Gaussian density functions $p(y \mid \omega_i)$, $i = 1, 2$ the two-class posterior probability can be evaluated at each non-leaf node

$$P(\omega_i \mid y) = \frac{p(y \mid \omega_i)P(\omega_i)}{\sum_{i=1}^{2} p(y \mid \omega_i)P(\omega_i)}, \quad i = 1, 2 \quad (7)$$

where $P(\omega_i)$ is the priori probability, which can be estimated from the training dataset empirically, and the denominator is the unconditional probability density function. Thereby, the dichotomic Bayesian classifier can be constructed at each non-leaf node by selecting the class ω_i having the largest posterior probability, so that x is assigned to class ω_i if

$$P(\omega_i \mid y) > P(\omega_k \mid y) \quad for\ all\ i \neq k \quad (8)$$

where y is the projections of x onto the discriminant w in the feature space. A Bayesian approach achieves the exact minimum probability of error based entirely on evaluating the posterior probability.

For classifying an unlabeled pattern, the evaluation starts from the root node of the binary tree, and then from top to down the synthesized dichotomic classifiers on the non-leaf nodes is used to assign the input pattern into one of child nodes. This procedure is iterated until the unlabeled pattern is finally classified into the class associated with one of leaf nodes, which determine a path from the root to one of leaf-nodes for each unlabeled pattern. Contrary to the conventional 'divide-and-combine' methods where all the dichotomic decision functions need to be calculated in evaluating an unlabeled pattern, only those dichotomic decision functions on the specified path need to be calculated in the proposed method.

In the realm of pattern recognition, there is general consensus that one of important technical challenges is how to estimate the multi-class posterior probability, which is more unwieldy than that for dichotomic classifier. However, in the algorithm developed in this paper, the multi-class posterior probabilistic outputs can be readily evaluated by capitalizing on the posterior probability estimated in (7) at each non-leaf node of the synthesized binary-tree. For the path along which an unlabeled pattern was classified from the root to one of the leaf nodes, each trained dichotomous Bayesian KFD on the path outputs the posterior probability, which is used to determine which child node the unlabeled pattern should be assigned to. Given that the path is determined by a sequence of dichotomous KFD successively, the posterior probability of classifying the unlabeled pattern into one of the multiple classes can be calculated by multiplying the posterior probabilistic outputs produced by each dichotomous KFD on the path. Contrary to the conventional methods, in which the values for all the decision functions need to be calculated in the phase of classification, it is not necessary to calculate the values of all the decision functions in the proposed method.

On the other hand, by taking advantage of the monotonicity of natural logarithm, the discriminant function induced by rule (8) on each non-leaf node can be expressed as

$$f(y) = \ell n\, P(\omega_1 \mid y) - \ell n\, P(\omega_2 \mid y) = \ell n \frac{p(y \mid \omega_1)}{p(y \mid \omega_2)} + \ell n \frac{P(\omega_1)}{P(\omega_2)} \quad (9)$$

Substituting the Gaussian density functions into $p(y \mid \omega_1)$ and $p(y \mid \omega_2)$ yields

$$f(y) = \frac{1}{2}\left[\frac{(y-\mu_2)^2}{\sigma_2^2} - \frac{(y-\mu_1)^2}{\sigma_1^2}\right] + ln \frac{\sigma_2}{\sigma_1} + ln \frac{P(\omega_1)}{P(\omega_2)} \quad (10)$$

If the variances for the macro-classes on the non-leaf node are equal, viz. $\sigma_1 = \sigma_2 = \sigma$, the equations (10) becomes

$$f(y) = \frac{\mu_1 - \mu_2}{\sigma^2} y + \frac{\mu_2^2 - \mu_1^2}{2\sigma^2} + ln \frac{P(\omega_1)}{P(\omega_2)} \quad (11)$$

The decision function $f(x)$ for data point x on each non-leaf node can be obtained by plugging equation (5) into the equation above as follows

$$f(x) = \frac{\mu_1 - \mu_2}{\sigma^2} \sum_{r=1}^{\ell} \beta_r k(x_r, x) + C \quad (12)$$

where the constant

$$C = \frac{\mu_2^2 - \mu_1^2}{2\sigma^2} + ln \frac{P(\omega_1)}{P(\omega_2)} \quad (13)$$

Hence, in this case the discriminant function can be represented in the form of kernel expansion (12), which is same as that in support vector learning. Whereas, for the case that the variances for the macro-classes on the non-leaf node are not same, viz. $\sigma_1 \neq \sigma_2$, the expression of discriminant function becomes more involved than (12), and it is no longer as simple as the linear combination of kernel functions.

The hierarchical structure of binary tree together with the kernel expansion (12) also shed light on the avenue to fulfill the polychotomous multi-scale Bayesian kernel Fisher discriminant. Hierarchical structures organize information into different levels and usually arrange it so that the higher in the hierarchy a level is, the smaller scale the information is analyzed. In the algorithm developed in this paper, the degree of separability between macro-classes on the non-leaf nodes of the binary tree decrease from top to down, and the synthesis of polychotomous classifier can be viewed as a mathematical process of hierarchically building classifier such that finer details are added to the coarser description at each level. This intrinsic conexus between hierarchical structure and multi-scale analysis sheds lights on the way to implement the polychotomous multi-scale Bayesian KFD via setting different kernel parameters on different levels of the tree. For the Gaussian RBF kernel used in this research

$$k(x, y) = exp\left(\frac{-\|x-y\|^2}{2\rho_n^2}\right) \quad (14)$$

The values of parameter ρ_n can be set as $\rho_1 > \rho_2 > \cdots > \rho_m$ at different levels n from top to down for controlling the scales. With the declining of the degree of separability between macro-classes from top to down, the scale parameter also decrease gradually. The larger scale parameters are adopted for the lower levels to prevent memorizing data, and the smaller scale parameters are employed for the higher levels for irregular localized features. In Ref. [34], two schemes, which use geometric sequence and arithmetic sequence respectively, have been invoked to adjust the scale parameters ρ_n for non-flat function regression.

5 Landsat satellite image data classification

The goal of image classification is to separate images according to their visual content into two or more disjoint classes [35]. In this section, the developed multi-scale parametric/nonparametric hybrid recognition strategy and multi-class posterior probability estimation algorithm are applied on the recognition of satellite image data [36], which is a benchmark problem from real-world and has been intensively studied. The experimental result is compared with those acquired from other popular multi-class pattern classification methods in terms of the generalization capability. The implementation of algorithms is on the strength of the *Statistical Pattern Recognition Toolbox* [37]. For the sake of fair comparison, the same training and validation datasets as those in Ref. [36] are used.

The satellite image database was generated by taking a small section from the original Landsat Multi-Spectral Scanner (MSS) image data from a part of Western Australia. In this database, each sample was featured by 36 attributes, which are numerical in the range 0 to 255. Namely, the input space is of 36 dimensions. Totally, 4435 samples are included in the training dataset and 2000 samples in the validation dataset. There are six categories of different soil conditions to be classified, and their distributions in the training and validation dataset are listed in Table 1.

For synthesizing the proposed polychotomous multi-scale Bayesian KFD classifier, the value and tuning scheme of scale parameter of the adopted kernel function need to be specified beforehand. In our experiment, the Gaussian radial basis function kernel with scale parameter $\rho_1 = 33$ is used at the root node, and subsequently the scale parameter is tuned as $\rho_{n+1} = \rho_n - \delta$, where δ is the common difference of the arithmetic sequence and n is the level of the hierarchical binary tree (root node is at the lowest level, i.e. level 1). The first step towards building the multi-class classifier is to induce the topology of the binary tree by taking advantage of macro-class partition algorithm described in section 2. For satellite image training database used herein, the topological structure of binary tree obtained via top-to-down induction is visualized in Fig. 1.

Upon determining the structure of the binary and the macro-classes on each non-leaf node, the algorithms developed in sections 3&4 can be brought to bear for training the dichotomic classifier at each non-leaf node and estimating the posterior probability.

To confirm the superiority of the proposed polychotomous multi-scale Bayesian KFD algorithm in terms of generalization capability, the testing error rate is calculated on the validation datasets, and then compared with those obtained from other popular classification strategies [36], such as Logistic regression, RBF neural networks, K-nearest-neighbor and multi-category SVM direct method [10], and so on. The results are listed in Table 2 and the details about the parameters setting and algorithmic implementation can be referred to the references [18,36]. From the test error rates in Table 2, it is salient that the polychotomous multi-scale Bayesian KFD excels other commonly-used pattern classification methods, including multi-class SVMs, in generalization capability. Also, for the Bayesian classification algorithms, the superiority in classification accuracy also implies the triumph in estimating the posterior probability. The uniqueness of path from root node to one leaf node enables us to calculate the multi-category posterior probability by multiplying the posterior probabilistic outputs produced by each dichotomous KFD on the path.

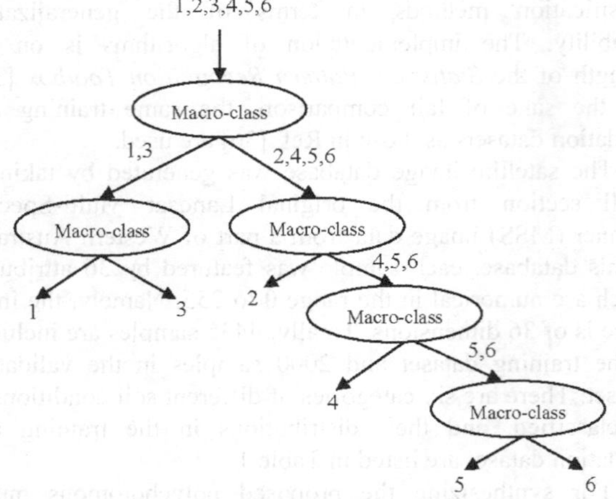

Fig. 1. Binary tree induced for Landsat satellite image datasets.

TABLE I
DISTRIBUTION OF TRAINING AND VALIDATION SAMPLES IN DATASET

Description	Training	Validation
1 red soil	1072(24.17%)	461 (23.05%)
2 cotton crop	479 (10.8%)	224 (11.20 %)
3 grey soil	961 (21.67%)	397 (19.85%)
4 damp grey soil	415 (9.36%)	211 (10.55%)
5 soil with vegetation stubble	470 (10.6%)	237 (11.85%)
6 very damp grey soil	1038 (23.4%)	470 (23.50%)

TABLE II
COMPARISON ON TESTING ERROR RATES OF VARIOUS ALGORITHMS

Pattern classification algorithms	Testing error rate (%)
Logistic discrimination	16.9
Quadratic discrimination	15.5
RBF neural networks	12.1
K-nearest-neighbor	9.4
Pairwise multi-class SVM	9.2
One-versus-rest multi-class SVM	9.65
Direct multi-class SVM	9.15
Method proposed in this article	8.55

6 Conclusions

The fact that the outputs produced by KFD can be interpreted as probabilities makes it possible to assign a confidence to the final classification. Based on this fact, in the polychotomous multi-scale classification algorithm developed in this paper, several key components are elegantly synergized together for synthesizing the multi-category Bayesian classifier in an nonparametric/parametric hybrid way: non-metric distance function for measuring inter-class separability; binary tree representation for nested macro-classes; Bayesian classification via class-conditional PDF estimation; multi-scale classification implemented in hierarchy.

The computations for constructing and evaluating the binary classifiers on non-leaf nodes are propagated from the root downwards through the binary tree. In the experiment on satellite image dataset, the excellent generalization capability and learnability are confirmed in terms of the testing error rate on validation dataset, which also corroborated the reliability of posterior probability estimation for multiple classes.

7 References

[1] P. Chaudhui, A. K. Ghosh, and H. Oja. "Classification based on Hybridization of Parametric and Nonparametric Classifiers," IEEE Trans. Pattern Analysis and Machine Intelligence, vol. 31, pp. 1153−1164, 2009.

[2] G. Zhai, X. Yang. "Image reconstruction from random samples with Multiscale hybrid parametric and nonparametric modeling," IEEE Trans. Circuits and Systems for Video Technology, vol. 22, pp. 1554−1563, 2012.

[3] S. F. Masri. "A hybrid parametric/nonparametric approach for the identification of nonlinear systems," Probabilistic Engineering Mechanics, vol. 9, pp. 47−57, 1994.

[4] J. Peres, R. Oliveira, and S. Feyo de Azevedo. "Bioprocess hybrid parametric/nonparametric modeling based on the concept of mixtures of experts," Biochemical Engineering Journal, vol. 39, pp. 190–206, 2008.

[5] L. Bruzzone, L., and R. Cossu. "A multiple-cascade-classifier system for a robust and partially unsupervised updating of land-cover maps," IEEE Trans. Geoscience and Remote Sensing, vol. 40, pp. 1984–1996, 2002.

[6] J. V. Black, and C. M. Reed. "A Hybrid Parametric, Nonparametric to Bayesian Target Tracking," in 1996 IEE Colloquium on Target Tracking and Data Fusion, pp. 178–183.

[7] B. Schölkopf, A. J. Smola. Learning with Kernels: Support Vector Machines, Regularization, Optimization, and Beyond, MIT Press, Cambridge, MA, 2002.

[8] J. Shawe-Taylor, N. Cristianini. Kernel Methods for Pattern Analysis, Cambridge University Press, 2004.

[9] N. Cristianini, J. Shawe-Taylor. Support Vector Machines and other Kernel-based Learning Methods, Cambridge University Press, 2000.

[10] J. Weston, C. Watkins. "Support vector machines for multi-class pattern recognition," in Proc. 7th European Symposium on Artificial Neural Networks, Belgium, 1999.

[11] C. W. Hsu, C. J. Lin, "A comparison of methods for multiclass support vector machines," IEEE Transactions on Neural Networks, vol. 13, pp. 415–425, 2002.

[12] K. Crammer, Y. Singer. "On the algorithmic implementation of multiclass kernel-based vector machines," Journal of Machine Learning Research, vol. 2, pp. 265–292, 2001

[13] Y. Lee, Y. Lin, G. Wahba. "Multicategory support vector machines: Theory and applications to the classification of microarray data and satellite radiance data," Journal of the American Statistical Association, vol. 99, pp. 67–81, 2004.

[14] E. L. Allwein, R. E. Schapire, and Y. Singer. "Reducing multiclass to binary: A unifying approach for margin classifiers," Journal of Machine Learning Research, vol. 1, pp. 113–141, 2000.

[15] J. Chen, C. Wang. "Combining support vector machines with a pairwise decision tree," IEEE Geoscience and Remote Sensing Letters, vol. 5, pp. 409–413, 2008.

[16] D. Casasent, Y.C. Wang. "A hierarchical classifier using new support vector machines for automatic target recognition," Neural Networks, vol. 18, pp. 541–548, 2005.

[17] Z. Lu, L. Liang, G. Song, S. Wang. "Polychotomous kernel Fisher discriminant via top-down induction of binary tree," Computers & Mathematics with Applications, vol. 60, pp. 511–519, 2010.

[18] Z. Lu, F. Lin, H. Ying. "Design of decision tree via kernelized hierarchical clustering for multiclass support vector machines," Cybernetics and Systems, vol. 38, pp. 187–202, 2007.

[19] S. Cheong, S. H. Oh, S.-Y. Lee. "Support vector machines with binary tree architecture for multi-class classification," Neural Information Processing – Letters and Reviews, vol. 2, pp. 47–51, 2004.

[20] T. Eiter. "Distance measures for point sets and their computation," Acta Informatica, vol. 34, pp. 109–133, 1997.

[21] D. W. Jacobs, D. Weinshall, and Y. Gdalyahu. "Classification with nonmetric distances: Image retrieval and class representation," IEEE Trans. Pattern Analysis and Machine Intelligence, vol. 22, pp. 583–600, 2000.

[22] I. Niiniluoto. Truthlikeness, D. Reidel Publishing Company, 1987.

[23] J.C. Platt. "Probabilities for SV machines," In Advances in Large Margin Classifiers, A.J. Smola, P. Bartlett, B. Schölkopt, and D. Schuurmans, Ed. Cambridge, MA: MIT Press, 1999, pp. 61–73.

[24] H.T. Lin, C.J. Lin, and R.C. Weng. "A note on Platt's probabilistic outputs for support vector machines," Machine Learning, vol. 68, pp. 267–276, 2007.

[25] B. Zadrozny, C. Elkan. "Transforming classifier scores into accurate multiclass probability estimates," in Proc. 8th Int. Conf. Knowledge Discovery and Data Mining, 2002, pp. 694–699.

[26] B. Fei, J. Liu. "Binary tree of SVM: A new fast multiclass training and classification algorithm," IEEE Trans. Neural Networks, vol. 17, pp. 696–704, 2006.

[27] J. Milgram, M. Cheriet, and R. Sabourin. "Estimating accurate multi-class probabilities with support vector machines," in Proc. Int. Joint Conf. Neural Networks, 2005, pp. 1906–1911.

[28] S. Mika. "Kernel Fisher discriminant," Ph.D. dissertation, Univ. of Technology, Berlin, 2002.

[29] J. Yang, Z. Jin, J. Yang, and D. Zhang, A. F. Frangi. "Essence of kernel Fisher discriminant: KPCA and LDA," Pattern Recognition, vol. 37, pp. 2097–2100, 2004.

[30] A. Shashua. "On the relationship between the support vector machine for classification and sparsified Fisher's linear discriminant," Neural Processing Letters, vol. 9, pp. 129–139, 1999.

[31] C. M. Bishop. Neural Networks for Pattern Recognition, Oxford University Press, 1996.

[32] S. Theodoridis, K. Koutroumbas. Pattern Recognition, Academic Press, 4th Ed., 2009.

[33] S. Mika, G. Rätsch, J. Weston, B. Schölkopf, K. Müller. "Fisher discriminant analysis with kernel," in 1999 Proc. IEEE Int'l Workshop Neural Networks for Signal Processing IX, pp. 41–48.

[34] D. Zhang, J. Wang, and Y. Zhao. "Non-flat function estimation with a multi-scale support vector regression," Neurocomputing, vol. 70, pp. 420–429, 2006.

[35] P. V. Gehler. "Kernel learning approaches for image classification," Ph.D. dissertation, Saarland University, Germany, 2009.

[36] R. King, C. Feng, and A. Shutherland. "Statlog: comparison of classification algorithms on large real-world problems," Applied Artificial Intelligence, vol. 9, pp. 289–333, 1995.

[37] V. Franc, V. Hlavac. Statistical Pattern Recognition Toolbox for MATLAB. [Software]. Czech Technical University, Czech. Available: http://cmp.felk.cvut.cz/cmp/software/stprtool/

SVM-Based Approaches for Predictive Modeling of Survival Data

Han-Tai Shiao and Vladimir Cherkassky
Department of Electrical and Computer Engineering
University of Minnesota, Twin Cities
Minneapolis, Minnesota 55455, U.S.A.
Email: {shiao003, cherk001}@umn.edu

***Abstract*—Survival data is common in medical applications. The challenge in applying predictive data-analytic methods to survival data is in the treatment of censored observations. The survival times for these observations are unknown. This paper presents formalization of the analysis of survival data as a binary classification problem. For this binary classification setting, we propose two different strategies for encoding censored data, leading to two advanced SVM-based formulations: SVM+ and SVM with uncertain class labels. Further, we present empirical comparison of the advanced SVM methods and the classical Cox modeling approach for predictive modeling of survival data. These comparisons suggest that the proposed SVM-based models consistently yield better predictive performance (than classical statistical modeling) for real-life survival data sets.**

***Index Terms*—classification, survival analysis, Support Vector Machine (SVM), SVM+, Learning Using Privileged Information (LUPI), SVM with uncertain labels, Cox model.**

I. Introduction

A significant proportion of medical data is a collection of time-to-event observations. Methods for survival analysis developed in classical statistics have been used to model such data. Survival analysis focuses on the time elapsed from an initiating event to an event, or endpoint, of interest [1]. Classical examples are the time from birth to death, from disease onset to death, and from entry to a study to relapse, *etc.* All these times are generally known as the *survival time*, even when the endpoint is something different from death. This statistical methodology can also be used in many different settings, such as the reliability engineering, and financial insurance. Even though the purpose of a statistical analysis may vary from one situation to another, the ambitious aim of most statistical analyses is to build a model that relates explanatory variables and the occurrences of the event.

The field of machine learning is also targeting the same or similar goals. Learning is the process of estimating an unknown dependency between system's inputs and its output, based on a limited number of observations [2]. However, the machine learning techniques have not been widely used for survival analysis for two major reasons.

First, the survival time is not necessarily observed in all samples. For example, patients might not experience the occurrence of event (death or relapse) during the study, or they were lost to follow-up. Hence, the survival time is incomplete and only known "up-to-a-point," which is quite different from the traditional notion of 'missing data.'

The second reason is methodological. Machine learning techniques are usually developed and applied under predictive setting, where the main goal is the prediction accuracy for future (or test) samples. In contrast, classical statistical methods aim at estimating the true probabilistic model of available data. So the prediction accuracy is just one of several performance indices. The methodological assumption is that if an estimated model is 'correct,' then it should yield good predictions. So the classical statistical methodology often does not clearly differentiate between training (model estimation) and prediction (or test) stages. This paper assumes a predictive setting, which is appropriate for many applications. Under this predictive setting, the survival time is known for training data, but it is not available during the prediction (or testing) stage. Thus, modifications are required for applying existing machine learning approaches to survival data analysis.

Previously, several studies applied Support Vector Machines (SVM) to survival data [3]–[5]. Most of these efforts formalize the problem under the regression setting. Specifically, the SVM regression was used to estimate a model that predicts the survival time. However, formalization using regression setting is intrinsically more difficult than classification. Further, practitioners generally use the modeling outputs as a reference and they are usually concerned with the status of a patient at a given time, such as six-month after surgery or two-year post transplant.

In this paper, we propose to use a special classification formulation that addresses the issues of incomplete information in the survival time. Instead of predicting the survival time, we try to estimate a model that predicts a subject's status at a time point of interest. This paper is organized as follows. The characteristics of the survival data are summarized in Section II. The predictive problem setting for survival analysis is introduced in Section III. The proposed SVM-based formulations are introduced in Section IV. Empirical comparisons for several synthetic and real-life data sets are presented in Section V and VI. Finally, the discussion and conclusion are given in Section VII.

II. Survival Data Analysis

This section provides general background description of survival data analysis and its terminology.

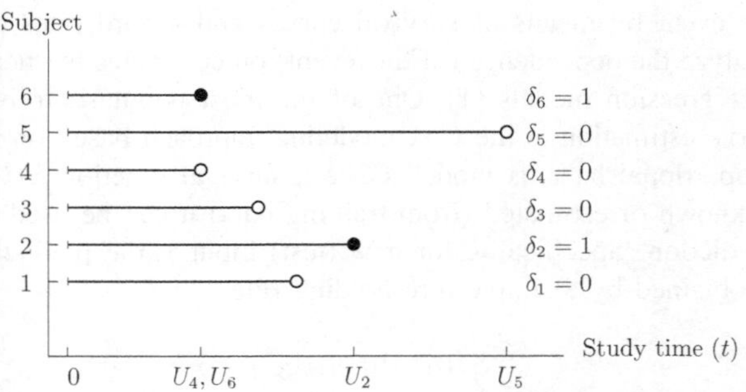

Fig. 1. Example of survival data in a study-time scale. The exact observations are indicated by solid dots, and the censored observations by hollow dots.

The survival data (or failure time data) are obtained by observing individuals from a certain initial time to either the occurrence of a predefined event or the end of the study. The predefined event is often the failure of a subject or the relapse of a disease. The major difference between survival data and other types of numerical data is the time to the event occurring is not necessarily observed in all individuals.

A common feature of these data sets is they contain censored observations. Censored data arise when an individual's life length is known to occur only in a certain period of time. Possible censoring schemes are *right censoring*, where all that is known is that the individual is still alive at a given time, *left censoring* when all that is known is that the individual has experienced the event of interest prior to the start of the study, or *interval censoring*, where the only information is that the event occurs within some interval. In this paper, we only consider the right censoring scheme.

The graphical representation of the survival data for a hypothetical study with six subjects is shown in Figure 1. In this study, subject 2 and 6 experienced the event of interest prior to the end of the study and they are the exact observations. Subject 1, 3, and 5, who experienced the event after the end of the study, are only known to be alive at the end of the study. Subject 4 was included in the study for some time but further observation cannot be obtained. The data for subject 1, 3, 4, and 5 are called censored (right-censored) observations. Thus, for the censored observations, it is known that the survival time is greater than a certain value, but it is not known by how much.

Suppose T denotes the event time, such as death or lifetime; C denotes the censoring time, *e.g.*, the end of study or the time an individual withdraws from the study. The T's are assumed to be independent and identically distributed with probability density function $\varphi(t)$ and survival function $S(t)$. For right censoring scheme, we only know $T_i > C_i$ with observed C_i. Then the survival data can be represented by pairs of random variables (U_i, δ_i), $i = 1, \ldots, n$. The δ_i indicates whether the observed survival time U_i corresponds to an event ($\delta_i = 1$) or is censored ($\delta_i = 0$). The U_i is equal to T_i if the lifetime or event is observed, and to C_i if it is censored. Mathematically, U_i and δ_i are defined as

$$U_i = \min(T_i, C_i), \tag{1}$$

$$\delta_i = I(T_i \le C_i) = \begin{cases} 0 & \text{censored observation,} \\ 1 & \text{event occurred.} \end{cases} \tag{2}$$

In Figure 1, subject 4 and 6 have the same observed survival time ($U_4 = U_6$), but their censoring indicators are different ($\delta_4 = 0, \delta_6 = 1$). Therefore, in the survival analysis, we are given a set of data, $(\mathbf{x}_i, U_i, \delta_i)$, $i = 1, \ldots, n$, where $\mathbf{x}_i \in \mathbf{R}^d$, $U_i \in \mathbf{R}_+$ and $\delta_i \in \{0, 1\}$. In contrast, under supervised learning setting, we are given a set of training data, $(\mathbf{x}_i, y_i)$, $i = 1, \ldots, n$, where $\mathbf{x}_i \in \mathbf{R}^d$ and $y_i \in \mathbf{R}$. The target values y_i's can be real-valued such as in standard regression, or binary class labels in classification.

Classical statistical approach to modeling survival data aims at estimating the survival function $S(t)$, which is the probability that the time of death is greater than certain time t. More generally, the goal is to estimate $S(t|\mathbf{x})$, or survival function conditioned on patient's characteristics, denoted as feature vector $\mathbf{x}$. Assuming that the probabilistic model $S(t|\mathbf{x})$ is known, or can be accurately estimated from available data, this model provides complete statistical characterization of the data. In particular, it can be used for prediction and for explanation (*i.e.*, identifying input features that are strongly associated with an outcome, such as death).

III. Predictive Modeling of Survival Data

In many applications, the goal is to estimate (predict) survival at a pre-specified time point τ, *e.g.*, survival of cancer patients two years after initial diagnosis, or the survival status of patients one year after bone marrow transplant procedure. Generally τ can be about half of the maximum observed survival time. Next we describe possible formalization of this problem under predictive setting, leading to a binary classification formulation.

Classification problem setting: Given the training survival data, $(\mathbf{x}_i, U_i, \delta_i, y_i)$, $i = 1, \ldots, n$, where $\mathbf{x}_i \in \mathbf{R}^d$, $U_i \in \mathbf{R}_+$, $\delta_i \in \{0, 1\}$, and $y_i \in \{-1, +1\}$, estimate a classification model $f(\mathbf{x})$ that predicts a subject's status at a pre-specified time τ based on the input (or covariates) $\mathbf{x}$.

The status of subject i at time τ is a binary class label through the following encoding

$$y_i = \begin{cases} +1, & \text{if } U_i < \tau, \\ -1, & \text{if } U_i \ge \tau. \end{cases} \tag{3}$$

Note that U_i and δ_i are only available for training, not for prediction (or testing stage). So the challenge of predictive modeling is to develop novel classification formulations that incorporate uncertain nature of censored data.

In a hypothetical study as shown in Figure 2, suppose a subject's status is given by (3), then there is no ambiguity in the statuses of subject 2 and 6. Likewise, the survival status of subject 5 is known, even though the observation is censored. However, the survival statuses for subjects 1, 3, and 4 are unknown since the observed survival times are shorter than τ.

There are two simplistic ways to incorporate censored data into standard classification formulation:

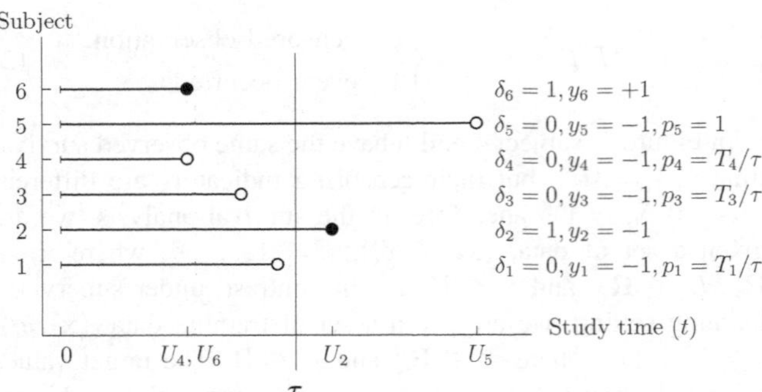

Fig. 2. Example of survival data under the predictive problem setting. The goal is to find a model that predicts the subjects' statuses at time τ.

- Treat the censoring time as the actual event time, *i.e.*, replace T_i with C_i. This approach underestimates the actual event time because $T_i > C_i$.
- Simply ignore the censored data and estimate a binary classifier using only exact observations. This approach yields suboptimal models, as we ignore the information available in the censored data.

This paper investigates two different strategies for incorporating censored data in SVM-based classifiers:

1) Note that censoring information is available/known for training data, but not known during prediction, the censored data can be regarded as the privileged information under the so-called Learning Using Privileged Information (LUPI) paradigm [6], [7].
2) We can assign probabilities to reflect the uncertain status of censored data samples. One simple rule is to set the probability of a subject being alive at time τ proportional to the (known) survival time, as indicated in Figure 2. That is, $\Pr(y_i = -1|\mathbf{x}_i) = U_i/\tau$ or $\Pr(y_i = +1|\mathbf{x}_i) = 1-U_i/\tau$. The idea is that if U_i is small, it is more likely subject i will not survive at time τ. On the other hand, if U_i is very close to τ, subject i will be alive at time τ with high probability. Therefore, the survival data $(\mathbf{x}_i, U_i, \delta_i)$, $i = 1, \ldots, n$, can be translated into $(\mathbf{x}_i, U_i, l_i)$, $i = 1, \ldots, n$. For exact observations, $l_i = y_i \in \{-1, +1\}$, $i = 1, \ldots, m$. For censored observations, $l_i = p_i \in [0, 1]$, $i = m + 1, \ldots, n$, where

$$p_i = \Pr(y_i = -1|\,\mathbf{x}_i) = U_i/\tau \tag{4}$$

considers the uncertainty about the class membership of $\mathbf{x}_i$. The concept of assigning probability to the uncertain status can be extended to the exact observations. For a exact observation, we have its status y_i with probability $p_i = 1$. Then the survival data are represented as $(\mathbf{x}_i, U_i, p_i, y_i)$, $i = 1, \ldots, n$. This formalization of censored data leads to the so-called SVM with uncertain labels modeling approach [8].

Both modeling approaches are presented later in Section IV.

Finally, we describe application of classical survival analysis under predictive setting (introduced earlier in this section). Classical survival analysis models describe the occurrence of the event by means of survival curves and hazard rates and analyze the dependence (of this event) on covariates by means of regression models [1]. One of the most popular survival-curve estimation is the Cox modeling approach based on the proportional hazards model. Once a survival function $S(t|\mathbf{x})$ is known or estimated (from training data) it can be used for prediction. Specifically, for new (test) input $\mathbf{x}$ the prediction is obtained by a simple thresholding rule

$$y_i = \begin{cases} +1, & \text{if } S(t|\mathbf{x}_i) < r, \\ -1, & \text{if } S(t|\mathbf{x}_i) \geq r, \end{cases} \tag{5}$$

where the threshold value r should reflect the misclassification costs given *a priori*. In this paper, we assume equal misclassification costs. Hence, the threshold level is set to $r = 0.5$. This approach will be used to estimate the prediction accuracy (test error) of the Cox model in empirical comparisons presented in Sections V and VI.

IV. SVM-Based Formulations for Survival Analysis

This section presents two recent advanced SVM-based formulations appropriate for predictive modeling of survival data. Presentation starts with a general description of these SVM-based formulations, followed by specific description of incorporating censored data into these formulations.

A. SVM+

One strategy to handle the survival data is the setting known as Learning Using Privileged Information (LUPI) developed by Vapnik [6], [7]. In a data-rich world, there often exists additional information about training samples, which is not reflected in the training data. This additional information can be easily ignored by standard inductive methods such as SVM. Effective use of this additional information during training often results in improved generalization [7].

Under the LUPI setting, we are given a set of triplets $(\mathbf{x}_i, \mathbf{x}_i^*, y_i)$, $i = 1, \ldots, n$, where $\mathbf{x}_i \in \mathbf{R}^d$, $\mathbf{x}_i^* \in \mathbf{R}^k$, and $y_i \in \{-1, +1\}$. The $(\mathbf{x}, y)$ is the 'usual' labeled training data and $(\mathbf{x}^*)$ denotes the additional *privileged* information available only for training data. Note that the privileged information is defined in a different feature space. This SVM+ approach maps inputs, $\mathbf{x}_i$ and $\mathbf{x}_i^*$, into two different spaces:

- *decision* space $\mathcal{Z}$ via the mapping $\Phi(\mathbf{x}) : \mathbf{x} \mapsto \mathbf{z}$, which is the same feature space used in standard SVM;
- *correcting* space $\mathcal{Z}^*$ via the mapping $\Phi^*(\mathbf{x}) : \mathbf{x} \mapsto \mathbf{z}^*$, which reflects the privileged information about the training data.

The goal of the SVM+ is to estimate a decision function $(\mathbf{w} \cdot \mathbf{z}) + b$ by using the correcting function $\xi(\mathbf{z}^*) = (\mathbf{w}^* \cdot \mathbf{z}^*) + d \geq 0$ as the additional constraints on the training errors (or slack variables) in the decision space. The SVM+ classifier is estimated from the training data by solving the following optimization problem:

$$\begin{aligned} \text{minimize} \quad & \frac{1}{2}\|\mathbf{w}\|^2 + \frac{\gamma}{2}\|\mathbf{w}^*\|^2 + C\sum_{i=1}^{n}\xi_i \\ \text{subject to} \quad & \boldsymbol{\xi} \succeq 0 \\ & y_i((\mathbf{w}\cdot\mathbf{z}_i)+b) \geq 1-\xi_i, \quad i=1,\ldots,n \\ & \xi_i = (\mathbf{w}^*\cdot\mathbf{z}_i^*)+d, \quad i=1,\ldots,n \end{aligned} \tag{6}$$

with $\mathbf{w} \in \mathbf{R}^d$, $b \in \mathbf{R}$, $\mathbf{w}^* \in \mathbf{R}^k$, $d \in \mathbf{R}$, and $\boldsymbol{\xi} \in \mathbf{R}_+^n$ as the variables. The symbol $\succeq$ denotes componentwise inequality and $\mathbf{R}_+$ denotes non-negative real numbers.

Predictive modeling of survival data can be formalized under SVM+/LUPI formulation (6) as explained next. Available survival data $(\mathbf{x}_i, U_i, p_i, y_i)$ can be represented as $(\mathbf{x}_i, \mathbf{x}_i^*, y_i)$, where $\mathbf{x}_i^* = (U_i, p_i)$ is the privileged information. Then the problem of survival analysis can be formalized and modeled using the SVM+/LUPI paradigm.

B. SVM with Uncertain Labels

This section describes novel SVM-based formulation [8] that introduces the notion of uncertain class labels. That is, some instances (training samples) are not associated with definite class labels. For such uncertain labels, only the confidence levels (or probabilities) regarding the class memberships are provided. In the context of survival analysis, exact observations have known class labels, and censored observations have uncertain class labels.

For the non-separable survival data, we have the following optimization problem,

$$\begin{aligned} \text{minimize} \quad & \frac{1}{2}\|\mathbf{w}\|^2 + C\sum_{i=1}^{m}\xi_i + \tilde{C}\sum_{i=m+1}^{n}(\xi_i^- + \xi_i^+) \\ \text{subject to} \quad & \boldsymbol{\xi} \succeq 0 \\ & y_i((\mathbf{w}\cdot\mathbf{x}_i)+b) \geq 1-\xi_i, \quad i=1,\ldots,m \\ & \boldsymbol{\xi}^- \succeq 0 \\ & \boldsymbol{\xi}^+ \succeq 0 \\ & q_i^- - \xi_i^- \leq (\mathbf{w}\cdot\mathbf{x}_i)+b \leq q_i^+ + \xi_i^+, \\ & i=m+1,\ldots,n. \end{aligned} \tag{7}$$

with $\mathbf{w} \in \mathbf{R}^d$, $b \in \mathbf{R}$, $\boldsymbol{\xi} \in \mathbf{R}_+^m$, $\boldsymbol{\xi}^- \in \mathbf{R}_+^{n-m}$, and $\boldsymbol{\xi}^+ \in \mathbf{R}_+^{n-m}$ as the variables. The first part of the constraints is for the exact observations. As for the censored observations, their decision values, $(\mathbf{w}\cdot\mathbf{x}_i)+b$, are bounded by q_i^- and q_i^+. The boundaries are functions of p_i, a, and η, *i.e.*,

$$q_i^- = -\frac{1}{a}\log\left(\frac{1}{p_i-\eta}-1\right), \quad q_i^+ = -\frac{1}{a}\log\left(\frac{1}{p_i+\eta}-1\right),$$

where $a = \log(1/\eta - 1)$ is a constant and η is the max deviation of the probability estimate from p_i [8], [9]. ,

The p_i values defined in (4) encode the information about survival time for both censored and exact observations, available in the training data. This formulation can be extended to nonlinear (kernel) parameterization using standard SVM methodology. This method is known (and will be referred to) as pSVM in this paper.

V. Empirical Comparisons for Synthetic Data

This section describes the empirical comparisons between the pSVM, SVM+/LUPI method and the Cox modeling approach [1]. Practical application of these methods to finite data, involves additional simplifications, as discussed next:

- For SVM+, the non-linearity is modeled only in the correcting space [10]. That is, in all experiments the decision space uses linear parameterization, and the correcting space is implemented via non-linear (RBF) kernels.
- pSVM uses either linear or non-linear mapping in the experiments.

Consequently, pSVM with RBF kernel has three tuning parameters, C, $\tilde{C}$, and σ (RBF width parameter), whereas SVM+ with RBF kernel has three tuning parameters, C, γ, and σ. Furthermore, pSVM with linear kernel has two tuning parameters (C and $\tilde{C}$). In contrast, there is no tunable parameter in the Cox modeling approach.

Empirical comparisons are designed to understand relative advantages and limitations of SVM-based methods for modeling the survival data sets with various statistical characteristics, such as the number of training samples, the noise in the observed survival times, and the proportion of censoring. The synthetic data set is generated as follows [11]:

- Set the number of input features d to 30.
- Generate $\mathbf{x} \in \mathbf{R}^d$ with each element x_i being a random number uniformly distributed within $[-1, 1]$.
- Define the coefficient vector as

$$\boldsymbol{\beta} = [1,1,2,3,3,1,1,1,1,0,2,0,2,2,0,\\ 2,0,0,0,0,0,0,0,0,0,0,0,0,0,0].$$

- Generate the event time T following $\text{Exp}((\boldsymbol{\beta}\cdot\mathbf{x})+2)$ distribution. The Gaussian noise $\nu \sim \mathcal{N}(0, 0.2)$ is also added to the event time T. Generate the censoring time C following $\text{Exp}(\lambda)$ distribution.
- The survival time and event indicator are obtained according to (1) and (2). The rate of the exponential distribution, λ, is used to control the proportion of censoring in the training set.
- Assign class label to each data vector by the rule in (3). The time of interest, τ, is set to the median value among the survival times. In this way, the prior probability for each class is about the same.
- Generate 400 samples for training, 400 for validation, and 2000 for testing.

This data set conforms to probabilistic assumptions (*i.e.*, exponential distribution) underlying the classical modeling approach. So the Cox modeling approach is expected to be very competitive for the synthetic data set.

The following experimental procedure was used in all experiments:

- Estimate the classifier using the training data.
- Find optimal tuning parameters for each method using the validation data. For the Cox modeling approach, the validation data are not used.

TABLE I
THE TEST ERRORS (%) FOR THE SYNTHETIC DATA WITH 400 TRAINING SAMPLES.

Trial	1	2	3	4	5	6	7	8	9	10
Cox	26.6	27.1	26.3	29.6	27.4	27.1	28.3	28.7	27.4	26.9
pSVM linear	25.7	**22.6**	**25.0**	**27.5**	**24.2**	26.5	26.1	**26.0**	25.6	**26.1**
pSVM rbf	**24.6**	25.7	25.8	27.9	25.7	**25.4**	25.7	26.9	26.2	26.8
LUPI	25.2	25.5	25.6	29.6	25.7	25.5	**25.6**	27.2	**25.0**	26.5

TABLE II
THE TEST ERRORS (%) FOR THE SYNTHETIC DATA WITH 250 TRAINING SAMPLES.

Trial	1	2	3	4	5	6	7	8	9	10
Cox	30.1	29.6	28.0	**27.6**	30.1	30.3	28.9	30.1	29.3	28.3
pSVM linear	**28.6**	**25.8**	**27.6**	28.1	29.8	**26.8**	**28.0**	28.1	27.3	29.0
pSVM rbf	28.9	26.9	30.4	**27.6**	30.5	28.1	27.5	**26.8**	27.7	28.1
LUPI	30.0	28.0	29.3	29.8	29.9	27.6	30.6	30.0	**25.0**	26.3

TABLE III
THE TEST ERRORS (%) FOR THE SYNTHETIC DATA WITH 100 TRAINING SAMPLES.

Trial	1	2	3	4	5	6	7	8	9	10
Cox	35.6	**31.3**	34.0	32.3	27.7	**30.6**	**30.6**	33.5	31.4	**28.4**
pSVM linear	**32.5**	33.0	33.5	30.0	**25.1**	33.5	36.9	**30.4**	31.4	30.8
pSVM rbf	**32.5**	32.0	33.8	**29.3**	32.2	32.2	34.2	31.4	33.1	29.9
LUPI	33.6	37.1	**32.0**	32.0	26.0	41.0	33.6	37.0	**30.9**	29.3

TABLE IV
THE TEST ERRORS (%) FOR THE SYNTHETIC DATA WITH 50 TRAINING SAMPLES.

Trial	1	2	3	4	5	6	7	8	9	10
Cox	35.0	**31.6**	37.5	39.3	33.7	46.5	40.2	41.2	**33.9**	42.1
pSVM linear	**34.3**	35.1	37.6	34.3	34.8	40.3	41.8	40.9	35.7	**38.1**
pSVM rbf	35.8	**31.6**	37.5	33.1	**34.1**	**38.0**	**38.1**	**35.5**	35.8	39.1
LUPI	37.8	35.4	**35.5**	32.0	39.4	41.3	41.5	39.3	38.4	42.0

- Estimate the test error of the final model using the test data.

The SVM+/LUPI has three tunable parameters, C, γ, and σ. These parameters are estimated using the validation data, and we consider C in the range of $[10^{-1}, 10^{2}]$, γ in $[10^{-3}, 10^{1}]$, and σ in $[2^{-2}, 2^{2}]$ for model selection. For pSVM with RBF kernel, we consider C and $\tilde{C}$ in the range of $[10^{-1}, 10^{2}]$, and σ in $[2^{-2}, 2^{2}]$.

Further, the experiment is performed ten times with different random realizations of the training, validation, and test data. In this experiment, the average proportion of the censored observation is 16.1% (or about 64 observations in the training set are censored). The test errors for ten trials are shown in Table I. The average test errors in percentage (along with standard deviations) for the Cox model, pSVM with linear kernel, pSVM with RBF kernel, and LUPI are 27.5±1.0, 25.6±1.4, 26.1±0.9, and 26.2±1.4, respectively.

The pSVM with linear kernel achieves the lowest test error among the methods in most trials. Comparing the pSVM method with different kernels, it is not surprising to find that pSVM with linear kernel performs better than that with RBF kernel. Because our synthetic data is generated from a nearly linear model and there is intrinsic linearity in the data. Methods with linear kernel are expected to perform better than those with RBF kernel.

The Cox model has the highest test error in most trails. The results illustrate potential advantage of using the SVM-based methods. Note that SVM-based methods yield similar or superior performance *vs.* classical Cox models, even thought the training and test data is generated using exponential distributions (for which the Cox method is known to be statistically optimal).

A. Number of Training Samples

To investigate the effect of training sample size on the test errors, the training sample size is reduced to 250, 100 and 50. The validation sample sizes are changed accordingly. The results are reported in Table II, III and IV.

For 250 training samples, the average test errors for the Cox model, pSVM with linear kernel, pSVM with RBF kernel, and LUPI are 29.2±1.0, 27.9±1.1, 28.3±1.3, and 28.7±1.9, respectively. The pSVM with linear kernel has the best performance in five trials. The relative performances between the pSVM with RBF kernel and LUPI are roughly the same. However, the performance gap between the Cox model and the pSVM with linear kernel is closing when the size of the training data is reduced. This observation is more evident when the sample size is reduced to 100. For 100 training samples, the Cox model has the lowest test error in four trials, whereas the pSVM with linear kernel has the best performance in three trials only.

When the training sample size is further reduced to 50, both the Cox model and the pSVM with linear kernel are outperformed by the pSVM with RBF kernel. This can be attributed to the high dimensionality of the input (feature) vectors. With high dimensional input vectors, methods with linear kernel fail to capture the linearity of the data when only 50 samples are available for training. It is also expected

TABLE V
TEST ERRORS AS A FUNCTION OF TRAINING SAMPLE SIZE.

Training size	50	100	250	400
Censoring	16.6%	15.9%	16.4%	16.1%
Cox	38.1 ± 4.6	**31.5 ± 2.4**	29.2 ± 1.0	27.5 ± 1.0
pSVM linear	37.3 ± 2.9	31.7 ± 3.1	**27.9 ± 1.1**	**25.6 ± 1.4**
pSVM rbf	**35.8 ± 2.4**	32.0 ± 1.5	28.3 ± 1.3	26.1 ± 0.9
LUPI	38.3 ± 3.2	33.2 ± 4.3	28.7 ± 1.9	26.2 ± 1.4

TABLE VI
TEST ERRORS AS A FUNCTION OF NOISE LEVEL.

Noise level	0	0.1	0.2	0.5
Censoring	15.9%	16.0%	17.2%	17.7%
Cox	**11.1 ± 0.4**	22.5 ± 1.7	28.7 ± 1.8	36.3 ± 1.3
pSVM linear	14.2 ± 1.0	**21.1 ± 1.8**	**27.1 ± 2.0**	34.8 ± 1.1
pSVM rbf	15.1 ± 1.5	22.5 ± 0.9	27.2 ± 2.1	36.0 ± 1.4
LUPI	14.3 ± 0.7	22.8 ± 1.7	27.5 ± 2.1	**34.7 ± 2.0**

that the estimated Cox model is not accurate due to the small sample size.

Table V shows the relative performance of the five methods, as a function of sample size. The pSVM with linear kernel outperforms all other methods when the training sample size is larger than 250. This is not surprising, because the linear space matches the synthetic data model. As expected, with increasing number of training samples, the relative advantage of the SVM-based methods is more noticeable. Nonetheless, the Cox model is more competitive for moderate training sample size (100).

B. Noise Level in the Survival Time

To examine the effect of noise level in the survival time on the test errors, noise with different variances are added to the survival time. The noise variance ranges from 0 to 0.5 and the training and validation sample sizes are kept at 250. The test errors are summarized in Table VI.

It is evident that the test errors are reduced in all methods when the noise variance is decreased. When there is no noise in the survival time, the data are generated from a distribution that follows the Cox modeling assumption. It is expected that the Cox model achieves the lowest test error under low-noise scenario. However, the increasing of noise level has much larger negative effect in the Cox modeling approach. The test error is increased from 11% to 36% when the noise level is raised from 0 to 0.5. Meanwhile, for the same changes in the noise levels, the test errors of the SVM-based approaches are raised from 14% to 35%.

Apart from the zero-noise scenario, the pSVM with linear kernel achieves the lowest average test error when the noise variance is less than 0.2. The LUPI, however, has the best performance when the noise level is higher than 0.2. It can be concluded that the SVM-based methods show more robustness to noisy data.

C. Proportion of Censoring

We also adjust the proportion of censoring in the training data to investigate the effect of censoring on the test errors. The percentage of censoring observations in the training data varies from 6% to 46% in our experiment. The noise variance is set to 0.2 and the training and validation sample sizes are kept at 250. The experiment results are summarized in Table VII.

TABLE VII
TEST ERRORS AS A FUNCTION OF CENSORING RATE.

Censoring	6.1%	30.6%	38.6%	46.0%
Cox	27.4 ± 2.0	33.8 ± 1.6	38.6 ± 2.2	42.0 ± 1.0
pSVM linear	**26.1 ± 1.6**	**31.5 ± 1.8**	36.8 ± 1.9	41.8 ± 2.4
pSVM rbf	26.9 ± 1.7	32.4 ± 2.5	**36.7 ± 1.3**	**39.9 ± 1.4**
LUPI	28.0 ± 2.7	32.5 ± 2.2	37.1 ± 2.1	41.3 ± 1.5

When less than 30% of the training data are censored, the pSVM linear gives the lowest test error. On the contrary, if a large portion of the observations are censored (about 40% or more), the pSVM with RBF kernel outperforms all other methods. With more censored observations in the training set, more observed survival times are obtained by the non-linear operator in (1). Hence, the linearity within the data is no longer maintained, and methods with non-linear parameterization (kernel) are expected to achieve better performances.

VI. Real-Life Data Sets

This section describes empirical comparisons using four real-life data sets from the *Survival* package in R [12]. For all comparisons, the common decision space for SVM+ uses the linear kernel while the unique correction space uses the RBF kernel. For the pSVM method, both linear and the RBF kernels are investigated. In all experiments, the time of interest τ was set to the median of the observed survival times. Our experiments for the four medical data sets follow the following procedure [2], [10]:

- Use five-fold cross-validation to estimate the test errors.
- Within each training fold, the parameter tuning (model selection) is performed through a five-fold resampling.

Our experimental set-up uses double resampling procedure [2]. One level of resampling is used for estimating the test error of a learning method, and the second level is for tuning the model parameters (or model selection). During the model selection stage, the possible choices of tuning parameters are C and $\tilde{C}$ in the range of $[10^{-1}, 10^{2}]$, γ in $[10^{-3}, 10^{1}]$, and σ in $[2^{-2}, 2^{2}]$. Since there is no definite class label for the censored observation with $U_i < \tau$, the test errors are reported based on samples with definite labels, *i.e.*, exact observations and censored observations with $U_i \geq \tau$. Further, model parameters are selected based on the performance with those samples with well-defined labels.

1) Veteran Data Set: The *veteran* data set is from the Veterans' Administration Lung Cancer Study which is a randomised trial of two treatment regimens for lung cancer. In the *veteran* data set, there are 137 instances (observations) and each instance has 10 attributes. Less than 7% of the instances are censored. Among the nine censored instances, one has the observed survival time less than the time of interest. In other words, only one instance is associated with the uncertain class label in the *veteran* data set.

2) Lung Data Set: The *lung* data set studied the survival and usual daily activities in patients with advanced lung cancer by the North Central Cancer Treatment Group (NCCTG). There are 167 instances in this data set, and each instance has 8 attributes. About 28% of the instances are censored, and 21 censored instances are linked to uncertain class labels.

TABLE VIII
SUMMARY OF THE *Survival* DATA SETS AND THE EXPERIMENT RESULTS.

Data set	Veteran	Lung	PBC	Stanford2
Size	137	167	258	157
Attributes	10	8	22	2
$\delta = 0$	9	47	147	55
Censored %	6.57	28.14	56.98	35.03
Uncertain cls	1	21	54	8
Cox	**23.4 ± 4.6**	43.3 ± 5.6	34.3 ± 7.1	51.9 ± 4.7
pSVM linear	27.2 ± 7.8	**38.3 ± 6.2**	26.2 ± 2.5	53.9 ± 7.4
pSVM rbf	32.0 ± 5.9	42.5 ± 8.0	**23.5 ± 5.2**	**34.3 ± 6.2**
LUPI	30.4 ± 4.5	38.3 ± 9.9	25.3 ± 10.6	42.4 ± 17.7

3) PBC Data Set: The *pbc* data set is from the Mayo Clinic trial in primary biliary cirrhosis (PBC) of the liver conducted between 1974 and 1984. The *pbc* data set contains 258 instances and each instance has 22 attributes. More than half of the instances are censored, and 54 censored instances do not have the definite class labels.

4) Stanford2 Data Set: The fourth data set is the *stanford2* data set from the Stanford Heart Transplant data, which contains 157 instances, each with 2 attributes. More than 35% instances are censored and 8 of them are associated with the uncertain labels.

The descriptions of the data sets are summarized in Table VIII. The fourth row indicates the proportions of censored observations in the data sets. The fifth row shows the number of censored observation with $U_i < \tau$ when τ is set to the median of the observed survival times. Table VIII also shows the test errors from different methods applied to the four data sets. Note that the SVM-based approaches achieve the lowest test error in three of the four data sets. On the other hand, the Cox model gives the best performance in the *veteran* data set. In these experiments, the number of training samples is fixed, so we cannot make any conclusions regarding the effect of sample size on methods' performance. However, we can make inferences about inherent non-linearity in some of the data sets. For example, for the *stanford2* data set, non-linear pSVM performs much better than other methods using linear parameterization. So we can infer this data set requires non-linear modeling.

These results illustrate the effect of censoring on generalization performance. For small proportion of censoring (such as 6%) in the data, the Cox model gives the lowest test error. However, the SVM-based methods show their advantages when the proportion of censoring is increased. Further, relative advantage of SVM-based approaches becomes quite evident for higher-dimensional survival data.

These results also show large variability of estimated test errors, due to partitioning of available data into five (training, test) folds. This variability is reflected in large standard deviations of test error rates. Direct comparisons suggest that SVM-based methods yield smaller or similar test error in each (training, test) fold. Another reason for variability of the SVM-based model estimates is due to model selection via resampling. Notably, standard deviations of error rates for all SVM-based methods shown in Table VIII are consistently higher than standard deviations for the Cox model (which has no tunable parameters). This underscores the importance of robust model selection strategies for SVM-based methods, which would be the focus of our future work.

VII. DISCUSSION AND CONCLUSIONS

This paper proposes predictive modeling of high-dimensional survival data as a binary classification problem. We apply the LUPI formulation and SVM with uncertain class labels to solve the problem. Both methods incorporate the information about survival time to estimate an SVM classifier. We have illustrated the advantages and limitations of these modeling approaches using synthetic and real-life data sets.

Advanced SVM-based methods appear very effective when the proportion of censoring in training data is large, or the observed survival time does not follow the classical probabilistic assumptions, *e.g.*, the exponential distribution [1], [11]. On the other hand, with fewer censored observations the Cox modeling approach may perform better. Further, the relative performance of LUPI and pSVM depends on the intrinsic linearity/non-linearity of the data itself. In particular, superior performance of the pSVM with RBF kernel for the *stanford2* data indicates an intrinsic non-linearity of this data set.

The equal misclassification cost is assumed throughout this paper; however, realistic medical applications use unequal costs. We will incorporate different misclassification costs into the proposed SVM-based formulations. Further, our methodology for predictive modeling of survival data can be readily extended to other (non-medical) applications, such as predicting business failure (aka bankruptcy) or predicting marriage failure (aka divorce).

REFERENCES

[1] O. Aalen, Ø. Borgan, H. Gjessing, and S. Gjessing, *Survival and Event History Analysis: A Process Point of View*, ser. Statistics for Biology and Health. Springer-Verlag New York, 2008.

[2] V. Cherkassky and F. Mulier, *Learning from data: concepts, theory, and methods*. Wiley, 2007.

[3] F. Khan and V. Zubek, "Support Vector Regression for censored data (SVRc): A novel tool for survival analysis," in *Data Mining, 2008. ICDM '08. Eighth IEEE International Conference on*, Dec. 2008, pp. 863–868.

[4] J. Shim and C. Hwang, "Support vector censored quantile regression under random censoring," *Comput. Stat. Data Anal.*, vol. 53, no. 4, pp. 912–919, Feb. 2009.

[5] P. K. Shivaswamy, W. Chu, and M. Jansche, "A support vector approach to censored targets," in *Proceedings of the 2007 Seventh IEEE International Conference on Data Mining*, ser. ICDM '07. Washington, DC, USA: IEEE Computer Society, 2007, pp. 655–660.

[6] V. N. Vapnik, *Estimation of dependences based on empirical data, Empirical inference science: afterword of 2006*. Springer, 2006.

[7] V. Vapnik and A. Vashist, "2009 special issue: A new learning paradigm: Learning using privileged information," *Neural Networks*, vol. 22, no. 5-6, pp. 544–557, July 2009.

[8] E. Niaf, R. Flamary, C. Lartizien, and S. Canu, "Handling uncertainties in SVM classification," in *Statistical Signal Processing Workshop (SSP), 2011 IEEE*, June 2011, pp. 757–760.

[9] J. C. Platt, "Probabilistic outputs for support vector machines and comparisons to regularized likelihood methods," in *Advances in Large Margin Classifiers*. MIT Press, 1999, pp. 61–74.

[10] L. Liang, F. Cai, and V. Cherkassky, "Predictive learning with structured (grouped) data," *Neural Networks*, vol. 22, no. 5-6, pp. 766–773, 2009.

[11] M. Zhou, "Use software R to do survival analysis and simulation. a tutorial," http://www.ms.uky.edu/ mai/Rsurv.pdf.

[12] T. M. Therneau, *A Package for Survival Analysis in R*, 2013, r package version 2.37-4. [Online]. Available: http://CRAN.R-project.org/package=survival

Large Scale Visual Classification with Parallel, Imbalanced Bagging of Incremental LIBLINEAR SVM

Thanh-Nghi Doan[1], Thanh-Nghi Do[2], and François Poulet[1,3]
[1]IRISA, [3]Université de Rennes 1, Campus Universitaire de Beaulieu, 35042 Rennes Cedex, France
[2]Institut Telecom, Telecom Bretagne, UMR CNRS 6285 Lab-STICC,
Université européenne de Bretagne, France, Can Tho University, Vietnam

Abstract— *ImageNet dataset with more than 14M images and 21K classes makes the problem of visual classification more difficult to deal with. One of the most difficult tasks is to train a fast and accurate classifier. In this paper, we address this challenge by extending the state-of-the-art large scale linear classifier LIBLINEAR-CDBLOCK proposed by Hsiang-Fu Yu in three ways: (1) improve LIBLINEAR-CDBLOCK for large number of classes with one-versus-all approach, (2) a balanced bagging algorithm for training binary classifiers, (3) parallelize the training process of classifiers with several multi-core computers. Our approach is evaluated on the 100 largest classes of ImageNet and ILSVRC 2010. The evaluation shows that our approach is 732 times faster than the original implementation and 1193 times faster than LIBLINEAR without (or very few) compromising classification accuracy.*

Keywords: Support Vector Machines, Incremental Learning Method, Balanced Bagging, High Performance Computing

1. Introduction

Visual classification is one of the important topics in computer vision and machine learning. The usual frameworks involve three steps: 1) extracting local image features, 2) building codebook and encoding features, and 3) training classifiers. These frameworks are evaluated on small datasets, e.g. Caltech 101 [1], Caltech 256 [2] and PASCAL VOC [3]. In step 3, most researchers choose either linear or nonlinear SVM classifiers that can be trained in a few minutes.

However, ImageNet dataset [4] with very large number of classes poses more challenges in training classifiers. ImageNet is much larger in scale and diversity than other benchmark datasets. The current released ImageNet has grown a big step in terms of the number of images and the number of classes, as shown in Fig. 1 - it has 21,841 classes with more than 1000 images for each class on average.

With millions of training examples or dimensions, training an accurate classifier may take weeks or even years [5], [6]. Recent works in large scale learning classifiers converge on building linear SVM classifiers, because it is possible to train linear classifiers (e.g. LIBLINEAR [7]) in order of seconds, even with millions training examples. However, when training data is larger and cannot fit into main memory, most existing linear classifiers encounter a problem. Yu [8] proposed a block minimization framework for linear classifier (LIBLINEAR-CDBLOCK), that can be applied to data beyond the memory capacity of computer. They show empirically that their method can handle data sets 20 times larger than the memory size. However, the current version of LIBLINEAR-CDBLOCK has two main drawbacks that prevent it scaleup to large scale dataset with many classes. Firstly, LIBLINEAR-CDBLOCK has not explored one-versus-all approach in the case of multi-class classification. Secondly, it does not take into account the benefits of high performance computing (HPC). On the dataset of ImageNet Challenge 2010 (ILSVRC 2010 [9]), it takes very long time to train classifiers. Therefore, it motivates us to study how to extend LIBLINEAR-CDBLOCK for large scale visual classification. Our key contributions include:

1. Improve LIBLINEAR-CDBLOCK for large number of classes by using one-versus-all approach.

2. Propose a balanced bagging algorithm for training the binary classifiers. Our algorithm avoids training on full data, and the training process of LIBLINEAR-CDBLOCK rapidly converges to the optimal solution.

3. Parallelize the training process of all binary classifiers based on HPC models. In the training step of classifiers, we apply our balanced bagging algorithm to achieve the best performance.

Our approach is evaluated on the 100 largest classes of ImageNet and ILSVRC 2010. The experiment shows that our approach is 732 times faster than the original implementation and 1193 times faster than LIBLINEAR without (or very few) compromising classification accuracy. Therefore, it can be easily applied to datasets with very large number of classes and the training data cannot fit into the memory of computer.

The remainder of this paper is organized as follows. Section 2 briefly reviews the related work on large scale visual classification. The incremental LIBLINEAR support vector machines is described in section 3. Section 4 presents its improvement for large number of classes. We describe how to speedup the training process of incremental LIBLINEAR by using balanced bagging algorithm and take the benefits of HPC. Section 5 presents numerical results before the conclusion and future work.

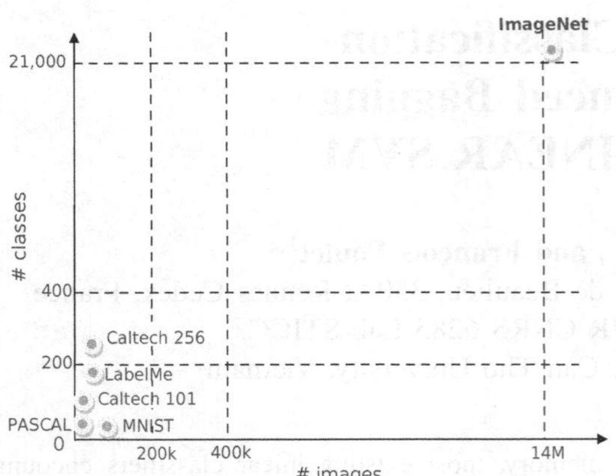

Fig. 1: A comparison of ImageNet with other benchmark datasets.

2. Related Work

Low-level local image features, bag-of-words model (BoW [10]) and support vector machines (SVM [11]) are the core of state-of-the-art visual classification systems. These may be enhanced by multi-scale spatial pyramids [12] on BoWs or histogram of oriented gradient [13] features. Some recent works consider exploiting the hierarchical structure of dataset for image recognition and achieve impressive improvements in accuracy and efficiency [14]. Related to classification is the problem of detection, often treated as repeated one-versus-all classification in sliding windows [15], [3]. In many cases, such localization of objects might be useful to improve classification accuracy performance. However, in the context of large scale visual classification with hundreds or thousands of classes, these common approaches become computationally intractable.

To address this problem, Fergus *et al.* [16] study semi-supervised learning on 126 hand labeled Tiny Images categories, Wang *et al.* [17] show classification experiments on a maximum of 315 categories. Li *et al.* [18] do research with landmark classification on a collection of 500 landmarks and 2 million images. On a small subset of 10 classes, they have improved BoWs classification by increasing the visual vocabulary up to 80K visual words.

The emergence of ImageNet makes the complexity of visual classification much larger and very difficult to deal with. Recently, many researchers are beginning to study strategies to improve the classification accuracy and avoid using high cost nonlinear kernel SVM classifiers. The prominent works are proposed in [5], [6], [19], [20] where the data are first transformed by a nonlinear mapping induced by a particular kernel and then linear classifier is trained in the resulting space. They argue that the classification accuracy of linear classifier with high-dimensional image signature is similar to low-dimensional BoW with nonlinear classifier.

In [6], the winner of ImageNet Challenge 2010, each local descriptor is encoded by using either Local Coordinate Coding [21] or Super-vector Coding [22]. Then, they perform spatial pyramid pooling and the resulting image signature is a vector in approximately 262K dimensions. To train classifiers, they propose a parallel averaging stochastic gradient descent (ASGD) algorithm. With 1K classes of ILSVRC 2010, it takes 4 days to train 1K binary SVM classifiers (one-versus-all) for one feature channel on three 8-core computers. However, their method involves training classifiers on a dataset in hundreds of giga-bytes. Therefore, it cannot be easily applied to the systems with limited memory resource. To tackle this challenge, Yu *et al.* [8] propose LIBLINEAR-CDBLOCK that can handle data larger than the memory size of computer. Nevertheless, LIBLINEAR-CDBLOCK has two main limitations: 1) multi-class classification with one-versus-all approach has not been explored, 2) it does not take into account the benefits of HPC. Therefore, the training time is very long on ILSVRC 2010 (at least 32 hours) due to learning 1K binary classifiers sequentially, independently.

3. Incremental LIBLINEAR Support Vector Machines

Let us consider a linear binary classification task with a training set $\mathbb{T} = \{(x_i, y_i)\}_{i=1}^n, x_i \in \mathbb{R}^d, y_i \in \{+1, -1\}$. SVM classification algorithm aims to find the best separating surface as being furthest from both classes. It can simultaneously maximize the margin between the supporting planes for each class and minimize the errors. This can be performed by solving the dual optimization problem (1).

$$\min_{\alpha \in \mathbb{R}^n} f(\alpha) = \frac{1}{2}\alpha^T Q \alpha - e^T \alpha$$
$$s.t. \begin{cases} y^T \alpha = 0 \\ 0 \leq \alpha_i \leq C, \ \forall i = 1, 2, ..., n \end{cases} \tag{1}$$

where $e = [1, \ldots, 1]^T$, C is a positive constant used to tune the margin and the error, $\alpha = (\alpha_1, \ldots, \alpha_n)$ are the Lagrange multipliers, Q is an $n \times n$ symmetric matrix with $Q_{ij} = y_i y_j K\langle x_i, x_j \rangle$, and $K\langle x_i, x_j \rangle$ is the kernel function.

The support vectors (for which $\alpha_i > 0$) are given by the optimal solution of (1), and then, the separating surface and the scalar b are determined by the support vectors. The classification of a new data point x is based on:

$$sign(\sum_{i=1}^{\#SV} y_i \alpha_i K\langle x, x_i \rangle - b) \tag{2}$$

Variations on SVM algorithms use different classification functions. No algorithmic changes are required from the usual kernel function K as a linear inner product other than the modification of the kernel evaluation, including a polynomial function of degree d, a RBF (Radial Basis Function) or a sigmoid function. We can get different support vector classification models.

LIBLINEAR proposed by [7] uses a dual coordinate descent method for dealing with linear SVM using L1- and L2-loss functions. And then, LIBLINEAR is simple and reaches an ϵ-accurate solution in O(log(1/ϵ)) iterations. The algorithm is much faster than state of the art solvers such as LibSVM [23] or SVM^{perf} [24].

Most SVM algorithms are designed by assuming that data can be stored in the main memory. Therefore, in the context of large scale classification, these approaches become intractable. To solve this problem, [25] and [8] propose incremental learning methods for solving the memory usage problem of linear classifiers. They show that training SVM classifiers can be performed on the successive subsets of the training set.

Let $\{B_j\}_{j=1}^{m}$ be a fixed partition of $\mathbb{T}$ into m blocks of rows. These blocks of rows are disjoint sets stored in m separate files. At each iteration, we consider a block of rows B_j and solve the problem (1) only for the samples in B_j, so the algorithm does not need to keep in memory the samples from other blocks of rows. According to memory size, we choose block size such that the samples in B_j can fit into memory. LIBLINEAR is used to solve the sub-problems and the solution is updated in growing training data without loading the entire data into memory at once. The incremental learning for LIBLINEAR is summarized in Algorithm 1.

Algorithm 1: Incremental learning for LIBLINEAR

```
input : A set of training samples T = {(x_i, y_i)}_{i=1}^n
output: The values α or w
Split T into B_1, ..., B_m and store data in m files accordingly
α ← 0 or w ← 0
for j ← 1 to m do
    Read x_r ∈ B_j from disk
    Solve the sub-problem (3) by using LIBLINEAR
    Update α or w
end
```

Solving dual SVM by LIBLINEAR for each block. The optimal solution of (1) can be obtained by solving the sub-problems (3).

$$\min_{d\in\mathbb{R}^n} f(\alpha+d) = \frac{1}{2}(\alpha+d)^T Q(\alpha+d) - e^T(\alpha+d)$$

$$s.t. \begin{cases} d_i = 0, \forall i \notin B_j \\ 0 \le \alpha_i + d_i \le C \ , \ \forall i \in B_j. \end{cases} \tag{3}$$

Let d_{B_j} be a vector of $|B_j|$ non-zero coordinates of d that correspond to the indices in B_j. The objective (3) is equivalent to

$$\frac{1}{2}d_{B_j}^T Q_{B_jB_j} d_{B_j} + (Q_{B_j,\bullet}\alpha - e_{B_j})^T d_{B_j} \ , \tag{4}$$

where $Q_{B_j,\bullet}$ is a sub-matrix of Q including elements $Q_{ri}, r \in B_j, i = 1,\dots,n$. Obviously, $Q_{B_j,\bullet}$ in Eq. 4 involves all training data. This violate the method presented in Algorithm 1. However, by maintaining $w = \sum_{i=1}^{n}\alpha_i y_i x_i$ into memory, we can compute $Q_{B_j,\bullet}$ by using the Eq. 5.

$$Q_{B_j,\bullet} - 1 = y_r w^T x_r - 1, \forall r \in B_j \tag{5}$$

where $w \leftarrow w + \sum_{r\in B_j} d_r^* y_r x_r$

This operation involves only the samples in B_j.

4. Improving incremental LIBLINEAR for large number of classes

Most SVM algorithms are only able to deal with a two-class problem. There are several extensions of binary classification SVM solver to multi-class (k classes, $k \ge 3$) classification tasks. The state-of-the-art multi-class SVMs are categorized into two types of approaches. The first one is to consider the multi-class case in an optimization problem [26], [27]. The second one is to decompose multi-class into a series of binary SVMs, including one-versus-all [11], one-versus-one [28] and Decision Directed Acyclic Graph [29]. Recently, hierarchical methods for multi-class SVM [30], [31] start from the whole data set, hierarchically divide the data into two subsets until every subset consists of only one class.

In practice, one-versus-all, one-versus-one are the most popular methods due to their simplicity. Let us consider k classes ($k > 2$). The one-versus-all strategy builds k different classifiers where the ith classifier separates the ith class from the rest. The one-versus-one strategy constructs $k(k-1)/2$ classifiers, using all the binary pairwise combinations of the k classes. The class is then predicted with a majority vote.

When dealing with very large number of classes, e.g. hundreds of classes, the one-versus-one strategy is too expensive because it needs to train many thousands of classifiers. Therefore, the one-versus-all strategy becomes popular in this case.

However, for multi-class classification, LIBLINEAR-CDBLOCK solves a single optimization problem by using [32]. Therefore, the current version of LIBLINEAR-CDBLOCK needs very long time to classify very large number of classes.

Due to this problem, we propose three ways for speedup the learning task of LIBLINEAR-CDBLOCK. The first one is to implement one-versus-all approach for multi-class case. The second one is to build the balanced bagging classifiers with sampling strategy. Finally, we parallelize the training task of all classifiers with several multi-core computers.

Balanced bagging incremental LIBLINEAR

In the one-versus-all approach, the learning task of incremental LIBLINEAR SVM is to try to separate the ith class (positive class) from the $k-1$ other classes (negative class). For very large number of classes, e.g. 1000 classes, this leads to the extreme imbalance between the positive class and the negative class. The problem is well-known as the class imbalance. As summarized by the review papers [33], [34] and the very comprehensive papers [35], [36], solutions to the class imbalance problems were proposed both at the data and algorithmic level. At the data level, these algorithms change the class distribution, including over-sampling the minority class or under-sampling the majority class. At the algorithmic level, the solution is to re-balance the error rate by weighting each type of error with the corresponding cost. Our balanced bagging incremental LIBLINEAR SVM belongs to the first approach (forms of re-sampling). Furthermore, the class prior probabilities in this context are highly unequal (e.g. the distribution of the positive class is 0.1% in the 1000 classes classification problem), and over-sampling the minority class is very expensive. We propose the balanced bagging incremental LIBLINEAR SVM using under-sampling the majority class (negative class).

For separating the ith class (positive class) from the rest (negative class), the balanced bagging incremental LIBLINEAR SVM trains T models as shown in algorithm 2.

Algorithm 2: Balanced bagging incremental LIBLINEAR SVM

input : B_+ the training data of positive class in B_j
B_- the training data of negative class in B_j
T the number of base learners
output: **LIBLINEAR SVM model**

Learn:
for $k \leftarrow 1$ **to** T **do**
  1. B'_- = sample(B_-) (with $|B'_-| = |B_+|$)
  2. LIBLINEAR(B_+, B'_-)
end
combine T models into the aggregated **LIBLINEAR SVM model**

We remark that the margin can be seen as the minimum distance between two convex hulls, H_+ of the positive class and H_- of the negative class (the farthest distance between the two classes). Under-sampling the negative class (B'_-) done by balanced bagging provides the reduced convex hull of H_-, called H'_-. And then, the minimum distance between H_+ and H'_- is larger than between H_+ and H_- (full dataset). It is easier to achieve the largest margin than learning on the full dataset. Therefore, the training task of incremental LIBLINEAR SVM is fast to converge to the solution. According to our experiments, by setting $T = \sqrt{\frac{|B_-|}{|B_+|}}$, the balanced bagging incremental LIBLINEAR SVM achieves good results in very fast training speed.

Parallel incremental LIBLINEAR training

Although the incremental LIBLINEAR SVM and balanced bagging incremental LIBLINEAR SVM deal with very large dataset with high speed, they do not take into account the benefits of HPC, e.g. multi-core computers. Furthermore, both incremental LIBLINEAR SVM and balanced bagging incremental LIBLINEAR SVM train independently k binary classifiers for k classes problems. This is a nice property for parallel learning. Our investigation aims to speedup the training task of multi-class incremental LIBLINEAR SVM and balanced bagging incremental LIBLINEAR SVM with several multi-processor computers. The idea is to learn k binary classifiers in parallel way.

The parallel programming is currently based on two major models, Message Passing Interface (MPI) [37] and Open Multiprocessing (OpenMP) [38]. MPI is a standardized and portable message-passing mechanism for distributed memory systems. MPI remains the dominant model (high performance, scalability, and portability) used in high-performance computing today. However, MPI process loads the whole subset (block) into memory during learning tasks, making it wasteful. The simplest development of parallel incremental LIBLINEAR SVM algorithms is based on the shared memory multiprocessing programming model OpenMP. However, OpenMP is not guaranteed to make the most efficient computing. Finally, we present a hybrid approach that combines the benefits from both OpenMP and MPI models. The hybrid MPI/OpenMP parallel incremental LIBLINEAR SVM algorithm is described in algorithm 3. The number of MPI processes depends on the memory capacity of the HPC system used.

Algorithm 3: Hybird MPI/OpenMP parallel incremental LIBLINEAR SVM

input : A set of training samples $\mathbb{T} = \{(x_i, y_i)\}_{i=1}^n$
P the number of MPI processes
output: The value α or w

Split $\mathbb{T}$ *into* $B_1, ..., B_m$ *and store data in m files accordingly*
$\alpha^t \leftarrow 0, w^t \leftarrow 0, \ 1 \leq t \leq k$
for $j \leftarrow 1$ **to** m **do**
  Read $x_r \in B_j$ *from disk* /* block j */
  Learn:
  $MPI-PROC_1$
  #pragma omp parallel for
  for $t_1 \leftarrow 1$ **to** k_1 **do** /* class t_1 */
    LIBLINEAR $(B_j^{t_1}, B_j \setminus B_j^{t_1})$
    Update α^{t_1} *and* w^{t_1}
  end
  ⋮
  $MPI-PROC_P$
  #pragma omp parallel for
  for $t_P \leftarrow 1$ **to** k_P **do** /* class t_P */
    LIBLINEAR $(B_j^{t_P}, B_j \setminus B_j^{t_P})$
    Update α^{t_P} *and* w^{t_P}
  end
end

5. Experiments and Results

In this section we compare our implementation with LIBLINEAR-CDBLOCK and LIBLINEAR in terms of training time, memory usage and classification accuracy. Our experiments were run on a cluster of ten computers with the same hardware architecture as shown in Table 1. The cores in the same processor share one L2 cache and the main

Table 1: The physical features of a multi-core computer.

# of CPUs	# of cores	Frequency	Memory	L2 cache
2	8	2.10GHz*16	47.26GB	256KB*2

memory is shared among all the cores. All the computers are running Linux 3.2.0-4-amd64 (x86_64).

The extended versions of LIBLINEAR are designed for large scale datasets, so we have evaluated our implementations on the two following datasets.

ImageNet 100. This dataset contains the 100 largest classes from ImageNet (183,116 images with data size 23.6GB). In each class, we sample 1K images for training and 150 images for testing. We construct BoW histogram of images by using libHIK [39] with SIFT descriptor [40], 1000 codewords and parameters "use both, grid step size 2 and split level 1". The image is encoded as a 12000 dimensional vector. We end up with 10.5GB of training data.

ILSVRC 2010. This dataset contains 1K classes from ImageNet with 1.2M images for training, 50K images for validation and 150K images for testing. Due to the memory restriction of computer, we take $\leq$ 900 images per class for training. We use the BoW feature set provided by [9] and encode every image as a vector in 21000 dimensions. Therefore, the total training images is 887,816 and the training data size is 12.5GB. All testing samples are used to test SVM models.

5.1 Memory usage

According to the memory size of the computer used, we have split data into small blocks of rows that can fit into memory in each incremental step of LIBLINEAR.

ImageNet 100. We have split this dataset into 3 and 6 blocks of rows. As shown in Table 2, our implementation can run on computer with the main memory less than 4GB (LIBLINEAR-B-3) and less than 2GB (LIBLINEAR-B-6).

ILSVRC 2010. Due to the large size of dataset, we have split this dataset into 8 and 24 blocks of rows, that allows training data to fit into 4GB RAM (LIBLINEAR-B-8) and 2GB RAM (LIBLINEAR-B-24) in each incremental step. As shown in Table 3, LIBLINEAR and LIBLINEAR-CDBLOCK-B-8 consume a large amount of main memory (16.70GB and 9.68GB), making it intractable on computers with limited memory. On the other hand, by splitting data into many small blocks of rows and using one-versus-all approach for multi-class case, our approach is found to be very suitable for this case. For instance, LIBLINEAR-B-8 uses only 3.23GB RAM to train 1K classifiers on ILSVRC 2010. That means our implementation can save from 66.63% to 80.66% memory usage, compared to LIBLINEAR-CDBLOCK and LIBLINEAR. Furthermore, by setting the block size appropriately, the program does not need to swap parts of the blocks of rows between main memory and secondary memory (on the hard disk), as shown in Fig. 2.

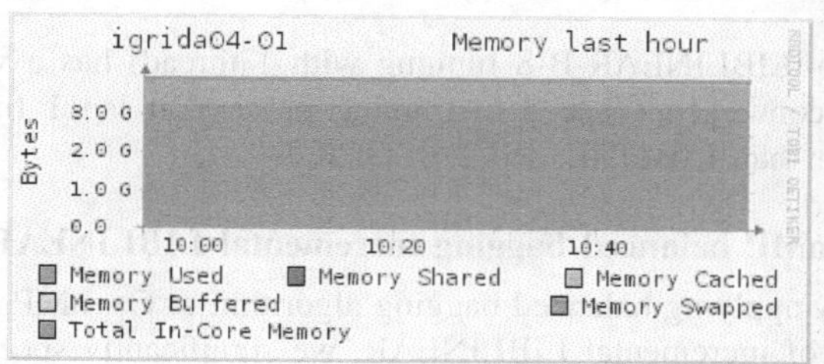

Fig. 2: Memory usage (GB) of the incremental LIBLINEAR (LIBLINEAR-B-8) on ILSVRC 2010.

Table 2: Memory usage (GB) of classifiers on ImageNet 100.

Method	ImageNet 100
LIBLINEAR	11.00
LIBLINEAR-CDBLOCK-B-3	3.78
LIBLINEAR-CDBLOCK-B-6	1.92
LIBLINEAR-B-3	3.71
LIBLINEAR-B-6	1.86

Note that the training time increases if we split the data into blocks of rows with smaller size. It is because the classifiers need to load and train more blocks (Table 4, 5).

5.2 Training time

We have implemented two extended versions of LIBLINEAR-CDBLOCK: 1) OpenMP balanced bagging incremental LIBLINEAR (omp-iLIBLINEAR-B), 2) Hybrid MPI/OpenMP balanced bagging incremental LIBLINEAR (mpi-omp-iLIBLINEAR-B). Incremental LIBLINEAR is designed to handle data beyond the memory size, so the training time is considered at disk-level:

training time = user time to run data into memory + time to access data from disk.

ImageNet 100. As shown in Table 4, on medium dataset ImageNet 100 our implementation shows a very good speedup in training process, compared to the original implementation. For instance, by splitting the dataset into 3 blocks of rows and use 10 MPI process and 16 OpenMP threads per MPI process, our implementation (10mpi-omp-iLIBLINEAR-B-3) is 494 times faster than LIBLINEAR-CDBLOCK-B-3.

ILSVRC 2010. Our implementations achieve a significant speedup in training process on this large dataset.

Balanced bagging incremental LIBLINEAR

As shown in Table 5, by splitting ILSVRC 2010 into 8 blocks, the balanced bagging incremental LIBLINEAR

Table 3: Memory usage (GB) of classifiers on ILSVRC 2010.

Method	ILSVRC 2010
LIBLINEAR	16.70
LIBLINEAR-CDBLOCK-B-8	9.68
LIBLINEAR-CDBLOCK-B-24	7.74
LIBLINEAR-B-8	3.23
LIBLINEAR-B-24	1.29

(omp-iLIBLINEAR-B-8 running with 1 thread) has a very fast convergence speed in training process, it is 11 times faster than LIBLINEAR-CDBLOCK-B-8.

OpenMP balanced bagging incremental LIBLINEAR

By applying balanced bagging algorithm to OpenMP version of incremental LIBLINEAR, we significantly speedup the training process of 1K binary classifiers. With the number of OpenMP threads set to 16, our implementation (omp-iLIBLINEAR-B-8) is 127 times faster than LIBLINEAR-CDBLOCK-B-8 (Table 5).

Hybrid MPI/OpenMP balanced bagging incremental LIBLINEAR

Although OpenMP balanced bagging incremental LIBLINEAR shows a significant speedup in training process, it does not ensure that the program achieves the most efficient high-performance computing on multi-core computers. Therefore, we explore this challenge by using a combination of MPI and OpenMP models. With this approach, our implementation achieves an impressive parallelization performance on a cluster of ten SMP (symmetric multiprocessor) nodes. For shorter, we use the technical term node instead of SMP node. The program first loads the whole block of data into nodes and each MPI process runs on one node. Therefore, each MPI process can work with their local data independently. However, we cannot increase the number of MPI processes exceed the memory capacity of a node. It is because each MPI process occupy the main memory during their computation process, resulting in an increase in the overall memory requirement. Unfortunately, OpenMP has been proven to work effectively on shared memory systems. It is used for fine-grained parallelization within a node. Consequently, in each node we can increase the number of OpenMP threads without demanding more extra memory. In this experiment, we have set the maximum number of OpenMP threads equal to the number of cores available on a node. As shown in Table 5, our implementation (10mpi-omp-iLIBLINEAR-B-8) achieves a significant speedup in training process by using 160 cores from ten nodes (10 MPI processes × 16 OpenMP threads). It is 732 times faster than LINEAR-CDBLOCK-B-8 and 1193 times faster than LIBLINEAR. We need only 2.62 minutes to train 1K binary classifiers, compared to LIBLINEAR-CDBLOCK-B-8 (∼ 32 hours) and LIBLINEAR (∼ 52 hours). This result confirms that our approach has a great ability to scaleup to full ImageNet dataset with more than 21K classes.

5.3 Classification accuracy

We have compared our implementations with LIBLINEAR-CDBLOCK and LIBLINEAR in terms of classification accuracy.

LIBLINEAR. The linear SVM from [7] with default parameter value $C = 1$.

LIBLINEAR-CDBLOCK-B. The block minimization framework for LIBLINEAR [8] with parameter $C = 1$, s = 4 (multi-class SVM by Crammer and Singer).

LIBLINEAR-B. The incremental LIBLINEAR with the same SVM parameters as LIBLINEAR (multi-class classification is implemented by using one-versus-all approach).

iLIBLINEAR-B. The balanced bagging incremental LIBLINEAR.

Table 4: SVMs training time (minute) on ImageNet 100.

Method	# OpenMP threads 1	8	16
LIBLINEAR	188.97		
LIBLINEAR-CDBLOCK-B-3	202.75		
LIBLINEAR-CDBLOCK-B-6	243.87		
omp-LIBLINEAR-B-3	56.45	9.12	7.50
omp-LIBLINEAR-B-6	72.55	11.28	8.82
omp-iLIBLINEAR-B-3	27.57	4.52	3.28
omp-iLIBLINEAR-B-6	30.07	4.88	3.43
5mpi-omp-iLIBLINEAR-B-3	6.08	0.98	0.70
10mpi-omp-iLIBLINEAR-B-3	3.32	0.55	**0.41**

Table 5: SMVs training time (minute) on ILSVRC 2010.

Method	# OpenMP threads 1	8	16
LIBLINEAR	3126.78		
LIBLINEAR-CDBLOCK-B-8	1917.37		
LIBLINEAR-CDBLOCK-B-24	2533.33		
omp-LIBLINEAR-B-8	1287.27	164.32	134.22
omp-LIBLINEAR-B-24	1716.00	238.42	202.17
omp-iLIBLINEAR-B-8	174.12	22.85	15.12
omp-iLIBLINEAR-B-24	210.22	29.82	23.42
5mpi-omp-iLIBLINEAR-B-8	38.14	5.10	3.96
10mpi-omp-iLIBLINEAR-B-8	23.89	3.22	**2.62**

As shown in Table 6, on medium dataset ImageNet 100, iLIBLINEAR-B (4GB) is 1.74% worse than LIBLINEAR-CDBLOCK-B (4GB) in terms of classification accuracy. However, on large dataset ILSVRC 2010, the classification accuracy obtained by iLIBLINEAR-B (4GB) is nearly the same as LIBLINEAR-CDBLOCK-B (4GB) (it is 0.89% worse than the original implementation). This result shows that our balanced bagging algorithm is very useful when one wants to speedup the training process of classifiers on large scale datasets without (or very few) compromising classification accuracy.

6. Conclusion and future work

In this paper, we have developed the extended versions of LIBLINEAR-CDBLOCK in three ways: (1) develop multi-class classification for LIBLINEAR-CDBLOCK by using the one-versus-all approach, (2) a balanced bagging

Table 6: Overall classification accuracy (%).

Method	ImageNet 100	ILSVRC 2010
LIBLINEAR	43.17	21.11
LIBLINEAR-CDBLOCK-B (4GB)	44.19	19.99
LIBLINEAR-CDBLOCK-B (2GB)	44.10	18.12
LIBLINEAR-B (4GB)	42.78	19.15
LIBLINEAR-B (2GB)	41.80	18.17
iLIBLINEAR-B (4GB)	42.45	19.10
iLIBLINEAR-B (2GB)	41.46	18.12

algorithm for training binary classifiers, (3) parallelize the training process of these classifiers with several multi-core computers. Our approach has been evaluated on the 100 largest classses of ImageNet and ILSVRC 2010. The experiment shows that our implementation is 732 times faster than the original implementation and 1193 times faster than LIBLINEAR with 160 cores. We need only 2.62 minutes to train 1K binary classifiers. Furthermore, our approach can be easily applied to dataset larger than the memory capacity of computer. Obviously, this is a roadmap towards large scale visual classification for systems with limited individual resource. The next step is to perform incremental LIBLINEAR on 10K classes of ImageNet. With this large dataset, the training data would be much larger than the capacity of many existing HPC systems.

Acknowledgements. This work was partially funded by Region Bretagne (France).

References

[1] F.-F. Li, R. Fergus, and P. Perona, "Learning generative visual models from few training examples: An incremental bayesian approach tested on 101 object categories," *Computer Vision and Image Understanding*, vol. 106, no. 1, pp. 59–70, 2007.

[2] G. Griffin, A. Holub, and P. Perona, "Caltech-256 Object Category Dataset," California Institute of Technology, Tech. Rep. CNS-TR-2007-001, 2007. [Online]. Available: http://authors.library.caltech.edu/7694

[3] M. Everingham, L. Van Gool, C. K. I. Williams, J. Winn, and A. Zisserman, "The pascal visual object classes (voc) challenge," *International Journal of Computer Vision*, vol. 88, no. 2, pp. 303–338, jun 2010.

[4] J. Deng, W. Dong, R. Socher, L.-J. Li, K. Li, and F.-F. Li, "Imagenet: A large-scale hierarchical image database," in *IEEE Computer Society Conference on Computer Vision and Pattern Recognition*, 2009, pp. 248–255.

[5] J. Deng, A. C. Berg, K. Li, and F.-F. Li, "What does classifying more than 10, 000 image categories tell us?" in *European Conference on Computer Vision*, 2010, pp. 71–84.

[6] Y. Lin, F. Lv, S. Zhu, M. Yang, T. Cour, K. Yu, L. Cao, and T. S. Huang, "Large-scale image classification: Fast feature extraction and svm training," in *IEEE Computer Society Conference on Computer Vision and Pattern Recognition*, 2011, pp. 1689–1696.

[7] C.-J. Hsieh, K.-W. Chang, C.-J. Lin, S. S. Keerthi, and S. Sundararajan, "A dual coordinate descent method for large-scale linear svm," in *International Conference on Machine Learning*, 2008, pp. 408–415.

[8] H.-F. Yu, C.-J. Hsieh, K.-W. Chang, and C.-J. Lin, "Large linear classification when data cannot fit in memory," *ACM Transactions on Knowledge Discovery from Data*, vol. 5, no. 4, p. 23, 2012.

[9] A. Berg, J. Deng, and F.-F. Li, "Large scale visual recognition challenge 2010," Tech. Rep., 2010. [Online]. Available: http://www.image-net.org/challenges/LSVRC/2010/index

[10] G. Csurka, C. R. Dance, L. Fan, J. Willamowski, and C. Bray, "Visual categorization with bags of keypoints," in *In Workshop on Statistical Learning in Computer Vision, ECCV*, 2004, pp. 1–22.

[11] V. Vapnik, *The Nature of Statistical Learning Theory*. Springer-Verlag, 1995.

[12] S. Lazebnik, C. Schmid, and J. Ponce, "Beyond bags of features: Spatial pyramid matching for recognizing natural scene categories," in *IEEE Computer Society Conference on Computer Vision and Pattern Recognition*, 2006, pp. 2169–2178.

[13] N. Dalal and B. Triggs, "Histograms of oriented gradients for human detection," in *IEEE Computer Society Conference on Computer Vision and Pattern Recognition*. IEEE Computer Society, 2005, pp. 886–893.

[14] G. Griffin and D. Perona, "Learning and using taxonomies for fast visual categorization," in *IEEE Computer Society Conference on Computer Vision and Pattern Recognition*. IEEE Computer Society, 2008.

[15] A. Vedaldi, V. Gulshan, M. Varma, and A. Zisserman, "Multiple kernels for object detection," in *IEEE 12th International Conference on Computer Vision*. IEEE, 2009, pp. 606–613.

[16] R. Fergus, Y. Weiss, and A. Torralba, "Semi-supervised learning in gigantic image collections," in *Advances in Neural Information Processing Systems*, 2009, pp. 522–530.

[17] C. Wang, S. Yan, and H.-J. Zhang, "Large scale natural image classification by sparsity exploration," in *Proceedings of the IEEE International Conference on Acoustics, Speech, and Signal Processing*. IEEE, 2009, pp. 3709–3712.

[18] Y. Li, D. J. Crandall, and D. P. Huttenlocher, "Landmark classification in large-scale image collections," in *IEEE 12th International Conference on Computer Vision*. IEEE, 2009, pp. 1957–1964.

[19] F. Perronnin, J. Sánchez, and Y. Liu, "Large-scale image categorization with explicit data embedding," in *CVPR*, 2010, pp. 2297–2304.

[20] J. Sánchez and F. Perronnin, "High-dimensional signature compression for large-scale image classification," in *IEEE Computer Society Conference on Computer Vision and Pattern Recognition*, 2011, pp. 1665–1672.

[21] K. Yu, T. Zhang, and Y. Gong, "Nonlinear learning using local coordinate coding," in *Advances in Neural Information Processing Systems*, 2009, pp. 2223–2231.

[22] X. Zhou, K. Yu, T. Zhang, and T. S. Huang, "Image classification using super-vector coding of local image descriptors," in *European Conference on Computer Vision*, 2010, pp. 141–154.

[23] C. C. Chang and C. J. Lin, "LIBSVM – a library for support vector machines," 2001, http://www.csie.ntu.edu.tw/$\sim$cjlin/libsvm.

[24] T. Joachims, "Training linear svms in linear time," in *proc. of the ACM SIGKDD Intl. Conf. on KDD*. ACM, 2006, pp. 217–226.

[25] T.-N. Do, V.-H. Nguyen, and F. Poulet, "Speed up svm algorithm for massive classification tasks," in *ADMA*, 2008, pp. 147–157.

[26] J. Weston and C. Watkins, "Support vector machines for multi-class pattern recognition," in *Proceedings of the Seventh European Symposium on Artificial Neural Networks*, 1999, pp. 219–224.

[27] Y. Guermeur, "Svm multiclasses, théorie et applications," 2007.

[28] U. Krebel, "Pairwise classification and support vector machines," *Advances in Kernel Methods: Support Vector Learning*, pp. 255–268, 1999.

[29] J. Platt, N. Cristianini, and J. Shawe-Taylor, "Large margin dags for multiclass classification," *Advances in Neural Information Processing Systems*, vol. 12, pp. 547–553, 2000.

[30] V. Vural and J. Dy, "A hierarchical method for multi-class support vector machines," in *Proceedings of the twenty-first international conference on Machine learning*, 2004, pp. 831–838.

[31] K. Benabdeslem and Y. Bennani, "Dendogram-based svm for multi-class classification," *Journal of Computing and Information Technology*, vol. 14, no. 4, pp. 283–289, 2006.

[32] K. Crammer and Y. Singer, "On the learnability and design of output codes for multiclass problems," *Machine Learning*, vol. 47, no. 2-3, pp. 201–233, 2002.

[33] N. Japkowicz, Ed., *AAAI'Workshop on Learning from Imbalanced Data Sets*, ser. AAAI Tech Report, no. WS-00-05, 2000.

[34] S. Visa and A. Ralescu, "Issues in mining imbalanced data sets - A review paper," in *Midwest Artificial Intelligence and Cognitive Science Conf.*, Dayton, USA, 2005, pp. 67–73.

[35] P. Lenca, S. Lallich, T. N. Do, and N. K. Pham, "A comparison of different off-centered entropies to deal with class imbalance for decision trees," in *The Pacific-Asia Conference on Knowledge Discovery and Data Mining, LNAI 5012*. Springer-Verlag, 2008, pp. 634–643.

[36] N. K. Pham, T. N. Do, P. Lenca, and S. Lallich, "Using local node information in decision trees: coupling a local decision rule with an off-centered entropy," in *International Conference on Data Mining*. Las Vegas, Nevada, USA: CSREA Press, 2008, pp. 117–123.

[37] MPI-Forum, "Mpi: A message-passing interface standard," 1995. [Online]. Available: http://www.mpi-forum.org

[38] OpenMP Architecture Review Board, "OpenMP application program interface version 3.0," 2008. [Online]. Available: \url{http://www.openmp.org/mp-documents/spec30.pdf}

[39] J. Wu, W.-C. Tan, and J. M. Rehg, "Efficient and effective visual codebook generation using additive kernels," *Journal of Machine Learning Research*, vol. 12, pp. 3097–3118, 2011.

[40] D. G. Lowe, "Distinctive image features from scale-invariant keypoints," *International Journal of Computer Vision*, vol. 60, no. 2, pp. 91–110, 2004.

Gaussian Process Regression with Dynamic Active Set and Its Application to Anomaly Detection

Toshikazu Wada [1], Yuki Matsumura [1], Shunji Maeda [2], and Hisae Shibuya [3]
[1] Faculty of Systems Engineering, Wakayama University, 930 Sakaedani, Wakayama, 640-8510 Japan
[2] Hiroshima Institute of Technology, 2-1-1 Miyake, Saeki-ku, Hiroshima, 731-5193 Japan
[3] Yokohama Research Laboratory, Hitachi Ltd., 292 Yoshida-cho, Totsuka-ku, Yokohama, 244-0817 Japan

Abstract - *Gaussian Process Regression (GPR) can be defined as a linear regression in high-dimensional space, where low-dimensional input vectors are projected by a non-linear high-dimensional mapping. Same as other kernel based methods, kernel function is introduced instead of computing the mapping directly. This regression can be regarded as an example based regression by identifying the kernel function with the similarity measure of two vectors. Based on this interpretation, we show that GPR can be accelerated and its memory consumption can be reduced while keeping the accuracy by dynamically forming the active set depending on the given input vector, where active set is the set of examples used for the regression. We call this method Dynamic Active Set (DAS). Based on DAS, we can extend the standard GPR, which estimates a scalar output with variance, to a regression method to estimate multidimensional output with covariance matrix. We applied our method to anomaly detection on real power plant and confirmed that it can detect prefault phenomena four days before actual fault alarm.*

Keywords: Gaussian Process Regression, Example based non-linear regression, Dynamic Active Set, covariance matrix estimation

1 Introduction

Gaussian Process Regression (GPR)[1][2][3] is a well-known non-linear regression method defined as a linear regression in high-dimensional space, where input vectors are projected by a non-linear high-dimensional mapping. Same as other kernel based methods, kernel function is introduced instead of computing the mapping directly.

Unlike the interpretation above, this paper shows another interpretation that GPR can be taken as an example based regression method, where each example consists of two components: input vector and output value. That is, output component of each example is simply weighted by the similarity value between a given input and input vector component of the example, and by summing up them, the output is estimated. Through this interpretation, kernel function is regarded as a similarity function between two vectors. For guaranteeing that input-output relationships in the examples are exactly kept in the regression, a normalization using inverse of gram-matrix is applied.

Based on this notion, we can reduce the size of active set consisting of examples to be used for regression, because only the examples with similar input components with the given input are dominant for output estimation. One contribution of this paper is to form active set dynamically depending on the given input. We call this method Dynamic Active Set (DAS). DAS drastically reduces the computational complexity and the memory consumption of GPR while keeping the accuracy of output.

DAS also breaks the limitation, shared by standard GPR, that only a scalar output and its variance can be estimated. According to the formulae, estimating the vector outputs in the framework of GPR is not a difficult problem. However, the covariance matrix estimation cannot be realized only by simple formula manipulation. Based on the notion above that output value is estimated as a weighted sum of the outputs examples, we propose a method to estimate covariant matrix from the output vectors in the active set with the same weight.

In the following sections, we first show the related works and the interpretation that GPR can be taken as a similarity weighted example based regression. Next, we introduce dynamic active set formation. Then, multivariate extension of GPR is proposed. In the experiments, we applied the resulted method, i.e. DAS based multivariate GPR, to anomaly detection problems and confirmed its efficiency and effectiveness.

2 Related Works

In this section, we first introduce the framework of GPR, and briefly explain some works on improving the computational cost and the memory consumption.

2.1 Gaussian Process Regression

In many literatures, Gaussian Process Regression is explained as a linear regression in a high-dimensional space where input vectors are projected by a non-linear mapping $\boldsymbol{\varphi}(\boldsymbol{x})$.

$$y(\boldsymbol{x}) = \boldsymbol{w}^T \boldsymbol{\varphi}(\boldsymbol{x}), \tag{1}$$

where $\boldsymbol{w}$ represents the coefficient vector obeying mean $\boldsymbol{0}$ isotropic covariance matrix $\sigma^2 I$ Gaussian. That is,

$$\boldsymbol{w} \propto N(\boldsymbol{0}, \sigma^2 I). \tag{2}$$

Providing N projected inputs: $\Phi = (\boldsymbol{\varphi}(\boldsymbol{x}_1) \ \cdots \ \boldsymbol{\varphi}(\boldsymbol{x}_N))^T$, and no information specifying the coefficient vector $\boldsymbol{w}$ is provided, the corresponding outputs: $\boldsymbol{y} = (y_1 \ \cdots \ y_N)^T$ can be represented as

$$\boldsymbol{y} = \Phi \boldsymbol{w}. \tag{3}$$

The distribution of $\boldsymbol{y}$ is also a Gaussian as shown below.

$$E[\boldsymbol{y}] = \Phi E[\boldsymbol{w}] = \boldsymbol{0}, \tag{4}$$

$$cov[\boldsymbol{y}] = E[\boldsymbol{y}\boldsymbol{y}^T] = \Phi E[\boldsymbol{w}\boldsymbol{w}^T]\Phi^T = \sigma^2\Phi\Phi^T = K, \quad (5)$$

where K represents gram matrix consisting of kernel functions between input vectors. That is, a kernel function $k(\boldsymbol{x}_n, \boldsymbol{x}_m)$ represents scalar product $\sigma^2\boldsymbol{\varphi}^T(\boldsymbol{x}_n)\boldsymbol{\varphi}(\boldsymbol{x}_m)$. That is,

$$\boldsymbol{y} \propto N(\boldsymbol{0}, K). \quad (6)$$

When training samples, information on the coefficient vector $\boldsymbol{w}$ is provided, and the estimation will be biased. Providing input-output training data $(\boldsymbol{x}_1, t_1), \cdots, (\boldsymbol{x}_N, t_N)$ consisting of input vector $\boldsymbol{x}_i$ and corresponding output scalar value t_i, the output mean and variance for input $\boldsymbol{x}$ are represented as below.

$$\mu_{GP}(\boldsymbol{x}) = \boldsymbol{k}^T(\boldsymbol{x})K^{-1}\boldsymbol{t}, \quad (7)$$

$$\sigma_{GP}^2(\boldsymbol{x}) = k(\boldsymbol{x}, \boldsymbol{x}) - \boldsymbol{k}^T(\boldsymbol{x})K^{-1}\boldsymbol{k}(\boldsymbol{x}), \quad (8)$$

where $\boldsymbol{t} = (t_1 \quad \cdots \quad t_N)^T$, $\boldsymbol{k}(\boldsymbol{x}) = (k(\boldsymbol{x}_1, \boldsymbol{x}), \ldots, k(\boldsymbol{x}_N, \boldsymbol{x}))^T$, $K = [k(\boldsymbol{x}_n, \boldsymbol{x}_m)]$.

In practice, training data may contain errors like

$$t_n = y_n + \varepsilon_n. \quad (9)$$

Here we assume that the error ε_n is a mean $\boldsymbol{0}$ variance β^2 Gaussian, which is independent of y_n. In this case, we need small modifications: redefine $K = [k(\boldsymbol{x}_n, \boldsymbol{x}_m) + \beta^2]$, and replace Equation (8) by

$$\sigma_{GP}^2(\boldsymbol{x}) = k(\boldsymbol{x}, \boldsymbol{x}) + \beta^2 - \boldsymbol{k}^T(\boldsymbol{x})K^{-1}\boldsymbol{k}(\boldsymbol{x}). \quad (10)$$

Same as other kernel based methods, kernel function can be selected from wide varieties of functions satisfying Mercer's condition. One widely used example is the RBF kernel shown below.

$$k(\boldsymbol{x}_n, \boldsymbol{x}_m) = \exp\left(\frac{-\|\boldsymbol{x}_n - \boldsymbol{x}_m\|^2}{\sigma_h^2}\right). \quad (11)$$

2.2 Fast and Memory Efficient GPRs

The dominant computation for the estimation is to compute K^{-1}. Its computational complexity is $O(N^3)$, and the spatial complexity to store the gram matrix K is $O(N^2)$. For the accuracy, the bigger N is the better, but smaller N is preferable for real-time applications.

For solving this problem, the following methods have been proposed [3].

1. Subset of regressors[4][5]: Pick up M examples out of active set consisting of N examples, and use the following approximations.

$$\mu_{SR}(\boldsymbol{x}) = \boldsymbol{k}_M^T(\boldsymbol{x})(K_{NM}K_{MN} + \beta^2 K_{MM})^{-1}K_{MN}\boldsymbol{t}, \quad (12)$$

$$\sigma_{SR}^2(\boldsymbol{x}) = \beta^2\boldsymbol{k}_M^T(\boldsymbol{x})(K_{NM}K_{MN} + \beta^2 K_{MM})^{-1}\boldsymbol{k}_M(\boldsymbol{x}), \quad (13)$$

where K_{NM}, K_{MN}, and K_{MM} represent $M \times N$, $N \times M$, and $M \times M$ gram matrices, respectively. $\boldsymbol{k}_M(\boldsymbol{x})$ represents a vector consisting of kernel functions between $\boldsymbol{x}$ and picked up M input examples.

2. The Nyström Method[6]: Pick up M examples, and approximate gram matrix by

$$\tilde{K} = K_{NM}K_{MM}^{-1}K_{MN}. \quad (14)$$

3. Subset of Datapoints: Pick up M examples, and simply approximate the gram matrix by K_{MM}.
4. Projected Process Approximation: Pick up M examples, and approximate the mean by equation (12) and variance by

$$\sigma_{PA}^2(\boldsymbol{x}) = k(\boldsymbol{x}, \boldsymbol{x}) - \boldsymbol{k}_M^T(\boldsymbol{x})K_{MM}^{-1}\boldsymbol{k}_M(\boldsymbol{x}) + \beta^2\boldsymbol{k}_M^T(\boldsymbol{x})(K_{MN}K_{NM} + \beta^2 K_{MM})^{-1}\boldsymbol{k}_M(\boldsymbol{x}). \quad (15)$$

5. Bayesian Committee Machine[7]: Partition the dataset into p subsets and estimate outputs and variances at multiple test points.
6. Iterative Solution of Linear Systems[8] : An acceleration using iterative conjugate gradient method.

Methods 1,2,3,4 requires the reduction of examples from N to M, which is done by random selection or greedy algorithm described in Algorithm1.

```
Input: M desired size of active set
Initialization: D := ∅, R = {1,⋯,N}
for j := 1 to M
    Create working set J ⊆ R
    Compute Δ_j for all j ∈ J
    i := arg max_{j∈J} Δ_j
    D := D ∪ {i}, R := R\{i}
endfor
return D
```

Algorithm1: Greedy algorithm to reduce the size of active set (extracted from [3] and modified.)

The big problem arose here is the computational cost of Δ_j, which represents the gain obtained by adding $\boldsymbol{x}_j$ into the active set $\mathcal{D}$. Foregoing researches propose *differential entropy score*[9], *information gain criterion*[10], as Δ_j. All of their computational costs are expensive, because the measure Δ_j is evaluated over all potential inputs.

Our idea is if the active set $\mathcal{D}$ is dynamically formed depending on a specific input $\boldsymbol{x}$, the measure $\Delta_j(\boldsymbol{x})$ can be more simple and $\mathcal{D}(\boldsymbol{x})$ is easily obtained.

3 GPR with Dynamic Active Set

This section presents our method that reduces the computational cost while keeping the accuracy and extends scalar output to vector output with covariance matrix.

3.1 GPR as a similarity weighted example based regression

$k^T(x)K^{-1}$ in Equation (7) can be regarded as a weight vector to the output examples $t = (t_1 \ \cdots \ t_N)^T$ (See Fig. 1).
From the viewpoint of similarity, the output for input x can be roughly estimated just by $k^T(x)t = \sum_{i=1}^{N} k(x, x_i)t_i$, because of the following facts.

If we regard $k(x, y)$ as a similarity measure between x and y, we can assume

$$k(x, x) \geq k(x, y). \quad (16)$$

Then the weight $k(x, x_i)$ is maximized at $x = x_i$, i.e., the weight of output example t_i is maximized at $x = x_i$.
However, this formulation does not keep the input-output relationship in the examples. That is, $k^T(x_i)t \neq t_i$, $(i = 1, \cdots, N)$.

For guaranteeing the input-output relationship, the weight vector for the input x_i should be

$$\delta_i = (\underbrace{0 \ \cdots \ 0}_{i-1} \ 1 \ \underbrace{0 \ \cdots \ 0}_{N-i})^T, \quad (17)$$

because $\delta_i^T x_i = t_i$, $(i = 1, \cdots, N)$.
We can show that $k^T(x_i)K^{-1} = \delta_i^T$ as follows.

For full rank gram matrix K,

$$KK^{-1} = I \quad (18)$$

always stands. By multiplying δ_i^T with both sides of Equation (13), we get

$$\delta_i^T KK^{-1} = k^T(x_i)K^{-1} = \delta_i^T. \quad (19)$$

For preserving the input-output relationship, $k^T(x)K^{-1}$ is the ideal weight vector at least for x_i.
Almost the same mathematical formula can be found in the works by S.W. Wegerich[11][12][13]in the context of anomaly detection. This method is called similarity based modeling (SBM). This method is almost the same as GPR except the following properties.

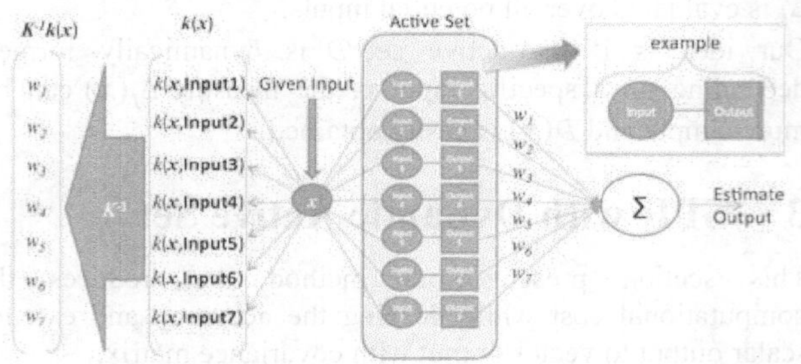

Fig. 1. An interpretation of GPR mean estimation

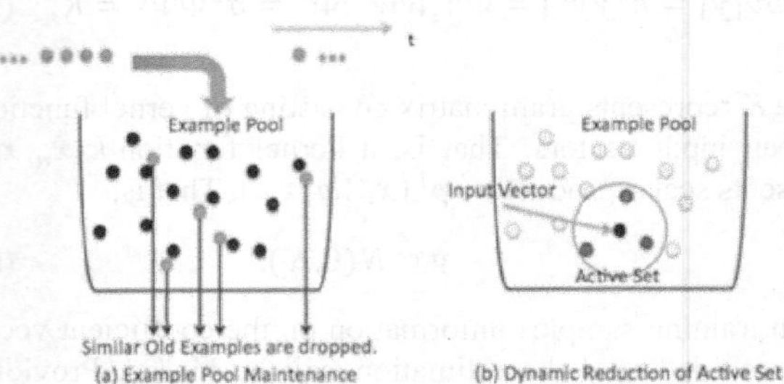

Fig. 2. Example pool and active set formation: (a) Excluding similar examples from the pool (b) Dynamic active set formation

- SBM can estimate vector values, but standard GPR can't.
- GPR can estimate output variance, but SBM can't.
- SBM normalizes the weight vector so that the sum equals to 1, but GPR doesn't.

Our question is whether the kernel function $k(x, x_i)$ can be an importance measure of x_i for estimating the output and variance for x or not. For the input $x = x_i$, the i-th components of $k(x)$ and $k^T(x)K^{-1}$ are the biggest as shown above. This implies that $k(x, x_i)$ can be an importance measure of x_i when $x \in \{x_j\}$.
The remaining question is: when an input example x_i is the nearest to the given input x, still the i-th component of $k^T(x)K^{-1}$ is the biggest or not? For answering the question, we introduce the assumption that the kernel function satisfies

$$k(x, y) \geq 0, \quad (20)$$

for any x and y. Under this assumption, the components in the vector $k(x) = (k(x, x_1) \ \cdots \ k(x, x_N))^T$ dissimilar with x will be close to zero. For such dissimilar input examples x_i, the corresponding weight w_i will be closer to zero, where $k^T(x)K^{-1} = (w_1 \ \cdots \ w_N)$.
As a consequence of above discussion, for kernel functions satisfying Inequalities (16) and (20), it is clear that kernel function can be used as Δ_j. That is,

$$\Delta_j(x) = k(x, x_j). \quad (21)$$

Note that the most distinguishing point from other Δ_j s, Equation (21) has an argument. This implies that the importance of an example cannot be defined apart from the given input x.

3.2 Dynamic Active Set

By using Equation (21), we can dynamically select an active set depending on the input x by gathering the examples x_i having bigger $k(x, x_i)$. Suppose that N and M are the sizes of all examples and reduced active set, we have to compute N kernel functions before the reduction and the computational complexity for computing inverse of gram matrix is $O(M^3)$. The advantage of this method is the computational cost of kernel function is much cheaper than *differential entropy score* or *information gain criterion*. Further, since $N \ll M^3$ stands in many practical problems, the total computational complexity including active set formation can be approximated by $O(M^3)$.

One thing we have to avoid is to include almost the same examples in the active set. If $\boldsymbol{x}_i = \boldsymbol{x}_j$, $k(\boldsymbol{x}_k, \boldsymbol{x}_j) = k(\boldsymbol{x}_k, \boldsymbol{x}_i)$ stands for all $\boldsymbol{x}_k$ in the active set. This means *i-th* and *j-th* row and columns in the gram matrix are the same, hence the gram matrix is singular and its inverse cannot be obtained. For avoiding this case, we introduce example pool that excludes almost the similar example.

For time series data, new examples are sequentially injected to the pool. When the kernel function between the injected data and an example in the pool exceeds the given threshold, the example in the pool is dropped and the injected data is stored in the pool as shown in Fig. 2. This pooling mechanism is intended to refer newer examples for representing recent trend.

The above pooling mechanism is an example design, but the most important function of the example pool is to exclude the similar data for stable computation of the gram matrix inverse.

3.3 Multivariate GPR

The extension of GPR to estimate vector output is very simple. By replacing the output example vector $\boldsymbol{t} = (t_1 \ \cdots \ t_N)^T$ in Equation (7) or (12) by matrix consisting of vector output examples $T = (\boldsymbol{t}_1 \ \cdots \ \boldsymbol{t}_N)^T$, the expected vector output can be estimated. However, in this case, we have to estimate the covariance matrix. Unfortunately, Equation (8), (10), (13), or (15) cannot simply be extended to estimate covariance matrix. The essential difficulty lies in estimating the covariance among the outputs.

The advantage of our method DAS is that we can reduce the input-output examples depending on the given input $\boldsymbol{x}$ and their weight vectors are computed as $\boldsymbol{k}^T(\boldsymbol{x})K^{-1} = (w_1 \ \cdots \ w_M)$. These fact implies a simple covariance matrix estimation: Suppose that $(\boldsymbol{x}_1 \ \cdots \ \boldsymbol{x}_M)$, $(\boldsymbol{t}_1 \ \cdots \ \boldsymbol{t}_M)$, $(w_1 \ \cdots \ w_M)$ are the reduced input examples, output examples, and weight values for given input $\boldsymbol{x}$. Then the output $\boldsymbol{\mu}$ and its covariance matrix Σ can be estimated as

$$\boldsymbol{\mu} = \frac{1}{\sum_{i=1}^{M} w_i} \sum_{i=1}^{M} w_i \boldsymbol{t}_i, \tag{22}$$

$$\Sigma = \frac{1}{\sum_{i=1}^{M} w_i} \sum_{i=1}^{M} w_i (\boldsymbol{t}_i - \boldsymbol{\mu})(\boldsymbol{t}_i - \boldsymbol{\mu})^T. \tag{23}$$

For those inputs same with one of the stored input components $\boldsymbol{x}_i$, $(i = 1, \cdots, M)$, $\sum_{i=1}^{M} w_i = 1$ automatically stands, because the weight vector will be $\boldsymbol{\delta}_i$. This means that the Equation (22) is essentially equivalent to Equation (7). This implies that the above equations are not far from the principle of GPR.

From these equations, since we can estimate the output vector and its covariance matrix, we can measure the Mahalanobis distance of the observed output from the expected output. This can be an anomaly measure of a system.

4 Experiments

In this section, we first show how DAS improves computational time while keeping the accuracy. Next, we examine the validity of the vector output and covariance estimation property by using 2D swiss roll data. Finally, our method is applied to an anomaly detection problem of a power plant, which is practically used in real world and stopped because of a fault. Among the sensor values attached to this plant, we picked up two sensor values and compared the sensitivities of the Mahalanobis distances for independent sensors and simultaneous analysis as 2D sensor values.

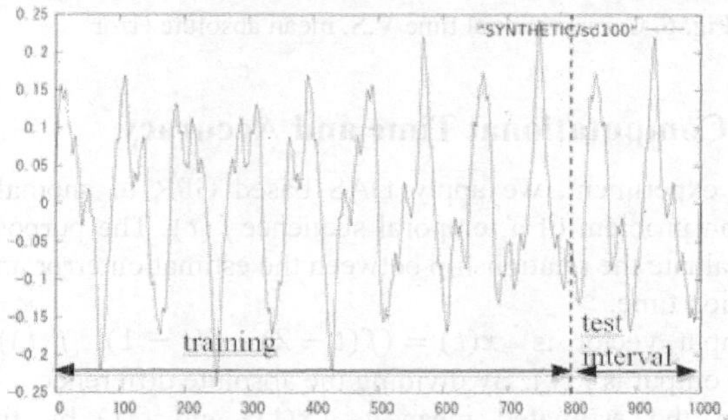

Fig. 3. Training and test intervals assigned on the artificial data [14]

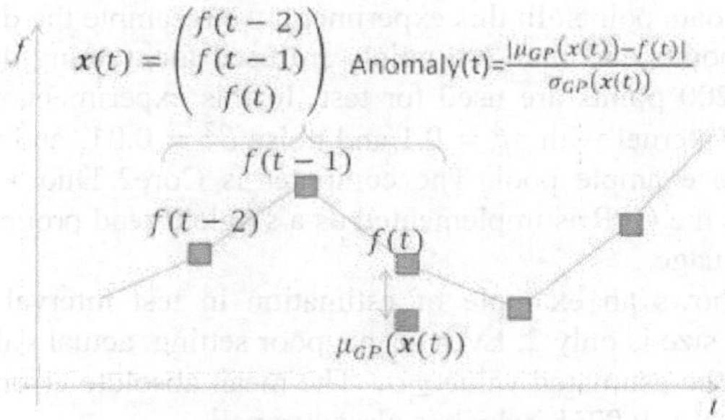

Fig. 4. Input-output assignment and anomaly measure.

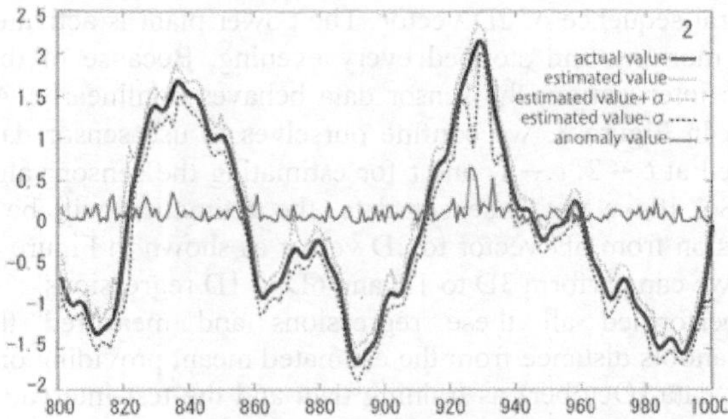

Fig. 5. Actual value, estimated value, estimated value ±σ, and anomaly value in test interval (Active set size = 2).

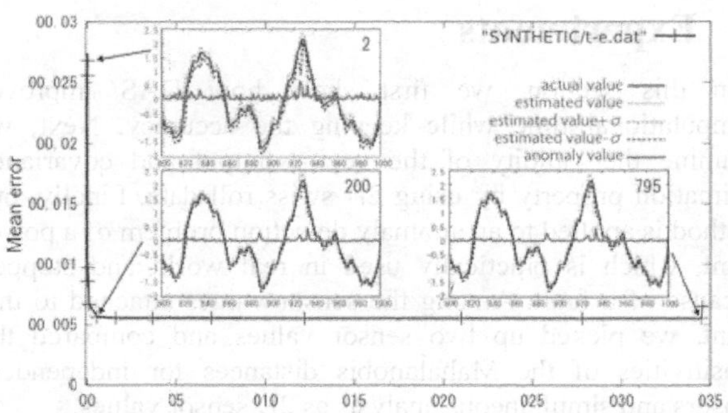

Fig. 6. Computational time V.S. mean absolute error

4.1 Computational Time and Accuracy

In this experiment, we apply DAS based GPR to anomaly detection problem of a temporal sequence $f(t)$. The purpose is to evaluate the relationship between the estimation error and estimation time.

The input vector is $\boldsymbol{x}(t) = (f(t-2) \quad f(t-1) \quad f(t))^T$ and the output is $f(t)$. By dividing the absolute difference between the estimated mean $\mu_{GP}(\boldsymbol{x}(t))$ and $f(t)$ by the estimated standard deviation $\sigma_{GP}(\boldsymbol{x}(t))$, we obtain the anomaly measure.

The sequence data is an artificially generated that was used in waveform retrieval research[14]. The original data consists of 10000 data points. In this experiment, we resample the data to 1000 points and first 800 points are used for training data and last 200 points are used for test. In this experiment, we used RBF kernel with $\sigma_h^2 = 0.1$ and noise $\beta^2 = 0.01$, and we didn't use example pool. The computer is Core2 Duo 1.86 GHz, and the GPR is implemented as a single thread program by C language.

Fig.5 shows an example of estimation in test interval at active set size is only 2. Even at this poor setting, actual value is within the estimated value $\pm\sigma$. The mean absolute error in this interval is 0.0268, which is already small.

Finally, we applied our multivariate GPR to a real power plant data. In this experiment, we used two sensor data. Both are sampled every 30 seconds. We take these sensor data as a temporal sequence of 2D vector. The power plant is activated every morning and stopped every evening. Because of this human intervention, the sensor data behaves nonlinearly. As shown in Figure 3, we confine ourselves to use sensor data sampled at $t-2$, $t-1$, and t for estimating the sensor value at t. So, if we use 2 sensor data, the estimation will be a regression from 6D vector to 2D vector as shown in Figure 8. Also, we can perform 3D to 1D and 6D to 1D regressions.

We performed all these regressions and measured the Mahalanobis distance from the estimated mean, providing one month data (October) as training data and the test interval is November 1-10, where embedded alarm system detected the fault during November 8-10.

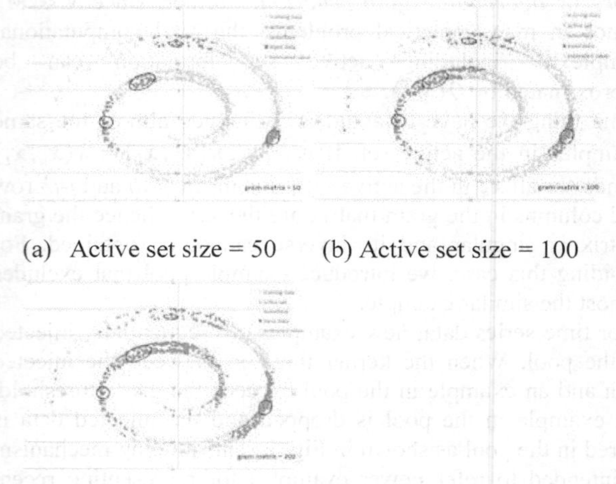

(a) Active set size = 50 (b) Active set size = 100

(c) Active set size = 200

Fig. 7. From 2D to 2D regression results on swiss roll data with Mahalanobis distance = 9 ellipses. Red brown points represent active sets

The results are shown in Figures 9-11. According to these results, prefault phenomenon seems occured from November Fig. 7 shows the results of ellipses whose Mahalanobis distances are all 9, which means . The active set size is changed 50, 100, and 200. From these plots, we can confirm that the ellipses fit the local point distributions representing local covariance, and the ellipses are almost insensitive to the active set size.

4 to 7, four days earlier than the actual alarm. Compared with the 3D→1D and 6D→1D results, 6D→2D regression provides us the clearest result.

One may think that Figure 9 (b) captures the prefault phenomenon like Figure 11. However, other 3D→1D and 6D→1D regressions are not congruent with each other. This means that only by Figure 9 (b), one cannot conclude that prefault is detected during November 4-7. On the other hand, Figure 11 is an integrated result of two sequences, and the Mahalanobis distance becomes bigger from November 4. Then one can notice something unusual phenomenon happening. These facts supports the superiority of our multivariate regression and anomaly detection.

By increasing the active set size, the computational time may increase but the mean absolute error will decrease. Fig. 6 shows the result.

This "L" shaped plot shows that the mean error is saturated at active set size greater than 200. It means we can accelerate the estimation speed almost 65 times faster in this case while keeping the accuracy. This is the effectiveness of DAS.

In this plot, we can also find that the mean absolute error increases at active set size bigger than 795. This is because the singularity of gram matrix caused by similar example inclusion.

4.2 Multivariate Regression

For testing the validity of our multivariate regression method defined in Equation (22) and (23), here we show some simple regression result.

In this experiment, we use 2D swiss-roll data and the input and the output examples are assigned to the same 2D data. We used RBF kernel with $\sigma_h^2 = 0.1$ and noise $\beta^2 = 0.01$. The data points are sequentially added to the example pool and those data points in the pool having kernel function greater than the threshold 0.998 are excluded from the pool.

The purpose of this experiment is to draw equi-Mahalanobis distance ellipses while changing the size of active set to verify 1) the ellipses represent the local distribution, 2) the shape and position of the ellipse are insensitive to the active set size.

4.3 Anomaly Detection on a Power Plant Data

Finally, we applied our multivariate GPR to a real power plant data. In this experiment, we used two sensor data. Both are sampled every 30 seconds. We take these sensor data as a temporal sequence of 2D vector. The power plant is activated every morning and stopped every evening. Because of this human intervention, the sensor data behaves nonlinearly. As shown in Figure 3, we confine ourselves to use sensor data sampled at $t-2$, $t-1$, and t for estimating the sensor value at t. So, if we use 2 sensor data, the estimation will be a regression from 6D vector to 2D vector as shown in Figure 8. Also, we can perform 3D to 1D and 6D to 1D regressions.

We performed all these regressions and measured the Mahalanobis distance from the estimated mean, providing one month data (October) as training data and the test interval is November 1-10, where embedded alarm system detected the fault during November 8-10.

The results are shown in Figures 9-11. According to these results, prefault phenomenon seems occured from November 4 to 7, four days earlier than the actual alarm. Compared with the 3D→1D and 6D→1D results, 6D→2D regression provides us the clearest result.

One may think that Figure 9 (b) captures the prefault phenomenon like Figure 11. However, other 3D→1D and 6D→1D regressions are not congruent with each other. This means that only by Figure 9 (b), one cannot conclude that prefault is detected during November 4-7. On the other hand, Figure 11 is an integrated result of two sequences, and the Mahalanobis distance becomes bigger from November 4. Then one can notice something unusual phenomenon happening. These facts supports the superiority of our multivariate regression and anomaly detection.

5 Conclusions

In this paper, we first show an interpretation that GPR is a similarity-weighted example based regression. Based on this interpretation, we next propose a computationally effective GPR with dynamic active set (DAS), which forms the active set depending on given input.

DAS is useful not only for the computational effectiveness but also for covariance estimation when estimating vector output. In the experiments, we have shown the following facts.

- DAS accelerates the GPR and reduces the memory use drastically while keeping the accuracy.
- DAS based multivariate GPR can estimate the local distributions around the estimated mean.
- DAS based multivariate GPR drastically improves the sensitivity of the anomaly measure, i.e., Mahalanobis distance from the estimated mean value.

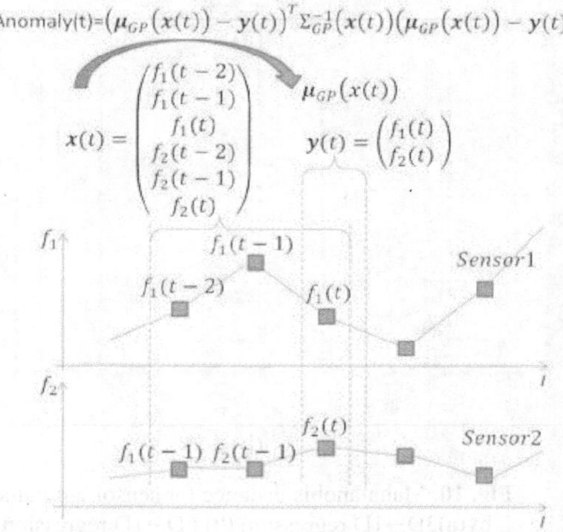

Fig. 8. Anomaly detection scheme for multiple sensor sequences.

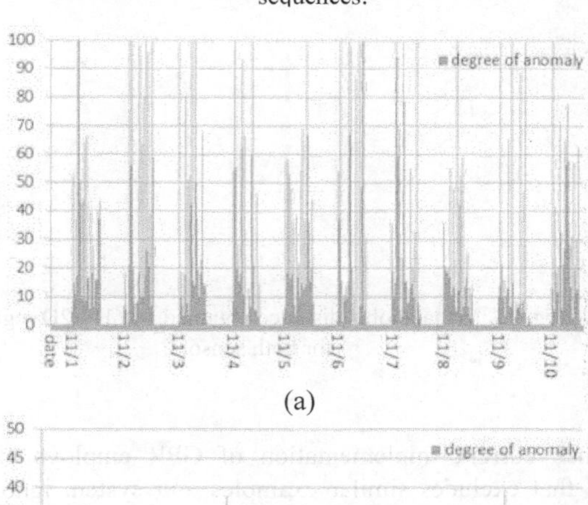

(a)

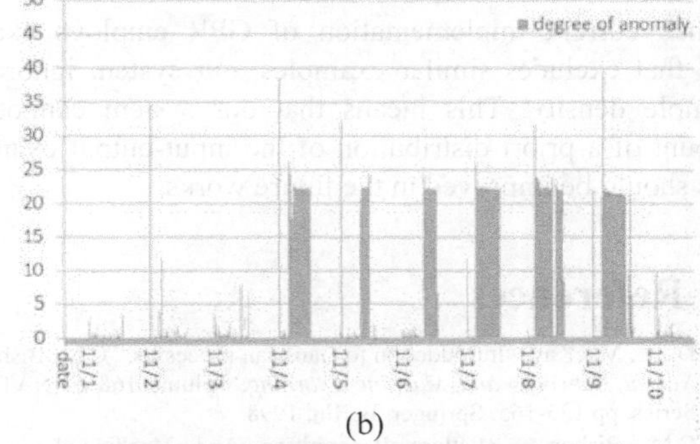

(b)

Fig. 9. Mahalanobis distance for sensor 1 obtained by(a)3D→1D regression (b) 6D→1D regression

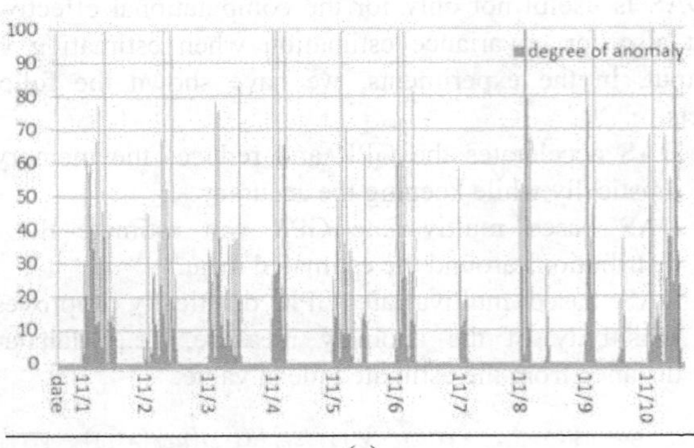

(a)

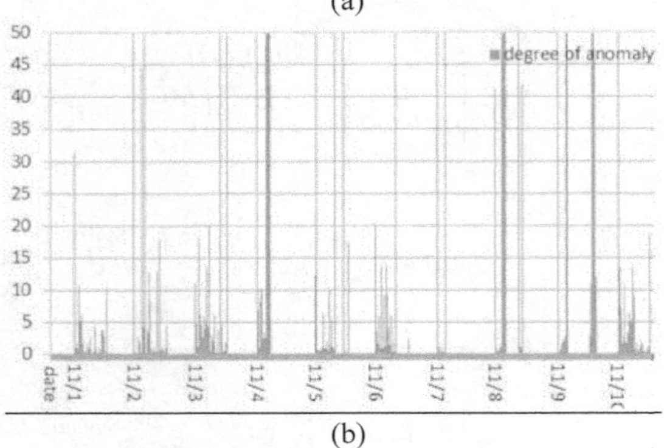

(b)

Fig. 10. Mahalanobis distance for sensor 2 obtained by(a)3D→1D regression (b) 6D→1D regression

•

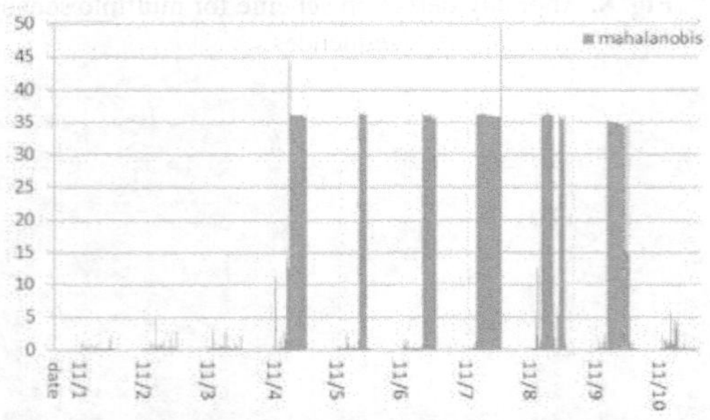

Fig. 11. Mahalanobis distance obtained by 6D→2D regression for both sensors.

Since current implementation of GPR employs example pool that excludes similar examples, our system ignores the example density. This means that our system cannot take account of a priori distribution of the input-output examples. This should be improved in the future works.

6 References

[1] D.J.C. MacKay, "Introduction to Gaussian processes," C.M. Bishop, ed., *Neural Networks and Machine Learning*, volume 168 of NATO ASI Series, pp.133-165, Springer, Berlin, 1998.

[2] C.M. Bishop, " Pattern Recognition And Machine Learning, " Springer-Verlag, Berlin, 2006

[3] C.E. Rasmussen, C.K.I. Williams, Gaussian Processes for Machine Learning, The MIT Press, Cambridge, MA, 2006.

[4] G. Wahba, "Spline Models for Observational Data," Society for Industrial and Applied Mathematics, Philadelphia, PA. CBMS-NSF Regional Conference series in applied mathematics, 1990

[5] T. Poggio, and F. Girosi, "Networks for Approximation and Learning," *Proceedings of IEEE*, Vol. 78, Issue 9, pp. 1481–1497, 1990

[6] C. K. I. Williams and M. Seeger, "Using the Nyström Method to Speed Up Kernel Machines," In Advances in Neural Information Processing Systems 13, eds. T. K. Leen, T. G. Diettrich, and V. Tresp, pp. 682–688. MIT Press. 2001

[7] V. Tresp, "A Bayesian Committee Machine," *Neural Computation*, Vol. 12, No. 11, pp. 2719–2741, 2000

[8] G. Wahba, D. R. Johnson, F. Gao, and J. Gong, "Adaptive Tuning of Numerical Weather Prediction Models: Randomized GCV in Three-and Four-Dimensional Data Assimilation," *Monthly Weather Review*, 123, pp. 3358–3369, 1995

[9] N. Lawrence, M. Seeger, and R. Herbrich, "Fast Sparse Gaussian Process Methods: The Informative Vector Machine," In Advances in Neural Information Processing Systems 15, eds. S. Becker, S. Thrun, and K. Obermayer, pp. 625–632. MIT Press, 2003

[10] M. Seeger, C. K. I. Williams, and N. Lawrence, "Fast Forward Selection to Speed Up Sparse Gaussian Process Regression," In *Proceedings of the Ninth International Workshop on Artificial Intelligence and Statistics*. Society for Artificial Intelligence and Statistics, 2003

[11] S.W. Wegerich, "Similarity based modeling of time synchronous averaged vibration signals for machinery health monitoring," *Proceedings of IEEE Aerospace Conference*, vol.6, no., pp. 3654- 3662 Vol.6, 6-13 March 2004.

[12] S.W. Wegerich, "Similarity-based modeling of vibration features for fault detection and identification", *Sensor Review*, Vol. 25 Iss: 2, pp.114-122, 2005.

[13] S.W. Wegerich, D.R. Bell, and X. Xu, "Adaptive modeling of changed states in predictive condition monitoring", US Pat. 7,233,886 - Filed 27 Feb 2001.

[14] E.J. Keogh, M.J. Pazzani, "An indexing scheme for similarity search in large time series databases," *Proceedings of the 11th International Conference on Scientific and Statistical Database Management (SSDBM)*, Cleveland, Ohio, 1999.

A Study of kNN using ICU Multivariate Time Series Data

Dan Li[1], **Admir Djulovic**[1], **and Jianfeng Xu**[2]
[1]Computer Science Department, Eastern Washington University, Cheney, WA, USA
[2]Software School, Nanchang University, Nanchang, Jiangxi, China

Abstract—*A time series is a sequence of data collected at successive time points. While most techniques for time series analysis have been focused on univariate time series data at fixed intervals, there are many applications where time series data are collected at irregular and uncertain time intervals across multiple input variables. The uncertainty in multivariate time series makes analysis difficult and challenging. In this research, we study kNN classification approach applied to ICU multivariate time series data for patient's mortality prediction. We propose three time series representation strategies to handle irregular multivariate time series data. The experiments show the performance of these three methods in different settings. We also discuss the impact of imbalanced class distribution and the effect of k in kNN classification.*

Keywords: Classification, kNN, Multivariate Time Series.

1. Introduction

Time series data have become available in many fields of study including signal processing, pattern recognition, weather forecasting, electroencephalography, scientific simulation, etc. Consequently, there have been increased interests in analyzing and predicting time series data using data mining techniques. Besides all the common features of data mining, the research on time series analysis has its unique challenges because of the high-dimensionality and multi-granularity features of time series data. Therefore, it is a non-trivial task to develop efficient and effective data mining solutions for time series analysis.

The research on time series analysis has been focused on two main areas [1]: (1) to find proper representation methods to reduce high dimensional time series data; and (2) to define effective similarity/distance measures to compare multiple time series sequences. Many dimensionality reduction techniques have been proposed and implemented to transform original raw time series data into lower dimensional representations. These techniques include Discrete Fourier Transformation (DFT) [2], Discrete Wavelet Transformation (DWT) [3], Piecewise Aggregate Approximation (PAA) [4], Principal Component Analysis (PCA) [5], Symbolic Aggregate approXimation (SAX) [6], Single Value Decomposition (SVD) [7], etc. Correspondingly, similarity/distance measures have been discussed in the literature focusing on the comparison of time series data. The commonly used measures include point-to-point distance measures such as Euclidean distance and Dynamic Time Warping (DTW) [8], and edit distance measures for strings such as the Longest Common Subsequences (LCS) [9].

A time series is a sequence of data typically measured at successive points over time at uniform time intervals. The time *granularity* determines the interval length between two adjacent time points [10]. While most time series representation methods have been focused on the analysis of time series data at fixed and stable time granularity, there are many applications where time series data are collected at irregular and uncertain time intervals. For instance, the Computing in Cardiology Challenge (2012) provides the data sets for predicting mortality of Intensive Care Unit (ICU) populations [11]. The input time series measurements are recorded in chronological order within each patient record. Some measurements are recorded at regular intervals ranging from hourly to daily, while others are recorded at irregular intervals as required [11]. This is an example of irregular time intervals caused by intended irregular data collection patterns. There are other cases when the uncertainty and the irregularity are caused by inherent imprecise data collection tools and privacy-preserving transformations [12].

There have been some studies on the analysis of imprecise and uncertain time series data [13], [14], [15], [16]. In these studies, various distance measures and probabilistic query models have been proposed to embrace the uncertainty and the incompleteness of time series data. However, most of these studies have been limited to the cases where the time series data are collected over **uniform time intervals**, and the time series itself is **univariate time series**. In this paper, we focus on the study of **multivariate time series** measurements being collected at **irregular time intervals**. We use the data collected from patients' ICU stays [11] as an example and the ultimate goal is to design proper analytical solutions to deal with multivariate time series data at irregular intervals for ICU patients' mortality prediction. The rest of this paper is organized as follows: Section 2 describes the notations and the concepts of the related work on multivariate time series representations; Section 3 discusses the methodologies we have proposed for representing irregular ICU multivariate time series; The experimental results and analysis are provided in Section 4; Finally, concluding remarks along with directions for future improvements are presented in Section 5.

2. Multivariate Time Series Representation

Typically, a *multivariate time series* instance can be represented as an $m \times n$ two-dimensional matrix D:

$$D = \begin{pmatrix} d_{11} & d_{12} & \dots & d_{1j} & \dots & d_{1n} \\ d_{21} & d_{22} & \dots & d_{2j} & \dots & d_{2n} \\ \vdots & \vdots & \ddots & \vdots & \ddots & \vdots \\ d_{i1} & d_{i2} & \dots & d_{ij} & \dots & d_{in} \\ \vdots & \vdots & \ddots & \vdots & \ddots & \vdots \\ d_{m1} & d_{m2} & \dots & d_{mj} & \dots & d_{mn} \end{pmatrix} \quad (1)$$

where m is the number of input variables, n is the total number of time points, and d_{ij} is the data point measured on input variable i at time point t_j ($1 \leq i \leq m$ and $1 \leq j \leq n$). This representation assumes that all m input variables are measured along the same time sequence $(t_1, t_2, ..., t_n)$ and the time intervals between each adjacent pair are equal. Here *time interval* is a time unit measuring the sampling rate of a time series. One example of such representation is for weather forecasting where the weather-related variables (temperature, precipitation, wind, etc.) are collected over an even time interval, e.g., every ten minutes.

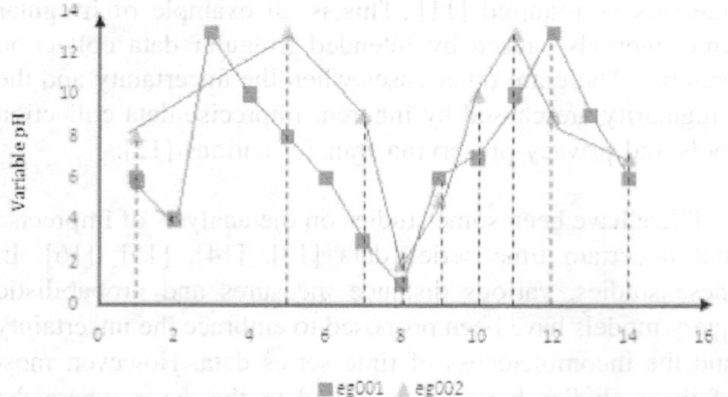

Fig. 1: Time Series at Regular and Irregular Interval

While the above matrix D is typically used to represent the multivariate time series at uniform time intervals, there are many real-world applications where the time series demonstrates various and irregular time intervals due to various data sampling rates. For instance, Figure 1 shows two time series sequences collected from two ICU patients (eg001 and eg002) on variable *pH* (a measure of the activity of a patient's hydrogen ion) [11]. The time series of patient eg001 has uniform intervals, while the time series of patient eg002 demonstrates various and irregular time intervals. Therefore, to be able to generally represent multivariate time series instances at either uniform or irregular time intervals, we modify the above matrix D into the following format:

$$D = \begin{pmatrix} (d_{11}, t_{11}) & \dots & (d_{1j}, t_{1j}) & \dots & (d_{1n_1}, t_{1n_1}) \\ (d_{21}, t_{21}) & \dots & (d_{2j}, t_{2j}) & \dots & (d_{2n_2}, t_{2n_2}) \\ \vdots & \vdots & \vdots & \ddots & \vdots \\ (d_{i1}, t_{i1}) & \dots & (d_{ij}, t_{ij}) & \dots & (d_{in_i}, t_{in_i}) \\ \vdots & \ddots & \vdots & \ddots & \vdots \\ (d_{m1}, t_{m1}) & \dots & (d_{mj}, t_{mj}) & \dots & (d_{mn_m}, t_{mn_m}) \end{pmatrix} \quad (2)$$

where m still denotes the number of input variables in a multivariate time series. Since the time series data are collected over uncertain intervals, the time series sequences from different input variables may end up with different number of data observations. To be more general, we use n_1, n_2, ..., and n_m to denote data observation numbers of each variable in an m-variate time series. Each pair (d_{ij}, t_{ij}) represents the data point of the ith input variable measured at the jth time stamp.

Note that D represents only one multivariate time series instance. If multivariate time series data are collected from multiple instances (e.g., data could be collected from multiple ICU patients, and the data set for each patient is a multivariate time series data set), we use $D_{all} = \{D_1, D_2, ..., D_p\}$ to represent a set of multivariate time series of p instances, where each D_i ($1 \leq i \leq p$) is an m-dimensional vector of the above structure.

Now let's introduce our problem definition: **Given an unlabeled multivariate time series Q, assign it to one of the two pre-defined classes {0, 1} by learning from a training set D_{all} of p multivariate time series instances.** Here, $D_{all} = \{(D_1, c_1), (D_2, c_2)...., (D_p, c_p)\}$ and $(c_1, c_2, ..., c_p) \in \{0, 1\}$ denote the known class labels of p training instances.

From the problem description, it is not hard to see that the problem itself is a typical classification problem. However, what makes this topic challenging is the needs of handling time series among multiple input variables and multiple instances. In other words, the number of available data observations varies among different input variables regarding each multivariate time series instance. Meanwhile, it also varies among different instances regarding the same input variable. Therefore, it is a non-trivial task to develop feasible solutions for the above classification problem.

3. Methodologies

Among many existing classification algorithms, we plan to use *k-Nearest-Neighbor* (*k*NN) approach because it is easy to implement and it handles numerical values conveniently and effectively. The key component of this research lies in how to define the distance measures among multivariate time series at various and irregular time intervals. The rest of this section discusses three approaches we have proposed and the basic idea of each approach is described as follows:

1) ***CaptureStatistics***: This approach captures the statistics of a time series using minimum, maximum, mean, and moving average and use these values to represent the time series.
2) ***DetectChanges***: This approach detects the key change-points in each time series, and uses these points to represent the entire time series.
3) ***AggregateSegments***: The main idea of this approach is to break a multivariate time series instance into multiple univariate time series, then each univariate time series is processed separately into disjoint segments and the aggregated distance is generated.

3.1 Capture Statistics

As shown in Figure 2, the *CaptureStatistics* algorithm is pretty straightforward. Step (1) is to normalize each time series using z-score normalization [17]. After normalization each time series has a mean of zero and a standard deviation of one. Step (2) is to capture the statistics including minimum, maximum, mean, and moving average for each variable in a multivariate time series. Remember that D_{all} denotes the entire training set of p time series data objects, and each object in D_{all} is a multivariate time series represented by Equation (2). Since each time series has variable number of observations at irregular time intervals, the mean and the moving average are calculated based on the existing observations in the time series. This process is repeatedly applied to all m variables in an m-variate time series. In Step (3), similar process is applied to the unlabeled test case Q. Step (4) compares each instance in D_{all} with Q and identifies the k-nearest neighbors using Euclidean distance (k is a pre-defined odd number). Step (5) uses the class label information from the k-nearest neighbors and applies majority vote to assign a class label to Q.

The *CaptureStatistics* algorithm transforms each variable-length time series into four numerical values. Thus, the variable number of observations from different time series instances is not a concern any more. We hope that these four statistical data values still capture the key features of a time series even though the temporal feature of the data is ignored.

3.2 Detect Changes

The main idea of the *DetectChanges* algorithm is to detect the key change-points in each time series and use these change-points to represent the time series. In other words, rather than focusing on the behavior of the entire time series, the trend of variations in the time series could be more informative than the time series itself. Even though the original multivariate time series has various numbers of data observations due to irregular measuring patterns, this approach uses the fixed number of change-points to represent each univariate time series. This makes the comparison between different data instances feasible.

Algorithm: `CaptureStatistics(`D_{all}`, `Q`, `k`)`

1) Apply z-score normalization to D_{all} and Q;
2) For each element in D_{all} = $\{D_1, D_2, ..., D_p\}$, find min, max, mean, and moving average;
3) Find min, max, mean, and moving average for Q;
4) Use kNN to find k-nearest neighbors of Q from D_{all};
5) Apply majority vote among k-nearest neighbors and assign a label to Q.

Fig. 2: ***CaptureStatistics* Algorithm.**

Figure 3 shows the *DetectChanges* algorithm. Comparing with *CaptureStatistics*, *DetectChanges* introduces one more parameter w which denotes the number of key points we plan to capture. The key of *DetectChanges* lies in Step (2) which detects w change-points in each time series by top-down piecewise segmentation approach [18]. These w representative data points are later used in Equation (3) to calculate the aggregated distance between each data object $D \in D_{all}$ and the test object Q, as shown in Step (3) of the algorithm. Here d_{ij} and q_{ij} denote the jth change-point in the ith univariate time series in D and Q, respectively.

$$ChangeDist(D, Q) = \sum_{i=1}^{m}\sum_{j=1}^{w}(d_{ij} - q_{ij}) \quad (3)$$

The last two steps of *ChangeDetection* are similar to the last two steps of *CaptureStatistics*, which find the k-nearest neighbors of Q and assign a corresponding class label to it.

Algorithm: `DetectChanges(`D_{all}`, `Q`, `k`, `w`)`

1) Apply z-score normalization to D_{all} and Q;
2) Detect w change-points in D_{all} and Q;
3) Calculate the aggregated distance between Q and each $D \in D_{all}$ using Equations (3);
4) Use kNN to find k-nearest neighbors of Q from D_{all}.
5) Apply majority vote among k-nearest neighbors and assign a label to Q.

Fig. 3: ***DetectChanges* Algorithm.**

3.3 Aggregate Segments

Figure 4 shows the *AggregateSegments* algorithm. The main idea of this algorithm is to preprocess each individual time series into a set of equal-width segments. This way, the temporal feature of a time series is kept in the data set. Meanwhile, the time series sequences with different number of observations are transformed into the same number of segments through dimensionality reduction.

Among many time series representation techniques introduced in Section 1, one of the most commonly used dimensionality reduction approach is *Piecewise Aggregate Approximation* (PAA) [4], because PAA is intuitive and easy to implement. At the same time, it provides competitive performance comparing to other sophisticated dimensionality reduction techniques [6]. In PAA, an n-dimensional time series $d = (d_1, d_2, ..., d_n)$ is transformed into w disjoint equal-width segments $\bar{d} = (\bar{d_1}, \bar{d_2}, ..., \bar{d_w})$ $(w < n)$, where the ith segment $\bar{d_i}$ is represented by finding the mean value of those data points falling into the ith segment [6].

Besides PAA, we employ another dimensionality reduction technique SAX (Symbolic Aggregate approXimation) [6], which transforms a numeric time series into a symbolic representation. The idea of SAX is to identify the breakpoints from a highly Gaussian distributed time series, and use ordinal symbols to represent the segments between each pair of breakpoints. The authors in [6] have demonstrated that SAX is an effective representation on the classic data mining tasks of clustering, classification, anomaly detection, etc.

Algorithm: AggregateSegments(D_{all}, Q, k, w)

1) Apply z-score normalization to D_{all} and Q;
2) Transform D_{all} and Q into w equal-width segments using PAA and SAX, respectively;
3) Apply linear interpolation to fill in the segments without data observations;
4) Calculate the aggregated distance between Q and each $D \in D_{all}$ using Equations (4) and (5) separately;
5) Use kNN to find k-nearest neighbors of Q from D_{all}.
6) Apply majority vote among k-nearest neighbors and assign a label to Q.

Fig. 4: ***AggregateSegments* Algorithm.**

Unlike the original raw data set D_{all} where the multivariate time series instances have various number of data observations recorded at various time intervals, both PAA and SAX methods transform the instances in D_{all} into a set of $m \times w$ fixed-size matrices. Here m is the number of univariate time series and w denotes the number of segments in each time series. Note that w is usually much smaller than the number of original data observations in a time series. Similarly, the unlabeled instance Q is also transformed into an $m \times w$ matrix using PAA and SAX respectively, as shown in Step (2) of the *AggregateSegments* algorithm.

Now all the time series sequences have the same number of segments, but some segments may not have any valid data due to the unavailability of data observations in the corresponding segments. Therefore, in Step (3) of the algorithm, linear interpolation is employed to fill in these missing segments.

After Step (3), we are ready to use kNN classification to evaluate the distance between Q and each element $D \in D_{all}$. Since both D and Q have been transformed into m-variate time series with w segments in each time series, the distance between D and Q is calculated as the aggregated distance between each pair of segments in each univariate time series from D and Q. Equation (4) shows the distance function when both D and Q are represented as PAA sequences. Here $\overline{d_{ij}}$ and $\overline{q_{ij}}$ denote the piecewise aggregated average of the jth segment in the ith univariate time series in D and Q, respectively.

$$PAADist(D,Q) = \sum_{i=1}^{m} \sum_{j=1}^{w} (\overline{d_{ij}} - \overline{q_{ij}}) \quad (4)$$

Equation (5) shows the distance function when both D and Q are represented as SAX symbolic sequences. Here sym_d_{ij} and sym_q_{ij} denote the symbolic representations of the jth segment in the ith univariate time series in D and Q respectively, and $dist(sym\_d_{ij}, sym\_q_{ij})$ is the subdistance function between two ordinal symbols, as illustrated in [6].

$$SAXDist(D,Q) = \sum_{i=1}^{m} \sum_{j=1}^{w} dist(sym\_d_{ij}, sym\_q_{ij}) \quad (5)$$

Again, the last two steps of *AggregateSegments* are similar to the last two steps of *DetectChanges*, which find the k-nearest neighbors of Q and assign a corresponding class label to it.

4. Experimental Results

We use the data sets for Computing in Cardiology (CinC) Challenge 2012 [11] to evaluate our algorithms. The focus of the challenge is to develop classification methods for patient-specific prediction of in-hospital mortality [11]. The training set for the challenge is a multivariate time series data set consisting of records from 4,000 ICU patients and there are 42 variables recorded at least once during the first 48 hours of a patient's ICU stay. However, not all 42 variables are available all the times. Six of these variables are general descriptors (e.g., ID, age, gender, etc.), and the remainder are time series, for which variable number of observations may be available [11].

4.1 Experiments with Imbalanced Data Set

In the original training set of 4,000 ICU records, there are 554 positive cases. In other words, about 14% patients did NOT survive their hospitalization. Our experiments are initially designed using this imbalanced data set and 10-cross validation with stratified sampling is use to evaluate the algorithms. Tables 1-3 show the experimental results from Algorithms *CaptureStatistics*, *DetectChanges*, and *AggregateSegments* with PAA5 (5 is the number of segments in PAA).

The tables show both the precision and the recall on negative and positive classes separately, and the overall system accuracy. We can see that the precision on negative class is as high as 88% and the recall on negative class is as high as 96% when 3NN or 5NN is used. However, when we look at the prediction for positive instances, the results are not promising. In the best case, the precision on positive class is only 38% (5NN with *DetectChanges* approach) while the recall is only 12% in that case. This means the false negative rate is very high. This is not surprising though, because for such an imbalanced data set, the nearest-neighbor method is hard to identify the instances with fewer number of samples in the training set, i.e., positive instances in our case.

Table 1: Results from *CaptureStatistics* using Imbalanced Data.

	Class 0		Class 1		Accuracy
	precision	recall	precision	recall	
k=1	0.88	0.89	0.24	0.21	0.80
k=3	0.87	0.95	0.30	0.13	0.84
k=5	0.87	0.97	0.37	0.10	0.85

Table 2: Results from *DetectChanges* using Imbalanced Data.

	Class 0		Class 1		Accuracy
	precision	recall	precision	recall	
k=1	0.87	0.88	0.21	0.19	0.79
k=3	0.87	0.95	0.28	0.12	0.84
k=5	0.87	0.96	0.38	0.12	0.85

Table 3: Results from *AggregateSegments* with PAA5 using Imbalanced Data.

	Class 0		Class 1		Accuracy
	precision	recall	precision	recall	
k=1	0.87	0.88	0.22	0.20	0.79
k=3	0.87	0.95	0.25	0.11	0.83
k=5	0.87	0.96	0.29	0.08	0.85

4.2 Varying Data Distributions

To deal with imbalanced data distribution and improve the performance for positive instance prediction, we vary the data distributions by undersampling negative instances in the original data set. Figure 5 shows the performance of Algorithm *CaptureStatistics* when the distributions between negative and positive class instances are 1:1, 2:1, 3:1, and 7:1, respectively.

We can see that the precision and recall on negative class and the overall accuracy increase steadily as the percentage of negative instances increases, but the performance on positive class prediction decreases dramatically as the percentage of positive instances decreases. This experimental result indicates that the class distribution in the training set is an important factor for system performance. We should choose an appropriate distribution based on the goal of the system. If the goal is to improve the overall prediction accuracy, or to improve the prediction on negative cases, we should keep more negative samples in the training set. If the goal is targeted at true positive rate, then the undersampling should be done on negative class samples. To balance between positive and negative classes, we determine to use the training set of 3:1 distribution rate between negative and positive samples. The rest experimental results are based on this setting.

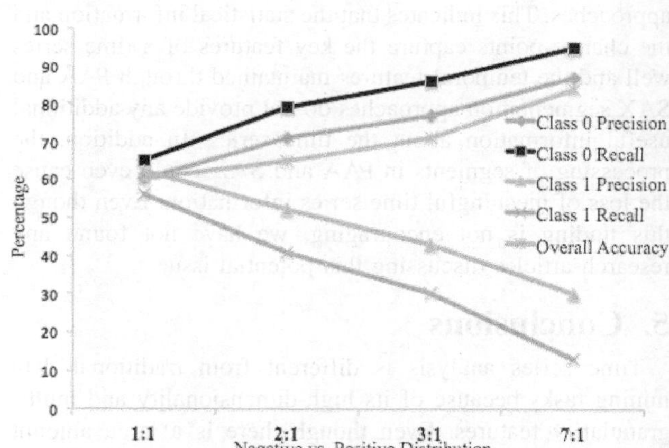

Fig. 5: Varying Data Distribution for *CaptureStatistics* Algorithm.

4.3 The Effect of k and the Comparison of All Algorithms

Table 4 demonstrates the effect of k in kNN classification. We can see that as k increases, the performance improves gradually until a certain point where the performance gets stable or slowly goes down. In particular, for Algorithms *CaptureStatistics* and *DetectChanges*, the overall results are best when k is set to 5. Under this setting, we have the highest recall on negative class, the highest precision on

Table 4: The effect of k and the comparison of all algorithms.

Method	k	Class 0		Class 1		Accuracy
		precision	recall	precision	recall	
Statistics	k=1	0.778	0.84	0.46	0.38	0.71
	k=3	0.78	0.88	0.52	0.34	0.74
	k=5	**0.77**	**0.97**	**0.63**	**0.24**	**0.76**
	k=7	0.78	0.92	0.59	0.31	0.75
Changes	k=1	0.77	0.82	0.42	0.35	0.70
	k=3	0.79	0.90	0.56	0.34	0.75
	k=5	**0.76**	**0.96**	**0.64**	**0.20**	**0.76**
	k=7	0.77	0.94	0.62	0.27	0.76
PAA10	k=1	0.76	0.80	0.38	0.34	0.68
	k=3	0.76	0.85	0.40	0.27	0.69
	k=5	0.76	0.88	0.45	0.26	0.72
	k=7	**0.76**	**0.90**	**0.47**	**0.22**	**0.72**
SAX10	k=1	0.77	0.80	0.39	0.35	0.68
	k=3	0.77	0.84	0.41	0.30	0.69
	k=5	0.76	0.87	0.42	0.25	0.70
	k=7	**0.76**	**0.89**	**0.43**	**0.23**	**0.71**

positive class, and the highest overall accuracy. For Algorithm *AggregateSegments* we test both PAA10 and SAX10 (10 denotes the number of segments), and the results show that setting k to 7 issues the best performance for both approaches while PAA slightly outperforms SAX.

Comparing all four approaches, the change-point detection and statistical approach have similar performance and both outperform PAA and SAX, the two piecewise segmentation approaches. This indicates that the statistical information and the change-points capture the key features of a time series well and the temporal features maintained through PAA and SAX segmentation approaches do not provide any additional useful information about the time series. In addition, the processing of segments in PAA and SAX could even cause the loss of meaningful time series information. Even though this finding is not encouraging, we have not found any research articles discussing this potential issue.

5. Conclusions

Time series analysis is different from traditional data mining tasks because of its high-dimensionality and multi-granularity features. Even though there is a large amount of research focusing on dimensionality reduction and representation of time series, there are a limited number of research papers discussing multivariate time series analysis, especially the time series at irregular and uncertain intervals.

This paper discusses the representations of irregular multivariate time series data and introduces a non-trivial classification problem using multivariate time series. We develop three kNN-based classification methods aiming at different time series representation strategies. ***CaptureStatistics*** uses minimum, maximum, mean, and moving average to capture the key features of a time series. ***DetectChanges*** uses the top-down segmentation approach to identify key change-points of a time series, and use these change-points to represent the entire time series. ***AggregateSegments*** is based on the piecewise aggregation approach and transforms each univariate time series into a fixed number of equal-width segments. We adopt both Piecewise Aggregate Approximation (PAA) and Symbolic Aggregate approXimation (SAX) approaches to segmenting the time series.

The experiments are conducted using ICU multivariate time series data for patient's mortality prediction. The original ICU data set is an imbalanced data set because most training instances have negative outcomes, i.e., most patients survive their ICU stays. This imbalanced data set has strong impact on the performance because kNN approach heavily depends on the class distribution of the data. With a small number of positive instances, the false negative rate would be inevitably high because kNN could not easily identify nearest neighbors with positive outcomes for a test case unless they present very strong common features of positive behavior. To deal with imbalanced data, undersampling method is used to change the distributions of positive and negative samples. The experiments show that as the distribution varies, the performance on positive and negative classes varies as well. The class with more samples usually has higher precision and higher recall than the class with fewer samples.

In addition, we conduct extensive experiments in different settings using our three time series handling algorithms. The experiments show the effect of k in kNN classification for each algorithm. Based on the results, we conclude that *CaptureStatistics* and *DetectChanges* outperform *AggregateSegments* in general. This indicates that the statistics and the change-points provide sufficient information to represent the time series and additional processing of time series could even downgrade the performance.

In future, we plan to develop weighted kNN approaches to handle imbalanced data distribution. We also plan to further investigate other sophisticated segmentation approaches and evaluate their effects on multivariate time series analysis.

References

[1] H. Ding, G. Trajcevski, P. Scheuermann, X. Wang, and E. Keogh, "Querying and mining of time series data: experimental comparison of representations and distance measures," *Proceedings of the VLDB Endowment*, vol. 1, no. 2, pp. 1542–1552, 2008.

[2] J. W. Cooley and J. W. Tukey, "An algorithm for the macine calculation of complex fourier series," *Mathematics of Computation*, vol. 19, pp. 297–301, 1965.

[3] K. Chan and A. W. Fu, "Efficient time series matcing by wavelets," in *Proceedings of the 15th International Conference on Data Engineering [ICDE'99]*, March 1999, pp. 126–133.

[4] C. Guo, H. Li, and D. Pan, "An improved piecewise aggregate approximation based on statistical features for time series mining," in *Proceedings of the 4th international conference on Knowledge science, engineering and management [KSEM'10]*, Northern Ireland, UK, September 2010, pp. 234–244.

[5] I. D. Var, "Multivariate data analysis," *vectors*, vol. 8, p. 6, 1998.

[6] J. Lin, E. Keogh, S. Lonardi, and B. Chiu, "A symbolic representation of time series, with implications for streaming algorithms," in *Proceedings of the 8th ACM SIGMOD Workshop on Research Issues in Data Mining and Knowledge Discovery [DMKD'03]*, San Diego, CA, June 2003, pp. 2–11.

[7] J. A. Cadzow, B. Baseghi, and T. Hsu, "Singular-value decomposition approach to time series modelling," *Communications, Radar and Signal Processing, IEE Proceedings F*, vol. 130, no. 3, pp. 202–210, 1983.

[8] E. Keogh and C. A. Ratanamahatana, "Exact indexing of dynamic time warping," *Knowledge and Information Systems*, vol. 7, no. 3, pp. 358–386, 2005.

[9] L. Bergroth, H. Hakonen, and T. Raita, "A survey of longest common subsequence algorithms," in *Proceedings of the 7th International Symposium on String Processing and Information Retrieval*, 2000, pp. 39–48.

[10] C. Bettini, C. E. Dyreson, W. S. Evans, R. T. Snodgrass, and X. S. Wang, "A glossary of time granularity concepts," *Temporal Databases: Research and Practice. Lecture Notes in Computer Science*, vol. 1399, pp. 406–413, 1998.

[11] CinC2012, "Predicting mortality of icu patients: the physionet/computing in cardiology challenge 2012," [Online] http://physionet.org/challenge/2012/.

[12] B. C. M. Fung, K. Wang, R. Chen, and P. S. Yu, "Privacy-preserving data publishing: A survey of recent developments," *ACM Computing Surveys*, vol. 42, no. 4, pp. 14:1–14:53, June 2010.

[13] M. Dallachiesa, B. Nushi, K. Mirylenka, and T. Palpanas, "Uncertain time-series similarity: Return to the basics," *Proceedings of the VLDB Endowment*, vol. 5, no. 11, pp. 1662–1673, 2012.

[14] D. Suciu, A. Connolly, and B. Howe, "Embracing uncertainty in large-scale computational astrophysics," in *MUD Workshop*, 2009.

[15] T. T. Tran, L. Peng, B. Li, Y. Diao, and A. Liu, "Pods: a new model and processing algorithms for uncertain data streams," in *Proceedings of the 2010 ACM SIGMOD International Conference on Management of data*, ser. SIGMOD'10, Indianapolis, Indiana, 2010, pp. 159–170.

[16] M.-Y. Yeh, K.-L. Wu, P. S. Yu, and M.-S. Chen, "Proud: a probabilistic approach to processing similarity queries over uncertain data streams," in *Proceedings of the 12th International Conference on Extending Database Technology: Advances in Database Technology*, ser. EDBT '09, Saint Petersburg, Russia, 2009, pp. 684–695.

[17] J. Han and M. Kamber, *Data Mining: Concepts and Techniques*. Morgan Kaufmann, 2006, ch. 6.

[18] E. Keogh, S. Chu, D. Hart, and M. Pazzani, "Segmenting time series: A survey and novel approach," *an Edited Volume, Data mining in Time Series Databases*, vol. 57, pp. 1–22, 2004.

Genetic Algorithms and Classification Trees in Feature Discovery: Diabetes and the NHANES database

Alejandro Heredia-Langner[1], Kristin H. Jarman[1], Brett G. Amidan[1], and Joel G. Pounds[1]

[1]Pacific Northwest National Laboratory, 902 Battelle Boulevard, PO Box 999 Richland, Washington 99352 USA

***Abstract*— This paper presents a feature selection methodology that can be applied to datasets containing a mixture of continuous and categorical variables. Using a Genetic Algorithm (GA), this method explores a dataset and selects a small set of features relevant for the prediction of a binary (1/0) response. Binary classification trees and an objective function based on conditional probabilities are used to measure the fitness of a given subset of features. The method is applied to health data to find factors useful for the prediction of diabetes. Results show that our algorithm is capable of narrowing down the set of predictors to around 8 factors that can be validated using reputable medical and public health resources. Key Words: Genetic Algorithms, Decision Trees, NHANES, Diabetes.**

1. INTRODUCTION

The National Health and Nutrition Examination Survey (NHANES) database (www.cdc.gov/nchs/nhanes.htm) contains a complete health survey for a sample of the U.S. Population. Included in the survey are nutritional, demographic, and socioeconomic data as well as results of medical examinations and laboratory analyses for the study participants. The survey, which began gathering data in the 1960s, contains information from around 5000 adults and children per year and results are presented in a biannual format, which means that each two-year dataset contains information from about 10,000 respondents.

The NHANES dataset is a rich environment in which a supervised learning algorithm can be applied. The dataset contains hundreds of features in a variety of formats. There are continuous features (age, body-mass index, cholesterol level), ordered categorical features (for example, annual household income value is expressed as integers where, in general, a higher number represents a higher level of income) and unordered categorical features (pregnancy, for example). Data gathered from the NHANES survey has been used in the past to inform and monitor the effects of public policy decisions [1], [2] and by researchers to help test relationships between lifestyle or nutrition levels and medical conditions or illness [3].

Although the vast majority of the NHANES related research uses the data to focus on testing hypotheses involving a small number of previously selected predictors, there has been recent development in applying data mining and pattern recognition algorithms [4], [5] to the information gathered from the NHANES survey. The work in [4] used 2005-2006 laboratory and questionnaire data for 10348 participants and constructed classification trees for an attribute of interest (the respondent has high blood pressure, for example) using the rest of the variables as potential predictors. The work in [4] used total accuracy of prediction as the objective function and discarded decision trees that result in too low (below 80%) or too high (above 95%) predictive accuracy. The work in [4] aimed at discovering predictive relationships among variables in the dataset that may shed new light on the association between health conditions and lifestyle choices, but its broad application produced a myriad of results that may be difficult to sift through and validate. The work in [5] used data for a subset of 4979 respondents. They develop a clustering approach to find associations between conditions of interest (high blood pressure and high cholesterol, for example). Their aim was to explore the data for new and interesting disease associations that could then be substantiated (or disproved) by searching literature in the appropriate field. The work in [5] was only reported for people with known illnesses or conditions, excluding respondents without the diseases, and their results show only disease associations, not associations between diseases and other factors.

The NHANES database contains hundreds of features, some of which may be useful for classification purposes. A key challenge is to find a small set of features whose combined use is optimal in some sense for a classification task, while at the same time avoiding the computationally impractical task of testing every possible combination of factors. The approach presented in this paper uses a combination of decision trees and a Genetic Algorithm (GA) to optimize the selection of a set of predictors that are useful to describe a condition of interest.

2. IMPLEMENTATION AND RESULTS

Genetic Algorithms (GA) are a heuristic optimization technique with mechanisms inspired by the process of evolution and natural selection. A solution to a problem is represented as a string of characters and a number of these solutions are generated, typically at random, to form the initial parent population. New, or offspring, solutions are created by recombining information from selected parents, and the best performing offspring individuals are then selected to form the new parent population. To avoid premature convergence, some solutions in the new parent population are subjected to a mutation mechanism, which may alter their contents. A GA works by repeatedly applying the mechanisms of recombination, selection and mutation to an initial population of solutions until some measure of convergence has been reached [6]. Genetic algorithms are well suited to explore large and complex problem spaces and are not deterred by noisy, constrained, or discontinuous objective functions. On the other hand, a GA cannot guarantee that an optimal solution will be found.

In this work, a GA is applied to a subset of the NHANES data to find a set of features that best predicts the presence of diabetes. At any given iteration, a solution to the feature selection problem consists of a vector with binary (1/0) entries, where a '1' indicates that the corresponding feature is present and may be used by a decision tree. The initial dataset includes 45 features (including demographic information, cholesterol data and body measures from 9965 respondents in the 1999-2000 NHANES database), and the initial population size is 35 solutions, each solution generated randomly. The recombination mechanism produces 175 offspring solutions (five times the size of the parent population). Each offspring solution is formed using two randomly selected individuals from the parent population. The new solution is created by joining alternating portions of each parent. Individuals in the offspring population are evaluated using a 90/10 train/test strategy, where the partitions are created anew in every generation to maintain, roughly, the proportions of (1/0) present in the overall dataset, and the best performing 35 individuals are selected for further processing. In the next step, up to 20% of the 35 individuals selected are mutated by having their contents randomly altered (it is possible that any given entry in a mutated solution remains unchanged). The GA was implemented in MatLab [7], using the CLASSREGTREE tree function.

A somewhat related approach was implemented in [8] who employed a GA for feature and instance selection using a support vector machine (SVM) and k-NN (nearest neighbor) classifiers on several datasets. The work presented in [8] focused solely on accuracy of prediction and their results suggest that in a dataset with many potential features, it is possible to greatly reduce the number of features without, in most cases, affecting classification performance. The work in [8] does not measure feature importance -- it is implicitly assumed that all features selected by their algorithm are equally important-- and their interest lies mostly in comparing accuracy of classification when feature and instance selection are used individually or together. The application of a GA for feature selection is also presented in [9].

During a run of the GA for the present work, the GA procedures are executed repeatedly, keeping track of the number of times each feature is present in every new parent population and the best objective function value in every new generation. The variable used for classification is the diabetes 1999-2000 set where the response was re-coded as follows: respondents with diagnosed diabetes or borderline diabetes are coded as '1', respondents without diabetes are coded as '0' and individuals that responded 'Don't know' or refused to answer are coded as 'N/A' (not available). The diabetes dataset is highly unbalanced, with around 5% of the respondents affected by the illness. Aside from cholesterol levels and body measures (such as waist circumference, height, weight), other demographic predictors (or features) include information about age, gender, ethnicity, education and income level, military veteran status, and others. Feature data were pre-processed to re-code values not useful for classification. This particular dataset was chosen to develop and test the optimization approach described in this document because findings on the relationship between diabetes and factors like age, ethnicity, socioeconomic and cholesterol data can be supported by numerous reputable sources (http://diabetes.niddk.nih.gov/dm/pubs/causes/#causes, and [10]).

The objective function developed for the GA produces conditional probability estimates of having diabetes or borderline diabetes for a given set of predictors and predictor levels. The simplest way of computing conditional probability estimates using binary classification trees involves computing the relative frequency of one of the classes at the leaves (terminal nodes) for a set of training data. Using relative frequencies as conditional probabilities is known to produce very poor estimates [11], because terminal nodes may have high purity (a single class assigned to it) but a very small number of observations. This is particularly true in highly unbalanced datasets like the one used for this work. Better probability estimates can be obtained by smoothing [12], curtailment [13], or averaging [14] probability estimates, or by applying a combination of these techniques. In this work, several different probability estimates were tested. These estimates were obtained using Laplace estimators, m-estimators and values from a Naïve Bayesian classifier, either alone or in combination. Probability estimates were used as inputs for an objective function in the form of the average negative cross entropy (NCE, [15]).

The task of developing and testing the algorithm was carried out including redundant predictors in the initial set of features. For example, NHANES contains several features related to family income. This approach was used to observe the behavior of the GA under different formulations of the objective function, as the goal is to develop an approach that can be applied to datasets that have received only a minimum of pre-processing. The objective function combined Laplace and binned Naïve Bayesian probability estimates [13], and aimed to minimize the average NCE of the test sets.

In total, the candidate set of predictors contained 45 variables, including demographic variables (age, ethnicity, gender, family income and others), results from blood analyses (total cholesterol, HDL cholesterol, C-reactive protein, Helicobacter pylori, fibrinogen, bone alkaline phosphate, N-telopeptides), and body measures (weight and BMI, waist circumference, arm circumference and others). Twenty generations of the GA produce the results shown in Figure 1.

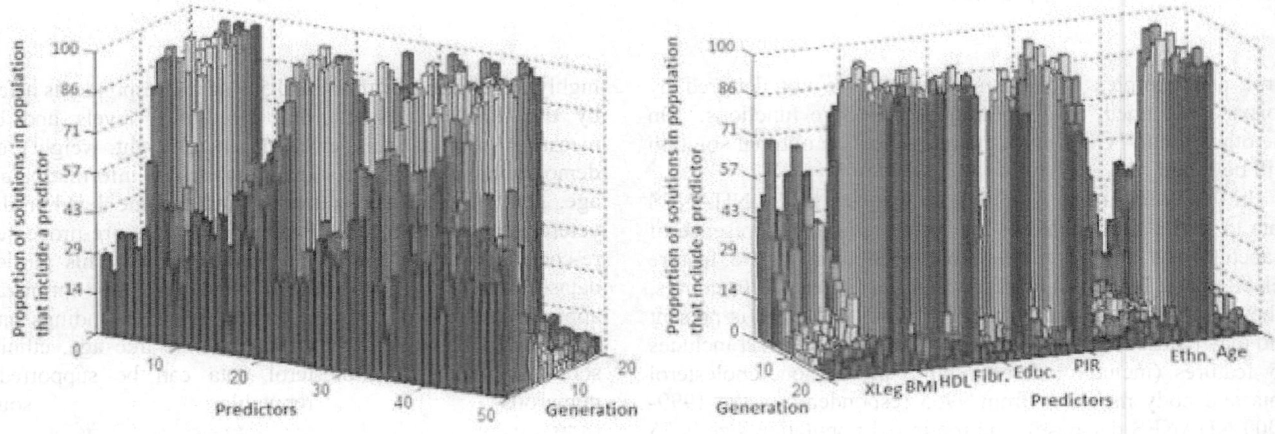

Figure 1. Proportion of predictors present in the population of solutions (z-axis) as a function of generation number (y-axis) with the first generation in the forefront (left panel) and the last generation in the forefront (right panel). The predictors that appear in a large proportion of the final population are Age, Ethnicity, Poverty income ratio (PIR), Education level, fibrinogen level, HDL cholesterol level, Body mass index (BMI), Upper leg length (XLeg).

Figure 1 shows the evolution in the proportion of predictors present in the parent population of the GA starting with the first generation (created at random) until the 20th generation. The first generation, shown in the left panel of Figure 1, contains all predictors in roughly the same proportion. As the run progresses, some predictors were effectively eliminated, while a few others tended to be present in nearly all the individuals in the population of solutions. Results shown in Figure 1 were obtained after evaluating $35\times5\times20 = 3500$ solutions, not necessarily distinct. The problem space consists of around 3×10^{13} possible solutions (a predictor is or is not present and there are 45 predictors available). This means that convergence has been achieved after exploring less than10^{-8} % of the problem space, in other words, a small fraction of all the solutions. Scientific support for the validity of the predictors selected by the GA can be found in [16],
[10], and
http://diabetes.niddk.nih.gov/dm/pubs/causes/#causes.

In addition to being efficient, the GA appears to be robust as well. The set of final features, shown in Figure 1 appears to be largely independent of the starting population. In particular, the GA was run several times with different, randomly selected starting populations and these runs produced essentially the same final population. The only notable differences were the substitution of a related variable for one of those listed above, for example waist circumference instead of body mass index (BMI). On the other hand, the final population doesn't necessarily contain only critical variables, those predictors that are important for the success of a classification tree. In fact, due to the way a GA processes information, it is possible for features to appear in the final population without having any role in the classification tree, simply because they happen to be chosen jointly with other, more critical predictors.

In the interest of finding the smallest, most critical feature set, it is useful to measure the relative importance of each predictor present in a given solution. In general, feature importance in decision trees is estimated by determining if the splitting variable improves the purity of the node (http://www.mathworks.com/ help/stats/classregtree.varimportance.html). Unfortunately, in some of our trials, calculating variable importance in this way produces results contrary to available information (ethnicity often appearing as having no importance as a factor affecting the incidence of diabetes, for example). A different approach to defining variable importance in decision trees is presented in [17]. In his approach, [17] proposes counting the predictor variables that direct an individual observation from the root to the leaf of the tree and apportioning importance accordingly. In this paper the approach proposed in [17] was implemented, using individuals in the test set to determine variable importance. Variable importance for a GA solution produced the results shown in Figure 2.

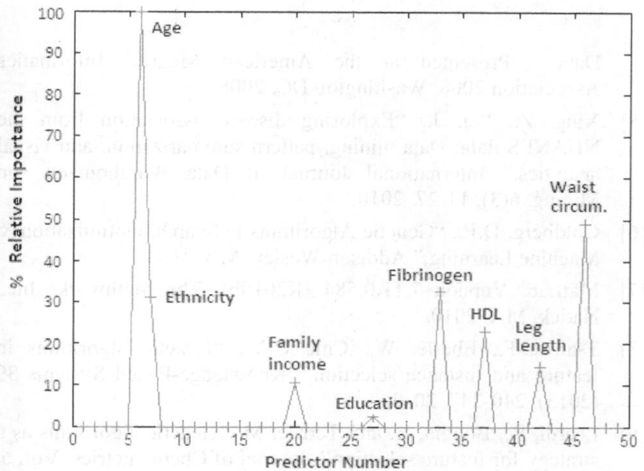

Figure 2. Relative importance of the predictors present in a GA solution. The y-axis represents the proportion of individuals in the testing set that are directed down the tree using the variables shown inside the box. HDL refers to HDL cholesterol. According to this analysis, age has, by far, the largest impact.

Combining the information from Figures 1 and 2 provides a much clearer picture of the importance of the predictors selected. Because Age was the variable at the root of the decision tree, it affected 100% of the individuals tested and is therefore the most important feature. At the other end, Education level impacted a relatively small percentage of the individuals in the testing set. Despite these differences, we are interested in all of these variables because the tree may identify relatively small portions of the space where an otherwise noncritical variable plays a big role in determining the presence or absence of the disease.

It is useful to compare the feature set obtained using this methodology to a situation where all the predictors are available for the construction of a decision tree. Figure 3 compares values of the average loss function applied to observations in the test sets used as the objective function of the 35 GA solutions in Figure 1 to results of 100 classification trees constructed from the complete set of predictors. In both instances, the same training/testing datasets, randomly created, have been used for every pair of GA/"all-available" solutions and the evaluation is over all folds, so that results can be directly compared.

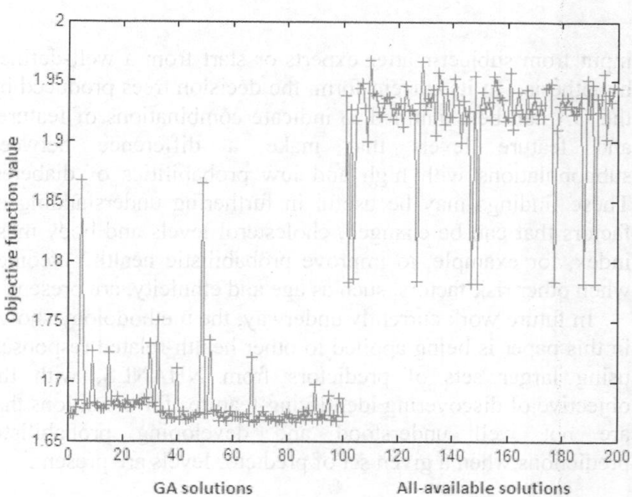

Figure 3. Average performance of GA-generated solutions (first 100 values shown) and "all-available" solutions using the same training/test sets. The objective function is the loss function described in the text. The GA solutions, in general, perform better than those for which all predictors are potentially available.

Figure 3 shows that, on average, the GA solutions are better than the "all-available" solutions. This conclusion is likely a consequence of the greedy nature of the splitting algorithm when confronted with a large number of predictors, especially if some of the predictors are categorical. In addition to reducing the average loss function as shown in Figure 3, the GA also produces much more parsimonious solutions, with many fewer variables than the "all-available" case. This result is important because the "all-available" solutions generally produce many non-zero importance values, resulting in a confusing picture and making it difficult to discriminate between more and less important predictors.

3. Conclusions

Using a dataset from the NHANES database, an optimization methodology that employs binary classification trees, genetic algorithms and a probability-based loss function has been employed to build decision trees with a small number of features, effectively and efficiently pruning a large number of variables down to a small number of highly important predictors. The predictors for diabetes found (age, ethnicity, income, education level, HDL cholesterol level, fibrinogen level, and two body measures) can be validated through reputable sources in the medical and public health fields. As implemented, the methodology allows for a more complete understanding of a complex variable space, including (1) the elimination of uninformative or redundant features, (2) the discovery of the most important predictors, (3) the level at which a given predictor is useful for discrimination, and (4) the relative importance of the predictors found. This approach allows to efficiently mine a database, identifying a small but important set of predictors for diabetes without having to elicit input from subject-matter experts or start from a well-defined hypothesis. In its current form, the decision trees produced by the GA can be examined to indicate combinations of features and feature levels that make a difference between subpopulations with high and low probabilities of diabetes. These findings may be useful in furthering understanding of factors that can be changed, cholesterol levels and body mass index, for example, to improve probabilistic health outcomes when other risk factors, such as age and ethnicity, are present.

In future work currently underway, the methodology shown in this paper is being applied to other health-related responses, using larger sets of predictors from NHANES, with the objective of discovering identifying features for conditions that are not well understood and developing probabilistic predictions when a given set of predictor levels are present.

ACKNOWLEDGMENT

The research described in this paper is part of the Signatures Discovery Initiative at Pacific Northwest National Laboratory. It was conducted under the Laboratory Directed Research and Development Program at PNNL, a multiprogram national laboratory operated by Battelle for the U.S. Department of Energy.

REFERENCES

[1] Annest, J.L., Pirkle , J.L., Makuc ,D., Neese, J.W., Bayse, D.D., Kovar, M.G, "Chronological trend in blood lead levels between 1976 and 1980," in New England Journal of Medicine, 308, 1373-1377, 1983.

[2] Yetley, E.A., Johnson, C.L., "Folate and vitamin B-12 biomarkers in NHANES: history of their measurement and use," The American Journal of Clinical Nutrition, May 18, 2011, 1S-10S, 2011.

[3] Li, C., Ford, E.S., Zhao, G., Croft, J.B., Balluz, L.S., Mokdad, A.H., "Prevalence of self-reported clinically diagnosed sleep apnea according to obesity status in men and women," National Health and Nutrition Examination Survey, 2005-2006. Preventive Medicine, 2010, 51(1), 18-23, 2010.

[4] Lee, J.W., Lin, Y.H., Smith, M., "Dependency mining on the 2005-06 National Health and Nutrition Examination Survey," Data. Presented at the American Medical Informatics Association 2008, Washington DC, 2008.

[5] Xing, Z., Pei, J., "Exploring disease association from the NHANES data: Data mining, pattern summarization, and visual analytics," International Journal of Data Warehousing and Mining, 6(3), 11-27, 2010.

[6] Goldberg, D.E., "Genetic Algorithms in Search, Optimization & Machine Learning," Addison Wesley, MA, 1989.

[7] MatLab. Version 7.11.0.584 (R2010b). The Mathworks Inc., Natick, MA, 2010.

[8] Tsai, C-F., Eberle, W., Chu, C-Y., "Genetic algorithms in feature and instance selection," Knowledge-Based Systems 39 (2013), 240-247, 2013.

[9] Leardi, R., Boggia, R. and Terrile, M. "Genetic algorithms as a strategy for feature selection". Journal of Chemometrics, Vol. 6, Issue 5, 267-281, 1992.

[10] Boyle, J.P., Honeycutt, A.A., Venkat Narayan, K.M., Hoerger, T.J., Geiss, L.S., Chen, H., Thompson, T.J., "Projection of diabetes burden through 2050," Diabetes Care, Vol. 24, Number 11, 1936-1940, November 2011.

[11] Provost, F., Domingos, P., "Tree Induction for Probability-based Ranking," Journal of Machine Learning, 52, 3, 199-215, 2003.

[12] Chawla, N.V., Cieslak, D.A., "Evaluating Probability Estimates from Decision Trees," American Association for Artificial Intelligence, 2006.

[13] Zadrozny, B., Elkan, C., "Learning and making decisions when costs and probabilities are both unknown," Proceedings of the seventh ACM SIGKDD International Conference on Knowledge Discovery and Data Mining. 204-213, 2001.

[14] Tumer, K., Ghosh, J., "Theoretical Foundations of Linear and Order Statistics Combiners for Neural Pattern Classifiers," Technical Report 95-02-98, The Computer and Vision Research Center, University of Texas, Austin, TX, 1995.

[15] Quiñonero-Candela, J., Rasmussen, C.E., Sinz, F., Bousquet, O., Schölkopf, B., "Evaluating Predictive Uncertainty Challenge," MLCW 2005, LNAI 3944, 1-27, 2006.

[16] Kafle, D.R., Shrestha, P., "Study of fibrinogen in patients with diabetes mellitus," Nepal Medical College Journal, 12(1), 34-37, 2010.

[17] Neville, P.G., "Decision Trees for Predictive Modeling," The SAS Institute, 1999.

SESSION

FILTERING, FEATURE SELECTION, INTEGRATION, ENSEMBLES

Chair(s)

Drs. Robert Stahlbock
Gary M. Weiss

Isolating Matrix Sparsity in Collaborative Filtering Ratings Matrices

Brian J. Pechkis and Eun-Joo Lee
Computer Science Department, East Stroudsburg University of Pennsylvania, East Stroudsburg, PA, U.S.A.

Abstract— *Collaborative filtering is a widely-used class of methods for providing recommendations of items that are personalized to each individual user's tastes. Although effective at providing easy access to the ratings of user-item pairs, the matrix data structure typically utilized for these tasks is often very sparse. Furthermore, the scalability of these systems suffers when performing operations on a large matrix with mostly null values. This paper proposes a method of reducing the size and sparsity of these matrices by rearranging the order of the rows and columns in such a way that the ratings are clustered into small, easily extractable submatrices. Experimental tests on a representative dataset show that, in addition to achieving those goals, the quality of the predictions within the densest submatrix is high, as indicated by a reduced error rate compared with the full, unaltered matrix.*

Keywords: collaborative filtering, recommender systems, data mining, matrix sparsity

1. Introduction

The continued expansion of the World Wide Web has made it easier to access a wide variety of products for purchase via e-commerce and media content providers, such as Amazon.com and Netflix. However, the large quantity of these products has made it more difficult for users to find products that are both pertinent to their preferences and that are of good quality. For this reason, collaborative filtering recommender systems have been developed to select products, or items, for recommendation to users based on a comparison of their purchase habits to those of other users [1] [2]. These recommendations often rely upon predicting a user's preference value, or rating, on items not previously purchased by the user [3]. Some algorithms for performing this prediction are more statistical in nature (memory-based), while others draw on techniques developed in the field of machine learning (model-based) [2] [3] [4] [5].

One data structure for storing user ratings is the user-item matrix, which contains one dimension for users and another for items, storing the rating of one user for one item where the two intersect. This data structure makes it simple to extract a vector containing the information for one user or one item and lends itself to linear algebra-based feature extraction techniques. However, the matrix tends to be very sparse, due to the users' inability to rate all of the millions of items available to them [4] [6] [7]. Dimensionality reduction through singular value decomposition has been proposed as a solution to this problem, but it has a high complexity due to the need to either compute or estimate eigenvalues and eigenvectors [6]. Other imputation-based or default voting techniques bias a user's average rating toward the imputated or default rating, compromising the effectiveness of the prediction algorithms [8] [9].

Therefore, this paper proposes a method that can effectively reduce the size of the original matrix prior to any preprocessing of the data. It will be shown that rearranging the matrix by creating a permutation of it can create denser regions that can be extracted and used for any further processing and collaborative filtering prediction. Results also indicate that producing a submatrix that is denser than the full, unaltered matrix results incorporates the user-item pairs that will yield more accurate predictions. The primary goal of this method is to reduce the effective size of the matrix.

2. User-Item Matrix Permutations

The goal of rearranging the user-item matrix in a collaborative filtering recommender is to isolate the sparsity of the matrix from newly-formed dense regions. Achieving this requires two steps. First, metrics are computed for each row or column to determine which half of the vector is denser, before they are grouped with vectors having a similar center of density. Second, as an optional additional step, isolation of a greater percentage of sparsity is ensured by preventing one group of vectors (either denser in lower indices or denser in higher densities) from being much larger than the other. A flow chart showing the steps of this algorithm is shown in Figure 1. This procedure produces approximately equal-size submatrices that are simple to extract and to be processed individually by collaborative filtering prediction algorithms.

2.1 Permutation Algorithm

In order to form dense matrix regions, there needs to be some means by which to judge which segments of a row or a column of the matrix are denser than others. Simplifying this idea, it would be beneficial to determine whether a row or a column contains more ratings in its lower-indexed elements or its higher-indexed elements. Two simple metrics have been developed to quantify which of these two ends of a row or a column is denser. Given a specific row or column

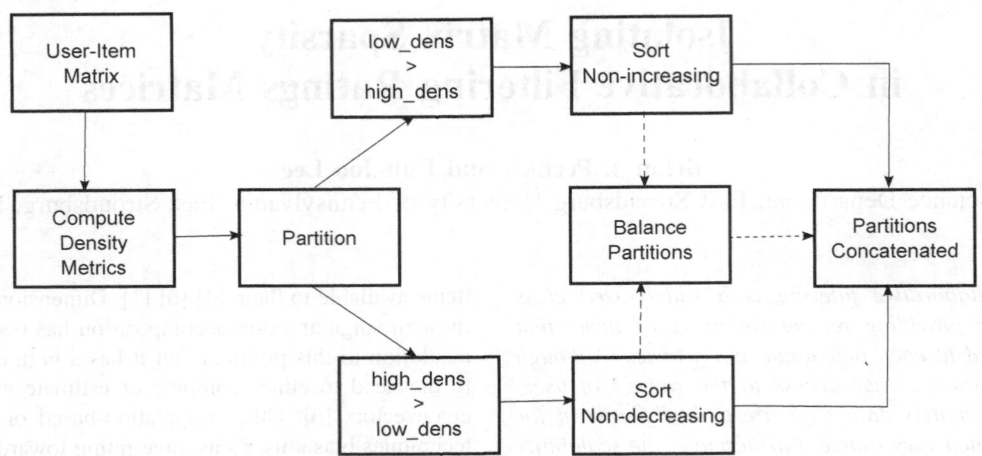

Fig. 1: Permutation algorithm flowchart

vector from the user-item matrix, v, of length n, we define Equation 1 and Equation 2.

$$low_{dens} = \sum_{i=1}^{n}((n+1)-1)^2 \quad \forall v(i) \neq null \qquad (1)$$

$$high_{dens} = \sum_{i=1}^{n} i^2 \quad \forall v(i) \neq null \qquad (2)$$

In Equation 1 , we see that, as $i \to \infty$, the terms in the summation become lower, resulting in higher overall values for vectors with larger numbers of lower-indexed ratings. Conversely, as $i \to \infty$, the terms within the summation in Equation 2 become higher, resulting in higher overall values for vectors containing more higher-indexed ratings. If these two metrics are computed for each of the rows and columns in the user-item matrix, a strong overall picture of the dense areas in the matrix is acquired.

This scheme of measuring vector density can be used to cluster vectors with similarly-located dense regions. Rows with greater density toward its lower-indexed elements can be grouped into one partition, and those with a greater density toward higher-indexed elements can be grouped into the other. Such a scheme can be duplicated for columns. In essence, this procedure examines each vector along one dimension of the matrix and decides which of the above-mentioned partitions to which it belongs. Then, it creates a permutation of the indices along the dimension by sorting the indices of vectors with a higher low_{dens} score by non-increasing order of low_{dens} metric and sorting the indices with a higher $high_{dens}$ score in non-decreasing order. If the dimension of interest is the rows of the matrix, we say that this algorithm performs a row permutation of the matrix, while it performs a column permutation if the columns of the matrix are considered.

The intent of this procedure is to create distinguishable regions with high numbers of non-null ratings in the matrix. A row permutation can be performed to create a matrix with a certain number of rows having more of its ratings to the left and a certain number of rows having more of its ratings to the right side of the matrix. A column permutation can be performed in addition to the row permutation to further solidify this pattern. The ultimate result is that we can find four clear regions in the matrix - two with a very high density of ratings and two with a rather sparse density of ratings. If these dense regions can be extracted from the matrix, the collaborative filtering algorithm can focus its efforts on them and have less exposure to sparsity, since many of the empty matrix elements have been moved to the sparse regions.

The efficiency of this algorithm comes from the fact that the ratings do not yet need to be in matrix form to perform the above-mentioned processing. It requires only a list of the non-zero elements of the matrix, which it adjusts once it has decided the proper ordering of the vectors along the specified dimension. When implemented in the C language, as was done for the tested implementation, the permutation algorithm becomes a simple exercise in list processing. Later, when processed as an actual matrix, the submatrices will exhibit the pattern described above. Therefore, assuming a dataset of w elements from an $m \times n$ matrix, this algorithm will only require w operations instead of the $m \times n$ needed to, at minimum, decide whether a matrix element is null or not. Although w could begin to approach $m \times n$ for denser matrices, this is unlikely to happen in the application of collaborative filtering. For instance, in the case of the MovieLens 100k dataset, $w = 100,000 << m \times n \approx 1.5M$. Therefore, the most computationally complex aspect of the algorithm is the sorting algorithm selected to sort the scores of the vectors in each partition. An efficient sorting algorithm designed for sorting numeric values can be utilized for this task.

2.2 Partition Balancing

The primary deficiency of the permutation algorithm is that it fails when faced with an imbalance in the data. For example, we may have many users (rows) who have rated more of the lower indexed items. Consequently, the balance of rows belonging to the low_{dens} partition will be very high. Should this same condition occur with the columns, we could be left with one very large submatrix and a few small ones. This would limit how many of the null values can be eliminated from consideration upon extraction of the submatrices. As a result, an add-on to this algorithm can help create a better balance between the partitions. After performing the initial partitioning of the vectors, the low_{dens} partition is sorted by non-decreasing order of $high_{dens}$ score or the $high_{dens}$ partition is sorted by non-increasing order of low_{dens} score, depending upon which has more member vectors. Then, the boundary marker is moved until there are an (approximately) even number of vectors in each partition. In effect, this process moves some of the vectors from the large partition that scores well in the other partition to that partition. The premise is that these vectors would still fit in well with the vectors of the other partitions, so it is acceptable to move them.

Once the permutation algorithm has been executed along both dimensions of the user-item matrix, the submatrices on which further processing and the collaborative filtering algorithms are run must be extracted. This process is simplified by the fact that the algorithm's execution has resulted in knowledge of where the boundary between the two density classes of vectors exists. If we divide the matrix along these boundary lines, it creates four submatrices of various densities that can be subjected to further preprocessing and to the collaborative filtering algorithms. Note that the full implementation of the permutation algorithm handles both the training and the corresponding test sets together. Once the submatrices are formed, the ratings that were part of the training set in the original matrix become part of the training set for the submatrix and likewise for the test ratings.

3. Experimental Setup

In addition to permutation algorithm described above, the system requires some additional components to constitute an operating collaborative filtering system. In this section, a description of the dataset used for the testing, as well as the preprocessing and collaborative filtering algorithms utilized are discussed.

3.1 Dataset

The chosen dataset for our testing was a widely-used, real-life dataset, the MovieLens 100k dataset [10]. It contains ratings data collected through the GroupLens research group's MovieLens movie recommendation website. The users of this website expressed their critique of various movies using a 1-5 scale, with 1 indicating a poor opinion of a movie and 5 indicating a high approval of the movie. The 100k dataset contains 943 unique users and 1682 unique movies (i.e. the "item" in this particular context), with its users submitting a total of 100,000 ratings out of a possible 1.59M ratings (a density of 6.3%). The MovieLens dataset contains a series of splits of training and test data, with each in the series containing a unique 20% subset used for test data, allowing for the use of 5-fold cross validation as the test method. This dataset meets the demands of testing collaborative filtering techniques by providing real-world data and, although not as large as many recommender systems, is large enough to discern the effects of the techniques in an operational setting.

3.2 Preprocessing

In collaborative filtering, it is rarely feasible to execute collaborative filtering algorithms on a raw set of ratings. These raw values usually are not numerous enough to be directly used to compute the Pearson correlations in a memory-based scenario nor do these alone serve as adequate features for training a model-based algorithm. As a result, a preprocessing of the data was needed to provide such features. The method used for preprocessing the training set parallels that described in [6]. Mean imputation is performed using the column mean, and then mean normalization is performed using the row mean. Once this was completed, the singular value decomposition could be computed for the matrix. Next, the element-wise square root of the matrix, S, was computed, so that any collaborative filtering prediction algorithm could use $U * \sqrt{S}$ as a set of features for each user and $\sqrt{S} * V^T$ could be used as a set of features for each item. Dimensionality reduction was delayed until execution of the collaborative filtering algorithms, so that the testing of multiple numbers of singular values to determine the permutation algorithm's effect on the optimal number of singular values. This procedure was performed in MATLAB, as its SVD routine was found to be faster than the one in the GNU Scientific Library used for implementing the collaborative filtering algorithms.

3.3 Collaborative Filtering Algorithms

After creating permutations of the user-item matrix, processing the matrix, and computing the singular value decomposition of the matrix, the process of producing predictions for each test rating in system can be performed. First, the training set for each submatrix is subjected to the training step for the algorithm while the test set is subjected to the prediction algorithm, producing the figures MAE and RMSE.

Three collaborative filtering algorithms were implemented. First, a user-based, memory-based algorithm was implemented that used the rows of $U * \sqrt{S}$ as the basis upon which Pearson correlation values were computed. The SVD-based algorithm described in [6] was also implemented. Fi-

Table 1: Percentage of non-null matrix elements (density) in submatrices extracted from permutation compared with density of original matrix

	No Balancing	Balancing
Unaltered	5.04%	-
Perm. submtx. 1	6.36%	3.36%
Perm. submtx. 2	3.11%	0.09%
Perm. submtx. 3	0.56%	14.92%
Perm. submtx. 4	8.41%	1.83%

Table 2: Number of non-null matrix elements in submatrices extracted from permutation compared with count from original matrix

	No Balancing	Balancing
Unaltered	80000.0	
Perm. submtx. 1	68424.0	13390.4
Perm. submtx. 2	6006.4	368.8
Perm. submtx. 3	1502.4	59027.2
Perm. submtx. 4	4067.2	7213.6

nally, a linear regression algorithm that learns the parameter matrix, λ, in the formula $P = (U * \sqrt{S}) * \lambda$ through a process of gradient descent was implemented to examine a more traditional model-based method.

4. Experimental Results

4.1 Evaluation Criteria

The testing of the permutation-enhanced collaborative filtering system required metrics through which to judge its effectiveness. This process was performed in two steps. First, it was evaluated how well the permutation algorithm clustered the ratings into dense submatrices, effectively isolating the sparsity to specific submatrices. This could be judged using two metrics - the density of the submatrices (i.e. what percentage of the submatrices' elements were non-null) and the number of ratings contained in the submatrix. The second of these two helped judge how many of the non-null elements from the original matrix were contained in each of the submatrices.

In addition, it needed to be determined whether performing these permutations had any effect on the error of the predicted ratings made by the collaborative filtering algorithm. The well-established collaborative filtering error metric - the mean absolute error (MAE) - was computed as shown in Equation 3.

$$MAE = \frac{1}{n} \sum_{R_{i,j} \neq null} |P_{i,j} - R_{i,j}| \quad (3)$$

4.2 Submatrix Density

The first step in evaluating the above collaborative filtering system was to fine-tune the parameters of the permutation algorithm. These parameters included the order in which the two dimensions of the matrix were permutated, the number of iterations of the algorithm, and whether the partition balancing routine was used or not. The primary means of evaluation was the density of the submatrices and the number of ratings in each submatrix.

The densities of the submatrices when partition balancing was used and was not used are shown in Table 1. The submatrices are numbered from left-to-right and top-to-bottom according to their position in the matrix. As anticipated, the permutation created when partition balancing is not used creates one large submatrix with a much greater density than the original matrix, but its size is very small compared to the second-densest submatrix. In addition, this second-densest submatrix contains a majority of the ratings in the original dataset, as shown in Table 2. When partition balancing was not used, the sizes of the submatrices are more uniform, and the largest one still contains a large percentage of the ratings from the original matrix while the others have a smaller density. However, the second-densest one contains enough ratings that, if combined with the densest, the number of ratings approaches that of the large, dense matrix in the other test, except that the total number of matrix elements (both null and non-null) is less. Our tests revealed that the order in which the dimensions were permutated did not alter the densities of the submatrices.

The permutation algorithm was also tested with a number of iterations varying between 1 and 20. Since it was found that the densities of the submatrices did not change significantly after 5 iterations, numbers of iterations between 1 and 5 were also tested. Overall the change in density was minute with a changing number of iterations, varying only by a fraction of a percentage point after the first few iterations. However, it appeared that 10 iterations maximized the densities of the two densest submatrices, and therefore, this number of iterations was used for any further tests. The optimal number of iterations was the same for the case in which the partition balancing was not used.

4.3 Collaborative Filtering Prediction Error

Submatrices created by the permutation algorithm were subjected to the three collaborative filtering algorithms mentioned above. A wide range of numbers of singular values was tested. The row permutation was performed first, and only the matrices created using the partition balancing routine were tested, as it was a goal to test the error rate of the concatenation of the two densest submatrices.

Table 3 on the final page shows the error rate of the linear regression collaborative filtering algorithm on the submatrices with changing numbers of singular values. The values between 10-20 were tested since the results in [6], upon which the SVD algorithm is based, indicates a minimum MAE within this range. Higher values were also tested to determine the difference in MAE with increasing numbers of singular values. The SVD-based algorithm demonstrated a similar trend in its results, although the MAE of submatrices 1 and 4 had a slightly higher MAE than in the linear regression case. It reveals a trend that, if the submatrix is of greater density than the original, full matrix, then the error rate will be lower, In addition, the concatenation of the two densest submatrices did not show an error rate that was as low as the densest submatrix alone. It appears that concatenating the second-densest submatrix (which by itself has a lower density than the original matrix) introduces enough sparsity back into the data that the error rates are slightly reduced. However, the one advantage is that these two submatrices permitted all of the users to be included in the combined dataset.

The memory-based algorithm was also tested with the same datasets. However, none of the submatrices had a lower error rate than the original matrix. This likely is due to the fact that memory-based algorithms compute predictions from the weighted averages of already-existing ratings. Therefore, predictions computed from a smaller subset of a user's or an item's ratings are based on less information, and the error rates are bound to be higher.

5. Conclusion

Creating permutations of a user-item matrix in a collaborative filtering recommender system has two primary benefits. First, the size of the matrix can be reduced by about half while losing only approximately 10% of the ratings in the original dataset. Furthermore, when such a permutation is created, the highest quality predictions are contained within the densest submatrix, as indicated by a lower error rate compared to the full, unaltered matrix. These more accurate predictions are ultimately more useful when making recommendations to the user. In conclusion, this method addresses two of the major drawbacks of collaborative filtering recommender systems - sparsity and scalability - in a simple algorithm.

References

[1] F. Ricci, L. Rokach, and B. Shapira, "Introduction to recommender systems handbook," in *Recommender Systems Handbook*, F. Ricci, L. Rokach, B. Shapira, and P. B. Kantor, Eds. U.S.: Springer, 2011, pp. 1–35.

[2] G. Adomavicius and A. Tuzhilin, "Toward the next generation of recommender systems: a survey of the state-of-the-art and possible extensions," *IEEE Trans. Knowl. Data Eng.*, vol. 17, pp. 734–749, Jun. 2005.

[3] J. Schafer, D. Frankowski, J. Herlocker, and S. Sen, "Collaborative filtering recommender systems," in *The Adaptive Web*, ser. Lecture Notes in Computer Science, P. Brusilovsky, A. Kobsa, and W. Nejdl, Eds. Berlin/Heidelberg, Germany: Springer, 2007, vol. 4321, pp. 291–324.

[4] J. Zhou and T. Luo, "Towards an introduction to collaborative filtering," in *Int. Conf. Computational Science and Engineering*, vol. 4, 2009, pp. 576–581.

[5] B. Sarwar, G. Karypis, J. Konstan, and J. Riedl, "Item-based collaborative filtering recommendation algorithms," in *Proc. 10th Int. Conf. World Wide Web*, ser. WWW '01. New York, NY, USA: ACM, 2001, p. 285âĂŞ295. [Online]. Available: http://doi.acm.org/10.1145/371920.372071

[6] B. M. Sarwar, G. Karypis, J. A. Konstan, and J. T. Riedl, "Application of dimensionality reduction in recommender system - a case study," in *ACM Web KDD Workshop*, 2000.

[7] J. A. Konstan, J. Riedl, A. Borchers, and J. L. Herlocker, "Recommender systems: A grouplens perspective," in *Proc. 1998 Workshop Recommender Systems*, 1998.

[8] X. Su, T. M. Khoshgoftaar, and R. Greiner, "A mixture imputation-boosted collaborative filter," in *Proc. 21th Int. Florida Artificial Intelligence Research Society Conf.*, 2008, p. 312âĂŞ317.

[9] J. S. Breese, D. Heckerman, and C. Kadie, "Empirical analysis of predictive algorithms for collaborative filtering," in *Proc. 14th Conf. Uncertainty and Artificial Intelligence*, ser. UAI'98. San Francisco, CA, USA: Morgan Kaufmann Publishers Inc., 1998, p. 43âĂŞ52. [Online]. Available: http://dl.acm.org/citation.cfm?id=2074094.2074100

[10] J. L. Herlocker, J. A. Konstan, A. Borchers, and J. T. Riedl, "An algorithmic framework for performing collaborative filtering," in *Proc. 1999 Conf. Research and Development Information Retrieval*, Aug. 1999.

Table 3: Prediction error of linear regression algorithm

Num. Singular Values	Unaltered	Perm. submtx. 1	Perm. submtx. 2	Perm. submtx. 3	Perm. submtx. 4	Perm. Submtx. 1&3
10	0.7658	0.8212	2.2212	0.7414	0.8329	0.7533
11	0.7656	0.8211	2.2227	0.7411	0.8324	0.7532
12	0.7654	0.8207	2.2216	0.7410	0.8324	0.7531
13	0.7653	0.8206	2.2211	0.7409	0.8324	0.7530
14	0.7651	0.8206	2.2216	0.7407	0.8323	0.7529
15	0.7651	0.8204	2.2214	0.7407	0.8323	0.7528
16	0.7649	0.8204	2.2210	0.7405	0.8322	0.7528
17	0.7648	0.8203	2.2217	0.7404	0.8321	0.7527
18	0.7647	0.8202	2.2214	0.7404	0.8319	0.7527
19	0.7646	0.8202	2.2199	0.7403	0.8320	0.7526
20	0.7645	0.8200	2.2197	0.7402	0.8318	0.7526
30	0.7639	0.8198	2.2218	0.7398	0.8306	0.7522
40	0.7636	0.8193	2.2194	0.7396	0.8294	0.7521
50	0.7632	0.8190	2.2198	0.7394	0.8283	0.7520
60	0.7629	0.8192	2.2206	0.7390	0.8273	0.7518
70	0.7626	0.8192	2.2198	0.7388	0.8267	0.7517
80	0.7625	0.8191	2.2198	0.7387	0.8259	0.7516
90	0.7623	0.8192	2.2198	0.7386	0.8252	0.7516
100	0.7622	0.8193	2.2198	0.7385	0.8247	0.7515

A Novel Randomized Feature Selection Algorithm

Subrata Saha[1], **Rampi Ramprasad**[2], **and Sanguthevar Rajasekaran**[1]*
[1]Department of Computer Science and Engineering
[2]Department of Materials Science and Engineering
University of Connecticut, Storrs
(*Corresponding author)
Email: {subrata.saha, rampi, rajasek}@engr.uconn.edu

Abstract— *Feature selection is the problem of identifying a subset of the most relevant features in the context of model construction. This problem has been well studied and plays a vital role in machine learning. In this paper we present a novel randomized algorithm for feature selection. It is generic in nature and can be applied for any learning algorithm. This algorithm can be thought of as a random walk in the space of all possible subsets of the features. We demonstrate the generality of our approach using three different applications.*

Keywords: Feature Selection (FS), Machine Learning, Data Integration (DI), Gene Selection Algorithm (GSA), Kernel Ridge Regression (KRR), Sequential Forward Search (SFS).

1. Introduction

Feature Selection is defined as the process of selecting a subset of the most relevant features from a set of features. FS involves discarding the irrelevant, redundant and noisy features. Feature selection is also known as variable selection, attribute selection or variable subset selection in the fields of machine learning and statistics. The concept of feature selection is different from feature extraction. Feature extraction creates new features from the set of original features by employing a variety of methods such as linear combinations of features, projection of features from the original space into a transformed space, etc. We can summarize the usefulness of feature selection as follows: (1) Shorter training times: When irrelevant and redundant features are eliminated, the learning time decreases; (2) Improved model creation: The model built is more accurate and efficient; and (3) Enhanced generalization: It produces simpler and more generalized models.

A generic feature selection algorithm employs the following steps: (1) Select a subset of features; (2) Evaluate the selected subset; and (3) Terminate if the stopping condition is met. The algorithm generates candidate subsets using different searching strategies depending on the application. Each of the candidate subsets is then evaluated based on an objective function. In the context of any learning algorithm, the objective function could be the accuracy. Note that for any learning algorithm there are two phases. In the first phase (known as the *training phase*), the learner is trained with a set of known examples. In the second phase (known as the *test phase*), the algorithm is tested on unknown examples. Accuracy refers to the fraction of test examples on which the learner is able to give correct answers. In the feature selection algorithm, if the current subset of features yields a better value for the objective function, the previous best solution is replaced with the current one. If not, the next candidate is generated. This process iterates over the search space until a stopping condition is satisfied. Finally, the best subset is validated by incorporating prior knowledge.

In this paper we introduce a novel randomized technique for feature selection. This technique can be used in the context of any learning algorithm. Consider the space of all possible subsets of features. We start with a random subset s of the features and calculate its accuracy. We then choose a *random neighbor*[1] s' of s and compute its accuracy. If the accuracy of s' is greater than that of s, we move to the new subset s' and proceed with the search from this point. On the other hand, if the accuracy of s' is smaller than that of s, we stay with the subset s (with some probability p) or move to the subset s' with probability $1 - p$. We proceed with the search from the point we end up with. This process of searching the space is continued until no significant improvement in the accuracy can be obtained. Our randomized search technique is generic in nature. We have employed it on three different applications and found that it is indeed scalable, reliable and efficient. Note that our algorithm resembles many local searching algorithms (such as Simulated Annealing (SA)). However, our algorithm is much simpler and differs from the others. For example, we do not employ the notion of *temperature* that SA utilizes.

The rest of this paper is organized as follows: Related works are summarized in Section 2. Some background information and preliminaries are presented in Section 3. In this section, from among other things, we provide a brief introduction to *Kernel Ridge Regression*, *Data Integration*, and *Materials Property Prediction*. In Section 4 we describe our proposed algorithm. The performance of the algorithm and the experimental results are presented in Section 5.

[1]The notion of a random neighbor is defined precisely in Section 4.

Section 6 concludes the paper.

2. Related Works

In this section we provide a summary of some well-known feature selection algorithms. These algorithms differ in the way the candidate subsets are generated and in the evaluation criterion used.

2.1 Selection of candidate subsets

Subset selection begins with an initial subset that could be empty, the entire set of features, or some randomly chosen features. This initial subset can be changed in a number of ways. In forward selection strategy, features are added one at a time. In backward selection the least important feature is removed based on some evaluation criterion. Random search strategy randomly adds or removes features to avoid being trapped in a local maximum. If the total number of features is n, the total number of candidate subsets is 2^n. An exhaustive search strategy searches through all the 2^n feature subsets to find an optimal one. Clearly, this may not be feasible in practice [1]. A number of heuristic search strategies have been introduced to overcome this problem. The branch and bound method [2] exploits exhaustive search by maintaining and traversing a tree, but stops the search along a particular branch if a predefined boundary value is exceeded. The branch and bound method has been shown to be effective on many problem instances.

Greedy hill climbing strategies modify the current subset in such a way that results in the maximum improvement in the objective function (see e.g., [3]). Sequential forward search (SFS) [4,5], sequential backward search (SBS), and bidirectional search [6] are some variations to the greedy hill climbing method. In these methods, the current subset is modified by adding or deleting features. SFS sequentially searches the feature space by starting from the empty set and selects the best single feature to add into the set in each iteration. On the contrary, SBS starts from the full feature set and removes the worst single feature from the set in each iteration. Both approaches add or remove features one at a time. Algorithms with sequential searches are fast and have a time complexity of $O(n^2)$. Sequential forward floating search (SFFS) and sequential backward floating search (SBFS) [7] combine the strategies followed by SFS and SBS. Some feature selection algorithms randomly pick subsets of features from the feature space by following some probabilistic steps and sampling procedures. Examples include evolutionary algorithms [8,9], and simulated annealing [10]. The use of randomness helps in the avoidance of getting trapped in local maxima.

2.2 Evaluation of the generated subset:

After selecting the subsets from the original set of features, they are evaluated using an objective function. One possible objective function is the accuracy of the predictive model. Feature selection algorithms can be broadly divided into two categories: (1) wrapper, and (2) filter. In a wrapper method the classification or prediction accuracy of an inductive learning algorithm of interest is used for evaluation of the generated subset. For each generated feature subset, wrappers evaluate its accuracy by applying the learning algorithm using the features residing in the subset. Although it is a computationally expensive procedure, wrappers can find the subsets from the feature space with a high accuracy because the features match well with the learning algorithm. Filter methods are computationally more efficient than wrapper methods since they evaluate the accuracy of a subset of features using objective criteria that can be tested quickly. Common objective criteria include the mutual information, Pearson product-moment correlation coefficient, and the inter/intra class distance. Though filters are computationally more efficient than wrappers, often they produce a feature subset which is not matched with a specific type of predictive model and thus can yield worse prediction accuracies.

3. Background Summary

In this paper we offer a novel randomized feature selection algorithm and demonstrate its applicability using three different applications. The applications of interest are: 1) the prediction of materials properties, 2) data integration, and 3) analysis of biological data. We employ the following learning algorithms: Kernel Ridge Regression (KRR) and Support Vector Machine (SVM). In this section we provide a brief summary on these applications and learning algorithms.

3.1 Kernel Ridge Regression (KRR)

Kernel ridge regression is a data-rich non-linear forecasting technique. It is applicable in many different contexts ranging from optical character recognition to business forecasting. KRR has proven to be better than many well-known predictors. It is not much different from ridge regression rather it employs a clever algebraic trick to improve the computational efficiency. The central idea in kernel ridge regression is to employ a flexible set of nonlinear prediction functions and to prevent over-fitting by penalization. It is done in such a way that the computational complexity is reduced significantly. This is achieved by mapping the set of predictors into a high-dimensional (or even infinite-dimensional) space of nonlinear functions of the predictors. A linear forecast equation is then estimated in this high dimensional space. It also employs a penalty (or shrinkage, or ridge) term to avoid over-fitting. It is called kernel ridge regression since it uses the kernel trick to map the set of predictors into a high dimensional space and adds a ridge term to avoid over-fitting.

Assume that we are given N observations $(x_1, y_1), (x_2, y_2), \ldots, (x_N, y_N)$ with $x_i \in \Re^d$ and $y_i \in \Re$, for $1 \leq i \leq N$. Our goal is to find a function f such that $f(x_i)$ is a good approximation of y_i for $1 \leq i \leq N$. Once we identify such a function we can use it on any unknown observation $x' \in \Re^d$ to estimate the corresponding y' as $f(x')$. Ridge regression calculates the parameter vector $w \in \Re^d$ of a linear model $f(x) = w.x$ by minimizing the objective function:

$$W_{RR}(w) = \frac{1}{2}\|w\|^2 + \frac{\gamma}{N}\sum_{i=1}^{N}(y_i - w.x_i)^2 \quad (1)$$

The objective function used in ridge regression (1) implements a form of Tikhonov regularisation [11] of a sum-of-squares error metric, where γ is a regularization parameter controlling the bias-variance trade-off [12].

A non-linear form of ridge regression [13] can be obtained by employing kernel trick. Here a linear ridge regression model is constructed in a higher dimensional feature space induced by a non-linear kernel function defining the inner product:

$$K(x_a, x_b) = \varphi(x_a).\varphi(x_b) \quad (2)$$

The kernel function can be any positive definite kernel. One of the popular kernels is Gaussian radial basis function (RBF) kernel:

$$K(x_a, x_b) = \exp\left(-\frac{\| x_a - x_b\|^2}{2\sigma^2}\right) \quad (3)$$

where σ is a tunable parameter. The objective function minimized in kernel ridge regression can be written as:

$$W_{KRR}(w) = \frac{1}{2} \| w\|^2 + \frac{\gamma}{N}\sum_{i=1}^{N}\xi_i^2 \quad (4)$$

subject to the constraints:
$\xi_i = y_i - w.\varphi(x_i), \forall i \in \{1, 2, \ldots, N\}$

The output of the KRR model is given by the equation:

$$f(x) = \sum_{i=1}^{N}\alpha_i\varphi(x_i).\varphi(x) = \sum_{i=1}^{N}\alpha_i K(x_i, x) \quad (5)$$

3.2 Gene Selection

Gene selection is based on SVMs [14-18] and it takes as input n genes $\{g_1, g_2, g_3, \ldots, g_n\}$, and l vectors $\{v_1, v_2, v_3, \ldots, v_l\}$. As an example, each v_i could be an outcome of a microarray experiment and each vector could be of the following form: $v_i = \{x_i^1, x_i^2, x_i^3, \ldots, x_i^n, y_i\}$. Here x_i^j is the expression level of the jth gene g_j in experiment i. The value of y_i is either *+1* or *-1* based on whether the event of interest is present in experiment i or not. The problem is to identify a set of genes $\{g_i^1, g_i^2, g_i^3, \ldots, g_i^m\}$ sufficient to predict the value of y_i in each experiment. Given a set of vectors, the gene selection algorithm learns to identify the minimum set of genes needed to predict the event of interest and the prediction function. These vectors form the training set for the algorithm. Once trained, the algorithm is provided with a new set of data which is called the test set. The accuracy of gene selection is measured in the test set as a percentage of microarray data on which the algorithm correctly predicts the event of interest. The procedure solely relies on the concept of SVM.

The gene selection algorithm of Song and Rajasekaran [19] is based on the ideas of combining the mutual information among the genes and incorporating correlation information to reject the redundant genes. The Greedy Correlation Incorporated Support Vector Machine (GCI-SVM) algorithm of [19] can be briefly summarized as follows: The SVM is trained only once and the genes are sorted according to the norm of the weight vector corresponding to these genes. Then the sorted list of genes are examined starting from the second gene. The correlation of each of these genes with the first gene is computed until one whose correlation with the first one is less than a certain predefined threshold is found. At this stage this gene is moved to the second place. Now the genes starting from the third gene are examined and the correlation of each of these genes with the second gene is computed until a gene whose correlation with the second gene is less than the threshold is encountered. The above procedure is repeated until end of the list of the sorted genes is reached. In the last stage, genes based on this adjusted sorted genes are selected. GCI-SVM brings the concept of sort-SVM and RFE-SVM [20] altogether which makes it more efficient.

3.3 Data Integration

Data integration involves combining data residing in different sources and providing users with a unified view of these data [21]. As an example, the same person may have health care records with different providers. It helps to merge all the records with all the providers and cluster these records such that each cluster corresponds to one individual. Such an integration, for instance, could help us avoid performing the same tests again and hence save money.

Several techniques [22-25] have been proposed to solve the data integration problem. In [26] the authors have proposed several space and time efficient techniques to integrate multiple datasets from disparate data sources. They employ hierarchical clustering techniques to integrate data of similar types and avoid the computation of cross-products. It can cope up with some common errors committed in input data such as typing distance and sound distance. Furthermore, it can deal with some human-made typing errors e.g., reversal of the first and last names, nickname usage, and attribute truncation.

3.4 Materials Property Prediction

If one wants to determine properties of a given unknown material, the traditional approaches are lab measurements or computationally intensive simulations (for example using the Density Functional Theory). An attractive alternative is to employ learning algorithms. The idea is to learn the desired properties from easily obtainable information about the material. In this paper we consider an infinite polymeric chain composed of XY_2 building blocks, with X = C, Si, Ge, or Sn, and Y = H, F, Cl, or Br. We are interested in estimating different properties of such chains including dielectric constant and band gap. We assume that an infinite polymer chain with a repeat unit containing 4 distinct building blocks, with each of these 4 blocks being any of CH_2, SiF_2, $SiCl_2$, GeF_2, $GeCl_2$, SnF_2, or $SnCl_2$. By plotting the total dielectric constant (composed of the electronic and ionic contributions) and the electronic part of the dielectric constant against the computed band gap, we find some correlations between these three properties. While some correlations are self-evident (and expected)—such as the inverse relationship between the band gap and the electronic part of the dielectric constant, and the large dielectric constant of those systems that contain contiguous SnF_2 units—it is not immediately apparent if these observations may be formalized in order to allow for quantitative property predictions for systems (within this sub-class, of course) not originally considered. For example, can we predict the properties of a chain with a repeat unit containing 8 building blocks (with each of the blocks being any of the aforementioned units)? In Section 5, we show that this can indeed be done with high-fidelity using our randomized search method.

We use specific sub-structures, or *motifs* or *scaffolds*, within the main structure to create the attribute vector. Let us illustrate this using the specific example of the polymeric dielectrics created using XY_2 building blocks. Say there are 7 possible choices (or motifs) for each XY_2 unit: CH_2, SiF_2, $SiCl_2$, GeF_2, $GeCl_2$, SnF_2, and $SnCl_2$. The attribute vector may be defined in terms of 6 fractions, $|f_1, f_2, f_3, f_4, f_5, f_6\rangle$, where f_i is the fraction of XY_2 type or motif i (note that $f_7 = 1 - \Sigma_{i=1}^{6} f_i$). One can extend the components of the attribute vector to include clusters of 2 or 3 XY_2 units of the same type occurring together; such an attribute vector could be represented as $|f_1, \ldots, f_6, g_1, \ldots, g_7, h_1, \ldots, h_7\rangle$, where g_i and h_i are, respectively, the fraction of XY_2 pairs of type i and the fraction of XY_2 triplets of type i. In Section 5, we demonstrate that such a motif-based attribute vector does a remarkable job of codifying and capturing the information content of the XY_2 polymeric class of systems, allowing us to train our machines and make high-fidelity predictions.

4. Our Algorithm

If we can identify a subset of the features that are the most important in determining a property, it will lead to computational efficiency as well as a better accuracy. It is conceivable that some of the features might be hurtful rather than helpful in predictions. Let $\vec{A} = |a_1, a_2, \ldots, a_n\rangle$ be the set of features under consideration. One could use the following simple strategy, in the context of any learning algorithm, to identify a subset of $\vec{A}$ that yields a better accuracy in predictions than $\vec{A}$ itself. For some small value of k (for example 2), we identify all the $\binom{n}{k}$ subsets of $\vec{A}$. For each such subset we train the learner, figure out the accuracy we can get, and pick that subset $\vec{S}$ that yields the best accuracy. Now, from the remaining features, we add one feature at a time to $\vec{S}$ and for each resultant subset, we compute the accuracy obtainable from the learner. Let $\vec{S}'$ be the set (of size $k+1$) of attributes that yields the best accuracy. Next, from the remaining attributes, we add one feature at a time to $\vec{S}'$ and identify a set of size $k+2$ with the best accuracy, and so on. Finally, from out of all of the above accuracies, we pick the best one.

We can think of the above simple technique as a greedy algorithm that tries to find an optimal subset of attributes and it may not always yield optimal results. On the other hand, it will be infeasible to try every subset of attributes (since there are 2^n such subsets). We propose the following novel approach instead: Consider the space of all possible subsets of attributes. We start with a random point p (i.e., a random subset of the features) in this space and calculate the accuracy q corresponding to this subset. We then flip an unbiased three sided coin with sides 1, 2, and 3. If the outcome of the coin flip is 1, we choose a random neighbor p' of this point by removing one feature from p and adding a new feature to p. After choosing p', we compute its accuracy q'. If $q' > q$ then we move to the point p' and proceed with the search from p'. On the other hand, if $q' < q$, then we stay with point p (with some probability u) or move to point p' with probability $(1-u)$. This step is done to ensure that we do not get stuck in a local maximum. If the outcome of the coin flip is 2, we choose a random neighbor p' by removing one feature from p and compute its accuracy q'. The next steps are the same as stated in the case of 1. Consider the last case where the outcome of the coin flip is 3. We choose a random neighbor p' by adding one feature to p and compute its accuracy q'. The rest of the steps are the same as above. If $q' > q$ then we move to the point p' and proceed with the search from p'. On the other hand, if $q' < q$, then we stay with point p (with some probability u) or move to point p' with probability $(1-u)$. We proceed with the search from the point we end up with. This process of searching the space is continued until no significant improvement in the accuracy can be obtained. A relevant choice for u is $\exp(-c(q-q'))$ for some constant c. In fact, the above algorithm resembles the simulated annealing (SA) algorithm of [30]. Note that our algorithm is very different from SA. In particular, our algorithm is much simpler than SA. Details of our algorithm can be found in Algorithm 1.

5. Results and Discussions

We have employed our randomized feature selection algorithm on three different application domains. These applications include but not limited to the prediction of properties of materials, data integration, and processing of biological data. Our algorithm is generic and can be used in conjunction with any learning algorithm.

Algorithm 1: Randomized Feature Selection

```
Input: The set F of all possible features and an Inductive Learning Algorithm 𝓛
Output: A near optimal subset F' of features
begin
    Randomly sample a subset F' of features from F.
    Run the inductive learning algorithm 𝓛 using the features in F'.
    Compute the accuracy A of the concept C learnt by 𝓛.
    repeat
        Flip an unbiased three sided coin with sides 1, 2, and 3.
        if (the outcome of the coin flip is 1){
            Choose a random feature f from F − F' and add it to F'.
            Remove a random feature f' from F' to get F''.
        } else if (the outcome of the coin flip is 2){
            Choose a random feature f from F − F' and add it to F' to get F''.
        } else if (the outcome of the coin flip is 3){
            Remove a random feature f from F' to get F''.
        }
        Run the inductive learning algorithm 𝓛 using the features in F''.
        Compute the accuracy A' of the concept C' learnt by 𝓛.
        if (A' > A ){
            F' := F'' and A := A'; Perform the search from F'.
        } else{
            With probability u perform the search from F' and
            with probability 1 − u perform the search from F'' with A := A'.
        }
    until no significant improvement in the accuracy can be obtained;
    Output F'.
```

5.1 Gene Selection

We have used the gene selection algorithm to identify some of the best features that can together identify two groups. The gene selection algorithm has two phases. In the first phase, the algorithm is trained with a training dataset. In this phase the algorithm comes up with a model of concept. In the second phase of the algorithm a test dataset is presented. The model learned in the first phase is used to classify the elements residing in the test dataset. As a result, the accuracy of the model learned can be computed. At first, we generated 4 datasets each having 200 subjects with 15, 20, 25, and 30 features, respectively. Each of the features has been given a random value in the range $[0, 99]$. We then randomly assigned a class label to each of the subjects residing in each dataset. Specifically, each subject is assigned to group 1 with probability $\frac{1}{2}$ and it is assigned to group 2 with probability $\frac{1}{2}$. We trained the classifier using a training set which consists of 50 percent of data from each of group 1 and group 2 (data being chosen randomly). The test set is formed using the other 50 percent from group 1 and group 2, respectively. GSA is trained with the training set and it builds a model of concept using SVMs. We have used LINEAR, and GAUSSIAN RBF to build the model of concept. The result is a $n \times m$ matrix where n is the number of subjects and m is the most influential features of the training dataset. Using the test data we have measured the accuracy. After employing our randomized search technique in conjunction with gene selection algorithm, the accuracy is greatly improved and at the same time the number of features is decreased significantly (please, see TABLE 1).

Table 1: GSA and modified GSA (GSA and mo-GSA) schemes

		GSA		Modified GSA	
System	Method	Accuracy	# of Features	Accuracy	# of Features
Dataset 1	GAUSSIAN	50%	15	54%	10
	LINEAR	49%	15	62%	12
Dataset 2	GAUSSIAN	52%	20	60%	13
	LINEAR	53%	20	65%	13
Dataset 3	GAUSSIAN	49%	25	58%	9
	LINEAR	50%	25	58%	11
Dataset 4	GAUSSIAN	50%	30	59%	13
	LINEAR	56%	30	62%	13

5.2 Data Integration

Data integration technique of [26] is used to detect similar types of data from a set of databases. To test the performance of our approach, we generated 4 datasets each having 10,000 subjects where each subject has 5 features. The features consist of a person's first name, last name, date of birth, sex, and zip code. In general, each person has multiple records. Since errors are introduced randomly in the features, instances of the same individual may differ from each other. Accuracy of any data integration method is calculated as the fraction of persons for whom all the instances have been correctly identified to be belonging to the same person.

We have employed our randomized feature selection algorithm on the data integration technique of [26]. The accuracy has been greatly improved and at the same time the number of features has also decreased (please, see TABLE 2).

5.3 Materials Property Prediction

We consider polymeric dielectrics created using the XY_2 blocks as described in Section 3. If we assume that our repeat unit consists of 4 building blocks, and that each building block can be any of 7 distinct units (namely, CH_2, SiF_2, $SiCl_2$, GeF_2, $GeCl_2$, SnF_2, and $SnCl_2$), we have a total of 175 distinct polymer chains (accounting for translational symmetry). Of these, we set 130 to be in the training set, and the remainder in the test set to allow for validation of the machine learning model.

Attribute vectors may be chosen in different ways. Consider the motif-based one as described in Section 3, i.e., our attribute vector, $\vec{A^i} = |f_1^i, \ldots, f_6^i, g_1^i, \ldots, g_7^i, h_1^i, \ldots, h_7^i\rangle$, where f_j^i, g_j^i and h_j^i are, respectively, the fraction of XY_2 units of type j, the fraction of pair clusters of XY_2 units of type j and the fraction of triplet clusters of XY_2 units of type j. Once our machine has learned how to map between the attribute vectors and the properties using the training set, we make predictions on the test set (as well as the training set). Furthermore, we considered several 8-block repeat units (in addition to the 175 4-block systems), and performed our machine learning scheme.

We have tested the above techniques on the KRR scheme presented in Section 3 with the systems represented using the motif-based attribute vectors. We refer to the greedy extension as the modified greedy KRR (mg-KRR) approach and the modified optimization version as mo-KRR. An assessment of the improvement in the predictive power when mg-KRR and mo-KRR are used for the three properties of interest (namely, the band gap, the electronic part of the dielectric constant and the total dielectric constant) is presented in Table 3. As can be seen, the level of accuracy of the machine learning schemes is uniformly good for all three properties across the 4-block training and test set, as well as the 8-block test set, indicative of the high-fidelity nature of this approach. In particular, note that the mg-KRR and mo-KRR methods, in general, lead to better accuracy. More importantly, typically, the number of attribute components decreases significantly. This means a significant reduction in the run times of the algorithms while predicting parameter values for an unknown material.

6. Conclusions

We have presented a novel randomized search technique which is generic in nature and can be applied to any inductive learning algorithm for selecting a subset of the most relevant features from the set of all possible features. The proposed scheme falls into the class of wrapper methods where the prediction accuracy in each step is determined by the learning algorithm of interest. To demonstrate the validity of our approach, we have applied it in three different applications, namely, biological data processing, data integration, and materials property prediction. It is evident from the simulation results shown above that our proposed technique is indeed reliable, scalable, and efficient.

Acknowledgment

This work has been supported in part by the following grants: NSF 0829916 and NIH R01-LM010101.

Table 2: DI and modified DI (DI and mo-DI) schemes

	Data Integration		Modified Data Integration	
System	Accuracy	# of Features	Accuracy	# of Features
Dataset 1	46.72%	5	89.71%	2
Dataset 2	85.50%	5	90.31%	3
Dataset 3	85.51%	5	90.32%	4
Dataset 4	85.50%	5	86.61%	3

Table 3: KRR and modified KRR (mg-KRR and mo-KRR) schemes

		Bandgap		Electric DC		Total DC	
System	Method	Accuracy	# of Features	Accuracy	# of Features	Accuracy	# of Features
4-Block	KRR	92.98%	20	93.75%	20	96.49%	20
	mg-KRR	93.07%	19	94.22%	11	97.23%	14
	mo-KRR	93.43%	16	94.23%	18	97.63%	14
8-Block	KRR	96.95%	20	90.58%	20	95.81%	20
	mg-KRR	96.95%	20	90.64%	15	95.99%	19
	mo-KRR	97.45%	17	95.17%	12	97.68%	13

References

[1] R. Kohavi, and G.H. John, *Wrappers for Feature Subset Selection*, In Artificial Intelligence, vol. 97, nos. 1-2, pp. 273-324, 1997.

[2] P.M. Narendra, and K.A. Fukunaga, *Branch and Bound Algorithm for Feature Subset Selection*, In IEEE Trans. Computer, vol. 26, no. 9, pp. 917-922, Sept. 1977.

[3] J.S. Russell, and N. Peter, *Artificial Intelligence: A Modern Approach (2nd ed.)*, In Prentice Hall, Upper Saddle River, NJ, pp. 111-114, ISBN 0-13-790395-2, 2003.

[4] A. Jain, and D. Zengker, *Feature selection: evaluation, application, and small sample performance*, In IEEE Transactions on Pattern Analysis and Machine Intelligence, vol. 19, pp. 153-158, 1997.

[5] J. Kittler, *Feature set search algorithm, Şin C.H.Chen, Ed., Pattern Recognition and Signal Processing*, In Sijthoff and Noordhoff, Alphen aan den Rijn, Netherlands, pp.41-60, 1978.

[6] H. Liu, and H. Motoda, *Feature Selection for Knowledge Discovery and Data Mining* In Boston: Kluwer Academic, 1998

[7] P. Pudil, J. Novovicova, and J. Kittler, *Floating search methods in feature selection*, In Pattern Recognition Letters, vol. 15, pp. 1119-1125, 1994.

[8] T. Jirapech-Umpai, and S. Aitken, *Feature selection and classification for microarray data analysis: Evolutionary methods for identifying predictive genes*, In BMC Bioinformatics, 6:148, 2005.

[9] M. Kudo, and J. Sklansky, *Comparison of algorithms that select features for pattern classifiers*, In Pattern Recognition 33, pp. 25-41, 2000.

[10] J. Doak, *An Evaluation of Feature Selection Methods and Their Application to Computer Security*, In Technical report, Univ. of California at Davis, Dept. Computer Science, 1992.

[11] A.A. Tikhonov, andV.Y. Arsenin, *Solutions of ill-posed problems*, In New York: John Wiley, 1977.

[12] S. Geman, E. Bienenstock, and R. Doursat, *Neural networks and the bias/variance dilemma*, In Neural Computation 4(1), pp. 1-58, 1992.

[13] C. Saunders, A. Gammerman, and V. Vovk, *Ridge Regression Learning Algorithm in Dual Variables*, In 15th International Conference on Machine Learning, Madison, WI, pp. 515-521, 1998.

[14] V.N. Vapnik, *The Nature of Statistical Learning Theory*, In Springer, 1995.

[15] C. Cortes, and V. Vapnik, *Support Vector Networks*, In Machine Learning, 20: 1-25, 1995.

[16] Y. Lee, Y. Lin, and G. Wahba, *Multicategory Support Vector Machines, Theory, and Application to the Classification of Microarray Data and Satellite Radiance Data*, In J. Amer. Statist. Assoc. 99, Issue 465: 67-81, 2004.

[17] T. Joachims, *Transductive Inference for Text Classification using Support Vector Machines*, In 1999 International Conference on Machine Learning (ICML), pp. 200-209, 1999.

[18] C.-W. Hsu, and C.-J. Lin, *A Comparison of Methods for Multiclass Support Vector Machines"*, In IEEE Transactions on Neural Networks, 2002.

[19] M. Song, and S. Rajasekaran, *A greedy correlation-incorporated SVM-based algorithm for gene selection*, In Proc. of AINA Workshops, pp. 657-661, 2007.

[20] G. Isabelle, J. Weston, S. Barnhill, and V.N. Vapnik, *Gene Selection for Cancer Classification using Support Vector Machines*, In Machine Learning, 46, pp. 389-422, 2002.

[21] *Data integration*, In http://en.wikipedia.org/wiki/Data_integration.

[22] P. Christen, and K. Goiser K, *Quality and complexity measures for data linkage and deduplication*, In Quality Measures in Data Mining. Volume 43. Edited by Guillet F, Hamilton H. New York: Springer, 2007, pp. 127Ű151.

[23] W.E. Winkler, *Overview of Record Linkage and Current Research Directions*, In [http://www.census.gov/srd/papers/pdf/rrs2006-02.pdf].

[24] A.K. Elmagarmid, P.G. Ipeirotis, and V.S. Verykios, *Duplicate Record Detection: A Survey*, In IEEE Trans Knowl Data Eng, 19:1Ű16, 2007.

[25] W.E. Winkler, *Improved Decision Rules In The Fellegi-Sunter Model Of Record Linkage*, In Survey Research Methods, American Statistical Association. Volume 1, Alexandria, VA: American Statistical Association, pp. 274Ű279, 1993.

[26] T. Mi, S. Rajasekaran, and R. Aseltine, *Efficient algorithms for fast integration on large data sets from multiple sources*, In BMC Med Inform Decis Mak, 12:59, 2012.

[27] Y. Sun, S. A. Boggs, and R. Ramprasad, *The intrinsic electrical breakdown strength of insulators from first principles*, In *Appl. Phys. Lett* 101, 132906, 2012.

[28] C.C. Wang, G. Pilania, and R. Ramprasad, *Dielectric properties of carbon, silicon and germanium based polymers: A first principles study*, In *Phys. Rev.* B, under review.

[29] C.S. Liu, G. Pilania, C. Wang, and R. Ramprasad, *How critical are the van der Waals interactions in polymer crystals?*, In *J. Phys. Chem.* C, 116, 9347, 2012.

[30] S. Kirkpatrick, C.D. Gelatt, and M.P. Vecchi, *Optimization by simulated annealing*, In *Science* 220(4598), pp. 671-680, 1983.

Fraud Detection Using Reputation Features, SVMs, and Random Forests

Dave DeBarr, and Harry Wechsler, *Fellow, IEEE*
Computer Science Department
George Mason University
Fairfax, Virginia, 22030, United States
{ddebarr, wechsler}@gmu.edu

***Abstract*—Fraud is the use of deception to gain some benefit, often financial gain. Examples of fraud include insurance fraud, credit card fraud, telecommunications fraud, securities fraud, and accounting fraud. Costs for the affected companies are high, and these costs are passed on to their customers. Detection of fraudulent activity is thus critical to control these costs. Last but not least, in order to avoid detection, fraudsters often change their "signatures" (methods of operation). We propose here to address insurance fraud detection via the use of reputation features that characterize insurance claims and ensemble learning to compensate for varying data distributions. We replace each of the original features in the data set with 5 reputation features (RepF): 1) a count of the number of fraudulent claims with the same feature value in the previous 12 months, 2) a count of the number of months in the previous 12 months with a fraudulent claim with the same feature value, 3) a count of the number of legitimate claims with the same feature value in the previous 12 months, 4) a count of the number of months in the previous 12 months with a legitimate claim with the same feature value, and 5) the proportion of claims with the same feature value which are fraudulent in the previous 12 months. Furthermore we use two one-class Support Vector Machines (SVMs) to measure the similarity of the derived reputation feature vector to recently observed fraudulent claims and recently observed legitimate claims. The combined reputation and similarity features are then used to train a Random Forest classifier for new insurance claims. A publicly available auto insurance fraud data set is used to evaluate our approach. Cost savings, the difference in cost for predicting all new insurance claims as non-fraudulent and predicting fraud based on a trained data mining model, are used as our primary evaluation metric. Our approach shows a 13.6% increase in cost savings compared to previously published state of the art results for the auto insurance fraud data set.**

Keywords—Fraud Detection; Reputation Features; One Class Support Vector Machine; Random Forest; Cost Sensitive Learning

I. Introduction

According to the most recent Federal Bureau of Investigation Financial Crimes Report to the Public [15], there is an upward trend among many forms of financial crimes including health care fraud. Estimates of fraudulent billings to health care programs, both public and private, are estimated to be between 3 and 10 percent of total health care expenditures. This estimate is consistent with the most recent Association of Certified Fraud Examiners Report to the Nations [2], which showed survey participants estimated the typical organization loses 5% of its revenue each year.

Common types of fraud include tax fraud [11], securities fraud [5], health insurance fraud [18], auto insurance fraud [19, 21], credit card fraud [9], and telecommunications fraud [4, 14]. For tax fraud, a taxpayer intentionally avoids reporting income or overstates deductions. For securities fraud, a company may misstate values on financial reports. For insurance fraud, the insured files claims that overstate losses. For credit card fraud, the credit card is used by someone other than the legitimate owner. Challenges for fraud detection include imbalanced class distributions, large data sets, class overlap, and the lack of publicly available data.

The novelty of our approach to fraud detection is the use of reputation features and one-class SVM similarity features for fraud detection. Reputation features have been used in [1] to analyze the previous behavior of Wikipedia editors for vandalism detection. For fraud detection, reputation features are used to characterize how often feature values from a claim have been associated with fraud in the past. Similarity features, derived from one-class SVMs, are then used to extend reputation from individual features to the joint distribution of features for a claim. Finally, a cost-sensitive Random Forest classification model is constructed to classify new claims based on reputation and similarity features.

Unfortunately there is not much publicly available fraud detection data available for research. Corporate victims of fraud are often reluctant to admit that they have been the victims of fraud, and transactional data is often sensitive (e.g. containing personally identifiable account information). The auto insurance fraud data set used in this study is the only publicly available fraud detection data set that we are aware of.

The remainder of this paper is organized as follows. Section II describes cost sensitive learning. Section III describes reputation and similarity features. Section IV describes the Random Forest classification algorithm. Section V describes our experimental design using the publicly available auto insurance fraud data set. Section VI provides experimental results, and Section VII provides conclusions.

II. Cost Sensitive Learning

The presence of an imbalanced class distribution is a common characteristic for fraud detection applications [5, 17], because fraudulent transactions occur much less frequently than non-fraudulent transactions. For some domains, fraud may occur 10 or more times less frequently than non-fraudulent transactions. Because there are relatively few fraudulent transactions compared to non-fraudulent transactions, larger data sets are required to learn to confidently distinguish fraudulent transactions from non-fraudulent transactions.

To make matters worse, fraudulent transactions often look like non-fraudulent transactions because the fraudsters want to avoid detection; i.e. the fraudulent and non-fraudulent classes overlap. Because fraudulent transactions look like non-fraudulent transactions (the classes overlap), standard pattern recognition "learning" algorithms will make fewer errors by simply declaring all transactions to be non-fraudulent. The resulting classification model is known as a "majority" classifier, because it simply declares all transactions to belong to the majority class (non-fraudulent transactions). Additionally, fraudsters may adapt their observed behavior in response to detection [5]. This leads to an adversarial game in which detection advocates must somehow adapt to changes made by fraudsters, which in turn leads fraudsters to adapt to changes made by detection advocates.

Consider two overlapping distributions: a bivariate Gaussian distribution (with 2 independent features) centered at (2,2) with a standard deviation of 0.5, and a second bivariate Gaussian distribution (with 2 independent features) centered at (0,0) with a standard deviation of 2. Suppose that the prior probability for the class centered at (2,2) is 1% and the prior probability for the class centered at (0,0) is 99%. In this situation, a majority classifier would be the optimal Bayes classifier [13] if the misclassification costs are equal! Bayesian risk for predicting class α_i for observation $\mathbf{x}$ is computed as:

$$R(\alpha_i \mid \mathbf{x}) = \sum_{j=1}^{C} \lambda(\alpha_i \mid \omega_j) P(\omega_j \mid \mathbf{x}) \quad (1)$$

where $\lambda(\alpha_i \mid \omega_j)$ is the loss (misclassification cost) associated with predicting class α_i when the actual class is ω_j and

$$P(\omega_j \mid \mathbf{x}) = \frac{p(\mathbf{x} \mid \omega_j) P(\omega_j)}{\sum_{k=1}^{C} p(\mathbf{x} \mid \omega_k) P(\omega_k)} \quad (2)$$

where $P(\omega_j \mid \mathbf{x})$ is the posterior probability of observation $\mathbf{x}$ belonging to class ω_j, $p(\mathbf{x} \mid \omega_j)$ is the likelihood (density estimate) of observing $\mathbf{x}$ within class ω_j, $P(\omega_j)$ is the prior probability of observing class ω_j, C is the number of classes (2 for fraud detection), and $\sum_{k=1}^{c} p(\mathbf{x} \mid \omega_k) P(\omega_k)$ is the evidence for observation $\mathbf{x}$.

Further suppose that the minority class represents fraud. The principal costs for fraud are the cost of investigations and the cost of paying claims. If an investigation costs $100 and a claim costs $5000, then the decision boundary for the optimal Bayes classifier is shown by the solid line in Figure 1. 95% of the fraudulent class distribution lies in the small dotted circle, while 95% of the non-fraudulent class distribution lies in the large dotted circle.

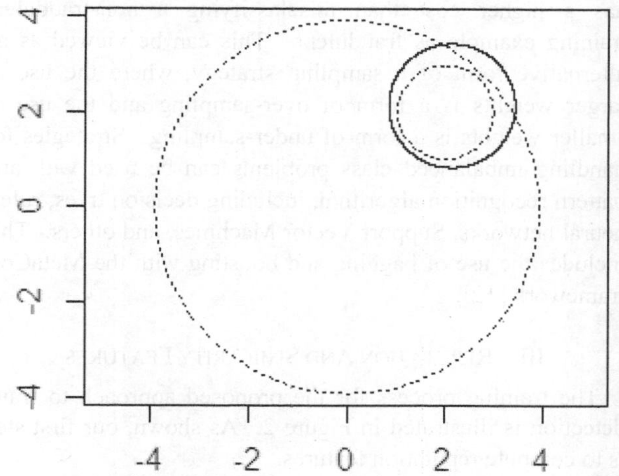

Figure 1. Optimal Bayes Decision Boundary

As shown in Table 1, this classifier would misclassify 4.4% of the fraudulent class distribution as non-fraudulent and 6.8% of the non-fraudulent class distribution as fraudulent; but overall costs would be minimized.

		Predict	
		Fraud	Not Fraud
Actual	Fraud	95.6%	4.4%
	Not Fraud	6.8%	93.2%

Table 1. Optimal Bayes Classification Errors

Strategies for overcoming the tendency to produce a simple "majority" classifier include sampling or cost sensitive learning [12, 17]. For sampling strategies, the training examples are "stratified" (partitioned) into two groups: fraudulent training examples and non-fraudulent training examples. Sampling from the training set can be performed "with" or "without" replacement. In sampling "with" replacement, each training example can be selected more than once, while in sampling "without" replacement, each training example can be selected at most once. In order to balance the fraudulent and non-fraudulent training examples, either the majority class can be under-sampled or the minority class can be over-sampled. Under-sampling involves selecting a subset of the non-fraudulent training examples, while over-sampling involves selecting a superset of the fraudulent training examples. Selecting a superset of the fraudulent training examples can be performed by sampling with replacement, or even synthesizing new fraudulent training examples similar to known fraudulent training examples [8].

In cost sensitive learning, the training examples are weighted to reflect different misclassification costs. Fraudulent training examples are given a larger weight than the non-fraudulent training examples, reflecting the notion that misclassifying a fraudulent example as non-fraudulent has a higher cost than misclassifying a non-fraudulent training example as fraudulent. This can be viewed as an alternative form of a sampling strategy, where the use of larger weights is a form of over-sampling and the use of smaller weights is a form of under-sampling. Strategies for handling imbalanced class problems can be used with any pattern recognition algorithm, including decision trees, rules, neural networks, Support Vector Machines, and others. This includes the use of bagging and boosting with the MetaCost framework [12].

III. Reputation And Similarity Features

The training process for the proposed approach to fraud detection is illustrated in Figure 2. As shown, our first step is to compute reputation features.

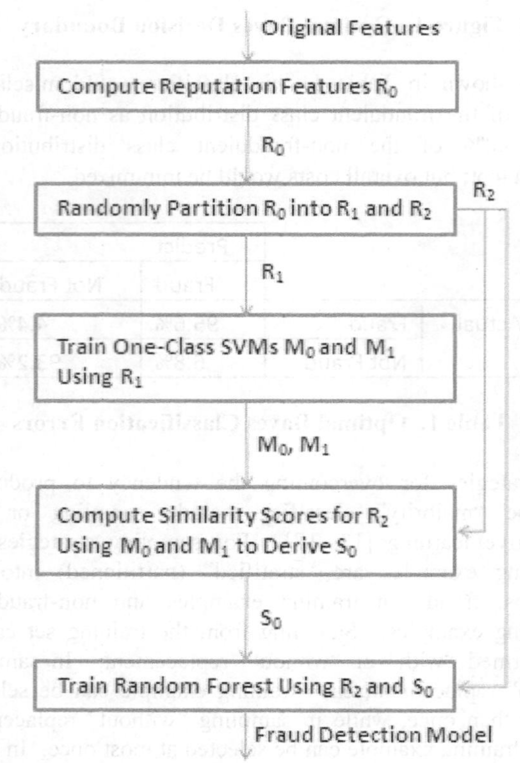

Figure 2. Training Process

We propose replacing each of the original features in the data set with 5 reputation features:

1. Fraud Count: a count of the number of fraudulent claims with the same feature value in the previous 12 months,
2. Fraud Months: a count of the number of months in the previous 12 months with a fraudulent claim with the same feature value,
3. Legitimate Count: a count of the number of legitimate claims with the same feature value in the previous 12 months,
4. Legitimate Months: a count of the number of months in the previous 12 months with a legitimate claim with the same feature value, and
5. Fraud Rate: the proportion of claims with the same feature value which are fraudulent in the previous 12 months.

These 5 values capture support and confidence values for each feature: how often a particular value is observed for a class (support) and what proportion of the time a particular value is associated with fraud (confidence). For the proportion feature we use a Wilson estimate [22] of the proportion to avoid the extremes of zero or one when we have not observed the value very often in previous months. The Wilson estimate is a weighted average of the observed proportion and one half:

$$\hat{p} = \frac{1 * \left(\frac{FraudCount}{FraudCount + LegitimateCount} \right) + \frac{1.96^2}{TotalCount} * \left(\frac{1}{2} \right)}{1 + \frac{1.96^2}{TotalCount}} \quad (3)$$

A training set is then randomly partitioned into two equal size subsets. The first subset is used to derive two one-class SVMs, while the second subset is used to construct a Random Forest classifier using the reputation and one-class SVM similarity features.

The two one-class Support Vector Machines (SVMs) measure the similarity of the derived feature vector to previously observed fraudulent claims and previously observed legitimate claims. One class SVMs [20] are used to estimate the probability of class membership. Given a set of observations $\{x_1, x_2, ..., x_n\}$, a one class SVM is trained by finding the corresponding α_i coefficient for each training observation such that the following expression is minimized:

$$\min_{\alpha} \left(\frac{1}{2} \alpha^T \mathbf{Q} \alpha \right) \quad (4)$$

subject to the following constraints:

$$0 \le \alpha_i \le 1 \quad (5)$$

$$\sum_{i=1}^{n} \alpha_i = \nu n \quad (6)$$

where

$$\mathbf{Q}_{i,j} = K(\mathbf{x}_i, \mathbf{x}_j) = \phi(x_i)^T \phi(x_j) \quad (7)$$

Training observations with a non-zero α_i coefficient are known as "support vectors", because they define the decision boundary. The kernel function K is used to measure similarity of two observations, which is the equivalent of measuring the dot product in a higher dimension feature space. The radial basis function was used as the kernel function:

$$K(\mathbf{x}_i, \mathbf{x}_j) = \exp\left(-\frac{\left\|x_i - x_j\right\|^2}{\sigma^2}\right) \quad (8)$$

where σ is the mean of the 10th, 50th, and 90th percentile of Euclidean distance values for a random sample of $n/2$ pairs of observations [7]. The hyper-parameter ν places an upper bound on the proportion of the training data that can be declared to be outliers and a lower bound on the proportion of the training set to be used as support vectors. The value of ν was chosen to be 0.05.

Once the α_i coefficients have been found, the distance of a new observation from the class boundary defined by the one-class SVM can be computed as:

$$\sum_{i=1}^{n}\left(\alpha_i K(\mathbf{x}, \mathbf{x}_i)\right) - \rho \quad (9)$$

where ρ is chosen as the offset that yields $1 - \nu n$ positive values for observations of the training set. The similarity feature of the one-class SVM is a measure of how well a new observation fits with the observed training distribution. The larger the similarity feature value, the more likely the observation belongs to the distribution characterized by the training data. The probability of membership can be estimated by comparing the distance for a new observation to the distance values computed for the training data.

To generate 2 new features for input to a classification model, two one-class SVMs are constructed using the first subset of training data. The first one-class SVM is constructed from fraudulent transactions in the first subset of training data, while the second one-class SVM is constructed from non-fraudulent transactions in the first subset of training data. Unlike the other reputation features, the one-class SVM similarity features consider the joint distribution of feature values when evaluating feature vectors.

IV. RANDOM FORESTS

The derived feature vectors for the second subset of training data, including the two one-class SVM similarity features, are used to construct a Random Forest classifier [6]. The Random Forest algorithm is an implementation of bootstrap aggregation (bagging) where each tree in an ensemble of decision trees is constructed from a bootstrap sample of feature vectors from the training data. Each bootstrap sample of feature vectors is obtained by repeated random sampling with replacement until the size of the bootstrap sample matches the size of the original training subset. This helps to reduce the variance of the classifier (reducing the classifier's ability to overfit the training data). When constructing each decision tree, only a randomly selected subset of features is considered for constructing each decision node. Of the k randomly selected features to consider for constructing each decision node, the yes/no condition that best reduces the Gini impurity measure g of the data is selected for the next node in the tree:

$$g = 1 - P(Fraud)^2 - P(NotFraud)^2 \quad (10)$$

The Gini impurity measure is largest when the classifier is most uncertain about whether a feature vector belongs to the fraud class.

To support cost sensitive learning, we used a balanced stratified sampling approach [10] to generate bootstrap samples for training the classifier. For training each tree, a bootstrap sample is drawn from the minority class and a sample of the same size is drawn (with replacement) from the majority class. This effectively under-samples the majority class.

To classify new feature vectors, the reputation features and two one-class SVM similarity features are derived, then each tree in the Random Forest classification model casts its vote for a class label: fraud or not fraud. The proportion of votes for the fraud class is the probability that a randomly selected tree would classify the feature vector as belonging to the fraud class. This is interpreted as the probability of a feature vector belonging to the fraud class.

V. EXPERIMENTAL DESIGN

The auto insurance data set [3] has been used to demonstrate fraud detection capabilities [16, 19]. As this is the only publicly available fraud data set, we use it for our experiments as well. It consists of 3 years of auto insurance claims: 1994, 1995, and 1996. Table 2 describes the distribution of fraud and not-fraud claims by year.

Year	Fraud	Not Fraud	Fraud Rate
1994	409	5,733	6.7%
1995	301	4,894	5.8%
1996	213	3,870	5.2%
All	923	14,497	6.0%

Table 2. Fraud Rates for Auto Insurance Data

The proportion of overall claims that are fraudulent is only 6%, so only 1 in 17 claims are fraudulent. Table 3 lists the features of the data. As shown, two of the features were not used for prediction. The Year attribute obviously does not generalize to future data. As we assume that policies associated with known fraudulent activity are terminated, we ignore the PolicyNumber attribute as well.

Month	RepNumber
WeekOfMonth	Deductible
DayOfWeek	DriverRating
Make	DaysPolicyAccident
AccidentArea	DaysPolicyClaim
DayOfWeekClaimed	PastNumberOfClaims
MonthClaimed	AgeOfVehicle
WeekOfMonthClaimed	AgeOfPolicyHolder
Sex	PoliceReportFiled
MaritalStatus	WitnessPresent
Age	AgentType
Fault	NumberOfSuppliments
PolicyType	AddressChangeClaim
VehicleCategory	NumberOfCars
VehiclePrice	~~Year~~
FraudFound	BasePolicy
~~PolicyNumber~~	

Table 3. Original Auto Insurance Fraud Features

Values in the data set have been pre-discretized (probably for anonymization); e.g. the distribution of VehiclePrice appears in Table 4.

Value	Frequency
Less than 20,000	1,096
20,000 to 29,000	8,079
30,000 to 39,000	3,533
40,000 to 59,000	461
60,000 to 69,000	87
More than 69,000	2,164

Table 4. VehiclePrice Distribution

We constructed Random Forest classification models for both the original features and the reputation features, as described in section III. To be consistent with previously reported results, claims from 1994 and 1995 were used as training data, and claims from 1996 were used as testing data. The primary evaluation measure is cost savings, as this was reported in earlier publications and it directly relates to the core goal for a fraud detection system: cost reduction. Table 5 shows an example of a confusion matrix describing the following counts:

- True Positives (TP): the number of claims in the test set that are predicted to be Fraud and are actually Fraud
- False Positives (FP): the number of claims in the test set that are predicted to be Fraud but are actually Not Fraud
- False Negatives (FN): the number of claims in the test set that are predicted to be Not Fraud but are actually Fraud
- True Negatives (TN): the number of claims in the test set that are predicted to be Not Fraud and are actually Not Fraud

		Predicted	
		Fraud	Not Fraud
Actual	Fraud	TP	FN
	Not Fraud	FP	TN

Table 5. Example of Confusion Matrix

Given classification results, as shown in Table 5, costs can be computed as follows:

$$\begin{aligned} &TotalCost = \\ &InvestigationCost * TP \\ &+ \left(InvestigationCost + ClaimCost \right) * FP \\ &+ ClaimCost * \left(FN + TN \right) \end{aligned} \qquad (11)$$

In [19], the average InvestigationCost was given as \$203 and the average ClaimCost was given as \$2,640. We use these values as well for consistency. We ran 10 trials for both the Original Features (OrigF) approach and the Reputation Features (RepF) approach.

Using the Original Features (OrigF), we constructed 10 Random Forests from the 11,337 original feature vectors from 1994 and 1995. Each of these 10 Random Forests was evaluated on the 4,083 original feature vectors from 1996.

Using the Reputation Features (RepF), we partitioned the 5,195 reputation feature vectors from 1995 into two subsets (as we used 12 months of history to construct reputation features). For 10 iterations, the first subset was used to construct our one-class SVMs and the second subset was used to construct a Random Forest classifier. Each of the 10 Random Forests was then evaluated on the 4,083 reputation feature vectors from 1996.

Balanced stratified random sampling was used for constructing Random Forests for both the original features and the reputation features. A total of 2,000 trees were constructed for each Random Forest model, with the ceiling of the square root of the number of input features used as the number of randomly selected features to consider for each decision node. For both Original Features (OrigF) and Reputation Features (RepF) the Out Of Bag (OOB) estimate of error from the training data [6] was used to select the classification threshold which minimizes cost.

VI. Experimental Results

Cost savings is used as our primary metric of interest. In [19], cost savings was recorded as the difference between the cost of paying all claims and the cost of using a fraud detection model (Equation 11). In addition to cost savings, we also report the following metrics:

1. Area Under the Receiver Operating Characteristic (ROC) Curve (AUC): the probability that a randomly selected claim from the fraud class will be viewed as more likely to be a fraudulent claim than a randomly selected claim from the not-fraud class
2. Precision: the probability that a predicted fraudulent claim is actually a fraudulent claim (TP/(TP+FP))
3. Recall: the probability that an actual fraudulent claim is predicted to be a fraudulent claim (TP/(TP+FN))
4. F Measure: the harmonic mean of Precision and Recall (2/(1/Precision + 1/Recall))

Table 6 shows evaluation metrics for our experiments. The values for the Reputation Features approach are marked as RepF, while the values for the Original Features approach are marked as OrigF. Standard Error (SD) values are listed to assess statistical significance.

	RepF	RepF SD	OrigF	OrigF SD
Cost Savings	$189,651	$2,665	$165,808	$748
AUC	82.0%	0.1%	73.8%	< 0.1%
Precision	13.3%	0.1%	11.2%	< 0.1%
Recall	80.3%	1.1%	94.2%	0.1%
F Measure	22.8%	0.1%	20.0%	0.0%

Table 6. Experimental Results

Table 7 shows the average confusion matrix for the Reputation Features approach.

		Predicted	
		Fraud	Not Fraud
Actual	Fraud	171.0	42.0
	Not Fraud	1,118.6	2,751.4

Table 7. Average RepF Confusion Matrix

Table 8 shows the average confusion matrix for the Original Features approach.

		Predicted	
		Fraud	Not Fraud
Actual	Fraud	200.6	12.4
	Not Fraud	1,591.4	2,278.6

Table 8. Average OrigF Confusion Matrix

Figure 3 compares the Receiver Operating Characteristic (ROC) curves for the two approaches to fraud detection.

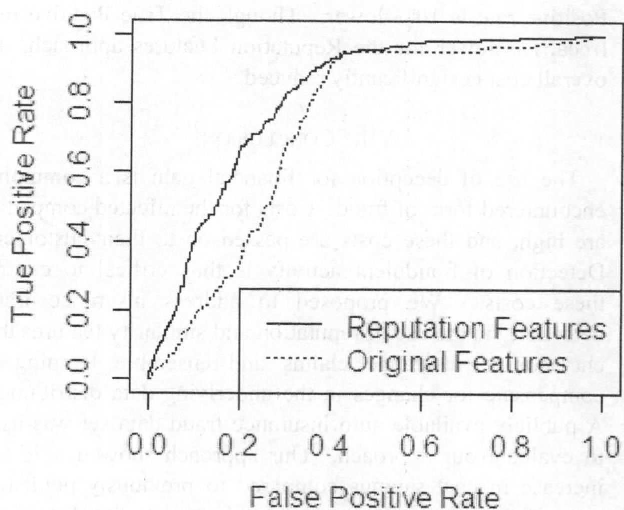

Figure 3. ROC Curves

Figure 4 identifies the most important classification features for the Reputation Features approach. Both the one-class SVM similarity feature for the Fraud class and the Legitimate class are identified as important features.

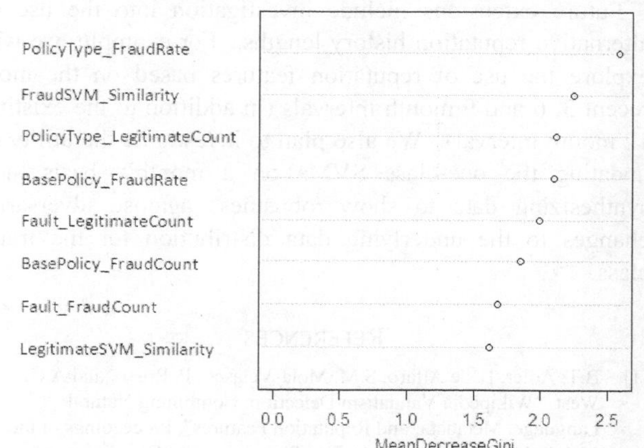

Figure 4. Most Important Reputation Features

As shown in Table 6, the Random Forest classifier constructed from the Original Features is competitive with previously reported state-of-the-art results. The previously reported state-of-the-art results for cost savings was $167,000, while the upper bound of the 95% confidence interval for the Original Features approach shown in Table 6 is $165,808 + 1.96 * 748 = $167,274. The cost savings for the Reputation Features approach is 13.6% higher than the previously reported state-of-the-art results:

($189,651 - $167,000) / $167,000 = 13.6%

It's interesting to note that the operating threshold for the Original Features approach occurs where the two ROC curves meet; but the operating threshold for the Reputation Features approach occurs in the region where the False

Positive rate is 10% lower. Though the True Positive rate (recall) is lower for the Reputation Features approach, the overall cost is significantly reduced.

VII. Conclusions

The use of deception for financial gain is a commonly encountered form of fraud. Costs for the affected companies are high, and these costs are passed on to their customers. Detection of fraudulent activity is thus critical to control these costs. We proposed to address insurance fraud detection via the use of reputation and similarity features that characterize insurance claims and ensemble learning to compensate for changes in the underlying data distribution. A publicly available auto insurance fraud data set was used to evaluate our approach. Our approach showed a 13.6% increase in cost savings compared to previously published state of the art results for the auto insurance fraud data set. Though an auto insurance fraud data set was used for this demonstration, reputation features could easily be applied to other fraud detection domains, including health care insurance fraud, credit card fraud, securities fraud, and accounting fraud. This approach could also be useful for other applications, such as credit risk classification [23] or computer network intrusion detection [24].

Future extensions include investigation into the use of alternative reputation history lengths. For example, we will explore the use of reputation features based on the most recent 3, 6 and 9 month intervals (in addition to the existing 12 month interval). We also plan to investigate the utility of updating the one-class SVMs on a monthly basis, and synthesizing data to show robustness against adversarial changes to the underlying data distribution for the fraud class.

References

[1] B.T. Adler, L. de Alfaro, S.M. Mola-Velasco, P. Rosso, and A.G. West. "Wikipedia Vandalism Detection: Combining Natural Language, Metadata, and Reputation Features", Proceedings of the 12th Intl Conf on Intelligent Text Processing and Computational Linguistics, 277-288, 2011.

[2] Association of Certified Fraud Examiners Report to the Nations, http://www.acfe.com/rttn.aspx, last accessed 2013-03-18.

[3] Auto Insurance Fraud Data, http://clifton.phua.googlepages.com/minority-report-data.zip, last accessed 2013-03-18.

[4] R.A. Becker, C. Volinsky, and A.R. Wilks. "Fraud Detection in Telecommunications: History and Lessons Learned", Technometrics, 52(1), 20-33, 2010.

[5] R.J. Bolton and D.J. Hand "Statistical Fraud Detection: A Review", Statistical Science, 17(3), 235-255, 2002.

[6] L. Breiman. "Random Forests", Machine Learning, 45(1), 5-32, 2001.

[7] B. Caputo, K. Sim, F. Furesjo, and A. Smola. "Appearance-Based Object Recognition Using SVMs: Which Kernel Should I Use?", Proceedings of the Neural Information Processing Systems Workshop on Statistical Methods for Computational Experiments in Visual Processing and Computer Vision, Whistler, 2002.

[8] N.V. Chawla, K.W. Boyer, L.O. Hall, and W.P. Kegelmeyer. "SMOTE: Synthetic Minority Over-sampling Technique", Journal of Artificial Intelligence Research, 16, 321-357, 2002.

[9] P.K. Chan and S.J. Stolfo. "Toward Scalable Learning with Non-Uniform Class and Cost Distributions: A Case Study in Credit Card Fraud Detection", Proceedings of the 4th Intl Conf on Knowledge Discovery and Data Mining, 164-168, 1998.

[10] C. Chen, A. Liaw, and L.Breiman. "Using Random Forest to Learn Imbalanced Data", University of California at Berkeley Tech Report 666, 2004.

[11] D. DeBarr and Z. Eyler-Walker. "Closing the Gap: Automated Screening of Tax Returns to Identify Egregious Tax Shelters", SIGKDD Explorations, 8(1), 11-16, 2006.

[12] P. Domingos. "MetaCost: a General Method for Making Classifiers Cost-Sensitive", Proceedings of the 5th Intl Conf on Knowledge Discovery and Data Mining, 155-164, 1999.

[13] R.O. Duda, P.E. Hart, D.G. Stork. "Bayesian Decision Theory", Pattern Classification, 2nd ed,Wiley & Sons, 20-83, 2001.

[14] T. Fawcett and F. Provost. "Adaptive Fraud Detection", Data Mining and Knowledge Discovery, 1(3), 291-316, 1997.

[15] Federal Bureau of Investigation Financial Crimes Report to the Public, Fiscal Years 2010-2011, http://www.fbi.gov/stats-services/publications/financial-crimes-report-2010-2011, last accessed 2013-03-18.

[16] A. Gepp, J.H. Wilson, K. Kumar, and S. Bhattacharya. "A Comparative Analysis of Decision Trees Vis-a-vis Other Computational Data Mining Techniques in Auto Insurance Fraud Detection", Journal of Data Science, 10, 537-561, 2012.

[17] H. He and E.A. Garcia. "Learning from Imbalanced Data", IEEE Transactions on Knowledge and Data Engineering, 21(9), 1263-1284, 2009.

[18] J. Li, K.Y. Huang, J. Jin, and J. Shi. "A Survey on Statistical Methods for Health Care Fraud Detection", Health Care Management Science, 11(3), 275-287, 2008.

[19] C. Phua, D. Alahakoon, and V. Lee. "Minority Report in Fraud Detection: Classification of Skewed Data", SIGKDD Explorations, 6(1), 50-59, 2004.

[20] B. Scholkopf, J.C. Platt, J. Shawe-Taylor, A.J.Smola, and R.C. Williamson. "Estimating the Support of a High-Dimensional Distribution", Microsoft Technical Report MSR-TR-99-87, 1999.

[21] S. Viaene, R.A. Derrig, and G. Dedene. "A Case Study of Applying Boosting Naive Bayes to Claim Fraud Diagnosis", IEEE Transactions on Knowledge and Data Engineering, 16(5), 612-620, 2004.

[22] E.B. Wilson. "Probable Inference, the Law of Succession, and Statistical Inference". Journal of the American Statistical Association, 22, 209-212, 1927.

[23] K. Bache and M. Lichman. "Statlog German Credit Risk Data Set", UCI Machine Learning Repository, http://archive.ics.uci.edu/ml/datasets/Statlog+%28German+Credit+Data%29, last access 2013-05-24.

[24] "KDD Cup 1999 Computer Network Intrusion Detection Data set, http://www.sigkdd.org/kdd-cup-1999-computer-network-intrusion-detection, last accessed 2013-05-24.

A Novel Ensemble Selection Technique For Weak Classifiers

Kung-Hua Chang[1], **and D. Stott Parker**[1]
[1]University of California Los Angeles
Los Angeles, CA, USA
{kunghua,stott}@cs.ucla.edu

Abstract - *Over the past decade ensemble selection has been proposed as an "overproduce and select" method for constructing ensemble classifiers from simpler individual classifiers. Many prior research papers suggest using the top performing 10%-20% of classifiers in an ensemble. In this paper, we simulate a duel between the top performing (strong) X% of classifiers and the bottom performing (100−X)% (e.g. the top 20% versus the bottom 80%). We propose an ensemble selection algorithm that can effectively use them to construct much stronger classifiers, and apply the algorithm to find the best ensemble (of top performing classifiers as well as of bottom performing classifiers). We also show that using the bottom performing classifiers can yield comparable and sometimes better performance. Furthermore the bottom classifiers can outperform top classifiers for many different values of X, and in some cases all values of X. Our algorithm is based on heuristic search algorithms for developing ensembles of diverse classifiers that optimize complementarity. These results are based on experiments made with 6 publicly available datasets and heterogeneous ensembles using 22 kinds of classifiers.*

Keywords: Ensemble Selection

1 Introduction

Ensemble methods have been shown both theoretically and empirically to outperform individual classification methods in a wide variety of settings and datasets [2][3]. For example, the winners [19][20] of the Netflix Challenge [18] used ensemble methods. Basically, in selecting an ensemble of classifiers, it is common practice to limit the candidates from classifiers with high performance under some evaluation metrics. This approach makes intuitive sense and generally delivers performance improvements. This paper was inspired specifically by experience with the strategy proposed in [3][4][5] of forming ensembles by selecting among only the top 10% of models yielding greatest accuracy. We began to wonder whether greater representation of models with lower accuracy scores might be beneficial. In our experience, strong classifiers can often make the same wrong classifications, particularly on minority examples and classes (because they often sacrifice minority examples/classes and embrace majority examples/classes).

As a result, ensembles built from strong classifiers often show limited improvement in classification accuracy. In order to improve this accuracy, ensembles must maintain a certain level of classifier diversity so as to avoid making the wrong classification altogether. That is, ensembles must have classifiers that can correctly classify minority examples/classes to offset the mistakes made by stronger classifiers. However, real improvement usually requires a high level of diversity – which we formalize as complementarity – that can be hard to produce in the first place. Thus, we need to understand the relationship between diversity, classification accuracy from individual classifiers, and the performance of ensembles. A premise behind this paper is that optimizing complementarity can benefit ensembles. In this paper we develop the idea of maximal complementary ensembles. “Complementary” here refers to the idea that in a teamwork environment, we usually do not put people with the same skills on the same team, but instead put together an ensemble using people with different skills as a way to diversify weaknesses. “Maximal complementary ensembles” mean that we search heuristically and explicitly for a minimal ensemble having maximally diverse classifiers..

2 Related Work

Data mining research usually considers only models that are optimal under some criterion. Choosing the top performing models has a history of success, but it has also introduces many serious problems, including overfitting and bias. A great deal of research in ensemble methods [1-6,13-16] has been aimed at these problems. Throughout this research, diversity has been recognized to be important in improving ensemble performance. Many measures of diversity have been considered in the literature for ensemble methods; cf. [16]. For example [17] suggested that an ideal ensemble consists of highly correct classifiers that disagree as much as possible. The use of "maximum diversity" was considered in [14], as a kind of generalized diversity seeking to develop ensembles in which incorrect labeling by one classifier is countered by correct labeling by another. Krogh & Vedelsby’s prior work [15] showed that ensemble error is directly related to the average accuracy of the ensemble plus a term measuring diversity (called ambiguity in the original paper). This particular property will be used in our paper to justify our algorithm.

3 Algorithms

3.1 Background

The heart of our strategy is to select excellent ensembles of classifiers from a large and diverse pool. These teams are deliberately kept as complementary as possible. By complementary here we mean that classifiers are selected incrementally so as to cover any remaining incorrectly handled cases in the training set. This can be done by selecting minimal sets of team members that correctly classify as many cases in the training set as possible. We employ the simplest classifier combination method – majority voting – and choose individual classifiers based on their training accuracy and on their misclassifications on the training set.

To communicate the basic idea let us limit our discussion to the simplest scenario: in majority voting during ensemble selection, if we have 1 incorrect vote (misclassification), we need 2 correct votes (correct classifications) to compensate. That is, if we have N bad votes, we need (N+1) correct votes to obtain the correct prediction outcome. Thus, a problem occurs when combining multiple classifiers together in which a majority cast incorrect votes. In order to offset them, we need to find enough classifiers to cast correct votes. In other words, the resulting ensemble will have at least N + (N+1) = 2N+1 classifiers. We can see that if we can reduce the number of incorrect votes at a much earlier stage, then we can greatly reduce the number of classifiers N needed. Intuitively, our strategy will be to identify where these incorrect votes are distributed while we are in the early stage of finding classifiers to add to the ensemble. We can then fill in correct votes accordingly in these soft spots to improve performance of the ensemble. However, the question is: how do we discover the way these incorrect votes are distributed?

3.2 Maximal Complementary Ensembles

Krogh & Vedelsby [15] proposed that ensemble error consist of the generalization errors of the individual classifiers plus a term measuring diversity (called ambiguity in the original paper). We will use representation from (Opitz and Shavlik, 1996) [17] below:

$$\hat{E} = \overline{E} - \overline{D}$$

Where $\overline{E} = \sum_i w_i E_i$ is the weighted average of the individual classifier's generalization error, and $\overline{D} = \sum_i w_i D_i$ is the weighted average of the diversity among these classifiers. (Opitz and Shavlik, 1996) [17] suggested that an ideal ensemble consists of highly correct classifiers that disagree as much as possible. If we want to have a near-perfect ensemble, we will need to have the ensemble generalization error as close to zero as possible. That is, in order to achieve

$$\hat{E} = \overline{E} - \overline{D} = 0$$

we must have:

$$\overline{E} = \overline{D}$$

$$\sum_i w_i E_i = \sum_i w_i D_i$$

In majority voting, if no individual classifier can predict everything correctly (that is, it has its own generalization error), then we need at least 3 classifiers (because 2 correct votes are needed for each incorrect vote). So we can divide $\hat{E}$ as $\hat{E}_1$, $\hat{E}_2$, and $\hat{E}_3$ where $\hat{E}_1$ is the weighted average of the generalization error of the first group of ensemble (called ENS_1), and $\hat{E}_2$ is the weighted average of the generalization error of the second group of ensemble (called ENS_2). $\hat{E}_3$ is simply an individual classifier's generalization error and we can name it as ENS_3 because a single classifier can form an ensemble by itself, so

$$\hat{E}_3 = \overline{E_3} - \overline{D_3}$$

Then we seek to achieve

$$\hat{E} = \hat{E}_1 + \hat{E}_2 + \hat{E}_3 = 0$$

$$\hat{E}_1 + \hat{E}_2 = -\hat{E}_3$$

$$\hat{E}_1 + \hat{E}_2 = \overline{D}3 - \overline{E}3$$

$$\hat{E}_1 + \hat{E}_2 + \overline{E}3 = \overline{D}3$$

This means that when we add the final individual classifier into the ensemble, we hope to have the combined averaged ensemble generalization error as close to the final individual classifier's diversity (the difference between ENS_{12} and ENS_3) as possible. We can discuss possible scenarios below.

Suppose we do a majority voting on the first and second groups of the ensemble to form a new ensemble (called ENS_{12}) having generalization error $\hat{E}_{12}$.

$$\hat{E}_{12} = \hat{E}_1 + \hat{E}_2$$

Then assuming majority voting, an ideal situation will be:

$$\hat{E}_{12} = \overline{D}3 - \overline{E}3$$

At this point, $\overline{D}3$ is the diversity between ENS_{12} and ENS_3. Figure 1 shows the ideal scenario when we select the final classifier in our ensemble.

ENS_{12}	Correctly Predicted Examples	Loss $\hat{E}_{12}$

ENS_3	Loss $\overline{E}_3$	Correctly Predicted Examples	$\overline{D}_3 - \overline{E}_3$

Figure 1. Ideal scenarios when measuring losses (incorrect predictions) in the training set. We intentionally display the losses as grouped together to simplify the presentation.

Since $\overline{D}3$ is the diversity between ENS_{12} and ENS_3, $\overline{D}3 - \overline{E}3$ is a set that differs from the losses ($\hat{E}_{12}$) in ENS_{12}.

That means $\overline{D}_3 - \overline{E}_3$ is a set that can cast correct votes for the final ensemble. Besides, ideally the losses $\overline{E}_3$ should have no impact at all on the final ensemble because there should exist enough correct votes in ENS_{12} such that the incorrect votes from $\overline{E}_3$ will be corrected. Figures 2, 3, and 4 are examples that illustrate the ideal situation:

ENS_1	1	-1	1	Correctly Predicted Examples
ENS_2	-1	1	1	Correctly Predicted Examples
ENS_3	1	1	-1	Correctly Predicted Examples

Figure 2. In this scenario, "correctly predicted examples" represent training examples for which there are sufficiently many correct votes, and 1 incorrect vote cannot change the outcome. "1" means currently we have one more correct vote than incorrect vote. "-1" means that we have one more incorrect vote than correct votes.

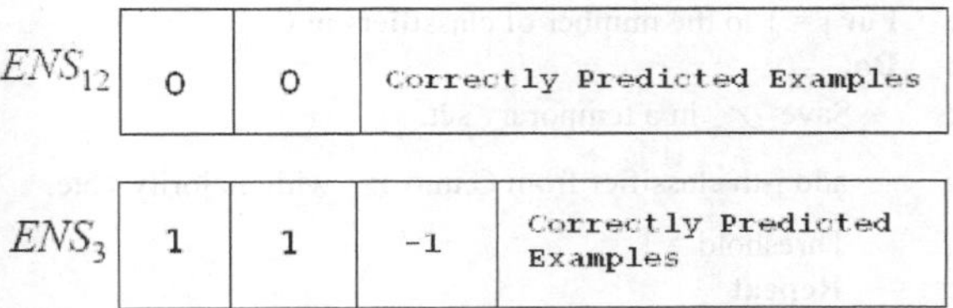

Figure 3. After we perform majority voting on the first and second ensemble, we can see that ENS_{12} has 2 places where 0 exists (0 means indecision due to equal number of 1 and -1); these places have the same number of correct and incorrect votes.

Final Ensemble

Correctly Predicted Examples

Figure 4. After we perform majority vote on ENS_{12} and ENS_3, we obtain a perfect ensemble.

An interesting phenomenon arises when we are adding the last classifier into our ensemble as illustrated in Figure 5.

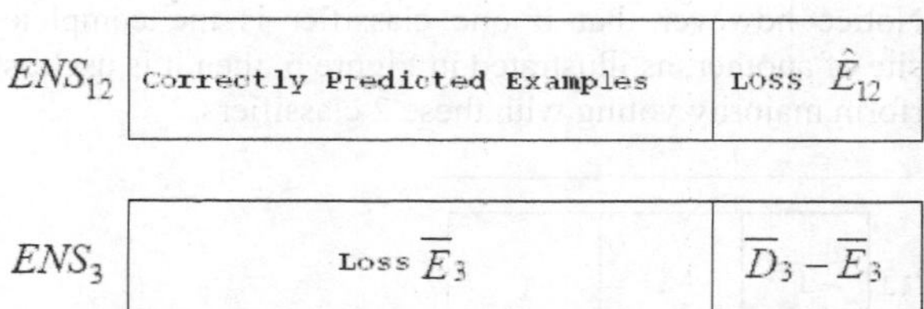

Figure 5. Problematic scenario in constructing a perfect ensemble.

If $\overline{E}_3$ is quite large, then this means ENS_3 is an ensemble (classifier) having very poor performance (we call it weak). However, this weak ensemble (classifier) can help our algorithm construct a perfect ensemble. This finding differs from what (Caruana et al., 2006) proposed, which was to set pruning levels only among the top 10-20% of models (classifiers).

(Krogh & Vedelsby, 1995) showed that "the generalization error of the ensemble is always smaller than the (weighted) average of the ensemble errors: $E < \overline{E}$." In particular, for uniform weights:

$$E \le \frac{1}{N} \sum_\alpha E^\alpha$$

Thus, if $\sum_\alpha E^\alpha = \sum_\alpha D^\alpha$, then $E = 0$.

3.3 Ensemble Selection Algorithm

We can construct an algorithm by extending the relationship between ENS_{12} and ENS_3 such that ENS_{12} can be an ensemble having only one classifier while ENS_3 is the next classifier we want to add into our ensemble. The algorithm will continue to add in new classifier if it satisfies certain conditions (described later) until either we have a perfect ensemble or we cannot improve performance further (beyond some predefined threshold). The algorithm will use the training set to measure diversity by comparing the differences of how well ENS_{12} and ENS_3 do on the training set. (Please note that the algorithm uses selection with replacement. That is, we allow a classifier to be added to the ensemble multiple times.)

The cost function is similar to a 0-1 loss function. If a classifier correctly predicts the true label for one example in training set, then we label it +1. Otherwise, we assign a -1 to it. Thus a classifier can be viewed as a set consisting of +1 and -1, and majority voting adds up the values from different classifiers. We can see that in an ensemble, a value of 0 reflects indecision due to the same number of +1 and -1 values.

Since the performance optimization problem is hard, we will propose an approximation algorithm. Rather than find exact matches of $\hat{E}_{12}$ and $\overline{D}_3 - \overline{E}_3$. We can instead add a classifier to the ensemble with $\overline{D}_3 - \overline{E}_3$ as close to $\hat{E}_{12}$ as possible.

Notice however that if one classifier is the complete opposite of another, as illustrated in Figure 6, then it is useless to perform majority voting with these 2 classifiers.

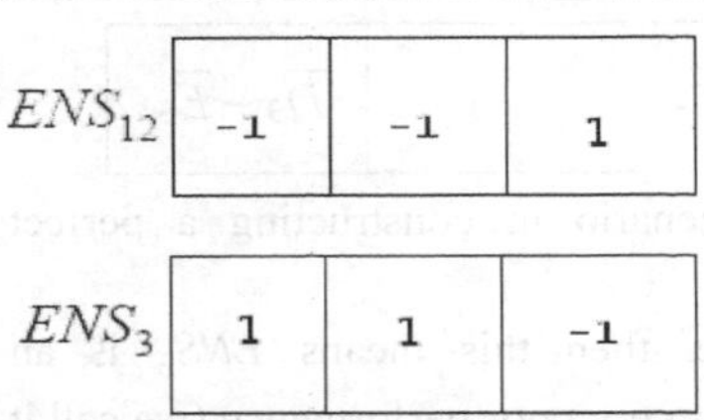

ENS_{12}	-1	-1	1
ENS_3	1	1	-1

Figure 6. Two classifiers that are complete opposites.

Figure 7 shows that another condition needed is for $\overline{E_3}$ to minimize damage to $(\overline{D_{12}} - \overline{E_{12}})$:

ENS_{12}	$\overline{D_{12}} - \overline{E_{12}}$	Correctly Predicted Examples	Loss $\overline{E_{12}}$

ENS_3	Loss $\overline{E_3}$	Correctly Predicted Examples	$\overline{D_3} - \overline{E_3}$

Figure 7. Relationship between ENS_{12} and ENS_3.

Algorithm 1 (shown in Figure 8) always chooses to add a classifier that can maximally correct the incorrectly classified instances in the current ensemble, while minimizing the damage the new classifier brings to the ensemble. Since the algorithm always corrects incorrect votes at the earliest possible stage, the total number of classifiers needed in an ensemble can be greatly reduced. Besides, since it always chooses a new classifier that differs most from the ensemble, it eliminates redundancy in the classifiers it selects.

The search method employed here is best-first search. However, it is computationally costly when the search depth is large (e.g. more than 30). So we adopt an alternative that searches both leaf nodes (the last classifiers added to the ensemble) and also next-to-root nodes (individual classifiers that are added to our ensemble second, as shown in Algorithm 1 as the set C). One reason is that it is infeasible to perform complete depth-first search in leaf nodes, and the other reason is that a next-to-root node usually has greater impact on ensemble selection than a leaf node. In other words, when we are selecting the last individual classifier (leaf node) for our ensemble, most of the votes are established and the last vote often has little effect on the outcome of the final ensemble. But the second selection (next-to-root node) can sometimes greatly change the outcome and can lead to very different selections in later individual classifiers.

3.4 Examples

Suppose we have a classification problem given training set T = [1, 2, 3, 1, 2, 3], which is a 3-class classification problem with the following 5 classifiers:

C1 = [1, 2, 2, 1, 2, 2] Training Accuracy = 4/6
C2 = [2, 2, 3, 2, 2, 3] Training Accuracy = 4/6
C3 = [3, 3, 3, 1, 3, 3] Training Accuracy = 3/6
C4 = [1, 1, 2, 1, 2, 1] Training Accuracy = 3/6
C5 = [1, 1, 1, 1, 1, 1] Training Accuracy = 2/6

We first transform the classifiers C1 to C5 (as G1 to G5) using the cost function we proposed as follows:

Algorithm 1 Maximal Complementary Ensemble

```
Input: M classifiers
For i = 1 to M
Do;
   Include the i-th classifier in initial ensemble set α .
   For j = 1 to M
   Do;
      A = argmax_j((D_j − E_j) ∩ E_α)
      B = argmin_j((D_α − E_α) ∩ E_j)
      C = A ∩ B
   End;
   For j = 1 to the number of classifiers in C
   Do;
      Save α in a temporary set.
      add j-th classifier from C into α with majority vote.
      Threshold = 1
      Repeat
         A2 = argmax_j((D_j − E_j) ∩ E_α)
         B2 = argmin_j((D_α − E_α) ∩ E_j)
         C2 = A ∩ B
         Add the best classifier from C2 to α with majority vote
         Record the performance of α (training/test)
         If the performance of α is improved then
            Threshold = 0
         Else
            Threshold = Threshold + 1
      Until we have a perfect ensemble or we cannot
            improve its performance after Threshold
            exceeds 10.
      Restore α from the temporary set.
   End;
End;
```

G1 = [1, 1, -1, 1, 1, -1]
G2 = [-1, 1, 1, -1, 1, 1]
G3 = [-1, -1, 1, 1, -1, 1]
G4 = [1, -1, -1, 1, 1, -1]
G5 = [1, -1, -1, 1, -1, -1]

Suppose we include G1 in the initial ensemble set α, so that $\alpha = \{G1\}$. The set A will choose classifiers 2 and 3 as possible classifiers to add to the ensemble.

$((D_1 - E_1) \cap E_\alpha)$ = [0, 0, 0, 0, 0, 0] Gain: 0
$((D_2 - E_2) \cap E_\alpha)$ = [0, 0, 1, 0, 0, 1] Gain: 2
$((D_3 - E_3) \cap E_\alpha)$ = [0, 0, 1, 0, 0, 1] Gain: 2
$((D_4 - E_4) \cap E_\alpha)$ = [0, 0, 0, 0, 0, 0] Gain: 0
$((D_5 - E_5) \cap E_\alpha)$ = [0, 0, 0, 0, 0, 0] Gain: 0

The set B will choose classifier 2 as possible classifiers to add to the ensemble.

$((D_\alpha - E_\alpha) \cap E_1)$ = [0, 0, -1, 0, 0, -1] Damage: 2
$((D_\alpha - E_\alpha) \cap E_2)$ = [-1, 0, 0, -1, 0, 0] Damage: 2
$((D_\alpha - E_\alpha) \cap E_3)$ = [-1, -1, 0, 0, -1, 0] Damage: 3
$((D_\alpha - E_\alpha) \cap E_4)$ = [0, -1, -1, 0, 0, -1] Damage: 3
$((D_\alpha - E_\alpha) \cap E_5)$ = [0, -1, -1, 0, -1, -1] Damage: 4

Since $C = A \cap B$, classifier 2 will be the only classifier included in set C. Thus, the algorithm will choose C2 to add to the ensemble set α and perform a majority vote, yielding α = [0, 1, 0, 0, 1, 0]. Here '0' means indecision due to equal number of correct and incorrect votes.

The algorithm continues this process until it hits the termination condition. The solution of this example is [C1, C2, C3, C5, C1, C3] such that

C1 = [1, 2, 2, 1, 2, 2]
C2 = [2, 2, 3, 2, 2, 3]
C3 = [3, 3, 3, 1, 3, 3]
C5 = [1, 1, 1, 1, 1, 1]
C1 = [1, 2, 2, 1, 2, 2]
C3 = [3, 3, 3, 1, 3, 3].

Here Majority_Vote of (C1, C2, C3, C5, C1, C3) = [1, 2, 3, 1, 2, 3]. So the training accuracy for the ensemble of these 6 classifiers is 100%, and test accuracy can simply be calculated accordingly. We can see that the weak classifier C5 does help bring the ensemble to 100% training accuracy.

4 Experimental Setup & Results

Table 1 shows the UCI KDD datasets [8] used in the experiment. All attributes in the datasets contain numeric values.

Dataset	#Training	#Test	# Attributes	#Class
balance-scale	417	208	4	3
bupa	230	115	6	2
iono-sphere	234	117	34	2
lung cancer	22	10	56	3
lymp	98	50	18	4
pima	512	256	8	2

Table 1. 6 UCI KDD datasets used in the experiment

4.1 Classifiers

For each dataset, we generated 500 different bagging results and applied 22 different kinds of classifiers (18 from Weka [11] and 4 from LIBSVM [7]) to them to overproduce enough classifiers. The kinds of classifiers considered were: NaiveBayesMultinomial, ComplementNaiveBayes, NaiveBayes, SMO, Logistic, Multilayer Perceptron, AdaBoostM1, LogitBoost, VFI, J48, NBTree, REPTree, RandomForest, ConjunctiveRule, DecisionTable, JRip, PART, Ridor, SVM (Linear), SVM (Polynomial), SVM (RBF), SVM (Sigmoid). Thus we overproduced 11000 classifiers and selected the best ensemble from among these 11000 classifiers for each dataset.

Since an ensemble-based method (e.g. AdaBoostM1 and RandomForest) usually yield better performance than individual learners using a single algorithm, we simply treated these methods as *strong* classifiers. This ensured having both strong and weak classifiers for our experiment.

4.2 Experimental Results

We set up the experiments by applying the same ensemble selection algorithm to the top X% of classifiers and compared the result to the remaining (100-X)%. For example, we started the experiment by comparing ensembles from the top 1% and the bottom 99%, then the top 2% versus the bottom 98%, until we reached the top 34% versus the bottom 66%. Below are graphs of test accuracy for all 6 datasets. The experimental results show consistently that bottom classifiers can yield comparable and sometimes better performance than top classifiers.

In the Balance-scale dataset, the bottom classifiers outperformed top classifiers for X values up to 79%. That is, we can discard the top 21% of classifiers and can still make an ensemble from the bottom 79% with better performance. In the Bupa dataset, the outperformance of bottom classifiers continued for the the entire range of X values, from 1% to 34%.

In the Ionosphere, and Lung cancer datasets, ensembles using only bottom classifiers consistently had comparable performance to ensembles using top classifiers. In the Lymphography dataset, bottom classifiers outperformed top classifiers up to 76%.

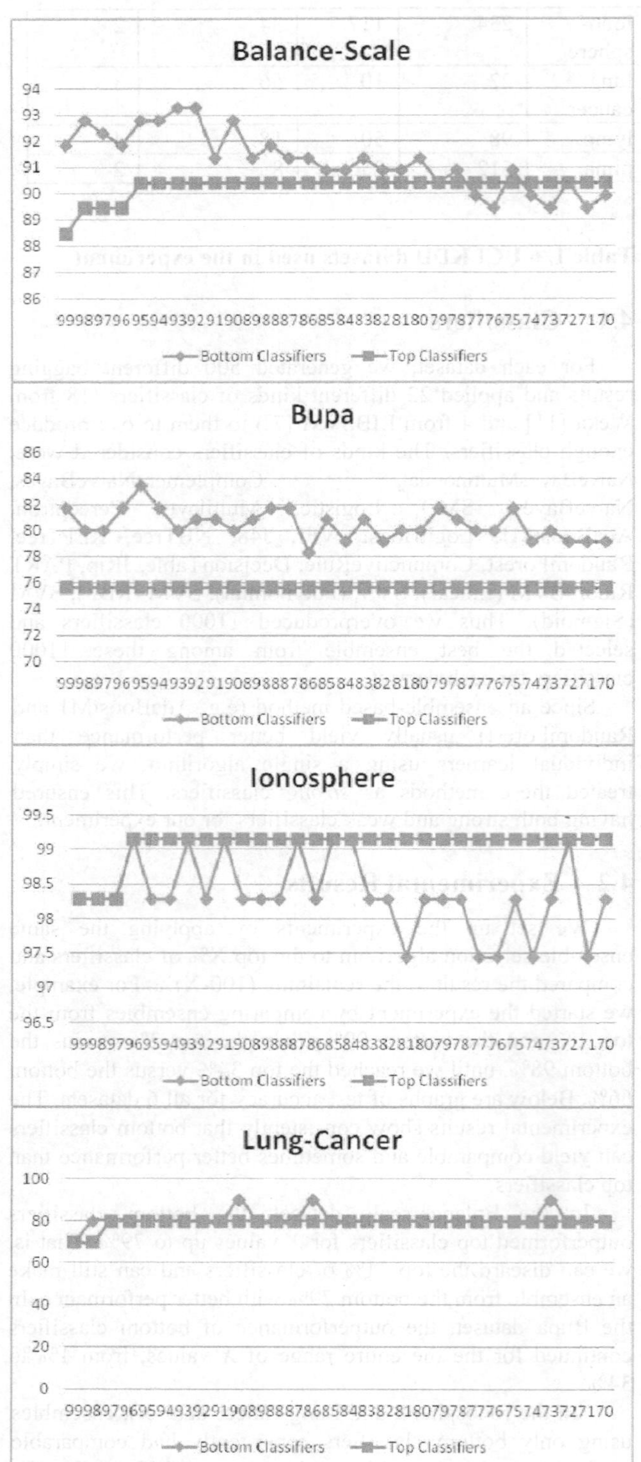

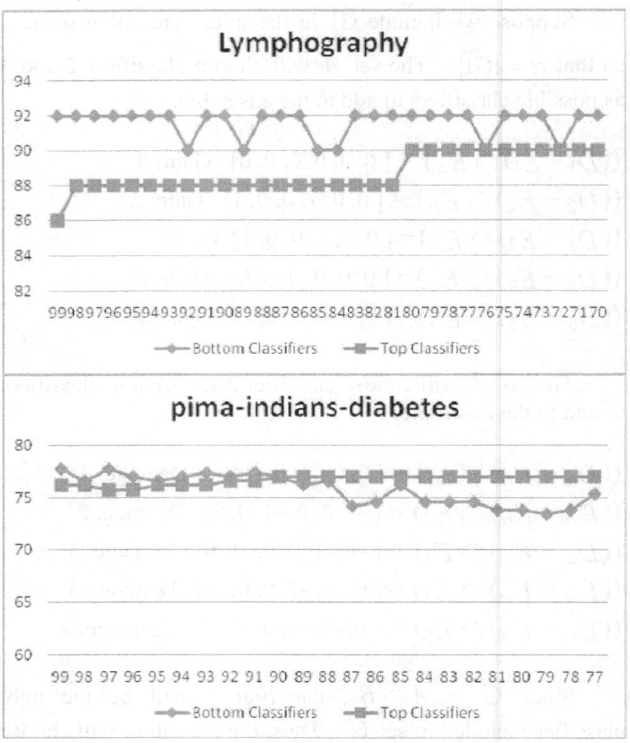

That is, we could omit the top 24% and still build ensembles with better performance. In the Pima Indian/diabetes dataset, we could reach 90% i.e., ensembles from the bottom 90% outperformed ensembles using the top 10% of classifiers.

It helps to study this phenomenon in detail to appreciate the way in which top performing classifiers can lower performance. For example, in the Balance-Scale dataset, if we use the top 1%-20% of all models, we just cannot achieve the highest possible test accuracy. It seems that the pruned bottom (weaker) classifiers can complement strong classifiers in a way that improves performance. This might seem to be an unusual situation, but in fact the same situation arises in the Bupa, Lymphography, and Pima Indian/Diabetes datasets. This suggests that as long as weaker/strong classifiers are included in the right places, then they are helpful. However, the top X% of classifiers are sometimes sufficient as long as they are complementary. Our experimental results suggest however that bottom (weaker) classifiers can help improve performance in terms of classification accuracy. The full experimental results can be found in our website in [12].

5 Conclusions

In this paper we have explored an ensemble selection strategy that finds complementary ensembles in the construction of ensembles of classifiers, comparing the test accuracy of the top performing X% of classifiers versus the bottom performing (100-X%), and emphasizing diversity in the kinds of classifier considered. The surprising successfulness of this approach has been explored in the experimental results.

A key aspect of our approach, and a primary contribution of this work, has been in the idea of maximizing diversity while minimizing ensemble size. BBBFS, our heuristic search algorithm, works precisely to limit redundancy among classifiers in an ensemble in this way. The result is a small ensemble of diverse classifiers whose complementarity has been optimized. Caruana et al noted in [3] that "While further work is needed to develop good heuristics for automatically choosing an appropriate pruning level for a data set, simply using the top 10-20% models seems to be a good rule of thumb. An open problem is finding a better pruning method." For example, taking model diversity [1] into account might find better pruned sets. Our algorithm, BBBFS, is a heuristic algorithm for maximizing diversity over the training set, and this approach has given interesting results for Caruana's open problem in the experiments.

Another key aspect of our approach is to highlight the cost of blindly cutting the bottom (weaker) classifiers. Our experiments contradict the validity of using only top classifiers,. We believe that further research is needed to consider factors such as complementarity structure among classifiers and the number of classifiers used in ensembles.

Future work should investigate further why an ensemble of bottom classifiers can sometimes outperform ensembles of top classifiers. We conjecture that overfitting could play a role here, as an ensemble of top classifiers could easily be misled in this way.

6 References

[1] L.I. Kuncheva and C.J. Whitaker, "Measures of diversity in classifier ensembles", Machine Learning 51: 181-207, 2003.

[2] T.G. Dietterich, "Ensemble Methods in Machine Learning", Proc. 1st Intl Workshop on Multiple Classifier Systems, Springer Verlag, LNCS #1857, 1-15, 2000.

[3] R. Caruana, A. Niculescu-Mizil, G. Crew, A. Ksikes, "Ensemble Selection from Libraries of Models", Proc. Intnl. Conf on Machine Learning, 2004.

[4] R. Caruana, A. Niculescu-Mizil, "An Empirical Comparison of Supervised Learning Algorithms Using Different Performance Metrics", ICML 2005.

[5] R. Caruana, A. Mnson, A. Niculescu-Mizil, "Getting the Most Out of Ensemble Selection", Technical Report 2006-2045, Dept. of Computer Science, Cornell University, 2006.

[6] L. Breiman, "Bagging Predictors", Machine Learning 24(2): 123-140, 1996.

[7] C-C. Chang, C-J. Lin, "LIBSVM : A Library for Support Vector Machines", 2001. Software available at http://www.csie.ntu.edu.tw/~cjlin/libsvm

[8] Bache, K. & Lichman, M. (2013). UCI Machine Learning Repository [http://archive.ics.uci.edu/ml]. Irvine, CA: University of California, School of Information and Computer Science.

[9] lymphography dataset: M. Zwitter, M. Soklic, University Medical Centre, Institute of Oncology, Ljubljana, Yugoslavia.
http://www.ics.uci.edu/~mlearn/databases/lymphography/lymphography.names

[10] primary-tumor dataset: M. Zwitter, M. Soklic, University Medical Centre, Institute of Oncology, Ljubljana, Yugoslavia.
http://www.ics.uci.edu/~mlearn/databases/primary-tumor/primarytumor.names

[11] Mark Hall, Eibe Frank, Geoffrey Holmes, Bernhard Pfahringer, Peter Reutemann, Ian H. Witten (2009); The WEKA Data Mining Software: An Update; SIGKDD Explorations, Volume 11, Issue 1.

[12] http://www.cs.ucla.edu/~kunghua/DMIN2013/

[13] L.K. Hansen, P. Salamon, Neural network ensembles. IEEE Trans. Patt. Anal. Mach. Intell. 12(10): 993-1001, 1990.

[14] D. Partridge, W.J. Krzanowski, Software diversity: Practical statistics for its measurement and exploitation. Information & Software Technology, 39, 707–717, 1997.

[15] A. Krogh, J. Vedelsby, Neural Network Ensembles, Cross Validation, and Active Learning, Advances in Neural Information Processing Systems, 231- 238, 1995.

[16] L.I. Kuncheva, Combining Pattern Classifiers: Methods and Algorithms, 2004.

[17] Opitz, D., and Shavlik, J. Actively searching for an effective neural network ensemble. Connection Science, 8(3/4):337–353, 1996.

[18] J. Bennet and S. Lanning (2007), "The Netflix Prize", www.cs.uic.edu/~liub/KDD-cup-2007/NetflixPrize-description.pdf.

[19] Y. Koren, "The BellKor Solution to the Netflix Grand Prize", (2009).

[20] A. Töscher, M. Jahrer, R. Bell, "The BigChaos Solution to the Netflix Grand Prize", (2009).

Labeled Subgraph Matching Using Degree Filtering

Lixin Fu and Surya Prakash R Kommireddy
Department of Computer Science,
University of North Carolina at Greensboro,
167 Petty Building, Greensboro, NC 27412, USA.
phone: 336-256-1137; fax: 336-256-0439; e-mail: lfu@uncg.edu

Abstract - *Subgraph isomorphism (SGI) is the problem to determine whether there is a subgraph in the given larger graph (called model graph) that is identical to a given smaller graph (called query graph). It is well known that SGI problem for an unlabeled graph in general is NP Complete. The famous Ullman's algorithm is still used in popular subgraph matching software package such as POSSUM. However, this algorithm handles unlabeled graphs. In this paper, we design and implement a new SGI algorithm that can handle graphs with labeled edges. Such graphs have important applications e.g. cheminformatics and pattern recognition. Our major contribution is to integrate degree filtering while comparing the node labels, so that the performance is greatly improved.*

Keywords: graph algorithms, subgraph isomorphism, labeled graphs, matching

1 Introduction

Many real world problems can be represented in term of graphs. From late seventies, graph-based techniques have been proposed as a powerful tool for pattern recognition. Pattern recognition in chemistry or biological databases is modeled as graph matching problem. Graph matching problems are of two types, they are exact graph matching and approximate graph matching. In this paper, we mainly concentrate on sub-graph isomorphism which is in category of exact graph matching.

The main use of the subgraph isomorphism in chem-Informatics is "the chemical similarity between any two molecules, either at the sub or superstructure level, and clustering of similar molecules are widely used to measure the diversity of chemical space and these methods are important as they can be applied towards discovering any new drug like molecules" In addition to cheminformatics, SGI has many other applications in bioinformatics, scene analysis, pattern recognition , image processing, etc. Related work is given in the next section. In sec. 3, Ullman's algorithm is discussed as the base for our algorithm (in sec. 4) to compare with. The experiment section of 5 shows that our new algorithm outperforms the traditional Ullman's algorithm. Lastly, the conclusion and further work are given.

2 Related Work

2.1 Exact Matching Algorithms

Subgraph isomorphism will come under the exact matching algorithms category. Exact graph matching is requires the mappings between the nodes of the two graphs to be edge-preserving. That is, if any two nodes in the first graph are linked by an edge then they are mapped to two nodes in the second graph that are linked by an edge as well. In the case of labeled graphs, the corresponding node and edge labels must match as well. There is a bi-directional one-to-one correspondence between each node of the first graph to the each node of subgraph of the second graph.

Most of the algorithms for exact graph matching are based on some form of tree search with backtracking. Many different implementations have been employed. Among them the recursive depth first search uses less memory.

Ullman"s algorithm was published as early as 1976, which is is still widely used today in the famous software package POSSUM (Protein On-line Substructure Searching – Ullman Method) [4]. Ullman proposes so-called refinement procedure that works on a matrix of possible future matched node pairs to remove. Many algorithms are proposed based on this algorithm.

Another similar algorithm is Corneil's breadth-first algorithm, which is presently the core component of Gemini and Sub-Gemini, which is still best performing package today for sub circuits extraction in VLSI layout verification. [2]. Cordella proposed a new algorithm for the subgraph isomorphism called VF [5] algorithm. In this algorithm, a heuristic is based on the analysis of the sets of nodes adjacent to the ones already considered in the partial mapping. The author redesigned and proposes another algorithm called VF2 [6] which is significant improvement over Ullman"s and work well for large graphs also.

Subgraph isomorphism has been proposed by the Larrosa and Valiente [7], authors changed slightly the problem and stated as constraint satisfaction problem (CSP), and this problem has been helpful in the framework of discrete optimization and operational research.

In this paper, we mainly modified Ullman's method so that in the case of labeled graph, the performance is greatly improved due to label matching and degree filtering. We will first present the simple enumeration algorithm and then the idea of Ullmann's method, and in coming section our algorithm called SGI-DF (Subgraph Isomorphism with Degree Filtering).

2.2 Simple Enumeration Algorithm for Finding Subgraph Isomorphism

This algorithm describes a brute-force enumeration procedure that is actually a depth-first tree-search algorithm. This algorithm is designed to find all the isomorphisms between given graphs G1 and the subgraphs of G2. The adjacency matrices for graphs G1 and G2 are A= [αij] and B= [βij].

These methods will use the representation of adjacency matrices. In this algorithm, we introduce the very important concept of permutation matrix, which is a key concept in Ullman's algorithm. We call the permutation matrix as M'. of size (rows of matrix A) X (rows of matrix B), such that the permutation matrix whose elements are 1's and 0's and such that each row contains exactly one 1 and no column contains more than one 1.

The permutation matrix is used to find the matrix C, where C= [cij] = $M'(M'B)^T$, and T represents transpose. Subgraph isomorphism exists if for all i and j's of α and β, $(\alpha_{ij}=1) = (c_{ij}=1)$.

2.3 Permutation Matrix

A permutation matrix, of N×M, has exactly one entry 1 in each row and each column and 0s elsewhere. For a 4×4 permutation matrix, 4! (Factorial of 4) permutation matrices are possible.

In the simple brute force enumeration procedure, it needs all the permutation matrices to be tried until the subgraph isomorphism exists. Here are just 3 of the matrices in all 24 matrices.

1 0 0 0 0 0 1 0 0 1 0 0 0 0 0 1	0 1 0 0 1 0 0 0 0 0 1 0 0 0 0 1	1 0 0 0 0 1 0 0 0 0 1 0 0 0 0 1

Example is given below for one of the permutation matrices [3 2 1 0], how it will be computed

3 2 1 0		0	1	2	3
3r column and 0th row- 1	0	0	0	0	1
2nd column and 1st row-1	1	0	0	1	0
1st column and 2rd row-1	2	0	1	0	0
0th column and 3rd row-1 (remaining all are 0's)	3	1	0	0	0

Table 1: permutation matrix showing each row and column

3 Ullman's Algorithm

To reduce the amount of computation, Ullmann proposed a refinement procedure to eliminate some of the 1's from the matrices M, thus reducing the number of the possibility matrices.

Ullman's algorithm mainly depends on permutation matrices to find all the isomorphism for given two graphs. Using permutation matrices, we find the matrix C and then compare it with a query graph. Ullmann's method is based on backtracking and a refinement procedure.

The inputs are the model graph and query graph, and the output will be a permutation matrix.

Query graph G= (V, E, L_V, L_E)

Model graph G1= $(V1, E1, L_V, L_E)$

Ullmann's algorithm:

ULLMANN (G= (V, E, L_V, L_E), G1= $(V1, E1, L_V, L_E)$)

1. Let P = (p_{ij}) be a n×n permutation matrix, n= |V|,
   m = |V1|,and M=adjacency matrix of G,
   M1=adjacency matrix of G1

2. Call Backtrack(M; M1;P;1)
3. Procedure Backtrack (adjacency matrix M, adjacency matrix M1, Permutation matrix P, counter k)
   (a) if k > m then P represents a subgraph isomorphism from GI to G. Output P and return.
   (b) For all i = 1 to n
      i. set $P_{ki} = 1$ and for all j = i set $P_{kj} = 0$
      ii. if $S_{k,k}(M1) = S_{k,n}(P)\, M\, (S_{k,n}(P))T$ then
         call Backtrack(M, M1, P, k +1)

Ullmann followed the backtracking procedure with the refinement steps. The refinement procedure is done by the idea of forward checking. The backtrack procedure in Ullmann's algorithm recursively builds permutation matrix element by element, checking for a match with input graph at each step.

The backtracking procedure stops whenever the match found or until all the possible matrices are over.

In comparison with the simple enumeration procedure, Ullmann's refinement method will reduce the number of permutation matrices. We will use the following example to explain.

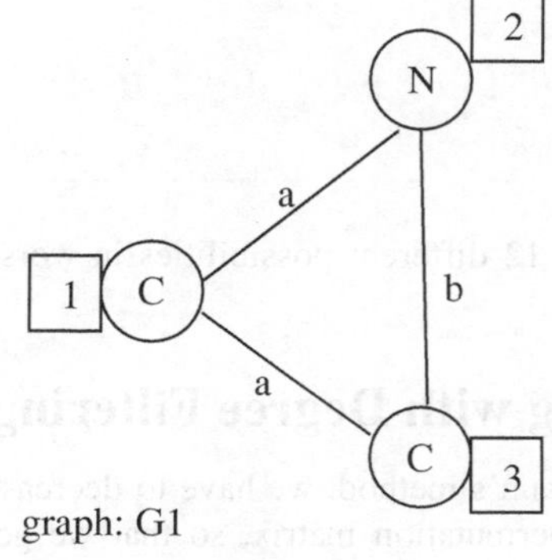

graph: G1

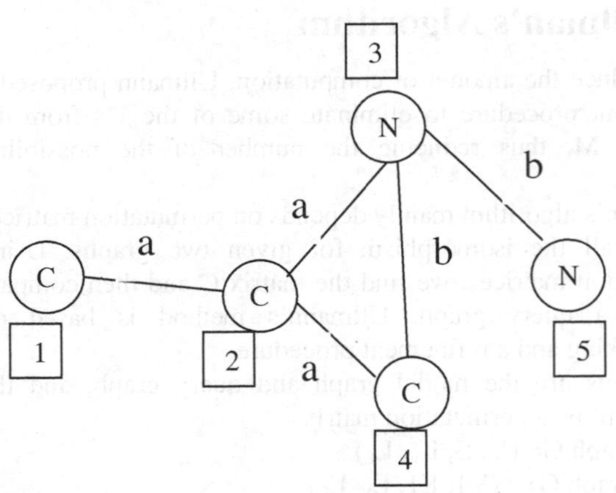

graph: G2

In the above figure, circles represent the node labels, squares represent indexes and remaining are the edge labels. For the simple enumeration procedure, the permutation matrix would contain of all 1's.

Indexes(labels)	1(C)	2(C)	3(N)	4(C)	5(N)
1(C)	1	1	1	1	1
2(N)	1	1	1	1	1
3(C)	1	1	1	1	1

In the above matrix, the total combinations would be 5*4*3=60 possibilities of permutation matrices. Because of its brute force approach it should have to try every possibility in worst case. For Ullmann's procedure, the permutation matrix would contain fewer 1's compared to the simple enumeration procedure.

Indexes(labels)	1(C)	2(C)	3(N)	4(C)	5(N)
1(C)	1	1	0	1	0
2(N)	0	0	1	0	1
3(C)	1	1	0	1	0

In this case, there are only 12 different possibilities in worst case.

4 Label Matching with Degree Filtering

To further improve Ullmann's method, we have to decrease the number of 1's in the permutation matrix, so that we get smaller number of combinations to check for the subgraph isomorphism. Our idea is to add degree filtering and label matching features for labeled graphs.

Using our algorithm we can reduce a lot of 1's in the permutation matrix than the 1's in the Ullmann's algorithm, thus reducing many unnecessary comparisons from query graph to the main graph.

The degree of a node is the total number of neighboring nodes connected to the node. For example, in Graph G2, the degrees of the nodes 1 through 5 are 1, 3, 3, 2, and 1 respectively.

4.1 Design of the algorithm

As we mentioned before, the aim of algorithm is to reduce the non-zero entries of matrix M to zeros. Suppose $\alpha\_1,\alpha\_2,\ldots\ldots\ldots\alpha\_n$ are in query graph and $\beta\_1, \beta\_2,\ldots\ldots\ldots$ B_m are in model graph. A and B are adjacency matrices of query and model graphs.

Step 1: Fast elimination

Before this step, we will find degree for each node in query graph and input graphs.

In this step, we will check the maximum degree of query graph and compare to that of the model graph, if there is no node having same label and not having higher degree than the maximum degree of query graph, then it's going to be terminated and say there is no subgraph form G1 to G2.

Step 2: Preprocessing

In this step, we preprocess the matrix and reduce as many entries of M to zero as possible by allowing only vertices with the same or greater degree to be mapped to each other as well as checking the label names.

We construct mapping matrix M as follows.

M(i,j) = 1, if Degree(α_i) $\leq$ Degree(β_j) and Label(α_i)=Label(β_j)

M(i,j) = 0, Otherwise

The above 2 steps are not in the Ullmann's method and so we improve the performance, and the remaining steps are very much similar.

Step 3: Changing Mapping matrix to the different arrays, and then using that arrays we will generate distinct arrays, each array for each possible matrix.

Step 4: Computing C according to this formula,

C=M(M*B)T, where M is the each possible matrix,

B is the input matrix

T is the transpose

C is the final matrix to check each time to the query matrix for every possible matrix.

Step 5:

If C=A, then the possible matrix matches the structure of query and main graphs, then it will check all the edges in query and main graph ,if they are same then print the result, If not then go to step 3 and get other possible matrices.

4.2 Flow chart of our algorithm:

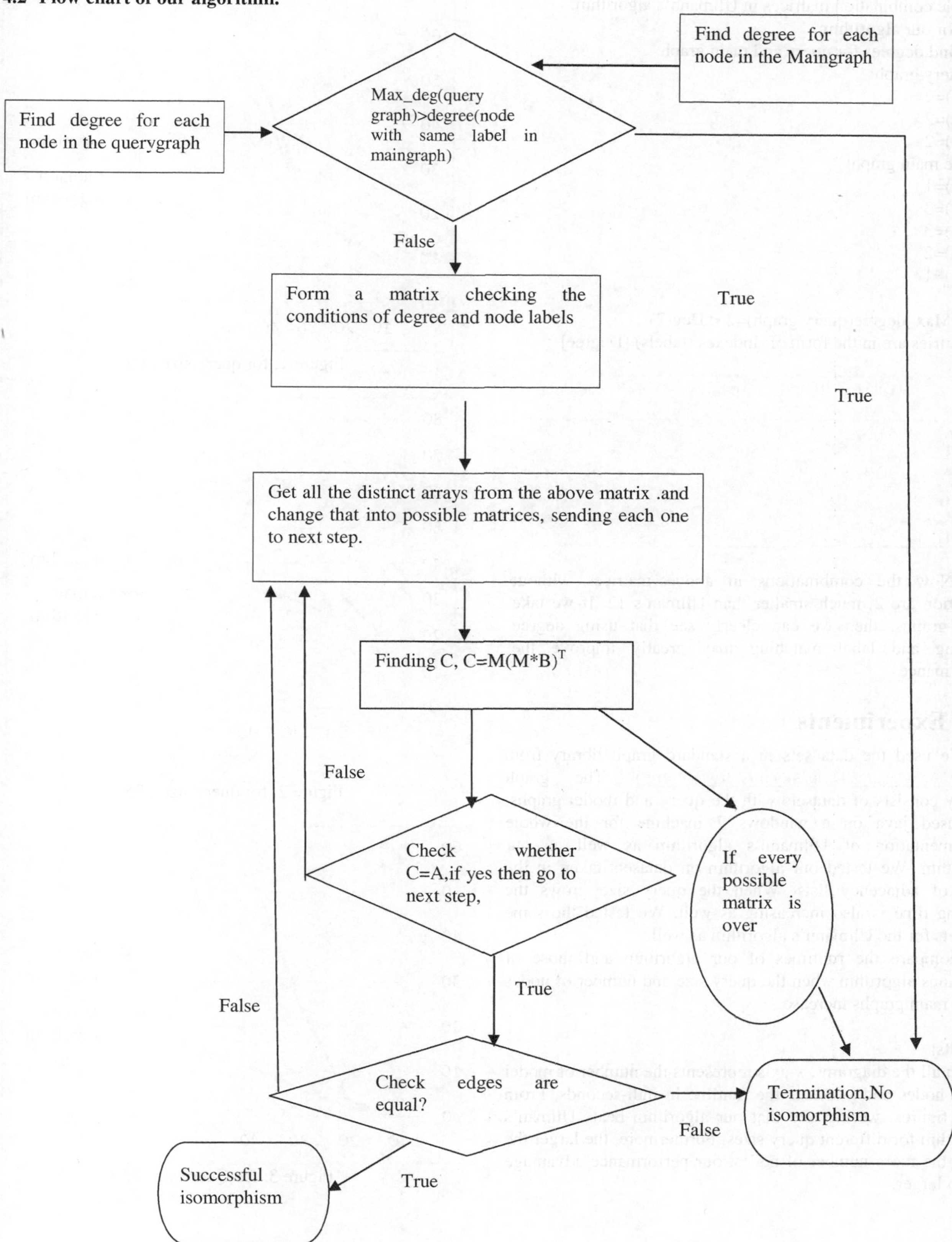

In the example of section III, we know that there are 12 possible combination matrices in Ullmann's algorithm.
Now for our algorithm:
First find degrees for query and main graph.
For query graph:
Deg(1)=2
Deg(2)=2
Deg(3)=2
For the main graph:
Deg(1)=1
Deg(2)=3
Deg(3)=3
Deg(4)=2
Deg(5)=1

Now, Max_degree(query graph)=2 < Deg(2)
The entries are in the form of: Indexes (labels) [Degree]

	1(C)[1]	2(C)[3]	3(N)[3]	4(C)[2]	5(N)[1]
1(C) [2]	0	1	0	1	0
2(N) [2]	0	0	1	0	0
3(C) [2]	0	1	0	1	0

Now the combinations in above matrices without repetition are 2, much smaller than Ullman's 12. If we take large graphs, then we can clearly see that using degree filtering and label matching may greatly improve the performance.

5 Experiments

We used the data sets in a standard graph library from (http://www.cs.ucsb.edu/~xyan/software.htm/). The graph library consists of datasets with the query and model graphs. We used java on a windows 7 machine for the whole implementation of Ullmann's algorithm as well as our algorithm. We tested our algorithm on datasets taken in the form of adjacency lists. When the query size grows the running time is also increasing as well. We tested the same datasets for the Ullmann's algorithm as well.
We compare the runtimes of our algorithm and those of Ullmanns algorithm when the query size and number of nodes in the main graphs increase.

Results:

In all the diagrams, x-axis represents the number of model graph nodes and y-axis is the runtime in mili-seconds. From these figures, we can see that our algorithm beats Ullman's algorithm for different query sizes. Furthermore, the larger the sizes, the more number of nodes, our performance advantage is also larger.

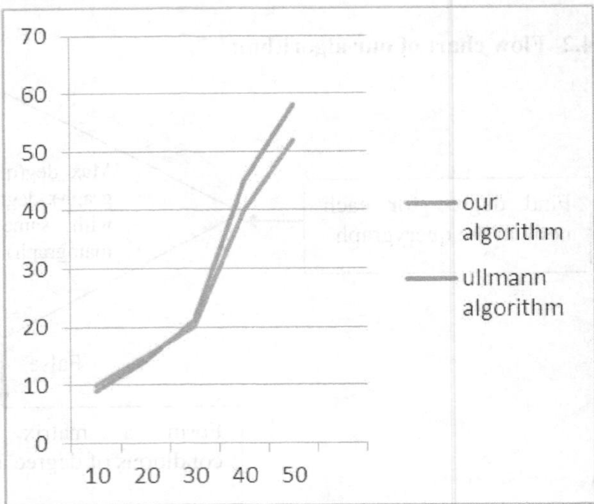

Figure 1: for query size of 3.

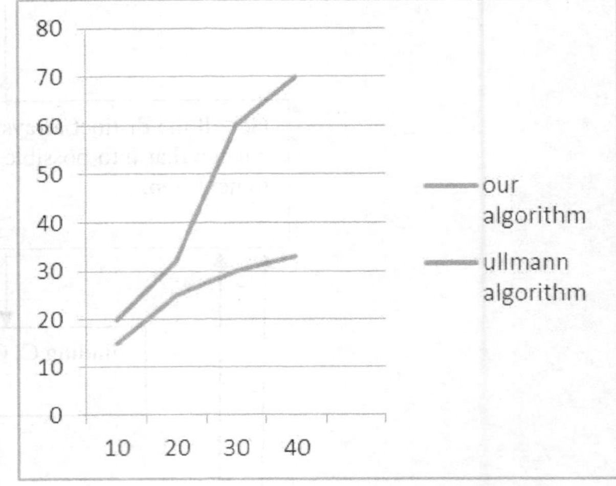

Figure 2: for query size of 5.

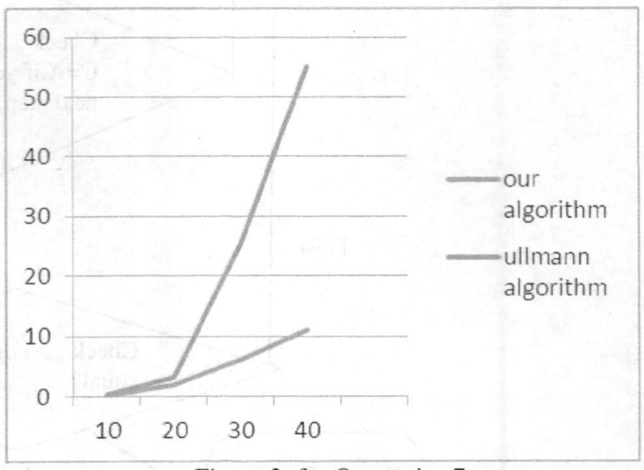

Figure 3: for Query size 7.

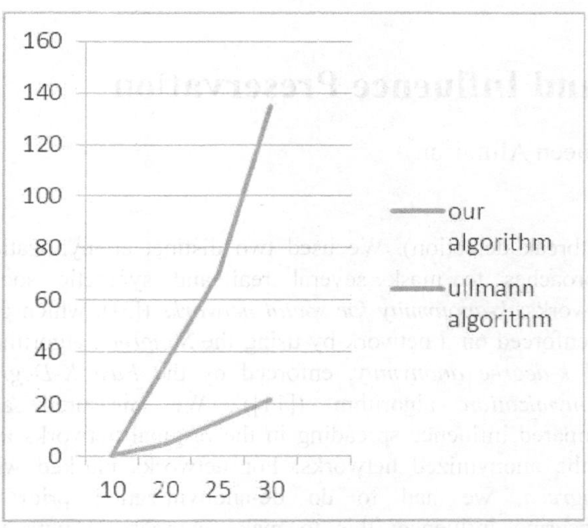

Figure 4: for query size 9.

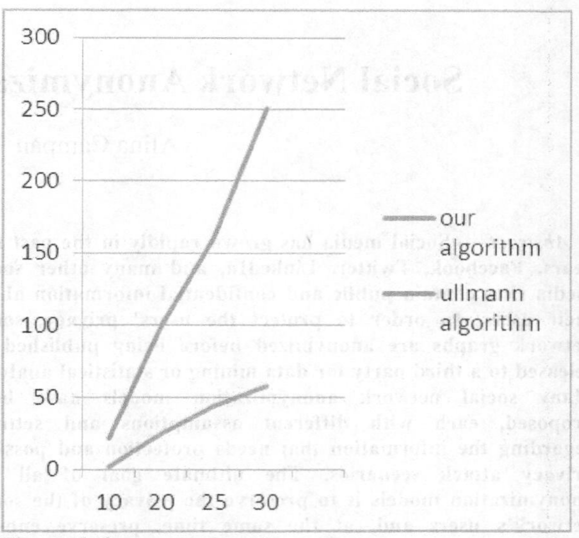

Figure 5: for query size 11.

6 Conclusion

We proposed a new algorithm called SGI-DF, which works for labeled graph subgraph isomorphism. Our conclusion from the experiments and results is that when the query size is smaller there would be no great difference but when the query size becomes bigger the runtime difference between Ullman's algorithm and SGI-DF becomes much larger. The reason is that our degree filtering feature added can eliminate many unnecessary computations. When the query sizes grow both algorithms run longer. In addition, our algorithm works for the labeled edges also which is very helpful in applications such as chem-informatics.

The scalability of this algorithm remains to be verified due to limited computing resources. One area is to extend the work here to accommodate large graphs stored in external disks. Further work on SGI computing on cloud environment is also desired.

References

[1] Taming verification hardness: an efficient algorithm for testing subgraph isomorphism, H Shang, Y Zhang, X Lin – proceedings of the VLDB Endowment, (2008)

[2] An Effective Approach for Solving Subgraph Isomorphism Problem- Zong Ling, Department of Electrical Engineering, University of Hawaii (1996)

[3] Parallel Subgraph Isomorphism, Aaron Blankstein, Matthew Goldstein, MIT Computer Science and Artificial Intelligence Laboratory (2010)

[4] J. R. Ullman, An algorithm for subgraph isomorphism, Journal of the association of computing machinery, 23(1976) 31-42.

[5] Performance evaluation of VF graph matching algorithm, LP Cordella, P Foggia, C Sansone, Image Analysis and processing, (1999) pp.1172-1177.

[6] A (Sub)Graph Isomorphism Algorithm for Matching large graphs- Luigi P. Cordella, Pasquale Foggia, Carlo Sansone, and Mario Vento, Proc. 3rd IAPR-TC15 Workshop Graph-Based Representations in Pattern Recognition, (2001), pp. 149-159.

[7] Liu and D. J. Klein. The graph isomorphism problem. Journal of Computational Chemistry, 12(10): 1243-1251, 1991.

[8]http://en.wikipedia.org/wiki/Subgraph_isomorphism_problem

[9] Subgraph Isomorphism in Polynomial Time – B.T. Messmer and H. Bunke, University of Bern, Neubruckstr. 10, Bern, Switzerland, Recent Developments in Computer Vision, (1996).

Social Network Anonymization and Influence Preservation

Alina Campan* and Yasmeen Alufaisan*

Abstract — **Social media has grown rapidly in the past few years. Facebook, Twitter, LinkedIn, and many other social media sites contain public and confidential information about their users. In order to protect the users' privacy, social network graphs are anonymized before being published or released to a third party for data mining or statistical analysis. Many social network anonymization models have been proposed, each with different assumptions and settings regarding the information that needs protection and possible privacy attack scenarios. The ultimate goal of all the anonymization models is to preserve the privacy of the social network's users and, at the same time, preserve enough information to enable a good analysis of the social network. In this work, we study how well we can preserve the important features in a social graph, specifically the nodes' influence in the network (as quantified by influence spread measures) while preserving privacy with different anonymization models.**

I. INTRODUCTION

As with other types of data (microdata, streams, location-based data etc.), social network graphs can be subjected to an anonymization process, before the social network data can be publicly released; the goal is to ensure the privacy of the social actors. Up until now, there are no standard models and algorithms for social network anonymization. Various solutions have been developed in the recent past, for different problem settings. Different anonymity approaches vary in their assumptions about: data available about the social actors and their relationships; private information that needs protection; background knowledge of an attacker [15]. Consequently, different anonymity models and methods to achieve them have been created corresponding to these problem settings. The resulting anonymized networks are very dissimilar, and so is the extent to which they preserve information inherent in the original network. For example, recent studies investigated how structural properties such as diameter, centrality measures, clustering coefficients, and topological indices are preserved between the original networks and their anonymized versions [14]. In this paper, we investigate how influence is preserved in social networks that undergo an anonymization process. Influence modeling has been studied with applications in understanding information diffusion, viral marketing ([6]), outbreak detection in networks ([9]). Influence spread was modeled and analyzed so that to find a small set of nodes in a network such that: their overall influence in the network is maximized (viral marketing), or they are able to detect most effectively the spreading of a process over a network (outbreak detection). We used two distinct anonymization approaches to mask several real and synthetic social networks: *k-anonymity for social networks* ([3]), which can be enforced on a network by using the *Sangreea* algorithm, and *k-degree anonymity*, enforced by the *Fast K-Degree Anonymization* algorithm ([11]). We measured and compared influence spreading in the original networks and in the anonymized networks. For networks masked with *Sangreea*, we had to do de-anonymization prior to measuring influence: this to make comparison with the original networks feasible, as we will explain later.

The paper is structured as follows. Next section reviews the two models we used for social network anonymization: *k-anonymity* and *k-degree anonymity*, and their respective anonymization methods. Section 3 presents our approaches to de-anonymize networks masked with *Sangreea*. We describe in Section 4 the influence spread measure we analyzed and the method we used to approximate influence. Section 5 describes how we measure influence preservation between an original network and its anonymized / de-anonymized version. Section 6 describes our experimental setup and results. The paper ends with conclusions.

II. ANONYMITY MODELS FOR SOCIAL NETWORKS

K-degree anonymity was proposed for protection against identity disclosure due to attacks that use background information about nodes' degrees. A social network modeled as a simple graph $\mathcal{G} = (\mathcal{N}, \mathcal{E})$, where $\mathcal{N}$ is the set of nodes and $\mathcal{E}$ is the set of edges, is said to be *k-degree anonymous*, for a given k value (5, 7 etc.), if for every node X in $\mathcal{N}$, there are at least k-1 other nodes with the same degree as X [10]. Lu et. al. proposed in [11] an efficient solution for enforcing *k*-degree anonymity on social graphs: *FKDA* (*Fast K-degree Anonymization Algorithm*). *FKDA* works by trying to anonymize groups of at least k nodes in one step. Nodes to be next in an anonymized group are selected in decreasing order of their degree, among the nodes which haven't been yet anonymized in previous steps. The anonymization consists in wiring new edges to nodes in the group, until all have the same degree, equal to the largest degree in the group at the beginning of the step. Wiring is attempted with nodes with smaller degrees than the highest one in the group, and which haven't therefore been put through anonymization before. If anonymization cannot be achieved for a group by following this procedure, a more relaxed wiring is allowed, which can destroy the anonymity of nodes processed in previous steps (then, the whole process is re-started). We used *FKDA* for enforcing *k*-degree anonymity.

* Department of Computer Science, Northern Kentucky University, USA {campana1, alufaisany1}@nku.edu

K-anonymity for social networks, introduced in [3], can protect against identity disclosure and against content (or attribute) disclosure. According to this model, both the data and the structure associated to nodes are anonymized such that a node becomes undistinguishable from at least *k*-1 other nodes in the network. The key to the anonymization process as applied by *Sangreea* consists in clustering the nodes into a partition with sets of cardinality at least *k*, and which are as similar as possible to each other in terms of their attributes and their neighborhoods. Nodes in each cluster are merged into a supernode in the masked network. For each supernode, there is some information that will be released: its cardinality (is *k* or greater), the number of edges internal to the cluster, and the generalized attribute values describing all nodes in the cluster. Connectivity information between supernodes is also released: for each pair of supernodes, a weight representing the number of edges with ends in the two clusters is published. *Sangreea* can be geared towards preserving more the attributes of the nodes or the structure of the graph, by using two user defined parameters. We used *Sangreea* to take into account only the structure of the network, and not the nodes' attributes.

A network masked with *Sangreea* will obviously have a number of supernodes at most the size of the original network divided to *k*. Such an aggregated network cannot be fairly compared w.r.t. influence preservation with the original network or the *FKDA* anonymized network. To be able to inspect how influence is preserved through *Sangreea* anonymization, we need to execute an extra-step: we try to reverse the anonymization process and create a replica of the original network. We called this process *de-anonymization*. De-anonymization is implemented based on the information packaged in the aggregated network and assumes certain statistical distribution of the nodes' degrees. The de-anonymization process is described next.

Let $\mathcal{G} = (\mathcal{N}, \mathcal{E})$ be an initial social network and $\mathcal{MG} = (\mathcal{MN}, \mathcal{ME})$ be a corresponding *k*-anonymous social network masked with *Sangreea*, where $\mathcal{MN} = \{Cl_1, Cl_2, \ldots, Cl_v\}$, and $Cl_j = [gen(cl_j), (|cl_j|, |\mathcal{E}_{clj}|)]$, $j = 1..v$. This anonymized network was built based on a partition $\mathcal{S} = \{cl_1, cl_2, \ldots, cl_v\}$ of the node set $\mathcal{N}$, $\bigcup_{j=1,v} cl_j$ such that $= \mathcal{N}$; $cl_i \cap cl_j = \varnothing$; $i, j = 1..v$, $i \neq j$; where nodes were grouped such that nodes within every cluster cl_i were as similar to each other as possible w.r.t. their attributes and neighbors. The corresponding ***masked social network*** $\mathcal{MG} = (\mathcal{MN}, \mathcal{ME})$ has:

- $\mathcal{MN} = \{Cl_1, Cl_2, \ldots, Cl_v\}$, node Cl_j corresponds to cluster $cl_j \in \mathcal{S}$ and is described by a "tuple" $gen(cl_j)$ (the generalization information of cl_j, w.r.t. quasi-identifier attribute set) and an intra-cluster generalization pair $(|cl_j|, |\mathcal{E}_{clj}|)$;
- $\mathcal{ME} \subseteq \mathcal{MN} \times \mathcal{MN}$; $(Cl_i, Cl_j) \in \mathcal{ME}$ iif $Cl_i, Cl_j \in \mathcal{MN}$ and $\exists\ X \in cl_j$ and $Y \in cl_j$, such that $(X, Y) \in \mathcal{E}$. Each generalized edge $(Cl_i, Cl_j) \in \mathcal{ME}$ is labeled with the inter-cluster generalization value $|\mathcal{E}_{cli,clj}|$.

For both anonymity models, we make the assumption that nodes' identities are released, as follows. For *k*-degree anonymity, we assume that identities of the nodes are released together with those nodes' degree in the anonymized network; for example, nodes *John*, *William*, and *Mary* have an anonymized degree of 4 – in this example, we assume *k* to be 3, therefore each group of nodes with the same degree has cardinality at least 3. We will call these groups of nodes with the same anonymized degree ***anonymity clusters***. Obviously, for random networks, the anonymity clusters will contain a rather large number of nodes from $\mathcal{N}$. However, for scale-free networks, it is expected that anonymity clusters for large degree values will have cardinality close to *k*, while anonymity clusters for small degree values will still have large cardinality.

For *k*-anonymity for social networks, we assume that the identities of the entities in each supernode are disclosed; for example, the supernode Cl_i in the 3-anonymous network consists of the nodes *John*, *William*, and *Mary*. In this model's case, each supernode is an anonymity cluster.

These assumptions about nodes' identities are not against the definitions of the two models, nor do they weaken the models' strength. These assumptions are necessary; otherwise a masked network would be unusable, for example, for viral marketing. Identifying, even accurately, the most influential nodes in an anonymized network would be useless if the nodes were unidentified, since they could not be targeted with different promotions without knowing who are the people represented by those nodes.

III. DE-ANONYMIZATION FOR *SANGREEA* NETWORKS

We used two procedures to de-anonymize a network masked with *Sangreea* to try to reconstruct the original social graph $\mathcal{G}$. Each one of these two procedures assumes a certain type of degree distribution for the nodes in the original network.

The first de-anonymization method, ***uniformReconstruct***, is based on the assumption that the node degrees, and therefore edges in the graph, are uniformly distributed among nodes. ***uniformReconstruct*** will then randomly reconnect with edges nodes that belong within each cluster, and then nodes in every pair of clusters. We are omitting the algorithm for ***uniformReconstruct*** due to space constraints.

Many real-world networks do not have a uniform distribution of the nodes' degrees. Instead, they are scale-free, and their node degree distribution follows a power-law. Our second de-anonymization method, ***rmatReconstruct***, is based on this assumption about node degree distribution. We use an *R-MAT* generation procedure ([4]) to de-anonymize an anonymous network $\mathcal{MG} = (\mathcal{MN}, \mathcal{ME})$.

```
Algorithm rmatReconstruct is
Input: MG = (MN, ME) - a k-anonymous social
         network for G = (N, E)
         MN = {Cl1, Cl2, ... , Clv}, where Clj has
         cardinality |clj|, and the identities of
         the nodes in clj ⊆ N are known (*)
         ME ⊆ MN × MN and each edge (Cli, Clj) ∈
         ME has a weight |Ecli,clj|, which is the
         number of edges in E ∩(Cli x Clj)
Output: G' = (N, E') a de-anonymized network with
         the same node set as G and |E'| = |E|
```

```
Set the adjacency matrix of G', AM', to be the
zero matrix; this is equivalent to E' = ∅;
For every Clj ∈ ME do:
  count = 0
  While count < |clj|:
    Use rmatEdgeGeneration on the restriction
    of AM' to the rows & columns representing
    nodes in clj to generate a random edge
    (X,Y): X,Y ∈ clj, X ≠ Y, (X,Y)∉ E'
    E' = E' ∪ {(X,Y)}
    Update AM' to reflect the newly added edge
    count++
For every (Cli, Clj) ∈ ME do:
  count = 0
  While count < |Ecli,clj|:
    Use rmatEdgeGeneration on the restriction
    of AM' to the rows & columns representing
    nodes in cli ∪ clj to generate a random edge
    (X,Y): X ∈ cli, Y ∈ clj, (X,Y)∉ E'
    E' = E' ∪ {(X,Y)}
    Update AM' to reflect the newly added edge
    count++
End uniformReconstruct;

Algorithm rmatEdgeGeneration is
Input: An adjacency matrix AM
       Parameters a, b, c, d: a + b + c + d = 1
Output: A (row, column) location in AM, chosen
        according to parameters a, b, c, d, that
        indicates a new edge (X,Y) to be added
        to the graph represented by AM.
If AM has a single row and column:
  Return that position in the matrix

Generate a random number r, in range [0, 1].
Divide AM in 4 equal-size partitions, top-left,
top-right, bottom-left, and bottom-right
If r < a:
  rmatEdgeGeneration(top-left, a, b, c, d)
Else If r < a + b:
  rmatEdgeGeneration(top-right, a, b, c, d)
Else If r < a + b + c:
  rmatEdgeGeneration(bottom-left, a, b, c, d)
Else:
  rmatEdgeGeneration(bottom-right, a, b, c, d)
End rmatEdgeGeneration
```

Note (*): we explained before why we assume that the identities of the nodes in the original network that belong to each supernode in $\mathcal{MN}$ are known for the corresponding released k-anonymous network $\mathcal{MG} = (\mathcal{MN}, \mathcal{ME})$.

The *R-MAT* procedure takes 4 probabilities, called a, b, c, d as input parameters, where $a + b + c + d = 1$. It works on a submatrix of the adjacency matrix of $\mathcal{G}'$ which is: a restriction of it to a cluster (to generate internal edges in that cluster), or a restriction of it to two clusters (to generate inter-cluster edges). ***rmatEdgeGeneration*** recursively determines the location of a new edge in this matrix: the algorithm divides the adjacency matrix into 4 equal-sized partitions and the location of the new edge is probabilistically selected in one of the 4 locations, based on the 4 probability parameters. Once a partition is found, it is again divided into 4 sub-partitions until there will be only one location left in the partition. If an edge was already placed on that location, we will repeat this procedure from the beginning (multiple edges between the same pair of nodes are not allowed in our graph model). For all our tests we used the following values for the 4 probabilities: 0.45, 0.15, 0.15, and 0.25. This choice seems to model better many real-world graphs that follow power-law degree distributions [4]. As explained in [4], this generation technique will create 2 large well-connected "communities" in the graph: one among the nodes in the first "half" of the node set (the top-left quadrant in the adjacency matrix), the other among the nodes in the second half of the node set (the bottom-right quadrant in the adjacency matrix). Edges are created with higher probability among nodes in those respective halves, since parameters a and d are higher. The two communities are more loosely connected, as decided by the lower probabilities b and c that command the placement of edges between nodes belonging to different halves. The process is repeated recursively in each quadrant such that larger communities are divided in smaller and smaller communities.

Since we need a symmetric adjacency matrix to reflect that our social network graph is undirected, the adjacency matrix produced with ***rmatReconstruct*** is finally processed once more. The matrix entries above (or below) the main diagonal are discarded and the other half is copied over it to make it symmetric. Since parameters b and c are equal, the number of edges that result by applying this transformation is fairly equal to the number of edges in the uncut matrix.

IV. Influence in Social Networks

Influence spreading, or propagation, has been studied in a number of fields for a while now: sociology, viral marketing ([6], [8]), outbreak detection in networks ([9]). The linear threshold influence model (*LTM*) and the independent cascade influence model (*ICM*) are among the most used models for influence spreading ([8]). Influence models are used in solving the influence maximization problem: given a network and a parameter k, find a set of k nodes in the network that, when activated, can spread their influence to more network nodes than any subsets of nodes of size k. Please note that k in this context has a different meaning, totally unrelated, from k as in k-anonymity.

We chose to use the *LTM* for influence spreading, and the degree-discount algorithm ([5]) for determining the subset of nodes that could maximize the spread of influence.

Under *LTM*, a social network is modeled as a directed graph, $\mathcal{G} = (\mathcal{N}, \mathcal{E})$. Note: the two anonymity models we are studying both employ undirected graphs; we cope with this difference between the influence model and the anonymity models by simply considering each undirected edge in the anonymity models to be equivalent to two directed edges between the same nodes, when computing the spread of influence. Each node in $\mathcal{G}$ can be either active or inactive. Nodes that are active (i.e. have adopted a product or embraced a new idea) can further activate other nodes, which are currently inactive. Each node is influenced in a certain degree by each one of its neighbors. The influence that a node w exerts over its neighbor node v (this means that (w, v) is a directed edge in $\mathcal{E}$) is denoted by $b_{v,w}$ where $b_{v,w} \geq 0$ and $\sum_{\text{w is a neighbor of v}} b_{v,w} \leq 1$. A choice for the weights $b_{v,w}$ for a node v is $1 / |\mathcal{N}_v|$, where $\mathcal{N}_v = \{w \in \mathcal{N}, (w, v) \in \mathcal{E}\}$ is the set of all nodes in $\mathcal{N}$ that are connected to v through edges pointing to v. This means that all v's neighbors have the same influence on v. Each node v chooses an activation threshold θ_v, uniformly at random from the interval [0, 1]; the node v will become active when the overall strength of all its active neighbors passes its threshold. In other words, v will become active when $\sum_{\substack{w \text{ is a neighbor of } v,\\ w \text{ is active}}} b_{v,w} \geq \theta_v$. The randomness in choosing the activation thresholds of the network nodes models our lack of knowledge regarding how susceptible to influence are the social actors in a network.

Given randomly selected thresholds for all nodes in $\mathcal{G}$, and a set of initially active nodes $\mathcal{S}$ (= the ***seeds***), the activation process proceeds in steps. In each step, the previously active nodes remain active, and inactive nodes that have enough active neighbors will be activated as well. The spreading process stops when no further nodes can be activated.

The influence maximization problem can be stated as follows. If $\sigma(A)$ denotes the expected number of nodes that will be influenced if the set A is initially activated, find the set of seeds $\mathcal{S}$, of size k, that has the maximum influence in the network. This set, called the ***seed set***, is a solution for the optimization problem $\max_{B \subseteq N} \sigma(B)$, such that $|B| = k$.

Kempe et al. showed in [8] that finding the optimum seed set under the *LTM* is NP-hard. They also proposed a greedy algorithm that is able to find an (1-1/*e*) approximation of the optimum solution; i.e. the solution found by the greedy algorithm will be at least 63% of the optimal one. This result is based on two significant properties that the influence function $\sigma(\cdot)$ has been proven to have: $\sigma(\cdot)$ is monotone and submodular (see [8] for definitions and proofs).

This greedy algorithm for the influence maximization problem has unfortunately a drawback, its efficiency. We therefore chose to use a different algorithm for the influence maximization problem, which is based on heuristics and has been proven to reduce the running time by more than six orders of magnitude ([13]). Chen et al. proposed the ***degree discount*** heuristic for estimating the most influential nodes in a network. Selecting a seed set based on the degree discount heuristics has been shown to be very efficient and to achieve, under the *ICM*, an influence spread almost as large as the one produced by the greedy algorithm; for other influence models (*LTM* included), degree discount has been said to have an improved performance compared to other heuristics, such as the pure degree heuristic.

Under the degree discount heuristic, the best k seeds for initial activation in the network are selected as follows. The selection proceeds in k steps, in each step a new seed is chosen, that has the highest discounted degree among the nodes not chosen yet. The discounted degrees of the nodes are initially, before the first selection is made, equal to the actual degrees of the nodes. After each seed selection, the discounted degrees of the nodes that are neighbors of that seed are decremented by 1. This alteration reflects the basic idea that it is not worth it to make a seed (i.e. initially active) a node that already has seed(s) in its neighborhood; this because that node will be potentially activated by the neighboring seeds, and then it will itself further spread its influence to its inactive neighbors.

V. Measuring Influence Preservation

In our experiments, we compared influence for the seed sets of the original social networks with seed sets of the corresponding *FKDA* anonymized network and the de-anonymized *Sangreea* networks. We describe next how the comparison can be performed, taking into consideration the point of view of a user attempting to do marketing targeted to the most influential nodes in an anonymized network.

Assume a user disposing of a budget for promoting products or services to p% of the network nodes. Of course, they would want the nodes they target to be the most influential in the network. Let's first assume the network they have has been anonymized with *Sangreea*. They can de-anonymize this network and determine the k most influential nodes in the de-anonymized network, where k is chosen to be a certain percentage of the network size. How is the k value to be chosen? k cannot be $|\mathcal{N}| * p / 100$, for the following reason. When we de-anonymize a network, we use information that we recorded during anonymization about the composition of each cluster: what node IDs belong to which cluster. However, the nodes within a cluster are anonymous and cannot be distinguished from each other, so a node restored from cluster $cl_j = \{X_j^1, X_j^2, \ldots, X_j^{|cl_j|}\}$ with id X_j^r will not necessarily be the same one that was identified by X_j^r in the original cluster; it could instead be anyone of the other nodes assigned to cluster cl_j. This further means that if X_j^r is determined as one of the seeds in the de-anonymized network, any one of the nodes in its cluster could actually be the real influential node, not necessarily X_j^r. Therefore, someone who wants to be sure they do not miss the real influential node(s) in a cluster containing a seed / seeds will have to basically target all the nodes in that cluster.

To stay in the allowed budget, one has to find less than or at most equal to p% most influential nodes. One would first search for the p% most influential nodes. If they happen to populate exhaustively their clusters, then the process would stop. If however, and this is much more likely, the clusters containing seeds also contain other nodes, one has to reduce the target percent, repeat the seed set determination, and check if they are in the allowed budget. The process will stop at the first p^*% found for which $\left|\bigcup_{s \in \mathcal{S}^*} cl^s\right| * 100 \big/ |\mathcal{N}| \leq p$, where $\mathcal{S}^*$ is the seed set with cardinality $|\mathcal{N}|$ x p^* / 100, and cl^s is the cluster containing the seed s. In our experiments, we computed p^* as follows: we started with p^* being equal to p; we then found the most influential p^*% nodes in the anonymized network; next, we determined the set of all nodes found in clusters containing seeds, $T(\mathcal{S}^*) = \left|\bigcup_{s \in \mathcal{S}^*} cl^s\right|$ - we call this set the ***targeted set***; if its size is greater than the budget of $|\mathcal{N}|$ x p / 100 nodes, then p^* is reduced to 0.95 x p^*; this adjustment process is repeated until the targeted set fits into the budget.

Once the seed set $\mathcal{S}^*$ is found, we can estimate and compare the spread of the most influential p% nodes in the original un-anonymized network, with the spread of the targeted set $T(\mathcal{S}^*)$. The loss incurred by targeting the nodes in $T(\mathcal{S}^*)$ instead of targeting the most influential p% nodes in the original network can also be computed as $loss = \sigma(\mathcal{S}) - \sigma(T(\mathcal{S}^*))$, where σ is the influence function defined under *LTM* and $\mathcal{S}$ is the seed set of size $|\mathcal{N}| * p / 100$, determined in the original network. σ is computed for both $T(\mathcal{S}^*)$ and $\mathcal{S}$ in the original network. The *loss* measure represents the estimated number of nodes that can be reached when activating $\mathcal{S}$ but cannot be reached when activating $T(\mathcal{S}^*)$. Theoretically, *loss* should be a positive measure, since $\mathcal{S}$ is the most influential set that could be found by the degree discount procedure; this set is obviously not the optimum solution for the influence maximization problem, but it is very likely to still be better than $T(\mathcal{S}^*)$.

The algorithm we used to estimate the spread of influence in a network, for an initial set of active seeds, under *LTM*, is based on a Monte-Carlo simulation.

```
Algorithm estimateSpread is
Input:    G=(N,E) and a set of seeds S ⊆ N
Output:   An estimate of σ(S) in G
R = 10000; spread = 0;
For i = 1, R do:
  Select random thresholds for nodes in G
  Perform a LT spread simulation in G, with
  seed set S; let count be the number of nodes
  activated in that simulation
  spread += count
Return spread/R
End estimateSpread.
```

For *Sangreea*, *loss* can be computed as the difference between the result of *estimateSpread*($\mathcal{G}$, $\mathcal{S}$) and that of *estimateSpread*($\mathcal{G}$, $T(\mathcal{S}^*)$). For *FKDA* networks, the loss in influence due to anonymization can be computed similarly as for *Sangreea*, with a modification: when determining p^*% and the seed set $\mathcal{S}^*$, the targeted set $T(\mathcal{S}^*)$ is computed as $T(\mathcal{S}^*) = \bigcup_{s \in \mathcal{S}^*} \{X \in \mathcal{N} \mid X \text{ has same degree as } s\}$.

Since every seed in the *FKDA* anonymized network is undistinguishable from the other nodes in the network with the same degree, when a seed is selected in $\mathcal{S}^*$, all nodes with the same degree should be targeted, to be sure that the true influential node is targeted. Compared to *Sangreea*, the clusters of anonymous nodes that *FKDA* creates are the subsets of nodes in $\mathcal{G}'$ with the same degree. Once $T(\mathcal{S}^*)$ and $\mathcal{S}$ are determined, *loss* could be again computed as the difference between the result of *estimateSpread*($\mathcal{G}$, $\mathcal{S}$) and that of *estimateSpread*($\mathcal{G}$, $T(\mathcal{S}^*)$).

VI. Experiments and Results

We study influence preservation (with degree discount) in the original, anonymized (for *FDKA*), and de-anonymized (for *Sangreea*) versions of three datasets.

The **Enron** dataset is a network of email exchanges available online at [7]. It is an undirected network with 36,692 nodes and 183,831 edges. Each node in this network represents an email address. And edge exists between two nodes if at least one email was sent from one node to the other from that edge. The **Random** dataset is synthetically generated using the Erdos-Renyi random network model [1] using the social network analysis program Pajek [12]. We used as input parameters for the social network generator 10,000 nodes and an average vertex degree of 20. The resulting network has 100,314 edges. The **ScaleFree** dataset is an undirected network generated based on the scale-free model [13]. This approach models real world social networks that follow a power-law degree distribution [2]. We generated this dataset using Pajek with the following parameters: the number of nodes 10,000, the average degree of nodes of 33, the number of nodes in the initial Erdos-Renyo graph 10. The generated graph has a significant number of multiple edges which were eliminated in a post-processing step. The final scale-free network that we used in experiments had 10,000 nodes and 152,909 edges.

The flow of our experiments is shown in Figure 1. This experimental framework consists of 6 steps. We start from the initial social networks (Enron, Random, and ScaleFree) previously described. First, the initial social networks are anonymized into *k*-anonymous social networks, using *FKDA* (step 1a) and *Sangreea* (step 1b) as described in Section 2. For each dataset we used the following values for *k*: 2, 3, 4, 5, 6, 7, 8, 9, 10, 15, 20, 25, and 50. Second, from each *k*-anonymous *Sangreea* network we generated two de-anonymized social networks, one following the *Uniform* de-anonymization strategy (step 2a) and the other the *R-MAT* de-anonymization strategy (step 2b). The need for performing de-anonymization on *Sangreea* networks was explained in Section 2. In Step 3, we computed the seed set $\mathcal{S}$ of the most influential p% nodes in the original networks, where p has values 2, 4, 6, 8, 10. In Step 4, we computed the seed set $\mathcal{S}^*$ of the most influential p^*% nodes in the *FKDA* networks and the de-anonymized *Sangreea* networks, where p^* is computed as described in section 5 for p values 2, 4, 6, 8, 10. Each of these sets $\mathcal{S}^*$ have the corresponding $T(\mathcal{S}^*)$. In Step 5, we also consider random selections for the seed sets in the original networks, denoted by $\mathcal{S}_{random}$, for the same p values 2, 4, 6, 8, and 10 – 5 random seed sets of each size, for each of the networks. In Step 6, we compare the influence of seed sets $\mathcal{S}$, $T(\mathcal{S}^*)$, and $\mathcal{S}_{random}$: the influence of these seed sets in the original network is estimated using the ***estimateSpread*** procedure, and is reported as a percentage of the network size. Since we generated 5 random seed sets for each original network, the influence determined in those cases is averaged.

Figures 2 a-f show the results of steps 5 and 6, for the Random, ScaleFree, and Enron datasets.

For the Random network, *FKDA* preserved reasonably well the spread of influence (Figures 2 a-b). The only situation where *FKDA* dropped rapidly is when $p = 8$ and k was 25 or 50 (not shown here). The reason for that behavior is that the targeting set $T(\mathcal{S}^*)$ kept decreasing by 5% of its size multiple times, until its size reached 578 nodes with

k=25 and 581 nodes with k=50 – by comparison, the size of the seed set for the original network was 800 (= 8% of 10000). Any significant difference in the size of the targeting set, compared to the current p% budget size, will definitely decrease the spread of influence for the targeted set; this happens regardless of the anonymity model. In this particular case, for k=25 and k=50, the size of the targeted set before the final 5% reduction might have been just a little bit over 800, and the last 5% adjustment was too drastic. With *Sangreea R-MAT(Reconstruct)*, the spread of influence was well preserved especially when k got larger. *Sangreea Uniform(Reconstruct)*, on the other hand, was the weakest in influence preserving, which indicates that it is not worth it to de-anonymize *Sangreea* networks with the *Uniform* algorithm for any random network.

For the ScaleFree network (Figures 2, c-d), *FKDA* and the original networks have almost identical spread of influence for all p values. *Sangreea* de-anonymization with *R-MAT* and *Uniform* have the same spread of influence until the anonymity parameter k reaches 10, for 2% the size of the seed set, and until k reaches 7, for the remaining p values.

For Enron, *FKDA* preserved well the most influential nodes with all the p values (similar behavior was recorded for the p values 4 and 8, which are not illustrated here).

However, *R-MAT* and *Uniform* de-anonymization for *Sangreea* have a similar behavior for all p values: the spread of influence decreased almost linearly, with p. In all these cases *R-MAT* had much better results than *Uniform*.

So, overall, *FKDA* preserved well the spread of influence in all networks. De-anonymized *Sangreea* networks weren't as good as *FKDA* networks, except for the Random network, where *R-MAT* over performed *FKDA* in about ½ of the cases. But always *R-MAT* behaved better than *Uniform*, even for the Random network. We also noticed that the random selection of the seed set didn't preserve the most influential nodes in any of the networks.

After all, the preservation of the spread of influence under the user's point of view assumption is almost entirely dependent on the purity of the anonymity clusters w.r.t. the most influential nodes in the network. If anonymity clusters

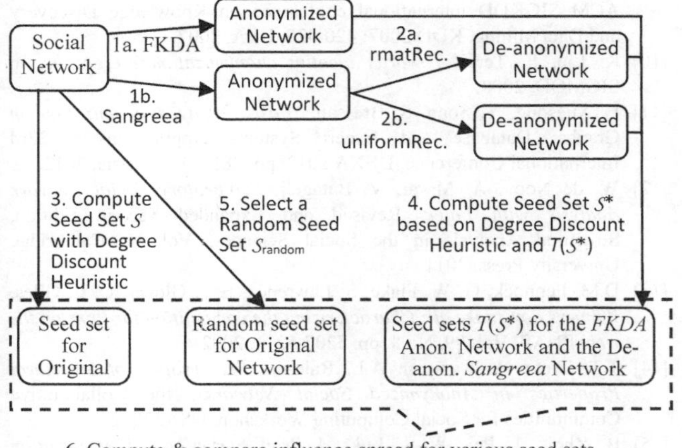

Fig. 1. Flow of Experiments

do not contain any residual nodes, meaning $T(S^*)$-S^* is close to ∅, then S^* is as big as the p% budget, and only real influential nodes are targeted. That would really ensure preservation of spread of influence compared to the original un-anonymized network. The question about the preservation of the influence spread is now reduced to how pure are the anonymity clusters produced by *Sangreea* or *FKDA* (purity from the point of view explained before). The *FKDA* anonymity clusters are induced by the groups of nodes anonymized together, which are nodes that have similar degrees. For high degrees, the *FKDA* anonymity clusters are small, since there are few nodes with high degrees, especially in scale-free networks. For smaller degrees and scale-free networks, the *FKDA* anonymity clusters could be bigger – and the chance of them becoming impure grows. On the other side, the degree discount procedure identifies the most influential seeds to be, more or less, the nodes with the highest degrees. Therefore, the most influential nodes will correspond to the anonymity clusters with the highest node degree, which are, as we discussed, small; their size should be about k, where k is the anonymity parameter, as in k- degree anonymity. Since we just look for p% of the most influential nodes, with p having small values in general, this means we never reach to the anonymity clusters with low node degree values, which could be larger than k and impure. Since the principle based upon which *FKDA* anonymizes nodes is so similar to the principle based upon which degree discount finds the most influential nodes, clearly the *FKDA* anonymity clusters, at least the ones that will be considered within the p% budget, tend to be very pure, for scale-free networks. For random networks, where nodes are more uniform in terms of their degrees, the *FKDA* clusters are not that pure anymore; this is reflected in smaller influence preservation scores. Only for the Random network had *FKDA* much smaller influence preservation; for Enron and ScaleFree, *FKDA*'s influence preservation was almost 100%. For Random though, *FKDA* had in 2 cases smaller preservation compared to *Sangreea R-MAT* (for p: 2, 10).

Sangreea attempts to put together in a supernode some of the original nodes that have the same neighbors, as much as possible. This could go somewhat against the way the degree discount procedure identifies the most influential nodes, and therefore it is expected to get more impure anonymity clusters compared to the ones created by *FKDA*. Also, in *Sangreea*'s case, more error is added to the one introduced by the anonymization itself, due to the de-anonymization process. As expected, *Sangreea* followed by *R-MAT* or *Uniform* de-anonymization will not preserve influence spread as well as *FKDA*.

VII. CONCLUSIONS

Anonymization models have been used to ensure the privacy of social networks. A conflicting goal with maintaining the privacy of a network's information is the preservation of the structural properties of the social network. The goal of this work was to investigate whether we can preserve privacy in social networks using anonymization techniques and in the same time preserve

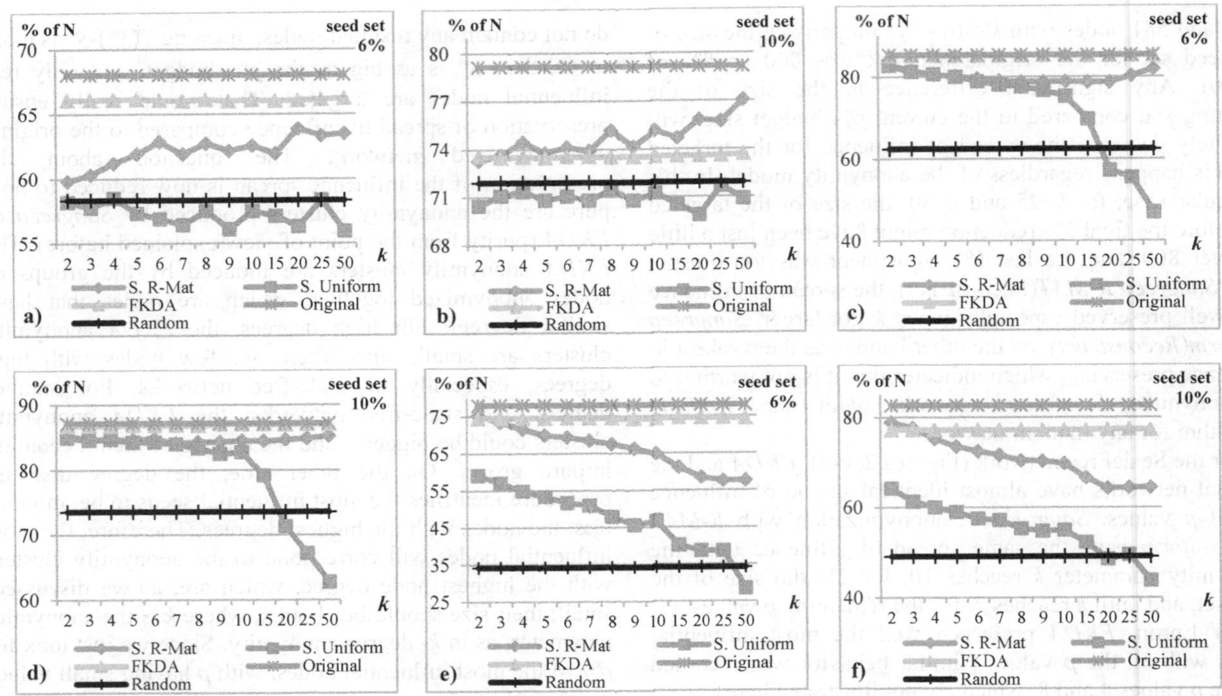

Fig. 2. Influence spread of most influential 6% (a, c, e) and 10% (b, d, f) nodes in the original network vs. influence spread of targeted sets T(S*) of size ≈6% and ≈10% in the FKDA Anonymized and the De-anonymized Sangreea networks – for the Random (a, b), ScaleFree (c, d), and Enron (e, f) networks

enough information to allow a good analysis of the properties of the social graph. We looked at how an influence spread measure changed between the original and the anonymized networks. *FKDA* had a better preserving for the spread of influence, compared with *Sangreea R-Mat* and *Uniform*. When comparing *R-Mat* and *Uniform*, the experiments showed that *R-Mat* is a stronger approach than *Uniform* – in the sense that better reconstructs the original networks, without disclosing information, but preserving well the influence spread from the original networks. This was to be expected at least for the scale-free networks, but it was also true for random networks; the explanation can be that, for small values of *k* that correspond to small clusters to be reconstructed, *R-Mat* and *Uniform* reconstruction produce sub-graph structures that are not very different, and therefore have similar influence spread. The better preservation of the spread of influence in *FKDA*'s case comes with a cost: *FKDA* is a much weaker model for preserving privacy than *Sangreea* is. An attacker with knowledge about the 2-radius neighborhood of a target node could still reidentify his target in an *FKDA* network, if the target's 2-radius neighborhood has some unique feature. *Sangreea*'s privacy preserving is stronger: an attacker won't be able to breach the privacy of a *Sangreea* network based on any structural properties knowledge.

REFERENCES

[1] B. Bollobás, *Random Graphs*, Cambridge University Press, 2011.

[2] B. Bollobás, O. Riordan, J Spencer, G. Tusnady, *The Degree Sequence of a Scale-Free Random Graph Process*, Journal of Random Structures and Algorithms, Vol. 18 (3), pp. 279-290, 2011.

[3] A. Campan, T.M. Truta, *A Clustering Approach for Data and Structural Anonymity in Social Networks*, 2nd ACM SIGKDD Intl. Workshop on Privacy, Security, & Trust in KDD, USA, 2008.

[4] D. Chakrabarti, Y. Zhan, C. Faloutsos, *R-MAT: A Recursive Model for Graph Mining*, SIAM Data Mining 2004, Orlando, USA, 2004.

[5] W. Chen, Y. Wang, S. Yang, *Efficient influence maximization in social networks*, Proc. of the 15th ACM SIGKDD Intl. conference on Knowledge Discovery and Data Mining (KDD '09), 2009.

[6] P. Domingos, M. Richardson, *Mining the Network Value of Customers*, Proc. of the 7th Intl. Conference on Knowledge Discovery and Data Mining (ACM SIGKDD), pages 57-66, USA, 2001.

[7] Enron Dataset, http://snap.stanford.edu/data/email-Enron.html.

[8] D. Kempe, J. Kleinberg, E. Tardos, *Maximizing the Spread of Influence through a Social Network*, Proc. 9th ACM SIGKDD Intl. Conf. on Knowledge Discovery and Data Mining, 2003.

[9] J. Leskovec, A. Krause, C. Guestrin, C. Faloustos, J. Vanbriesen, N. Glance, *Cost-effective outbreak detection in networks*, Proc. of the 13th ACM SIGKDD international conference on Knowledge Discovery and Data Mining. KDD 2007: 420-429, USA, 2007.

[10] K. Liu, E. Terzi, *Towards identity anonymization on graphs*, in SIGMOD, 2008.

[11] L. Xuesong, Y. Song, S. Bressan, *Fast Identity Anonymization on* Graphs, Database and Expert Systems Applications - 23rd International Conference, DEXA 2012, pp. 281-295, Austria, 2012.

[12] W. de Nooy, A. Mrvar, V. Batagelj, *Exploratory Social Network Analysis with Pajek,* Revised and Expanded Second Edition, Structural Analysis in the Social Sciences, Vol 34, Cambridge University Press, 2011.

[13] D.M. Pennock, G. W. Flake, S. Lawrence, E. J. Glover, C. L. Giles, *Winners don't take all: Characterizing the competition for links on the web*, PNAS, Vol. 99, No 8, pp. 5207-5211, 2002.

[14] T.T. Truta, A. Campan, A.L. Ralescu, *Preservation of Structural Properties in Anonymized Social Networks*, the Collaborative Communities for Social Computing Workshop, USA, 2012.

[15] B. Zhou, J. Pei, W.-S. Luk, *A Brief Survey on Anonymization Techniques for Privacy Preserving Publishing of Social Network Data*, ACM SIGKDD Explorations, 10(2):12–22, 2008.